HEP-CATS,
NARCS,
AND
PIPE DREAMS

A History of

America's

Romance

with

Illegal Drugs

JILL JONNES

SCRIBNER

SCRIBNER
1230 Avenue of the Americas
New York, NY 10020

Designed by Jenny Dossin
Photo insert designed by Sam Potts
Set in Adobe Trump Medieval

Manufactured in the United States of America
10 9 8 7 6 5 4 3 2 1

Library of Congress Cataloging-in-Publication Data is available.

ISBN 0-684-19670-0

Portions of chapters 2, 3, and 19 first appeared as "The Rise of the Modern Addict" in *American Journal of Public Health*, vol. 85, no. 8, August 1995.

Portions of chapters 1, 2, and 15 first appeared as "American Drug Culture" in *Civilization*, vol. 3, no. 4, 1996.

Portions of "Everybody Must Get Stoned" first appeared in *Maryland Historical Magazine*, vol. 91, no. 2, 1996.

FOR MY DAUGHTER HILARY

CONTENTS

Hep-cat. A jazz "fiend" (swing music)
—*Eric Partridge's Dictionary of Slang*, 1984

Narc. U.S. slang for a narcotics agent
—*Brewer's Dictionary*, 1992

Pipe dream. Originating with opium smoking;
an impossible, imaginary, and fanciful hope or
plan
—*Brewer's Dictionary*, 1989

From the schoolhouse to the crack house, the problem of illegal drugs permeates our society. Suburban brick junior highs sport DRUG-FREE SCHOOL ZONE signs. Drug testing for work and in the military are accepted—if resented—staples of our world. The daily toll of minority youth gunned down in drug-dealing disputes no longer shocks.

This book tells the history of America's romance with illegal drugs, a complex and extraordinary tale peopled by those as august as Sigmund Freud, as brilliant as Charlie Parker, as vicious as "Legs" Diamond and the Colombian cartels, and as misguided as Timothy Leary. It is the history of how a small, deviant subculture took root and eventually spread throughout our whole society. By the early 1990s, an estimated 37 percent of Americans age twelve and older (75 million citizens!!) had used marijuana, cocaine, and/or heroin. Considering this, it is astonishing how woefully ignorant—historically, sociologically, and scientifically—we are about these substances that have so altered our world for the worse.

Few of us know we had a serious heroin and cocaine problem in the early decades of this century. Otherwise well-informed friends are amazed when told that city youth used heroin back in 1910 and called it "happy dust"; or how in that same year President William Howard Taft identified cocaine as "more appalling in its effects than any other habit-forming drug in the United States" and urged Congress to restrict its availability; or that empty cocaine vials littered city streets in the early years of this century. The original "war" on drugs in the early years of this century was so successful that we have no collective memory of that era.

Although the historical ignorance is not so surprising, our lack of real understanding about the pharmacology of drugs is. Despite the huge numbers of contemporary Americans who have used and abused illegal drugs, few fully appreciate their true nature. Time and again people make direct analogies between drugs and alcohol on television talk shows or in letters to the editor. The fact is that drugs are very different from alcohol—and far more dangerous.

To understand why, it is necessary to understand the concept of "reinforcement." How "reinforcing" a substance is reflects how driven people (or laboratory animals) are to use it again. This is the crux of addiction. Part of what makes one substance more reinforcing than another has to do with routes of administration. Alcohol, for instance, can only be taken orally, a very inefficient way to reach the brain and induce a high. However, cocaine and heroin can be snorted or shot into the veins, which provide much more direct and powerful doses (and therefore are more reinforcing) to the brain. But the fastest and most dose-intensive of all routes to the brain is smoking, which helps explain the extraordinarily addictive qualities not only of crack but of cigarettes.

Therefore, scientists now class alcohol as a "moderately reinforcing" substance. In notable contrast, people (and laboratory animals) who use heroin and cocaine often seem highly driven to use them again and again. Therefore, scientists class these drugs as "highly reinforcing." A May 1992 issue of *Trends in Pharmacological Sciences* noted that it is now clear that opiates and cocaine act by "hijacking reward pathways [in the brain] that exist to ensure survival of the species. . . . Understanding of how different abused drugs feed into these circuits is starting to lead to a clearer appreciation of why some drugs (e.g., cocaine) are, at the purely scientific level, more reinforcing than others."

As the United States continues to struggle with the pernicious power of the drug culture, there is great need to understand that culture's historical origins and growth, and then to connect that history to present and future policy. Studying the history of drug use and drug culture in the United States makes clear that—like all commodities—

supply and demand are key factors. Availability is fundamental, for wherever there are drugs to be had, use and addiction will *always* rise. One need only look at Pakistan, which had virtually no heroin problem before the 1980s, when the Afghan guerrillas and corrupt local officials flooded the nation with heroin, creating 1.3 million heroin addicts in three short years. (The United States, with its infamous drug problems, has 500,000 heroin addicts and three times the overall population.)

But history shows that demand can vary, depending on several mediating factors. Taking the widespread availability of drugs as a given, certain people and groups always will be most vulnerable. These are the poor and socially marginal, people who feel they have no stake in society, especially those with weak families and little connection to other institutions, such as schools or religious congregations. Also vulnerable are the young and alienated, typically middle and upper-class youth in pursuit of a superficial bohemianism. And so our worst drug problems have arisen at those times in our history when we have had widespread availability intersecting with large numbers of poor people living in slums and facing dead-end prospects and/or large numbers of young people.

The third factor that can substantially affect demand is the phenomenon of learned experience, first noted by Dr. David Musto of Yale University. When people see firsthand the pernicious qualities of illegal drugs, they shy away. In the United States, this has created historical thirty-year cycles of tolerance and intolerance.

As the Spanish film director Pedro Almodovar explained when speaking of his own experience with drugs: "You know, the first period of drugs was very stimulating. But this is a lesson you learn with time: that drugs only work in the first stages. The second and third stages are just a nightmare." One can certainly see that this lesson was absorbed by the younger generations in the United States, who grew up heavily exposed to the negative consequences of the drug culture. They have shunned drugs much more than their baby-boomer parents, who had a lot of romantic notions about drugs when they first encountered them in the sixties and seventies. The younger generations have seen what drugs, even the milder marijuana, can do over time. But even today's lower levels are still too high, and youthful drug use is once again rising as we allow the lessons of the recent past to fade.

Illegal drugs as we know them today in America—cocaine, heroin, marijuana, LSD—all came into popular use only in the last century or half century. They are phenomena of the modern, industrial world. The story of how the contemporary drug culture came to permeate and corrode our society all begins in the nineteenth century, when the whole strange idea of addiction was first introduced.

PART I

America's First Drug Epidemic 1885–1925

"We Are the Drug-Habit Nation."
—H. W. WILEY, 1911

"One Day You Find Yourself in Hell."

—*Long Day's Journey Into Night*,
EUGENE O'NEILL

In 1821 the obscure and impecunious English writer Thomas De Quincey created a minor sensation with his *Confessions of an English Opium Eater*. Graced with an elegant, labyrinthine style, De Quincey's autobiography described in disturbing detail his tortured love affair with laudanum, a liquid form of opium dissolved in alcohol. Here for the first time the Western world was presented with a extraordinary new concept: drug addiction. Since Englishmen and women of the period, both high and low, thought nothing of dosing themselves with various forms of opium for sundry aches and pains, De Quincey's tale was rather unsettling.

Like countless of his countrymen, De Quincey had begun using opium to alleviate an ailment, in his case rheumatic pains that struck in 1804 when he was a student at Oxford. From the moment he first drank laudanum, he was smitten: "[H]ere was the secret of happiness, about which philosophers had disputed for so many ages, at once discovered: happiness might now be bought for a penny, and carried in the waistcoat pocket: portable ecstacies might be had corked up in a pint bottle: and peace of mind could be sent down in gallons by the coach mail."

Despite this memorable first experience, De Quincey did not become "habituated" then and there. More than a decade would pass before the writer took up laudanum as an "article of daily diet." Instead, he initially reserved this "exquisite pleasure" for his cherished monthly outings to the opera or certain dolorous days. After university, De Quincey lived in the Lake District with the Wordworths, reading and writing before strains in the friendship drove him to London and a halfhearted stab at lawyering. He moved on, ever restless, until by his late twenties he had used up the last of a small inheritance playing an Edinburgh gentleman scholar.

Then, much to the dismay of his friends, De Quincey fathered a child with a farmer's daughter, married her, and embarked upon a precarious family life. Financially beset as he tried to support his growing brood as a journalist, De Quincey at age twenty-eight was "attacked by a most appalling irritation of the stomach." From this time on he was "a regular and confirmed opium-eater, of whom to ask whether on any particular day he had or had not taken opium, would be to ask whether his lungs had performed respiration, or the heart fulfilled its function."

And while pain was the original reason for treasuring his daily laudanum, De Quincey freely described how opium's other qualities made him an addict. Much of the *Confessions* is a long and loving panegyric, a paean to the power of a mere draught of laudanum to bring wondrous peace to the harried breadwinner and writer. Or—given a high enough dose—how the opium-eater could experience the fabulous dreamlike reveries that he termed "the paradise of opium."

But soon enough opium showed its treacherous nature. And like every addict, De Quincey found that what had begun as profound pleasure gradually became deepest torment. The drug had "ceased to found its empire on spells of pleasure; it was solely by the tortures connected with the attempt to abjure it, that it kept its hold . . . I saw that I must die if I continued the opium: I determined, therefore, if that should be required, to die in throwing it off. . . . Think of me as . . . agitated, writhing, throbbing, palpitating, shattered; and much, perhaps, in the situation of him who has been racked."

When De Quincey wrote these desperate words in the early nineteenth century, the medicinal qualities of the opium poppy, *Papaver somniferum*, had been known for millennia. Western doctors of the time argued endlessly about how and why this extraordinary drug acted, but it had earned the sobriquet "God's Own Medicine" for its incomparable power to still the suffering of the sick. In 1680, the eminent English physician Thomas Sydenham had pronounced, "Among the remedies which it has pleased Almighty God to give man to relieve his sufferings, none is so universal and efficacious as opium." This was still true in De Quincey's time, but until his *Confessions*, opium's "habituating" qualities were little considered by doctors or ordinary folk. And while readers of De Quincey's 1822 work finished the book reassured that he had overcome his opium eating, in truth he wrestled with his addiction for another twenty-six years.

As for the concept of opiate addiction, deemed "chronic opium intoxication," it would be decades before it was taken seriously as a bona fide hazard of medical treatment. In the United States, despite the notoriety of De Quincey's *Confessions* and repeated warnings in medical journals, physicians and patients flocked to use the seemingly miraculous opiate drugs. Morphine, codeine, laudanum—all were readily available without prescription. All-purpose patent medicines, with reassuring names like Children's Comfort or Carney's Common Sense Cure, were loaded with opiates. In the 1850s, doctors adopted the newfangled syringe, whose potent delivery of morphine produced virtually instant surcease of pain. Nineteenth-century America's huge appetite for opiates shows in the almost fivefold increase in per capita crude opium imports, from twelve grains per capita in the 1840s to fifty-two grains per capita by the 1890s.

Not surprisingly, by the late nineteenth century a great many Americans had come to recognize and understand the concept of opiate addiction. Generally, the problem was blamed on "the unpardonable carelessness of physicians" who were accused of "relieving every ache and pain by the administration of an opiate." So concluded one J. M. Hull in 1885 for the Iowa Board of Health. He further observed that most of the addicted were to be found "among the educated and most honored and useful members of society; and as to sex, we may count out the prostitutes so much given to this vice, and still find females far ahead as far as numbers are concerned."

White, middle-class women were specially prone to opium eating, basically because they could afford the doctors who then treated them with opiates for painful "female problems" and that characteristic Victorian complaint, neurasthenia. Keep in mind the primitive state of medicine. The typical American nineteenth-century doctor began practicing after one year of book learning. He (and occasionally she) had never trained in a hospital, but learned about patients during a brief apprenticeship before embarking on a career in medicine. There was little understanding of hygiene or infection, and surgery was extremely perilous. Under these circumstances of gross medical ignorance, it's no wonder that morphine, codeine, and laudanum were doled out liberally to all patients.

This was especially true for female patients, who were given opiates for "practically everything, even for such unlikely disorders as masturbation, photophobia, nyphomania, and 'violent hiccough.' " But above all, it was childbearing and its aftermath that lead "more ladies to fall into the habit, than all other diseases combined." A variety of surveys showed that anywhere from two thirds to three quarters of opiate addicts were women.

There is probably no more famous example of these early genteel addicts than playwright Eugene O'Neill's mother, Ella O'Neill. After the difficult delivery of Eugene in 1888 and a slow recovery, her doctor prescribed morphine, a typical treatment for such a patient. For not only was the thirty-four-year-old Mrs. O'Neill in physical pain, but she was still melancholy over the loss of an earlier baby and unhappy about her actor-husband's peripatetic career and the world of dreary hotel rooms. Ella O'Neill clung to the morphine, continuing it so quietly that her own husband did not realize at first that her new "dreaminess and detachment" was a sign of addiction.

For the next quarter of a century Ella O'Neill tried again and again to free herself from morphine. Her husband cursed it as "that damn poison," hating how it transformed her into a pathetic, wraithlike figure, a semirecluse who had to be hidden from the outside world. Only when Ella's sons reached adolescence did they discover why their mother was so odd, the elder son walking in when Ella was using the hypodermic. On occasional visits home from boarding school, the boys cringed as Ella O'Neill spewed torrents of wounding words, blaming her husband for engaging a "cheap quack" who prescribed morphine, as if it was not then standard medical practice. In O'Neill's *Long Day's Journey Into Night*, the mother wails, "I hate doctors! They'll do anything . . . to keep you coming to them. They'll sell their souls. What's worse, they'll sell yours, and you never know it till one day you find yourself in hell."

No one knows how many times Ella O'Neill went for "cures" at rural sanitaria, only to relapse. But finally in 1914 she essayed to try again, this time in a Brooklyn convent, and broke free of morphine's grip for good. The serene, expensively dressed gentlewoman who now went daily to Mass gave no hint of the phantom existence she had left behind. But her second son never forgot, transforming it into one of the great American tragedies, one that had played out across the land again and again during the nineteenth century.

The growing awareness of drug addiction led a few American addicts to present themselves as native De Quinceys. A typical effort was one penned in 1903 by a wealthy Missouri scion named Reuben Blakey

Eubank. His was the sorry tale of a stomach ailment that led to *Twenty Years in Hell: The Life, Experience, Trials and Tribulations of a Morphine Fiend*: "With each recurring attack I would send for the doctor and have the morphine injection repeated. Never for a moment did I suspect that I was laying the foundation for a habit which I would carry with me to the grave. At first, habit only binds us with silken threads, but alas! these threads finally change to links of strongest steel."

A whole industry of sorts arose to offer hope (at a stiff price, of course) to these unfortunates, ranging from secret-formula patent medicines used in the privacy of one's home to lengthy stays at private sanitaria. The most eminent of the cure doctors was one Leslie E. Keeley, whose nationwide chain of Keeley Institutes treated addicts (and alcoholics) with Keeley's much-bruited Bichloride of Gold formula.

Physicians and others regularly trotted out new possibilities for curing addiction. In early 1880 Dr. Edward C. Huse of Rockford, Illinois, wrote in the Parke-Davis–sponsored journal, *The Therapeutic Gazette*, of "Coca-Erythoxylon—A New Cure for the Opium Habit," describing how he had weaned two addicts off opium through use of Parke-Davis & Co.'s fluid extract of coca. Dr. W. H. Bentley of Valley Oak, Kentucky, reported in the September 1880 issue of similar success treating addicts with coca syrups, including one elderly lady who had long cultivated a tenth-acre of poppies to supply her opium habit.

Across the Atlantic, a young Viennese neurologist named Sigmund Freud would eventually read these reports from the New World with great interest. Not only was one of his dearest friends in the grips of a dreadful morphine addiction, but Freud was, as he wrote his fiancée, Martha Bernays, furiously "chasing after money, position, and reputation" so he could marry her as soon as possible. In 1884 Freud, then an impatient twenty-eight years old, sensed the possibilities of glory in the little-known drug, coca, after reading how it had been used by a military doctor to boost the energy of Bavarian soldiers on maneuver. As he wrote Martha, "We do not need more than one such lucky hit to be able to think of setting up house."

Freud determined that the soldiers had been using a new product of the Merck pharmaceutical firm, a white powder derived from the leaves of the South American coca plant. First isolated by the German scientist Albert Niemann of Göttingen in 1860, this cocaine alkaloid was only now being produced commercially in Darmstadt. Freud read the meager medical and scientific literature on the products of the coca plant and ordered a gram. In keeping with the medical style of the times, he immediately began experimenting on himself, carefully calibrating dosage and observing and recording his own reactions. He snuffed a twentieth of a gram and found it lifted him right out of a bad mood and filled him with energy. As for Freud's addicted friend, Ernst von Fleischl-Marxow, he embraced cocaine "like a drowning man" and was soon off morphine.

Next, Freud found that cocaine dramatically improved a case of painful gastric catarrh. (Catarrh is the inflammation of the mucous membranes.) Using cocaine himself "regularly against depression and indigestion, and with the most brilliant success," Freud began proselytizing for what he called this "magical drug," pressing it upon his colleagues, friends, relations, and patients. Gathering evidence from some quick animal studies and a few clinical cases, young Dr. Freud became convinced coca might even supersede opiates in medical practice. By July 1884 Dr. Freud was in print with his long and enthusiastic review, a "hymn of praise" entitled *Uber Coca*.

Freud proposed cocaine as a promising treatment for a whole host of medical problems: melancholy, neurasthenia, digestive ailments, wasting diseases, asthmas, and (based on Fleischl) morphine and alcohol addiction. He concluded that using coca syrups to cure opium habits must already be a well-established practice in the United States "judging by the advertisements of drug dealers in the most recent issues of American newspapers."

Shortly after Freud's "hymn of praise" stimulated medical interest in cocaine, his colleague Carl Koller discovered the drug's anesthetic value for eye surgery. The twenty-six-year-old Koller swiftly became famous (to Freud's chagrin) for showing that cocaine solution could completely anesthetize the surface of the eye, making possible painless ophthalmological surgery. By 1885, a much-truncated version of Freud's major review appeared in the *St. Louis Medical Journal*. That and Koller's discovery provoked a flood of interest in cocaine. Whereas the 1883 *Index Catalogue of the Library of the Surgeon General* listed a handful of medical articles on coca erythoxylon, a mere six years later, the 1889 edition overflowed with hundreds and hundreds of articles, filling nine pages and touching on every aspect of the drug.

And little wonder when one considers that respectable pharmaceutical firms such as Parke-Davis were promoting coca to physicians in 1885 with assurances that it would "make the coward brave, the silent eloquent, free the victims of alcohol and opium habit from their bondage, and, as an anesthetic render the sufferer insensitive to pain." Both doctors and dentists began enthusiastically trying out coca products for everything from melancholia to toothache to masturbation. The patent medicine industry swung into action, marketing hundreds of coca tonics, elixirs, and syrups promising to cure whatever ailed one, from sinus trouble and headaches to "sexual apathy" to "diseases of the blood."

Knowing the enormous popularity of the European coca wine cordial, Vin Mariani, enterprising Americans formulated the logical alternative for a temperance-minded society: coca-based soft drinks that promised to pep you up. Koca Nola, Celery Cola, Wiseola, Rocco Cola, Dope Cola, and Coca Cola (to name but a few) all billed themselves as ideal beverages for the tired masses, and delivered their punch with several milligrams of cocaine (about a third of a line). Powdered cocaine for snuffing became the official remedy of the Hay Fever Association. In 1906, an American population of 90 million consumed almost eleven tons of cocaine.

But even as Americans embraced cocaine in all its manifold guises, reports filtered in of cases of cocaine addiction and intoxication. Over in Europe, Dr. Freud was attacked roundly for his injudicious popularizing of what one doctor condemned as the "third scourge of mankind," especially for asserting that cocaine could cure opium addiction. Certainly, Freud had seen with his own eyes the fate of his beloved friend, the handsome and brilliant von Fleischl-Marxow. He had given up morphine, but was soon injecting huge doses of cocaine, suffering dreadful hallucinations of white snakes writhing over his body. Within seven years Fleischl-Marxow was dead. Freud would concede only that confirmed "morphinists" were prone to "cocainism."

This early dispute about cocaine, whether it was brain food or curse, was vividly illustrated in some of Sir Arthur Conan Doyle's early and wildly popular Sherlock Holmes tales. In *The Sign of Four*, set in the fall of 1888, the faithful Dr. Watson begins by describing the brilliant Holmes taking his

> bottle from the corner of the mantelpiece, and his hypodermic syringe from its neat morocco case. With his long, white nervous fingers he adjusted the delicate needle and rolled back his left shirtcuff. For some little time his eyes rested thoughtfully upon the sinewy forearm and wrist, all dotted and scarred with innumerable puncture-marks. . . .
>
> "Which is it today," I asked, "morphine or cocaine?"
>
> He raised his eyes languidly from the old black-letter volume which he had opened.
>
> "It is cocaine," he said, "a seven-percent solution. Would you care to try it?"

Watson chastises Holmes and warns that cocaine could damage him physically. Dr. Watson admonishes, "Surely the game is hardly worth the candle. Why should you, for a mere passing pleasure, risk the loss of those great powers with which you have been endowed?"

Holmes replies, "My mind rebels at stagnation. Give me problems, give me work, give me the most abstruse cryptogram, or the most intricate analysis, and I am in my own proper atmosphere. I can then dispense with artificial stimulants."

The dispute over cocaine—useful medicine or addictive scourge—dragged on throughout the late 1880s and 1890s. After all, no less a personage than Dr. William Alexander Hammond, Surgeon General of the U.S. Army at age thirty-five (albeit dismissed under a cloud by Lincoln), an international neurological authority, author, playwright, director of his own private hospital in Washington, D.C., strongly endorsed cocaine in the most glowing terms. As the good doctor told a meeting of the New York Neurological Society in late 1886, not only had cocaine been most beneficial and effective for a variety of patients, he himself had tried it and found it akin to several glasses of champagne. As for the so-called cocaine habit, it was no worse than the caffeine habit.

Another society member, Dr. J. B. Mattison of Brooklyn, rose from the audience to strongly suggest that the great doctor was misguided, pointing out that in the past few months alone he personally had in his care seven cases of the cocaine habit, five physicians and two druggists. His patients had suffered hallucinations, delusions, and marked emaciation. In general, Dr. Mattison was already convinced that cocaine addiction was worse than morphine addiction. And so it went, back and forth.

Certainly one of the most notorious cases of cocaine addiction was that of Dr. William Halsted, a socially prominent New York surgeon who was famed not only for his medical skill but for his vivacious personality and exuberance. Trained in Europe, Halsted was thrilled by the news of Carl Koller's work using cocaine as an anesthetic and promptly launched his own experiments in late 1884 with injected cocaine, seeking to find whether it worked as an anesthetic on other parts of the body. He enlisted numerous friends and colleagues, and the consequences were swift and devastating. Several doctors, including Halsted, became addicted.

One need only read a small bit of Halsted's one short article about cocaine to sense the disaster. This surgeon, author of dozens of articles admired for their clarity and precision, composed the following: "Neither indifferent as to which of how many possibilities may best explain, nor yet at a loss to comprehend, why surgeons have, and that so many, quite without discredit, could have exhibited scarcely any interest in what, as a local anesthetic. . . ."

From one year to the next, this rising surgical star with appointments at the city's best hospitals, the jolly companion whose elegant townhouse was the scene of much merriment, had suffered a social disintegration, becoming a strange and remote recluse. Several of Halsted's colleagues would die of their cocaine habits. Perhaps fearing the same fate for Halsted, his friend Dr. William Welch hurried north from Baltimore (where he was establishing the Johns Hopkins Hospital) and spirited the broken Halsted away in a schooner to the Windward Islands, hoping to end the cocaine habit. During the next few years, a strange and subdued Halsted worked quietly in Baltimore at a Hopkins laboratory between stays at the Butler Psychiatric Hospital in Providence, Rhode Island. Somewhere along the line, Dr. Halsted substituted a morphine habit for the cocaine habit.

While Dr. Halsted remained as remote and eccentric as ever, he returned to the operating table and established himself as one of the brilliant surgeons of modern medicine, becoming chairman of the Johns Hopkins Department of Surgery. Nevertheless, he still disappeared without explanation for long periods and secluded himself each summer in remote European hotels. The bon vivant was gone forever. His addiction remained the great secret of his career, unrevealed until 1969 when a "secret history" of the hospital was opened.

However hushed-up Halsted's habit was, there were other more spectacular cocaine collapses in the medical world that put to rest the issue once and for all. By 1898, the *Medical News* prominently featured a six-page article on "The Abuse and Dangers of Cocain [sic]," detailing all the possible clinical pitfalls, including the "development of the cocain [sic] habit." Numerous cases were cited, including a physician who developed "an irresistible craving for the drug and abandoned himself entirely to its toxic influence. He lost his practice, squandered his property, and was brought to the brink of ruin. After four attempts at abstinence within two years he finally succeeded, but still remains an attendent at the asylum where he was treated." The journal author ended the article by flatly declaring, "cocaine should never be placed in the hands of the patient under any circumstances, as the habit is so easily acquired."

Despite the enormous hopes it had aroused, cocaine turned out to have only one truly valuable medical purpose: as a local anesthetic. It had not made the cowardly brave or the silent eloquent, and it had certainly not freed those in bondage to opium and alcohol. In fact, it had turned out to be thoroughly addicting in its own way.

As the twentieth century began, Americans and their doctors, who had enthusiastically embraced the beneficial effects first of opiates and then cocaine, had very gradually come to recognize that the possible price of these wonder drugs was a new kind of thralldom: drug addiction. Understandably, there was rising concern about the American appetite for habit-forming drugs. So much so that public attention was now focused on a major but hidden source of opiates and cocaine—the ubiquitous and extremely popular patent medicines.

With the excesses of the Gilded Age giving way to the reform spirit of the Progressive era, "muckraking" journalists began in the early years of the new century to investigate the nation's festering social problems: the horrific city slums, rampant prostitution, the brutal labor exploitation of small children, and the overall corruption of the body politic. The rising tide of drug use naturally attracted attention, especially the role of the huge and lucrative patent medicine industry. Most Americans had not a clue that the vast array of heavily promoted soothing syrups and cures were loaded with opiates and/or cocaine. The homey and reassuring-looking boxes and bottles usually offered little hint of the active ingredients. Given that the dangers of opiates and cocaine were well established in the medical world, this was an outrageous and insidious deception. Worse yet, the nation's newspapers, deeply beholden to the patent medicine industry's copious advertising, displayed no interest at all in enlightening their readers. To doubly ensure that craven journalistic silence, patent medicine advertising contracts actually stipulated that they would be canceled if any state law were passed affecting the industry.

It was only when that greatest of muckrakers, Samuel Hopkins Adams, began exposing the villainy of the industry in 1905 in *Collier's Weekly* that horrified Americans learned how they had been regularly dosing themselves (and often their children) with significant amounts of opiates and cocaine. And the lowest of the low among the patent medicine quacks, declared Adams, were those occupying the very bottom of this "noisome pit of charlantanry," the "drug habit specialists." In any newspaper or magazine of the day one could easily find their come-ons, typically along the confident lines of: "Opium, morphine, cocaine habits absolutely cured." So promised the Coats Cure, which like most was a mail-order outfit. Adams wrote in and received the "remedy" by mail. Availing himself of a chemist, Adams showed that Coats Cure contained a whopping 2.5 grains of morphine per dose.

Or there were the more elaborate and genteel ads, such as that for the Richie Co. of Brooklyn. Picturing a kindly looking minister (conveniently deceased), it featured this endorsement: "The suffering caused by the Johnstown Flood is not to be compared to that caused by Drug Habit. The Richie Cure is an effective remedy for the Drug Habit." Adams and his chemists demonstrated that the Richie Cure—along with every single other drug habit remedy he bought—contained morphine.

Presumably the extraordinary furor that followed Adams's exposé shamed the nation's newspapers into action. That same year, *The National Druggist* complained that "while the daily newspapers of the country, from one end to the other, teem with articles on the 'cocaine evil,' or the 'morphine habit,' or the 'narcotic curse' . . . [n]o hint is given that ninety-nine druggists out of every hundred . . . bitterly condemn the trade, and despise and loathe the men guilty of engaging in it."

Between Adams's scandalous revelations about dangerous patent medicines and Sinclair Lewis's exposé of unsafe food in his novel *The Jungle*, Progressive reformers rode a wave of middle-class outrage to enact the federal Pure Food and Drug Act in 1906. During the Congressional debate, one legislator declaimed, "For every case of ptomaine poisoning from meat, there are a hundred cases of poisoning from hurtful drugs masquerading as helpful medicines." A landmark piece of reform, this federal law forced manufacturers of patent medicines for the first time to reveal drug content above a certain amount. The middle class now learned just how many of its favorite nostrums were heavily laced with cocaine and opiates. And so in one fell swoop, federal legislation eliminated a significant source of inadvertent genteel drug use. A great many patent medicine brands either removed drugs altogether, cut down the dose, or went out of business. Several weeks after the new law had gone into effect, the *New York Times* remarked, "The operation of the new law in the grocery and the liquor store is trifling compared with the widespread effects of the act on manufacturers of patent medicines."

Public health officials would later conclude that in 1900 about 250,000 Americans in a population of 75 million were opiate addicts, or about one American in three hundred. As for cocaine addicts, in 1902 the American Pharmaceutical Association estimated there were about 200,000, or 1 American in 375. Assuming there was some overlap in these two groups of addicts, one might guess that at the turn of the century, 1 American in about 200 was a drug addict. And the bulk of these were genteel, middle-class women.

CHAPTER 2

"Had the Dope Habit
and Had It Bad."

—From "Willie the Weeper,"
VAUDEVILLE SONG (C. 1904)

In 1895 William Rosser Cobbe, a former navy chaplain and longtime medical opiate addict, complained that the United States was too complacent about addicts because they were mainly well-behaved ladies, "the noblest and best brought low." He predicted, "If opium habitués were noisy, demonstrative, brutal, wicked, and criminal, they would excite legislation and popular hostility." And indeed, when society became aware of a growing subterranean world of pleasure users—initially mainly opium smokers—they were viewed with nothing but contempt and loathing. Cobbe, the educated morphine addict, denounced opium smoking in no uncertain terms: "It is entered into with deliberation. The surroundings are always repulsive and the inmates of these resorts are criminals or petty offenders against police regulations. They are ignorant, illiterate, vulgar, brutal, and wicked." Even one of Chicago's most notorious barons of vice, Bathhouse John Coughlin, drew the line at "hop": "Opium-smoking don't go in the First Ward." Like Cobbe, he thought it beyond the pale.

Nor was "hitting the pipe" tolerated in the most rip-roaring mining town of the Wild West, the nationally notorious Deadwood, South

Dakota. Deadwood gloried in its depraved reputation for wide-open brothels, saloons, anything-goes gambling, and street brawls. But when the Deadwood sheriff's office learned in 1877 that ten opium dens were thriving not just on the patronage of the usual Chinese, but whites too, this caused "scandal even among the reckless adventurous spirits . . . of a rich mining camp."

The Deadwood deputy sheriff marched over to the Sin Lee Laundry to conduct an undercover investigation. There he found a Chinese in "a gaily coloured quilted silk robe with wide-flowing sleeves, wide trousers, and shoes peculiar to this race of people, standing behind the primitive counter." The deputy paid a half dollar sack of gold dust and "our Celestial friend produced a card, on which he placed a very small quantity of opium, and called an attendant to conduct us to a smoke room." Entering a small, murky pine-board room with simple pallets, the deputy was almost overcome by stale opium smoke. Exploring further, he found room after room with "one, two, three, and sometimes four 'fiends' of both sexes, either dreaming off the effects of the deadly drug, or else smoking." Fearful of this seductive substance that would quickly "rob a [white] man of all semblance of manhood," Deadwood shuttered the dens.

As this story suggests, Chinese immigrants introduced opium dens to America. Arriving originally to work the California gold rush of the 1850s, the Chinese soon fanned out across the nation, armies of lonely, single sojourners settling in impoverished enclaves offering cheap lodging, fan-tan gambling, prostitution, and spartan opium dens. Perhaps because the Chinese appeared so insular and alien, no whites seem to have ventured into a Chinatown den for a good twenty years. Or so concluded one H. H. Kane, who in 1882 tried to trace how opium smoking among whites got started. Kane credited "a sporting character named Glendenyn" as the first American to smoke opium back in California in 1868. From there, this new vice spread swiftly among the white sporting demimonde, a raucous world of gamblers, prostitutes, sharpers, and theatrical types.

In 1877, the same year that Deadwood shuttered its dens, a Dr. Winslow Anderson of San Francisco reported in alarm that a large proportion of that city's white sporting class, or demimonde—perhaps as many as ten thousand people—had taken up smoking opium, "hitting the pipe" as often as three times a day. The doctor reported "the sickening sight of young white girls from sixteen to twenty years of age lying half-undressed on the floor or couches, smoking with their 'lovers.' Men and women, Chinese and white people, mix indiscriminately in Chinatown smoking houses."

Thoroughly alarmed by this development, San Francisco had passed the first antidrug law in the United States, an 1875 city ordinance aimed squarely at the ever more popular opium-smoking dens of Chinatown. For several years a floating white underworld had patronized the dens, and by the time local authorities cottoned on, the gamblers, thieves, and prostitutes were being joined there by otherwise respectable white people out for exotic adventure. When an investigation convinced city leaders that innocents experimenting with opium smoking were being "ruined morally and otherwise," they began using vagrancy laws and something called the Cubic Air Ordinance to discourage addicts and opium dens, and then passed a tough law "forbidding the practice [for whites] under penalty of a heavy fine or imprisonment, or both."

Within a few years San Francisco police had ended "the visits of white men and girls to opium hells in Chinatown." (No one cared if the Chinese smoked opium as long as they kept the habit and their hands to themselves.) But nonetheless, wrote the supervisor of San Francisco's Methodist Chinese Mission in 1892, "the vice is spreading amongst depraved white people of both sexes . . . carried on in private houses or in rooms secretly kept by white people."

From his own window he could see into a nearby house occupied by "two dissolute-looking young white women, upon whose besotted faces opium has stamped its indelible brand. . . . The window shade is sometimes up and I can see a bed, an opium tray and lamp. The light falls upon the faces of a young man and a young woman reclining near, with opium pipes in their hands." As a missionary in China, the supervisor had seen firsthand how opium smokers "lost all capacity for business and interest in work. . . . If you discover[ed] your domestic servant to be an opium smoker, go and count your spoons at once, and send him off." The easy availability of opium in China had led a good third of the population to smoke opium regularly, with half of those becoming hopeless "sots."

Similar circumstances unfolded again and again across the nation. In Virginia City, Nevada, as elsewhere, the sporting classes and demimonde happily embraced opium smoking and then were joined by a "younger class of boys and girls, many of the latter of the more respected class of families. The habit grew very rapidly, until it reached young women of more mature age." At that point, the city stepped in with an ordinance against opium smoking. When, as in San Francisco, that proved inadequate to quell the fast-spreading habit, the state legislature enacted yet harsher laws, aimed not just at smokers, but at those keeping dens. What roused civic ire was not Chinese immigrants' opium smoking, but the patronage of their opium dens by whites.

And even then it was not as much the fact that low white characters were degrading themselves further as it was the alarming participation of curious but otherwise respectable youth. Ultimately, twenty state legislatures—from Alaska to Connecticut—felt compelled to shield citizens and society by specifically outlawing smoking opium and opium dens. In 1892 the American Medical Association worried about rising imports of smoking opium (as opposed to medicinal opiates) since "its sole uses are as an intoxicant or as an aid to the perpetration of illegal and vicious acts. . . . The time has come to call a halt, and if necessary to prohibit the entry of the material altogether."

All over nineteenth-century America, whether in the booming big cities or frontier towns, so-called tenderloins and red-light districts served up a variety of not-so-genteel diversions and entertainments— powerful whiskey, loose women, high-stakes gambling—for men rich and ragged. The desperate plight of the Gilded Age lower classes guaranteed an endless supply of whores, pimps, gamblers, and thugs to service the sin districts that catered to human greed, lust, and loneliness. While shrewd robber barons such as Carnegie and Morgan and Gould accumulated vast riches, the immigrant poor—the Irish, the Italians, the Eastern Europeans (Christian and Jewish)—flooded daily off the boats and struggled to survive. Many floated into the hardscrabble and exciting life of gambling, sex for sale, vaudeville, and crime.

Muckraker Jacob Riis revealed to middle-class America in 1890 just how brutalizing that struggle could be. His reports and photographs from the ghastly tenements of New York, an instant classic called *How the Other Half Lives*, showed how those teeming, filthy, airless warrens were "the hot-beds of epidemics that carry death to rich and poor alike; the nurseries of pauperism and crime that fill our jails and police courts; that throw off scum of forty thousand human wrecks a year to the island asylums and workhouses year by year; that turned out in the last eight years a round half million beggars to prey upon our charities; that maintain a standing army of tramps with all that implies." From such tough precincts as these—whether in New York, Chicago, or a thousand smaller locales—emerged the citizens of the sporting world and vice districts.

The denizens of this itinerant underworld found smoking opium to be a companionable and novel form of intoxication, best learned in the relaxed social setting of the disreputable den. Preparing and cooking crude opium for the long bamboo pipe was something of an art, usually performed by resident "chefs." (Americans called the gooey black opium "dope," a generic term of the time—derived from the Dutch word *doop* for sauce—that applied to anything thick and viscous.) Neophytes to the den were shown how to smoke laying on the hip, and introduced to all the rituals and accoutrements described by precise Chinese argot: the *yen hop* was a box that contained the "cheffing" paraphernalia; the *sui dow* was a sponge for cleaning the pipe; the *yen yen* described the physical craving of the addict, etc. Solidarity was instantaneous.

The appeal of smoking opium was eloquently described by H. H. Kane, who tried smoking himself. Six to ten pipes would evoke "a condition of dreamy wakefulness . . . a state in which the devotee feels himself on a stratum above his fellowmen and their pursuits—at peace with himself and all mankind—a pleasant, listless calm and contentment steals over him. . . . This waking dream, this silken garment of the imagination, will take its shape and its coloring from the most cherished and most brilliant strands . . . and puts out of sight the real and unpleasant crudities of life." However, this honeymoon did not last long. Kane was just as eloquent in describing the pitfalls. He warned sternly, "Then the good spirit of the pipe disappears, giving place to a demon who binds his victim hand and foot."

By the turn of the century, opium dens had become commonplace throughout America. In the fall of 1886, after Denver police raided a den, a reporter from the *Denver Daily News* was dispatched to dig up more on this exotic and supposedly outlawed vice. He easily located several bustling Chinese-run "joints." He concluded that "the number of slaves to the hop habit in Denver" was 145, with 27 of those being women. "The habit is principally confined to gamblers and prostitutes, though there are at least six who move in different walks of life."

The reporter made the acquaintance of a loquacious former "hophead" who confided, "An opium smoker is a peculiar creature. He will pawn the clothes from his back for money to buy the drug. He will do even worse—steal, lie or betray any confidence for half a dollar with which to replenish the empty 'hop toy.' . . . They are a society in themselves and care nothing for the outside world. A fiend full of 'hop' is as happy as a clam at high tide."

Reformers visiting New York City's Chinatown in 1901 reported that local cigar and cigarette stores were generally fronts for opium dens. At one Mott Street brothel, American girls could be "seen in nude forms, some of them in their undershirts, others in short silk dresses which come to their knees and then their long stockings, all smoking cigarettes or long pipes which I was informed had opium in them. . . . In all these places the prostitutes have opium and pipes and charge 25 cents for smoking." On that same visit, one Annie Gilroy offered to show the reformers an opium den "where society women from the uptown districts—some women from families of refinement—were reclining on couches under the influence of opium and generally had the bosoms of their dress open." (One wonders if this was one of the fake dens expressly operated to titillate voyeuristic tourists into visiting the sin districts.)

But in fin de siècle New York, one did not have to travel to Chinatown to find opium dens. In 1896 writer Stephen Crane described how, before the "hammer of reform struck," whole streets in the midtown tenderloin were lined with opium dens. "Splendid 'joints' were not uncommon then in New York," he advised. "There was one on Forty-second Street which would have been palatial if it were not for the bad taste of the decorations. An occasional man from Fifth Avenue or Madison Avenue would there have his private 'layout,' an elegant equipment of silver, ivory, gold." Crane estimated that there were twenty-five thousand regular opium smokers in Manhattan, which then had about a million and a half residents.

Somehow, there was great irony in all this. For throughout the latter decades of the nineteenth century, Americans had continually berated doctors and patent-medicine makers for creating armies of innocent addicts by too casual attitudes toward opiates and cocaine. The typical addict memoir, such as a *McClure's* article titled "In the Gray Land of Drugs," inevitably featured the careless physician, as in, "Months earlier a doctor had left them [morphine tablets] with me, saying I might take one in an extreme case." Years of these cautionary tales and much firsthand experience had finally driven home the very real dangers of inadvertent addiction from medical treatment. Doctors and patients alike became much more cautious, while the Pure Food and Drug Act of 1906 forced unscrupulous patent-medicine makers to reveal the heavy doses of opiates and cocaine, allowing upright consumers to avoid these products. Now, society was faced with people who wanted drugs, a whole new group of users who purposefully pursued the pleasurable sensation of the altered state. And opium smoking was just the beginning.

In 1896, a St. Louis physician described the disturbing advent of a backroom "cocaine joint" in a local drugstore. A woman reporter who had peeked into the dimly lit rear had been able to make out a dozen prostitutes, black and white, sprawled about snuffing pulverized cocaine crystals. When they wanted more, they rang the bell and the clerk came out with another ten-cent purchase wrapped in white paper. The physician did not doubt that this was just the visible tip of a whole new kind of debauchery.

And one worse than alcohol. For as *Everyday Life* pointed out, "A drunkard may retain his moral equilibrium between debauches; a libertine may have ideals apart from his indulgences; but the 'dope fiend,' once thoroughly addicted, inevitably drops into utter debasement." The fact was that drug addiction could rapidly become a full-time and debilitating matter. Unlike an alcoholic, an addict was not only out of it while high, but also tended to be highly preoccupied in between drug sessions with securing his or her next dose or the money to purchase it.

By 1900, Chattanooga, Tennessee, had an infamous area known as "Cocaine Alley . . . a den of vice and filth." One concerned pharmacist making a nocturnal inspection there reported hundreds of blacks and a few whites, many milling around "snuffing" small bits of cocaine, while others lay around "in every conceivable state of depravity." The *American Druggist* also expressed concern about "the widespread addiction of the colored and vicious white population of the larger cities to cocaine and other narcotic drugs. . . . Many lives have been wrecked."

Southern blacks apparently first began using cocaine in New Orleans, where longshoremen found the drug could help them tolerate the "extraordinarily severe work of loading and unloading steamboats, at which, perhaps, for seventy hours at a stretch, they have to work without sleep or rest, in rain, in cold, and in heat. . . . Whiskey did not answer and cocaine appeared to be the thing needed." White bosses throughout the South were soon routinely supplying it to black crews hired for the backbreaking work of picking cotton and building railroads and levees. When the drug moved from being a work aid to an after-hours high at juke joints and parties, providing what a medical journal called a "coke drunk," the consequences were not long in coming. As one blues song of the time declared, "Well, that cocaine habit is might' bad. It kill ev-ybody I know it to have had." Once southern sheriffs began complaining that cocaine-crazed Negroes were running amok, forcing the law to shift to higher caliber bullets to contain the menace, the enthusiasm of whites palled.

Up in the fast-growing northern cities with their mushrooming tenement slums, the sporting classes who had patronized the opium dens for a good decade were also busy experimenting with cocaine. For while cocaine had first been available to the public initially as an expensive elixir infused into liquid coca wines and syrups, by the turn of the century cocaine manufacture had been so perfected that it was sold in various cheap, powdered products, especially the catarrh remedies. In New York City, Birney's Catarrh Cure, with its cocaine content as high as 5 percent, became extremely popular, and not for its advertised purpose of calming inflamed noses and throats. The white powder "cure" with its eight grains of cocaine came handily packaged in a small glass bottle with a glass tube and rubber hose to snuff the powder. Local cocaine addicts became known as "Birney blowers" and the disreputable Lafayette Hotel at West Fortieth Street and Seventh Avenue even had a Birney Tree in its back room, fancifully bedecked with tiny discarded black rubber hoses. Some prostitutes explained to an inquisitive reformer that "they had used drugs because it gave them a wonderful feeling and helped to pass away hours when they became too pensive."

In Chicago, veteran policemen observed in amazement the sudden vogue among the white sporting classes for cocaine and morphine. These new-style addicts flocked to certain drugstores on the West Side levee, there to openly snuff cocaine or shoot it up by syringe. "It produces an extravagant feeling of buoyancy and well-being," noted one observer, and "is very attractive to persons who are unfortunate and despondent." Another explained that cocaine created "a mood of well-being and expensiveness, a dream of unlimited wealth and power, a feeling of nonchalant cheerfulness." With abstention from the drug one felt a "great emotional longing, a profound depression, a bitter homesickness which only more cocaine will relieve." Before long Chicago cracked down, assigning a plainclothes detective to police the pharmacies and keep track of the city's growing legions of sporting-world dope fiends (estimated at eight thousand).

But what was far more alarming than the perhaps predictable appetite of the sporting classes for "hitting the pipe" and "blowing the Birney," was the growing enthusiasm for recreational drugs among plain working-class boys. In 1904, Chicago social activist Jane Addams watched in horror as neighborhood kids who had grown up in and around Hull House became cocaine addicts. She was haunted by one case of a "vivacious boy . . . animated and joyous and promising. . . . When I last saw him in his coffin, it was impossible to connect that haggard shriveled body with what I had known before." Hull House campaigned successfully to end the outright sale of pure cocaine, but the infamous catarrh powders were still in every drugstore.

So, for instance, in 1909 the dean of the Chicago's Cathedral of Saints Peter and Paul watched out his rectory window as local youths openly snorted Gray's Catarrh Powder with its eight grains of cocaine. Each morning the trim rectory lawn was strewn with hundreds of small empty Gray's vials. Elsewhere in Chicago's squalid "dope district," empty catarrh bottles were scooped up by the bucketful from the gutters. Cocaine consumption was soaring. By 1907, U.S. coca leaf imports had risen twentyfold over what they had been in 1900.

The Pure Food and Drug Act was effective mainly for alerting those who *wanted* to avoid drugs. The infamous catarrh powders, such as Birney's and Gray's, now just stated forthrightly on their labels: "Eight grains of cocaine hydrochloride to the ounce." (This translates to about 4 or 5 percent purity, comparable to the street cocaine of the 1980s.) Some brands had even greater amounts. And while conscientious druggists now shunned the catarrh powders, not wishing to traffick in something grown so notorious, the expanding ranks of cocaine addicts—the Birney blowers and Graymen—simply found others less scrupulous. Enterprising street peddlers took to selling "bindles" of cocaine in pool rooms and public parks. Cocaine, once celebrated as a brain food and overall tonic, was falling into thorough disrepute. In 1907, the makers of Maltine Coca Wine informed the FDA that they were withdrawing this product "because all the cocaine preparations are getting into such bad odor. . . . We feel it would hurt our other products to have a coca wine on the market."

In 1909 *Everyday Life* lamented, "In every slum it [cocaine] is the favorite 'dope': it leads men and women, boys and girls, into the stews [brothels], and it keeps them there. . . . Squalor, poverty, starvation, theft, prostitution and murder: these are the inevitable concomitants of cocaine." It described one twenty-four-year-old man, "fairly intelligent and decently bred," whose forays to the tenderloin had involved him in cocaine. He left Chicago to work on a farm and escape the drug's allure. After three years, he returned to Chicago. "Two hours after he reached the city, he was 'floating' madly, his savings all invested in a store of cocaine. He had gone back to the drug like a homing pigeon." In 1917, the Provincetown Players, who prided themselves on dramatizing real life, put on a play by Pendleton King called *Cocaine: A Play in One Act*. The characters were a down-and-out fighter named Joe and a journalist-turned-whore named Nora earnestly discussing their desperate need for a "blow" of cocaine.

Soon, the vaudeville houses were poking fun at addicts in songs such as "Willy the Weeper":

Did you ever hear about Willy the Weeper,
Willie the Weeper, yes, the chimney sweeper,
Had the dope habit and had it bad,
Listen and I'll tell you 'bout the dream he had.

"Got a ruby-bush, a diamond-mine,
An emerald-tree, a sapphire-vine
Hundreds of railroads that run for miles,
A thousand dollars' worth of coke stacked up in piles."

But in the morning, where am I at?
I thought I was in my sweet baby's flat.
But in the morning I'm right in line.
Mister Hop Sing Toy you're no friend of mine.

Willie the Weeper and his ilk had alarmed American society sufficiently so that many cities and states finally concluded that, as with smoking opium, they had little choice but to pass antidrug legislation. There was a general rising concern about the American appetite for habit-forming drugs in all their guises. Historian David Courtwright has estimated that in 1896 70 million Americans were consuming almost seventy thousand pounds of medicinal opiates annually. Not to mention the 230,000 pounds of imported opium that were smoked. Contrast that to Europe, where 60 million Germans were consuming only seventeen thousand pounds of medicinal opiates. Or 33 million Italians consuming only six thousand pounds. Why was Europe so different? Essentially because those nations had strong centralized governments that exercised strict controls on drugs. The United States had no controls at all. American doctors and druggists prescribed however they pleased. Unlike Europe, drugs were available readily to Americans for the asking, whether through physicians, druggists, or the mails. It was the old story. Where drugs are plentiful, plenty will be used and abused.

No one could possibly attribute America's large drug imports to legitimate medical use. This meant, concluded the American Pharmaceutical Association (APA), that far too many druggists were abusing their right to sell whatever drugs they wished and "pandering to this most unfortunate, this man-destroying appetite." Consequently, the APA announced that it now was backing some kind of uniform and restrictive narcotic and cocaine legislation in every state. It also joined the AMA in proposing the "absolute suppression" of smoking opium by ending all imports.

In New York State, legislators were pressed to act on cocaine in the spring of 1907, making it legally available only through a doctor's prescription. "Over four thousand letters of friends and relatives of cocaine takers in New York have been received. . . . On the Lower East Side the habit is said to be spreading rapidly." By 1910, virtually every city and state had antidrug laws. Which is not to say they were well enforced or highly effective. But they expressed society's belief that cocaine and the opiates, when used outside of legitimate medical practice, constituted a "drug habit evil." Typical were raids made in 1907 by Newark, New Jersey, police to arrest a hundred cocaine dealers after it was found that schoolboys were snuffing coke. As authorities cracked down and made both smoking opium and cocaine harder to get, those seeking altered states began turning to another product of the pharmacopoeia, one that was still legal and reasonably affordable: heroin.

Introduced in 1898 by the Fredrich Bayer Company of Eberfeld, Germany, heroin was an essence of morphine whose name was a play on the German word *heroisch*, meaning powerful. Heroin was marketed all over Europe and the United States, often in tandem with Bayer's other popular preparation, aspirin. A typical Bayer ad for heroin billed it as "a respiratory stimulant, sedative, expectorant and analgesic in the treatment of coughs, bronchitis, laryngitis, pneumonia, dyspnoea, phthisis, corzya, whooping cough, asthma, hay fever, colds, etc." Free samples were liberally available to doctors and druggists.

The greatest pharmaceutical emphasis—in this era before antibiotics and basic public health measures—was on anything effective against the respiratory diseases that were both rampant and deadly. Consequently, when pharmacologist Heinrich Dreser of Bayer synthesized this new essence of morphine, diacetylmorphine, that seemed to have a sedating effect on hacking coughs and no habituating qualities, he had high hopes. Diacetylmorphine had actually first been synthesized in 1874 by C. R. Alder, who reported it in the London *Journal of the Chemical Society*, but nothing more had come of it.

But now Dreser, seeing diacetylmorphine's effects in animal studies, believed the drug could quiet the chronic wracking cough that plagued victims of pneumonia and tuberculosis, the most deadly diseases of the day. When a local doctor tried it out in a nearby factory clinic, he got a very favorable response from the sixty patients. "Immediately after taking the powder, I felt relief," reported one. "I had to cough a lot less and in general the cough improved a great deal." Dr. Floret of the clinic found it very effective on his own hacking cough.

And so it was a highly gratified Dreser who traveled to Dusseldorf in 1898 for the seventieth congress of German naturalists and physicians. There he delivered a paper describing diacetylmorphine as a marvelously effective treatment of respiratory diseases, ten times more potent than codeine in stilling chronic cough and respiratory discomforts. A major advantage of diacetylmorphine over codeine, he explained, was that it was not habit forming.

In America, one of the earliest champions of heroin was Dr. Morris Manges of Mount Sinai Hospital in New York. He found the drug to be just as promised, and his article "Treatment of Coughs With Heroin," in an 1898 issue of the *New York Medical Journal*, reported that "the remedy was very prompt and effacacious in a large number of cases."

Just as important to conscientious physicians of the day was the fact that "apparently there was no habituation to the drug."

Between Bayer's aggressive marketing and the genuine need for a powerful cough suppressant, heroin was soon a commonly used medication. In 1900 Dr. Manges weighed in with a second enthusiastic report based on a survey of 141 doctors around the country. They considered heroin to be a "valuable remedy for allaying coughs, especially in pharyngitis, laryngitis, bronchitis, pulmonary tuberculosis, and emphysema." At the end of his thorough review, Dr. Manges briefly cautioned that "habituation has been noted in a small percentage (six to eight) of the cases. . . . All observers are agreed, however, that none of the patients suffer in any way from this habituation, and that none of the symptoms which are so characteristic of chronic morphinism have ever been observed."

Three years later, drug addiction specialist Dr. George E. Pettey minced no words in his call to alarm: "The Heroin Habit: Another Curse" in *The Alabama Medical Journal*. He had noticed that among 150 patients with drug habits under his treatment, eight were heroin addicts, including three who he started off on it. "I am prepared to say that the prolonged use of Heroin does result in the formation of a habit and that when that habit is formed it is to all intents and purposes the opium habit."

Typical of these patients was a woman who was given heroin every four to six hours for "relief of cough in incipient phthisis." Her doctor noticed he had to increase the dose over time to allay the cough. After seven months on the daily cough medication the patient was faring well, and so the physician ended the heroin treatment. Within hours the doctors recognized all the classic signs of opiate withdrawal: restlessness, nausea, shooting pains through the legs and back, profuse sweating.

By 1906, heroin was officially recognized as yet another addictive form of opium. The *Journal of the American Medical Association* (*JAMA*) warned its readers that with heroin "the habit is readily formed and leads to the most deplorable results." However, practitioners of medicine were still so professionally fragmented that many doctors— having prescribed heroin with no untoward results—resisted the warning that it was addictive. Why were so many doctors unconvinced? Unlike morphine, heroin was generally taken not by syringe, but orally, meaning that addiction occurred gradually. Furthermore, since many heroin users had chronic conditions, there was no reason to stop taking the drug and exhibit withdrawal symptoms. Consequently, it would be a few more years before the revised status of heroin as an addictive narcotic warranting careful use was accepted completely.

And while overall consumption of opiates and cocaine was declining thanks to growing restrictions, by 1912 the first full-fledged reports of street use of heroin began to roll in. A Cleveland doctor felt impelled to report in *JAMA* that "heroin is being used extensively by means of 'snuffing' in the tenderloin districts of large cities. . . . [One young patient] said he knew at least twenty of his associates, many of whom work at soda-water fountains in drugstores, who used the drug in this manner."

In June 1913 the *New York Times* reported that "scores" of young men in the Morrisania section of the Bronx (a neighborhood of immigrants who had escaped the slums of lower Manhattan) were addicted to heroin. These youths were known to "sneak into hallways with small quantities of the drug and sniff it up their noses." Of four young men picked up by police, one was a clerk and the other three had no occupation. Too many of the new addicts seemed unable to maintain even menial jobs once they got going with drugs.

Then, at the end of 1913, physicians speaking at a Philadelphia medical meeting on the study of alcohol and other narcotics described growing drug use, as reported by the *New York Times* in an article headlined SAY DRUG HABIT GRIPS THE NATION. A Boston doctor spoke of "the ravages of a new drug which, he said, was making victims by the hundred in his own city. This new chemical is called heroin . . . and is sold so openly in one district . . . that it has become known as 'heroin square.' "

Just as Ella O'Neill or Dr. Halsted typified the old-fashioned genteel morphine addicts with their private habits, so fifteen-year-old Leroy Street of New York typified the new-style heroin addict—the city boys who gathered together on stoops and in local pool rooms and used drugs socially for enjoyment. Street, the son of a postman, first sampled "happy dust" in 1910, viewing it as a rather daring and cosmopolitan venture.

When Street took his first "blow," he "expected something very stimulating, a feeling of excitement and joy. Actually the reaction was much more insidious, a smug complacency that began to steal over me in the most delightful manner." After a month of using heroin, he was hooked, regularly "snuffing" heroin and then also cocaine. It was an easy enough matter to buy pure Bayer heroin tablets in small bottles, crush them, and dilute them somewhat with lactose, or the sugar from milk. All told, Street guessed, a hundred other kids from his West Village neighborhood became addicted. These were by no means the usual fodder of the sporting world, but many ordinary boys whose days had typically centered around school and work and family. Now they gravitated toward other drug users, odd jobs, and the petty theft that fast became necessary to pay for their growing habits.

In Philadelphia, a doctor marveled in 1915 that the heroin habit was "a mushroom growth which has reached huge proportions in the congenial soil of the tenderloin within the last three years." A Brooklyn psychiatrist (or "alienist" as he billed himself) observed that the addicts hc had treated "appeared to be without ambition at their work and took less interest in life. It also seems to have occurred frequently that after a time the patients had to give up their positions because of their inability to do satisfactory work."

In 1916, psychiatrist Pearce Bailey concluded in *The New Republic*, "The heroin habit is essentially a matter of city life. . . . The majority are boys and young men who . . . seem to want something that promises to make life gayer and more enjoyable. . . . It would almost seem that their desire for something to brighten life up is at the bottom of their trouble and that heroin is but a means." He speculated that heroin had been discovered as a popular street drug after New York City police shuttered the opium smoking dens in 1909, and those original pleasure addicts had then switched to heroin.

CHAPTER 3

"The Congress

Should Take

Immediate Action

on the Antinarcotic

Legislation."

—*President William Howard Taft,*
December 1912

While the Pure Food and Drug
Act of 1906 had tackled the worst excesses of patent medicines heavily laced with opiates and cocaine, it would take another eight years for Congress to pass the first broad federal antidrug legislation, the Harrison Narcotic Act of 1914. Oddly enough, it was not the states or the national reform movements that launched the fight for federal antidrug laws and pushed them through. Instead, it was the U.S. State Department.

Why ever for? one might well ask. Initially, the State Department's surprising interest in drugs had everything to do with designs on the vast China market and currying favor. But it was also motivated by genuine altruism and the American desire to promote a better world. A handful of American reformers had trained their energies on the international scene, with widespread opium addiction in China (sustained by Western opium imports) a burning issue.

The origins of this unlikely crusade went back to our victory in the Spanish-American War of 1898. The United States happily had become a colonial power, assuming control of Puerto Rico, Guam, and the Philippines. In this last island nation, the Spanish had long had in place a government opium-smoking monopoly that sold only to the local Chinese. When future president William Howard Taft became civil governor of the Philippines, he appointed the local Episcopal bishop, one Charles Henry Brent, to visit other Asian countries and see how they handled opium smoking.

Ultimately, the Philippine situation was resolved by simply outlawing smoking opium. But along the way Brent and Taft decided the whole issue presented a great opportunity for the United States in the Far East, especially in China. After all, for years, the Dowager Empress and the Chinese government had made clear their fierce desire to end opium imports and attack rampant addiction among their people. (When the empress was warned that 3 million of her addict-subjects would surely die without opium, she declared the price well worth the larger benefit.)

China was a country of surpassing interest to the United States, for the simple capitalist reason that it represented the biggest market in the world. American businessmen had been eyeing the Chinese multitudes hungrily for years, but the British and the Europeans dominated the scene. Now American businessmen and reformers saw a natural opportunity to advance their respective causes by actively supporting China's desire to end all opium imports. In 1906 President Theodore Roosevelt endorsed this strategy for improving U.S. trade relations with China. As Dr. David Musto relates in *The American Disease*, thus began a long and circuitous path to active federal involvement in the drug problem on both an international and national level.

To demonstrate American sincerity in helping China suppress opium, the State Department proposed an international conference in Shanghai to discuss the issue. Up until this point, Bishop Brent was the principal instigator of events, a man who ardently believed it the duty of the European colonial powers to forswear this lucrative but debilitating trade. Being a man of the world, Brent also recognized that moral suasion would not sway the powerful, while commercial interests would.

It is here that Dr. Hamilton Kemp Wright, a dashing man with bristling mustachios and a fervid manner, entered the picture. Born in Ohio, young Wright grew up in Boston, earned his M.D. at McGill University in Montreal, and obtained further training as a researcher-pathologist first in Europe and then in Malaysia. He also served in "three crack Canadian regiments," earning a medal for his military service. Then, after a peripatetic and reasonably distinguished medical career, Wright settled in Washington with his wealthy, politically connected wife, Elizabeth Washburn Wright, and began a family.

Mrs. Wright, a Radcliffe College graduate, had traveled extensively in the Far East before she ever met her husband and married him in 1899 at age twenty-three. At age nineteen she had already authored a book of "impressions," titled *The Colour of the East*. But plans for a literary career soon gave way to visions of government service, perhaps inevitable considering her family background: her father, a Minneapolis industrialist, and three uncles had served in both the U.S. House and Senate. A Colonial Dame and staunch Republican, Mrs. Wright found when she settled in the nation's capital with her husband, two sons, and three daughters that she had a built-in network of powerful government friends. When her husband entered the political fray, she happily joined him.

The dashing Dr. Wright discovered his life's work almost accidentally one May morning in 1908. The good doctor was pleasantly strolling through Scott Circle when he ran into a *Chicago Tribune* reporter who asked if Wright was interested in being appointed to a new opium commission that was to organize an international conference on the opium problem. Apparently the journalist had heard Wright's name mentioned. Wright was looking for a worthy project, and so hustled down to the White House later that day to talk to President Roosevelt's secretary. The job was his.

With Bishop Brent in Manila and the third opium commissioner in Peking, it fell to Wright (aided always by his equally energetic wife) to pull together the American end of things. This he did with characteristic gusto, spending the lovely spring combing first the musty shelves of the Library of Congress and then the State Department files. There was ample information on the Chinese situation, for the history was well known and scandalous. Although contemporary Westerners assume opium smoking was an ancient Chinese tradition, it was not. As China scholar Jonathan Spence explained, "The habit of opium smoking in China was an offshoot and development of tobacco smoking," which did not become widespread in the celestial kingdom until the early eighteenth century. At that time, a weak opium goo was mixed with tobacco, a smoke known as *madak*. But once the British East India Company began importing large amounts of smoking opium to China in 1773, hoping to rectify a huge trade imbalance, the weaker *madak* was soon replaced by the purer product. The Manchu imperial court became extremely alarmed when in "1832 it was finally proven beyond doubt that opium addiction in certain parts of the army had become so serious that the troops were incapable of combat." In 1836 one high-placed Chinese official reported opium smoking "[had spread] to the mercantile classes [and] has gradually contaminated the inferior offi-cers, the military, and the scholars. Those who do not smoke are the common people of the villages and hamlets."

In 1840, as another history detailed, "the Chinese government, rec-ognizing the terrible ascendency the vice of opium-smoking, . . . [issued] an edict . . . by the emperor against the traffic in any form, and forbidding any vessel having opium on board to enter port."

When the British failed to comply, the Chinese seized and destroyed twenty thousand chests of opium worth $11 million. In this first Opium War, the victorious British compelled the Chinese to make restitution and allow the opium trade. In 1860, the British declared yet a second Opium War, this time forcing the Chinese, among other con-cessions, to legalize the trade. Now Chinese farmers began to expand vastly their own fields of opium poppies. "This domestic production," writes Spence, " . . . came to cater mainly to Chinese workers—espe-cially the coolie laborers, chair-bearers, and boatmen who seemed to have become addicted on a massive scale by the 1870s." So in fact, Chi-nese opium smoking was essentially a modern phenomenon, and the West's role in China's severe opium problem—many believed a third of the population smoked habitually, and that a half of those smokers were hopeless "sots"—had become a source of great shame. Helping China was an opportune means to promote American interests.

As the sweltering Washington summer heated up, Wright wrote up a general memorandum and sent it directly to President Roosevelt. This earned a severe rebuke from Secretary of State Elihu Root, who warned Wright (technically an employee of the Department of State) to go through proper channels in the future. To prepare for the Shanghai commission (now scheduled to begin the first day of 1909), the United States had requested that each attending nation provide information on its use and control of opium and coca. Wright, who had found plen-tiful material on China, had far more difficulty gathering comparable data for the United States. It didn't take long to appreciate the highly inconvenient truth. The United States had no national controls at all, nothing whatsoever on the federal level that limited or prohibited the importation, use, sale, or manufacture of opium or coca or any of their derivatives.

This was an uncomfortable situation for the State Department, but completely consonant with the nature of American governance then, for states at this period still retained exclusive police powers. That being the case, it was natural that American restrictions on drug use were expressed through a patchwork of municipal and state laws. Nonetheless, this presented a diplomatic problem. Secretary of State Elihu Root worried that other countries would point to America's lack of central controls as evidence that the United States was not serious about opium. He felt it imperative to have in hand some sort of national antidrug legislation before the Shanghai meeting. Congressional leaders believed it would not be too difficult to ban the importation of all smoking opium. And so, under the proddings of the State Department, the Smoking Opium Exclusion Act became in 1909 the first piece of national antidrug legislation.

The Shanghai commission—a preliminary to a full-fledged conference—was highly gratifying to the Wrights. Even though the other nations had no palpable interest in restricting their respective lucrative drug trades, virtually all reluctantly agreed to resolutions stating that nonmedicinal use of drugs should be discouraged and that nations should not export opium to nations with laws against it. Afterward, Hamilton and his formidable wife, Elizabeth, meandered home via Peking, Moscow, St. Petersburg, and London. When they arrived back in Washington in April, he immediately began planning the actual international conference. After certain factions in the State Department balked, Wright wrote to Secretary Root: "Our move to help China in her opium reform gave us more prestige in China than any of our recent friendly acts. If we continue and press steadily for the Conference, China will recognize that we are sincere in her behalf, and the whole business may be used as oil to smooth the troubled waters of our aggressive commercial policy there." Root agreed wholeheartedly.

And so Wright redoubled his efforts to obtain the domestic legislation that would mark America as the international moral leader in this arena. He authored a major report that amply documented the "large misuse of opium" in the United States and the worrisome problem of cocaine. While the general thrust of Wright's 1910 report was correct, the doctor-diplomat knowingly hyped the threat of cocaine-debauched Negroes in the South (presumably to galvanize the staunch states-rights Southern Dixiecrats), while also knowingly exaggerating various figures on imports and use.

Confident that Congress now would do its domestic and international duty, Wright worked up draft legislation based on federal powers of taxation. For as he wrote a colleague, "it would be perfectly absurd for us to go to the Conference with our stable only partly cleansed." Under his proposed law, everyone who handled opiates, cocaine, chloral hydrate, and cannabis would have to register, pay a small tax, and record all transactions, at peril of fines and imprisonment. Wright's legislation was introduced in April 1910 by the chairman of the House Committee on Foreign Affairs, Representative David Foster of Vermont, and was known as the Foster bill.

Much to Wright's dismay, the medical and pharmaceutical interests were extremely cool to any legislation. At a number of hearings, hostile emissaries from various druggists associations actively denounced the Foster bill as a "tremendous financial burden," an unfair saddling of honest patent medicine makers and dispensing pharmacists with piles of pointless paperwork. Of course, everyone wanted a stricter law to thwart the addicts, but a law that would be simpler. As Congress concluded in 1911, the Foster bill died an intended death. For as Musto notes, "In his enthusiasm and political naivete, Wright had not taken into consideration the great threat his bill posed to everyday routine and sales in the drug trades."

With domestic legislation a rout for the moment, Wright turned his forceful personality to organizing the next international conference. And he was so enjoying this line of work that he sought a real diplomatic post, and he asked Brent to help. The bishop put in a good word, but cautioned Wright, "I would hate to see you enter diplomacy without a pretty sure chance of success, which I doubt." As a torrid summer enveloped Washington, Wright became worried about his children, for the "scourge of infantile paralysis" was again loose. And so the Wrights headed north to their Maine summerhouse, Topside, in Livermore Falls.

From there he continued to pressure and cajole the various nations to schedule a definite date for the opium conference. The diplomatic badgering worked, and in December 1911 the first International Conference on Opium duly convened at The Hague. There Wright was so self-righteous and intemperate in his denunciations of the other attendees that he alienated the archbishop of Canterbury, an important leader in the antiopium movement. From an ocean liner heading toward Hong Kong, an exasperated Bishop Brent wrote the offending Wright that while he knew "your earnestness, your knowledge, your persistence have kept things going in the face of grave difficulties, . . . [nonetheless,] I sometimes feel that you ought frankly to face the possibility of retiring for the sake of the cause." Wright refused.

The issue at The Hague had been how best to control and regulate international narcotics traffic. This was no simple matter when every country had its own agenda and many were reaping large revenues from drugs. Yet consensus emerged that restriction was the proper route. The conference produced a document known as the Opium Convention, which stipulated that each of the forty-six nations expected to sign and ratify the protocol would control narcotics through internal, domestic legislation.

As the New Year began in 1912, Hamilton Wright sailed back to Washington, D.C., determined to see the United States do the right thing and enact domestic legislation. This time round Representative Francis Burton Harrison, a Tammany Democrat from New York, was the congressional point man. As Wright girded for legislative battle on Capitol Hill, so did the wholesale drug trade, the patent medicine makers, the pharmacists, and the physicians, organizing into the National Drug Trade Conference. While courting China had been the original impetus for national antidrug legislation, now there was domestic pressure, too. Rising grassroots alarm over antisocial drug abuse, especially in northern cities, had convinced the drug trade and the medical profession that some kind of restrictive bill was inevitable and even necessary. After all, when Wright first had introduced the Foster bill three years earlier in 1910, authorities had not yet been aware of heroin as a recreational drug. Now heroin was everywhere in the big city tenderloins.

It was distinctly worrisome the extent to which heroin—known on the street as "happy dust"—was attracting legions of young users such as Leroy Street, boys from solid families who had never tried any drug previously. An army doctor at Fort Strong outside Boston discovered in 1913 that dozens of young soldiers were using heroin, the "pioneers" having discovered it in Boston's red-light district. Never before had the military doctor encountered "this practice among soldiery . . . or heard of this derivative of morphine being used in this way." When the U.S. Army investigated further, it found a handful of other bases where drugs had made inroads. At a time when it was almost certain the United States would be entering the Great War in Europe, it was determined quickly that "no man known to be, even to a small extent, addicted to the use of cocaine or opium or any of its derivatives, should, at any time, be permitted to remain in the service or return to it after discharge. . . . [Drug use has] resulted in much inefficiency on the part of enlisted men and, I think, caused the moral and mental ruin of many of them." The issue was no longer whether national antidrug legislation was needed, but what kind?

In spite of this shift in attitude, Wright remained as difficult as ever. As Bishop Brent had once observed to him, "You are never happy except when you are unhappy, by which I mean that you rather revel in problems and scraps!" All his diplomatic and legislative experience had failed to temper the righteous Wright. His abrasive style soon united the disparate drug trade lobby on one issue: their intense dislike of him. When Wright stormed out of a meeting at the luxurious Willard Hotel, the druggists dug in their heels. Several days later, Congressman Harrison, as practical as every Tammany politician, informed Wright that if the Harrison bill was not modified to suit the druggists, he would not shepherd it through the House. Wright compromised grudgingly.

Yet the Harrison bill then stalled in the Senate. When Wright sailed for the Second Opium Conference in The Hague in the summer of 1912, he still could not produce the promised domestic legislation. Fortunately, that embarrassment was mitigated by United States ratification of the Opium Convention. Thirty-four of the forty-six nations ratified the Convention, but such critical signatories as Turkey, a major opium producer, and Switzerland, a major pharmaceutical producer, had not.

Wright got a much needed political boost when Woodrow Wilson assumed the presidency in 1913. Secretary of State William Jennings Bryan was an ardent reformer, and the new administration directed the State and Treasury departments to collaborate with the drug and medical professions to produce an acceptable bill. The new version required that all physicians and retail druggists handling cocaine and opiates (chloral hydrate and cannabis were no longer included) register with the Internal Revenue Service, which would monitor their activities through yearly tax stamps and standard order blanks. Patent medicines containing small amounts of opiates and cocaine were exempt and could still be sold by mail order and in stores.

Finally, on December 14, 1914, Congress passed the Harrison Narcotic Act. Unlike the push for national prohibition, which set off a ferocious political battle before the temperance movement triumphed in Congress in 1917, one congressman noted that "no individual has ever represented to the Committee on Ways and Means that the present extensive traffic in narcotics should be allowed to continue." It is further noteworthy that a week after Harrison passed with minimal public comment, a full-dress debate on liquor prohibition raged in the Congress, as wets and drys engaged in spirited argument before packed galleries. Unlike cocaine and opiates, which had brief histories in Western culture, alcohol and drinking were embedded deeply in Anglo-Saxon and European social custom.

Just as significant were the differences in experience with alcohol versus drugs. It generally takes many years to create a serious drunkard, but only weeks or months to create a drug addict. And while all but the worst alcoholics could function quite well when not drunk, such was not the case with drug addicts, who could not function well when high or when the need for drugs propelled them to focus on the next snuff or shot. Furthermore, addicts required constantly increasing doses of drugs to remain "normal" even a portion of any day. As one Philadelphia doctor who saw a great many "narcomaniacs" explained, "Practically all of the addicts under our observation who had been engaged in occupations requiring any real effort, either mental or physical, had been forced to abandon them, and were living as dependents on their relatives or friends, or else as purveyors of vice and petty crime." In an age much taken with efficiency and purity, this was intolerable.

So, while there had been packed galleries for liquor prohibition, and hours of debate, the Harrison Narcotic Act stirred little furor, except with the pharmaceutical and medical lobbies, and their main concern was to limit onerous record keeping. With Europe descending into the maelstrom of war, the advance of the Harrison Act received minor newspaper coverage. The story was typically sandwiched between items on orphans getting their first chance to see a motion picture and a dancing policeman whose vigorous fox-trot propelled him through a second-story window. The bill was barely mentioned in the *New York Times*, whose pages were overflowing with terrible news from across the Atlantic. The day the Harrison Act was signed, the lead story relayed fast-escalating hostilities: GERMANS SHELL THREE ENGLISH TOWNS; SCORES ARE KILLED AND MORE HURT; RAIDING SHIPS ESCAPE ENGLISH FLEET.

Hamilton Wright, who had pressured and lobbied and cajoled five hard years for this national legislation, had little personal reason to celebrate. In July 1913 Secretary Bryan had fired him to placate various congressmen, and then had been forced to recall him temporarily to help prepare for the 1914 conference at The Hague. No one else had such grasp of this complicated material. Part of Wright's bad relations with State centered on money, for he had long been disgruntled about his remuneration, and this dispute had come to a head under Bryan. Wright claimed to be owed more than eight thousand dollars, but State cooly rejected this out of hand. Nor would Bryan console the faithful if irritating Wright with some other appointment. Instead, the man who effectively had established an international system of narcotic controls and would later be known as the "father of American narcotic laws" sought a new mission by volunteering for civilian relief work in wartime France. There, in 1915, he was in a bad automobile accident, from which he never recovered. He died at home in Washington two years later of pneumonia, only forty-nine. Wright left behind five children and his powerhouse wife, Elizabeth Washburn Wright, who vigorously carried on the cause she and her husband had championed so long.

During this period when drug addiction was first recognized and then addressed, no American individual or group had ever stepped forward to defend the nonmedical use of drugs. Unlike alcohol prohibition, which a great many respectable citizens and organizations condemned as bad legislation, drug restrictions were viewed as a necessary and uncontroversial measure. Not only would they quash a worrisome development in the cities, but they upheld America as a moral leader on the international front. Once the Harrison Act took hold, often in concert with state laws passed to complement it, the public and the authorities clearly believed that a disturbing social problem had been addressed properly. The *New York Sun* avered after a mere six weeks that the antidrug law was "so carefully drawn that the shrewdest drug fiend is precluded from continuing the miserable habit."

On March 1, 1915, when the new federal Harrison Act went into effect, drugs became more difficult to obtain, and addicts were all-but-branded social outcasts. Complained young Leroy Street, the New York heroin addict, "Now I was one of a band set apart by the will of society, too, and harried for our nonconformity. At least it seemed to me that we were being persecuted only because we were different, not because we were dangerous."

But it was for precisely this reason—that the nation had come to perceive "vicious" drug use as a definite danger to society—that the United States was now embarked on a determined campaign to root out addicts and addiction forever. The new laws definitely succeeded in convincing a great many addicts to eschew now illegal drugs and discouraged others from experimenting. They also gradually forced those who could not or would not give up drugs into a furtive and perilous existence, pursued by authorities on one side and exploited by traffickers and shady doctors and druggists on the other. And so, slowly but surely the new-style addicts retreated into a nascent illegal drug subculture in the urban tenderloins, complete with its own argot.

Once the new antidrug laws went into effect, many addicts—such as Street—were also forced to try treatment, thereby providing the first significant information about the new-style U.S. addicts. Doctors at various municipal and county hospitals were soon publishing studies to answer such basic questions as: Who exactly were the drug addicts? Why and how had they acquired such "efficiency destroying" habits? How best could they be cured and returned to society as useful citizens?

At Philadelphia General Hospital, a study of 130 habitués found the preponderance were young males using heroin. A second study from the same hospital a year later in 1916 amplified this finding. Of 147 patients, 103 were male, 44 female, all white save two Chinese and three Negroes. Thirty-eight used only morphine, 27 only heroin, 21 heroin and cocaine, while the remaining 61 used combinations. (Quite a few "began the use of heroin as a substitute for the habit of opium smoking. These were perhaps the pioneers . . . [as they turned] to something less expensive.") About 30 of the 147 blamed their addiction on medical treatment. Virtually all the rest took to drugs for pleasure and social diversion. "The majority of the women were prostitutes. . . . A number were notorious crooks and thieves. In all, over fifty occupations were represented, among the number being one physician, two nurses and three druggists. The majority were dwellers in, or frequenters of, the 'tenderloin.' "

In a Cleveland study of 62 patients, virtually all the addicts worked or had worked at ordinary jobs: as bellboys, waiters, machinists, clerks, salesmen, housewives. Again, mostly young men; fully two thirds admitted starting drugs, especially heroin, out of indulgence or through curiosity piqued by companions.

None of these early medical reports found any permanent physical consequence from drug use, and all described similar opiate withdrawal symptoms of extreme restlessness, bad insomnia, and cramping of the arms and legs. Invariably, once withdrawal was complete, patients ate heartily and regained a healthful appearance. But to the dismay of the physicians, true cure was neither simple nor certain. After dealing with a thousand New York City addicts, one doctor wrote, "I wish to state most emphatically that there is no treatment which will cure a drug fiend in two weeks or even two months." The medical consensus was that left unchecked, these young male addicts posed a menace to society and only severe restrictions on habit-forming drugs might save them from themselves.

In retrospect, it is amazing that the Harrison Act in no way spelled out—despite all the years of dickering among the druggists, doctors, and politicians—one highly critical issue: What exactly did the new law expect of those most affected, the drug addicts? Abstinence or continuous maintenance of their habits? Clearly, most doctors assumed that those colleagues willing to deal with addicts (and already many doctors wanted nothing to do with them) could treat them as any patient, providing drugs as deemed necessary. The U.S. Public Health Service obviously assumed this, for it reassured one concerned woman that she could indeed continue to receive morphine regularly if her doctor felt it necessary. After all, the Harrison Act stated that those legally allowed to possess the specified drugs included any person who obtained them with "a prescription given in good faith."

But before long, the Treasury Department, which enforced the law, made clear what "in good faith" meant. And it was that prescriptions could be written only for ever-diminishing amounts as the physician promoted a permanent cure. In short, addicts would not be viewed by the government as ordinary patients needing indefinite care. Maintenance would not be tolerated. This hard-line policy was predicated on the belief that once addicts came under the professional care of a physician, the doctor should be able to wean and cure all but frail and elderly addicts. And even when hard experience with addicts revealed the discouraging reality of relapse rates as high as 90 percent, some optimistic strain in the American polity refused to acknowledge that a great many addicts either could not be cured or were not interested in being cured.

And so, the government's hard-line policy established, Treasury agents began pursuing druggists and physicians maintaining addicted patients. In the first four months of enforcing the new Harrison Act, 257 physicians and 40 dentists were charged with violations. Among those was Dr. Jin Fuey Moy of Pittsburgh, who had prescribed 1/16 of an ounce of morphine sulfate to one Willie Martin, an addict. Treasury agents arrested Dr. Moy (who had a reputation as a "dope doctor"), charging that he was providing opiates not for medical purposes, but "for the purpose of supplying one addicted to the use of opium." As the arrests mounted, an astonished and outraged medical community swiftly turned to the courts. And in *United States* v. *Jin Fuey Moy* (1916) the U.S. Supreme Court sided (7 to 2) with the doctors, ruling it unlawful for the government to interfere with the practice of medicine, in this instance a doctor prescribing morphine for an addict-patient. Treasury saw no recourse but to secure new amendments to the Harrison Act from Congress.

Congress, however, was preoccupied with the anarchic state of the world. In Europe, the great nations were bogged down in murderous trench warfare, while in Russia a workers' revolution had plunged the empire into civil strife. In the United States itself, American socialists and anarchists were advocating similar revolt. As the country moved inexorably toward a declaration of war against Germany in March 1917, a mood of self-sacrifice and patriotic fervor swept the nation. All patience was gone for anything that undermined the national will.

This mounting alarm over the state of the nation was nowhere more decisively demonstrated than in the about-face of the U.S. Supreme Court on Harrison and doctors and drugs. In the fearful year of 1919, with the war in Europe mercifully over, the United States had entered a state of near panic over its own social unrest. Four million American workers now struck in 3,600 strikes, ruthlessly opposed by big business. A spring of terrorist bombs, including one at the U.S. Attorney General's house, made Bolshevism all too real. In this jittery atmosphere, the Eighteenth Amendment was ratified, bringing on liquor prohibition.

Not long after, the Treasury Department contributed to the sense of national panic with its report, *Traffic in Narcotic Drugs*, which asserted postwar America harbored a million addicts. New York City alone was said to have three hundred thousand addicts. (Five years later, the U.S. Public Health Service quietly repudiated these absurd figures, putting the national total at a more likely 110,000.) And this, rather than being an increase, was a huge decline, two thirds of what it had been when drugs had been widely available at the turn of the century. Most who followed the issue believed that while youthful antisocial drug use was a growing problem, overall drug use and addiction had peaked in the early years of the century at about 250,000. If one added in the cocaine addicts (some of whom overlapped), it reached 350,000.

But in 1919 the Supreme Court had seen Treasury's dire report and presumably took it to heart when making two crucial rulings that March. The Court ruled first in *Doremus* (1919) that Harrison did not exceed federal constitutional powers and, just as important, ruled further in *Webb* that physicians did *not* have the right to maintain addicts. In the first case, Dr. Charles T. Doremus of San Antonio had been charged after providing five hundred tablets of morphine to a known addict. The Texas courts held that the Harrison Act was a revenue law, not a police law, and such enforcement therefore exceeded its constitutional bounds. But now the Supreme Court disagreed.

Furthermore, to underscore its shift, the Supreme Court ruled the same day in the second case that Dr. Webb and Goldbaum, a retail pharmacist, who had routinely supplied known addicts in Memphis with large quantities of morphine "for the sake of accustomed use," were so clearly not engaged in legitimate medical practice that "no discussion of the subject is required." A year later the same Dr. Moy who had triumphed in 1916 was back again before the Supreme Court. This time around the court found his practice of charging "according to the amount of the drug prescribed, being invariably one dollar per dram" convincing evidence that Dr. Moy essentially was peddling drugs. His conviction under Harrison was upheld.

Armed with *Webb* and *Doremus*, Treasury agents all over the country cracked down on physicians who catered to addicts. In New York City, on April 9, 1919, agents swooped down on six physicians and four druggists. Some of these doctors had been writing up to two hundred prescriptions a day, and one druggist had fifty thousand prescription forms in his basement, all filled in the past ten months. Another druggist had filled one hundred thousand prescriptions, mainly for heroin, in the preceeding year. Altogether these six doctors wrote prescriptions for about eight hundred addicts.

New York officials worried that some of these hundreds, deprived of their easy prescriptions, might resort to violent crime to obtain heroin. Not long before a drug addict looting a Madison Avenue jewelry store had shot and killed someone. So after the April raid, officials hurriedly met and agreed to set up a special clinic for addicts at the New York City Health Department. Treasury agents earlier had suggested similar clinics to health and police officials in other cities with sizable addict populations.

Of all the clinics, none was so large or so thoroughly studied as New York City's Worth Street Clinic. Started as an emergency measure, Worth Street opened on April 10, 1919, to huge lines of young men, many already wearing the straw boaters of summer. The anxious, pushing crowds circled around the block, creating a circus atmosphere that quickly attracted sight-seeing buses whose conductors yelled through megaphones to behold "New York's dope line!"

One of the principal doctors at the clinic, S. Dana Hubbard, systematically gathered information on the 7,464 people who passed through in the course of the year the clinic remained open. The vast majority of the Worth Street Clinic addicts—70 percent—were in their twenties and had been taking drugs (mainly heroin) for pleasure for six or seven years. Eighty percent were men, in contrast to the old-time medical addicts, who were usually women. No longer were doctors or patent medicines at fault. Now it was young men and boys (mainly working class) hanging around the stoop or the poolroom, casually offering a pal a little "blow." And indeed, Leroy Street, age twenty-four and nine years an addict, was among those jostling, anxious crowds waiting in line. Hearing the stories of these lost souls led Dr. Hubbard to conclude, "Drug addiction spreads like a pestilence through association."

Every day in the early months of the clinic about a thousand addicts jammed in. Heroin was far more restricted and expensive now, and most addicts had switched from snuffing to shooting up, since injected drugs gave more bang for the buck. Dr. Hubbbard watched in amazement at the addicts' peculiar methods, which involved a small, simple spoon and matches to heat and liquify the powdered heroin in water. Then they rigged up cheap medicine droppers as makeshift syringes.

What especially impressed Dr. Hubbard was what he termed the "free-masonry of the drug addict," a secretive world in which drugs—obtaining them and using them—was the central and defining feature. He was astonished at how many of the addicts knew one another—usually by strange nicknames. "They meet in places convenient for secret conference, toilets being most often selected, and in such dens of iniquity as will tolerate such lounging and loafing. Their hours are as irregular as a stray cat, and neither day nor night is of any particular consequence. . . . All that this class of drug addicts—the confirmed habitué—appears to care for is to have a supply of 'dope,' and a place where it can be obtained. . . . [E]verything that would be natural in the usual daily life of the ordinary man, to him, is unnecessary."

In short, the new urban addicts largely ignored the traditional values of community, family, hard work, and deferred pleasure. Instead, they sought out like-minded addicts and created their own separate and secret ritualistic world centered on self, personal freedom, the hedonism of drugs, and steering clear of the law. As Dr. Hubbard observed, "One very peculiar and universal characteristic is that they, one and all, are insistently selfish and self-concerned. For others they care not at all."

The Worth Street Clinic offered so-called "ambulatory" treatment aimed at weaning the addict off dope. Most of the clientele, however, displayed little interest in this agenda. When daily doses got too small, addicts generally just returned to the street peddlers or dubious doctors and druggists. Less than 2,000 of the 7,464 patients at Worth Street accepted the city's offer of supervised withdrawal and recovery at a hospital. Most discouraging was that even those who did accept hospital treatment failed—with few exceptions—to stay off drugs for long. Since the official government and medical goal was cure, not maintenance, the clinic could not justify itself easily. By the end, only 150 addicts bothered to appear each day at the Worth Street Clinic.

Moreover, many nonaddicts, including friends, street pushers, and Treasury agents, found it simple to get drugs at the clinic. The top federal narcotics official, Colonel Levi G. Nutt, personally stood in line and obtained drugs at Worth Street. Meanwhile, the neighborhood was complaining bitterly that addicts had taken over a local park and were shooting up openly and loafing about. All concluded that perhaps it was better to send addicts for prolonged treatment at some rural sanitarium, and then make sure that when they got out, they had no place to obtain drugs—not from doctors, druggists, clinics, or street peddlers. Thoroughly discouraged by this failure, the City Health Department closed the clinic after about a year.

All told, as many as fifty American cities opened clinics to accommodate addicts. Half were located in Connecticut and New York, while the rest were in such diverse states as Louisiana, California, Ohio, Texas, and Tennessee. Often it seemed the only reason a municipal clinic opened was to reward a well-connected physician with a city salary, since they served but a handful of clients. Other clinics—in places such as California—often served a couple of hundred addicts. Some were run by fairly blatant physician profiteers who seemed concerned only in writing as many prescriptions as possible; others by highly reputable and devoted doctors who sincerely tried to wean the addicts off drugs or provide minimal doses so addicts could get on with their lives.

For instance, in New Haven, police surgeons operated a narcotic clinic out of City Hall for an hour each morning and evening. This had been organized after local complaints about a particular private doctor. His "fees (fifty cents a prescription) were too high, the parade of addicts to the physician's residential office offended his neighbors, patients were said to resort to petty thievery to pay their fees, drug peddling still thrived, and not one addict was cured." And so the clinic was established and eventually served about ninety addicts.

In Houston, the clinic was open only six months before the doctor who ran it shut the doors. He complained that "when the clinic opened, the dope fiends or addicts increased in great numbers, coming in from out of town, that there subsequently appeared a wave of crime in the City of Houston, which disappeared immediately after the closing of the Clinic."

In contrast, the clinic in Shreveport, Louisiana, was hailed as a model by everyone in its community, including the police. Run by Willis P. Butler, a respected graduate of Vanderbilt Medical School, the Shreveport clinic discouraged addicts from elsewhere and maintained strict records on its 198 patients. Probably Shreveport's most unique feature was requiring addicts to work and maintain their appearance or be cut off. One suspects that this probably weeded out most of the "sporting" addicts and other unsavory types who so frustrated the New York doctors. However, unlike New York City, the Shreveport clinic also made little attempt to diminish doses and wean addicts. Nonetheless, because the clinic effected no cures and supplied drugs to addicts—contrary to stated federal policy—it eventually was forced to close in 1923.

Once total abstinence was declared to be the official U.S. government drug policy, no legitimate source, not doctors, not druggists, not clinics, was allowed to supply anyone any longer with drugs for non-medical purposes—especially those who were known drug addicts. And those who tried would feel the full wrath of the new Narcotics Unit federal agents. To administer the Volstead Act and the Eighteenth

Amendment laws prohibiting the sale (but not possession) of alcohol, the U.S. Treasury Department had set up a Prohibition Unit in December 1919 that featured a new and separate Narcotics Division. This was headed by Colonel Levi G. Nutt, a pharmacist and former official with the Alcohol Tax Division.

By 1919, government had decided that the only way to cure addicts and stop the further spread of addiction was to cut off all nonmedical access to drugs. Based on the unhappy experience of the New York clinic and the embarrassment of the dubious dope doctors, the AMA had condemned any "ambulatory" treatment. Treasury not only began closing all the municipal clinics, it cracked down on drug-dispensing doctors. Only those addict-patients who were very aged or infirm could be maintained. Private doctors—no matter how respectable and cautious their dosage—found themselves at risk if they persevered in treating otherwise healthy addicted patients or even arguing their cause.

Treasury's crackdown reflected an official decision about an ongoing and heated debate. Were addicts victims of an actual physical disease or moral turpitude? Could they be cured? Treasury concluded (as did most doctors) that there was no physical evidence of disease and that left to their own devices many addicts—especially the new young male addicts—would use drugs forever, steadily recruiting others to their benighted ranks.

There is no question that over the years the local laws and then Harrison dramatically cut down on overall nonmedical drug consumption. It is probably no coincidence that Ella O'Neill, for instance, finally had overcome her morphine addiction as the Harrison Act went into effect. And so the government felt quite justified in continuing to restrict access.

As the twenties progressed, Treasury sought and obtained ever greater restrictions on opiates and cocaine. In 1922 the Supreme Court ruled in *Behrman* that it was not legitimate medical practice to prescribe for an addict even in diminishing amounts with intention of cure. Known addicts could no longer legally be prescribed drugs for their addiction by a private physician. That same year the Congress passed the Jones-Miller Act, aimed at establishing a high-level Narcotic Control Board that would monitor drug manufacture. Just as important, it ended a loophole that had allowed American drug manufacturers to export large quantities of narcotics with no proof that they were for legitimate medical purposes. A substantial trade had developed with Canada, from whence drugs were then smuggled back into the United States for illegal sale.

And then in 1924, the preeminent and powerful Congressman

Stephen Porter held hearings on banning opium imports to manufacture heroin, as a parade of witnesses testified to that drug's alarming spread "over a vast section of the country, particularly among the younger generation of the large cities." Various physicians confirmed that heroin, now as stigmatized as cocaine, largely had been eliminated from the standard medical practice. Military service doctors were not allowed to use it. Heroin, introduced a quarter century earlier as a non-addictive cough medicine, had become associated exclusively with youthful addiction and crime.

The hearing also revealed that Harrison Act violators were swelling the prison rolls. This was most evident at the federal penitentiary in Leavenworth, Kansas, where of 1,482 prisoners sentenced in 1923, fully half, or 717, were drug act violators, and of these, 299 were addicts. Authorities viewed this as disturbing testimony to the need for tighter restrictions. The Porter bill was passed, and in 1925 heroin became completely illegal in the United States, permanently removed from the medical pharmacopoeia.

Historian David Courtwright believes that the dying-off of the old-fashioned medical addicts meant that by 1930 the majority of American addicts were pleasure addicts. The new-style American addicts were young lower-class men in the northern industrial cities who mainly used heroin. One of the most detailed social portraits of these modern addicts was compiled by a graduate student named Bingham Dai, writing his dissertation at the University of Chicago's famed sociology department in the early thirties. Dai's own fascination with drugs had its origins in China, where his uncle was an opium addict who had also worked on opium suppression in the city of Nanking. Dai himself was an active member of Shanghai's National Anti-Opium Association and editor of its reform-minded journal, *Opium, a World Problem*.

The most striking finding of Dai's study of 2,500 addicts in the Chicago of the thirties was their rootlessness. Fully four fifths of the addicts had migrated from some other urban area. They tended to live in slum neighborhoods and work erratically at a variety of menial jobs, often as waiters in the amusement business. About 60 percent began using drugs in their twenties even though drugs by then were illegal, with morphine by needle the drug of choice for most. By 1933 most were, however, switching to heroin at $38 to $40 an ounce, versus morphine at $90 to $110.

Dai was struck that not only had most Chicago addicts come to the city as migrants and strangers, but most "did not seem to have much of what might be called familial ties." Only a third of the males, but two thirds of the females, were married. Only a third of any of those addicts had children. In short, they were mobile, rootless, erratically employed, and poor. About a fifth already had criminal records. As newcomers to Chicago, they settled in marginal areas where drugs were available and most of the other residents were unattached men "constantly moving from place to place. . . . [H]ere the control of traditional mores and of what are ordinarily called primary-group associations, such as family and local community, is practically nil, and the individual's life, thereby, often lacks organization or direction."

Once arrived, the newcomers hung out in poolrooms, brothels, gambling houses, and dubious dives, where they made new friends who urged them to have a "blow" or a "shot." Most started using drugs as a way of cementing new friendships and being part of a new crowd. Once addicts, they took up the drug culture's argot—still full of Chinese opium-smoking terms—and values of hedonism and self above all. What is notable in retrospect is that these addicts did not take drugs as any conscious expression of rebellion. Drugs were a specific illicit urban pleasure and pastime that could (and generally did) dominate one's life.

Leroy Street finally would give up heroin when he was twenty-eight, after thirteen years of addiction. For him, the motivation was falling in love and getting married. In middle age, Street would write, "Of more than 100 addicts in my neighborhood [the West Village of Manhattan] whom I knew, boys who acquired the habit a little sooner or a little later than I, all are dead except myself. Some died in prison and were buried in potter's field. Some died in insane asylums. Others died as gutter bums in streets and flophouses and public washrooms. A few even died in their homes with physicians to sign certificates that death was due to heart disease or pneumonia. They are all gone."

CHAPTER 4

"A Cinema Crowd

of Cocaine-Crazed

Sexual Lunatics."

—*Visitor to Hollywood, 1916*

As the sun rose over the palmettos and wisteria of Alvarado Court in Hollywood on February 2, 1922, silent film star Edna Purviance heard a voice yell, "Mr. Taylor's dead. Help! Help! Mr. Taylor's dead!" She and a dozen other neighbors in the charming Spanish-style enclave—mainly movie people—rushed downstairs to find Paramount Studios director William Desmond Taylor sprawled on his back in the front hall of his bungalow. Clothed in the elegant English gentleman style he always favored, only a small crust of blood on Taylor's mouth and his rigid face suggested he was dead. Even as the owner of the Alvarado Court called the police and soothed the butler who had raised the alarm, Taylor's shocked chauffeur alerted Paramount. Several studio staff raced over, intent on removing anything that might cause posthumous scandal—bootleg liquor, incriminating diaries, racy letters, or questionable photographs.

They left just as the police and coroner arrived to begin the routine examination of the body. Meanwhile, Edna Purviance (Charlie Chaplin's female lead) returned to her bungalow to call Mabel Normand, a beautiful devil-may-care star who had blazed to international renown with Fatty Arbuckle in the Keystone comedies. Mabel, the last person to see Taylor alive the previous evening, became hysterical. Not only was Taylor, forty-nine, a good friend of hers (and maybe even a lover), Mabel already had been tarred in one shocking scandal, the Fatty Arbuckle rape and murder case being retried for a second time in San Francisco. Then Edna Purviance called again, this time to report that William Desmond Taylor had not keeled over from a heart attack as originally assumed. He had been shot and murdered. Mabel barely had digested this horrendous news when a mob scene of reporters and police invaded her opulent mansion.

Up at the Arbuckle retrial in San Francisco, the Chicago *Tribune's* hard-charging West Coast reporter, Edward Doherty, was ordered back to Hollywood ASAP. Taylor's murder was front-page news coast to coast. Doherty and another Chicago reporter and friend, Wallace Smith, quickly became convinced that the murder was drug-related. For not only were the nation's urban slums awash in illegal cocaine, heroin, and morphine, so too was that glamorous never-never land, Hollywood.

It was an open secret in the movie colony that the beauteous Mabel Normand had a debilitating cocaine habit. It was also well known in the industry that director William Desmond Taylor had tried to save Mabel, one of America's top box office draws in dozens of wholesome slapstick comedies, by dispatching her to a sanitarium in New England. Taylor actively opposed Hollywood's pushers and dealers. He had met with law enforcement officers—both local and federal—and urged them to crack down on the drug trade. He had asked Assistant District Attorney Tom Green personally for help with studio-based drug dealers. One federal drug agent told a friend of Mabel's that she was mixed up with an East Coast drug ring and warned, "Before she's through, somebody's going to get killed on her account." There were rumors that Taylor had even turned in Mabel's dealer after her most recent relapse. The two Chicago reporters, well-steeped in the underworld and its ways, firmly believed Taylor had been ordered "hit" by drug syndicates angered by his zealous crusade.

All this high drama could easily have come right off the silver screen, for since 1912 Hollywood had churned out a couple of hundred silent movies on this sordid yet fascinating issue: illegal drugs, addiction, and the drug trade. The many real-life dramas reported in the nation's newspapers and magazines about narcotics and cocaine had provided plentiful inspiration for early filmmakers. One of the first drug movies, *For His Son*, was made by D. W. Griffith in 1912, and told the story of a doctor who seeks quick riches by creating a cocaine-based soft drink ("knowing how rapid and powerful is the hold obtained by cocaine") called Dopokoke. As Biograph Films described the plot, "The drink meets with tremendous success . . . but [the doctor's] son cultivates a liking for it. The father discovers his son's weakness too late, for he soon becomes a hopeless victim of the drug."

Another drug story filmed in 1914 by the Lubin Company was called *The Cocaine Traffic* and was made with the help of the Philadelphia police. Here Spike Smith is a cocaine addict who persuades his former boss to get into dealing the drug in the tenderloin. It is only a matter of time before the dealer's daughter and son-in-law are soon hooked, too. The same year *The Drug Traffic* featured an ostensibly respectable druggist doing big business selling cocaine and morphine to selected furtive clientele. Another character, Kurson, is making a fortune selling Kurson Consumption Cure, a patent medicine loaded with morphine. The druggist's daughter becomes an addict and dies a terrible death, while Kurson goes to jail.

Invariably, as these plot summaries suggest, Hollywood portrayed its cinematic addicts (hooked for a variety of reasons, some medical, some pleasure) as once decent citizens who would now betray family, work, and honor for a sniff or a shot. Their fate was a grim demise. The sellers and pushers were unscrupulous sorts looking to get rich quick and were sure to be punished severely. In a later film made in 1918, *A Romance of the Underworld*, a young girl from the convent school rejoins her brother on the Lower East Side, only to see him exposed as the lieutenant of a notorious drug trafficker.

The one notable exception to these usual plots was an utterly bizarre comedy, *The Mystery of the Leaping Fish*. This 1916 release written by Tod Browning starred Douglas Fairbanks, Sr., as Coke Ennyday, a manic and wacky detective who is shooting up drugs constantly, even as he battles to thwart drug traffickers using inflatable rubber fish to smuggle in the goods. One suspects that all this seemed hilariously madcap to those on the set (inspired perhaps by the product in question?), but completely dumb to those in the audience. An embarrassed Fairbanks tried, but failed, to keep it from being released.

There was often something of a mixed message delivered in many of these early Hollywood drug films (virtually all of them now lost). Because before these silver screen addicts and pushers paid the price for their sins, they often frolicked through glamorous locales, from plush opium dens to sleek nightclubs. As one New York doctor complained in 1918, "Publicity has thrown an appealing glamour of romance about the addict."

The riches and glamour up on the screen were not so surprising, for the movie colony was engaged in its own intense romance with illegal pleasure drugs. Here in the natural fantasyland of early Los Angeles, ringed by lovely mountains, bathed by perennial sunshine, the movie actors and actresses worked arduous hours for high pay and then cavorted endlessly. None of Hollywood's high jinx or scandals surprised screenwriter Anita Loos (she supplied the captions for *Mystery of the Leaping Fish*), who felt you couldn't expect much from the undereducated and overenergetic citizens of filmdom. Or as one Keystone director so bluntly put it, "That's what comes of taking vulgarians from the gutter and giving them enormous salaries and making idols of them. . . . They are the ones that resort to cocaine and the opium needle and who participate in orgies that surpass the orgies of degenerate Rome."

Here the California sun shone steadily on a lush and sensuous landscape of pepper trees, swaying palms, fragrant eucalyptus. Nearby citrus groves scented the warm air, while roses ran riot over pastel bungalows and instant chateaux. As if this were not exotic enough, the multitude of ever more elaborate movie sets transported one instantly to other continents and other eras. On one location squadrons of actors and actresses wandered around dressed as Sioux Indians. Nearby, starlets were disembarking from sporty chauffeured cars costumed as Marie Antoinette and her court. Over the next hill, one could contemplate the vast sands of the Sahara, a make-believe sheik leading real camels toward a distant walled city. On yet another set rose Hollywood's notion of Lhasa, sacred city of Tibet. A huge crowd dressed as high priests were chanting and marching up the steps to witness a religious sacrifice. This surreal film capital was buzzing with good-looking, ambitious youth hoping to earn huge sums of money and have a rollicking good time. As early as 1916, a visitor passing through Hollywood had described a "cinema crowd of cocaine-crazed sexual lunatics."

Mabel Normand epitomized the new screen royalty. Remembered actress Madge Kennedy, "Many of us became queens overnight, but Mabel became a goddess." Heady stuff indeed for a poor girl from Staten Island barely scraping by as an artist's model when she wandered into a movie studio in New York. Normand's dewy good looks, natural athletic ability, and zany screen antics catapulted her to stardom as a comedienne with a six-figure salary. When the silent filmmakers headed west to the reliably sunny climes of southern California, Mabel Normand followed.

Audiences were not the only ones who loved her effervescence. Left and right, men fell in love with Mabel, who delighted in being the "wildest girl in Hollywood." Chided for her perennial lateness on the set, she sat on director Mack Sennett's lap and peed on him. Faced with the dumb publicity questions, Mabel answered, "Say I love dark, windy days when trees break and houses blow down; and what I like best to do . . . just say I love to pinch babies and twist their legs."

Normand's biographer Betty Fussell speculates that the actress began using cocaine in 1917 to counteract an opiate she was taking for a lung problem. But Anita Loos paints a less innocent scenario unfolding at the Vernon Country Club, where, said Loos, the underworld stationed "pushers of dope. They had an easy time converting those simple young drunks into drug addicts."

While most new addicts were the lost young men, Leroy Streets scuffling to avoid the police, a tiny but influential cadre of Bohemian or artsy users existed, typified by Mabel and other Hollywood addicts. For the rich and arty, pleasure drugs were just part of a larger rebellion against the old Puritan morality. From the start, Hollywood symbolized the sybaritic life, a place that celebrated conspicuous consumption in every possible form. The new stars—former bootblacks, bartenders, wrestlers, vaudevillians, etc.—almost overnight had achieved the pinnacle of the American Dream. Swathed in silks and furs, they suddenly owned "large estates, and stables full of costly motor cars and yachts and blooded horses and dogs and more clothes than they can wear. Some of them live in palaces and keep platoons of servants." Life was to be lived at top speed, wildly, amplified with whatever was at hand, including drugs.

In a place dedicated to make-believe and high spirits, drugs seemed to intensify already intense lives. Explained one self-proclaimed "drug fiend" of the time, the British writer Aleister Crowley, about morphine: "It kills all pain and worry like a charm. But at the very moment when you have the most gorgeous ideas, when you build golden palaces of what you are going to do, you have a feeling at the same time that nothing is really worth doing, and that itself gives you a feeling of terrific superiority to everything else in the world."

Mabel was but one of numerous movie people whose sybaritic indulgence in recreational drugs eventually came to exact a serious toll. Mabel's dewy good looks faded. She appeared wasted even on screen. Cocaine dulled her appetite and she couldn't eat enough. She alarmed friends with her strange behavior. All this must have been much on Hollywood's mind when William Desmond Taylor was found dead in his bungalow. And certainly the murder investigation itself had to prove unsettling, degenerating as it soon did into a Keystone Kops sort of operation. It began with the Paramount Studio minions riffling through the whole house and racing off with anything they deemed dicey. Then, some of the things Paramount snatched reappeared, specifically a pile of silly letters from Mabel Normand. Taylor himself, considered an aristocrat by Hollywood standards, turned out to have abandoned his real name, wife, daughter, and antiques business in New York City years earlier. Nor was his departed larcenous valet the proper servant he said he had been, but a former convict. And then there was the mysterious brother, who had also decamped from the East Coast, leaving behind a wife and family. The black butler just had been arrested for trying to pick up young boys. These sorts of unsavory revelations made Hollywood distinctly nervous, for they undermined the whole glamorous image of the place. Taylor had been viewed as one of the class acts, a suave and cultured man who earned $88,000 a year making high-toned films such as *Huck Finn* and *Tom Sawyer*. Here was a real Englishman who actually had read books, hunted, put in a romantic stint in the Yukon mining gold, and looked natural in his hand-tailored clothes. But he was not who he had said he was.

Within days of Taylor's funeral (a near riot of thirty thousand fans beseiging St. Paul's Cathedral), a new "development" in the investigation was acknowledged tersely. From the start, neighbors had given eyewitness accounts of a man in a plaid cap and heavy muffler leaving Taylor's house the night of the murder, just after what sounded like a gunshot. But the man, even when he knew he had been seen, acted so unruffled they felt no suspicions. If he had indeed fired the fatal shot, why? Now, here were the first official hints that maybe the issue was drugs. Reported the *New York Times*, "The police were reticient as to the details concerning their search for the man, a peddler who was believed to have sought patrons for his contraband drugs among the employees of motion picture studios, but they intimated their belief he had attempted to make a delivery through Taylor to an actress who found it difficult to make her purchases in person."

A week later, Doherty of the *Chicago Tribune* offered a far more detailed scenario, one where an unnamed actress had asked Taylor for help against blackmailing drug dealers. Without mentioning Mabel Normand's name, Doherty described an actress who "went to an eastern sanitarium and remained there until the luster came back to her eyes, the tint to her cheeks, the ambition into her system. She returned to the studios and made a smashing success in her first picture. But the blackmailers and venders of narcotics kept after her, gave her no peace." Doherty suggested that the actress turned to Taylor, as a "man not afraid to use a gun" and quoted him as having said of blackmailers, "The only way to get rid of them is to kill them."

The *Chicago Herald-Examiner* actually named Mabel in reporting this new possible murder motive. She had been questioned for four hours by the district attorney, and the paper explained that a new "supposition" was that "Miss Normand, during her last sojourn in New York, was made the objective victim of a blackmailing gang—perhaps that of 'Dapper Dan Collins.' "

When the two Chicago reporters continued emphasizing the drug angle, an undersheriff called them into his office and warned them they were in danger. "Let me furnish you each a bodyguard. Hollywood's crazy mad at the stuff you've been writing." When they pointed out the truth of their articles, the undersheriff responded, "That isn't the point. The industry has been hurt. Stars have been ruined. Stockholders have lost millions of dollars. And a lot of people are out of jobs, and incensed enough to take a shot at you."

Ultimately, the Taylor murder was never solved, and many concluded that that was just fine with the Hollywood powers-that-be. Doherty wondered why "not one cent" was offered by the movie magnates as a reward for finding Taylor's murderer. Publisher Robert Giroux, whose book about the case, *Deed of Death*, argues strongly for the Doherty version of events, wonders why the Los Angeles authorities made no attempt at all to find the man seen leaving the murder scene. No composite drawing was ever circulated. Instead, dozens of other irrelevant leads and speculations swirled about uselessly.

If drugs were indeed the cause of Taylor's murder, the scandal would have been hard to contain. Any drug dealers put on trial might have felt free to reveal their considerable clientele among the movie colony. And America was unlikely to feel friendly or sympathetic to such goings-on. The studios literally could not afford further airing of their dirty linen. Studio head Mack Sennett's first reaction when he heard of Taylor's murder was, "There goes half a million dollars. . . . And nothing to do but sit and take it." For Mabel Normand was starring in his current film, *Molly O*, and Sennett didn't believe her career could ride out two huge scandals, especially if this one exposed Mabel's own cocaine addiction.

Even before Taylor's murder, the moguls of the fledgling motion picture industry had felt compelled to do something dramatic to reassure America that Hollywood was not the hopeless den of iniquity it might seem. The problems began with Olive Thomas's strange death in Paris in late 1920. The beautiful actress, wife of the dissolute Jack Pickford, had died amid rumors of "drug and champagne orgies," her name on a client list of a U.S. Army officer sentenced for selling cocaine. Just as that was hushed-up, along came the Fatty Arbuckle scandal, where Virginia Rappe died after an Arbuckle party that lasted several days. Not only was Arbuckle's highly lucrative career destroyed (even though ultimately he was found completely innocent of all charges of rape and murder), but the whole mess generated a torrent of unflattering stories about Hollywood's wild parties and evil ways.

Vanity Fair gaily reported on a playful gathering where "the pool was specially filled with scotch and soda, in which the merrymakers took many an exhilarating bath, after which they ran pajama races round the tessellated pavement." All this might have been amusing before Olive Thomas and Virginia Rappe. But now, it smacked of wanton and dangerous debauchery. Disgusted citizens of Main Street, U.S.A., did not approve and began staying away in droves from the movies made by such depraved sorts. All through 1921 box office receipts suffered a steady decline.

Sensing the groundswell of outrage, legislators introduced nearly one hundred movie censorship bills in thirty-seven states. Writes A. Scott Berg in *Goldwyn*, "One day, Louis B. Mayer confided to young director King Vidor, 'If this keeps up there won't be any motion picture industry.' " Casting about for some way to restore Hollywood's good name and box office, the studio heads recruited Will Hays, the upright Hoosier postmaster general of the Harding administration. The Motion Picture Directors Association, then headed by William Desmond Taylor, already had promised that Hollywood was "cleaning house" and vowed to produce only the "cleanest of films." Yet the Arbuckle debacle dragged on (all told there were three trials), and Taylor, that very spokesman for wholesomeness, had been murdered, perhaps by drug dealers.

The Taylor murder investigation lurched nowhere, but Hollywood went its jolly way, or so one would have to assume from the following dispatch in the May 1922 *Vanity Fair*, mere months after the murder: Entitled HAPPY DAYS IN HOLLYWOOD, the writer burbled,

> With the brightening influence of spring there has been a distinct quickening of the social pace. Drugs are not as much in evidence as during the more trying days of winter, but they still spread their genial influence at some of the more exclusive functions. Last week little Lulu Lenore of the Cuckoo Comedy Co. gave a small house dance for the younger addicts. "Will you come to my 'Snow'-ball?" read the clever invitations. In one corner of the living room was a miniature "Drugstore," where Otho Everard kept the company in a roar as he dispensed little packages of cocaine, morphine and heroin. The guests at their departure received exquisite hypodermic nee-

dles in vanity boxes which have caused many heart-burnings among those who were not invited.

Such gossip (however spurious) cannot have pleased the moguls. Much less Will Hays, who had just arrived to take over as president of the Motion Picture Producers and Distributors of America. The first order of business, as movie receipts continued to decline, was the "morality clause" (also known as the Arbuckle clause), aimed squarely at the loose-living denizens of filmdom. Basically, any performer "tending to shock, insult, or offend the community or outrage public morals and decency" was subject to immediate firing. New motion picture codes also would dictate what *kinds* of movies would be made. Films about drugs were soon officially discouraged and ultimately banned outright.

In the wake of the Taylor murder, movie executives drew up a "black list" of 117 "unsafe" Hollywood drug users. All over town, dabblers and addicts were called in and warned to cease and desist or face cancellation of their contracts. At Paramount, Cecil B. DeMille had the unpleasant duty of speaking with that studio's top star, Wallace Reid, a dashingly sexy Gibson Boy type. Edward Doherty described Reid as "the biggest box-office attraction in the world." DeMille must have felt a bit sheepish, for he himself had served his guests drugs as a chic after-luncheon treat. Reporter Adela Rogers recalled, "It was HMC, a combination of hyacine, morphine and cactine." Furthermore, the studio had been complicit in Reid's drug addiction, sending doctors to the set with morphine when necessary to get a picture finished. But now, Reid's addiction was affecting his looks and stamina. Fans were asking openly what was wrong with their idol. Reid agreed to enter a sanitarium, telling DeMille, "I'll either come out cured or I won't come out."

The problem, of course, was what to say for public consumption. Wallace Reid was a star of the first magnitude. Having first gained real public notice as a blacksmith in D. W. Griffith's *The Birth of a Nation* in 1915, the tall, darkly handsome Reid had become the nation's strapping ideal of young American manhood in dozens of features. Son of two well-known theatrical parents, Reid was an actor of many talents. Not only did he look wonderful in a tuxedo or a cowboy getup, but (as the fan magazines lovingly showed) he also knew a lot about fast cars, could play the sax well, painted passably, and possessed a doting wife, actress Dorothy Davenport, and two adorable children. How then to tell America that this top star and family man was a drug addict?

At first, Paramount tried very hard not to. In late October 1922, when the press and fans wondered why their idol was not churning out the usual picture every other month, a variety of excuses were offered up. First, the word was "Wally" was a victim of Kliegeyes, "a burning of the eyeballs caused by bright Klieg lights used in studios, . . . a common illness in motion picture studios." He was said to be on a three-week vacation in the mountains. Two months later, when Reid still was not back on the set, the rumors had become so rampant the studio issued a press release saying he was in a sanitarium because his "health had been failing for three years." A few days later another press release insisted that Reid was suffering from a severe case of influenza, not "from overindulgence in alcoholics or the use of narcotics." In fact, Reid was dying.

His doctors could not say why. Kicking opiates was horrible, but not something that would generally kill you. But Reid had lost sixty pounds, spiked high fevers, and was too weak to walk. Endless medical tests revealed no explanation for the fevers or failing lungs and kidneys. Dorothy Davenport asked permission to tell reporters that Reid had been addicted and was now in treatment. Will Hays agreed. The whole story was designed to elicit maximum sympathy while portraying Hollywood and Reid as utterly blameless. According to Davenport, Wallace Reid had been injured physically while working on a film in New York City in late 1921 and given morphine for his pain. In short, he was not one of the odious new pleasure addicts undermining society, but an old-fashioned accidental medical addict.

Moreover, she emphasized, "It is a queer coincidence that while all the world frowns on 'horrible Hollywood' and whispers of its 'orgies,' Wally Reid had to go all the way to New York to become a drug addict. Isn't that a splendid answer to the colony's critics?" Davenport also insisted that Wally had never had to buy illegal drugs and always used his opiates orally. His legendary charm had beguiled doctors and druggists to prescribe whatever he needed.

Hollywood's official version of events generated tremendous sympathy when the bombshell of Reid's addiction and death hit the front pages on January 18, 1923. But no one in Hollywood believed the official version for a moment. The thirty-one-year-old Reid had been addicted long before he went to New York. Just as Mabel's addiction to cocaine was an open secret, so was Reid's addiction to opiates, whether morphine or heroin. Anita Loos describes in her autobiography, *A Girl Like I*, how

> when he took to using heroin Wally also adopted a few gangster methods of behavior, one of which was blackmail. He used to hide out during the shooting of a scene and send word to the

director, "If you want to bring this picture in on schedule, it'll cost you a thousand dollars to get me on the set." The money would generally be sent to Wally, and he would come out of hiding to give a convincing performance of an upstanding, clean-cut, clear-eyed, square-shooting American hero of the type that was his specialty.

One cameraman who frequently worked on Reid's films described studio doctors arriving on the set to provide morphine. But Reid clearly did not obtain all the drugs he wanted this way. His own mother, not obligated to the studios for her survival, said, "I know there are 'dope' parties in Hollywood—everyone knows that—and I suppose Wally has attended some of them." His wife, perhaps forgetting the official line for a moment, acknowledged the "mysteriously worded telegrams and messages which came to our home late of nights," presumably drug dealers doing lucrative business with her husband. Reid's name was reportedly on the client list of a major New York drug dealer, William Williams, arrested in December 1922. (The final Reid estate of less than $100,000 strongly suggested that Reid, who had made $1 million in just the previous three years, threw away a great deal on drugs.) Nor did Wallace Reid only take his drugs orally. Always a lover of gadgets, Reid was inordinately proud of his trick golf club: inside the handle was a hypodermic syringe that he showed off to others.

After the huge brouhaha surrounding Reid's death subsided, Dorothy Davenport announced that she would produce, as "a memorial to my Wally's great fight," an antinarcotic film to be called *Human Wreckage*. Will Hays, who had been privately furious about this latest scandal, gave special permission. The film begins with the arrest of a twenty-year-old thief caught stealing a watch from a pawnshop. It turns out the thief is a heroin addict. The addict's mother is helped to find an attorney for the hapless youth. This attorney persuades the court to send him for a cure. Meanwhile, the attorney, under great stress in his own career, tries some morphine at the urging of a doctor he knows socially at his club. Next, it seems that another young female neighbor, a mother nursing a young child, is also an addict and even uses morphine to quiet her baby.

About this time in the plot, the federal narcotic squad swings into action, arresting various members of the local drug ring. But the movie makes clear that influential people will guarantee that the pushers are found not guilty and returned to their lucrative trade. The attorney, representing one of the dealers, is still struggling with his own morphine addiction. Dorothy Davenport, playing his wife, finally persuades him to give up morphine. In the end, the drug ring—even those high up—is about to be exposed and the worst pushers die in a collision with a locomotive. *Human Wreckage* opened in June 1923 and became one of the year's big screen hits.

However, official Hollywood had concluded that neither its films nor its stars could afford to be even remotely linked with such stigmatized substances as illegal drugs. It had been just over a decade since recreational use of cocaine and opiates had been taken up heavily by the sporting classes and then begun spreading elsewhere, and the public clearly had come to fear everything about drugs, addiction, and addicts. Once the Reid scandal blew over, no further drug films were sanctioned. The Motion Picture Code of 1930, when talkies began, stated unequivocally, "Illegal drug traffic must never be presented. . . . The existence of the trade should not be brought to the attention of the audiences."

And under the watchful eye of the Hays Office, Hollywood's own drug scene gradually quieted down. Occasional minor scandals—washed-up stars such as Juanita Hansen being arrested or others found dead of overdoses—were the only reminders of the wide-open years when Hollywood churned out drug films and frolicked at "Snowballs." In 1926 Barbara LaMarr, an early Hollywood beauty, veteran of six husbands, dozens of lovers, and untold quantities of drugs—her cocaine was kept in a gold casket on her piano—fatally overdosed at age twenty-six. The lovely Alma Rubens, who had played an opium smuggler's mistress in the bizarre *Mystery of the Leaping Fish*, died not long after LaMarr, another casualty of the early Hollywood drug culture. Juanita Hansen was forced out of films and busied herself as an antinarcotics crusader. Presumably others, such as Tallulah Bankhead, handled their drugs better and more quietly. While companion Estelle Winwood tried to keep Bankhead away from cocaine, complaining, "It made her dirty and rude to people," the drug did not ruin her. One of Tallulah Bankhead's famous remarks, reported by Louise Brooks, was, "Don't tell me cocaine is habit-forming. I've been taking it for seventeen years and I ought to know."

The Taylor murder hurt Mabel Normand's career, but did not destroy it. She was a big enough star that it took yet a third scandal—one involving more gunplay—to do that. On New Year's Day of 1924 Mabel's chauffeur used Mabel's gun to shoot Edna Purviance's millionaire oilman boyfriend. The boyfriend was okay and refused to press charges, but the chauffeur was revealed to be an ex-con and cocaine addict. After that, even Mack Sennett refused to use her. In 1930, Mabel Normand, thirty-eight, died. The front-page obituary cited tuberculosis, but others assumed it was the cumulative effect of her longtime cocaine addiction.

The legacy of Hollywood's drug films and real-life scandals was to link drugs not only to perdition, but also to a certain loose and glamorous high life. Screens and newspapers across America had been filled with the powerful image of the high-class drug user, the hedonistic rebel and Bohemian enjoying exotic pleasures while frolicking in glamorous locales. Imprinted on the collective consciousness, it would linger on.

"Arnold Rothstein, Financial Genius of the Underworld Plutocracy."

—*historian Lloyd Morris*

Very late on the night of November 4, 1928, New York gambler Arnold Rothstein, forty-six, was found shot inside the service entrance of the stately Park Central Hotel. Blood coursed down the trouser leg of his pin-striped suit as Rothstein resolutely groped his way toward the Fifty-sixth Street door. A bellhop spotted the wounded man and alerted the hotel detective. He, in turn, ignored Rothstein's request for a taxi, instead summoning police and medics. Rushed to the Polyclinic Hospital, Rothstein held tight to the code of the underworld, refusing to identify the man who had shot him in the groin or otherwise shed light on the attack. He brushed off police detectives with a mumbled, "If I live, I'll tend to it; if I die, the gang will." Rothstein lingered silently on for two days, while out in the hospital corridors, friends and hangers-on held furtive whispered conferences. Reportedly a millionaire from racetrack winnings and shrewd investments, Rothstein died Election Day, unable to collect five hundred thousand dollars won on the election of Herbert Hoover, the new president.

The *New York Times* identified Arnold Rothstein as "Broadway's greatest chance-taker" and the accused-but-acquitted fixer of the 1919 World Series. The *Herald Tribune* called him the "most spectacular gambler Broadway has known" and described a soft-spoken man who frequently played ultra–high stakes poker till dawn, returned home to his Fifth Avenue apartment to sleep briefly, and then put in a busy day at the West Fifty-seventh Street office building he owned. A man who routinely carried a huge cash bankroll, as much as $100,000, Rothstein had $6,500 on him when he died. At the Saratoga track, he won $825,000 in a single day.

But these early newspaper articles describing Rothstein merely as a clever and extraordinary gambler had assigned him far too modest a role. Only Hearst's *New York American* came close when it proposed that "Arnold Rothstein remained the most powerful personality outside official life in the city or the State, and perhaps the nation." In truth, Rothstein was an all-round criminal genius, one whose prodigious energy, imagination, and intellect had catapulted him to supremacy in an underworld he would change forever. New York chronicler Lloyd Morris called him the "[J. P.] Morgan of the Underworld," while historian Arthur Goren credits Rothstein with permanently transforming American crime "from petty larceny into big business."

Moreover, Rothstein's final criminal enterprise was also his most nefarious and long lasting: organizing and bankrolling big-time international narcotic trafficking. Arnold Rothstein's extensive involvement in drug trafficking was virtually unknown until his murder. New Yorkers were astonished to learn that this Broadway denizen, famed for his marathon gambling sessions, chauffeured Rolls-Royce, and huge cash bankrolls, was the brains and capital behind what federal prosecutors described as "a gang of international criminals who in recent years had smuggled millions of dollars in drugs into this country."

But this was indeed the case. Rothstein had seen an enormous opportunity in the local and federal governments' escalating (and successful) campaign to end easy access to addicting drugs and had moved ruthlessly to exploit it. Even though Rothstein died in 1928, the system he established retained much the same form through the 1970s, when the Colombian cartels brought cocaine and chaos to the American drug markets.

The Brain, as writer Damon Runyon dubbed Rothstein, thought big, inventing whole new ways to get rich exploiting society's weaknesses. And so, Rothstein had risen swiftly to criminal glory and enormous political influence: At a time when other gangsters were still working the traditional rackets, he masterminded the million-dollar stolen-bond business, pioneered and financed the first rum-smuggling from Europe during Prohibition, and brought blackmail to new heights through labor racketeering. And then, finally, there was the organizing of big-time drug trafficking. All of which required the active collusion of a corrupt New York political system, the Tammany Hall Democrats who controlled police and courts happy to go easy on the underworld.

Lloyd Morris describes in *Incredible New York* New York Mayor Jimmy Walker's response to Rothstein's shooting. Walker was at a Westchester speakeasy when an underworld type "went to the Mayor's table and whispered something in his ear. Jimmy . . . prepared to depart immediately . . . [T]he Mayor explained his perturbation. Arnold Rothstein had been shot; that meant plenty of trouble. As things turned out, it did."

Unlike most of his criminal cronies, the "wise guys" who idolized him, Rothstein seemed in no way destined to become a gangster. His prosperous, Orthodox father Abraham was a revered pillar of the community, much honored by Governor Alfred E. Smith and Supreme Court Justice Louis D. Brandeis for ending the garment industry's bitter 1919 union wars. But young Rothstein never cared for his father's pious ways and disliked school (except math, where he was brilliant). By his teens he largely had embraced the exciting life of the sporting man and the underworld. Rothstein was an outstanding professional gambler, specializing in fast-moving games of three-card monte, craps, poker, and "stuss." When he had a bankroll, he lent it out at high interest, insuring repayment through Monk Eastman, one of Gotham's most notorious thugs, another Jewish-boy-gone-bad.

Of medium height, five-seven, and pale complexion, Rothstein dressed in tasteful dark suits. His most notable features were his brown eyes, which missed nothing, and his nonstop nervous energy. When he gambled, he fidgeted and sipped endless glasses of water. He did not drink or smoke cigarettes. Like others of the sporting classes, he tried opium smoking, but he was not ensnared. Seated somewhere holding court, Rothstein had the odd habit of plucking at his sock garter as he talked in his soft, well-modulated voice. At age twenty-four, he married a blonde *shiksa*. He viewed himself as a devoted husband, but spent little time at home. The couple maintained separate bedrooms, and never had any children.

By his early twenties, Arnold Rothstein had enough political clout to open a string of gambling houses in the midtown theatrical district known as the Tenderloin (for here the payoffs were juiciest). He became renowned for his prowess at marathon gambling. By his late twenties, Rothstein was powerful enough to open a plush gambling casino in Saratoga Springs, summer home of thoroughbred racing, high society, and the sporting crowd. Bribes to local officials to guarantee "wide open conditions" alone cost fifty thousand dollars.

All this wealth and fame produced an arrogant man contemptuous of others. He once said, "The majority of the human race are dubs and dumbbells and have rotten judgment and no brains. . . . I wasn't fifteen years old before I learned my limitations. I never played with a man I wasn't sure I couldn't beat. I knew how to size them up. I still do. That is all there is to making money."

What so distinguished Arnold Rothstein (or A.R., as he was also known) from so many other underworld types was the ambitious scope of his criminality. Familiarizing himself with the world of big business, in 1919 Rothstein immediately saw that it did not take much to persuade the young, poorly paid messengers who ferried around millions of dollars worth of negotiable Liberty bonds to pretend they had been robbed. Then someone such as Rothstein could use the bonds as collateral for other deals or quietly dispose of them elsewhere. And while many believed Rothstein was the brain behind the rash of notorious bond robberies, others went to jail.

A regular on the colorful New York nightlife circuit, Rothstein was the first to exploit the possibilities of Prohibition, pioneering the original overseas rum-running organization. He made a fortune smuggling high-quality scotch whiskey from the British isles before stepping aside to let more violent, reckless gangsters do battle with the federal revenue agents and one another. He then backed and patronized some of New York's most famous speakeasies, including the Cotton Club and the Silver Slipper.

But Rothstein's real genius was in understanding how to further leverage those millions. By investing his ill-gotten gains in legitimate stocks, bonds, and real estate, Rothstein acquired the collateral for borrowing substantial sums from reputable banks. The Brain soon parlayed that advantage into a lucrative role as the underworld's investment banker. Rothstein loans backed a myriad of enterprises and featured unique guarantees—life insurance policies with Rothstein as beneficiary. Crooks, politicians, businessmen on hard times, showbiz types, all sought out Arnold Rothstein for his ability to come up with big money fast. For some, such as certain judges or politicians, it seemed no payback was expected, just the convenience of acquaintance.

As Rothstein became richer and more powerful, his reserved manner and quiet sartorial elegance set a gangster standard. Mobster Charles Lucania, later known as "Lucky" Luciano, apprenticed under Rothstein and credited A.R. with teaching him "how to dress, how not to wear loud things but to have good taste. . . . He was the best etiquette teacher a guy could have—real smooth." F. Scott Fitzgerald immortalized Rothstein in *The Great Gatsby* as Jay Gatsby's shady business partner and patron, Meyer Wolfsheim, "the man who fixed the World Series back in 1919." Was it Rothstein (described by an unadmiring Fitzgerald as a "small, flat-nosed Jew") who paid eighty thousand dollars to the Chicago White Sox to throw the World Series? Everyone believed it, but no one could prove it, and in real life Rothstein walked out of the Chicago courthouse unscathed by the Black Sox scandal.

Fitzgerald captured as no other writer the restless hedonism of the Roaring Twenties, Rothstein's heyday, an era when America found a certain racy glamour in illicit liquor, philandering, and mingling in the "speaks" with denizens of the underworld. Malcolm Cowley identified the twenties as the decade that marked the shift from prewar America, where the Protestant ethic of saving and self-denial and production prevailed, to the postwar America of prosperous consumerism, where citizens were encouraged "in a thousand ways to buy, enjoy, use once and throw away."

As Prohibition and the new ethos made local gangsters rich and powerful, Rothstein biographer Leo Katcher speculates that A.R. worried that other mobsters were becoming big enough to challenge his longtime preeminence as "the man uptown," the banker-gangster with the biggest bankroll and best political connections. Rothstein, having abandoned rum-running, was casting about for a new and less violent source of significant income. Illegal drugs looked highly promising. He knew something about them, having personally patronized the opium dens that had been so popular with the sporting class. His longtime personal secretary, Sidney Stajer, was an opium smoker.

Moreover, Rothstein had done business with Irving Wexler, a.k.a. Waxey Gordon, another Jewish-boy-gone-bad and one of the bigger names in New York's pre–World War I cocaine trade. Gordon had been identified back in 1917 by the New York Jewish community's own reform agency, the Kehillah Bureau of Social Morals, as an all-round local criminal and prominent cocaine wholesaler-importer. When federal narcotics agents showed too much interest in Waxey (an early nickname from his pickpocketing skills), he had switched first to transatlantic bootlegging, and then to beer breweries with A.R.'s financial backing.

And like every other New Yorker, Rothstein certainly had seen the newspaper stories in 1919 about the thousands of addicts lining up outside the brief-lived Worth Street Clinic. And no doubt, as an active member of the underworld, he also knew how popular heroin had been for a decade, and how difficult it was becoming for addicts to find it. Federal and city narcotics agents had continued to crack down hard on druggists and doctors. And while some still risked selling addicts drugs, the trade largely had reverted to the street peddlers, who had always been around for those willing to pay more. (Rothstein employee Charles Lucania a.k.a. Lucky Luciano had been arrested first in 1916 for selling heroin on the street to addicts.) These peddlers, like the druggists and doctors, had long obtained their supplies of morphine, cocaine, and heroin from the dozen or so American pharmaceutical plants then holding licenses to manufacture narcotic drugs.

Some of the peddler's supply of drugs came through pilfering, some through big heists, as when the American Drug Syndicate Company's Long Island plant was robbed in 1920 of 150 pounds of heroin tablets. But the bulk of street drugs came simply enough by placing orders with U.S. companies via dummy firms in Mexico and Canada. The Treasury Department complained during a 1920 congressional hearing that "drugs are exported from this country for the purpose of reentry through illicit channels." One federal narcotics official confirmed that much "confiscated opium bears the labels of reputable manufacturers of this country, particularly that we get from Canada." Plugging up this major source of illegal drugs had been the purpose of the Miller-Jones Tariff Act of 1922, but it was not much enforced for a couple of years.

By the mid twenties, Rothstein well knew, the easy access to the opiate and cocaine products of the American pharmaceutical firms was finished at both the retail and wholesale levels. The Miller-Jones Act of 1922 largely had constrained the pharmaceutical firms from exporting drugs to dubious front companies in Canada and Mexico, the 1924 Porter bill outlawed the domestic manufacture and medical use of heroin, while pure cocaine generally had been replaced in the medical pharmacopoeia by such variants as eucaine and novocaine. This left smuggling from Europe or Asia, heretofore minor, to supply virtually the whole illicit market. It was this opportunity that so obviously attracted Rothstein.

Rothstein's criminal genius was not just in recognizing that an established and lucrative market of drug users and addicts had lost its ultimate source of supply—American pharmaceutical firms—but in swiftly creating a whole new system to replace it. The moment for big-time international drug trafficking was ripe, and Rothstein now established a basic system that would survive for decades. Rothstein possessed—as no other gangster of his era—the capital to finance such an enterprise, the political clout to operate with impunity, and the connections to big-city criminal gangs around the country for street-level distribution to what the U.S. Treasury Department estimated were one hundred thousand addicts nationwide.

Rothstein dispatched a number of employees with experience purchasing liquor in Europe to locate major sources of supply. They found buying narcotics on the Continent ludicrously easy. Legitimate pharmaceutical firms—in France, Germany, and Holland—were still happy to sell huge orders of heroin, morphine, or cocaine, no questions asked. Dealing in one and two thousand–pound lots, Rothstein arranged for these giant orders to be shipped back as innocuous sea freight. We know that A.R.'s longtime personal secretary, Sidney Stajer, described as "slightly built, cherubic of countenance, taut of nerves," was acting as a buying agent in France in 1927 because French police arrested him and one Abraham Stein on narcotics charges. Once the drugs were smuggled successfully into New York, they then were distributed by Rothstein's people to the wide network of big-city Prohibition gangsters. After all, the modern addict generally was a young urban male easily served and cultivated through the Prohibition gangster's natural terrain of marginal neighborhoods and nightspots.

But Rothstein's many years of colluding with Tammany Hall had made him arrogant and careless. Indifferent even to appearances, A.R. freely engaged in blatant, frequent bailing out of arrested drug traffickers (who presumably were working for him). As can be imagined, this brazen activity attracted official federal interest, especially as it coincided with a corresponding quantum leap in the amounts of smuggled drugs seized by federal Customs agents. In the year ending June 30, 1926, U.S. Customs had confiscated 449 pounds of opium, 42 pounds of morphine, 3.5 pounds of heroin, and 10 pounds of cocaine. By mid 1928, those figures had soared to 2,354 pounds of opium, 91 pounds of morphine, 27 pounds of heroin, and 30 pounds of cocaine.

Obviously convinced that he was safely beyond reach, Rothstein made no effort at all to hide his intense concern over the biggest narcotics smuggling case of 1926. On July 13 of that year, Charles Webber and William Vachuda had been arrested at a New York toy company. Federal agents had barged in just as the two were opening five crates, containing 1,220 pounds of heroin, morphine, and cocaine identified as "bowling balls and pins," off the newly docked transatlantic liner *Arabic*. This was just one of numerous such deliveries originating in Germany and supposedly in transit to Japan, charged prosecutors. The retail value was $4 million. Not only did Rothstein immediately post twenty-five thousand dollars bail each for Webber and Vachuda (the latter a former city cop), the Brain personally attended the trial in federal court in January 1927. During the seventeen hours that the jury deliberated before finding the two guilty, Rothstein paced the court's marble corridors relentlessly.

Court regulars (and no doubt Rothstein) were stunned when the judge sentenced Webber to fourteen years and Vachuda to eight. No one could recall "a sentence so severe for such a crime." Federal prosecutors said they had reliable information that "from Feb. 1 to Aug. 1, 1926, more than two tons of narcotics were introduced by this ring into the traffic of this country." Federal prosecutors also had tantalizing but incomplete evidence that Jack "Legs" Diamond, another Rothstein employee, had been in Paris arranging the purchase of the drugs from Berlin and their shipment to New York. While that specific link was not brought up in court, or ever proved legally, Diamond subsequently was arrested on other narcotic charges in 1927 up in Mt. Vernon, New York. Here again, Rothstein boldly posted fifteen thousand dollars bail.

Rothstein may have pioneered large-scale international trafficking, but as with bootlegging, he possessed no personal monopoly. Furthermore, he still had his fingers in many other pies. One reporter described the frenetic routine of Rothstein in his office: The "telephone was ringing from minute to minute and he was constantly barking out instructions on buying real estate and selling it, buying and selling stocks, placing bets on the horses, lending or calling in money and paying or demanding pay for gambling debts. He bet on everything and boasted he was ready to take a chance on any transaction where money was to be made."

Once Rothstein blazed the way with drug trafficking, other gangsters quickly saw the possibilities. Three years after Rothstein's murder New York trafficker "Ike" Berman—disgusted by an undercover agent's reluctance to make a ten-kilo purchase of heroin—burst out, "Do you know who I used to do business with? Arnold Rothstein, Jack Diamond and Oscar and Sam Weiner. . . . [W]e used to bring back a million dollars worth of junk from Merck's factory in Berlin. I once went there with a hundred thousand dollars of Rothstein's dough and sixty thousand of my own and went to the main connection of the factory." Berman also revealed that "at another time he was facing twenty years and had to do some heavy fixing and called on Arnold Rothstein for fifty thousand dollars for that and saved doing that term."

In trying to reconstruct Rothstein's first forays into trafficking, one wonders just when the young Italian mobster Charles (Salvatore) Lucania entered Rothstein's orbit and the drug business. Lucania, the child of struggling Sicilian immigrants, was much more typical of the New York underworld than Rothstein. The impoverished Lucanias had arrived in lower Manhattan in 1907 when their son was already ten and young Salvatore quickly took to the streets. Unlike the brainy Rothstein, who rose to the pinnacle of criminal power without ever being convicted of a crime or spending a day in prison, Luciano had a much rougher rise. A chronic truant, he spent four months as a youngster in the Brooklyn Truant School.

Then he dropped out of sixth grade, ostensibly to work as a clerk for the Goodman Hat Company at six dollars a week. But his real interest was learning the criminal ropes, and as an eighteen-year-old punk he had his first serious run-in with the cops. He was caught selling heroin and served a six-month sentence at the New Hampton Farms Reformatory in 1916. Shunned by his shamed parents, he emerged to master the ins and outs of illicit gambling, stickups, and then bootlegging. (Like a great many immigrant families, the Lucanias must have wondered often why two sons and a daughter led honest lives and Salvatore turned to the underworld.) Once he became a regular at the racetracks and crap games, Lucania evidently met Rothstein.

For we know that the thirty-year-old Lucania was working for him when A.R. was murdered in 1928, and almost certainly in some aspect of the drug business. The morning after Rothstein was shot, Lucania and one of Rothstein's drug buyers, George Uffner, were picked up by police when they walked into Rothstein's office. What one wonders is whether Lucania already was connected to A.R. in some capacity in 1923, when he was arrested (the second time) for selling heroin to what turned out to be a federal informant. City and federal narcotics officers who had been watching the transaction on East Fourteenth Street grilled Lucania for several hours. Finally he directed police to 163 Mulberry Street, where he said they'd find a trunkful of narcotics. For this cooperation, the narcotics charges were dropped. Lucania's probation record shows that he was picked up again for "violating the Harrison Act" on March 1, 1926. The details are not known, but again the charges were dropped. The trunkful of narcotics, the leniency of dropped charges, all suggest a higher-up of Rothstein's stature.

While we can't say exactly when Arnold Rothstein first took up big league drug trafficking, his full-blown involvement definitely can be dated to 1926. This is when he began regularly bailing out drug traffickers. After Rothstein's high-profile presence at Webber and Vachuda's 1927 trial, the U.S. Attorney's Office in New York (a Republican entity hostile to Tammany) sent several federal agents to talk

with him. The Brain blandly "admitted lending money to those suspected . . . of trafficking in drugs," but denied knowing what they were
spending it for. The agents were not impresssed, and in March 1927
U.S. Attorney Charles H. Tuttle, a lanky, ambitious, crusading Republican WASP freshly appointed by Calvin Coolidge, decided to go after
Rothstein on narcotics. Tuttle, a graduate of Columbia Law School,
seasoned corporate lawyer, and lifelong trustee of City College,
delighted in twisting the tail of the Tammany Tiger. And since no one
better exemplified the corrupt alliance between the underworld and
Tammany than Rothstein, he made an irresistible target. The gung-ho
prosecutor reportedly was preparing a federal narcotics indictment
when Rothstein was murdered.

The city police investigation of Rothstein's murder was pure Keystone Kops. The official explanation of the gangland hit was that Rothstein was shot for welshing on a gambling debt, a theory few insiders
bought. The police were so patently unwilling to probe *anything*
linked to Arnold Rothstein, much less his murder, that Tammany
Mayor Jimmy Walker had to rebuke the police commissioner publicly
and finally fire him. Embarrassed into action, the police located and
questioned certain Rothstein associates, including various gamblers,
his wife, Carolyn, and his showgirl companion, Inez Norton, a flapper
who looked fetching in cloche hat, bobbed hair, and plush mink coat.
The Manhattan District Attorney's major endeavor in the murder—an
offer of immunity for any witness who stepped forward—was played
for big laughs by Will Rogers, who nightly repeated the offer to his
Broadway audiences.

Two bemused observers would comment a decade later, "[The
police] fell all over themselves backing away from whatever evidence
there might have been to indicate the slayer. Not only was Rothstein a
very powerful man, but he had many dealings with other very powerful men. Whatever a detective might have found out about the murder
was likely to be the wrong thing for him to know. The officers of the
law . . . did a very resourceful job of bungling." When Long Island
Republicans proposed making hay over the Rothstein scandal, Gotham
Republicans were oddly cool to the idea. So scant was the evidence
against a small-time gambler and hoodlum railroaded for the murder
that the judge in the much-delayed trial directed a verdict of acquittal.

But the loss of Rothstein himself could have been well-compensated
for by the incredible windfall of his meticulous "secret" files. Found in
his apartment at 912 Fifth Avenue, his office, and a number of safe
deposit boxes, these detailed all manner of business dealings and loans.
When the main files were discovered in Rothstein's apartment by the

office of the Manhattan District Attorney, they were not impounded immediately, thereby allowing Rothstein factotum Sidney Stajer time to make a hurried purge. Nonetheless, those sixty thousand documents promised to yield, as one assistant prosecutor crowed, "startling indications of Rothstein's connection in the past with murders, robberies and gambling and labor feuds in this city." But by the next day, District Attorney Banton, a good Tammany stalwart, had announced that the files were proving of little use and were being returned to the estate. Rothstein's personal lawyer and executor was one Maurice F. Cantor, Tammany regular and state assemblyman. (Cantor was deposed as executor when Polyclinic nurses testified that he had helped the comatose Rothstein sign an "X" on a new will that made Cantor the major beneficiary.)

But even as the Tammany DA hastened to rid himself of the red-hot files found in Rothstein's home, the crusading Republican Tuttle unleashed federal agents to search the premises of Rothstein's offices at 45 West Fifty-seventh Street. Using leads from papers found there in the files of the Rothmere Mortgage Corporation, federal agents (operating without informing local police) seized on December 7 several trunks full of opium, cocaine, heroin, and morphine with a street value of $2 million from an unnamed Manhattan hotel.

Having definitely connected Rothstein to financing "the biggest drug ring in the United States," U.S. Attorney Tuttle now demanded from Tammany DA Banton any and all files he had on the Rothmere Mortgage Corporation, the front for Rothstein's narcotics business. An internal FBI letter explained Tuttle's separate investigation by noting a "lack of confidence" in the city's efforts to "unearth the narcotic features of Rothstein's alleged activities." When the Rothmere files from the apartment reluctantly were turned over and studied, the *New York Times* reported, "these folders revealed Rothstein's close connection with drug peddlers and distributors, for whom he provided bail and lawyers after their arrests by Federal agents or the police."

Armed with new leads, federal narcotics agents swooped down two days later in New York, Buffalo, and Chicago, seizing four suspects and three steamer trunks filled with drugs said to be worth more than $3 million. "This is the single biggest raid on a narcotic ring in the history of this country," declared Tuttle, thus launching the hyperbolic style of assessing drug raids that has continued to this day.

In the wake of these sensational events, the preeminent congressional activist on the issue of narcotics, Stephen G. Porter, hurried north to Manhattan to confer personally with "Tiger Tamer" Tuttle. Porter, a Pennsylvania Democrat, was a member of the powerful House

Ways and Means Committee and chairman of the important Foreign Relations Committee. It was the so-called Porter bill that had ended the legal manufacture of heroin in this country in 1925. After meeting with Tuttle, Congressman Porter held a press conference with Colonel Levi G. Nutt, head of the federal Narcotic Bureau, at his side. "It was perfectly obvious to anyone," said Porter, that the European countries whose drugs were turning up in such huge quantities were not adhering to the Hague Opium Convention of 1912. "I have been gathering evidence in this phase of the matter for a long time and I am hopeful that the Rothstein homicide will add materially to the data which I have collected." The congressman added that he had given Tuttle information that he felt might help his grand jury investigation.

On December 19 came the largest seizure "in the history of the country," five crates off the French liner *Rochambeau*. Ostensibly a shipment of brushes bound for Philadelphia, the crates held one ton of drugs from legitimate European pharmaceutical factories. In March 1929 four gangsters, including Irving "Little Itch" Halper, were charged in New York as part of a "syndicate of illicit drug distributors in this and other states financed by Arnold Rothstein, the slain gambler."

Meanwhile, perhaps to no one's surprise, the Rothstein affair dragged on unsolved. Occasionally, there was a revelation from the secret files that hinted at the explosive nature of the scandals still hidden. In fall 1929, mayoral candidate Representative Fiorello LaGuardia revealed just one small tidbit: Bronx City magistrate Albert H. Vitale had gotten a $19,940 loan from Rothstein, a fact the judge freely acknowledged. A lawyer for the Rothstein estate said frankly, "If the Rothstein papers are ever made public, there is going to be a lot of suicides." But New Yorkers of the Jazz Age were still in high spirits and happy to wink at such shenanigans. Tammany's mayor Jimmy Walker was reelected handily with more than twice the votes of the upright LaGuardia.

Two months later in December, Tuttle swooped down again, rounding up fourteen people running "three huge narcotic rings. . . . The roundup was the culmination of an investigation based upon evidence of the 'Rothstein ring' seizures." Among those arrested was the proprietor of a Harlem speakeasy where drugs were sold as openly as liquor. The same man was said to supply (via the mails) "a good part of the cocaine, morphine and opium used in Hollywood." No federal or city narcotics agents based in New York had known of or participated in the raids; Tuttle had imported federal agents from Washington, D.C.

The reasons for this would eventually become clear. The next month, on January 30, Tuttle convened another federal grand jury and prosecutors promised "to show how sinister was the influence of Rothstein in the drug racket. . . . The persons involved thus far, we believe, will seem like small fry." A later story mentioned "prominent attorneys and politicians." Then, on February 20, Tuttle's first bombshell finally landed: GRAND JURY AACCUSES HIGHEST OFFICIALS IN NARCOTIC BUREAU.

Not only was the New York federal narcotics bureau padding its cases and getting cozy with traffickers, but one last scandal had slithered out of the secret Rothstein files and into public view. Arnold Rothstein had hired as his lawyers the relatives of Colonel Levi G. Nutt, deputy commissioner of the U.S. Treasury's Prohibition Unit in charge of narcotics. Nutt's son, a Washington tax attorney, had taken on a (successful) tax appeal for Arnold Rothstein before the U.S. Treasury, his father's place of business.

Even more incriminating was the revelation that son-in-law L. P. Mattingly had gone to Rothstein repeatedly for personal loans, which at the time of Rothstein's death totaled $6,200, a sizable sum for the time. Colonel Nutt testified that he knew nothing of any of this. The grand jury concluded that while the younger generation had been indiscreet, "We find no evidence that the enforcement of the narcotic law was affected thereby."

Equally embarrassing to Colonel Nutt were the dubious practices of his New York agents, who had pumped up federal arrest statistics by claiming city arrests as their own. Agents insisted that this was done on direct telephone orders from Washington. Certain agents also had allowed traffickers to evade arrest or prosecution in circumstances so suspicious as to reek of corruption. In one instance, the agent had changed his testimony suddenly, midway in a trial, ruining the prosecutor's case.

This was juicy enough, but where was the really big stuff? "Tiger Tamer" Tuttle virtually had promised to unmask crooked high-level politicians and attorneys growing fat on the drug trade, "startling disclosures" that would shock and dismay the public. The grand jury had sat for months and netted only a couple of small-fry lawyers. Rothstein's biographer, Katcher, credited Tuttle with being completely sincere. "But he could not get witnesses to talk. And when he sought fresh access to Rothstein's papers many of the papers could not be found."

While none of the grand jury's charges lived up to the advance billing, they were more than sufficient to wreck Colonel Nutt's not very glorious career. Ten days after the grand jury report was released, Colonel Nutt was demoted to field supervisor of Prohibition agents, and banished to the icy north of Syracuse, New York. One Harry J.

Anslinger, an assistant commissioner of the Prohibition Division, was appointed interim commissioner.

All this perfectly suited Congressman Stephen G. Porter. He long had wanted to separate the Narcotics Bureau from its hugely unpopular Prohibition parent and see it reorganized. He found Tuttle's damaging grand jury report very useful to his cause, and by March 1930 easily had persuaded Congress to go along. The powerful Porter felt it imperative not only to revamp the Narcotics Bureau, but for the new bureau's head to shine in the world of diplomacy. International control was essential to keeping drugs out of America and the United States needed to present a more forceful and impressive persona overseas. Nutt's failure to impress even the State Department, a key ally in the drug fight, marked him as a liability. But before Porter could ensure that his own choice for commissioner was installed, the congressman became ill with cancer and died.

Meanwhile, back in New York City, the Rothstein murder trial, with its directed verdict of acquittal, had come and gone, providing no further elucidation of that mysterious and fatal event. Rothstein's estate, initially valued at $1.8 million in stocks and real estate, was worth half that after the 1929 crash. Katcher's explanation of the small estate, considering Rothstein's reputed wealth, was that with Rothstein dead, few borrowers felt any compulsion to pay back their loans. Moreover, there was no way for the estate legally to retrieve all the money invested in drugs. "Tiger Tamer" Tuttle, much hailed for his vigorous pursuit of Tammany corruption in its various guises, ran on the Republican ticket against Governor Franklin Delano Roosevelt in the 1930 election. FDR reacted to this crusading candidate by appointing Judge Samuel Seabury to clean up the embarrassing odor of Tammany. Tuttle had little talent for campaigning, and the charismatic FDR easily swept to reelection, leaving Tuttle to return to corporate law and a lifetime of civic activism.

And so who did kill Rothstein? Or, as one of his gang was overheard to say into a pay phone, "gave it to Arnold"? Chroniclers of the underworld nominate "Legs" Diamond. Though Diamond claimed publicly that he barely knew Rothstein and had spoken to him on "perhaps twelve occasions," in fact it was well known that both Diamond and his tubercular brother, Eddie, had worked for Rothstein for one thousand dollars a week. Diamond seems a plausible assassin. Depending on who's doing the recounting, Rothstein double-crossed the Diamonds, or they him, over a drug deal, which led to Rothstein's murder.

Even by the lax standards of the underworld, "Legs" was crazy and out of control, a loose cannon. From the start, reporters wondered when "Legs" would be questioned. But authorities insistently denied his importance as a suspect. For if "Legs" was crazy enough to bump off Arnold Rothstein, who knew what he might say if brought in? A bungled attempt on Eddie Diamond's life sparked a bloody feud between Diamond and Rothstein loyalists that left eight dead. Yet, as the *New York Times* reported, "After Rothstein died Diamond had a chance to jump into a commanding position in the underworld, but he muffed it. . . . [H]e drank too much and when he was drunk he lost all control of himself." Federal prosecutors were trying to assemble enough evidence to indict Diamond for international drug trafficking when they read at the end of 1931 that "Legs" had been slain, his body riddled with five bullets. Evidently, the underworld had decided "Legs" was too dangerous and ordered him killed.

Other gangsters moved in to take over drug trafficking, and the basic system Rothstein had established survived for decades. Generations of New York mobsters handled America's illegal drug traffic much as The Brain had. They cultivated overseas sources, either smuggling the goods home themselves or acting as receivers here and then distributing drugs through fellow gangsters in other cities. But it would never again be as easy as it had been in the twenties.

CHAPTER 6

"It Can Be Safely Stated That the Days of the 500-Kilo Deliveries Have Passed."

—*police statement*
of trafficker Elie Eliopoulos,
September 1932

On December 5, 1930, the SS *Alesia* sailed into Brooklyn's Thirty-first Street pier from Izmir, Turkey, and unloaded, among other cargo, twenty-five tin-lined wooden containers consigned as furs. Still unclaimed ten days later, they were removed to a nearby warehouse. Not long after, federal Customs and narcotics agents, who had been keeping the boxes under continual surveillance, arrived and began cracking open the crates. There they found more than a thousand pounds of morphine cubes.

On April 24, 1931, New York narcotics detectives pulled onto Pier 84 at West Forty-fourth Street, shortly followed by federal agents. The SS *Milwaukee*, having arrived several days earlier from Hamburg, towered over the quiet dock. To one side, seventeen crates marked IN TRANSIT sat. Rather than the woolens declared in the Customs papers, the first opened crate revealed zinc sheets separating three layers of narcotics. Nervous police drew their guns against possible lurking hijackers, hustled the crates onto trucks, and zoomed off to the safety of a Brooklyn army base. When inventoried, the crates yielded almost a ton of opiates.

It would be decades before such huge drug seizures were made again in this country. In 1930 and 1931 a few such losses drove home indelibly to American drug traffickers that the easy days were over. A new regime had begun. The Rothstein drug scandals, which had shown how simple it was for gangsters to breeze over to the Continent and buy thousand-pound lots from legitimate firms, also had brought about the professional demise of the head of the Treasury Department's Narcotic's Unit, Colonel Levi Nutt. Powerful Republican Congressman Stephen G. Porter seized this opportunity to remake America's federal antidrug agency.

Representative Porter, who spent two years in medical school before becoming a lawyer and Pennsylvania politician, had for almost a decade been the preeminent congressional authority on drugs. Elected from Pittsburgh in 1911, Porter had risen to a high position on the House Ways and Means Committee and to chairmanship of the House Foreign Relations Committee. From these perches of power, Porter had shepherded through first one bill creating federal narcotics farms for treating addicts and a second bill ending all legal use and manufacture of heroin in the United States.

Since 1923 Porter had lead the American delegations to the League of Nation's Opium Advisory Committee. This had not been a happy experience for the idealistic congressman, who had nothing but contempt for the many Western (and Eastern) governments happy to earn fat revenues from opium monopolies that drugged their own people or those of other nations. Porter's wranglings with the League's Opium committee convinced him it was imperative for the United States to separate the Narcotic Unit from its hugely unpopular Prohibition parent and see it reorganized as an independent agency. This would then serve as a model for every other nation. The thought was that if such agencies existed worldwide they would work together to provide information and restrict drug use.

Moreover, the crusading antidrug congressman had concluded that a new and independent Bureau of Narcotics should be headed by someone who could shine in the world of diplomacy. International control was essential to keeping drugs out of America, and the United States needed to present a more forceful and impressive persona overseas. The prosaic Colonel Nutt's failure to impress the State Department, a key player in the international drug fight, marked him as a liability. Consequently, Porter found U.S. Attorney Charles Tuttle's damaging grand jury report on Colonel Nutt and the corrupt Narcotic Unit very useful to his cause. By the spring of 1930, when Porter was gravely ill with cancer, he easily convinced his congressional colleagues to go along with spinning off a whole new Bureau of Narcotics to be located in the Treasury Department. Congressman Porter's choice for narcotics commissioner was Rear Admiral Mark L. Bristol.

Elizabeth Washburn Wright, who had been extremely active in the international drug field since her husband's untimely death, also backed the rear admiral. As her longtime ally Porter lay dying, Wright made several forays to talk to the Treasury official appointed to run the Narcotic Unit following Nutt's exile. This was Harry J. Anslinger, a tall, good-looking man with a cleft chin and pomaded hair parted in the middle. Anslinger, thirty-eight, a dynamic Pennsylvania Dutchman, was an assistant commissioner of Prohibition who had made a favorable impression at Treasury by using diplomatic channels to put an end to flagrant rum-running from English and French islands in the Caribbean. With Colonel Nutt gone, Anslinger was dispatched from alcohol to run the show temporarily.

Although Wright was backing Admiral Bristol to become the new narcotics commissioner, she wrote President Herbert Hoover's secretary to say she found Anslinger to be a "very alert and intelligent man, . . . [someone who could be] a most valuable lieutenant or assistant to the Admiral." Wright, it should be noted, very much expected to have a job in the new narcotics bureau. Anslinger, a longtime and loyal Republican, however, had little interest in serving as Admiral Bristol's second in command, for he had his own ambitions. Moreover, he well knew that the admiral had offended President Hoover deeply with impolitic congressional testimony. As spring turned to hot Washington summer, Anslinger quietly began marshalling his own allies and admirers to bombard the Hoover White House with letters arguing that he above all others possessed the proper combination of diplomatic skills and administrative experience to be narcotics commissioner.

On July 1, 1930, just days after Congressman Stephen G. Porter died from cancer in Pittsburgh, the new Bureau of Narcotics was formally established. U.S. Treasury Secretary Andrew Mellon thoughtfully waited until after Congressman Porter's funeral before making Anslinger acting commissioner, because he knew Anslinger was not Porter's choice. On September 23, President Hoover formally nominated Anslinger to the job, a nine thousand dollar post overseeing all laws regulating habit-forming drugs—legal and illegal—in the United States. While the Bureau with its 250 agents would be best known for fighting American and foreign traffickers and harrassing addicts, it also regulated all domestic manufacture of opiates and cocaine and their legitimate use. Drug companies, physicians, and pharmacists all were licensed to dispense narcotics by the Federal Bureau of Narcotics, or FBN.

On September 20, the day that Anslinger was informed that the commissionership was his, he relayed to the president's secretary the latest on Elizabeth Wright, who was lobbying hard for a job. "I pointed out that [if she worked for the Bureau of Narcotics] she could not formulate international policy nor participate in European negotiations, since such matters rested entirely within the Department of State. . . . She said she would be humiliated by such an arrangement." Knowing Mrs. Wright's influence within Congress, where her father and four uncles once had served, and of her close ties to numerous influential Republicans, Anslinger shrewdly made amends by dispatching her to the Philippines on a mission to study the opium problem. Thus Mrs. Wright not only was placated, but far, far away while Anslinger consolidated his new position.

Anslinger's deft handling of Mrs. Wright revealed early on his notable talent for finessing any situation that might undermine him. Mrs. Wright presented exactly such a threat to the neophyte commissioner because she had become a respected expert in international drug diplomacy. Historian Arnold Taylor credits Elizabeth Wright's "energy, zeal, and uncompromising dedication" with shaping "American drug policy in the 1920s. She was regarded by American officials as perhaps the most knowledgeable of the Americans in the [reform] movement. . . . The great emphasis which the United States placed on the theme of limitation of production, after World War I, was to a considerable degree the result of the persuasion and activities of Mrs. Wright. She had early concluded that restriction at the source was the only way to deal with the opium question."

In 1923 she traveled (with the State Department's blessings) to report firsthand on the opium situation in Turkey and Persia. The next year she was part of Congressman Porter's American delegation to the Second Geneva Opium Conference, an assignment that made her the first American woman to receive plenipotentiary powers as a diplomat. Clearly, Anslinger viewed her as a potential rival and made sure that she never gained a foothold in his new agency. Narcotics Commissioner Harry J. Anslinger would again and again prove himself the consummate bureaucrat, an ambitious and canny politician who excelled at promoting himself, protecting his turf, and above all, surviving.

Anslinger's was the classic American story of the bright boy of humble origins determined to make good. He had grown up the eighth of nine children in a solid working-class family in Altoona, Pennsylvania, a place he described as quintessential small-town America, a "mixture of new immigrants, rolling farmlands and new factories, miners and road-workers, foremen and factory heads." Here his Swiss émigré father struggled along as a barber, before finding steady work and security with the Pennsylvania Railroad. Young Anslinger was recognized early on in his own small universe as someone special, someone with promise, and he was determined to make a name for himself in the larger world.

Certain experiences in small-town Altoona would shape forever Anslinger's views as narcotics commissioner. The first occurred in 1904 when he was twelve,

> visiting in the house of a neighboring farmer. I heard the scream-
> ing of a woman on the second floor. I had never heard such cries
> of pain before. The woman, I later learned, was addicted, like
> many other women of that period, to morphine. . . . All I remem-
> ber was that I heard a woman in pain, whose cries seemed to fill
> my whole twelve-year-old being. Then her husband came run-
> ning down the stairs, telling me I had to get into the cart and
> drive to town. I was to pick up a package at the drug store and
> bring it back for the woman.
>
> I never forgot those screams. Nor did I forget that the mor-
> phine she had required was sold to a twelve-year-old boy, no
> questions asked.

A few years later, when Anslinger was a teenager, he saw a "young pool player, the best in Altoona, a bright-eyed, grinning youth who wanted to be a world's champion" and who also sang in "the choir—a pool player who sang tenor like an angel" succumb to opium smoking. "Within two years he was dead."

Like almost every American of that turn-of-the-century era, Anslinger personally saw the tragedy of the old-style medical addiction, presumably the consequence of careless doctoring. But he also saw the tragedy of the new-style addict, the young pool player who took up opium smoking, not because of illness, but because of the enjoyable altered state it initially produced. It was clear even to young Anslinger that dangerously addictive drugs were available too easily.

Anslinger's interest in police work dated back to high school, when he worked part-time for the Pennsylvania Railroad debunking fraudulent claims. (Hence his fraternity nickname at Pennsylvania State College of "Holmes.") On a later "Pennsy" job (supervising a group of mostly Sicilian immigrant laborers) Anslinger also first encountered organized crime. One day the most energetic workman was found bloody and full of bullets, a warning to those who might refuse to hand over a cut of their pay to the local version of the Mafia, known as the Black Hand. The worker survived, and Anslinger warned off the local racketeer. "Such was my first direct encounter with this transplanted brotherhood of plunder, extortion, thievery, and murder."

When America entered World War I, Anslinger was rejected for military service due to blindness in one eye (a brother throwing a rock). Instead, he got a job in Washington, D.C., in 1918 on the Efficiency Board of the War Department's Ordnance Division. But young Anslinger knew the road to glory was not to be found as "assistant to the Chief of Inspection of Equipment." Anslinger parlayed his fluent German into a consular position in Europe with the State Department.

Just as the Great War was ending, Anslinger was assigned to the American legation at The Hague in the Netherlands. The child of a railroad worker found himself part of a delightful diplomatic social whirl—glittering, formal dinners, gracious garden parties, and a general high-class camraderie. Aside from the usual work routine, Anslinger undertook a whole range of intelligence gathering. The high point was his successful infiltration of Kaiser Wilhelm II's entourage, where he acted as an American liaison.

In the wake of this professional triumph, Anslinger was then transferred to Hamburg, a tough port replete with intrigue and evil doings. In a letter, he crowed that he had "succeeded in uncovering a new Communistic organization in the United States, a bed of counterfeiters; disclosing illegal financial transactions of New York bank; revealing a grafting Consulate employee; bringing a crooked bank to justice; discovering ships engaged in wholesale illicit liquor traffic, uncovering several large cases of dope smuggling; finding a false passport bureau and numerous things too lengthy to mention."

Then Anslinger was assigned to the dismally quiet backwater of La Guaira, Venezuela (population 6,000). He dutifully put up with three dull years, unable even to bring over his new wife, Martha, because there was no school for Joseph, the child of her first marriage. Anslinger's marriage was not only long and loving (though childless), but highly advantageous. For Martha Denniston had family money and connections, both of which the Pennsylvania Dutchman singularly lacked.

Anslinger's languishing career revived during his next posting, Nassau in the Bahamas. This picturesque port had become a stopover for oceangoing ships loaded with liquor and en route to Prohibitionist America. Anslinger persuaded the English to put a stop to the blatant rum-running and then worked out similar deals with Canada, France, and Cuba. The reward was a new job in the Treasury Department (where his wife's relative Andrew Mellon was secretary) as chief of the Prohibition Bureau's Division of Foreign Control. In 1929 Anslinger was advanced to assistant commissioner.

About the same time that Anslinger ascended to the top job at the new Bureau of Narcotics in 1930, a quiet, pipe-smoking diplomat named Stuart J. Fuller returned from a decade in turbulent China to work in the State Department. There, in the Far Eastern Division, Fuller joined John K. Caldwell to work full-time on narcotics issues. By 1932 the energetic Fuller would become State's key man on habit-forming drugs, supervising as many as three other officers. A native of Keokuk, Iowa, Fuller had a law degree from the University of Wisconsin and several years in railroads and the export business. In 1906 he had joined the State Department, serving as consul in various exotic locales—everywhere from Hong Kong to Naples to Durban to Tientsin. For seven years during the 1920s Fuller again had been in business overseas. Now at forty-nine he had returned home to rejoin the State Department.

Fuller proved to be an extraordinary stroke of good fortune for Anslinger, because, as the new commissioner had pointed out to Mrs. Wright, the State Department generally handled the international aspect of drug trafficking. And Fuller, having seen firsthand the ravages opiates had wrought on war-torn, beleaguered China, was passionate in his hatred of drugs. By the early thirties, opium had become ubiquitous throughout that vast land. As one Treasury attaché stationed in Shanghai observed in 1934, "It has been an established fact with Chinese politics during the past twenty years that opium cultivation has served as the main source of revenue for various militarists. Almost every militarist has been dependent on poppy and opium revenue to build up his army and to continually support his political machinery."

A traveler going to Chungking in 1930 marveled at the ethereal beauty of mile after mile of vast silky poppy fields. In the city itself the traveler found "opium smoking shops on every hand, practically every fourth building. Curious, I entered [to see] a frightfully dirty interior, rows of bunks occupied by filthy smokers and the air almost deadening to the sense in the density of the smoke." The communists retreating on the Long March through Guizhou province were appalled by the local situation. "This was opium country. Here, as Peasant Zeng observed, almost everyone of the age of fifteen and above smoked opium. They sat outside their huts puffing their pipes with glazed eyes, men, women and teenagers. The men and teenagers often wore nothing but loincloths, the women not even that. The opium was piled up in brown stacks in the sheds like cow dung put to dry." With scenes like that fresh in his memory, Fuller was as determined as Anslinger to bring a halt to the flagrant trafficking throughout Europe and the Far East.

The international drug situation at this time could only be described as outrageous. For not only was China overwhelmed with native-grown smoking opium pushed by revenue-hungry warlords, imperialist Japan had begun saturating the benighted celestial kingdom with manufactured opiates such as morphine and heroin. The Treasury attaché in Shanghai passed along this dispiriting report from a female missionary in northern Manchuria.

> There is a brisk trade springing up in morphine and heroin which is almost entirely run by Japanese. . . . [T]he country is being flooded with morphine, heroin and opium where little or none existed before. In her small village where before there was just one or two opium dens, there are now forty-seven, all managed and run by Japanese and Koreans under the official monopoly. She declared that it was her firm conviction that the Japanese are flooding Manchuria with dope deliberately and maliciously—not [just] for the sake of the revenue derived from it, but equally to shatter the morale of the people. In Jehol the Japanese are carrying forward a hundred fold the work of General Tang Yu-ling, the ex-opium-war-lord.

Nor was it just ruthless imperialists such as the Japanese who were inundating the Far East with habit-forming drugs. Fuller himself would describe in a 1935 speech the numerous "ostensibly respectable European firms who during these years were engaged in the illicit traffic on an enormous scale. . . . [They were] able, through defects in the . . . system of control, to export . . . enormous quantities. . . . The greater part of the exports were to the Far East." Fuller also cited the French firm of Rossler Fils, which in little more than three years exported six and a half tons of heroin and a ton of morphine. "The United States was the principal victim. . . . As a result of these scandals, a fresh impetus was given to the international movement. The control exercised by governments in central and western Europe became more strict."

As historians Terry Parssinen and Kathryn B. Meyer have noted, the major target of international traffickers in the twenties and thirties was not the United States with its one hundred thousand addicts. The real money was in China. Colonel Joseph W. Stilwell, then a U.S. military attaché in China, "estimated that there were eight million Chinese heroin and morphine addicts and another 72 million Chinese opium addicts. . . . American addicts represented less than five percent of the world market for illicit narcotics . . . a small and relatively unimportant secondary market."

The ultimate and oft-stated goal of the United States at the League of Nation's Opium Advisory Committee was to limit international commerce in habit-forming drugs to those amounts necessary for medical treatment. However, this did not particularly suit such great colonial powers as England, France, Holland, and Portugal, which enjoyed rich revenues from opiates sold in the Far East opium monopolies, drugs that also kept the natives docile. For much the same reasons, the ruling classes in such producer nations as Turkey, Persia, and Thailand also were not anxious to cooperate. As for China, the little progress against drugs made under the Manchus had been swept away after the 1911 revolution. Now all the factions (save the communists) depended upon drug sales to fill their war chests and hence had no interest in controls.

Disgusted by the whole scandalous scene of rampant self-interest, Congressman Porter had at one point back in the mid-twenties decreed it pointless for Americans to participate in the League's Opium Advisory Committee. But the fact was that the twenties saw a major advance in international control with the 1928 establishment of a Permanent Control Board as part of the Opium Advisory Committee "to survey drug factories, to collect and analyze national quarterly reports on imports and exports of proscribed drugs, and to conduct other similar surveying and statistical tasks."

Congressman Porter's passing was not mourned by the State Department, which had resented the assertive, activist congressman's domination of American drug policy. Displeased to lose control over international drug matters to the politician from Pittsburgh, the State Department lost no time in swiftly reasserting its historic domination of the opium question. To ensure that it would control the American agenda at Opium Advisory Committee meetings, State now assigned its own officers to represent the United States. By these preemptive actions, the State Department made it unlikely that any other congressman could assume what they saw as Porter's interfering role. For most of the thirties, Stuart J. Fuller would be the U.S. representative to the Opium Advisory Committee. U.S. Narcotics Commissioner Anslinger, who reveled in diplomatic palaver and the attendent elegant socializing, was always an important and active member of the delegation.

While the opium situation in China was outrageous, the immediate challenge for new Narcotics Commissioner Harry J. Anslinger and his colleagues at the State Department was to do something on the home front. The Arnold Rothstein drug scandals, which had shown how effortlessly large amounts of drugs were procured overseas and smuggled back in, provided part of the diplomatic ammunition to embarrass the Europeans into action. The other part came from the Opium Advisory Committee's Permanent Control Board, whose newly gathered facts and figures allowed Fuller and Anslinger to demonstrate some unpleasant truths. One of which was France's dubious preeminence as a manufacturer of tons of narcotics that far exceeded any possible medical needs. Thanks to the Permanent Control Board, it was possible to see that in 1928 "France imported 251.5 tons of Turkish opium, almost three times the amount reportedly imported by the rest of the world. This figure confirmed that France was Europe's major producer of opium derivatives and thus the likeliest center for diverting narcotics into the underground economy."

The biggest and more flamboyant of the Paris-based traffickers when Anslinger and Fuller came onto the scene was Elias Eliopoulos, a Greek bon vivant who claimed to be the son of a "prominent and respectable family of Piraeus" and a graduate of the prestigious Roberts College in Istanbul. A tall and elegant man impeccably turned out in striped pants, gray spats, and kid gloves, Eliopoulos's trademark was his gold-topped cane. Accustomed to wealth and the good life of the boulevardier, he was very unhappy when his family's import business incurred a large loss supplying the Greek army during World War I. In 1927, Eliopoulos, lounging around a café as was his wont, heard of great opportunities in the booming Chinese opiate market. He voyaged to Tientsin (Peking's port) himself to confirm the stories of vast armies of Chinese addicts needing to be supplied. With a few crucial and shady connections arranged, Eliopoulos returned to France, invited his brother, George, to join him, and hooked up with two French drug firms, Paul Mechelaere's Comptoir Français des Alcaloides and George Devineau's Société Industrielle de Chimie Organique (SICO).

While the Eliopoulos's major customers were in China, the brothers were happy to sell to others, including the American gangsters. So widespread had Elie's business become within three years that at the 1930 London conference of the Opium Advisory Committee, the Paris-based Eliopoulos drug empire merited a heated and separate discussion. While the French delegate tried hard to stifle Harry J. Anslinger's description of how the Eliopoulos brothers openly flouted supposed restrictions on international drug sales, the damning documentation forced the reluctant French to crack down hard.

When French officials revoked the licenses of the two firms that had supplied the Eliopoulos empire, Eliopoulos simply helped them to relocate lock, stock, and barrel to Istanbul, Turkey, where they jointly opened a new factory. Eliopoulos would later explain in a 1932 police statement:

> At the end of August, 1930, it became practically impossible to obtain any considerable quantity of drugs in France. Beginning in September, 1930, the French authorities granted licenses to deal in narcotic drugs solely to 15 or 16 reputable firms, and this was the first effective measure of control adopted in France.... [It became] practically impossible to obtain for other than legitimate needs any considerable quantities of narcotic drugs in Europe. An exception may have to be made in the case of the new small drug factories in or near Sofia, but it can be stated safely that the days of the 500 kilo deliveries have passed.

The centralized nature of European governments made it fairly simple for these nations to assert true control over the sale for export of habit-forming drugs produced by their pharmaceutical industries. The governments simply had to be shamed into taking meaningful action.

And it was not just such European actions that were bringing to a close the era of the five hundred–kilo deliveries. U. S. Treasury officials also began establishing effective secret intelligence networks overseas. One of Anslinger's first acts in Washington had been to hire several confidential Treasury agents to work overseas, including his old friend Charlie Dyar in Europe. Dyar, Harvard man and veteran multilingual Foreign Service officer, had a notable flair for intelligence work. He had been invaluable to President Woodrow Wilson during World War I, who began each morning by reading Dyar's daily report from Berlin. Anslinger described the chess-playing Dyar as "tall, well-groomed, taciturn, with remarkable composure. He looked a little like Gary Cooper and was called 'The Sphinx.' He almost never smiled." Anslinger credited Dyar with uncovering the "startling tie-ins" between the Eliopoulos brothers and various notorious American traffickers.

The advent of these undercover Treasury agents signaled a whole new direction for international narcotics enforcement. Colonel Nutt certainly had never launched any such ventures. But now Anslinger had Dyar and several others roaming Europe and the Middle East, as well as Treasury attaché M. R. Nicholson in China, cultivating friends, acquaintances, and informants in the strange underworld of drug traffickers. Informants were rewarded according to how much was seized.

In 1930 the going rate could reach as high as forty dollars per kilo for morphine or heroin, twenty dollars per kilo of cocaine, and 10 dollars per kilo of crude opium.

Anslinger and Fuller also launched another semisecret project through the Opium Advisory Committee, something called the International Black List. Conveniently organized as a small loose-leaf notebook, each page featured a known or suspected trafficker, complete with mug shot, aliases, police record, and whatever else was known. Constantly updated, it was circulated to embassies and police colleagues around the world. Many of the lawmen had been recruited by Anslinger in 1931 into the so-called Committee of One Hundred, a top secret panel of narcotics officers in London, Cairo, Ottawa, Rotterdam, Berlin, and Paris.

Meanwhile, in Fuller's small office at the State Department, observed one colleague, he worked "incessantly at it, seven days a week, and with definite and great efficiency." Fuller was amassing more than eight hundred confidential files on everyone remotely associated with the illicit international drug traffic. (Presumably so did Anslinger, but the Drug Enforcement Agency has not—as the State Department has—put theirs into the National Archives.)

This new strategy of intensively cultivating intelligence began paying immediate dividends. For it was Charlie Dyar who alerted Anslinger that the SS *Alesia* was en route from Turkey with a thousand pounds of morphine cubes. (Dyar's informant was duly paid twenty-two thousand dollars, a munificent sum in those Depression years, but still a bargain for the government, which just added the morphine to its legal stockpile available to military hospitals in the event of war.) And it was Dyar again who alerted New York that the SS *Milwaukee* was coming in from Hamburg with almost a ton of opiates. (That time the informant was paid only $8,800.)

It was a promising start, and from the beginning of their working partnership, Anslinger and Fuller meshed well, peppering one another with a constant flow of notes and information on the world's narcotics traffic. Whenever a significant drug seizure was made in the United States, Anslinger's Bureau of Narcotics would furnish Fuller's Division of Far Eastern Affairs with details or clues as to the origins of the shipment. The State Department then swung into action, using these leads to pressure foreign governments to tighten up. Typical of this interplay was the case of the SS *Innoko*, which arrived from Antwerp in late July 1930 with more than two hundred pounds of morphine in crates manifested as electrical apparatus.

Since the morphine was shipped from Antwerp, Fuller's office contacted the Belgian government and tartly asked them to investigate. Then the wrapping paper from the morphine was dispatched to the American embassy in Turkey with instructions to see whether it was a local brand. If so, it was the necessary proof that Turkish drug factories had produced the morphine. In that case, the evidence would be presented to Turkish officials.

The U.S. government's dramatically tougher tone and tactics were noted not only by official counterparts overseas, but by the extraordinary cast of criminal characters who trafficked in illegal drugs. Straight out of an early Alfred Hitchcock film, this shifting and duplicitous ensemble of suave Greeks, Eastern Jews, questionable Peruvians, crooked Frenchmen, and American gangsters suddenly found itself scrutinized and pursued. When Rothstein's emissaries first had ventured across the Atlantic in the twenties, Paris was the preferred wide-open business locale. Aside from the obvious delights of the City of Light, especially its racetracks, the Gallic authorities had been pleasantly indifferent to local factories producing prolific amounts of drugs. The going wholesale price for a kilo (2.2 pounds) of heroin in those carefree days was about eighty dollars, with even cheaper deals for large orders.

But once someone like Eliopoulos had to relocate his main factory so far from Paris—the preferred business venue for most American traffickers—the trafficker also had to engage a number of diplomats with their valuable diplomatic passports to ferry drugs from Istanbul to Paris, and sometimes even to New York. The most infamous of these diplomat couriers was the dapper Carlos Fernandez Bacula, a Peter Lorre type whose stated employment was as a Peruvian chargé d'affaires posted around Europe. When the United States first became suspicious of the slight, mustachioed Bacula in 1931, the American embassy in Lima looked into him and sent along a report. The report gives a flavorful feeling for the shadowy nature of these international traffickers:

> Señor Bacula's father apparently was a Peruvian, but his mother, the Minister [for Foreign Affairs] informs me, came from some place in Eastern Europe and is a Slav or a Slovak or some thing. . . . His father was a considerable land owner in Peru, . . . however, [Bacula the son] is a good deal of a mystery. . . . [He is] very close to Cornejo, the former Peruvian ambassador in Paris. Doctor Galvez thinks Leguia may have used Bacula as a sort of spy, but he cannot be sure of this. He says he thinks Bacula is an extremely acute, astute, and intelligent man, but that he has lived separate from Peru and abroad for many years and that he does not know much about him.

Traffickers of the thirties were bedeviled not only by tightening international controls but their own rotten venality. The crooks were double-crossing one another constantly. The American traffickers were virtually all of the Prohibition gangster class, murderous toughs who had graduated to international crime: Such infamous names as "Legs" Diamond, Waxey Gordon, Louie Lepke, and such complete unknowns as Little Augie Del Gratio, Sam Bernstein, and the Neiditch, or Newman, Brothers. Individuals and groups continually fell in and out of alliances (and the market itself) based on current feuds, betrayals, and fortunes.

Typical of American traffickers in the twenties and thirties was one Augie Del Gratio, a ruthless New York mobster who had grown up on the Lower East Side, acquiring a long rap sheet of discharged assaults, unproven homicide, burglary, etc., and a couple of prison stints. By 1928, Little Augie, or Augie the Wop, as he was known to some, had become a very good customer of Eliopoulos's, though he bought from other sources, too. In post-Rothstein New York, for a while Little Augie supplied the low-profile Neiditch, or Newman, brothers, best known as gamblers and owners of unsavory hotels, until they had a falling out. The huge SS *Milwaukee* shipment spirited off to the Brooklyn army base had been Little Augie's, opiates purchased from Eliopoulos's new Istanbul factory and shipped from Hamburg for the Newman brothers.

Another active American trafficker was one Jacob Polakiewitz, an unassuming naturalized American Jew of numerous aliases and Polish origin. He operated all over Europe as a salesman for Eliopoulos, according to a police statement by a disgruntled former associate, hanging out with such unsavory types as a "white slaver said to own a brothel in Buenos Aires." The disillusioned associate told police, "I know for a fact that Jack's inventory early in 1931 comprised 500 kilos of morphine cubes and 150 kilos of heroin received via the Simplon Express, all supplied by Elie. In addition to this, Noury and [Corsican gangster Paul] Carbone had brought 140 kilos of drugs to Jack in Bremen." Even though he supposedly had an exclusive arrangement with the Newman brothers of New York, Polakiewitz still solicited alternate deals on the quiet with other New York criminals.

One of these was Sam Bernstein, who started his career as a street peddler of illegal drugs on the Lower East Side, then moved up in 1917 to wholesaling five-, ten-, and twenty-ounce lots. Caught, he served a brief sentence, and then turned to the bootlegging business, where he was a "pipefitter" who specialized in building stills. Then, in 1929, Bernstein and three other bootleggers decided to try drug trafficking again. They sailed to Paris and soon made contact with Polakiewitz and the Eliopoulos brothers. To show they had the goods, the wholesaling Eliopoulos brothers escorted Bernstein to a warehouse. Later he would describe it: "I saw a lot of trunks and cases and different kinds of bags—balled up goods. . . . They really started to show me quantities of narcotics and morphine and opium and different cases that was packed." Once they agreed to do business, the new partners whiled away many a pleasant afternoon at the Café Du Barry on the Champs Élysées, regrouping in the evenings for drinks and dinner at Claridge's Hotel Grill.

Bernstein soon paid his new friends the Eliopouloses in cash for a hundred kilos of heroin. He packed it up in a new steamer trunk and shipped it through on a transatlantic liner in the name of an unsuspecting passenger. Once in New York the trunk went unclaimed until Bernstein or a partner would appear to take it away. He shipped about 1,200 kilos during 1929 in this fashion until he was caught, the police perhaps tipped off by jealous rivals.

"There is no honor among thieves" never was truer than with this crowd of international drug traffickers. Elie Eliopoulos complained (without a hint of irony) to police, "My privileged position was known to American and other traffickers, who frequently brought pressure on me, threatening to denounce me, etc., in order to obtain drugs through me." When Jack (Yasha) Katzenberg, a heavyset and somewhat hapless New York criminal with owlish spectacles arrived in Paris in 1930 on a liquor-buying mission for a group of gangsters, the unassuming Polakiewitz convinced him to buy some heroin, too. Lukewarmly interested, Katzenberg finally agreed. What followed was a first shipment of bad quality heroin, a second shipment "knocked off by U.S. Customs," and yet another shipment that was talcum powder. With that, Katzenberg wisely abandoned the business.

Or consider the experience of the notorious Peruvian diplomat and international courier Bacula when he ferried 150 pounds of heroin to New York in 1931, using his special Hartmann trunks bought near the Paris Opéra and outfitted with a secret compartment. Ensconced in a Manhattan hotel room, the dapper Bacula dispatched the first fifty pounds of heroin, only to have the local courier reappear beaten and bloody, reporting the drugs hijacked. Next, the handsome but intimidating "Legs" Diamond appeared at the door to offer his services. Legs then munificently "retrieved" thirty pounds and earnestly advised a terrified Bacula (a refined man unused to such violent thuggery) to move to another hotel and entrust the remaining one hundred pounds to one Wilhelm Kofler. The next day, Kofler was dead and all the heroin was gone. The whole thing smelled suspiciously of the classic "Legs" heist, complete with casual killings. Such double-dealing and violence were endemic to trafficking.

As international law enforcement—led by the Americans—cracked down, the traffickers began going further afield to manufacture or buy drugs, first Turkey, then the Far East. As business became more time consuming and riskier, prices rose accordingly. By the early thirties, wholesale prices had more than quadrupled, to $350 a kilo. In France, some of those denied licenses when the government got tough on dubious pharmaceutical firms just went underground. French Corsican criminals based in Marseille (but also active in Paris and the French colonies) eventually would exploit this new criminal terrain. The legendary Corsican gang leader Paul Carbone took time out from other gangsterly pursuits to sponsor clandestine heroin labs right in France—presumably using some of the newly unemployed chemists. The first one was discovered near Marseille in Bagnol in 1937.

International drug traffickers found they could no longer operate with complete impunity. When Little Augie, number eighty-nine on the League's Black List, presented himself in 1931 to an American consul in Istanbul to extend his passport, the consul recognized him from the list. He wired Treasury for instructions, and Anslinger, who had a Committee of One Hundred colleague in Berlin, alerted the Germans that Little Augie was on the Simplon Express coming their way. One thing and another, Augie Del Gratio was picked up, arrested in Berlin on December 2, 1931, and eventually sentenced to two years. This, in turn, flushed out a worried Elie Eliopoulos, who made a statement in Athens to Charlie Dyar and an Egyptian narcotics official and insisted he was now getting out of the business. The prolific Turkish factories soon closed, thanks again to American diplomatic pressure. In June 1932 Polakiewitz was arrested in Paris with almost a dozen pounds of morphine on him. He was extradited to the United States, where he pleaded guilty and went off to serve two years in Lewisburg.

Official persistence of this sort by the United States also bore real fruit on the home front. In late October 1931, Anslinger had been able to write a somewhat self-serving letter to George Z. Medalie, the U.S. attorney in Manhattan, that narcotic agents all over the country were reporting that "New York has never been as tight as it is at the present time, and that it is almost impossible to get shipments through there." (While Republican Medalie was a revered public servant and political godfather to the still-unknown Thomas Dewey, he also had been the attorney for both "Legs" Diamond and Arnold Rothstein. In fact, he had been one of the defense lawyers for the traffickers Webber and Vachuda in their 1927 trial.)

On the diplomatic front, the United States had scored a major breakthrough in 1931. In Geneva that summer, fifty-seven nations agreed to a new convention for the Limitation of the Manufacture of Narcotic Drugs. Finally, each nation was committed to state each year how much drugs it would need for medical and scientific purposes. To give some real meaning to this groundbreaking agreement, each country agreed to provide a detailed annual report of its own production, export, import, and use of narcotics and cocaine. With this stricter monitoring mechanism, governments could no longer pretend not to be aware that their factories were producing tons of opiates, or concede that they knew, but pretend they thought it was going for medical use elsewhere. Each year, the Opium Advisory Committee—prodded by the Americans—would confront those nations who had not played by the rules, declaring them renegades if they did not conform. By the summer of 1933, the new convention was ratified. Thanks to these American diplomatic efforts, first launched by Hamilton Wright two decades earlier, legal worldwide production of opium had plummeted from forty-two thousand tons in 1906 to eight thousand tons by 1934.

After chalking up this series of successes against traffickers and governments reluctant to honor treaty obligations in his first three years in office, U.S. Narcotics Commissioner Harry J. Anslinger found himself stymied and beseiged. Democrat Franklin Delano Roosevelt had ascended to the presidency in 1933, and almost immediately a budget-cutter proposed merging the Bureau of Narcotics with what was left of the Prohibition Bureau over in the Justice Department. Stuart J. Fuller laconically pointed out that this was not allowed under the 1931 convention, which obligated every country to maintain a separate narcotics bureau. Anslinger then desperately rallied old friends such as Reginald Wright Kauffman, a foreign correspondent who churned out numerous outraged articles from Geneva. In May 1933 Anslinger wrote his thanks, noting that the bureau was saved, but he was not, saying "the axe will fall in due course." But, in fact, Anslinger the Republican was already so popular with old-time reform groups and conservative newspaper publishers that he survived to be reappointed in this most liberal of administrations.

However, having survived that threat, Anslinger found life under the New Dealers decidedly trying. In November 1933, Henry Morgenthau, Jr., became Secretary of the Treasury and Anslinger's boss. (Not to mention also a neighbor of sorts since both resided in the exclusive Shoreham Hotel.) Morgenthau was a dedicated gentleman farmer, a neighbor of FDR's, and a like-minded squire from rural Dutchess County. Morgenthau had taken on the herculean task of trying to resuscitate the nation's collapsed economy. But the Bureau of Narcotics was part of his Treasury domain, too, and when he got around to scrutinizing it, he did not like what he found.

For despite being reappointed and his early successes, Anslinger's agency now was faltering seriously. The drug traffickers were no longer complacent and the easy pickings of the early thirties were over. Not one major trafficker was apprehended in 1934 or early 1935. The Bureau of Narcotics' annual report for 1934 showed only seventy-two pounds of heroin, the smuggler's drug of choice, had been seized in the whole year.

Anslinger, forty-two, would complain privately that his nerves felt jangled, and in the fall of 1934 he was horrified to realize his hair was falling out. Almost certainly Anslinger was anxious about his new boss, Henry Morgenthau. The Narcotics commissioner did his best to appear productive, orchestrating a steady stream of blowhard publicity in the newspapers, preferably with a photo of a stern-looking Anslinger leading drug raids. The truth was that Anslinger had developed an unseemly appetite for publicity that was not being matched by solid results at the bureau. To keep his name in the news, Anslinger launched a crusade against the evils of racehorse doping. None of this impressed the no-nonsense Morgenthau.

Then in early 1935 a Washington scandal sheet called *Inside Stuff* went after Anslinger, accusing the commissioner of talking big but failing to deliver. "To publicize the [narcotics] racket and the Government's drive against it is the Commissioner's forte. It is not enough forte, however, to conceal the weakness of the actual detection and suppression of the narcotics trade." The caption under his photograph read, "No bushel hides his light." Harsh medicine, indeed.

Six weeks later Anslinger suffered something of a nervous breakdown. On April 1, 1935, a distraught Anslinger checked himself into the U.S. Marine Hospital at Norfolk, Virginia (well removed from the capital's gossip mills). During a ten-day workup, he told doctors that his hair loss was "tremendous," his work "very difficult and trying," and that he "recently has noticed insomnia after 3 or 4 A.M. Wakes up early and can't go back to sleep." While the official diagnosis was hypothyroidism, the medical director concluded that Anslinger was "suffering from a form of nervous strain incident to his professional duties." The doctor ordered Anslinger to take two months off, eat better, and exercise daily.

After Secretary Morgenthau saw the doctor's report, he sent Anslinger a brief note reassuring him "that you must not worry about your job. It is here waiting for you when you come back. The important thing is for you to stay away as long as is necessary to make a complete recovery." It's not certain how long Anslinger was gone, but while he was away Morgenthau proposed folding the Bureau of Narcotics into one super Treasury enforcement agency, but FDR nixed this in March 1936. A month later, United States Attorney for Manhattan Lamar Hardy visited Morgenthau's Treasury office to complain about the Bureau of Narcotics' New York office. He protested that they brought in "only the peddlers." Hardy proposed an "intensive drive to get at the source of distribution," conducted, however, without the New York agents of the FBN. Perhaps they would use FBI agents or other Treasury investigators.

Morgenthau was delighted. "That's swell! More power to you! . . . I think you are the first one [prosecutor] who has come in and wanted to bring pressure. Nothing pleases me more . . . we will give everything we have to help you." There is no sign that Secretary Morgenthau informed Narcotics Commissioner Anslinger about the meeting or the ensuing plans. Instead, Treasury Special Agent E. C. Palmer went quietly to Manhattan with IRS agents to see what was up.

What Palmer found in the New York Bureau, the FBN's front line against international and domestic trafficking, was a moribund and corrupt office. This was no small matter, for New York was the center of American trafficking, the port where the vast majority of smuggled drugs entered. It was also (not coincidentally) the city with the biggest addict population. And yet, reported Palmer, for the 1936 fiscal year ending June 30, in New York "seizures of narcotics in illegal traffic were negligible. There seems to have been very little effort directed towards the matter of apprehending major violators." Palmer blamed this pathetic track record on "incompetent agents or agents suspected of corruption; the absence of intelligent and up to date investigative methods; and the lack of aggressive and competent leadership in the field service."

When Morgenthau summoned the Narcotics commissioner to his office on August 18, 1936, the New York investigation was still under wraps. No one had as yet enlightened Anslinger about the untoward events in his major field office. The secretary just told Anslinger that he "was not satisfied with the work being done by the Bureau of Narcotics either in this country or abroad." The time had come to reorganize. Anslinger gamely defended the bureau, pointing out (as he always did) that the bureau had "put more criminals in Federal penitentiaries per agent employed than any other enforcement organization of the Federal government."

The brusque secretary was utterly unswayed. Impatiently, he pointed out to Anslinger that "the bulk of the Bureau's defendants are petty violators, chiefly peddlers and addicts." Morgenthau informed Anslinger that as far as he was concerned the Bureau "had not made a sufficient effort against the criminal organizations responsible for the distribution of narcotics in wholesale quantities." This was no small matter, for Morgenthau viewed addicting drugs as utterly pernicious, as did FDR, who saw narcotic offenses as "the worst of all crimes except murder . . . [and perhaps] an even more severe offense against society than murder itself. In the case of murder you take away the life of a fellow human being. In the case of distributing narcotics you take away the mind of the individual and make his future life intolerable for the good of his own soul."

Having berated Anslinger for doing a bad job of enforcement against major traffickers, Secretary Morgenthau personally assigned a Treasury agent temporarily to the bureau to oversee criminal investigation and enforcement work. Still, no mention was made of the New York investigation. Presumably Anslinger remained in the dark.

That scandal did not break until the fall. The whole Manhattan office stank of corruption, but it was too difficult to develop court-worthy cases. Three New York–based agents were fired outright for lying. Another nine agents, including the New York supervisor, were demoted and exiled to other offices, replaced by those "believed to be competent and trustworthy." A Customs man named Garland Williams was installed as head of the office, and by late December 1936, it was reported that in the one month since the shake-up, "the agents under the direction of Mr. Williams have seized more heroin in illegal traffic than was seized by the prior organization in New York City for the twelve month's period ended June 30, 1936." The beleaguered Anslinger seems to have taken this surprisingly well, and many of the people thrust upon him by Morgenthau—including Garland Williams—would become valued colleagues. A shrewd judge of bureaucratic politics, Anslinger apparently decided his survival entailed going along humbly.

Naturally, one wonders: Why didn't Secretary Morgenthau simply fire this somewhat inept Republican political appointee? Probably it wasn't worth stirring up Anslinger's ardent and vocal supporters in reform and conservative circles. Moreover, Anslinger's weaknesses in antitrafficking efforts were presumably outweighed by his diplomatic abilities in the international arena of narcotic control. Anslinger happily attended the long and ponderous diplomatic sessions of the Opium Advisory Committee and various subcommittees as a member of the U.S. delegation, and then engaged in the essential follow-up work, prodding governments on "leaks," requesting extraditions. When Morgenthau was secretary the axe never fell.

As for what Commissioner Anslinger thought about Morgenthau's revamping, we don't know, for he never acknowledged this unhappy time. Thirty years later, Anslinger would describe Morgenthau as a "fine law enforcement official." The only suggestion of the severe humiliations was the mild remark that "Mr. Morgenthau and I didn't always see eye to eye."

The irony in all this was that while the beleaguered commissioner's forte was diplomatic wrangling, he was far too savvy to think such effete talents would rate space in the nation's press or rally popular support. Anslinger so skillfully portrayed himself as a tough cop attacking the "dope evil" that few realized that his real strength was in the tedious but necessary diplomatic realm. To retain his beloved, but appointive, post of narcotics commissioner, Anslinger worked relentlessly to foster his tough cop image. He regularly sallied forth on high-profile raids, his commanding presence emphasized by snappy fedora and double-breasted topcoat. This "implacable foe of the dope evil" image generated enormous support from influential civic groups and conservative newspapers, especially the powerful Hearst chain. Yet it was essentially a false front. Anslinger, as Morgenthau had concluded, was not very aggressive at going after traffickers. He was, however, a reasonably skilled diplomat who enjoyed the dull intricacies of complex international treaties.

Once Secretary Morgenthau felt that the domestic situation was in hand, he then turned his attention to the Treasury's narcotics work overseas. Personal assistant Commander B. M. Thompson was deputized to revamp and expand the undercover network. In March 1937, he disembarked at Le Havre with three new agents and began his task by "having a nice visit at the Café des Fleurs, the reported narcotic traffickers rendezvous." Thompson was a jaunty, upbeat sort who relished his assignment and for several months sent back high-spirited, detailed assessments of the trafficking scene, the efficacy of the Treasury agents, and the local police. In his first report from Paris, he wrote, "I presented the doctrine to the boys that what we wanted was *information* that would lead to *seizures*. Some of them seemed a little surprised that we should take such a severely practical viewpoint, but they got the idea and I think will get down to brass tacks in that direction." (Somehow Fuller's policy of rewards based on seizures had been changed to regular monthly stipends to informers.)

While the original handful of agents, such as Charlie Dyar, had delivered some initial, spectacular tips, wary traffickers now appeared to be smuggling numerous smaller lots through a variety of channels to minimize losses. Consequently, Treasury felt it needed more hard-charging agents and many more informers to work the territory. Thompson's mission was to scope out the "hottest" spots, staff them

ASAP, and cultivate new sources. By the end of March he was writing from Marseille, a very "hot" port, advising that on the matter of narcotics agents, "We don't want any tourists over here or white collar guys. We want agents . . . with guts and talent for skullduggery."

By mid May, Commander Thompson had crisscrossed the Continent several times, and he was writing the Secretary, "A good guess as to what part of the 10 tons of narcotics estimated smuggled into our country per year is cargo and what is not, would be eight tons in cargo and two tons in personal carriers, including their baggage."

From his room at the stately Hôtel de la Paix in Geneva, Commander Thompson reported to Secretary Morgenthau on the 1937 Geneva meeting, "The line of demarcation is quite apparent, between those who are here to cover up, or, let us say, tone down the report of, what has happened in the way of seizures of narcotics originating from, or taking place in, their own countries. . . . I would . . . class Mondanel of France in this group." Thompson drily noted that when Portugese Macao authorities were asked why a half ton of seized heroin was still sitting there, they said "it is in their museum as an exhibit. It would be interesting to know how much is some type of white powder substitution."

After the good commander had spent a couple of fruitful weeks in Geneva observing the various sessions and networking with enforcement officers and delegates, he concluded, "There is no question that the Geneva conferences do a lot of good in keeping down the volume of world illicit traffic. This is done through the 'washing of dirty linen' in the Seizure Committee meetings, which identifies the countries at fault as sources. . . . In other words, the fear of publicity at Geneva should be a deterrent to such countries as Iran, Portugal (Macao), Japan, and others, with regard to tacitly or otherwise sponsoring smuggling."

Stuart J. Fuller, the official American delegate to the Opium Advisory Committee, delighted in using these open sessions to expose and embarrass the worst offenders. The previous summer he had risen and read into the record one Japanese exporter's written instructions for drug smuggling: "In using members of ships' crews for this business, we will supply them with double-cased soles on their shoes. This method has been adopted in our business with India and China and proved so successful that not a single case has been discovered. By this method each person can carry one pound ashore."

A few years earlier, Fuller blandly had inquired what Bulgaria had done with the six thousand kilos of acetic anhydride it had imported in 1933 since it manufactured no dyestuffs, aspirin, or rayon? The assumption was that it had been used to produce about six tons of heroin, four of which had ended up in the United States. In 1935, Fuller had caused great umbrage during a discussion of the various existing opium monopolies in the Far East by stating, "Monopolies are merely another device for poisoning one's fellow man for gain." These sorts of frank pronouncements had earned Fuller the reputation of a diplomat who "did not suffer fools gladly, and could on occasions display a somewhat violent temper."

As the ever-cheery Commander Thompson headed home in mid 1937, his official peregrinations and presence at Geneva had advertised strongly that the United States was determined to restrain drug trafficking into its own territory. The reorganized network of overseas agents now featured five men in Paris (including Dyar), and one each in Sofia, Milan, and Vienna. Along with dozens of new informers, Treasury was up and running and began once again to bag the big ones. In 1938, Zurich police arrested the elusive Peruvian diplomat-courier Carlos Fernandez Bacula, shortly after Paris police arrested his politically connected partner, French restaurateur Louis Lyon. Dozens of accomplices were picked up in the aftermath, for this was one of Europe's major trafficking gangs. Bacula alone was charged with having smuggled one and a half tons of heroin into the United States on six visits.

As such pressures built in Europe, most illegal drug production shifted to the chaotic and corrupt Far East. And it was there, when Prohibition ended in 1933, that some American gangsters headed to buy narcotics. The hapless Jake Katzenberg, who had been so burned by Polakiewitz and Eliopoulos in 1930, decided to try again. This time, Katzenberg sent various friends and relations on luxury liners to China, *the* reliable marketplace for illegal narcotics. In just the month of January 1935, authorities in Shanghai had raided five small factories and confiscated more than two hundred kilos of heroin. Katzenberg's smugglers found they easily could purchase a few dozen kilos or as much as 120 kilos. They packed it in steamer trunks and escorted it back to New York. Once on the busy docks they made sure to be cleared by certain Customs inspectors who had been bribed to append the right stickers for safe exit. All told, in six trips, they brought in almost 1,500 pounds of heroin. Then one load was hijacked somewhere along the line. Once again, Katzenberg was getting upset. He was also having trouble with the quality of the drugs, and associates were being murdered right and left, five in all. Just when Katzenberg announced in 1937 that he would run no more loads, one of his chemists converting morphine base to heroin caused a fire in a Bronx apartment. The invigorated New York bureau uncovered the trafficking setup, and Katzenberg fled. But recent diplomatic agreements gave him little shelter, and soon he was back in New York being sentenced to ten years in prison.

The escalating risks and changing economics of trafficking in the thirties drove American smugglers to develop a marked preference for trafficking in heroin, because all its pharmaceutical properties made it a far superior street drug to the still highly popular morphine. Not only was heroin three to four times as strong as morphine, its crystalline structure made it ideal for adulteration. Heroin's high water solubility also made it easier to inject than morphine. Moreover, while morphine could *only* be injected, heroin could be swallowed, sniffed, smoked, or injected. As for cocaine, by 1942 its role in the illicit markets was "so small as to be without significance." The traffickers' preference for the far more profitable heroin eventually would force almost all American drug addicts to use it, whether that was their drug of choice or not.

As one longtime opium smoker, a New York woman, explained, "Then I couldn't get opium no more . . . about 1930, 1935, somewhere in there. I just couldn't buy it no more. When I couldn't get opium, I took heroin. I was skin popping. It's true that opium was bulky and heroin was easier to smuggle in." Even the Chinese who patronized the few remaining opium dens found it difficult to obtain smoking opium. Remembered one Chinese seaman who lived in Manhattan, "Sometimes you couldn't get opium, maybe no ship had come in. So I changed to the white stuff—heroin. This was when I was about thirty-five years old [around 1935.]"

Morphine addicts too were forced gradually to switch drugs. Bingham Dai, the young Chinese graduate student at the University of Chicago, found when interviewing drug addicts for his thesis that half of all Chicago addicts preferred morphine, but virtually all were switching to heroin. "One reason . . . is the exacting price of morphine compared to that of heroin [$90 to $110 an ounce for morphine versus $38 to $40 an ounce for heroin]. . . . [H]eroin is a more profitable drug for peddlers." In effect, the business decisions of the drug syndicates, hard-pressed by authorities, were shaping illegal drug habits, forcing a steady shift over to heroin. The street prices did not rise much in the thirties, but quality and purity declined so much that many addicts who had been smoking or sniffing began using a hypodermic. The purity of street heroin plummeted from 27 percent in 1938 to 10 percent in 1939 to 3 percent by 1940.

Washington's determined attack on drugs really was bearing fruit. Successful diplomacy and law enforcement had limited availability severely, the most important cause for once widespread drug use. Then the Progressive movement, prosperity in the twenties, and the New Deal successfully had alleviated early immigrant city slums, further shrinking the pool of potential users. And then there was learned experience. By the thirties, most Americans personally had witnessed the debilitating and sometimes fatal consequences of drug use, and there had been a collective repudiation of drugs. It appeared that young people—specifically teenaged urban males—were no longer falling prey to drugs in anywhere near the numbers that had prompted such determined enforcement of the drug laws from 1915 on.

There were no longer reports that certain neighborhoods were awash with drugs. Medical committees no longer worried that heroin was menacing a generation of city youth. One New York addict, a Puerto Rican who began shooting up at twenty-three, remembers of the thirties, "You didn't see no kids selling or using drugs. If a kid came around, fifteen or sixteen years old, they'd chase them away. They'd say, 'What do you want? Get out of here! You want a lollipop or something?' The kids were definitely not involved in the Thirties and Forties." This encouraging anecdotal evidence never was substantiated officially because the few studies done in the thirties all were flawed seriously for various reasons, most notably for leaving out New York and other major cities.

The thirties were marked not only by significant federal progress against trafficking, but also by long delayed progress on an equally important but much neglected front: treatment. As part of the New Deal's huge public works projects, the federal government finally built the long promised federal treatment centers, another part of the legacy of Congressman Stephen G. Porter. Dedicated in the spring of 1935, the first hospital-prison-sanitarium was located on 1,100 acres of rolling bluegrass outside Lexington, Kentucky. Run by the Public Health Service, the U.S. Narcotics Farm was an Art Deco campuslike affair with barred windows that had taken three years and $4 million to complete. Neighboring farmers expressed concern when the promised tall fence topped with barbed wire did not materialize, for they worried about escaping addicts.

Not since the demise of the ill-fated city clinics had any organized, official effort actually addressed the persistent (albeit shrinking and less visible) problem of drug addicts. With no one in Congress carrying on Porter's concern about drugs (in part because the problem was so less pressing), and with Anslinger absolutely indifferent to treatment, that aspect of the solution had received short shrift. Most attention and resources had been focused on trafficking. And, thanks to Morgenthau and international cooperation, that had been quite effective.

Up until Lexington opened, authorities simply had dispatched addicts convicted of possessing drugs off to federal prisons, where they proved great pests to wardens. Well aware of this gap back in the twenties, Congressman Porter had introduced legislation that Congress passed providing for two narcotic "farms." This had delighted the beleaguered wardens, and promised to provide physicians a captive group to test the belief that a prolonged stay in healthful environs would cure an addict. (A wholesome sojourn in the country was the classic Progressive solution to all evils of the city.) Aside from Harrison Act violators being sent to Kentucky, other addicts could voluntarily commit themselves.

In its early years, Lexington was literally a working farm operated by the patient-inmates, with "chicken hatcheries, slaughter houses, . . . four large dairy barns, a greenhouse and a utility barn." When not farming, inmates could work in the sewing, printing, or woodworking shops. And because medical director Dr. Lawrence Kolb believed that most addicts were psychopaths to one degree or another, all addicts were evaluated psychologically and provided therapy. After the first year, the name "Narcotic Farm" was changed to U.S. Public Health Service Hospital, "in part due to the confusion and kidding resulting from the logical question asked so many times, 'Where do you grow the narcotics?' "

Lexington became the site for the first national research laboratory on narcotics and addiction, the Public Health Service's Addiction Research Center. In addition to research on the pharmacology, physiology, and neurology of addiction and a decades-long fruitless quest for a nonaddicting painkiller, Lexington scientists and physicians developed the standard techniques for withdrawal from morphine and heroin, as well as techniques for confirming opiate addiction. The research center also took advantage of the huge pool of addicts to conduct clinical and epidemiological research.

The inaugural study of the thousand-plus patient-inmates revealed that by this time the typical American addict was a thirtyish white male from a "deteriorated metropolitan section" working at a menial job, addicted for ten years, and engaging in petty crime to support his habit. Presumably, many of these were the same youthful addicts who had so alarmed authorities in previous decades.

Among this first group studied, three fourths admitted previous unsuccessful attempts at cure. Whatever it was that drew addicts into the quicksand of addiction, it exercised the same allure in drawing them back again. Lexington graduates blamed perennial relapse above all on the "return to former associates and the effort to recapture the beginner's thrill," followed by "relief of physical discomfort." The addicts of the thirties had acquired a pessimistic assessment of their prospects. As Bingham Dai noted, the "general belief among drug addicts is that once an addict, always an addict, and that there is no cure for drug addiction."

While many young men and women drifted into drug use out of curiosity or a desire to sample this forbidden and dangerous pleasure, the ensuing addiction was all too real and extremely difficult to shed—especially once one was an active member of the drug subculture and comfortable in its ways. Much of the medical profession now shared the same conclusion about the dismal prospects for cure, but some hoped that earlier efforts had just been insufficiently comprehensive.

Ironically, the very government treatment meant to help addicts of the thirties to give up drugs—going to Lexington, or KY as it was known—simply became part of the addict ritual and experience. Or, after 1938, going to Fort Worth, Texas, where the second farm opened to serve the western states. Anybody with a serious habit seemed to end up at one or the other eventually, and apparently the difficulties and drawbacks of life in the narcotic farms were mitigated by the chance to freely and endlessly talk about drugs and addiction. Even as Public Health Service doctors strove to find ways of erasing addiction, the main effect of going to KY for most addicts was to expand their network of addict pals. In time, the farms doused any last, flickering hopes that the robust rural retreat would prove the elusive cure for addiction. While KY doctors had a variety of kind things to say about these early patients, the postdischarge prospects were summed up thus: "He will probably relapse." Sadly this was proven decades later when Lexington follow-up studies showed a typical relapse rate per effort at cure of 90 percent. Nonetheless, the very age of the Lexington addicts was testimony to the success of the government's determined twenty-five-year war on drugs. The generation represented at the Narcotics Farm had grown up when cocaine and opiates were still fairly cheap and plentiful.

By the early forties illegal drugs were hard to find in America and heavily diluted. When World War II came, illegal drugs virtually disappeared. The legitimate needs of the war wounded absorbed large amounts of drugs—which Anslinger prudently had stockpiled. And wartime sea blockades made smuggling almost impossible. The war finally would force a great many addicts, despite themselves, to give up drugs.

Recalls one addict of this time, "There were no drugs in New York during World War II, no drugs in Philadelphia, no drugs in Chicago—there were no drugs on the East Coast. *No drugs.*" Confirms another, "There was no heroin. . . . I mean you couldn't buy a bag anywhere. . . . Then they started using morphine. . . . They'd get it from doctors, and some from drugstores. . . . We'd write scrips [prescriptions]." When notorious New York gangsters known as the 107th Street gang began running drugs from Mexico, they were soon caught. Lexington saw its patient population plunge from 1,533 new admissions in 1940 to 772 new admissions by 1945. With so many free beds, Lexington and Fort Worth began taking psychiatric cases from the wartime services.

The war also provided certain other satisfactions to those long engaged in fighting drugs and addiction. Bacula, the diplomat-trafficker who had been enjoying life after a short prison term, was imprisoned again as an "undesirable" at the Tourelles concentration camp in France. And the notorious Eliopoulos brothers, who had grown rich from their admitted role as major league traffickers but had never spent a day in prison for any crime, now washed up in New York City with thousands of others escaping the Nazis. The Federal Bureau of Narcotics soon summoned them for a chat. They were indicted on May 5, 1943, for selling the thousand-plus pounds of morphine seized thirteen years earlier from the SS *Alesia*. One of their betrayed customers, trafficker Sam Bernstein, happily testified against them. Convicted a month later in Brooklyn federal court, the brothers appealed. In October, the judge dismissed the case, ruling that the statute of limitations had passed.

The United States had better luck with the Newman brothers, major New York traffickers whose extraordinary discretion had made them highly elusive quarry. Finally, in early 1940 they were indicted and pleaded guilty. Treasury concluded that their two-year sentences and five thousand dollar fines were the best that could be done considering "the extreme difficulty experienced in assembling competent evidence against the defendants."

But perhaps most satisfying of all, as the United States war machine rescued Europe from the Nazis and Asia from the Japanese, Congressman Walter Judd, a former American missionary to China, saw a great opportunity. At his urging, as one State Department historian relates, the United States "waged a diplomatic war on behalf of a sort of narcotics Emancipation Proclamation in the Far East. It extracted the agreement from its European Allies that when their colonial territories were recovered from the Japanese, the drug traffic and official monopolies in particular would be eliminated." This was the United States at its idealistic best, obliging far more cynical colonial governments to cease and desist exploiting their most vulnerable citizens.

When the United States first recognized the widespread problem of addiction in 1900, public health officials estimated that one in three hundred Americans was an opiate addict. Adding in cocaine users and assuming a certain overlap one would have increased that to one in two hundred. Now, after four decades of growing restrictions that had made drugs a scarce and difficult commodity, the addict population was growing in only one way—older. By World War II, when the U.S. population had almost doubled to 140,000,000, the number of opiate addicts (cocaine had almost disappeared) was about forty thousand, or one in three thousand, a tenfold decline. So successful had governmental action been against the nation's first drug epidemic that it was virtually forgotten. When illegal drugs reappeared in fearsome quantities again, few remembered the first American experience with habit-forming drugs.

PART II

America's Second Drug Epidemic 1950–1970

"Heroin had just about taken over Harlem."
—CLAUDE BROWN,
Manchild in the Promised Land, 1965

CHAPTER 7

"The Sky Is High
and So Am I"

— "You'se a Viper,"
STUFF SMITH, 1936

When World War II ended, a
new kind of illegal drug culture began to develop in the United States.
Highly subterranean, it would be distinguished by two things. Foremost would be heroin's new cultural significance as a "badge" of hipsterism and alienation. For the first time, heroin acquired a powerful, articulated cultural meaning, joining marijuana as an essential of the hip life: "Heroin abuse became a symbol, one of the trappings affected by the boppers, just as dark glasses and pegged cuffs were, except that heroin was potentially lethal." Hipsters used heroin, squares didn't. Asserted musician Red Rodney, who played with Charlie Parker on numerous tours, "[Heroin] was our badge. It was the thing that made us different from the rest of the world. It was the thing that said, 'We know. You don't know.' It [heroin] was the thing that gave us membership in a unique club, and for this membership we gave up everything else in the world. Every ambition. Every desire. Everything. It ruined most of the people."

The second big difference in this postwar American drug culture was the identity of the marginal males who now peopled the traditional northern urban marketplaces for heroin. At the turn of the century, when addicting drugs such as heroin first became a problem in northern industrial slums, the biggest users were marginal young white men— waiters, teamsters, clerks. After World War II, as the Italian-American gangsters reactivated the old drug trafficking routes, the marginal city neighborhoods were slowly but surely becoming black. As Nicholas Lemann described in his book, *The Promised Land*, five million south- ern blacks were beginning the diaspora north.

Black hipster culture had been evolving since the twenties, serving as an instant niche for young black men trying to find their place in northern cities. But now the postwar hipster stance moved beyond the old standard marijuana into heroin, projecting a much more alienated and bitter edge. One Baltimore black veteran just back from the war described his frame of mind at the time: "I wanted something more out of life, something to grab hold of me and get me out of the mud of rou- tine." But nothing promising presented itself. Lacking any larger inspi- rational framework, a political or social movement that spoke to his hopes or his alienation, he turned to Life Style as Statement. By 1949 he had become a hipster and taken up heroin. "I liked the hipsters' appearance. They were very slick. I liked the way they talked, the slang. You chose sides between the squares and the hipsters." The heroin, he explained, was just part of the "glamour" of hipsterdom.

To get an idea of how subterranean the early black hipster culture with its use of marijuana was, we have only to look back to a *New Yorker* story written in early 1938 by one of Gotham's savviest reporters, Meyer Berger. It took Berger many weeks of negotiation just to gain access to a Harlem "tea pad" operating out of a graystone tenement on 140th Street. As he described it in *The New Yorker*, he and a friend arrived around midnight on a Saturday night, rang the bell, and were admitted warily to a ground-floor apartment. Dimly lit by blue lights, the air was close and thick with marijuana smoke and incense. The four- room pad was furnished with nine broken-down sofas and various easy chairs. Lounging in the first room were a half-dozen black "vipers" smoking "tea" (at fifteen cents a reefer), giggling, and keeping beat to the jazz music playing on the jukebox.

Meyer Berger was a legendary New York journalist who specialized in covering the city's Damon Runyonesque characters—whether high- profile gangsters such as "Legs" Diamond or obscure vipers patronizing tea pads. It demonstrates how extremely subterranean smoking mari- juana was that an old pro like Berger—familiar with the city's lowest dives and its colorful "sporting" life—had to negotiate for weeks sim- ply to gain entry to a tea pad. But even more telling is that having spent an evening there, he missed the real story, which was not the existence of exotic tea pads, but the thriving new subculture of black hepsters.

Up in Harlem, young black men were declaring themselves conscientious objectors to an American Dream that never had included them. While white Americans as a matter of course toiled, planned, saved, and nurtured families with expectations of better things to come, some young blacks—shut off from such prosaic bourgeois prospects—were flocking to an urban underworld of jazz and fast living. Black hepsters derided the very notion that a man's daily job (and its accompanying income and prestige) defined him. Instead, hepsters made creativity, spontaneous pleasure, freedom, and excitement central goals. In spurning the traditional values of organizing life around secure work and family, they rejected the central tenet of Western Protestant society: "the subordinating and disciplining of present conduct in the interests of future rewards." As the Romans would say, carpe diem. Live for today.

The black hero of Ralph Ellison's *Invisible Man* articulated the profound sense of exclusion and alienation that fueled the hepster world: "I am a man of substance, of flesh and bone, fiber and liquids—I might even be said to possess a mind. I am invisible, understand, simply because [white] people refuse to see me. . . . Irresponsibility is part of my invisibility. . . . Responsibility rests upon recognition." The classic 1945 study of Chicago, *Black Metropolis*, observed how certain blacks assessed their limited prospects and adopted "a pattern of conspicuous behavior and conspicuous consumption." Lacking any bona fide political outlet for their discontent, some turned to the stylishness and creativity of the hep lifestyle to express their alienation. Integral to this new subculture was marijuana, which was viewed as the special inebriant of the hep world.

But the larger symbolism of marijuana was not readily apparent to journalist Meyer Berger and his friend as they settled awkwardly in at the tea pad, watching a steady stream of customers entering, some to buy reefers and leave, others to stay and hang out and get high. One can well understand Berger's uneasiness, for he had been warned by federal narcotics agents that "vipers are always dangerous; that an overdose of marijuana generates savage and sadistic traits likely to reach a climax in axe and icepick murders." Naturally concerned, Berger had checked with a few New York cops, who knew of no such dangers. Broached on the same issue, the resident vipers were bemused: "They said reefers only made them happy. They didn't know a single viper who was vicious or mad."

Indeed the mood was languid and otherworldly, what with the low blue light and the viper songs, blues and jazz whose subject was marijuana and getting high. "Above the throb and beat came the words of the viper song, low and soothing. . . . 'I dreamed about a reefer five feet long/Mighty, immense, but not too strong.' " Soon, couples rose to dance. Wrote Berger: "They jerked to the music's beat, her slender form bending at sharp angles, in perfect rhythm with the tune. Her head shot back in an ecstatic fling. The blue bulb lighted their laughing faces. . . . The recumbent vipers moaned in voodooistic chorus: . . . 'Then you know yo' body's sent./You don't care if you don't pay the rent./Sky is high and so am I,/If you're a viper.' "

Had Meyer Berger properly understood the first line of Stuff Smith's tune, "You'se a Viper," he would have heard not "five feet long, mighty, immense . . ." but "five feet long, mighty mezz . . ." "What," Berger might well have asked "is mezz?" The answer would then have put him onto the real story of tea pads and the rise of hepsterism and a new kind of drug use. For Mezz was Milton (Mezz) Mezzrow, a minor luminary of the jazz world whose fame in Harlem was *not* based on his musical talents.

Rather, Mezzrow was reknowned for introducing marijuana to the black masses (back when it was still legal in 1929) and for selling only the highest quality tea. Something "mezz" was supremely good, especially good marijuana. More than anyone, Mezzrow (who believed himself black though he had started off life white and Jewish) could have explained to a middle-class white man such as Berger about this whole new subterranean black world of hepsters thriving in Harlem. And how marijuana had become one of its essential accoutrements.

Mezzrow, like the rest of mainstream America, had never heard of marijuana until he entered the jazz world in the 1920s. Born in Chicago in 1899, Mezzrow was from a family "as respectable as Sunday morning." Yet he liked the streets, and so when caught in a stolen Studebaker, his family thought Pontiac reform school might be salutary. There Mezzrow discovered jazz and black people. When released a year later, he had decided that "from then on [I was] sticking close to Negroes. . . . And I was going to learn their music. . . . I was going to be a musician, a Negro musician, hipping the world about the blues the way only Negroes can." Jazz became his life and world.

Chicagoan Mezzrow first smoked "muggles" in 1924 when playing a roadhouse near Gary, Indiana. Another musician had just come up from New Orleans with a stash and urged the hesitant Mezzrow to try some. Known also as "muta" and "grefa," marijuana was a commonplace around the melting-pot port of New Orleans, the birthplace of jazz. It had been introduced there around 1910 by Caribbean sailors and was soon quite popular. All of New Orleans's marijuana "supply was drawn from Havana, Tampico and Vera Cruz and a small quantity from Texas. Quite a few sailors went into the business with great enterprise. . . . Traffickers were found at every dock."

The "weed" was *Cannabis sativa*, or the hemp plant (long culti-vated for use in making rope) and its dried leaves were smoked, though with deeper, longer inhalation than tobacco cigarettes. Marijuana use was soon firmly established in New Orleans, where "the drug's peculiarly fas-cinating effects are so generally known, especially among the negro population." When the city's Storyville red-light district was shut down during World War I, many of the musicians headed north up the Missis-sippi, bringing with them the local custom of smoking marijuana.

Mezzrow became an instant convert because he felt it dramatically improved his playing. "Suddenly there wasn't a sour note or a discord in the world that could bother me. . . . I began to preach my millenni-ums on my horn, leading all the sinners to glory." After all, didn't the great genius of Dixieland jazz, New Orleans native Louis Armstrong, smoke marijuana? Remembers one saxophonist, "We thought, 'Man, Louis gets high and blows and blows.' So we all used to get high."

Slowly, the still-legal drug acquired a cultural meaning beyond merely getting high. As Mezzrow later would explain in his 1946 auto-biography, *Really the Blues*, "Us vipers began to know we had a gang of things in common. . . . We were on another plane in another sphere compared to the musicians who were bottle babies. . . . We liked things to be easy and relaxed, mellow and mild." In the world of jazz, those musicians who viewed their music as part of a wider revolution against staid society, what Mezzrow called "a collective improvised nose-thumbing at all pillars of all communities," embraced marijuana. The "nose-thumbers" smoked marijuana.

When South Carolina trumpeter John Birks "Dizzy" Gillespie arrived in Harlem in 1937 via Philadelphia, innocent of both alcohol and marijuana, another musician promptly "turned me on to smoking pot," warning that otherwise, " 'You gonna be a square mothafucka.' " For the early distinction that Mezzrow had delineated between the vipers and "bottle babies" still held true. Said jazz musician Chubby Jackson: "There were two cliques in a musical organization, the whiskey drinkers and the pot smokers, and n'er the twain ever met."

Louis Armstrong once explained that his own enthusiasm for mari-juana went beyond its role in music: "It makes you feel good, man. It relaxes you, makes you forget all the bad things that happen to a Negro. It makes you feel wanted, and when you're with another tea smoker it makes you feel a special sense of kinship." New York authorities inves-tigating the spreading use of marijuana in that city—mainly in Harlem—noted that among users (largely blacks), "[T]here was common agreement that a feeling of adequacy and efficiency was induced by the use of marijuana and that current mental conflicts were allayed."

Yet smoking marijuana had remained virtually unknown in the North outside jazz musician circles until Mezzrow began selling in Harlem. He had arrived there flat broke right after the Great Wall Street Crash in 1929 and decided to sell marijuana cigarettes to make ends meet. To his own astonishment, Mezzrow overnight became, he would recall, "the most popular man in Harlem, . . . the Man that Hipped the World, the Man that Made History. . . . [In short,] marijuana took Harlem by storm." Mezzrow certainly did not look like a cultural revolutionary. He had neatly shorn wavy hair and, like every man of the era, sported a suit and tie. In the few photos of him, he looks like anybody's nebbishy uncle. Yet by the mid thirties, marijuana had become so woven into northern black hepster life that allusions to it abounded in dozens of jazz tunes, and tea pads (so reminiscent of opium dens) were part of the scene in northern ghettos. By the time Meyer Berger reported on this phenomenon in 1938 to the upper-class readership of *The New Yorker*, marijuana had been illegal for a year.

Bernie Brightman, an inquisitive Jewish high school student from Brooklyn, discovered this new black hepster world in 1936 when he daringly visited Harlem's famous Savoy Ballroom. The availability of marijuana added an air of the exotic to this already glamorous place, its huge dance floor packed with elegant lindy hoppers swirling to the famous swing bands. Even when reefers were legal, Brightman remembers they were still purchased discreetly and smoked in the bathrooms. Once the law changed in 1937, the Savoy bouncers put an end to that. It was then that Brightman was introduced by a black girlfriend to the subterranean tea pads.

"Kaiser's was the crème de la crème of tea pads," recalls Brightman, now in his seventies, sporting a white goatee and aviator glasses, and heading Stash Records. "You literally had to go through a couple of basements to reach the place. I remember they served the reefers on a tray and it was all very mellow, maybe fifteen or twenty people on easy chairs and sofas, just listening to the music from a jukebox. There was no alcohol. You just wanted to get high, listen to music, and not be bothered." Typically a quarter of the clientele was white and, Brightman says, "I'd be surprised if there had been two-hundred white vipers in all the boroughs at that time." And while Meyer Berger and a later New York City report spoke of "hundreds" of tea pads, Brightman disputes this. "At most, maybe there were a dozen." On the jukeboxes, aside from many standards of the day, were dozens of viper songs, everything from "Smoking Reefers," "Reefer Head Woman," "A Viper's Moan" to "The Stuff Is Here and It's Mellow."

Like Mezzrow, Brightman came to see himself as the privileged participant in a superior hepster subculture. "You did not drink booze and lose control. You were in on the music and in on marijuana and you were simply a more aware person." Marijuana smokers, black and white, prided themselves on being deliberate outsiders, scornful of a square world. Making marijuana illegal only enhanced its special role as the inebriant of choice of what were now known in Harlem and the jazz world as "hep-cats."

Harlem in the thirties was the undisputed epicenter of hep. The liberating air of New York and the critical mass of black creative talent had elevated Harlem from crowded urban ghetto to magical mecca for music, dancing, and writing, attracting blacks and whites, high and low, to nightclubs, saloons, and soirees. It was here in the twenties and early thirties that northern blacks, freed from the worst racism of their southern past but still frozen out of traditional American routes to success, furiously were creating their own vibrant alternatives.

On the high end presided the "Talented Tenth," the elite literary cadre of the Harlem Renaissance—Langston Hughes, Claude McKay, Jean Toomer, et al.—who wrote poems, novels, and published all manner of highbrow magazines and journals. These new Harlem intellectuals fervently promoted black art, but (with the exception of Hughes) were "so fixed on a vision of *high* culture that they did not look hard or well at jazz." This was most ironic, because while the jazzmen represented the "low" end of the Harlem Renaissance and were far less respectable than the writers, they were also ultimately far more influential.

The jazzmen presided as the high priests of hep, venerated and emulated, living examples of creativity, personal style, and fast wits. Below the jazz musicians in this hep world's hierarchy came the hustler-hepsters, the "sharp-dressed young cats who hung on the corners and in the poolrooms, bars, and restaurants," and manned the numbers and other shady enterprises. But for the many acolytes who were never going to be jazzmen or hustlers, part-time hep was also possible. Thus, a black man might spend his days downtown as a janitor or scrounging for a day's work, but come home to Harlem and assume part-time brotherhood among the hep.

Within the new black urban hepster subculture, marijuana was key. One only had to peruse jazzman Cab Calloway's tongue-in-cheek *A Hepster's Dictionary*, issued in 1939, to see how entrenched marijuana was in hep lingo, with all its slang names listed. And then there was the word "hip," still obscure enough to the world at large to require explication. Though this certainly appears to be an old piece of drug argot, going back to the days of opium dens and opium smoking (performed recumbent and "on the hip"), Calloway explained "hip" as meaning, "wise, sophisticated, anyone with boots on." The latter odd phrase referred to blacks who had had the good sense to abandon the cotton fields for the North, don city shoes, and become thereby someone who "know[s] what it is all about, you are a hep cat, you are wise."

The hepsters, however, were not the first Americans to sing the praises of *cannabis* in public. Back before the Civil War, the young Fitz Hugh Ludlow of Poughkeepsie, New York, had written enthusiastically in *Putnam's Magazine* of his euphoriant experiences with the fluid extract of marijuana, a medical product often prescribed for migraine headaches. Ludlow's article, which justified his short-lived, exotic pursuit as the experiments of a sensitive soul, was then expanded into his 1857 book, *The Hasheesh Eater*. But as the 1863 letters of New York stockbroker Edward Homans to his fiancée make clear, using *cannabis* (or what he called the "Divine Weed") was not approved of. For Homans wrote earnestly to his sweetheart, "I've remembered your injunctions darling about smoking and am remarkably temperate in my use of the 'Divine Weed.' Smoking in bed and after dinner have been renounced entirely—also smoking early in the morning—the most pernicious time of all—and the greatest privation, too. Ain't I good?"

Apparently those nineteenth-century New Yorkers who indulged in the perfectly legal "Divine Weed" and hashish did so very quietly, for the same H. H. Kane who had documented the extraordinary proliferation of opium smoking and opium dens was quite amazed to discover the existence of a hashish den in New York City. In a November 1883 article in *Harper's*, he described visiting an extraordinarily plush den patronized by the better classes, including many ladies. Dark and decrepit on the outside, the atmosphere and furnishings within "brought to my mind the scenes of the *Arabian Nights*." First, visitors donned silk smoking robes, tassled hats, and felt slippers. Then they paid two dollars for the hashish and ascended to the main smoking room, a dazzling space. Underfoot was a rich "velvety carpet, . . . above, a magnificent chandelier, consisting of six dragons of beaten gold, . . . all about the sides of the spacious apartment were mattresses covered with different-colored cloth, and edged with heavy golden fringe, . . . and soft pillows in heaps. Above the level of these divans there ran, all about the room, a series of huge mirrors framed with gilded serpents intercoiled, effectually shutting off the windows. The effect was magnificent." In the center of the room a fountain tinkled gently. Kane initially enjoyed his hashish reverie, but then was plunged into terrifying dreams of pursuing packs of dogs and hissing serpents that left him weeping. He departed into a gray and drizzling dawn, still amazed. Yet there is little indication that nineteenth-century *cannabis* use spread much or endured long in New York City.

It was another half century before Meyer Berger reported on spending an evening in the far more prosaic Harlem tea pad. But already the hep-cat and the hep world had so evolved that the truly hip black hepster could find significant psychic refuge from square and racist America in the distinctive and prestigious world of northern urban jazz culture. There the hep-cat could make a virtue of rejecting the bourgeois square world and all its values. He could actively pity the poor square: the dull, sober wage-slave too preoccupied and constricted by the daily rat race, family, home, car, pet to really savor life in all its pleasures and excitements. However, this was clearly still such a subterranean subculture and mind-set that even a terrific reporter hanging out in the middle of it completely missed the story. The world of black pot-smoking vipers and hepsters in 1938 was just too alien and weird even to a journalist steeped in the city's lowlife.

However, five years later, when Berger reported on the phenomenon of the zoot suit in the *New York Times*, he had caught up, noting the suit's popularity with "the hep-cats or swing-mad kids." Now not only music, but fashion was moving up from the streets. Berger wrote that a young black man working as a busboy in Georgia had dreamed up the zoot. The man's tailor found the zoot so extraordinary—with its superwide trousers, narrow cuffs, and big, draped jacket—that he sent pictures to *Men's Apparel Reporter*. Within eighteen months, the zoot was the rage all over the country. The idea that such a major style had "originated among financially poor people" was astonishing to the garment industry, for "most men's styles are copied from high-priced models made by top-drawer designers for men." Berger was much closer now to the real story: the phenomenon of the black hepster and the growing influence of this lower-class black culture on the rest of America.

Amazingly, it was not the black hep world's adoption of marijuana that brought authorities down on the weed. Rather, it was its popularity with Mexican immigrant workers in the western and southern border states, where uneasy officials increasingly linked marijuana with crime and violence. *Cannabis* had initially been targeted—along with the opiates and cocaine—in the early versions of what eventually passed as the Harrison Narcotic Act in 1914, but its medical uses for migraine and glaucoma had convinced lawmakers to keep it legally available.

Nonetheless, complaints from the southern border regions about "loco weed" smoking by the lower classes caused the U.S. Treasury to outlaw the importation of any marijuana except for medical purposes in 1915. When a department aide named Reginald Smith traveled to eleven Texas cities in 1917 to see whether this had helped, he reported widespread marijuana smoking for pleasure by Mexicans and "sometimes by Negroes and lower class whites." He strongly recommended that marijuana be added to the Harrison Act to make it illegal. But in this period before the favorable 1919 Supreme Court rulings on Harrison, the act was viewed as too shaky to tamper with. Furthermore, hard-pressed federal officials had little enthusiasm for policing marijuana. By 1926, New Orleans newspapers were expressing special concern over the "large numbers of boys of school age [who] buy and smoke 'mootas.' . . . Most of these children were of poorer family and of foreign parentage." An aroused Louisiana legislature made marijuana illegal in 1927 and local police went into action. Repeated sweeps gradually brought the marijuana situation "under better control than it had been in the past."

Throughout the early thirties, most of the western states outlawed marijuana. But politicians and newspapers in Texas, Colorado, and Louisiana clamored for federal help. Just as with opium, cocaine, and then heroin, the new laws came in the wake of local experience that showed drug use exacerbating antisocial behavior. A 1935 *American Mercury* article, "The Menace of Marijuana," asserted that using the drug led to "disintegration of personality" and quoted a Denver report saying, "Most crimes of violence in this section, especially the country districts, are laid to users of marijuana." The article concluded that marijuana was "no less vicious than opium, cocaine, morphine or heroin." The editor of the Alamosa, Colorado, *Daily Courier* wrote in 1936 to the Treasury Department on behalf of local leaders: "Is there any assistance your Bureau can give us in handling this drug? Can you suggest campaigns? Can you enlarge your Department to deal with marijuana? Can you do anything to help us?" When Meyer Berger wrote his 1938 article on tea pads, he summed up expert medical opinion this way: "Marijuana, while no more habit-forming than ordinary cigarette smoking, offers a shorter cut to complete madness than any other drug."

Narcotics Commissioner Harry J. Anslinger wanted nothing to do with federal marijuana laws. After all, the early thirties were the depths of the Depression and his agents had plenty of work reining in opiates without taking on a drug that grew like a weed in whole sections of the country. Anslinger stiffly suggested the states handle the problem themselves. But Southwest governors lobbied the Treasury Secretary and finally an unenthused Anslinger agreed to some federal action.

There ensued a series of interagency meetings. At one, Anslinger point-blank asked Dr. Carl Voegtlin, chief of the Division of Pharmacology of the National Institute of Health, if smoking marijuana caused insanity. The doctor answered: "I think it is an established fact that prolonged use leads to insanity in certain cases, depending upon the amount taken, of course." Drawing on such expert opinions and bloodcurdling reports from southwestern lawmen, Anslinger thunderously denounced "Marijuana: Assassin of Youth" in a 1937 article in *American* magazine. He described marijuana as "dangerous as a coiled rattlesnake," an addictive drug that rivaled heroin in its dangers. He cited the case of "a whole family murdered by a youthful addict in Florida" and another grisly case in California.

Nonetheless, the American Medical Association, which resented the FBN's monitoring of doctors and wanted to preserve access to marijuana's medically useful qualities, testified against the Marijuana Tax Act before Congress. Such was the pressure from the Southwest, however, that it passed and became the law of the land on October 1, 1937. While not explicitly making marijuana illegal, it had that effect. Anyone who grew, transported, sold, prescribed, or used marijuana had to register and pay a one-dollar tax, with all nondoctors required to pay a one-hundred-dollar-per-ounce tax each time the drug changed hands. As marijuana had now been made illegal in every state, such filings would only alert local authorities to one's nefarious doings, while failing to file was a federal offense.

With marijuana effectively outlawed, federal authorities did begin to crack down. Yet, it seems it was not until during the war that Anslinger became fully aware of the jazz-marijuana connection. In 1943 he instructed his agents: "Because of [the] increasing volume of reports indicating that many musicians of the swing band type are responsible for the spread of the marijuana smoking vice, I should like you to give the problem some special attention in your district." What he really hoped to pull off was a splashy nationwide roundup of major jazz musicians, but the bureau failed, mainly because agents could never find "anyone inside the jazz world to become an informant."

Among the lesser knowns snagged (though not by federal agents) was Mezz Mezzrow, arrested in 1940 by New York City police with sixty joints as he entered the back door of a jazz club at the New York World's Fair. It was the final straw in a tough decade, much of it spent so wrapped up in smoking opium that Mezzrow barely played music at all. Mezzrow served a seventeen-month sentence in the "colored" cell block at Riker's Island, where he played in a prison band, and found a new calling as a musical arranger. Though Mezzrow said he never returned to dealing thereafter, marijuana would remain readily available in Harlem, a staple of the hep world. Eventually, Mezzrow followed the great American jazz migration to Europe and died there in 1972. He is ensconced in the Père Lachaise cemetery in Paris, sharing immortality in this shady city of the dead with such other expatriates as Gertrude Stein and Isadore Duncan.

Among the many Harlemites who peddled illegal reefer, probably none ever achieved such subsequent reknown as Detroit Red. A Michigan country boy, he quickly had transformed himself into the complete urban hepster in Boston, working there briefly at legitimate, low-paying jobs amid galling racist slights. Once he moved on to Harlem, he left behind the square world and by 1940 was making big money hustling marijuana. "I sold reefer like a wild man. I scarcely slept; I was wherever musicians congregated. . . . In every band, at least half of the musicians smoked reefers."

Embittered by the negligible prospects for a black male in mainstream America, and repelled finally by the empty hedonism of the petty hustler-hepster, Detroit Red embraced a whole new black alternative, one discovered while serving prison time for burglarizing houses. Espousing the squarest of values—sobriety, religion, work, family—Detroit Red took up the Black Muslim way of life, which shunned both whites and hepsters. By 1950, Detroit Red had become Malcolm X, the radical black Muslim leader, offering not only a lifestyle, but a political agenda of self-respect, responsibility, and self-sufficiency to counter white racism.

Now, you might think that the white addicts of this era, many of whom were in New York, would have found common ground with their black, tea-smoking brethren, especially once marijuana became illegal in 1937 like heroin. But as one observer of the time noted, the white opiate addicts completely "excluded the 'weed-heads' or marijuana addicts from their company." By the same token, such venerated hepsters as Louis Armstrong disdained as lowlifes addicts using what he called the "drastic stuff." They were, he complained, "dirty-grimey all the time. Show most addicts a bucket of water and they'll run like hell to keep it from touching them." In contrast, explained Louis Armstrong, marijuana was a positive force and "when you're with another tea smoker it makes you feel a special sense of kinship."

Among the many jazz musicians who flocked to New York's hep scene in the late thirties was a young alto saxophonist named Charlie (Yardbird) Parker. A large, shambling, charismatic personality, Parker was a prodigious and original instrumentalist who dazzled his peers with sheer speed and inventiveness and changed American music forever by fathering bebop. Born in 1920, Charlie Parker was the only child of Charles and Addie Parker. Seven years later the respectable churchgoing Mrs. Parker relocated alone to the Kansas City, Missouri, where she supported her child as a charwoman.

When as a young teen Charlie discovered Kansas City's notorious wild side—its honky-tonks, clubs, bootleg liquor, and fabulous jazz—he took up the alto sax. He showed so little early promise that his first appearance at a local club brought gales of derisive laughter. After that debacle, Parker did little but practice for two years. By high school, he was a regular in local jazz bands.

At sixteen he had married Rebecca Ruffin, who was soon pregnant. One July evening Charlie summoned her upstairs. Things had not been going well between them, and she sat staring glumly toward the mirror. There she saw her husband, dressed for work in a dark suit, pull his tie around his arm and stick a needle in. When she screamed, Parker smiled benignly, put his necktie back on, kissed her, and headed out. The next morning his mother chastised him for using that "stuff." Parker became more and more haggard. Household objects began disappearing: jewelry, a radio, even an iron. Not long after Parker's son was born in January 1938, Boss Tom Pendergast was indicted and Kansas City's wide-open vice districts were shuttered, throwing most of the jazz bands out of work. Charlie Parker took off to New York City.

Parker made little initial impression in the Big Apple jazz scene and survived at first washing dishes at Jimmy's Chicken Shack. Slowly Parker picked up small gigs and began sitting in on sessions. He dated his radical discovery of improvising around chords—rather than melody—to a December 1939 jam session in the back room of Dan Wall's Chili House. "That night I was working over 'Cherokee' and, as I did, I found that by using the higher intervals of a chord as a melody line and backing them with appropriately related changes, I could play the thing I'd been hearing. I came alive." The boy who had been laughed off the stage in Kansas City was turning into a virtuoso, a saxophonist whose speed and imagination amazed his peers.

When the war came, numerous young jazzmen rebelled against military service, telling army psychiatrists that they might be tempted to use their guns on white Americans. Parker's track marks, the unmistakable stigmata of the addict, earned an instant 4F, leaving him free to spend the war collaborating with other 4Fs—Dizzy Gillespie and Thelonious Monk—on bebop. Bebop caused a sensation. Remembers one musician, "We used to play those records—we'd get in a room and live with them all night. It was unbelievable. Something from outer space."

When the veteran jazzmen and their legions of fans returned home from the war, bebop was a bafflement. "They came back and couldn't figure out what was happening," remembers trumpeter Howard McGhee. "A lot of cats looked at Bird with their mouths wide open. 'What's he doing?'" Bernie Brightman had flown fifty-two bombing missions over Europe. He got out of the Air Force service and headed straight to the jazz clubs. "I couldn't relate to bebop at all," he said, "so I stopped going." He also stopped smoking marijuana. "What's the good of it if it's just laying back? What did they do with that more aware consciousness? Did they somehow advance the world?" By the fifties, Brightman had become an active communist.

Many of the veteran jazz musicians responded with hostility to the new bebop music. Cab Calloway dismissed it as "Chinese music." The great Louis Armstrong called it "slop" lacking any melody. If the veterans were scornful, the younger musicians enshrined Charlie "Bird" Parker as the genius of the bebop world, the Supreme Hipster whose virtuoso playing and cool, dignified delivery expressed the basics of the hipster ethos: complete freedom from convention, an intense pursuit of life in its most pleasurable aspects, untrammeled creativity, and, as ever, contempt for the square world. (There had been a subtle linguistic shift to "hip" and "hipster" as squares started using the term "hep" and "hepster.") The young found bebop the perfect expression for a new, cooler, atomic age.

The irony was that bebop was *so* different that the multitudes who loved dixieland and swing simply balked at it—white and black. Wrote Leroi Jones, "Bebop was the coup de grace, the idea that abruptly lifted jazz completely out of the middle-class Negro's life. . . . It was for him, as it was for any average American, 'deep' or 'weird.'"

Charlie Parker became the living symbol of that bebop rebellion, a hipster who lived as intensely and freely as he played. He was notorious for his hedonism, indulging insatiable appetites for women, food, and all forms of inebriation. (He would ultimately have four wives—two black, two white—but after the second he no longer bothered with legal niceties.) As Parker found growing success in the jazz world, he began a lifelong habit of disappearing on pleasure sprees, lost to hedonistic excess.

Yet this enormous desire to devour life also manifested itself in a more highbrow way, through a love of books and knowledge. In a given evening he might spend hours discussing Nietzsche and Stravinsky with strangers at a club, and then when leaving share a few bottles of Thunderbird with winos on the corner. Explained one awed follower, "That's what you hear when you listen to him play: he can reach the most intellectual and difficult levels of music, then he can turn around—now watch this—and play the most low down, funky blues you ever want to hear."

Parker's relentless pursuit of pleasure became, despite the glamorous gloss conjured up by devoted fans, pathologically destructive to himself and everyone near him. He slept wherever, often in his clothes, was always pawning his saxophone or borrowing someone else's and never returning it. He shamelessly mooched money, meals, drinks, and grew alarmingly run down. Years later one musician still vividly remembered the shock of a late-night encounter, "Bird was thin and drawn. He looked like an unmade bed. It was six degrees below zero and Bird was wearing a T-shirt, no socks and an expensive black overcoat."

Musician Max Roach remembers playing in a combo that included Gillespie and Parker. "Bird came in late and instead of coming right in and going to the bandstand . . . went right to the bathroom. . . . Dizzy went to the bathroom and peeped over into the stall. . . . 'Do you know what that mothafucka is doing?' he said. 'He's in there shooting shit!' " For the heroin habit that Parker had begun in 1937 in Kansas City was worse than ever. "When you have a bad day," he would try to explain to his third wife, Doris, "there's nothing you can do about it. You have to endure it. When I have a bad day, I know where to go and what to do to make a good day out of it."

As this aspect of Parker—his serious heroin addiction—got around, it made him seem only more incredible, more enigmatic. Even in the hard-living world of jazz and hip cats, heroin was virtually unknown. Marijuana was commonplace, almost de rigueur, a familiar part of the subculture, but heroin was something highly exotic. Recalls saxophonist Budd Johnson, "The [hard] drug users as far back as I can remember were always white." Now here was a black jazzman, the Supreme Hipster, who was a heroin addict. "A lot of younger people were so amazed and fascinated by the likes of Charlie's playing," remembers Chubby Jackson, "that something told them inside that if they were to assume his personal habits that they could get close to him." So profound was Parker's influence in the jazz world that the mere fact of his addiction embued heroin with a cachet it had never possessed before.

Recalls musician Frankie Socolow, "Bird was a big junkie, and to be like Bird you had to be a junkie. I mean everybody smoked pot, but when it came to hard shit, it didn't really become popular, if that's the right word to use, until Bird and his emulators." The equation now moved up from hepsters smoked marijuana, squares didn't, to hipsters shot heroin, squares didn't.

Heroin exacted an enormous price as it swept through the bebop world, leaving in its wake a sad debris of jazzmen dead on overdoses, broken families, and shattered careers. Howard McGhee remembers, "I know a lot of cats just tried to act like [Bird], and they was found layin' on the side of the road somewhere, fuckin' with shit like Bird was. Little alto player, I don't know his name, from out of Chicago, he was gonna be like Bird, and he came to play a dance. He followed Bird around. Two days later he was dead." Parker—ever the original—was exempt from some of the typical problems plaguing opiate addicts. Rarely did heroin dampen any of his appetites—for sex, for food, and, above all, for music. Yet heroin was his central preoccupation and slowly but surely it destroyed him.

In 1946, Dizzy Gillespie put together a bebop band to storm Los Angeles. Charlie Parker, whom he viewed as both a genius and "musically, the other side of my heartbeat," was signed up. But because he was so unreliable, Gillespie hired an additional person. A good move, as it turned out, for Parker was frequently absent or late and disappeared completely toward the end of the two-month engagement. Try as they might, the band members could not find him. Parker remained in Los Angeles, badly strung out and only occasionally capable of real work.

One night that summer in California, Parker twice wandered naked into the lobby of his seedy hotel. Then he fell asleep in bed while smoking. As the mattress billowed smoke, policemen and firemen swarmed into his room. Finally roused, Parker fought with everyone and ended up in jail. Ten days later his friends found him and had him transferred to the Camarillo State Hospital, where he spent six months. He returned to New York City off drugs, restored to health, the triumphant, conquering hero.

The next few years were some of Parker's most brilliant. To his fans, Parker was an unparalleled force, soaring, free, inspirational, and intimidating in his talent. Remembers tenor saxophonist Sonny Rollins, "He was definitely the messiah, no doubt about it." Mused one fan, "I guess the only thing he never did was invent an A-bomb." Adulation of Parker could take amusing turns, as when fans began appearing in rumpled suits because they saw Parker in his "unmade bed" look and thought it was a new hip style. Or there were the berets he and Gillespie sported after a European tour or the dark glasses he often wore on stage. Remembers one fan, "The first time I ever saw anyone wearing sunglasses at night was in the Deuces. To me, that was the absolute zenith of hipsterism."

But, ultimately, adulation of Parker became a tragedy, as Bird's genius and cool came to be inextricably equated with heroin use. One musician remembered watching Parker down whiskey, pills, smoke pot, shoot up, and then play "strong and beautiful. . . . We felt we'd be willing to do anything to warm ourselves by that fire, get some of that grease pumping through our veins." Addicts on the West Coast signaled one another discreetly by whistling the opening three notes of "Parker's Mood."

When Frankie Socolow returned to New York in 1950 after being away a couple of years, he was shocked: "Everybody, everybody was a junkie." Nor was it only New York. In Chicago one nonaddicted jazzman left because "all the players . . . were wiped out most of the time." Jazz historian Lincoln Collier concludes, "It is probable that 50 to 75 percent of the bop players had some experience with hard drugs, that a quarter to a third were seriously addicted, and that perhaps as many as 20 percent were killed by [heroin]. . . . In the end, the carnage was immense." Recalls saxophonist Gerry Mulligan bitterly, "A lot of guys died during that period. These people just didn't have any kind of sense of responsibility to each other or for what they were doing." If they weren't overdosing, they were getting arrested. Soon, there was the sardonic saying, "To get the best band, go to KY," meaning Lexington, Kentucky, at the narcotics farm. Surveying the scene, Artie Shaw said, "Jazz was born in a whiskey barrel, grew up on marijuana and is about to expire on heroin."

Parker, who had emerged from Camarillo in fine fettle, was slowly but surely being dragged down by his habit. With each passing year he grew more troubled, manipulative, and unreliable. Still the idol of the hipsters, Bird faltered even in his music. His career was in parlous condition, as band leaders and club owners grew weary of his destructive antics. When *Life* ran a short, silly feature in 1948 on bebop, explaining this strange music to the square world, Parker was not so much as mentioned. It was Gillespie, a tremendous talent with a head for business, who garnered the national press with his hipster stance, signature goatee, beret, and jive talk. Disciplined, ambitious, and determined to reap the full benefits of his talent, Gillespie had no patience with the heroin users.

Parker was extraordinarily lucky that he was never jailed over narcotics. Federal agents were well aware of his reputation and kept close tabs on him. On June 15, 1948, two agents questioned him in his room at the Dewey Square Hotel. While talking, they saw on top of a table sixty-seven empty capsules, two syringes, three hypodermic needles, one spoon, and one empty glassine envelope containing traces of heroin. "Parker admitted ownership of the equipment and said that he had been using narcotics for the past several years, but that he had never been addicted. He got his supply, he said, from the many peddlers in the neighborhood of 112th Street and Fifth Avenue." Naturally, Parker was arrested and taken downtown, but the federal prosecutors deemed the evidence insufficient to bring a case. Then in 1950 Parker "was convicted of possession of heroin in the New York State Court of Special Session in December," but there is no sign he served any time.

In the spring of 1955, Gillespie was at a Fifty-second Street club listening to a band when Charlie Parker made his way through the audience. Parker's life had been spiraling rapidly downward since the death in 1952 of a two-year-old daughter from pneumonia. Parker looked bad: bloated, fat, tired. He said, "Diz, why don't you save me?" Gillespie, who had been burned again and again by Parker's erratic behavior, did not know how to answer. He looked at his longtime friend, his musical other-half, and asked how he could do that. Parker pleaded, "I dunno but just save me, save me, man." Gillespie had seen too many drug casualties to harbor any illusions. "I didn't know what to do. I just didn't know what to say to that man. . . . When a dude is using drugs, no one can help him. You have to have the determination to pull yourself up."

Parker's death at age thirty-four on March 12, 1955, was a fitting coda to a life that so straddled the highs and lows. He was struggling with tough times, unable to find enough work, drinking heavily in hopes of conquering his heroin addiction. Yet he died in a luxury suite at the Stanhope Hotel on Fifth Avenue tended to by minor royalty, the Baroness Nika De Konigswarter, Rothschild and jazz patron. The coroner guessed Parker's age as mid fifties and attributed his death to lobar pneumonia, cirrhosis of the liver, a perforated ulcer, and possibly a fatal heart attack brought on by all of these.

Charlie Parker's legacy was twofold. He was an artistic genius who successfully set out to forever change the musical landscape. For however disdained bebop was at first, its long-term influence would be immense and its "sense of rhythm, challenging, dangerous and always confident, is now heard in [popular American] music everywhere, from rock to Muzak to movie scores." But Charlie Parker also—despite himself—linked incapacitating drug use to being hip. Unlike his fans and acolytes, Parker had no romantic illusions about heroin. Once when shooting up in front of an appalled Gerry Mulligan, Parker said dolefully, "This is something I have to do. It's terrible but I'm stuck with it."

Blues chanteuse Billie Holiday, though not part of the bebop world, also found solace in heroin and cocaine. Arrested on May 16, 1947, in New York in front of the Hotel Compton, Holiday had been a heavy user for three years. When the judge asked Lady Day, then twenty-nine, how she started, she replied laconically, "You know how show business is. Always looking for a thrill." When he wondered what she used and where she started, she said, "Heroin caps. In Washington." In and out of jail and treatment centers, Billie Holiday's deteriorating health undermined her extraordinary voice, which was losing its vibrancy. Deprived of her

New York cabaret license and increasingly unreliable and manipulative, Holiday had trouble finding work. On May 31, 1959, she collapsed and was taken to Metropolitan Hospital. At age forty-one she was dead.

When the Newport Jazz Festival quietly sponsored a Musicians' Clinic in 1957 to help addicted musicians, all of fifteen people (out of the estimated seven hundred jazz musician heroin addicts) presented themselves. This was the same year that the young Dr. John the Night Tripper (Mac Rebennack) began using heroin down in New Orleans. A high school student with his own band, he recalls, "When I looked around, most of the famous musicians I'd heard of were junkies. That was a heavy influence on me. [Using heroin] was my way . . . of joining the set I dug." The musician Professor Longhair, recalls Dr. John, "warned me against heroin. . . . [He said] that stuff is going to turn on you." Yet Dr. John and tens of thousands of other young men blithely ignored this sound advice.

The stage was now set for a revived and transformed urban drug culture. With each postwar year, more heroin (with its new association with hip) flowed into the northern cities. Availability was rising. The postwar heroin was peddled much as the prewar heroin had been, in the hangouts of poor and working-class neighborhoods—the pool halls, bars, street corners. And as many of these neighborhoods became black, a new generation of socially marginal young men—the Leroy Streets of the forties and fifties—began experimenting with and becoming addicted to drugs. These brand-new city dwellers had had little firsthand experience with heroin or other drugs and therefore little appreciation at first of their perils. Saxophonist Stan Getz, a New Yorker from the working-class Bronx, recalls that when he first tried heroin, "I didn't even know that smack was habit-forming. In two weeks I was hooked and spent ten years trying to get off." The swiftness with which heroin swept northern black ghettoes was terrifying, and not so dissimilar from "happy dust's" rapid dispersal through white immigrant slums four decades earlier.

As Claude Brown wrote in wondered dismay about the Harlem of the 1950s in *Manchild in the Promised Land*, "Heroin had just about taken over Harlem. It seemed to be a kind of a plague. Everytime I went uptown, somebody else was hooked, somebody else was strung out . . . cats would say . . . 'Look here, I got some shit,' meaning heroin. 'Let's get high.' They would say it so casually, the way somebody in another community might say, 'C'mon, let's have a drink.' "

"I'd tell them, 'No, man, I don't dabble in stuff like that.' They'd look at me and smile, feeling somewhat superior, more hip than I was because they were into drugs."

Leroi Jones would make the same observation, that heroin appealed to the black working class and poor because the "drug itself transforms the Negro's normal separation from the mainstream of society into an advantage. . . . It is one-upsmanship of the highest order. Many heroin addicts believe no one can be knowledgable or 'hip' unless he is an addict."

In 1951, just one three-block area of East Harlem was described during a congressional hearing as having twenty places selling drugs. In a local social athletic club of fifty boys, at least eighteen or twenty were heroin addicts. A welfare official declared black teenage drug use at "epidemic proportions," saying, "Boys have a term describing what happens to them. They say they go from Sneaky Pete [cheap wine] to pot, to horse, to banging [mainlining heroin]."

Just as when "happy dust" swept the urban ghettoes the first time, young men and teenage boys were the most susceptible to heroin, experimenting at first with sniffing and then advancing to using needles. Certainly not every young black man who began using heroin in this era could articulate its "hip" meaning as did the bebop musicians. But they were aware of heroin's connection to hip, as they wandered into addiction through curiosity and the urgings of friends and acquaintances. Unlike their white predecessors, however, the new young black addicts generally got their first initiation to drugs by smoking marijuana. Then, as *Newsweek* reported, "Jaded on marijuana, [they] had found a greater thrill in heroin." As one teenager was quoted, "We felt grand, like we were ruling the world."

A Detroit grand jury examining the surge in addiction found that youthful drug users were often followers of the "so-called 'be-bop' music. . . . It was in such associations that most of the marijuana users were introduced to heroin, and once introduced to heroin, they were hooked." One Brooklyn detective infiltrating the local drug scene made his way to an apartment where he "could hear the throbbing, screaming cacophony of 'be-bop' records . . . [and] couldn't help but sense the weird atmosphere as he entered the room to find four young men sitting around a table and gesticulating to the tempo of the music as they prepared to 'take a fix.' "

Also like the white prewar addicts, the new black addicts often were marginal young men within their own community. Compared with the black population at large, the new heroin addicts were more likely to have come from a broken home, dropped out of school, and engaged in crime. A twenty-year-old East Harlemite in treatment after four years of addiction was typical. From a chaotic home life, he had abandoned school, and while hanging around had tried heroin and liked it. To support his habit, he tended bar, peddled heroin, and occasionally mugged people. But as he said, "When you're on horse [heroin], you ain't worrying about nothin'."

Adults were nonplussed by these juvenile lost souls. Professor David Maurer, a linguist whose scholarly specialty was drug argot, was taken aback in the early fifties to find the tight, secretive world of older white opiate addicts

> invaded by literally thousands of newcomers, many of them youngsters under 21 who, ten years ago, could never have penetrated the underworld circles where they now circulate freely. . . . Ten years ago, most drug addicts were over 30, and a juvenile addict had yet to be encountered. All this activity has . . . introduced a vast new class of addicts . . . [including] an increasing number of zoot-suited needle-pushers and marijuana smokers who are not only playing havoc with the drugs of addiction, but with the argot as well, . . . [because] the marijuana smoker has not only adopted much of the slang and argot characteristic of swing music, but has contributed heavily to it. . . . Compared to the argot of opiate users [marijuana slang] appears to the authors to be thin, obscure and affected.

For the mainstream bourgeois world, this was all baffling and disturbing—young men throwing their futures away as slaves to a white powder. Especially since the new hipster-addicts so completely failed to see things this way. As one sociologist noted, "The common image of the young colored drug addict pictures him as a pitiful figure, a trapped unfortunate." But in the inverted values of the black hipster, nothing could be further from his own self-conception. Instead, the new hipster-addict viewed his whole situation with a "certain zest" as he "recounted his search for 'kicks,' the adventure of his life on the streets, and the intensity of his contest against the whole world to maintain his supply of drugs." This was not just an alternative subculture, but an oppositional subculture, one that actively opposed and despised the "square" world.

Authorities could only feel perplexed and alarmed as the casualties of this new wave of heroin surfaced in New York, Chicago, Washington, D.C., Detroit, and virtually every northern city with growing black slums. But as Nicholas Lemann points out in *The Promised Land*, public policy experts of the fifties in no way viewed the new black slums or race as an issue or a concern. And so, even though by 1950 newspapers and magazines were reporting that illicit hard drugs were resurgent, few made much of the disturbing new twist: this set of users were young and disproportionately black.

Dr. Victor Vogel, the chief medical officer at Lexington, looked at the rapidly changing profile of narcotic patients at KY and declared a new heroin epidemic. The numbers were startling and graphic: In 1947, there were 2,943 admissions to Lexington, and 214, or 7.3 percent, were black; in 1950, admissions soared to 4,534 and now 1,460, or 32.2 percent, were black. By 1957, when treatment facilities began to open in affected cities and states, overall admissions at Lexington declined to 4,089, but 1,826, or 44.7 percent, were black. Moreover, the Federal Bureau of Narcotics estimated that of the 46,266 active narcotic addicts it had tracked in 1958, 27,016, or 59 percent, were black. But the FBN, too, made little of this fact. Not only had the problem of modern American addiction—considered largely to be licked—sprung back to monstrous life, but in these postwar years it was embedding itself in America's oldest and most enduring dilemma: race.

CHAPTER 8

"His Fame Spread
Throughout
the World."

—*Commissioner Harry J. Anslinger*
on himself.
UNDATED MS, CA. 1950S

On a cold February evening in 1946, one chauffeured car after another pulled up to a dark Brooklyn dock. Ignoring the few guards, organized crime notables such as Frank Costello stepped forth and boarded the battered Liberty ship SS *Laura Keene*. Holding court in a modest cabin was Charles "Lucky" Luciano, long-ago protégé of Arnold Rothstein. Stripped of his citizenship, Luciano was being deported to his native land, Italy, on a cargo ship carrying flour for war-ravaged Europe. But on this, Luciano's last night, various thuggish friends had come to share a farewell feast of lobsters, spaghetti, and wine. About five-foot-nine and slender, Luciano in his youth had been conventionally good-looking, the dark, wavy hair framing a handsome face. But the thick knife scar slicing across his neck and a drooping right eye, souvenirs of a 1929 gangland "ride," had altered his appearance, marking him with a deserved aura of underworld menace.

Earlier in the day, hostile longshoremen had barred journalists trying to board the ship for a final interview with the "vice king." Luciano
had declined to come out, saying he "had had enough of the press." The
next morning, as the SS *Laura Keane* left New York Harbor, a small
group—mainly reporters—watched, obviously hoping Luciano would
come on deck. Standing back from the crowd was Charles Siragusa,
federal narcotics agent, tall, brown-haired, wearing horn-rimmed
glasses, and sporting a pencil-thin William Powell moustache. Having
joined the FBN's New York office in 1939, Siragusa was just back from
wartime service in Italy with the Office of Strategic Services (OSS). As
a cop and native New Yorker, Siragusa was curious to witness one of
Gotham's most infamous gangsters depart these shores. And to see
who else was there, for throughout the war Luciano's 107th Street gang
had remained the major source of what little illegal heroin there was.

Deprived of their European connections by sea blockades, members
of the 107th Street gang had turned to Mexico, where they had bought
crude opium, smuggled it back to New York, and refined it into heroin.
The quantities were small and the quality poor. In any case, in the
coming year, the FBN would infiltrate the East Harlem gang and convict all its major members. But as the *Laura Keene* steamed off across
the wintry harbor waters, the FBN had good reason to believe that
Luciano—who had not been personally caught with narcotics since
1926, but whose associates were involved deeply—would reenter the
field now that he was free and the war over.

Luciano, routinely dubbed the city's, the nation's, even the world's
number one criminal, had risen very swiftly since Arnold Rothstein's
murder in 1928. At that time, those newspapers that even mentioned
Luciano misidentified him as a waiter. After A.R.'s death, Luciano had
turned to another powerful patron, becoming assistant and bodyguard
to Giuseppe "The Boss" Masseria. One of the old-fashioned Moustache Petes, Masseria was a transplanted Black Hand Sicilian Mafiosi,
creator of East Harlem's 107th Street gang. The lucrative Italian lottery, cheap bootleg liquor, and generic extortion/protection were their
specialties.

In the spring of 1931, Luciano was playing a postprandial game of
cards with his boss at a trattoria when he excused himself to go to the
men's room. Four men entered the Coney Island seafood restaurant and
blasted away at Masseria. The *New York Times* reported in a front-page
story that this big boss of the underworld ("bigger than Al Capone")
was found dead on his back, clutching in his left hand "a brand new ace
of diamonds." Previous assassination attempts over the years had left
twelve innocent bystanders wounded and two dead. Consequently,

Masseria had taken to driving around in a steel-armored sedan with "plate glass an inch thick in all its windows."

This murder (immortalized first by writer Mario Puzo and then by filmmaker Francis Coppola in *The Godfather*) was followed six months later by the murder of Salvatore "Boss of Bosses" Maranzano, creator of the five-family system in New York. With that, the restive young American gangsters seized power from the conservative old Sicilians. Luciano's ruthless role in this bloody transition entitled him to a position of primacy in an American-style underworld. Aside from the continuing gold mine of Prohibition and traditional gambling, the young Turks expanded the old-fashioned Italian lottery into the illegal numbers game, organized prostitution, began taking over drug trafficking from the aging Jewish gangsters, and extended extortion and racketeering to new fields. But Luciano's domination of the New York underworld was rudely interrupted in 1936 by Special Prosecutor Thomas Dewey.

For even as Luciano and his lieutenant, Vito Genovese, had expanded their New York criminal empire into new spheres, public mood was changing dramatically. With the thirties came not only Repeal, but a renewed zeal for reform. During the laissez-faire and prosperous Jazz Age, society had winked at gangsters growing fat on Prohibition. But with the hard times of the Depression, public tolerance evaporated. The great party had ended badly, and now many a willing guest felt the hosts should pay penance. And the politically astute moved to capitalize on the new mood. A year after the Great Crash, New York Governor Franklin Delano Roosevelt had set in motion Judge Samuel Seabury's investigation of corruption in New York City.

A year later, unknown Republican Thomas E. Dewey began riding reform to political glory. An upper-class WASP out of the Midwest, Dewey had graduated from Columbia Law School and been comfortably launched as a Wall Street lawyer when public service called. As a prosecutor for the Southern District of New York, the smart, disciplined, and highly determined Dewey led a series of successful federal tax evasion prosecutions against gangsters. His first case targeted Rothstein protégé Waxey Gordon; by 1933 a wealthy Prohibition beer baron and America's Public Enemy Number One indicted on tax charges. The federal judge in the Waxey case, who sentenced the gangster to ten years in jail, pronounced the trial "astounding" for the prosecutor's virtuoso legal performance. Modestly, Dewey demurred, saying, "This is in no sense a personal victory. It is the result of three years of constructive work by the overworked and underpaid government servants who carried on this investigation against genuinely unbelievable odds." Organized crime had become so entrenched and so politically powerful, the law-abiding public—and the gangsters—were openly astonished to see justice done.

In 1935, Dewey was appointed special rackets prosecutor in New York. He immediately went after Luciano, who was flabbergasted to find himself extradited from Hot Springs, Arkansas, and hauled into court like a common criminal. There he was charged with running whorehouses. After all, in the twenty years since Luciano's six-month 1916 stint for selling heroin, the man had been arrested nineteen times in New York alone for every crime from bootlegging, drugs, grand larceny, shooting, and felonious assault to gambling. Yet again and again the cases were discharged, or laughable fines of two dollars or three dollars or five dollars imposed. Luciano paid no greater price for these serious crimes than he did for dozens of speeding citations.

The documents Dewey assembled to make his case against Luciano—the first mob case that did not depend on tax evasion—show how assiduously the Tammany-connected New York City police and judiciary of the day had ignored a man the press clamorously identified as the city's preeminent "vice overlord." The police had compiled virtually no information at all on Luciano, except the skeletal facts on his arrest record, while judges released him time after time. It was obviously not wise to be too curious or too harsh toward such a man—a violent, influential criminal who spent many hours each week relaxing at the 107th Street Nestor Democratic Club, a stalwart outpost of Tammany. (The FBI were no more aggressive. Their slender file on Charles Lucania began only in 1936. While the FBI classified him as an "outstanding criminal" and "general gangster and racketeer" and listed the basics of his rap sheet, they evinced no further interest or concern. "Outstanding criminals" were obviously someone else's problem.)

Dewey's monthlong prosecution provided numerous entertaining moments, as when Luciano, "the 39-year-old droopy-eyed boss racketeer of New York," had to concede he had never filed any state taxes, and had only bothered to pay six years of federal taxes (those covered by the statute of limitations) after being arrested. The testimony explained the origins of his nickname, acquired after the infamous gangland "ride" in 1929 that ended not in murder, but with Luciano's release in Staten Island. There a police officer found him alive but "badly beaten up and cut up . . . [with] tape over your eyes and mouth." The Staten Island grand jury that insisted on investigating the "kidnapping" heard that Luciano claimed to be a chauffeur, but "could not give the names of persons whom he had driven." When found by police, Luciano had three hundred dollars in cash, and a diamond-studded watch and chain worth four hundred dollars. (The average wage during the Depression was ten dollars a week.)

Luciano dressed for the Dewey trial in a "gray flannel double-breasted suit, with a faint check; his soft white collar almost the only unwilted one in the court room." When he took the stand, he reluctantly admitted to the hard-driving prosecutor that "he had had no legitimate occupation since 1920." That, however, had not prevented Luciano from living the high life, with his own Lockheed plane, an apartment at the Waldorf-Astoria under the name of Charles Ross (just upstairs from Bugsy Siegal), and regular attendance at famous racetracks. Luciano was utterly disdainful of the average working stiff. "I never was a crumb [a worker] and if I have to be a crumb, I'd rather be dead." Star reporter Meyer Berger was just as full of scorn for Luciano's nouveau riche affectations, writing, "Whenever possible he appeared in the latest in cutaways, a weakness that makes him look somewhat like that other public enemy—Dracula."

However suave his sartorial appearance, Luciano on trial came across like a truculent tough, sulkily insisting, "I says I am telling the truth now." (Even as he lied on such basic facts as where he was born; he claimed it was in the United States.) After Luciano was convicted of running chains of whorehouses and sent up for thirty to fifty years to Clinton Prison in Dannemora, impressed voters rewarded Dewey with the office of District Attorney of New York County, which served as a useful launching pad for yet more racket-busting and his 1942 election to governor of New York State. Dewey would serve in that office until 1955, running twice for president and losing, first to Franklin Delano Roosevelt in 1944 and then to Harry S. Truman in 1948.

When Lucky Luciano's lieutenant, the plain, bespectacled Vito Genovese, saw how relentlessly Dewey the prosecutor was pursuing mobsters, he did not wait for a turn in the dock. He instead fled to Italy and warm friendships with the Fascist higher-ups, including Benito Mussolini, who bestowed the honorary title of *commendatore*. The wisdom of fleeing became apparent, as back in New York yet another major gangster, Louis (Lepke) Buchalter of Murder Inc. infamy, was indicted and convicted for narcotics trafficking and then murder. Only Dutch Schultz's murder by other gangsters in late 1935 had saved him from prosecution.

When the United States entered World War II, the imprisoned Lucky Luciano quickly grasped the possibilities for his own liberation. Authorities were approached on Luciano's behalf by various gangsters, including none other than Augie Del Gratio, the longtime international trafficker back in New York after his two-year German jail term for narcotics smuggling. The general proposition was that the imprisoned Luciano could contribute his unique talents and connections to the war effort. Reports vary on what exactly this entailed. *Reader's Digest* wrote that Naval Intelligence in New York accepted Luciano's offer to use his waterfront racketeering contacts to set up "a counterespionage and antisabotage system among the longshoremen."

But the *New York Times* reported that Luciano's lawyer, one Moses Polakoff, credited his client with "aiding military authorities for two years in the preliminaries leading to the invasion of Sicily," a place filled with Mafiosi—both native Italian and deported Americans. Whatever the details of the quid pro quo, the upshot was a postwar commutation of Luciano's remaining decades of imprisonment. When Governor Dewey announced on January 3, 1946, that Luciano would be freed and immediately deported to Italy, he acknowledged Luciano's cooperation but questioned its "actual value."

When FBI Director J. Edgar Hoover heard of Luciano's pardon, he was astounded. He immediately unleashed his agents to investigate, marveling in a memo, "This is an amazing and fantastic case. We should get all the facts, for it looks rotten to me from several angles." Of course, one can assume—from the FBI's continuing indifference to gangsters and their nefarious activities and the FBI's infamous denial that organized crime even existed—that Hoover was interested mainly in acquiring dirt for his secret files on government officials. (As late as 1959, the FBI's New York office had four hundred agents investigating communists and four investigating organized crime.) When an FBI agent duly reported that the Office of the Chief of Naval Operations "acknowledges that Luciano was employed as an informant," Hoover scrawled across the report, "A shocking example of misuse of Navy authority in interest of a hoodlum. It surprises me they didn't give Luciano the Navy Cross."

Luciano's pardon dogged Dewey for years, as the U.S. government refused to publicly admit being cozy with gangsters, and Dewey's enemies made political hay, charging (falsely) during Senator Estes Kefauver's 1950–51 organized crime hearings and elsewhere that Luciano somehow had bribed Dewey to let him go. For reasons unknown, Commissioner Anslinger actively promoted this smear against a fellow Republican, and historians have concluded that the FBN investigators on loan to Kefauver—including Siragusa—gave perjured testimony harmful to Governor Dewey.

Dewey tried to avenge himself when fellow Republican General Dwight D. Eisenhower was elected president in 1952. Dewey summoned FBI Director J. Edgar Hoover to the governor's mansion in

Albany right after Christmas and strongly urged that Anslinger be replaced as narcotics commissioner, perhaps with someone from the FBI. As Hoover wrote in a memo, "Governor Dewey was quite disturbed about Anslinger and Anslinger's statements over a period of years associating Governor Dewey with Lucky Luciano." But Anslinger had many ardent Republican backers (especially in the pharmaceutical industry that the FBN monitored) and their plaudits prevailed. Still angry and determined to clear his name, Dewey finally took matters into his own hands in 1954. William B. Herlands, New York State Commissioner of Investigation, conducted a thorough hearing and exonerated Dewey completely. But much to the governor's chagrin, an embarrassed Office of Naval Intelligence invoked national security and insisted that Herlands's report be kept secret. And so it was until 1977, when it became the basis of a book exposé by Rodney Campbell, *The Luciano Project: The Secret Wartime Collaboration of the Mafia and the U.S. Navy*.

As for Luciano, he found banishment to dry, dusty, impoverished southern Italy less than congenial. Homesick for New York, he sat with his new mistress in the better cafés of a ramshackle Naples still pocked with bomb craters and collapsed war ruins. The notorious gangster was reduced to socializing with young American sailors on shore leave and going to the local track. A half year in war-weary Italy sufficed. Soon Luciano sailed off to Batista's Cuba, a tropical playground of swaying palms, elegant racetracks, and sexy casino nightlife for sin-seeking Americans. Once more in his element, Luciano relaxed with old underworld pals and began courting the local powers. Over in Washington, Commissioner Anslinger was convinced that the debonair as ever Luciano was setting up not just a new life on this lush island, but a new narcotics smuggling route. Washington requested that Luciano be deported back to Italy. When Cuba dawdled, the Treasury Department cut off the island's supply of legal medical narcotics from the United States. Luciano was asked to leave.

Soon thereafter, charged the FBN, large shipments of heroin began to arrive in the United States from Europe, where Luciano had once again settled in, now joined by a growing community of other deported mobsters. In New York on February 5, 1947, the first big postwar seizure was made: seven pounds of heroin found on a Corsican seaman leaving a vessel just arrived from France. On March 17, 1947, twenty-eight pounds of heroin was found on the French liner *St. Tropez*. A year later, fifteen pounds of morphine was seized off a ship just arrived from France. In late June 1948, eight pounds of heroin were found in the tail assembly of an Air France plane. On October 2, 1948, sixteen pounds of pure heroin was seized from the Italian liner *Vulcania*. On January 7, 1949, more than fifty pounds of opium and heroin were discovered on the French ship *Bastia*.

With the war over, the international traffickers were clearly back in business. Both U.S. Customs and the Bureau of Narcotics specifically blamed Luciano, "deported underworld leader," for the *Bastia* and *Vulcania* cases. But the Corsican hand was also notably visible, since almost everyone actually arrested in these early cases was a Corsican (identifiable by the French first name and Italian last name, as in Lucien Ignaro or Angi Marie Poggi).

Before World War II, independent operators such as Elie Eliopoulos and Carlos Fernandez Bacula based in France had been the major heroin suppliers in Europe for American gangsters, collaborating at times with the French Corsican mobs based in Marseille. The Bureau of Narcotics had been way ahead of the rest of federal law enforcement agencies in its identification of the American Mafia as a major criminal force on this side of the Atlantic. But the FBN failed to do much with this valuable information, neglecting to publicize this or somehow galvanize public opinion. For while Americans were familiar with Prohibition gangsters and racketeers (both Italian and Jewish in those days), it would be the 1960s before the concept of organized crime, by then dominated by the American-Italian Mafia, sank in, thanks to the sensational congressional testimony of small-time hood Joey Valachi.

Yet as early as the autumn of 1939 a New York narcotics agent named Anthony Piazza had written in a detailed memo:

> The Italian [American] Underworld is a well organized and fully controlled syndicate with sectional bosses in absolute control of their immediate districts. These bosses control every racket within their jurisdiction such as: lottery, mutual numbers, horse betting, cigarette machines, pin ball machines, exacting tribute from business people, and sundry other items. These bosses are also directly and indirectly concerned with the narcotic traffic, in as much as they will finance large narcotic deals, exact tribute or receive a "cut" on a large narcotics transaction, settle disputes between narcotics dealers, designate a narcotic peddler to a certain territory within their district, and at times establish a contact for narcotic buyer.

To maintain its criminal dominance, explained Piazza, the Mafia paid graft to "police or to politicians. . . . [They] operate brazenly and keep a firm hold on members of the underworld. . . . [I]t must be understood that the major narcotic violators are bosses in their own right, operating with the sanction of the underworld bosses." The agent noted that "due to the European War, there is very little narcotic smuggling going on, and as a result the narcotic dealers are having difficulty in getting enough narcotics to carry on their business."

In the mid and late thirties enterprising American gangsters knew that the easiest place to buy heroin was wide-open Shanghai, but getting there had become increasingly hazardous. And once World War II was over, the Chinese communists, determined to end mass addiction, went after the drug trade ruthlessly. The vast and ethereal poppy fields were destroyed and the heroin factories shuttered. So if American organized crime was reactivating the old trafficking networks and developing new ones, the obvious question was, "Where are they getting their heroin?", heroin that was increasingly plentiful in the black slums of New York, Chicago, Detroit, Philadelphia, and Washington, D.C.?

The first real clue came from an American seaman hurt in a hit-and-run accident in New York on July 18, 1948. When hospitalized, it became apparent that he was an opiate addict. FBN agents searched his hotel room and found more than a pound of high-quality heroin. Where had it come from? Trieste, confessed the sailor. This port north of Italy was then an occupation zone under U.S. and British administration. The two top law enforcement officials there happened to be former FBN agents. But the lead was a dead end.

Not long after, Anslinger dispatched Garland Williams to Europe in 1949 on something of a scouting expedition to see what he could learn of the postwar situation. Colonel Williams was not only the man brought in to lead the New York office after the 1936 corruption scandal, he was now also the much admired veteran of a wide variety of wartime assignments, ranging from counterintelligence and training OSS officers to working with the Joint Chiefs of Staff. What an exasperated Williams encountered in Italy was not encouraging. He informed Anslinger that in that post-Fascist nation "narcotic law enforcement is actually non-existent."

As Williams proceeded from one ornate law enforcement ministry to another, each one disclaimed any responsibility. All referred him to the "Deputy Chief of Questura in charge of International Police matters," also Italy's representative on INTERPOL. Wrote Williams, "All police officials are constantly saying, 'Dosi handles all drug matters. You will have to take that up with him.' The man has an office that is a miniature museum and he literally talks you to death. . . . He is a man of a few million words and you cannot stop him from talking. . . . When you ask him any specific question, he jumps at conclusions and goes off on the wildest tangents and you actually have to outholler him to get him to stop." After further descriptions of the bizarre Dosi, a real-life character to rival any official in a Marx Brothers movie, Williams stated unequivocally, "It is my opinion that Dosi is a mental case." Garland Williams came back to New York not much reassured.

When a year later a bigger trafficker was picked up in California, again, the word was Trieste. This time Agent Charles Siragusa was heading overseas on temporary assignment to stir up leads on trafficking. (It seems that the network of agents installed by Morgenthau aide Commander Thompson in the late thirties had been disrupted by the war and not yet reinstated for lack of money.) At age thirty-seven, Siragusa was embarking on an extraordinary career as an international drug agent. He was the son of Sicilian parents who had immigrated to the teeming tenements of the Lower East Side at the turn of the century. In 1914, when Charlie was just a year old, the family of nine fled the crime and chaos of those immigrant slums for the then bucolic Bronx. Siragusa had few illusions about ruthless gangsters such as Luciano and Genovese. His own uncle had been murdered by Mafia thugs when he refused to hand over part of his pay in a shakedown. An excellent student, Siragusa got his B.A. from New York University, joining the U.S. Immigration Service in 1935. After four years he was bored and decided to try the Bureau of Narcotics. Here he truly found his métier—investigator and undercover agent extraordinaire. He possessed an amazing intuitive sense about criminals and their ways, spoke fluent Sicilian, and had a chameleonlike quality that allowed him to penetrate virtually any world.

On his first overseas narcotics mission in 1950, Siragusa easily entered the trafficking scenes in Istanbul, Beirut, and Athens before meeting up with another agent who was undercover already in Trieste, masquerading as a California mobster. Now Siragusa, with his thick Bronx accent, high-strung New York manner, and habit of chain-smoking, introduced himself on the waterfront as one of the 107th Street mob from Manhattan, desperate to buy heroin. His act was convincing, and within days he and the other agent were escorted to an apartment, there to hand over five thousand dollars in American dollars (scraped together with some difficulty) to a distinguished older man, a pharmacist, and receive back about twelve pounds of heroin. They left the apartment, let the door close, and then rang the buzzer. When the door opened, they flashed their badges, and arrested the astonished pharmacist.

A search of the apartment turned up labels showing that the heroin had come from Schiaparelli of Turin, one of Italy's top pharmaceutical houses. As for the arrested man, this highly respectable citizen was one of the owners of a bona fide Trieste pharmaceutical wholesaling house, and he and the other corporate officers admitted to having diverted almost five hundred pounds of heroin to the underworld in the previous two years. Numerous arrests of confederates ensued, and the FBN asked the Italian government to investigate Schiaparelli. Here, finally, was the first serious evidence about the origins of the growing stream of heroin.

In February 1951 Siragusa arrived back at the U.S. embassy in Rome, a white marble pallazzo located on the fashionable Via Veneto. Siragusa wanted to follow up the Schiaparelli business. The Italians admitted that their annual medical need for legal heroin, for cough medicines and such, was about fifteen pounds a year. Yet they acknowledged that total licensed heroin production was 350 pounds a year. After the Trieste episode, Siragusa naturally wondered where all that legal Italian heroin was going. At this time, five Italian pharmaceutical firms were licensed to produce legal narcotics. But one, the Società Anonima Stabilimenti Chemici Riuniti Schiaparelli in Turin, actually manufactured about 90 percent of the 350 pounds of legal heroin allowed annually. These narcotics were then sold to drug wholesalers, who dispatched them to hospitals, pharmacists, and for export.

What Siragusa soon found was that wholesalers who bought heroin had no obligation to keep records of who *their* customers were. He also found out that one well-respected Milanese wholesaler, Egidio Calascibetta, had been visited numerous times by the ever sociable Luciano, on one occasion accompanied by New York gangster Joseph Biondo. Italian police conceded the situation was sufficiently suspicious to warrant investigation and raided Calascibetta's SACE wholesaling firm in Milan. The books showed that Calascibetta had diverted almost eight hundred pounds of legal Italian heroin to the illegal trade during the previous four years. As a jubilant Agent Siragusa wired Anslinger in May 1951, "This is concrete evidence Luciano connected with Calascibetta in heroin racket." But this was not—as Siragusa obviously hoped—sufficient cause to charge him, at least not under Italian laws.

While Siragusa was a highly productive workaholic ever in pursuit of traffickers, he also quickly developed a taste for la dolce vita. One British writer asked in the mid 1950s, "Who is this elegantly-dressed man . . . seen dancing the mambo with Italian starlet Elsa Martinelli in a Rome night club? Who is this gentleman in impeccable evening dress lighting a cigarette in a restaurant for Italian film star Silvana Pampanini? Who is this man in the neat bow tie hurrying after the great Italian actress Anna Magnani? Why, they are all one and the same man, Charles Siragusa."

However much Siragusa enjoyed such glamorous flirtations and the attendant publicity in local papers, his real love was narcotic investigation. And in the Calascibetta case, he soon discovered that the general manager of the firm's laboratories, the shady Professor Carlo Migliardi, clandestinely had been producing (at night) more than two hundred pounds of pure heroin annually since 1948. Federal agents concluded that Schiaparelli, Italy's foremost producer of legal heroin (and, as it turned out, illegal heroin), had been a significant source of America's rising tide of postwar narcotics. And this was just what had been uncovered. Siragusa strongly suspected that some of the other Italian pharmaceutical firms also were churning out large lots of heroin and offering them to the underworld.

At one point Siragusa reported to Anslinger that "the Alfa concern located at Via Pia No. 1, Savona, Italy had during the year 1950 purchased 134 kilos of heroin from the five heroin manufacturers. Although these purchases were ridiculously excessive, representing almost the entire estimated yearly consumption for all of Italy for 1950, no control was ever made. . . . This concern is unquestionably engaged in selling practically all of their supply of heroin to illicit channels." Once in underworld hands, the heroin headed to U.S. shores in a myriad ways—via traveling gang members, Italian or Corsican, itinerant sailors, crew members on commercial airlines, and secreted in legitimate cargos.

When pressed on specifics, the Italian authorities cooperated on this or that. After all, the Americans had just won World War II and Italy was a vanquished nation. Moreover, the U.S. government was helping to rebuild the country and stave off the communists through the beneficence of the Marshall Plan and sub rosa funneling of CIA funds to the Christian Democrats. Nonetheless, the justly famous Italian bureaucracy seemed capable of endless stalling. The London *Times* reported on September 19, 1951, that "Italy appears to be the world's largest producer of narcotic drugs. Italian chemical plants can easily obtain licenses for the production of heroin, allegedly destined for medical use. Very large amounts of this drug are diverted to illegal channels." Yet Italy made only the most token gestures to reduce or eliminate legal heroin production. One suspects that it was not unpleasant to spite one's conqueror.

While the Schiaparelli scandal remains interesting for what it reveals about early postwar trafficking patterns, its real importance is how clearly it illustrates the enormous shift in postwar U.S. government drug policy. Historically, the prestigious and powerful U.S. Department of State had dominated American antidrug policy, especially overseas. After all, it was the State Department that had dispatched Hamilton Wright in 1909 to wrest a federal drug law from Congress. And the patrician, WASPy State Department long had prided itself on being the leader in the international reform campaign against opiates and cocaine, an overseas expression of noblesse oblige. All through the thirties, American diplomats such as the vigorous Stuart J. Fuller, aided by a four-person staff, had led a relentless campaign against international drug traffickers and complacent or corrupt foreign governments. But as the Schiaparelli scandal makes clear, after World War II the State Department lost interest in anything not directly relevant to the Cold War. Its own historians would later conclude: "In view of the near-constant atmosphere of crisis caused by the Cold War, narcotics control received a low priority in American foreign policy." This "low priority" dovetailed nicely with Commissioner Harry J. Anslinger's own fierce ambition to single-handedly control American antidrug activities and personally dominate the field.

For more than a decade, Commissioner Anslinger and the Federal Bureau of Narcotics had been supervised closely by Treasury Secretary Henry Morgenthau, who obviously thought Anslinger was adequate as commissioner as long as someone kept a skeptical eye on the overall effectiveness of the agency. Furthermore, Secretary Morgenthau must have been reassured by the presence at State of Stuart J. Fuller, who ran a tight ship and kept the heat on internationally. Fuller was much admired as the U.S. representative to the League of Nation's Opium Advisory Committee and he and Anslinger worked well together.

However, Stuart J. Fuller died in February 1941 from cancer, just as America entered the war, while Secretary Morgenthau resigned from Treasury not long after Harry Truman assumed the presidency in 1945. With these two forceful and knowledgeable men gone and illegal drugs an almost vanquished problem as the war ended, Commissioner Anslinger had little trouble establishing himself as *the* preeminent government power on drugs. During the war, Anslinger had arranged for the League of Nation's Opium Advisory Committee to be headquartered in the United States and also to have himself appointed American representative to replace Fuller. State's waning interest, obvious in its acquiescence in this appointment, was made explicit in its 1944 reorganization, when State formally consigned drug policy to the backwaters of its division of International Labor, Social, and Economic Affairs.

When the old Opium Advisory Committee was reconstituted in 1946 as the U.N. Commission on Narcotics Drugs, Anslinger continued as the U.S. representative. In agreeing to that, the U.S. State Department effectively ceded its historical role as a dominant force in the shaping and promulgating of American drug policy. At State, "a modest narcotics program . . . served largely to backstop the operations of Commissioner Anslinger. . . . [The State Department officer] did not coordinate U.S., or even State Department, international narcotics policy."

All this must have been highly satisfactory to Anslinger. He was, after all, an ambitious man who had been humiliated at times by Morgenthau. He was also a political appointee who needed to show he was indispensable so he could continue in what he once proudly called his "fabulous, fantastic career." In a typed rough draft for a self-composed author's note, Anslinger's increasingly swelling head was embarrassingly obvious. He immodestly wrote: "His fame spread throughout the world. His great contributions to rid the world of the worst plague of mankind have won him many awards. He was the first Federal Commissioner of Narcotics. . . . Many foreign officials publicly called him 'the world's greatest living expert on the international narcotic traffic.' " Anslinger made sure that this particular plaudit, first bestowed by Britain's Sir Leonard Lyall in the thirties, became a virtual appendage to any public mention of him as commissioner. Any article about him, his entry in various *Who's Who*, any introduction, always always included that phrase, "the world's greatest living expert on the international narcotic traffic."

Presumably, if no other official of stature knew as much as Anslinger did about events at the United Nations and overseas (much less what went on in the Bureau of Narcotics), the commissioner could preempt even the idea of being replaced. Illegal drugs were, after all, a complex issue with a long and convoluted history, and after sixteen years in office the commissioner could legitimately claim enormous expertise, especially on the diplomatic front. And indeed, as the hostilities with Governor Dewey confirm, Anslinger was sufficiently entrenched sufficiently by 1952 to ward off Dewey's efforts to purge him. He had succeeded in becoming *the* dominant official on American drug policy. But Anslinger's continuing professional triumph would eventually exact a considerable public cost. On the international scene, nothing would compensate for the loss of the State Department's prestige and power, something perfectly illustrated by the Schiaparelli scandal.

Before World War II, one can imagine easily the State Department's Stuart J. Fuller scornfully confronting the Italians on the issue of heroin manufacture with the full heft of official American outrage, combining in one person the might of both the State Department and the Opium Advisory Committee. In notable contrast, neither Commissioner Anslinger nor his agent in Italy, Charles Siragusa, even informed the U.S. embassy in Rome or the State Department in Washington that the Italians (recipients of millions in Marshall Plan aid) were producing large amounts of heroin that was fueling drug epidemics in America's growing northern ghettoes. And, furthermore, that the Italians evinced little interest in curbing this outrageous conduct by their pharmaceutical houses and wholesalers.

Then, in June 1955 a magazine called *Bluebook* burst on the scene with an exposé titled, How ITALY'S GOVERNMENT LETS HEROIN FLOOD U.S. The magazine's editors sent copies to high administration officials, every member of Congress, and the U.S. ambassador to Rome. With great verve, author Henry Jordan related the whole Schiaparelli scandal, concluding with the notably tepid response of the Italian government. He detailed how Schiaparelli had been closed down briefly but was now open again, its license to make heroin reinstated. Jordan told readers that the enterprising Professor Migliardi, who had been churning out illicit heroin at night in the Schiaparelli factory, was out on bail and back at work. "More than two years have passed and there is no sign that his case will ever go to trial." As for Calascibetta, the Milanese wholesaler friendly with Luciano and caught red-handed, his case had been thrown out of the courts completely.

And even though the Italian government had signed an international protocol in 1953 that aimed to end legal heroin production throughout the world, author Jordan observed that when "submitted to the Italian Parliament as a matter of routine—it was promptly buried." In short, the embarrassed Italians had made a few gestures and then continued with business as usual. Concluded Henry Jordan, "As far as can be determined, at no time have there been any definite negotiations between U.S. and Italian representatives about heroin. If there have been, they deserve a prize for the vaguest diplomatic palavers in history."

The U.S. ambassador to Rome at this time was the indomitable Clare Boothe Luce, glamorous wife of *Time* publisher Henry Luce and a political powerhouse in her own right. She was, to put it mildly, highly incensed. It was not that she was completely and totally in the dark. Before Ambassador Luce left Washington, a Treasury aide close to Anslinger, Malachi Harney, had told her "of the tremendous diversions from Italian pharmaceutical houses which had contributed so heavily to the illicit market in this country, and of the work of American narcotics agents in Italy which had uncovered this."

But one has to assume that after this courtesy briefing, Luce was not kept apprised further. For a secret State Department cable dated June 8 reported that Luce was horrified to learn in this manner [from the *Bluebook* article] of an apparently serious situation in Italo-American relations. [She] called in the U.S. Narcotics Agent in Rome [Siragusa] who said that in general the contents of the article were true, though he did not explain why he had not previously brought the matter to her attention or that of any of her predecessors. Before leaving Rome on vacation, Ambassador Luce discussed the article with Italian Foreign Minister Martino. Last week she presented a memorandum on this subject to the President and the Secretary of State. . . . The Department [also] has several Congressional inquiries to answer.

U.N. Ambassador Henry Cabot Lodge was equally shocked by the *Bluebook* article. He quickly passed his copy along to U.S. Secretary of State John Foster Dulles with an offer to do something at the United Nations if necessary. Dulles wrote back, "Apparently the situation was as new to Ambassador Luce as it was to the Department. On the face of it, the situation seems deplorable." Dulles went on to propose vaguely that the situation required "careful exploration and thought."

After Dulles complained to Anslinger's new boss at Treasury, the Narcotics commissioner was obliged to appear at the State Department's white marble offices on June 21, where he mollified several undersecretaries by presenting two documents: testimony before the United Nations by the Italian delegate averring better control and his own congressional testimony averring better behavior by the Italians. Those present discussed the fact that the Italian Ministry of Health was completely under the sway of the pharmaceutical industry, which wished to continue producing large amounts of heroin. Anslinger expressed his belief "that there is no evidence to indicate that the Italian government at present condones or protects illicit heroin manufacture or traffic. The difficulty is mainly inefficiency, inertia, and the fact that the actual prosecution of law violations is not the province of the police but the Magistracy who, as the case of the notorious heroin trafficker Calascibetta demonstrated, could be bought off."

Later when Treasury checked back to make sure State was placated, an undersecretary of State complained again about no one informing Ambassador Luce about the heroin trafficking, which came as "quite a bombshell." He further observed, "Years ago there had been close cooperation between the State Department and the Bureau, but such liaison had dwindled away over the years until the State Department is pretty much in the dark about what is going on in this field." Treasury promised it would "have a talk with Mr. Anslinger to see that there is no repetition of this kind of situation."

The Schiaparelli scandal showed how successfully Anslinger had isolated the State Department (which evidenced no real interest in retrieving its lost influence), and how damaging this would be to the greater public interest. It was only because of the *Bluebook* exposé that State felt compelled to press the issue. By the following year, under the persistent diplomacy of Ambassador Luce, the Italians finally ended all legal heroin production. And the enterprising Professor Migliardi suddenly was brought to trial and sentenced to eleven years in jail.

Certainly the new U.N. Commission on Narcotic Drugs had failed to rein in the Italians, in part because it was nowhere as hard-hitting and aggressive as its predecessor. The commission "has not, unfortunately, dealt with [illicit narcotic traffic] as effectively and as ruthlessly as did the Opium Advisory Committee," lamented Bertil A. Renborg, a Swedish lawyer who had long served in the international drug policy field. Instead, he noted, "There has been a discernible tendency to soft-pedal criticism in order to save the national pride of certain governments; there has not been the same frank publicity concerning unsatisfactory conditions."

Nor was there any reason to imagine that Anslinger's own tiny (three hundred some agents) and little-known agency, the Federal Bureau of Narcotics, or even its parent agency, Treasury, could begin to exert the kind of influence in Washington or overseas that the State Department did. Yet Anslinger, in his zeal to control U.S. narcotics policy with an iron fist, specifically instructed his agents abroad to steer clear whenever possible of anything that would let the State Department know what they were doing. A furious Ambassador Luce had wondered why Narcotics Agent Siragusa "had not previously brought the [heroin] matter to her attention or that of any of her predecessors." The reason was simple: He almost certainly had been ordered specifically by Anslinger not to. Andrew Tartaglino, who began serving as a narcotics agent overseas under Siragusa in 1956, recalls, "Anslinger was always very clear on one thing, 'Stay away from the State Department. No diplomatic passports. Don't tell them what you're doing, where you are. Stay away from the striped-pants set.' "

In the early fifties Anslinger was very much in his political prime, a big, physically imposing man whose bull-like neck and total baldness gave him an uncanny resemblance to Mussolini. He favored gangster-style double-breasted suits and a brusque public manner. Subordinates largely remember Commissioner Anslinger with fear-tinged respect as a gruff, ruthless, remote figure utterly in charge of his domain.

Anslinger was "the consummate bureaucrat," recalls one Treasury aide, a shrewd practitioner of the bureaucratic arts. So even as he avoided the State Department, Anslinger carefully cultivated other powers in the capital. Longtime Washington attorney Rufus King, who met Anslinger while the former was Kefauver Committee staff counsel, remembers, "No one was ever more attentive or did more stroking on the Hill than Anslinger."

Even more important, recalls James Bennett, onetime director of the Justice Department's Bureau of Prisons, Anslinger "had the Hearst newspapers behind him a hundred percent, and he had the California legislatures, California congressmen behind him." All of this contributed to a large ego. Anslinger no doubt thought it his due when FBN Philadelphia District Supervisor Joseph Bransky nominated him in 1958 for the Nobel Prize as "the undisputed leader in the world in suppressing the abuse of narcotic drugs."

Nor was Anslinger above collecting useful political dirt. After agents raided a high-class New York whorehouse in the mid fifties where drugs were available, "the case kept getting postponed, so we raided the place again," recalled one former agent. "We found a letter from Senator John Kennedy to the Mayor of New York asking if he could do anything for the two women arrested the first time. Anslinger did what Hoover did. He put it away, and the case didn't go anywhere."

Yet even as Commissioner Anslinger built up power and influence around Washington, he never used it for his own agency. Decade after postwar decade, Anslinger failed to secure adequate manpower to confront the growing heroin flow. When a reporter criticized the bureau for concentrating on small-fry peddlers in 1952, Anslinger lamely said, "We'd like to concentrate on big importers, but it would take men we haven't got." Yet he never even asked for them. In 1953, a Scripps-Howard journalist wondered before Congress why Anslinger was so complacent, reporting, "One high narcotics official told me that he could use 260 men, or his entire force, in the city of New York alone." The journalist said the narcotics force should be quintupled at minimum.

Yet the "consummate bureaucrat" preferred not to rock boats. "I believe he kept the size of the agency very small and didn't ask Congress for extra money so he could retain this secure pulpit. He really enjoyed the prestige of his job," says John Ingersoll, a well-regarded police executive who ran the U.S. Bureau of Narcotics and Dangerous Drugs (a successor agency to the FBN) from 1968 to 1973. "The thing I do know is that the old Federal Bureau of Narcotics did not grow with the problem or the economy." Moreover, the agency lacked any overall enforcement strategy besides generating a certain level of arrests.

Anslinger's domination of the field let him frame the drug issue as a glamorous struggle between his swashbuckling agents and wily, depraved traffickers and addicts. After the war the Bureau fed a steady diet of tarted-up tales to the popular pulp magazines. Typical was a July 1949 story in *Argosy* entitled "Nemesis of the Dope Gangs" that described "a beach-side villa on the southern California coast, [where] three figures of the movie industry peer through the smoke of opium pipes." All was melo-drama and, of course, the ever present Commissioner Anslinger, identi-fied as the "directing genius behind every dope raid."

Anslinger's self-image and that of his agency were deeply dependent on this glamorous tough-guy mentality, painfully evident in his own postwar writings. Typical of the tone of his work is the following: the "flaxen-haired eighteen-year-old girl sprawled nude and unconscious on a Harlem tenement floor after selling herself to a collection of cus-tomers through the afternoon."

If the facts did not fit Anslinger's racial and class notions, he just invented them. In his papers, a chapter-length manuscript entitled *Underworld Slaves* purports to tell about a 1931 case out of Cleveland, Ohio. The actual FBN report describes a middle-aged Chinese man selling small amounts of heroin to local young (white) women of no great repute. Nowhere is there mention of parties or sex. Yet in Anslinger's version "an unknown Chinese was luring respectable white girls to his rooms and administering drugs that launched them on unspeakable orgies . . . [Soon] she slipped off her dress and was danc-ing in her smart little silken shorts and brassiere. She was very beauti-ful." Of course, what it all led to was: "Everywhere now the girls were in the arms of Chinese men."

Not surprisingly, a commissioner so enamoured of seeing himself and his agency in such wrought-up terms had little interest in devel-oping genuine national expertise about addiction. It was not until the FBN's 1956 annual report that the agency even offered in writing an estimate of the number of addicts, which it then put at thirty-six thou-sand. Yet just the previous year, Anslinger had testified before a con-gressional subcommittee, saying "The total number of addicts in the United States today is estimated at between 50,000 and 60,000, or an incidence of 1 in 3,000 in the population." As public concern mounted in the fifties, Anslinger became actively hostile to any serious study of the drug problem. He discouraged independent scientific and medical research into such basic questions as the nature of addiction and the problems of treatment. Dr. Vincent Dole of Rockefeller University, who defied the bureau and developed methadone maintenance treat-ment, would observe years later, "The Federal Bureau of Narcotics had an iron clamp on the field and had essentially driven out physicians for thirty years or more. . . . [W]hat a shame it was that there was none of the scientific thought in the field of addiction that I had encountered in my other researches. It didn't have recognition as a scientific problem. Certainly there wasn't any research talent in it. Such talent as there was was limited to people who were in the main part pharmacologists and studied animals."

With few other experts out there to challenge him, Anslinger felt free to say whatever he pleased. Thus, he proclaimed in speeches, "The prolonged use of marijuana—hashish, Indian hemp—usually leads to insanity, as well as to crime." And though his own agency's reports showed at least a postwar doubling of addicts, Anslinger would write in 1961 in the obscure *Military Police Journal*: "Contrary to erroneous reports, addiction in the United States since the war has declined every year and continues to decline."

Anslinger also exhibited no concern with epidemiology or more accurate statistics. One suspects this was partly because of what such figures would have shown. During the late fifties, as Anslinger reassured Congress that the northern heroin epidemic was subsiding, addiction rates in central Harlem doubled from 22.1 per 10,000 in 1955 to 40.1 in 1961. Nor did Anslinger back serious inquiry into treatment. In a 1947 article in *True Detective* called "Freeing the Drug Slaves," Anslinger declared the only possible treatment was compulsory hospitalization, yet he well knew the dismal relapse rates from Lexington.

Claude Brown described them graphically in *Manchild in the Promised Land*: "Heroin had been the thing in Harlem for about five years and I don't think anybody knew anyone who had kicked it. They knew a lot of guys who were going away, getting cures, and coming back, but never kicking it. Cats were even going into the army or jail, coming back, and getting strung out again." Yet Anslinger insisted that hospitalization was *the* treatment solution. In 1953, he advocated warehousing addicts permanently who had taken three "cures" and relapsed. He was adamantly against any kind of drug education, believing it would encourage experimentation.

Anslinger was just as simplistic in his public discussions of trafficking. For years, Anslinger insisted that Lucky Luciano was *the* mastermind behind international trafficking. By blaming one demonlike figure, Anslinger sounded as if his agency had a handle on the situation. This denied the fluidity of the traffic and justified his agency's failure to stem the rising tide of heroin in American cities. Certainly the bureau's own secret Black List featured literally hundreds of traffickers, making clear that no one person could possibly control or direct the illegal drug trade into America. Yet the Black List and the agency's annual reports, while meant to show the FBN's diligence and inside knowledge in gathering all these names and histories of traffickers, only underscored the agency's failure to analyze its own files intelligently and put together a coherent larger picture of who the major trafficking gangs were and how they operated.

It's hard to know if Commissioner Anslinger really did believe what he said about Luciano. Somewhere along the line, the bureau's drawers full of files on Luciano largely have disappeared. But Lucky provided the commissioner and other American officials with an extremely famous villain whose very physical remoteness could excuse their inability to bring him to justice.

Certainly Anslinger personally was quite obsessed with Luciano. Yet Siragusa and Anslinger never got any closer than the Calascibetta case. Circumstantial evidence—typically Luciano's friendliness with other Italian criminals and deported American mobsters who did get caught trafficking—implicated Luciano, but provided nothing legally solid. The Italian police, egged on by the Americans, pestered Luciano and larded on various irksome restrictions—he had to reside in Naples, he had a 10:00 P.M. curfew, etc. But such meager official files on Luciano as have survived tend to consist of reports from Italy along the lines of this one from the Naples police: "Lucania maintains a brilliant standard of living, spending great amounts of money and often taking trips to this city (Naples) with a speed boat that he hires for his own private use. . . . [H]e is not, at least apparently, engaged in any suspicious activity."

Anslinger's fascination and frustration with Luciano was such that the commissioner even wrote a never published and truly dreadful manuscript chapter based loosely on Luciano's life entitled *Il Capo*. In this he writes:

> As a young man, we caught Il Capo cold several times in heroin transactions. In exchange for a light sentence on one count and dismissal on another charge, he became our special employee and caused the arrest and conviction of so many competitors and associates that he took over as head of the gang. We unwittingly helped him to this end. He branched out into other rackets and always went to the top. He was sent up for white slavery for a long, long time. He was paroled for purpose of deportation.

As the heroin flowed in after the war and addiction rose relentlessly, Anslinger, true to form, insisted that all that was needed was tougher trafficking penalties. The commissioner long had been angered and annoyed by what he saw as lenient or corrupt judges, but he had never been able to do anything about it. Now, suddenly, as youthful addiction was back in a way not seen since the early tumultuous decades of the century, Anslinger seized the moment to push for tougher laws.

A number of FBN agents on loan to Senator Estes Kefauver's Special Committee to Investigate Organized Crime in Interstate Commerce helped organize the hearings, lining up dozens of anonymous addicts to testify. One eighteen-year-old boy who had moved up from South Carolina ("They don't have no drugs down there at all.") to Baltimore was disturbingly laconic about his addiction: "I smoked reefers for a while, just for the kick of it, and then I started using heroin to get a kick out of it."

Another young Baltimorean, a black woman, described how her friends had laughed at her because she was a "square." Then they took her to a party where every kind of drug was available for the buying. She related admiringly of the other guests, "They will go to the limit to have a good time. They will steal up a breeze to satisfy their habit. . . . [The party] was terrific; it was jumping. . . . [She describes smoking her first marijuana cigarette and explains:] Reefers make you like and just love music." The next week she tried heroin and was soon hooked. This was most unnerving, graphically showing how easily undirected young people succumbed without a thought to the allure of drugs.

Even as such testimony was receiving nationwide press coverage, Anslinger stood before an American Legion conference on narcotics in June 1951, and vowed that he "could put an end to narcotics peddling if adequately equipped with 'tools' in the form of laws providing compulsory prison terms." Numerous lawmakers rushed to comply, but Congressman Hale Boggs of Louisiana authored the final measure whose chief feature was mandatory minimum sentences. First offenders caught with marijuana, cocaine, or opiates would get two to five years, second offenders five to ten, and third offenders, ten to twenty.

But the mandatory sentencing of the Boggs Act still failed to stem the rising tide of heroin flowing into northern ghettos. Statistics from the U.S. Narcotics Farm in Lexington, Kentucky, confirmed the drug disaster sweeping these urban slums. Half empty during the war, most of Lexington's beds had then been assigned to mental patients and shell-shocked soldiers. By the mid fifties Lexington was logging in four thousand addicts a year, triple and quadruple the rates of the thirties. Furthermore, new treatment facilities in some of the hardest-hit states—New York and California—meant that the situation was even worse than the Lexington admissions indicated. Almost half of these postwar addicts were black. New York's chief magistrate, John M. Murtagh, blasted the federal government for "failing miserably" to deal with the fast-spreading heroin epidemic, the worst since the days of "happy dust" back in the 'teens and twenties. In 1954, President Dwight D. Eisenhower became the second of numerous postwar presidents to declare a halfhearted war on drugs. The Senate Judiciary Committee decided to dispatch Senator Price Daniel of Texas to find out just what was happening via hearings on the drug problem in Washington, Philadelphia, New York, Texas, California, Chicago, Detroit, and Cleveland. His chief investigator was a fellow Texan named Wayland L. Speer.

Senator Daniel, who used the hearings (especially those in Texas) to drum up publicity for a coming run for governor, returned convinced that spreading addiction and crime required yet more draconian laws and bigger appropriations to law enforcement. Commissioner Anslinger fervently agreed, and the ensuing Narcotics Control Act of 1956 toughened the Boggs Act, significantly stiffening the minimum mandatory sentences. Most notably it stipulated two to ten years for a first-time drug possession (still meaning opiates, cocaine, or marijuana), five to twenty for a second offense with no possibility for parole, and ten to forty years for a third, again with no possibility for parole.

As for traffickers, the penalties for the first offense were five to twenty years, no parole, and thereafter ten to forty years, no parole. A Texas stripper, for instance, caught with a marijuana joint was sentenced to fifteen years in jail. Pushers caught selling heroin to minors were even liable for the death penalty. Naturally, Commissioner Anslinger felt vindicated and delighted by the tough new sentences.

But the reality was that things got worse, not better. The flow of heroin grew steadily, and so did the ranks of the addicts. In 1956, the bureau said in its annual report that there were 35,835 addicts. Four years later, that figure was 44,906. The reasons for this worsening situation were in certain ways straightforward and visible: The FBN did not begin to have enough agents to do their job against the traffickers, while the paucity of medical and scientific knowledge meant there was no meaningful treatment for addicts. These were the consequences of Anslinger's stranglehold on the field of narcotics control. And as long as most of the new addicts were urban minorities, there was little public outcry for concerted action. As one retired narcotics agent and a former high-level Treasury official both succinctly expressed it in the exact same phrase, "Nobody gave a shit." But there were other less straightforward and visible reasons for the growing flood of heroin, reasons that would never be publicly discussed before congressional committees at the time nor in the press.

"Marseille is Unquestionably the Most Important Narcotics Smuggler's Haven in . . . All of Europe."

—Letter dated March 3, 1953,
FBN Agent Charles Siragusa to
Commissioner Anslinger

In the years before World War II,
American international narcotics policy had been extremely straightforward. The United States was righteously against anything that promoted or sustained the nonmedical use of addicting drugs. But the
Cold War created not only new national security priorities, but a new

shadow world that accepted a far more ambivalent attitude toward drugs and drug trafficking. The clear-cut moral outrage that had fueled a Stuart J. Fuller and his relentless crusade against traffickers—governmental and underworld—now yielded quietly to the perceived needs of realpolitick. And so even as the United States maintained a public stance of implacable opposition to international drug trafficking, the new Cold War atmosphere made battling communism the overriding concern. And Commissioner Harry J. Anslinger, the consummate bureaucrat, adjusted swiftly to that new reality.

An ardent patriot who adored cloak-and-dagger stuff, Anslinger happily had put himself and his agency at the service of the fledgling intelligence community organized during World War II. Businessman and World War I hero General William J. Donovan had long known the commissioner and he quickly recruited Anslinger to the cause of establishing the Office of Strategic Services (OSS) in 1940. It's not known what Anslinger himself did, but his agency lent numerous narcotics agents (including Charlie Siragusa) to teach the clandestine arts of gathering information and how to engage in so-called counterintelligence. Garland Williams, head of FBN's New York office, became director of OSS special training. George Hunter White, one of the FBN's crack agents, became "director of all OSS counterespionage training," at what he called the "Oshawa School of mayhem and murder."

After the war, Anslinger maintained close and cordial relations with OSS's successor agency, the Central Intelligence Agency (CIA). White, "a heavily built man with the shoulders of an ox," for instance, held a cover job as the roving district supervisor for the FBN's New York office while engaging in CIA mind-control research (more on that later), and the FBN and CIA jointly operated safe houses in Greenwich Village in New York and San Francisco. The FBN (like many other agencies) also provided overseas cover jobs for CIA agents. Nor was it unusual for bona fide narcotics agents abroad to feed information back to the CIA or to turn to the much richer Agency for thirty thousand or forty thousand dollars in "flash" money needed to impress traffickers. No doubt everything about the CIA appealed to Anslinger's longtime love of the covert. But far more important, he and his agency were now aligned with *the* great shadow power of the postwar era, even though the CIA's own goals almost certainly subverted those of the Federal Bureau of Narcotics.

For as historian Alfred W. McCoy writes in his monumental *The Politics of Heroin*, the OSS and CIA "created a situation that made it possible for the Sicilian-American Mafia and the Corsican underworld to revive the international narcotics traffic." While the postwar State

Department paid little attention to international drug trafficking, the OSS and then the CIA actively aided and abetted groups overseas who were zealously anticommunist, even if they also were engaged in the criminal activity of international drug trafficking. The tragic truth is that the United States government covertly played a crucial role in strengthening the very organizations that fed the postwar drug plague, a plague that began on the streets of Harlem and other northern ghettoes, and spread eventually throughout the country.

The first criminal group the United States allied itself with and reinstated into power was the Sicilian Mafia. When World War II began, the "venerable society" was but a wraith of its former fearsome self. For twenty years Mussolini's government had pursued the Mafia relentlessly, determined to eradicate its power. McCoy explains why: "During a state visit to a small town in western Sicily in 1924, the Italian dictator offended a local Mafia boss by treating him with the same condescension he usually reserved for minor municipal officials. The mafioso made the foolish mistake of retaliating by emptying the piazza of everyone but twenty beggars during Mussolini's speech to the 'assembled populace.' Upon his return to Rome, the outraged Mussolini appeared before the Fascist parliament and declared total war on the Mafia." A "reign of terror" followed that reduced "the venerable society to its weakest state in a hundred years."

So these very same beleaguered Mafiosi were viewed as an invaluable resource by the American military, reliable natives who would merrily help depose Mussolini's Fascists. As the Allies geared up to invade Sicily, agents from the U.S. Office of Naval Intelligence actively cultivated New York Mafiosi through Luciano. And once the agents landed in Sicily as the advance guard, they sought out Mafia contacts, presumably using information provided by Luciano and his ilk. The surviving Sicilian Mafia were more than eager to assist in overthrowing their persecutors. When Sicily was captured, the Mafia were well rewarded with numerous political appointments. Colonel Charles Poletti, former Democratic lieutenant governor of New York, personally appointed numerous Mafiosi as mayors. Lord Rennell, commander of the British occupation forces, became concerned that the Allies had "appointed a number of Mafia 'bosses' or allowed such 'bosses' to propose suitable malleable substitutes."

This blatant favoritism toward the Italian underworld so alarmed Allied headquarters, "a review committee was sent out from Washington and there was a thorough shake-up. Scores of intelligence agents working for Secret Intelligence were sent to other parts of the Mediterranean. An official report made at the time stated, 'The SI Italy section was the Principal unit investigated. Its personnel, predominantly Sicilian American, had tended to form a clique reluctant to concede authority to others.' " But by then, the damage was done. The Sicilian Mafiosi once again occupied positions of power.

However, it is important to keep in mind that the traditional Sicilian Mafia had *not* been drug traffickers. It was the separate U.S. policy of deporting its Italian-born American gangsters that introduced international drug trafficking as a new and lucrative criminal activity. As Sicilian writer and political activist Michele Pantaleone explains:

> Certain "undesirables" such as Lucky Luciano, Frank Coppola, Nicola Gentile, Joseph De Luca, Antonio Schillaci and Giovanni Caputo had been repatriated to Sicily together with other well-known American gangsters. These men, who had emigrated to America when they were very young, had been denaturalized. . . . Once back in Italy they resumed their smuggling activities. They organized the New Mafia to work with them and so made Sicily a bridge for the traffic in drugs from the Near East via Sicily to France and America. The American gangsters who came to Italy with the Allied troops, ostensibly as liberators, were friends of the Old Mafia, but the "undesirables" allied themselves with the New Mafia and taught it the methods used by American criminals.

While the deportation policy saved the United States the cost of imprisoning these criminals, it also provided a regular supply of American Mafiosi to strengthen the local criminal ranks and teach new underworld specialties to their Italian cousins, avid and eager learners. A *Rome Daily American* article in 1951 said, "An estimated 50 men deported from the U.S. to Italy on narcotics charges since the war are believed to have formed the nucleus of a far-flung dope smuggling network."

And so, the United States government had unwittingly helped set the stage for a new and powerful postwar trafficking alliance. First by cultivating the Mafiosi as allies for the assault on Sicily, secondly by installing them in power, and thirdly by eventually deporting about four hundred American gangsters, who introduced Sicilian criminals to narcotics trafficking. And as the political scandals of the 1990s in Italy have revealed, the Christian Democrats who dominated postwar Italian politics were longtime secret allies of the Mafiosi, ensuring that they and the heroin trade flourished.

In the aftermath of the Calascibetta scandal, the new Italian heroin traffickers had to develop some fresh sources of product. Legal Italian heroin would continue to be diverted, but not in hundred-pound lots. In July 1952 the American consul general in Palermo, Sicily, reported that those known as traffickers apparently had gone "so far as to make plans for the actual manufacture of refined drugs from raw opium here in Sicily rather than, as heretofore, in northern Italy and Trieste, in order that the opium could be smuggled directly to this island by water route and leave the same way. For this purpose, sites in the country had been selected, and a qualified chemist was to supervise the work in Sicily." However, he noted, a few arrests had made "the narcotics gang centered in Palermo particularly watchful." And the plan had apparently been put aside.

The consul general concluded, "Although a great deal has been done here to control drug traffic, arrests and jail sentences of a handful of criminals could hardly affect the overall operations of a gang with perhaps 150 important members sheltered and assisted at every turn in Sicily by the vast network of the Mafia." A network the United States had helped bring back to monstrous life through its own wartime and judicial policies.

Italian-American gangsters had to rethink their trafficking strategy. The biggest issue was where to obtain raw opium or morphine base to manufacture heroin. Very few countries grew opium poppies. And, by the next year, the United Nation's Opium Protocol of 1953 would limit production for export to seven countries: Yugoslavia, Greece, Bulgaria, the USSR, Turkey, Iran, and India. Greece had stopped growing poppies, while the USSR kept tight controls, as did Yugoslavia and Bulgaria. Iran stopped production in 1955, and India used her production domestically. That left Turkey, which had vast poppy acreage and great resentment of outsiders suggesting restraint. Lebanese businessmen in Beirut were happy to act as go-betweens. The problem for the Mafiosi supplying the American market was processing the morphine base into heroin, especially once they had abandoned early plans to locate laboratories in Sicily.

Instead, the American gangsters in Italy (and their new Sicilian confreres) broadened their long-standing collaboration with the Corsican underworld in Marseille, criminals already experienced in narcotics trafficking and smuggling. The Corsicans, like the Sicilians, were clannish islanders. Both groups spoke an Italian dialect. The Corsicans were also renowned sailors and smugglers, happy to match wits with authorities. And many American gangsters knew the Corsicans from their prewar drug trafficking days. When Commander E. B. Thompson (Treasury Secretary Henry Morgenthau's personal emissary) had scoped out Marseille,

France's second biggest city, back in 1937, he had reported, "This is a hot port. I find that narcotics have moved here in a big way in the past. At one time, the French knocked off over two tons of opium (Turkish) here at one crack. Also that they have made other seizures of 50 kilos, 100 kilos, etc."

Set on a series of low hills encircling the picturesque Vieux Port, the old city of Marseille long had exuded a certain shabby and sinister Mediterranean charm. A relentless southern sun beat down on the urban tumble of washed-out pastel buildings with sloping-tile roofs. Perched above the tough old port was the monumental wedding-cake cathedral Nôtre-Dame de la Garde, its tower topped since 1931 by a gleaming golden statue of the Virgin and child visible for miles. Across the narrow harbor on a lower hill sat the large and elegant Byzantine-style church, Le Major. A block from this spiritual landmark loomed the city's central police station, itself a mere stone's throw from the notorious Le Panier district, a Corsican stronghold. Marseille's polyglot citizenry reflected the many nations and colonies connected to the city's port and shipping lines—everywhere from far Indochina to nearby Algeria. Consequently, this bustling, run-down French city had long had a highly foreign flavor. And a distinctly international cast of criminals.

Thanks to the port and the frequent arrival of ships from opium-producing countries, it had always been easy enough to smuggle in morphine base to Marseille from the Far East or the Near East. And while it was predictable that a major port's underworld would be skilled in such time-honored criminal activities as smuggling, Marseille criminals also showed an enterprising side by organizing the actual manufacture of heroin. The leading narcotics traffickers of the late thirties, Francois Spirito (a Naples transplant) and Paul Bonaventure Carbone, were known to have opened a heroin conversion laboratory near Marseille in Bandol.

During the war years, however, Spirito and Carbone (unlike most of the criminal milieu) were active collaborators with the Nazis, going so far as to provide lists of resistance fighters. Carbone died in 1943 in a train wreck attributed to the Maquis, the French resistance. Not long after the liberation of France, Spirito felt compelled to disappear. He headed to New York City, where he renamed himself Charles-Henri Faccia. One late fifties version of Spirito's fate has "the all-powerful boss of Marseille . . . reduced to stealing his married sister's jewels (she had been married to an American since 1905) and selling them in hockshops. With the proceeds, he bought a tiny supply of heroin, milked it down with lactose, and peddled it from bar to bar, rather naively as if he were selling peanuts. He was picked up by agents of the Treasury

Department Narcotics Bureau within a few days, and sent down to Atlanta Peniteniary in Georgia for two years." However, agency documents from the time and a much later internal Drug Enforcement Agency (DEA) review of French Corsican trafficking describe Spirito in his New York years as a significant player importing kilo lots of heroin and working closely with fellow fugitive Joseph Orsini and such major American gangsters as Salvatore Shillitani before they were all arrested in 1951. Spirito was released and deported to France in 1954, where he was wanted for crimes connected to collaborating. He was sent to prison briefly.

With Spirito and Carbone absent from Marseille in the immediate postwar years, the underworld came to be dominated by the Corsican Guerini brothers, whose courageous service in the resistance made them local heros. However, the Corsicans found their longtime political influence challenged by the rise of the local communist movement, a high-minded group with little use for gangsters. In bomb-cratered Marseille—as elsewhere in impoverished postwar France—labor strikes and demonstrations were escalating. An American government troubled by rising communist influence watched uneasily. Years later State Department eminence George Kennan would recall, "We were alarmed particularly over the situation in France and Italy. We felt that the Communists were using the very extensive funds that they then had in hand to gain control of key elements in France and Italy." Through the new CIA, a "secret operation to fund French non-communist unions was begun in 1947." The United States threw its covert support behind the French Socialists, who broke with the communists and urged patience on the nation's suffering workers. Marseille, a major Mediterranean port and the entryway for large amounts of Marshall Plan aid, was a key city in this struggle for France's political soul.

And so, as McCoy reports in *The Politics of Heroin*:

> The CIA, through its contacts with the Socialist party, had sent agents and a psychological warfare team to Marseille, where they dealt directly with Corsican syndicate leaders through the Guerini brothers. The CIA's operatives supplied arms and money to Corsican gangs for assaults on Communist picket lines and harrassment of important union officials. During the month-long strike the CIA's gangsters and the purged CRS [Compagnies Républicaines de Sécurite] police units murdered a number of striking workers and mauled the picket lines. . . . The Guerinis gained enough power and status from their role in smashing the 1947 strike to emerge as the new

leaders of the Corsican underworld. . . . This combination of political influence and control of the docks created the ideal environment for the growth of Marseille's heroin laboratories.

The United States government now effectively had used its prestige and power to inadvertently create and/or revive the two major groups of international drug traffickers: the American-Sicilian Mafia and the French Corsican underworld.

As early as 1951, French police began to encounter the first of the Corsican-run postwar heroin labs. The United Nation's *Bulletin on Narcotics* noted that in May of that year a clandestine lab was found in Marseille. The next spring the French found a crude kitchen lab in Paris. That summer French police scored a major coup in Paris when they swept down on Marius Ansaldi, a veteran drug trafficker known from before the war in Marseille. Rumors of heroin available in sizable lots through a small Paris café led the French to send in two undercover agents. Purportedly shoe salesmen, they gradually became viewed as regulars at the small establishment. They took to drinking with Marius Ansaldi, who confided one night after numerous Pernods that he was a chemist. Police tailing his girlfriend back to the Villa Castebian in suburban Montgeron noticed her habit of patronizing numerous pharmacies en route, purchasing basic chemicals for manufacturing heroin. When police stormed the villa, vaulting over the garden walls, they caught Ansaldi and two assistants in the act of making heroin. That July another lab was found in Marseille. These developments were viewed "as a consequence of the cessation of diversions in Italy during the previous years."

Since 1928, French police often had worked together with American narcotics agents on cases. After all, France had been *the* center for prewar trafficking from Europe. Now, those prewar contacts were reestablished with France's Police Judiciaire Central Narcotics Office, a Paris-based agency that in 1950 consisted of a chief, an assistant, and six to eight agents. Two low-ranking agents were dispatched to Marseille to combat the reviving French connection. For Turkish opium and/or morphine base was flowing steadily in, being converted to heroin in local processing labs and smuggled to U.S. markets either directly or via Canada or South America. And after this early string of laboratory busts, the French police hit a long, long dry spell.

Once FBN agent Charles Siragusa had established the Rome office, he eventually was joined by several other agents, including John T. Cusack and Andrew Tartaglino. Cusack was a Fordham grad in economics with intense blue eyes and thinning hair. Tartaglino, short, reserved in manner, had graduated from Georgetown in biology before serving in the navy. Cusack, one of the Bureau's smartest and most admired agents, would explain that in the fifties, American agents "regularly visited Paris and Marseille to assist the French Police Judiciaire in the development of investigations, as well as narcotic arrests and seizures in the traffic affecting the United States." He recalled that the French police "welcomed the participation of their American counterparts and participated in a very active exchange of reports, information, intelligence, and evidence." Starting in 1956 French police began coming periodically to the United States to help develop cases, especially in New York City.

However, this tiny French police agency—however excellent and enthusiastic—was obviously vastly inadequate to the task of taming the rapidly reviving Marseille heroin industry. Moreover, what successes the French did have in Marseille were negated by the local courts. In early 1953 Charles Siragusa learned that two Corsicans caught in Marseille with a kilo of heroin had received suspended sentences of three and six months and small fines. Utterly disgusted, Siragusa decided to stir up some international pressure and proposed a story to a friendly *Herald Tribune* correspondent.

In a long and detailed letter, Siragusa described Marseille as

> unquestionably the most important narcotics smugglers' haven in France and probably of all of Europe . . . there are at least 5 large heroin laboratories. . . . [The Corsicans] exercise a virtual monopoly of the illicit narcotic traffic in France . . . [smuggling] opium, morphine base and heroin from Beirut and Indo-China into Marseille. . . .
>
> Corsican criminals residing in the United States . . . have long been prominent narcotic suppliers. Since the war, they accelerated their activities. . . . The Marseille courts nullify the excellent enforcement efforts of the French police. . . . As long as these ridiculously shocking sentences are meted out, heroin smuggling to the United States will get progressively worse.

Nor could the French police agency's reasonable cooperation with the Americans disguise the outrageous reality of the situation—what the same savvy John Cusack would later describe to the U.S. Congress as the "obstinate refusal for ten years [actually more like twenty years] by France to assign the necessary manpower, equipment and funding to bring the illicit manufacture and traffic of heroin at Marseilles under control." Why, one feels compelled to ask, should that have been?

Were the French not our allies? Had we not helped save them from the Germans in two World Wars? Had we not helped revive their economy with the Marshall Plan?

Well, there were the mundane explanations. President Charles de Gaulle heartily disliked the United States and Americans. This well-known animosity no doubt had its effects. And then there was plain old graft. One U.S. agent working in Marseille reported that his French colleague "explained that it is impossible for the police to operate effectively in Marseille because of the degree of corruption existing in that city." Also, there was the general feeling that the French people did not abuse and become addicted to heroin, so why should the French police care? As this same French policeman bluntly told the American, "No member of his family and none of his friends are addicted. He regretted the narcotics problem facing the United States but added that, as France has no such problem, he does not see any reason for him to lose any sleep over this enforcement problem."

But there was also a more sinister reason. For just as our own military and the CIA were perfectly prepared to collaborate with the Sicilian and Corsican underworlds if that suited their Cold War agendas, so was French intelligence, an agency known as the Service de Documentation Extérieure et de Contre-Espionnage, or SDECE. Before World War II, the French colonial government long had operated an opium monopoly in Indochina without any moral qualms, supplying 2,500 opium dens and retail shops with about sixty tons of smoking opium routinely imported from Iran and Turkey. The taxes provided about 15 percent of colonial revenues. When the war cut off traditional opium supplies, French colonial administrators actively and successfully encouraged peasants in the Golden Triangle—where Laos, Burma, and Thailand intersect just below China—to cultivate enough opium poppies to supply Indochina's one hundred thousand addicts.

After World War II, the French and other colonial powers in the Far East agreed to the American demand that they end their legal opium monopolies. When the French officially outlawed opium smoking in 1946, the First Indochina War was just beginning. The Vietminh were determined to wrest their country back from the French, while the colonials were just as determined to remain in power. As the unpopular war dragged on, the French National Assembly cut military funds to the bone. And so, writes historian Alfred McCoy, "Desperately short of funds, French intelligence and paramilitary agencies expropriated the opium traffic to finance their covert operations during the First Indochina War. . . . The opium monopoly had gone underground to become Operation X." Wrote *Le Monde* correspondent Lucien Bodard in *The Quicksand War,* "Opium was a military objective for both the Vietminh and the French. . . . The possession of the opium crop meant that the Vietminh were denied the opportunity of filling their coffers; and what was more it allowed the Expeditionary Force and the administration to add to their secret funds, which, officially, were absurdly meager."

Colonel Maurice Belleux, the highest ranking SDECE officer in French Indochina, sanctioned Operation X. Major Roger Trinquier of the Mixed Airborne Commando Group supervised the purchasing of the opium from Laotian tribes and his paratroopers flew it to a French air base near Saigon. Local gangsters known as Binh Xuyen took it from there, preparing the opium and marketing it, initially through the old opium dens now renamed "detoxification clinics." When the clinics were closed in 1948, less conspicuous dens opened to replace them. The considerable opium revenues were used mainly by Major Trinquier and Captaine Antoine Savani, a Corsican, to pay the heavy counterinsurgency expenses of numerous hill tribes, pirates, and assorted guerrilla armies. If the Binh Xuyen still had surplus opium on their hands, says McCoy, it was "sold to local Chinese merchants for export to Hong Kong or to Corsican criminal syndicates in Saigon for shipment to Marseille." In short, Turkey and the Near East were not the sole source of raw opium in the 1950s for manufacturing heroin. The hill tribes of the Golden Triangle, under the prodding of the SDECE, also were producing large crops, with surpluses sufficient at times to supply the French Corsicans.

When Colonel Edward G. Lansdale of the American CIA toured Indochina for six weeks in the summer of 1953, he was appalled to discover French military intelligence up to its neck in drug trafficking. When he found that opium actually was being sent to Saigon for further export, he suggested to his superiors that an investigation was in order. Interviewed by Alfred McCoy almost twenty years later, Lansdale still recalled that the U.S. government reacted something like this: "Don't you have anything else to do? We don't want you to open up this keg of worms since it will be a major embarrassment to a friendly government. So drop your investigation."

Did Commissioner Anslinger know that the French in Indochina were trafficking beyond their own borders with the Corsican mob, who in turn were supplying American traffickers? We have no way of knowing. Very few files of the Bureau of Narcotics have ever been deposited in the National Archives. Even though the Bureau's successor agency, the Drug Enforcement Administration, was quite cooperative (in the Clinton era) in responding to Freedom of Information requests, it did not locate any of the Indochina folders in its stored "Country file" boxes. But even if Anslinger did know that the colonial French were trafficking, what would he have done? The State Department would have been the logical avenue of complaint, but its priority was containing communism, not drugs. Nor had Anslinger displayed any interest in diluting his hard-won postwar autonomy by conferring with State. Moreover, Anslinger was already an enthusiastic cold warrior, who fervently embraced the new rules that gave total priority to the shadow world of "national security." Those unspoken rules now began to compromise our antitrafficking efforts. The United States, which historically had been implacably opposed to anything that promoted nonmedical drug use, had started to turn a blind eye to certain trafficking activities if they involved those friendly to our cause in the Cold War.

When the French withdrew from Indochina in 1954 in the wake of their defeat at Dien Bien Phu, French intelligence does not seem to have abandoned its drug trafficking. For while it no longer had to pay for guerrilla armies in Indochina, the SDECE moved onto colonial struggles elsewhere, especially in Algeria. No doubt these, too, were expensive endeavors underfunded by the French National Assembly. And no doubt the drug revenues were helpful when segments of the military disagreed with their government's decision to relinquish their colonies, notably Algeria in 1958, and expressed that displeasure with a bloody terrorist campaign in Africa and France that was not suppressed until 1962.

This virtual civil war produced a new and ruthless pro-Gaullist group known as SAC, for Service D'Action Civique. A Pulitzer Prize–winning Newsday series on French heroin traffickers concluded, "Born out of the Algerian turmoil and terror, SAC quickly became a haven for underworld toughs, milieu strongmen who saw in it an opportunity for protection under the cover of political action." SAC, said Newsday, developed into "an organization of toughs, of killers, of heroin merchants. But also the protected offspring of some of France's most powerful politicians."

All through the fifties and sixties, one has to strongly suspect that not only were the Italian-American Mafiosi provisioning Marseille heroin labs with Turkish morphine base, but that French Corsicans with connections (however tangential) to French intelligence and SAC also were funneling in Golden Triangle opium. And all of it was then likely processed into high-grade heroin and directed toward North America and U.S. cities, smuggled by a multitude of couriers. Corsicans long had been at home in the criminal activities of French colonial Southeast Asia. In 1960, for instance, a Time correspondent in

Laos described "the boys" hanging out at the Snow Leopard hunting lodge in Laos, where they sipped *pastis* (a traditional Marseille drink) and waited for the colorful Meo tribesmen with their red-and-blue turbans to come down from the hills to sell the annual opium crop. Most of those waiting had "vaguely French antecedents—Petit Père, La Sèche Noire (the Black Cigarette), Le Gorille Gris (the Grey Gorilla)." Almost certainly, they were the Corsicans. A biography of Pop Buell, a legendary American known as a helper of Laotian hill tribes, describes how in 1960 he had "watched from the side of the [Phong Savan] airstrip as a modern twin-engined plane took on a huge load of opium. Beneath the wing, talking heatedly with the plane's Corsican pilot was a slender woman, . . . [the] grande madame of opium from Saigon."

Bodard of *Le Monde* also alludes to the powerful presence of the Corsicans in the French stronghold of Saigon, a highly corrupt city he describes in this era as revolving around rue Catinat, which

> began splendidly at the Plateau, among the fine houses and palaces, and ended squalidly half a mile further down at the port. The last stretch was the domain of the Corsican underworld. There one might see the dark, suspicious faces of the tough guys from the Isle of Beauty: their headquarters were the shiny bars, full of chrome and neon lighting, with their espresso machines, and roaring music. Endless mirrors reflected everything, from the manner of the boss's greeting (the true barometer of that particular world) to the long speculative stares of the habitual clients. Beyond the watchful, Junoesque cashier, beyond the doors that common mortals never entered, lay all the mysteries of the racket.

Yet this French connection that spanned the globe and poured heroin into the United States was not what Commissioner Anslinger denounced when using the bully pulpit of public office. After initially tagging Lucky Luciano the mastermind of the international drug traffic, Anslinger the loyal Cold Warrior took a new tack, targeting communist China. The commissioner first denounced China in a 1951 speech to the American Legion, claiming that "Communist China is producing and shipping large quantities of heroin which is finding its way into this country. We have presented this fact to the United Nations." Anslinger kept on loyally in this vein for the next decade. (After all, this was an era when the Los Angeles County Museum had to take down paintings by Picasso and Magritte because the city council said they were communists. So anticommunist attacks played well.)

In April 1953, Anslinger again formally accused the Chinese at the United Nations, stating, "There can be little doubt of the true purposes of Communist China in the organized sale of narcotics. These purposes include monetary gain, financing political activities in various countries, and sabotage." The Chinese scornfully rejected the accusations as "malicious slander" and "shameless dissemination of lying rumors." By 1955 Anslinger was claiming that communist China was "the greatest purveyor in history of habit-forming drugs, . . . reaping tremendous amounts from its network of narcotics smugglers operating on a world-wide basis."

In May, the Senate Judiciary Committee's Subcommittee to Investigate the Administration of the Internal Security Laws even held hearings entitled, "Communist China and Illicit Narcotic Traffic." There Anslinger testified to "a great concentration of Communist heroin in California. Some of it has come east of the Rockies. We have identified it in a certain way, which I can't disclose to you." He even went so far as to estimate that the Chinese were earning $60 million a year from the heroin trade. That August, Anslinger once again formally charged China at the United Nations with trafficking, much to the satisfaction of those opposed to China's entry into the United Nations. The Committee of One Million quickly filled the nation's major newspapers with full-page ads featuring Anslinger's charges and his photo.

At the United Nations, these accusations were greeted with puzzlement by the British representative to the Narcotic Drug Commission, who said that the "narcotics smugglers named by Anslinger as [Chinese Communist traffickers active in] Hong Kong were unknown in the colony." British officials responsible for Hong Kong "believed that Anslinger's accusations were 'ridiculous and completely unfounded.'" Anslinger's biographer, John C. McWilliams, describes the commissioner as allowing "international politics to distort and greatly exaggerate his assessment of narcotics trafficking in southeast Asia. . . . [N]o evidence supports his theory of a communist-organized heroin invasion originating in China." John Ingersoll, who headed one of the successor agencies to the FBN, was asked whether he found anything in agency files to support the charges against China when he took over in 1968. Ingersoll just rolled his eyes and said dismissively, "That was the sort of thing that went on in politics in those days. It was all just McCarthyism and making Communist China the bogeyman."

It was not China pumping heroin into America in the fifties and sixties. It was democratic, capitalist France. France had regained the dubious distinction as *the* center for international trafficking. Yet when it came to the French, Anslinger was mum. In his 1961 book, *The Murderers: The Story of the Narcotics Gangs*, Anslinger alludes to the French Corsicans only tangentially in a two-page account (in a three-hundred-page book) of one spectacular drug bust. Nor did anything in the public record suggest the French harbored the world's major heroin industry all through the fifties and sixties and up through the early seventies.

As early as 1955 Anslinger was writing privately to Siragusa in Europe that "the enormous amounts of heroin being smuggled into the United States and Canada on French vessels could not all come from clandestine laboratories. . . . I have been strongly of the opinion that there was some large diversion somewhere [from a legitimate French pharmaceutical factory]." The dapper Siragusa rushed off to Paris, where Charles Vaille, chief of the Central Pharmacy Service in the French Ministry of Public Health, assured Anslinger this could not be.

But the extraordinary quality of Gallic heroin made the Bureau of Narcotics certain that some had to be from the legitimate trade. On several subsequent occasions during the late 1950s, the bureau formally requested the French to investigate, always to no end. In 1963 agent Andrew Tartaglino noted in a memo that a French colleague strongly suspected a civil servant of Corsican background (known to be "closely allied to Corsican traffickers in Marseille") of diversion. The fishy activities in question were taking place at a major chemical company headed by the Comar family. As Tartaglino noted, "Raymond Comar is a close and intimate friend of the Minister of Public Health." Further, opined Tartaglino, "Should this phase develop into anything concrete, the French will most certainly conceal as much as possible, particularly since Giovanetti [the suspected Corsican] was in their files as mentioned above since 1957, and no action was ever taken." This ongoing American suspicion was, of course, never made public, anymore than the overall American concern with the huge volume of French trafficking.

We do not know if licit French heroin was being diverted. We do know that amateur Corsican chemists were turning out heroin so extraordinarily pure it could have been mistaken for factory made. Preeminent among these skilled, malevolent transformers of morphine base was one Joseph Césari, a Corsican born in Bastia in 1915. Like many a countryman he left his poor, barren island as a teenager and shipped out as a sailor from Marseille. Immediately after World War II, Cesari could be found working in his aunt and uncle's cheese store off Marseille's most fashionable avenue, the broad, shop-lined *la Canebière*. A tall, quiet, slender soul, Joseph Césari seemed incapable of doing much more than slicing Gruyère and reliably opening and closing up the store. His uncle was quite stunned when one day in 1948 this mouselike nephew offered to sell eight kilos of an extremely rare and valuable essence used for perfume manufacturing. The uncle recoiled at this criminal prospect and soon Joseph had disappeared altogether.

It seems that Césari then apprenticed himself to a half brother renowned for his skills as an underworld chemist. Soon the self-effacing shop helper had embarked on his own discreet but lucrative career manufacturing heroin. Transforming the thick brown morphine base into the pure white powder of heroin is potentially highly dangerous. The necessary noxious chemicals and ensuing fumes steadily undermine human health—in his later years Césari looked more like an emaciated, yellowed cadaver than a live person—while missteps in the cooking process can lead to horrific explosions. As underworld chemists such as Césari in and around Marseille perfected their malevolent craft and increased their output, their Corsican and Mafiosi colleagues provided a steady supply of raw morphine base and a guaranteed outlet in the United States for the finished product, heroin.

Dr. John the Night Tripper, a musician, remembers fondly the New Orleans heroin of the late fifties. "One of the reasons those highs were so tremendous was that the stuff that came through New Orleans was real, 100 percent Corsican junk that came straight off the boats from Cuba uncut. . . . I recall that dope that originated from the Corsicans was sometimes molded in hard cakes with the face of a little boy on it—an innocent face, indicating purity."

The extraordinary magnitude of the Marseille underworld's heroin operation only became hinted at publicly in 1960 with the first major French connection case, which painfully confirmed what two high-level informants had been telling skeptical FBN agents for several years: While the bureau had been seizing about two hundred pounds of heroin in a typical year, usually in three-to-five-pound lots, Corsican traffickers alone were smuggling in two hundred pounds every other *week*. The breakthrough case was the first of the "Ambassador" cases, that of Mauricio Rosal, age forty-eight. "Like all good cases," recounts Andrew Tartaglino, who worked on this one, "it started with an informant in Beirut, someone very reliable. In June of 1960, the informant told our agent in Lebanon about a diplomat named Mauricio Rosal [the Guatemalan ambassador to Belgium, the Netherlands, and Luxembourg], who was smuggling morphine base from Beirut to Marseille. We informed the French and they knew him. He was in their files as a pedophile who had a young Lebanese waiter as a boyfriend." An American Customs agent further discovered that in 1941, while Rosal was married to the daughter of the president of Honduras, he had performed various diplomatic chores for that nation. In the course of those duties he apparently had been caught smuggling "essential oils valued at $48,000 as well as $37,000 worth of diamonds. Rosal had managed to extricate himself from that one and the earlier smuggling venture never became generally known."

But far more important, the French reported that Ambassador Rosal's Corsican connection was one Etienne Tarditi, fifty-eight, ostensibly the proprietor of an electronics business in Paris. Tarditi, despite his veneer of respectability, once had served a jail term and had been observed with at least one known member of the Corsican underworld. The French Sûreté began keeping an eye on Tarditi, an Alfred Hitchcock look-alike right down to the protruding lower lip, double chin, and huge belly. On August 17 the French called Tartaglino, by then the FBN's Paris agent, to report that Tarditi had just flown back to Paris from New York. The bureau in New York scrambled on their end and found that Ambassador Rosal had been on that same flight with Tarditi. The hunt was on.

About six weeks later, on Saturday October 1, Monsieur Tarditi headed out to Orly, where agents watched him board a flight to New York. When he emerged from Customs at Idlewild (as Kennedy Airport was then known) wearing a trenchcoat and dark porkpie hat, the American surveillance team went into action. Tarditi was steered toward a cab driven by a narcotics agent. He said he was going to the Sherry Netherlands Hotel. The cabbie–narcotics agent repeated this loudly enough for nearby undercover agents to hear. The bureau needed time to install an electronic bug in Tarditi's hotel room. But as the agent was approaching the Queensboro Bridge, Tarditi leaned forward and said in French-accented English, "I've changed my mind. Take me to the Savoy Hilton." The agent quickly scribbled this on a piece of paper, crumpled it up, and dropped it out the window while signaling to the agents trailing the taxi. They coasted to a halt and retrieved the note. Soon they pulled ahead and indicated that the taxi should proceed slowly. The agent-driver managed to catch every red light and backup from there on in. By the time Tarditi checked in at the Savoy Hilton, agents had installed an eavesdropping bug and were occupying the adjacent rooms.

The agents knew Rosal was coming Sunday (because he had booked a room at the Plaza) but not when or from where. After a long, tense day at Idlewild they finally sighted Rosal at 7 P.M. striding toward Customs, one of the disembarking passengers on a flight from Brussels. Ambassador Rosal, a tall, elegant man with a high, receding hairline, looked every inch the diplomat, with dark homburg hat, impeccable suit, maroon tie, and slender attaché case. At the baggage carousel, he retrieved three black suitcases and headed toward Customs. But first he stopped to fit a cigarette into a long holder. Then the ambassador watched haughtily as his bags were whisked through, standard courtesy to all diplomats. The skycap piloting Rosal's bags to the curb stopped briefly in the crowded airport so an FBN agent surreptiously could make a tiny identifying penknife mark on each bag.

Meanwhile, Rosal was overheard telling a fellow passenger he would not be taking a cab because he had a ride. Forty minutes later, as the patrician diplomat looked more and more irate, a stationwagon suddenly emerged from the clotted airport traffic. The three suitcases were loaded in swiftly and as the stationwagon roared off, the tailing FBN agent followed, sideswiping a limousine in his haste. What if they disappeared with the suitcases? What if Rosal did not go to the Plaza, where they knew he had a reservation? But Rosal did proceed to the luxurious hotel overlooking Central Park. Little did Rosal guess as he checked into room 944 that his next-door neighbors were narcotics agents, busily listening in.

The next morning, a crisp fall day, agents tried to blend into the Plaza's lobby, luxurious with thick carpets and huge floral arrangements. Suddenly Tarditi strolled in carrying a small brown paper bag. Upstairs on the ninth floor, eavesdropping agents heard the bag being opened and Tarditi saying in French that it contained $16,500 in cash for Rosal and $10,000 for Tarditi. Then the Frenchman directed Rosal on how to deliver the heroin.

A few hours later, at 12:25 P.M., waiting agents watched anxiously as Rosal walked out the Plaza's front door, the bellboy carrying three suitcases. The doorman hailed a taxi and Rosal directed it toward the chic shopping district of East Seventy-second Street and Lexington Avenue. There, waiting on the corner, stood Etienne Tarditi, watched by almost two dozen undercover agents from FBN and Customs. The cab pulled over, the Corsican slid in to join the ambassador, and the taxi pulled out. Worried about losing their quarry, the narcotics agents decided this was it. They cut off the cab and from every side agents swooped down. Rosal and Tarditi were obviously stunned as they were pulled out and handcuffed. In the trunk lay three black valises—with the identifying knife marks—holding 110 pounds of pure heroin and their courier payment of $26,500 in cash.

Also arrested in a nearby stationwagon holding $70,000 in cash were a TWA purser who worked the Paris–New York run, Charles Bourbonnais, a Frenchman with U.S. citizenship, and a New York longshoreman with mob ties named Nick Calamaris. The FBN was astounded at the amount of heroin they had just confiscated, the biggest such seizure on U.S. soil since 1931. And TWA purser Bourbonnais had another 110 pounds hidden in the garage of his Long Island estate.

(Bourbonnais's neighbors were quite surprised to hear he was not an airline pilot, since he took great pains to arrive home always in a pilot's uniform. Apparently he did not want his fancy neighbors to wonder how he could afford the life he led. When one took a flight where Bourbonnais served him drinks, the other neighbors would not believe it.)

Not only had the FBN just seized more than two hundred pounds of heroin, the biggest of all postwar seizures, they soon confirmed just what the informants had been insisting: similar amounts had been smuggled into New York every other week in recent years. According to a later confidential study of worldwide trafficking patterns, Bourbonnais, the TWA purser, had been working with the Corsicans for a decade, making heroin deliveries in New York for French traffickers and then smuggling back drug money. After spending a year in prison, Bourbonnais began to talk, presumably hoping for leniency. His trafficking career began in 1951, he said. That year he couriered eight separate deliveries of four kilos each on TWA from Paris to New York. By the following year the heroin packages weighed in at five kilos and Bourbonnais typically made six to eight deliveries each year, from 1952 through 1956. In 1957 the usual heroin package weight rose to twelve kilos and Bourbonnais made four runs. By 1958 the weight of the smuggled packages had risen to fifty kilograms. All told he personally smuggled in almost a half ton of heroin. What Bourbonnais's testimony made clear was the steeply escalating quantities being trafficked. Drug criminals seemed willing to risk losing larger and larger shipments. By 1960 an average load was ten times heavier than it had been a decade earlier.

Ambassador Rosal only admitted to being a courier for a year, using his diplomatic passport to bring in fifty-kilo, or 110-pound, lots on three previous occasions. Based on what they were hearing from Bourbonnais and Rosal, the FBN had to revise completely (way, way upward) its official estimates of how much heroin was entering the United States. Before the Rosal case, French police had figured that Marseille, which was believed to supply four fifths of the total market, was smuggling about a thousand pounds of heroin a year. But Rosal alone in one year had used his diplomatic status to bring in 440 pounds. And no one deluded themselves that the Corsicans relied on only one or two people to smuggle in heroin. So now the FBN's 1960 annual report estimated that 2,600 pounds to 5,000 pounds was coming in annually from France. Years later, in 1982, Cusack would testify that it was 5,000 pounds. And even that was probably still way too low. Agents today say that within the agency the credible figure was 8,000 to 10,000 pounds, or four to five tons. And that figure did not include heroin coming in from other sources, such as Mexico and Asia.

But these huge inflows of Corsican heroin were not admitted to outside the inner sanctums of the FBN. It would have been too public and too humiliating an admission of failure, especially when annual seizures averaged about two hundred pounds. And so when a presidential advisory commission began looking at the whole drug situation, from trafficking to treatment, in 1963, Treasury officially reported that it estimated that "one and a half tons are smuggled annually into this country." Yet it knew the Corsicans alone were bringing in far more than that, and its own annual reports showed that Mexican and Chinese gangs were active in the Southwest and on the West Coast. In short, the bureau had simply begun to dissemble about the huge flow of heroin.

A congressional study done in 1970 concluded that the postwar Marseille trafficking scene consisted of

> five, and possibly ten, groups operating at any one time with up to 100 individuals employed. Each group appears to have its own courier and trafficking and purchasing operations. Over the past 10 years every narcotics case in Marseille has involved one or more of four Corsican families: the Venturi brothers (Jean and Dominic), Marcel Francisci, Antoine Guerini and Joseph Orsini. (Orsini himself served a prison term in the United States and was deported in 1958.) There are offshoots of these four families and ad hoc groups may appear from time to time, but these four families are the heart of illegal heroin production in Marseille.

When a Johnson administration task force on narcotics surveyed the trafficking situation in the mid sixties, it expressed wonder that no one had registered a single word of high-level diplomatic complaint to our Gallic friends about the tons of heroin their criminals were exporting to our criminals. The task force noted, "Approximately 85–90% of the heroin illegally sold in the United States comes from France, . . . [yet] we are not aware that there has been any political level discussion of this problem with the GOF [government of France]." The task force proposed in its late 1966 report that the American ambassador in Paris "convey the serious concern of the [American] President over the illegal export traffic in heroin, . . . suggesting that France has both moral and treaty obligations to throw a great deal more resources into its domestic enforcement program. . . . The matter would be raised, pursuant to this proposal, at a political level for the first time of which we have any knowledge."

In fact, Commissioner Anslinger *had* written to the French ambas-

sador in Washington within weeks of the 1960 Rosal case and diplo-
matically expressed concern that "such enormous quantities of heroin
are reaching the United States from France." Then, in early February of
1961, Charles Siragusa, by now an assistant deputy commissioner, had
an extremely blunt discussion with the French representative to the
U.N.'s Commission on Narcotic Drugs, complaining "that almost all
the heroin smuggled into our east coast directly, or via Canada, Mexico
and Cuba, originates in France." That same month the French consul
general in New York was sent out with the NYPD narcotics squad to
see firsthand the effects of the heroin manufactured by his countrymen. According to a report from the FBN's number three man, Wayland L. Speer, to Anslinger, "The minister [consul general] asked one of
the addicts where the narcotics were coming from and the addict
replied. 'And you are from the French government and you're asking
me? It all comes from Marseille, of course.' The minister was visibly
shaken and was disturbed to know that even the lowest echelon of the
underworld realizes that France is the source of the heroin reaching the
United States."

But in the meantime, the Rosal case had wiped out whatever illusions anyone harbored at the FBN that they had a handle on trafficking.
As Andrew Tartaglino recalled, "Four or five tons of heroin was coming into the U.S. and we hadn't had an inkling [about the amounts].
Whatever the reason, all this stuff was coming in and we had our heads
in the sand." One is struck by the lack of any public reaction by Commissioner Anslinger to what was the most important postwar case on
American soil.

While Anslinger remained largely silent, Wayland Speer began to
raise a ruckus. A heavyset man with close-cropped blond hair and a
thick Texan accent, Speer retained close ties to powerful Texas Democrat Price Daniel, for whom he had once worked. Recalls Tartaglino, "I
think Speer was feeling that JFK was coming in and Anslinger's days
were numbered and that the job would be his. I'm in Paris in early 1961
and Speer starts shooting off all these cables and saying that the State
Department must do something and starts blasting the French over all
these drugs pumping into the States. What happens is that Speer
pushes the French into increasing the narcotics staff in Marseille from
two to twelve and in Paris from twelve to eighteen. The French do
react to Speer. Anslinger, during this time, was silent."

In the spring of 1961, Treasury Secretary Douglas Dillon wrote to
Secretary of State Dean Rusk saying, "I would be grateful if you could
have our Embassy in Paris instructed to raise this problem with the
appropriate French authorities at an early date. If these further repre-

sentations do not produce results, I think we should consider raising the matter during the President's visit to Paris next month." The matter never reached the presidential level, and midlevel Treasury officials visiting Paris were brushed aside by French officials stating "that there was no manpower available for increased narcotic enforcement until the Algerian problem was solved." The U.S. narcotics agent in Paris affirmed this stance in September 1961, saying that his French counterpart explained that "all normal law enforcement activities . . . are being neglected during the present crisis, . . . the continuing and recently intensified emergency caused by terrorist attacks on police stations, the attempt to assassinate the President of the Republic, and other disorders." But even once Algeria was a moot issue in 1963 and political peace returned, the French still refused to confront their own traffickers seriously.

Anslinger's successor, Commissioner Henry Giordano, explained the intransigent Gallic stance in a 1966 memo. The French, he wrote, "take the position that the illicit production problem in their country, which does not affect them, is artificially created by their accidentally being astride the route of the raw materials in the Near East and the market in North America. They . . . conveniently overlook their actual position as a vast clandestine producer, a role created and sustained by their organized underworld which they also, for their purposes, tend to ignore." Years later, Giordano would say that complaints were made to the French yearly at the United Nations (obviously not in public session) and also through Interpol, but that France chose to ignore them.

Just as disturbing as the magnitude of the French trafficking were the forces linked to it. When Etienne Tarditi was interrogated after being plucked unceremoniously from the chic venues of the Upper East Side, he declared that "he had highly placed friends in the French government. He mentioned belonging to Gaullist anticommunist political groups and intimated that he was involved in intelligence work beneficial to American interests." The Corsicans were part of the postwar French shadow world where drug trafficking was either a direct form of raising funds or a deliberately ignored means of rewarding part-time agents and criminal allies.

Tarditi was one of those second-echelon French Corsicans who claimed connections to French intelligence front groups. He had recruited not only Rosal, but other diplomats as well to smuggle heroin. To keep the ambassadors completely insulated, a Corsican always met the diplomat-courier in the United States to retrieve and personally deliver the heroin to American mobsters. "That first night, Tarditi was in a state of shock and just wanted to get out of this jail, and so he said he'd cooperate," recalls Tartaglino. "But after giving a certain amount of information, he got nervous that he would end up being killed. The next day he got a lawyer and clammed up."

Meanwhile, each passing year provided more and more egregious examples of this rampant French trafficking. On January 18, 1962, French television talk-show host Jacques Angelvin, thirty-four, and François Scaglia, thirty-four, a Corsican who managed a Paris nightclub, were arrested ten days after disembarking from the SS *United States*. They were charged with smuggling in twenty-four pounds of heroin, which they were caught delivering to one Anthony Fuca, thirty-one, in the Bronx. But city and federal narcotic agents were certain there was still more heroin that had come across with Angelvin, who had brought along his Buick Invicta. In the Academy Award–winning movie *The French Connection*, the New York cop is shown triumphantly finding the heroin by dismantling the car. In real life, the heroin was found by round-the-clock surveillance of Anthony Fuca, who was out on bail. On February 24, an NYPD narcotics detective literally tackled Fuca as he emerged from the basement of his Bronx apartment house with three plaid airline bags holding eighty-eight pounds of heroin.

Yet in May 1962, when Commissioner Anslinger made his yearly pilgrimmage to the civilized pleasures of Geneva and the seventeenth session of the United Nations Narcotics Commission, there was no public upbraiding of the French. Instead, the *New York Times* reported, in a short article headlined, NARCOTICS RISE LAID TO CHINA AND CUBA, that Anslinger had (as usual) accused communist China and Cuba of "obtaining badly needed foreign currency by traffic in narcotics. . . . The Chinese are regularly running mule caravans loaded with millions of dollars worth of opium from Yunnan Province into Burma, Mr. Anslinger said. Much of it finds its way to the United States as processed heroin." That was almost certainly news to Anslinger's own agents, who had never seen any evidence of Chinese heroin.

Whatever Anslinger the cold warrior might be saying, the working agents of the bureau were focused fully on the French. For Etienne Tarditi, the Corsican arrested in the first Ambassador case, and Bourbonnais had talked, implicating various members of the French underworld as suppliers. One arrested trafficker based in Paris was extremely distraught because *Le milieu*, as the Corsicans were known, had informed him he had to make good on the fifty kilos of heroin lost in New York. *Le milieu* did not just say *"dommage"* ("too bad") and swallow its losses. It expected those involved to make good—or else. The trafficker had been so fearful he had sold a small hotel and handed over thirty million old francs, only to be told, "Don't think this covers everything. You still owe." Pleading calls to Barthelemy Guerini, one of the reigning powers of the Corsican mob, got him nowhere.

Tarditi's late-night jail cell indiscretions in New York also had implicated yet another diplomat, one who apparently had recruited Rosal for Tarditi. In his state of nervous shock, Tarditi had provided several clues: This diplomat-trafficker was from a Spanish-speaking country, had once served at the United Nations, and in the fifties had been accredited to a country in the British commonwealth. "So," recalls Tartaglino, who had in the interim been transferred back to Washington (in part because his supervisor, Wayland Speer, felt he was too close to the French) and would supervise this case, "we decided to look at all Spanish diplomats, of which there are many, who were coming into New York. Four people were sent down to Immigration and spent four months just going through I-94s [immigration forms] on microfilm. We began to whittle it down until we had twenty or twenty-five people." The major suspect was one Salvador Pardo-Bolland, fifty-five, an aristocratic-looking Mexican diplomat with a thick silver streak in his combed-back hair. Pardo-Bolland and his American wife traveled frequently to New York, often only staying one night.

Not certain where Pardo-Bolland was assigned then, "We asked the CIA for help on that and it turned out he was the Mexican ambassador to Bolivia and playing bridge on a regular basis with the ranking CIA man there," recalls Tartaglino. Oddly, the French showed no record of Pardo's entering France, even though he stayed often at the elegant Hotel Meurice in Paris. Then everyone realized that Pardo-Bolland, as ambassador, easily could issue himself passports under any name. Edgy and watchful, Pardo often met his contacts in nearly empty churches, quiet and dim but for the sputtering flames of memorial candles. If he thought he was being followed, he would get down on his knees to pray. If he made no such signal, then necessary communications or even delivery of the heroin took place in the sacristy. One time when narcotics agents "peeked" into Pardo-Bolland's checked luggage they found not heroin but weights. Obviously, it was a dry run.

In early February 1964, Ambassador Pardo-Bolland appeared at his usual hotel in Paris, and then continued on some days later to Cannes, where he met up with Juan Ariztí, sixty, a diplomat from Uruguay. Ariztí was an old drug-smuggling colleague from the fifties when both were posted in the Middle East. Ariztí was no minor diplomatic functionary. He was about to be appointed Uruguay's ambassador to Moscow.

Unaware of being watched, the two old friends relaxed in a Riviera café with two notorious Corsican traffickers. Then Pardo-Bolland returned to Paris and flew on to New York, arriving on February 15. Juan Ariztí flew straight from Nice to Montreal, stashing four suitcases in a locker at the train station before going to his hotel. The Royal Canadian Mounted Police opened the locker, removed the bags, and confirmed that they held heroin—120 pounds worth. They substituted flour for all but two pounds and returned the bags to the locker.

The next day, Ariztí arrived in Manhattan, four bags in tow, and registered at the same hotel as Pardo-Bolland. Narcotics agents listened in from adjoining rooms. On February 20, Pardo-Bolland met another French trafficker, who had come over to act as the go-between, shielding the diplomats from American traffickers. When narcotics agents picked up the go-between the next day, he had the four precious baggage claim checks in his possession. Agents arrested Ariztí and Pardo-Bolland shortly thereafter. This created a real diplomatic embarrassment, for even as Pardo-Bolland was brought to court in handcuffs, kicking and screaming at the news photographers, President Lyndon Baines Johnson was meeting with Mexican President López Mateos in Los Angeles. One of the points for discussion was rampant drug trafficking by Mexican nationals across the border. The Mexicans neatly finessed the situation by insisting that Pardo-Bolland had been "dismissed" from the diplomatic corps weeks earlier.

In any case, Pardo-Bolland showed that if the French connection accounted for five tons of heroin annually, and the typical smuggled load was one hundred pounds plus, this meant one hundred times each year couriers of some kind—diplomatic or otherwise—were entering the country.

The Pardo-Bolland case also showed how completely communication had lapsed between the State Department and the Bureau of Narcotics. When the story broke, bureau officials complained loudly to the media that crooked diplomats were responsible for smuggling in 75 percent of America's underworld heroin. Journalists, of course, eagerly bounced this off State Department officials, who immediately contacted the bureau to set up a meeting. There a junior State official loftily explained what was what:

> Diplomats who enter the United States as visitors or tourists do not enjoy immunity from search. . . . [D]iplomats who enter this country on official business, or in transit to their posts in other countries do enjoy immunity from arrest, search, etc. . . . However, the Vienna Convention of 1961 and international practice, permit search of property owned by a diplomat who enjoys immunity when there is reasonable evidence or suspi-

cion that items are being brought in by the diplomat which are detrimental to the security or health of a nation.

One might well wonder why the bureau did not know something so important to its basic enforcement duties.

Throughout the sixties, one seizure after another only confirmed the growing magnitude of the unchecked stream of French heroin flowing out of Marseille—and the trafficker's disturbing links to the French government. Etienne Tarditi in the Rosal case had claimed intelligence connections. But the case of Michael Mertz was even more egregious. The case began when a known Corsican trafficker arrived in New York. As the FBN tailed Jean Nebbia, he checked into the posh Waldorf-Astoria, while his traveling companion, Louis Jacques Douheret, headed to his mistress's apartment at 309 West Fifty-fourth Street. The next morning they were seen meeting with two American Mafiosi in the elegant Waldorf bar. Then, improbably, Nebbia and Douheret flew to Columbus, Ohio, where they were met by a retired U.S. Army major who had been posted in Orléans, France.

Now, even more strangely, the two Frenchmen rented a car, drove to Opelika, Alabama, bought three suitcases and a footlocker, and drove back to Columbus. Once again they met with the retired military man, who introduced them to yet another American, army officer Herman Conder, just transferred back from Orléans, France. Two days later on December 20, 1965, FBN agents walked into Conder's trailer near Fort Benning, Georgia (located on land owned by the retired American military man) just as he was transferring almost two hundred pounds of heroin from secret compartments in the family freezer into suitcases. Up in New York, Nebbia and Douheret, second-echelon French traffickers, were arrested as they waited to pick up Conder's heroin and then sell it to the Americans they had met with in the Waldorf bar. The French revealed when arrested that the freezer was a new twist for the gang, which had been smuggling in heroin regularly since 1960 using cars. Following the chain of traffickers in the Conder case led back to French army captain Michel Victor Mertz, a resistance hero whose military title was a cover for his real work in SDECE, French intelligence. It would take another four years and several more heroin-in-automobile cases connected to Mertz before the French finally arrested him in 1969.

In the meantime, this purported army captain lived in a luxury apartment on Boulevard Suchet in Paris, weekended at his 1,445-acre hunting lodge (complete with private landing strip) in Loiret, maintained two apartments in Metz, a villa outside Paris, and a summer house in—of all places—Corsica. Each year during the late sixties, the flow of Corsican heroin grew. When seizures of one hundred and two hundred pounds had been made from Rosal, Angelvin, and Pardo-Bolland in the early sixties, they had had a visible impact on the retail market, creating shortages and panics for addicts on the streets. But by the late sixties, this was no longer true.

To combat the numerous Corsican organizations, the French government had assigned all of thirty French police officers. Their inadequacy was obvious from one simple statistic: From 1950 to 1970, a period of twenty years, the French had located and closed all of thirteen heroin labs. Yet at any one time at least five to ten laboratories were busy manufacturing heroin.

As veteran agent John Cusack would describe later, following the profound shock of the Rosal case, "the U.S. government began a series of requests to the government of France to increase the manpower and resources of its narcotics enforcement effort, and increase the maximum penalty of five years for narcotics trafficking." When these low-level requests had no effect, and as the situation worsened notably, the "requests" went higher. Says Cusack,

> These interventions extended through 1968 and were made with the French Ambassador in Washington, the Consul General in New York, the Minister of Interior, the directors of the Sûreté Nationale and Police Judiciaire, and Ministry of Justice officials at Paris. These requests were made by successive assistant secretaries of the Treasury, commissioners of narcotics, and U.S. Ambassadors at Paris. They were also made in cordial and informal discussions between the United States and French delegations to the UN Commission on Narcotic Drugs to the ICPO Interpol General Assemblies.

But still the drugs flowed in and the French connection flourished. By 1969, the Federal Bureau of Narcotics estimated that the Marseille Corsicans were flooding the United States with eight to ten tons of heroin annually. As devastating as this was, it was not the only factor in the great heroin plague.

CHAPTER 10

"Agents Were
Engaged in
Illicit Activities."

—Chief Inspector Andrew Tartaglino
testifying before Congress

On the cold evening of February
7, 1959, police from Manhattan's Forty-third Precinct were summoned
to the Watson Bar & Grill, where they found a federal narcotics agent
sprawled in a comatose state. Rushed to Jacobi Hospital, the agent was
found to be suffering from narcotic poisoning. Since there were no needle marks, doctors concluded that the heroin or morphine had been
administered orally. The agent, it turned out, had been drinking with
several colleagues. When searched, his car yielded a quantity of heroin
secreted in the glove compartment. Within thirty-six hours, following
the agent's recovery, he had resigned from the bureau. Ten years later,
investigators were told the agent "had been given an overdose of drugs
in a drink." Not by the traffickers, but by fellow narcotics agents.

"Reportedly," wrote the investigators, "this agent made the unforgivable error of trying to solicit funds from members of the narcotic
underworld without clearing it with the appropriate corrupt individuals

in our New York office." Newly transferred from Philadelphia in late 1958, the young narcotics agent apparently had approached two New York traffickers and tried to sell information on a case pending against them. When other FBN agents found out, they turned him in. Faced with dismissal, the agent had contacted U.S. Representative Francis Dorn (a member of a House subcommittee that handled federal employee grievances) to arrange a meeting between Commissioner Anslinger and the agent. For unknown reasons, Anslinger agreed to give the crooked agent another chance. (So much for the vaunted hard line.) When the reprieved agent returned to active duty in January 1959, he warned his colleagues not to meddle with him again, saying, "If I go down, I'll take others along with me." This threat had proven near fatal.

As this extraordinary episode makes clear, corruption was well entrenched in the all-important New York FBN office in 1958. But only the reckless actions of this new agent had forced the issue momentarily to the surface. Looking back, this is the first *documentable* instance of growing corruption in the New York office after World War II.

In the postwar shadow world, the Federal Bureau of Narcotics was compromised not only by international traffickers with intelligence connections to a major but intransigent ally, but by its own severe internal problems, problems of corruption that remained resolutely hidden from outsiders. Because Commissioner Anslinger was such a commanding and generally respected figure, few suspected that his agency was going rotten. And certainly no one could have dreamed that the agency would choose to ignore and deny the outrageous criminality of its own agents.

At first, a gung-ho New York FBN agent named Edward J. Coyne viewed the Watson Bar & Grill episode as an aberration, for the new agent had struck him as a "little flakey. Four quarts in a five quart car." But by 1960, Coyne began to suspect that that strange event was just the tip of the proverbial iceberg. The New York office was organized into three groups of about twenty working narcotics agents, each quite autonomous in its antitrafficking activities. And even within the groups, two or three agents often partnered together, making it quite possible to be unaware of others' activities.

The New York office physically was located in lower Manhattan at 90 Church Street, a huge Depression-era building near the Hudson River. The post office occupied the first five floors, the Bureau of Narcotics half the sixth floor, and the U.S. Navy the remaining six floors. Narcotics agents worked in a large, open office littered with old coffee cups and tossed debris, oblivious to the constant background noise of postal trucks pulling in and out of huge ground-floor bays.

Coyne, the tall, innocuous-looking sort who does so well blending in during undercover operations, had been an agent for about six years when approached by a corrupt colleague in early 1960. "I became aware that drugs were being seized and not turned in, money was being stolen and apartments looted during raids. The agent would claim the money was given to an informant and then just keep it or the agent would give confiscated drugs to informants to sell. I started listening more and more and paying more attention. Other agents told me similar stories." He rallied a number of agents who were also disturbed by blatant signs of corruption. In April 1960, Coyne approached his superiors in the New York office with specific allegations against ten other agents, all of whom worked together in one group. His superiors were ostensibly receptive, but it soon became clear nothing substantive would be done. Meanwhile, Coyne and his wife began receiving threatening and obscene phone calls at their home.

Then, one day a superior called him in and said in a jocular way, "Were you up to something with a woman clerk in a car?" Coyne, very shocked, said, "Absolutely not." His boss laughed and said, "Somebody told me that, but I didn't believe it. You can't believe everything people tell you." As an unnerved Coyne walked out, he concluded this was a not-so-subtle threat and began looking for a new job. Coyne had been Anslinger's New York driver from 1951 to 1955 and had quite admired his agency's boss. Yet now, he was profoundly disillusioned. "Anslinger ran the bureau with an iron fist and he had to have known. Corruption cannot occur on that widespread a scale without higher-ups being aware of it. When you have the things that happened in the Bureau of Narcotics, it was impossible for it to happen without superiors knowing it." Within the year, Coyne had transferred to U.S. Customs. (There he would have a distinguished career as a narcotics agent, going on to become supervisor of the New York office.)

Things remained placid on the surface in New York for well over a year, until August 31, 1960. On that hot summer evening, an agent came home complaining to his wife that he did not feel well. When she went to bed, her husband was still watching television in the living room. At 4:00 A.M. she awoke and went downstairs to find him slumped over. She called another agent, and then a doctor, who came and pronounced her husband dead. Even though the medical exam listed as the cause of death "possible narcotics overdose," there was no investigation into this bizarre incident for seven months, and only then because the upset wife approached her congressman. Many years later, investigators were told that this agent had attempted "to go it alone and extort monies from indicted narcotics traffickers." Other corrupt agents had murdered him by administering opiates in a drink.

Finally, in July 1961 Wayland L. Speer, still number three in the agency's hierarchy, was dispatched from Washington to the New York Office. A big man whose blond buzz cut went back to his days in the military in the Far East, Speer presumably was sent to Manhattan by Anslinger in response to these strange goings-on. Speer, it should also be noted, was a pushy, ambitious fellow with his heart set on becoming commissioner when Anslinger retired the next year. Furthermore, he was resented within the agency because he had not come up through the ranks, but had entered at a high level as a protégé of Texas politician Price Daniel. Moreover, Speer also had been stirring up trouble by complaining steadily within the agency and to the French about the outrageous indifference of French officials to Corsican trafficking. Though Ed Coyne was gone by the time Speer arrived to investigate, he knew Speer. Coyne assumed Speer "certainly went to New York because Anslinger wanted him there. Speer was about fifty then and very, very straight."

Tartaglino, well aware that Speer's major preoccupation was getting some kind of action out of the French, heard his boss had come to New York on special assignment. (Tartaglino was now back in New York from Paris and working out of the federal prosecutor's office on the ambassador cases, looking for Pardo-Bolland.) "The next thing I knew his career was ruined," recalls Tartaglino. Speer, who had little experience as an investigator, was trapped by his own carelessness and naivete, completely outwitted by the street-smart New York agents.

Speer's downfall began early one morning when he telephoned one of the accused agents, a black former D.C. cop named Charles McDonnell, and summoned him to his hotel room for a talk. McDonnell exploited this circumstance—a private meeting in a hotel room—to devise a strategy to bring down Speer. He would accuse Speer, obviously a southerner, of lewd and racist conduct toward him, specifically, questioning McDonnell while exposing himself. McDonnell went straight to Senator Jacob Javits to complain about Speer. Javits rightly wondered what kind of professional investigation gets done in a hotel room? Meanwhile, the other corrupt agents happily backed up McDonnell and piled on their own complaints—that Speer was making false accusations, that they hadn't been warned of their rights. Speer had left himself vulnerable by conducting confrontational interviews in private and alone. Tartaglino says, "Speer never did anything he was accused of. Maybe he was getting dressed or something while talking to McDonnell." Tartaglino could say this with certainty because seven years later McDonnell himself described what happened after getting caught in a sting. McDonnell was crooked and admitted it freely after he sold an undercover agent first a quarter kilo and then a half kilo of heroin on a Baltimore golf course. McDonnell then explained how he and the other agents had conspired to successfully smear and destroy Speer.

Consequently, all that came out of Speer's thwarted investigation—aside from his own downfall—was a mild report conceding "many areas of misconduct, particularly with regard to the payment and use of informants." Meanwhile, the corrupt agents emerged unscathed, having successfully sabotaged Speer with complaints about improper behavior and civil rights. Years later Congress would be told, "Mr. Speer was demoted and sent to the Southwest. . . . He was the target of an obvious effort to get him to resign." Coyne's theory was that Speer "uncovered so much it may have been an embarrassment. And so he got sent off to Texas." Worse yet, those whom Speer suspected in the New York bureau were soon promoted. The message was clear. Corruption would not be pursued seriously. And there may have been additional messages, too. Perhaps that those who complained too loudly about France jeopardized their careers, as did those who showed too much initiative and eyed the commissioner's job.

Twenty years earlier, the New York office had been rendered largely ineffective by corruption. In that situation, the U.S. Attorney for the Southern District had gone personally to Treasury Secretary Morgenthau to complain about the problem. It was notable at the time that Morgenthau said nothing to Anslinger, presumably viewing the then young commissioner as either somehow incapable of dealing with it or simply derelict in not recognizing and resolving the problem himself. Unfortunately, when corruption metastasized this time around, there was no Morgenthau to take decisive action and instigate an investigation and cleanup. Instead, you had a far more seasoned Commissioner Anslinger, a consummate bureaucrat who operated largely as he pleased within his own small fiefdom, and who still displayed little interest in confronting corruption.

A far more minor instance in 1952 similarly had been swatted aside. In that case a janitor at the FBN's Washington headquarters was discovered by a local assistant DA named Thomas A. Wadden to be stealing cocaine and marijuana right out of the FBN vaults and then selling it to several major local traffickers. Anslinger actively discouraged Wadden from taking the case to trial, publicly stating, "The bureau could see no reason for all the fuss." As Wadden prepared to round up five dealers fingered by the janitor before a grand jury, Anslinger preempted him, sweeping out on a high-profile raid executed with dozens of agents and reporters to ensure maximum coverage. The commissioner then sent a clear message to the ranks by dispatching the FBN agent who'd had the misfortune to cooperate with D.A. Wadden to some remote and dangerous posting. Clearly, Anslinger was as reluctant in the fifties to confront corruption as he had been in the thirties.

And by late 1960 there was quite a bit to ignore. For not only had narcotics agents in the all-important New York office been poisoned (and in one case murdered) in a highly suspicious fashion, informants were being killed at a steady clip, too. Unlike any other branch of law enforcement, narcotics work depends heavily on informants, and the New York bureau had about two hundred active informants at any time. They ranged from down-and-out street junkies to seemingly respectable businessmen allowed to remain free on parole if they worked off trafficking convictions by providing leads.

John Ingersoll, who took over the agency in 1968, would later testify before Congress:

> Because of arrest quotas and poor controls over the use of informants, informants had too much freedom and too much influence in determining who would be arrested and when. In some cases one could and did wonder who was in charge of the investigation, agents or informants. Informants were not screened by supervisors, there was no provision for supervisors or management to debrief them and evaluate their continuing value to the organization. On the other hand, ironically, there was no particular security over the files that revealed the identities of informants.

Obviously, these largely unsupervised informants posed both an opportunity and a threat to corrupt agents. For instance, an agent who had stolen a kilo of heroin during a raid on a trafficker's apartment always needed someone to sell that for him. He could give it to an informant with impunity, partly in payment for services rendered, with the rest to be sold and the profits divided. But now the informant had damaging evidence that the agent was corrupt. But probably even more dangerous for the informants was the sloppy security in the New York office files. Corrupt agents easily could find out which informants (working with honest agents) were passing along information dangerous to the drug traffickers with whom these rogue agents were collaborating.

For corrupt agents were not just holding on to seized drugs and looting apartments, they were actively engaged in big-time heroin trafficking with certain gangsters. For instance, when agents were closing in on Mauricio Rosal and Etienne Tarditi in the first Ambassador case, a corrupt New York agent was running at full tilt up Lexington Avenue to the stakeout site to warn off Nick Calamaris. The agent, working with Calamaris's underworld boss, arrived too late. When talkative informants threatened partnerships between rogue agents and Mafia traffickers, the quick and easy solution was murder. Over the course of a decade, about forty or fifty informants working with the New York office were murdered. (The investigation was done so long after many of the deaths, it was hard to determine the exact number.) Since the official report from the corruption investigation eventually done in the late sixties (known popularly as the Wurms Report) is still sealed, this incredible slaughter has never been made public officially.

What did come out eventually was that almost sixty of the FBN's three hundred agents nationwide actively were corrupt, many colluding with major traffickers and making major heroin sales personally. Yet this huge corruption scandal finally brought to light by Chief Inspector Andy Tartaglino received almost no public airing. Treasury had little desire to broadcast its failings, and so the full official report remains sealed. (A copy was viewed by the author.) And those few details made public came out in congressional testimony only in 1975. By the standards of daily journalism, it was all ancient history. Consequently, almost nothing was ever written about what remains the worst case of corruption ever to hit a federal law enforcement agency.

No one has ever suggested that Anslinger himself was corrupt. But he clearly was not prepared to confront his agency's poor performance. One can only speculate about why Anslinger did not act as he approached seventy and retirement. Though often absent from Washington in 1960 and 1961 caring for his dying wife, it's unlikely that this was a factor. Anslinger already had a history from the thirties and again in 1952 of doing nothing. Moreover, he was clearly someone who cared more about appearance than effectiveness.

Ramsey Clark, U.S. attorney general when the corruption investigation finally was launched in 1968, said in an interview, "The least you can make of it is that Anslinger was derelict in being so unaware of what was happening in his own agency. Apparently he had decided as a matter of self preservation not to address it."

In the old days, Anslinger scornfully had dismissed his few critics as kooks and cranks, head-in-the-cloud academics. But in 1958, a joint committee of the American Bar Association and American Medical Association on narcotic drugs issued an interim report asserting that Anslinger's punishment-only approach to drug addiction was not working. The report proposed five modest projects ranging from opiate maintenance at one city clinic to looking at using education as a preventive technique. Anslinger, who had refused to participate, angrily denounced the report draft as full of "glaring inaccuracies, manifest inconsistencies, apparent ambiguities, important omissions and even false statements."

Anslinger even sent an agent to the foundation slated to publish the report to suggest they step aside. (As a nonprofit whose tax status was determined by Treasury, they quickly agreed.) Anslinger then cobbled together his *own* opposing U.S. Treasury report, which *Harper's* opined "may well be the crudest publication yet produced by a government agency. The tone ranges from thudding, pretentious irony to upper-case italicized hysteria." These heavyhanded manuevers to undermine critics deeply angered the brand new Kennedy White House. The new administration believed in a more scientific, medical approach. A presidential aide shot off a tart, reproving note to Treasury about Anslinger, advising that "close supervision of [Anslinger's] operation is essential."

For the first time ever, critical articles began to appear in prestigious publications. *The Nation* ran a profile of Anslinger subtitled, "Zeal Without Insight," *The Yale Law Journal* featured, "The Narcotics Bureau and The Harrison Act: Jailing The Healers and The Sick," while *Harper's*, in its article, "The Great Narcotics Muddle," pronounced, "The federal Narcotics Bureau is in trouble. For decades this agency lived high in the bureaucratic fastnesses where FBI men and other Jovian characters dwell. It sighed and Presidents groveled; it uttered and critics gaped; it asked and Congress gave. But all that is ending now." In 1959 Chief Magistrate John M. Murtagh of New York had advocated publicly clinics for addicts, as well as for Anslinger's retirement and replacement with "a distinguished public-health administrator of vision and perception and, above all, heart." Anslinger struck back, crudely calling Murtagh "a gas bag."

The irony was that none of these critics realized that Anslinger was failing to deliver the very thing he said mattered: effective and honest law enforcement. *The Nation*, in an otherwise critical article, noted, "Although many critics deplore Anslinger's attitude toward the addict, few disparage his zealous efforts to wipe out the illegal traffic. One has described him as an honest, hard-working cop. . . . He has carried out the federal narcotics laws as honestly and effectively as possible." The article went on to note that "the bureau has been untainted by any significant scandal in its thirty-year history." In fact, heroin was entering in a steady stream from the French connection and Commissioner Anslinger was not addressing it. He was raising no public alarms, instead insisting that things were under control or even getting better. He did not ask for more agents. Worse yet, he knew he had serious corruption in the all-important New York office and he was not pursuing it.

The consequences of the FBN's failure were real and profound. With each passing year, the heroin plague worsened, poisoning the lives of addicts, their families, and their communities. In New York, heroin had been readily available in Harlem ever since 1950. Now, it was spreading slowly but surely to other boroughs. As more and more young men in urban neighborhoods tried heroin and got hooked, rising crime—especially muggings and burglaries—brought real fear. The story of a long-time clothing merchant near Charlotte Street (in what became known as the South Bronx) is emblematic. In 1960 the merchant, a Mr. Lefkowitz, began to notice heroin addicts (identifiable by the telltale scratching of the nose and eyes) hanging around this old working-class neighborhood. One day a junkie he knew wandered into his small store and Lefkowitz gave him fifty cents "just to get him out of my hair."

Later that night, the clothing store owner got a call at home saying this very same junkie had been caught breaking into his business. "I said, 'Why did you pick on me?' and he said, 'Charlie, I was so hopped up I didn't know what I was doing.' But I prosecuted him, and he threatened, 'When I get out I'm coming back to burn your place up.' Sure enough, when he got out, he came back and started a fire in the window. They called me at three in the morning." As the junkies multiplied, longtime merchants such as Lefkowitz, fearful of growing crime, closed their doors for good. In a neighborhood such as Charlotte Street that had never seen even a mugging from one year to the next, predatory addicts became commonplace. While urban decay has many causes, heroin addicts and pushers were often the final, fatal blow for whole blocks and neighborhoods. The decent working poor who had stoically suffered through substandard housing, filthy streets, and lousy schools often would give up and move when they saw the addicts and the pushers. They posed too much of a risk to their children's futures.

Nor was this grassroots fear exaggerated. When two professors of psychiatry studied a sample population in St. Louis, they were astounded to find 10 percent of the cohort (235 young men in their early thirties selected from elementary school records and then tracked down and interviewed) had become heroin addicts. They reported, in their study "Drug Use in a Normal Population of Young Negro Men," that the young men in question had all "lived in St. Louis between 1959 and 1964 . . . and all had exposure to the same drug market." Moreover, the researchers were amazed to find, "Every man who reported using heroin *more than six times* had been addicted." And once addicted, their lives had begun a precipitous downward spiral.

Even as criticism of Anslinger mounted, he was often not present in Washington. His wife was dying of cancer and he was nursing her at their home in Hollidaysburg, Pennsylvania, until she died in October 1961. As he turned seventy, Anslinger quietly retired, submitting his resignation as commissioner to President Kennedy in July 1962. He retained his appointment as the American representative to the U.N. Narcotic Drug Commission. The Kennedys appointed as the new commissioner Anslinger's choice, a deputy supervisor named Henry Giordano. The appointment was baffling both to critics, who had hoped for a reformer from the outside, and to the old-timers in the Bureau of Narcotics. A pharmacist by training, Giordano was seen as a decent administrator, but not as commissioner material. Moreover, he had no experience at all in the agency's two most important working arenas—New York and overseas.

Anslinger's final years must have been painful. Long used to respect and admiration from the press and public, his ideas, and even his very style—that old newsreel tone of bombast and high dudgeon—were now the subject of growing scorn. For the first time, his expertise was publicly questioned by others than academics, his worldview challenged. He was simply out of touch with a zeitgeist that more and more preferred to see addiction not as a crime, but as a social problem or even a disease.

The new Kennedy administration, despite having reappointed Anslinger and then his chosen successor, obviously viewed him and his agency as a throwback to a less enlightened era. In the fall of 1962 the administration convened a White House conference on narcotics, even though a retired Anslinger dismissed such endeavors as "a waste of time." Moreover, U.S. Attorney General Robert Kennedy's remarks were an open rebuke to Anslinger and his legacy. RFK told the five hundred gathered scientists and law enforcement officials, "This conference can be an historic beginning, for it embodies two important principles which for too long have been missing in this field: Reliable information and sustained cooperation. For all that is said, argued, or believed and written about narcotics, . . . the depressing truth is that we don't know very much about them."

Anslinger never had been much interested in the social causes of drug use, but he well knew when he retired that the typical postwar addict was a young black man living in a northern slum. When questioned about this over the years, he had proffered various explanations. In a 1951 *Reader's Digest* article he said, "Most of the juvenile addicts come from families in which there is no proper parental control or training in decent personal habits." And, in fact, the St. Louis study showed men who grew up without fathers at higher risk of heroin addiction. However, availability was a far more important factor.

Then, in a later speech, Anslinger said, "Perhaps the most important factors contributing to the spread of narcotic drug addiction are (1) association with hoodlums and (2) the availability of narcotics. Association with criminals is responsible for most of the addiction which is found in the police precincts of areas having a high percentage of crime. Low social and economic status is the major contributing cause, particularly broken families and inadequate parental control, and substandard housing." In the spring of 1962, Anslinger appeared on CBS News's *New York Forum*. When asked specifically why there was such a high rate of addiction among young blacks, Anslinger repeated his usual assertion that addiction was an issue "only in Northern cities where there are bad economic and social conditions in certain police precincts." When the interviewer pressed again about why there were so many young black addicts, Anslinger demurred, retreating to the good bureaucrat's standby, saying, "I think a study should be made as to the reason for this large rate of addiction in the negro population."

But what really perplexed him in his waning years was why middle-class white youth—and not just the bohemian rebels—had started experimenting with marijuana, something new called psychedelics, and even heroin.

PART III

The Counterculture 1960–1975

"Turn On, Tune In, Drop Out."
—TIMOTHY LEARY, 1963

CHAPTER 11

"Burning for the Heavenly Connection."

— "Howl," Allen Ginsberg, 1956

On May 21, 1957, San Francisco police sauntered into the City Lights bookstore in North Beach and bought a slender book of poetry entitled *Howl and Other Poems*. Shortly thereafter they returned to arrest the book clerk and charge the absent store owner, poet Lawrence Ferlinghetti, with publishing and selling "obscene and indecent writings." The author, a seemingly nice Jewish Ivy League graduate named Allen Ginsberg, had written a wild hipster anthem brimming with despair and sex and drugs. In what would become one of the most famous (and bestselling) poems of its times, Ginsberg denounced corporate, conformist, atomic America and celebrated the personal quest through drugs, jazz, and sexual freedom (even between men). Ginsberg bemoaned the "best minds of my generation . . . dragging themselves through the negro streets at dawn looking for an angry fix/angelheaded hipsters burning for the heavenly connection to the starry dynamo in the machinery of night."

Across the continent, in New York's longtime enclave of self-conscious bohemia, Greenwich Village, an arty young woman named Diane DiPrima was handed a copy of Ginsberg's controversial poem.

She remembers reading it with "a sweeping sense of exhilaration, of glee: someone was speaking for all of us, and the poem was good. I was high and delighted. . . . I read it aloud to everyone. A new era had begun." Indeed it had. The tiny hipster subculture, replete with drugs as a badge of self-important alienation and experience, was about to begin spreading into the culture at large via a new group of white bohemians known as the Beats.

For DiPrima, *Howl* immediately joined Mezz Mezzrow's 1946 auto-biography, *Really the Blues*, as a critical anti-Establishment screed. Mezzrow, with his detailed (and sometimes hilarious) descriptions of black hipster life, had been an important how-to book, said DiPrima, filling "our heads with a way of talking and a way of being. . . . As far as we knew, there were only a handful of us—perhaps forty or fifty in the city—who knew what we knew; who raced about in Levi's and workshirts, smoked dope, dug the new jazz, and spoke in a bastardiza-tion of the black argot. We surmised that there might be another fifty living in San Francisco and perhaps a hundred more scattered through-out the country." All of this, as DiPrima proudly explains, was still highly subterranean, little known in the dull mainstream world. And, as is also made clear, she and her coterie were hip long before anyone else, already preoccupied with maintaining a sense of superior know-ingness toward the world of squares.

However ardent the young Beats, few of the nation's cultural tastemak-ers paid them much mind at first. American families were too busy ful-filling the American Dream—buying a suburban house, raising children, working hard at getting ahead, and enjoying such new pleasures as big cars, grassy backyards, barbeques, and washer-dryers. Amid this unprece-dented prosperity, the Cold War got colder and the atom bomb became a national leitmotiv even as the record number of births testified to a firm belief in the future. Commentators of the time—even in the most all-American and bullish publications—frequently ruminated that this long-sought, long-awaited peace, prosperity, and mass-market abun-dance seemed to entail a disturbing degree of social conformity, not to mention the dross of mass-produced culture. Writes historian Warren Sus-man, "In the very hour of achievement, of triumph over fascism and total-itarian government, doubts began to arise. . . . [P]eople in the period from 1945 onward actually talked about living in an 'age of anxiety.' " Soci-ologist William H. Whyte articulated these concerns and had a bestseller in his 1956 classic *The Organization Man*.

Ginsberg had stirred up a tiny storm with *Howl*, but it was Jack Ker-ouac's *On the Road* that irretrievably launched the growing white hip-ster subculture out into the mainstream, shocking the elders and captivating youth. Published in September 1957, six years after it was first submitted, *On the Road* depicted the ever-restless cross-country wanderings of these new beings, the Beats. Writer Joyce Johnson, then twenty-one, recalls feeling that all over America young people like her "were waiting for a prophet to liberate them from the cautious middle-class lives they had been reared to inherit. *On the Road* would bring them the voice of a supreme outlaw validated by his art, visions of a life lived at dizzying speed beyond all safety barriers, pure exhilarating energy."

Kerouac aspired to describe the other, hipper, better world he believed he heard in bebop and black America. Wistfully he wrote of walking through Denver's "colored section, wishing I were a Negro, feeling that the best the white world had offered was not enough ecstasy for me, not enough life, joy, kicks, darkness, music, not enough night." By the time *On the Road* was published, Kerouac was a rather sad and frequently inebriated thirty-five, a man who yearned for new places and new travels, only to be disappointed always by the reality.

Just months before the hugely popular *On the Road* came out, novelist and self-appointed Angry Young Man Norman Mailer took it upon himself to articulate Hip for other intellectuals in the pages of *Dissent*. Mailer solemnly argued in a piece entitled, "The White Negro" that real life was to be found via jazz clubs, liberated sex, all-night sprees, coffeehouses, and other havens from square America. "One is Hip or one is Square (the alternative which each new generation coming into American life is beginning to feel), one is a rebel or one conforms, one is a frontiersman in the Wild West of American night, or else a Square cell, trapped in the totalitarian tissues of American society, doomed willy-nilly to conform if one is to succeed." White hipsters naturally would seek out black hipsters for their authentic company and wisdom, and the true white hipster, pontificated Mailer, had to become a "white Negro."

Many intellectuals were skeptical. Sociologist Ned Polsky declared the current hipster bohemia "greatly inferior to its predecessors of at least the last four decades. . . . Most hipsters scarcely read at all. . . . [And the hipster worship of blacks had its own obvious pitfall.] The white Negro accepts the real Negro not as a human being in his totality, but as the bringer of a highly specified and restricted 'cultural dowry,' to use Mailer's phrase. In so doing he creates an inverted form of keeping the nigger in his place."

Certainly black writer James Baldwin was infuriated that Mailer was retailing what Baldwin described as "so antique a vision of the blacks." And he was just as disgusted with Kerouac's romantic maunderings on race, which he dismissed as "offensive nonsense." Wrote Baldwin, "I would hate to be in Kerouac's shoes if he should ever be mad enough to read this aloud from the stage of Harlem's Apollo Theatre."

Many years later Ginsberg would dismiss "The White Negro" as square and dated. Ginsberg asserted that by then everything "going on with the Beat thing had to do with American tenderheartedness," though it would have been very hard for any outsider to have discerned that. The extraordinary number of personal calamities among the early Beats—three killings, numerous suicides, divorces, abortions, jail terms, and institutional commitments—had apparently convinced Ginsberg that "the whole notion of being smarter, more psychotic, beating the world at its own game was no longer of interest."

The utterly unlikely avatars of this new era of deliberate outsiders— the Beats—had all first met at Columbia College in New York City in the last months of World War II. Most important (and personally most influential over the long haul) would be poet-seeker Allen Ginsberg. Ginsberg was a bright, mixed-up English major from New Jersey who hoped to become a labor lawyer. Ginsberg's father was a minor poet, high school teacher, and old-style Jewish leftist, his mother a committed communist and frequent inmate of mental institutions. The young Allen, coming to terms with his homosexuality, displayed a positive talent for getting into scrapes. But his earnest charm always saved him. Finally suspended from college (in those far more innocent times) for writing "Fuck the Jews" on a window, Ginsberg retreated to the off-campus apartment of a married Barnard student named Joan Adams. There he spent a great deal of time discussing books and writing with another disenchanted Columbia dropout, the boyishly handsome athletic hero Jack Kerouac.

Before long, an older Harvard grad named William Burroughs joined their small scene. Tall, cadaverous, fiercely intellectual, Burroughs had gotten himself ejected from the wartime army "on my nut-house record" before wandering through a variety of jobs. Extremely well read, he quickly earned their intense admiration. The grandson of the inventor of the adding machine, Burroughs had a small trust fund of $150 a month and, like many a well-off young man before him, enjoyed slumming.

When Burroughs finally managed to meet some real New York criminals—men who pulled payroll heists—he found them enthralling. He happily bought a stolen tommy gun and sixteen morphine ampules, and then arranged to sell the goods. His contact was Herbert Huncke, petty thief and junkie, then occupying a Henry Street railroad apartment decked out like a fancy opium den. Burroughs liked both the morphine and Huncke, a Times Square hustler the police had dubbed The Creep. After a bit, Burroughs introduced his Times Square curiosity, Huncke, to the Columbia boys. Huncke became "a crucial figure, a sort of Virgilian guide to the lower depths, taking them into another world." Of course, Huncke was the first junkie-hipster the college boys had met. Huncke had no illusions about his role as tour guide to middle-class intellectuals. "I felt as though at best they were patronizing toward me."

Kerouac had first heard the term "beat" from Huncke, who used the word to mean down and out. Beat then mingled in Kerouac's mind with the word beatific, but all that was lost instantly once Beat entered the mainstream. Beat thus became, said a later chronicle of the Beats, a rebellion against the conditions "which fatigued the ordinary citizen's soul, . . . all the ways in which mass society and corporate employment had inhibited one's energy and appetite for experience."

The Columbia boys' nocturnal explorations began just as bebop burst on the New York jazz scene, propelling Charlie Parker to Supreme Hipster. The effect on Kerouac, a child of French-Canadian factory workers from Lowell, Massachusetts, was profound. He had been searching for something outside the academy and its literary traditions, something earthier. He quickly came to identify "more with musical geniuses like Bud Powell, Charlie Parker, Billie Holiday, Lester Young, Gerry Mulligan and Thelonious Monk than he did with any established literary scene," writes biographer Ann Charters. "[He began to experiment with a] method of spontaneous composition [that] was meant to do the same thing with words that he heard bop musicians doing with their instruments." But above all others towered Charlie Parker, and Kerouac now "consciously modeled his writing after Parker's magnificent music. . . . [He] felt myriad connections of subject, style, and approach and tried to reflect that aural perfection in his own prose."

Writer Albert Goldman remembered years later how amazed he was when he moved to Brooklyn in 1950 from Chicago to find the "hip" kids smoking something called marijuana, part and parcel of a general fascination with black jazz life. Wrote Goldman, "They called [marijuana] 'tea,' 'boo,' 'grass' and 'pot,' but the preferred word was 'shit.' That the word for heroin in the black ghetto had been appropriated by the sons and daughters of Jewish storekeepers and garment-center workers for the milder drug is suggestive of the passion with which these young men and women admired the black culture of jazz."

As the black bebop/hipster culture was discovered and appropriated by middle-class whites, they added their own cultural layers—first off was prose and poetry composed in what they viewed as a whole new literary form, "bop prosody." Dubbed "write as you breathe," it meant (in theory) never rewriting after the initial rush of creation. Using illicit drugs remained, of course, a basic part of the hipster subculture, and the Columbia crowd was soon dabbling in marijuana and various pills, including Benzedrine. The young Allen in this period systematically catalogued in his journal "the various drugs he found interesting (including morphine, opium, marijuana, cocaine, codeine, and Benzedrine), along with detailed notes about the differing effects of the drugs." Kerouac would recall this as a "year of evil decadence." For the first time since the English Romantic poets and such French literary figures as Genet and Céline, aspiring writers deliberately were experimenting with drugs to alter and heighten consciousness and, thereby, presumably, their artistic creations.

Burroughs, however, evinced little interest in the actual bebop-hipster scene, even though it was he who produced the entrée via Huncke. He was far more attracted to criminals than jazz. His own experience was more that of the marginal males who appeared after the 1914 Harrison Act. When he tried drugs, Burroughs skipped that hipster perennial, marijuana, instead plunging right in with opiates. Years later, he would write, "I tried it [morphine, then heroin] as a matter of curiosity. I drifted along taking shots when I could score. I ended up hooked." His biographer, Ted Morgan, rejects this explanation, believing Burroughs deliberately took up heroin, a move designed to give him entrée into the criminal-junkie-outcast class that fascinated him. "Using junk made him part of the group, it was sort of a rite of passage."

Once mainlining heroin, Burroughs found his $150-a-month trust fund no longer sufficed. He rolled subway drunks before experimenting with pushing. Soon, authorities descended to arrest Burroughs for writing false narcotics prescriptions and Huncke for hot goods. Huncke the Creep went to jail, while Burroughs's respectable family got him off. Though he was an acknowledged misogynist and homosexual, Burroughs then married Joan Adams and retreated to rural Texas with Joan's child to farm and cool out.

With Burroughs and Huncke gone, Ginsberg and Kerouac took up with another wild man of the streets. In early 1947, Neal Cassady, twenty, had blown into New York from Denver, a supremely charming, athletic human dynamo, son of a skid-row bum, veteran of ten arrests for stealing cars. "He fit right into their cast of characters, as a creature of appetite and instinct who hungered after experience and was ready to try anything. Neal was a perpetual motion machine, investing every moment with his own brand of manic intensity." Kerouac and Cassady soon departed on a maniacal cross-country jaunt.

Left on his own, Ginsberg took an apartment in East Harlem, where in 1948 he had the defining experience of his life: While reading Blake, he was suffused by an extraordinary vision of almost being swallowed by God. His father, his professors, his former analyst, and many of his friends feared he might be going mad like his mother. But Ginsberg would say later that he was convinced he had been given a mission: "I thought for many years that my obligation was to annihilate my ordinary consciousness and expand my mystic consciousness." The early means to that expansion would be drugs.

But even in the midst of such transcendental events, Ginsberg had a practical side that led him to take the prosaic job of nighttime copy boy at the Associated Press. Meanwhile, Huncke was out of jail and stashing hot goods at Ginsberg's. Again, the police descended, and the Columbia professors rallied to save their former student from the "clank of iron." This time they persuaded authorities Ginsberg was crazy and to prove it helped have him committed to the Columbia Presbyterian Psychiatric Institute.

When Ginsberg emerged seven months later, Burroughs and his family had fled to Mexico to avoid drug charges brought in Texas. Although he was now a married man with two children, Burroughs espoused as his life philosophy what he called "factualism," or "The only possible ethic is to do what one wants to do." In Mexican exile, Burroughs's intellectual fascination for the outcast and criminal and Joan's self-destructive bent took a fatal turn. After a long afternoon of drinking, she perched a glass on her head, Burroughs aimed at it with a loaded gun, and shot and killed her. Joan Burroughs thus became one of the earliest casualties among the middle-class whites experimenting with the alternative hipster subculture. A philosophy that enshrined the Kick and the Self above all else exacted its own price.

Burroughs, devoted to doing what he wanted to do, fled Mexico, dispatched his young motherless children to be raised by their grandparents, and completed the autobiographical *Junky*. One of the first American contributions to the addict-confessional genre since the turn of the century, *Junky* was the straightforward story of a young man who takes up opiates and his adventures in the subterranean world of junkies. It described the endless "making" of doctors for narcotics, the inevitable pilgrimmage to Lexington for the "cure," and "Lee's" arrest in New Orleans just as the nation becomes convinced its teenagers are all in danger of becoming addicts. In this unfriendly atmosphere, he says, "I saw my chance of escaping conviction dwindle daily as the anti-junk feeling mounted to a paranoid obsession, like anti-Semitism under the Nazis. So I decided to jump bail and live permanently outside the United States."

Junky's subtitle, *Confessions of an Unredeemed Drug Addict*, made clear Burroughs's hope that he was a worthy claimant to the De Quincey mantle, but his modern tale possessed none of the elegance of the original. This was a matter-of-fact description of the junkie's world: the sly, thieving addicts as well as the corrupt doctors, cops, and stool pigeons. Ginsberg convinced an editor friend to publish the book, but the editor offset Burroughs's enthusiasm for opiates by combining the book into a paperback volume with a reissue of Maurice Helbrant's 1941 autobiography, *Narcotic Agent*. Understandably ignored by critics when published as a lurid pulp paperback in 1953, *Junky/Narcotic Agent* had the very respectable first-year sale of 113,170 copies.

America alternately was fascinated, amused, and appalled by the Beats. San Francisco columnist Herb Caen quickly coined the term Beatnik, inspired by Sputnik and hinting at a silly, alien way-outness. Suddenly any so-inclined youth could don a black turtleneck, shades, and head off to Beatnik nights sprouting up at local clubs and featuring cool jazz (bebop had been superseded by an even cooler style), free-style poetry, and maybe even bongo drums. Comic strips, television shows, and movies all began featuring Beatniks.

Allen Ginsberg, his earnest charm as potent as ever, proved a genius at self-promotion and what would later be called "networking." The young Joyce Johnson watched admiringly as, "Like a guerrilla general, Allen ambushed the world of the established literati—presenting himself to be interviewed at the *New York Times*, *Time*, *Life*, and the *Village Voice*; turning up at publishing houses and cocktail parties to convert agents, editors, critics into supporters of his revolution. He exhorted, charmed, raged, stripping himself naked on occasion to prove his point, as he'd done at a reading in Los Angeles in response to a heckler."

But many literati were put off by the Beats. Writer Dan Wakefield recalls of *Howl*, "My own antipathy to the poem . . . began with the very first line, where the poet states he has seen the very best minds of his generation destroyed by madness. Another blow to our much-maligned generation! First we were 'silent,' and now we were not only 'beat' but crazy!" One of Wakefield's novelist pals noted "tongue in cheek that one of the best minds of *his* generation (the same as Ginsberg's) was a scientist friend who had not gone mad at all but was working in Toledo, Ohio."

For Norman Podhoretz, "there is a suppressed cry in those [Beat] books: Kill the intellectuals who can talk coherently, kill the people who can sit still for five minutes at a time, kill those incomprehensible characters who are capable of getting seriously involved with a woman, a job, a cause." The young Truman Capote found their work boring and observed on one of the new TV talk shows that it wasn't "writing at all—it's *typing.*"

Amid all this highbrow disputation, "culture and demography began to intersect," Russell Jacoby writes in *The Last Intellectuals.* "As the beats and would-be beats took to the road they stumbled on new youth centers, college campuses crammed with the baby boom generation. Almost by virtue of numbers, youth on these campuses formed a critical mass, a unique social formation." The once invisible subculture of black hipsters now was spreading everywhere via the white Beats.

One of the great ironies as hip entered the larger world was that some of hip's major values—especially hedonism and instant gratification—happened to dovetail neatly with emerging mainstream corporate advertising culture, which used just such messages to promote the burgeoning consumer culture. Capitalism remained brilliant at coopting and exploiting such situations.

In 1959, Lawrence Lipton's exegesis of Beat life, *The Holy Barbarians,* turned into one of the summer's bestsellers. Unlike *On the Road,* a novel that celebrated the wanderings of various young men, the nonfiction *Barbarians* laid out the nature of daily Beat life, the philosophy of hip cats and chicks rejecting what that old bohemian Henry Miller had called the "air-conditioned nightmare" of materialistic America. "It is important to make a living," intoned Lipton from the Beat settlement of Venice, California, "but it is even more important to make a life."

Unlike the Columbia Beats, who seemed to have little interest in the historical antecedents of their lifestyle rebellion, Lipton did, in part because he was old enough—sixty-one—to have been a rebel in the Jazz Age of the twenties. What these rebels wanted from the usual target of revolutions—the upper classes—were "the only things they had which we felt had any value for us: their leisure, their access to the arts—to music, literature, painting—their privilege of defying convention if they wanted to, of enjoying their vices and sinning with impunity." Even back in the twenties, the American rebels were perplexed by Russian revolutionaries obsessed with power and production and material goods. It all seemed pointless. Wrote Lipton, "We were expropriating the things of inner gratification and lasting value, *and we were* doing it without overthrowing the rich." Lipton saw the twenties bohemians and now the Beats as engaged in the continuing and desirable "democratization of amorality."

The apolitical quest for a freer way of life certainly connected the twenties bohemians and the fifties Beats, but the black hipster antecedents of the Beats accounted for the more populist and intellectual nature of the later group. It also accounted for the Beats' deep involvement in illegal drugs, an interest largely absent from the American bohemia of the twenties. Lipton was forthright about their importance for Beats: "Everything the shamans of jazz do is legendary material for the beat: the gargantuan [drug] user, the cat who kicked it, the martyr-hero who died of it. Dead, he becomes, like Charley Bird Parker, a cult hero on the order of James Dean and Dylan Thomas"

Life, the most flag-waving of the big American magazines, soon weighed in on the Beats, leaving no doubt that the white hipster subculture had penetrated the heartland. *Life* was repelled to find their very manner of speaking was "mostly stolen from jazz musicians, narcotic addicts and prostitutes." Somehow "these dirty people in sandals," who gleefully rejected clean living, work, conventional marriage, and sobriety, had garnered "wide public attention" and "astonishing influence." Such leading Beats as Ginsberg had by now, one sensed, thoroughly honed their bad boy personas. An infamous-and-much-in-demand poet who was openly homosexual, Ginsberg told *Life*, "I have seen God. I saw him in a room in Harlem." He liked to imply that he was a heroin addict, though he was not, and to complain vehemently that all drugs—marijuana, heroin, morphine, cocaine—should be legalized.

Like Lipton, Ginsberg made quite clear that illegal drugs were still an integral part of the hip life—something that sociologist Ned Polsky confirmed after spending the summer of 1960 in the Village studying Beats. He concluded, "Few outsiders realize that it [drug-taking] is a totally pervasive part of beat life, both as an activity and as a topic of conversation. The illegal use of drugs is one of the handful of things that characterizes all male beats with very rare exceptions." Polsky estimated that about one in twelve Beats had become heroin addicts. The rest mainly smoked marijuana and complained to Polsky that local supplies of pot were diminishing because marijuana smoking was "spreading rapidly in the worlds of advertising, radio-TV, college students—the *Playboy* readership, essentially—and that some suppliers formerly in the Village have shifted to the favorite hangouts of these groups because they pay more."

With illegal drugs playing so prominent a role in the ever-growing Beat world, there was naturally great interest in Burroughs. By his own admission, he recently had hit bottom. Holed up in Tangier, he wrote that he "had not taken a bath in a year nor changed my clothes or removed them except to stick a needle every hour in the fibrous grey wooden flesh of terminal addiction. . . . [B]oxes and garbage piled to the ceiling. Light and water long since turned off for non-payment. I did absolutely nothing. I could look at the end of my shoe for eight hours. I was only roused to action when the hourglass of junk ran out."

Somehow he pulled himself together to publish *Naked Lunch* in Europe. In the book's repulsive, wildly surrealistic world, all was driven by addiction. Here macabre doctors, cops, a wide assortment of lowlifes, even cars and kitchen mix-masters all whirled through time and place and bizarre sexual escapades to illustrate the "Algebra of Need," Burroughs's theory that heroin addiction was a metaphor for all other addictions, whether crossword puzzles or material goods or money. "Junk," he explained "is the ideal product, . . . the ultimate merchandise. No sales talk necessary. The client will crawl through a sewer and beg to buy."

Once *Life* had heaped scorn on the Beats in all their manifestations, it also was forced to concede that the grubby Beats expressed something important in "questioning the values of contemporary society, in feeling spiritually stifled by present-day materialism, and in growing restive at the conformity which seems to be the price of security."

As the fifties ended, Allen Ginsberg began to develop grandiose visions of a whole new spiritual movement, drawing heavily upon a watered-down Zen and aimed ultimately at an altered consciousness. Ever since his catalytic encounter with God in Harlem, Ginsberg had been searching to recapture that spiritual intensity. To expand his "mystic consciousness," writes Ginsberg's biographer, Barry Miles, Ginsberg had since 1948 steadily pursued "a series of experiments. . . . He took every powerful hallucinogen he could find, from laughing gas to mescaline; he sniffed ether and shot heroin. He disappeared into the upper reaches of the Amazon to take ayahuasca with the Indian witch doctors and smoked hashish all night with naked sadhus on the burning grounds on the bank of the Ganges."

And so, slowly but surely the white Beats enlarged the repertoire of hip drugs and the "meaning" of using them. They believed that drugs had a major and significant role to play in opening closed minds to higher experience and religiosity. Thus, the Beats began pushing illegal drugs beyond their longtime role as part and parcel of the socially marginal life, trying to imbue them with new meaning as spiritual aids. The Zen lunatic so admired by the Beats was one who pursued a "deliberate derangement of all the senses in order to open oneself to the larger reality to which convention is blind. One plays the fool for God." Drugs were presented as not just helpful, but integral to the quest.

Looking back, one has to wonder why exactly had the very society that the Beats so despised given them so much attention—bestowing fame, fortune, and influence? Certainly, the vast majority of American families by the late fifties believed themselves to be living the good life—finally well housed, well clothed, well fed in a rich and powerful country that was at peace. Jazz musician David Amram remembers older artists "always reminded us how lucky we were to be around in the fifties—not selling apples, like in the Depression, or making money painting apartments or selling sketches for a dollar." Yet there hovered a sense of unease. Was the mass culture of consumer capitalism exacting too high a price in conformity? Had affluence itself rendered its beneficiaries uncertain of what to do with all this new money and time? The Beats became the most visible and vocal challenge to the established order, for they not only spurned monogamy and marriage (like the ever more popular *Playboy*), but a socially acceptable job.

America was entering an era of unprecedented prosperity when growing numbers of young middle-class whites would rebel against the traditional values and expectations of American society, a time when a great many young people *elected* to become socially marginal, rejecting established ties and values as they sought to refashion society. The earlier drug users—the traditional post–Harrison Act white male opiate addicts and the black hipsters—truly were socially marginal, generally rootless men with few commitments to family or community and few future prospects.

The new white middle-class drug users *chose* to become outsiders and hipsters. And by this time, an almost inevitable part of that stance was using illegal drugs. The coming of age of a huge middle-class generation that would choose (however briefly) to be deliberate outsiders meant the creation of a vast new pool of potential drug users who had little knowledge in this arena. It had been a great many years since most middle-class Americans had had any dealings with habit-forming or mind-altering drugs, and therefore they lacked the "learned experience" of earlier generations. That the dangers of such drugs generally far outweighed their pleasures was largely forgotten.

By 1959, the police drug raid on Beatnik enclaves had become a staple of big-city newspaper coverage. As the *New York Herald Tribune* reported in November of that year, "Five narcotics detectives, posing for a month as Greenwich Village beatniks with beards, berets, bop odes, and bongo drums, took part yesterday in a roundup of nearly 100 alleged dope pushers and users." In Washington, D.C., late-night police raids of the Coffee n' Confusion Club and the Java Jungle led to twelve drug arrests. The new-style drug culture had made its public debut.

CHAPTER 12

"One Pill Makes

You Larger."

— "White Rabbit,"
Jefferson Airplane song, 1968

One November day in 1960, Allen Ginsberg—still seeking to replicate his encounter with God in Harlem—took the train to Boston and met Harvard clinical psychologist Timothy Leary, then living in Newton Center in a rented "three-story mansion on a hill with trees, lawns, a four-car garage, a garden gazebo, and 185 stone steps up to the front door. It was luxuriously furnished: wood paneling, thick rugs, plush sofas, Moroccan metalwork lamps. There was a wide staircase winding up from the entrance hall."

Through the grapevine, Ginsberg had heard Leary was in Cambridge studying the hallucinogen psilocybin. Leary's crew cut, academic appearance belied his tumultuous past, which included abandonment by an alcoholic father and a difficult adolescence that culminated in being driven out of West Point over a drinking incident (but not before surviving a long campaign of "silent treatment") and expulsion from the University of Alabama after getting caught in the girls' dormitory. But ultimately the handsome and charismatic Leary had settled down, earned his Ph.D. in clinical psychology from the University of California at Berkeley, married, fathered two children, and become a well-respected expert in personality assessment and behavior change.

Then, on Leary's thirty-fifth birthday, his wife had committed suicide. Several months later Leary, hair gone gray, resigned his prestigious job as research director at Oakland's Kaiser Hospital and took off to Europe with his son and daughter, six and eight, and mounds of research notes that were to be used in writing a book. Instead, he drifted, landing in Florence in the spring of 1958. There he ran into an old friend, Professor David McClelland, who suggested Leary take a position at Harvard and come home to the States. Leary did just that and was a big success at Cambridge, impressing students and fellow faculty at the Center for Personality Research with his intelligence and charm.

In the summer of 1960, while vacationing in Mexico, the forty-year-old Leary, feeling weary and depressed despite his apparent accomplishments, sampled "magic" psilocybin mushrooms at the behest of a friend. Overwhelmed by the ensuing visionary experience, he felt transformed, and began telling anyone who would listen "how he devolved back through millions of years until he became a single solitary cell." In one of several autobiographies, Leary remembers wanting to tell the world, "Listen! Wake up! You are God! You have the divine plan engraved in cellular script within you. Listen! Take this sacrament! You'll see! You'll get the revelations! It will change your life! You'll be reborn!"

Professor Leary returned to Harvard convinced that he had found an extraordinary healing tool, an instant means for deep insight, a new method for breaking through internal barriers that would lead to personal awareness and positive personal change. As Jay Stevens relates in his history of psychedelics, *Storming Heaven: LSD and the American Dream*, Leary the clinical psychologist would argue that "it's an axiom of psychology that true insight would lead to true change; why not test that proposition?" Leary drew up an ambitious research program, obtained a special research supply of psilocybin (the psychoactive ingredient of the Mexican mushrooms) from the Sandoz pharmaceutical company, and began charting his and others' expeditions to what he was soon calling The Other World.

By the time Ginsberg, his lover Peter Orlovsky in tow, came to suburban Newton to meet this well-respected Harvard expert, Leary ostensibly was researching whether patients using hallucinogenic psilocybin made easier breakthroughs to personal awareness and positive change. (Leary was, after all, the admired author of *The Prediction of Interpersonal Behavior in Group Psychotherapy* [1955] and *Interpersonal Diagnosis of Personality; a Functional Theory and Methodology for Personality Evaluation* [1957].) The professor and the poet hit it off immediately and began regaling one another with tales of altered consciousness. Ginsberg, his short black hair tousled, his signature heavy black frame glasses sporting a crack, sat chain-smoking and drinking tea, describing his fantastic psychedelic, spiritual experiences with Indian healers deep in the Peruvian jungle, while Leary described his own visionary ideas of changing the world through drugs.

Leary already had discussed his hopes and dreams with the grand old man of psychedelics, Aldous Huxley, visiting professor that fall at neighboring M.I.T. and author of two thoughtful and enthusiastic essays—"The Doors of Perception" (1954) and "Heaven and Hell" (1956)—about his own experiments with the hallucinogen mescaline (a synthetic drug derived from the peyote mushroom). It so happened that the immensely erudite Aldous Huxley, best known as the chronicler of Britain's Bright Set and author of *Brave New World*, had had a delightful experience taking psilocybin with Leary. The two lounged before a cozy fire at Leary's house and discussed how the drug conferred an overwhelming sense of enlightenment. Huxley, so tall, thin, and naturally elegant that he often was likened to a stork or an egret, was charmed with Leary's persona and credentials, and before long was convinced that this was the man to prepare the world for "psychedelics," substances which both men passionately believed were potential agents of historic evolutionary change.

Huxley, however, strongly cautioned Leary to focus initially only on the elites. "The artistic elite, the intellectual elite, the economic elite. 'That's how everything of culture and beauty and philosophic freedom has been passed on,' " Huxley advised. The gist of his plan as described in *Storming Heaven* was: "Use Harvard's prestige to artfully spread the word about these mind-changers. But do it shrewdly and cautiously, always staying within the medical model. . . . [Leary was exhilarated] to think one might be playing a crucial role in the evolution of the species."

When Allen Ginsberg descended on the fledgling Harvard psilocybin project that winter, he quickly grasped the magnitude of Leary's vision, and he was committed instantly. After an afternoon of getting to know Leary, Ginsberg then settled into an upstairs bedroom and took the small pink psilocybin pills. At first, he felt nauseous, but as the drug took hold, Ginsberg removed his clothes and wandered forth naked. At this, Leary's embarrassed teenage daughter fled to the third floor. Ginsberg then proceeded downstairs, where he announced, "I'm the Messiah. I've come down to preach love to the world. We're going to walk through the streets and teach people to stop hating." Dissuaded from that, Ginsberg instead telephoned Kerouac at his mother's house and raved at him about this new drug. There ensued pronouncements about calling Kennedy and Khrushchev and Burroughs and Mailer and arranging world peace. Leary thought it all amusing and wonderful.

"It seemed to us," said Leary, "that wars, class conflicts, racial tensions, economic exploitation, religious strife, ignorance, and prejudice were all caused by narrow social conditioning. Political problems were manifestations of psychological problems, which at bottom seemed to be neurological-hormonal-chemical. If we could help people plug into empathy circuits of the brain, then positive social change could occur." The psychedelic revolution would change people intrinsically and thereby the world.

Ginsberg, catapulted to prominence in the few short years since *Howl*, would prove to be an extraordinarily important convert. From that moment on, he devoted much prodigious energy and ambition to the cause of psychedelics. Ginsberg began by providing Leary entrée to the influential Beats, and from there made introductions to a high-powered crowd of New York artists, musicians, and Beautiful People. In January 1961, Ginsberg was writing Leary, "I spoke to Willem de Kooning yesterday, and he was ready to swing, too, so please drop him an invitation. I figure [Franz] Kline, de Kooning, and [Dizzy] Gillespie are the most impressive trio imaginable for you to turn on at the moment, so will leave it at that for a while, til they can be taken care of."

However, as Ginsberg's biographer Michael Schumacher writes in *Dharma Lion*, "the effects of psilocybin were not quite as universal as Allen had hoped they would be. [Jazz musician Thelonious] Monk was unimpressed, asking Allen if he had anything stronger. Publisher Barney Rosset had a bad, anxiety-ridden trip," while Kerouac remarked that "walking on water wasn't made in a day."

Enthralled with the prospect of all these new connections, Leary began commuting down to New York on weekends, pills at the ready. Writer Dan Wakefield describes his first Leary encounter at Ginsberg's East Village pad. There to interview Ginsberg on an article about marijuana, Wakefield soon was buttonholed by Leary. When Ginsberg stepped out to go grocery shopping, Wakefield and Leary tagged along, and all three stopped for beers at a corner bar. There, recalls Wakefield,

> Leary regaled me with stories of the wonders of psilocybin. . . .
> It was a wonderful stimulant to creativity, he said, which was
> why he was so excited about trying it out on some of the poets
> and writers gathered at Ginsberg's that day. He was going to
> give them pencils and paper and see what they wrote after tak-
> ing the drug—that's what I gathered was the essence of his
> "scientific experiment."

With his crew cut and bubbly manner, Leary seemed more like an overeager salesman than an experimenter seeking data. . . . Leary sounded like a pitchman for a cure-all elixir as he told me this drug not only stimulated creativity, it made people feel so good they lost their old hostility.

Wakefield was curious about this last claim, because when he arrived at Ginsberg's pad, he had deliberately avoided the famous Jack Kerouac, who appeared angry and sullen. After Kerouac took the small pink pills, Wakefield waited a while and then approached. Kerouac threatened to toss Wakefield, whose writing he didn't like, out the window. When Leary pressed paper and pencil upon Kerouac for the creativity session, Kerouac contemptuously drew a grid and returned it. Later, he would write that psilocybin "stupefies the mind and hand for weeks on end." Worse yet, he told some friends that he "believed the psilocybin had had a more permanent damaging effect, that after taking it he 'hadn't been right since.' " Kerouac returned to his mother and Lowell to drink himself slowly to an early death in 1969 at age forty-seven.

Neal Cassady, still a great monologuist and enthusiast for anything coming down the pike, appeared in the East to try this new hallucinogen and eagerly talked it up. Eventually even Burroughs, cadaverous, mordant, never removing his beloved fedora, brought his dour presence to the rah-rah Newton scene. Burroughs, however, found nothing to like in psilocybin. And since his own obsession with drugs had abated somewhat, he displayed little patience with Leary's grand but inchoate agenda. After a month, Burroughs departed amid considerable acrimony. From New York drifted back Burroughs's sarcastic parody of Leary: "Listen to us. We are serving the garden of delights immortality cosmic consciousness the best ever in drug kicks. And love love love in slop buckets." Undaunted, Ginsberg and Leary pressed on, continuing to ply the famous and accomplished with Leary's wares.

But an equally important aspect of this partnership was Ginsberg convincing Leary to alter his strategy. Leary would recall years later, "Allen, the quintessential egalitarian, wanted everyone to have the option of taking mind-expanding drugs. . . . It was at this moment that we rejected Huxley's elitist perspective and adopted the American open-to-the-public approach." As Leary personally took more and more trips to The Other World, he developed an increasingly ambitious agenda, in his own mind nothing less than a new Great Awakening that would sweep the nation: "Leary wanted to spread the word of mind expansion, which he saw as a tool for 'cracking the psychotic crust' that covered America. The Tree of Knowledge, he thought, had been the first controlled substance, which Adam and Eve had been expelled from paradise for using. The Bible had enforced food and drug prohibitions."

But even as word spread of Leary and his researches into the effects of psilocybin (which included a formal investigation of whether the drug would help rehabilitate local convicts), other Harvard clinical psychology faculty were becoming uneasy. They felt Leary was too personally involved in this powerful drug (by March 1961 he had taken the drug fifty-two times). Moreover, his original inquiries into how psilocybin could help people work through their psychological problems seemed to be taking a backseat to a different, heavily spiritual agenda, an instant drug-induced enlightenment. In this atmosphere of growing concern, an Englishman named Michael Hollingshead appeared in Leary's life in suburban Newton with ten thousand doses of something called lysergic acid diethylamide-25. Hollingshead, a balding fellow in his mid thirties, had telephoned Aldous Huxley from New York City wondering how to proceed with this potent psychedelic, and Huxley, unaware of Leary's new common-man direction, had recommended the Harvard professor as his best contact.

Trade-named Delysid, LSD-25 first had been offered in 1947 to selected researchers interested in matters psychological and psychiatric by the Swiss pharmaceutical firm Sandoz. LSD-25 itself was the synthesized active ingredient of the rye fungus ergot, which had driven whole villages mad during the Middle Ages. It had been discovered accidentally in 1943 by Albert Hofmann, research director of Sandoz, the same company that already was supplying Leary with psilocybin. Hofmann had discovered LSD when he accidentally swallowed some and went home feeling dizzy. "I experienced fantastic images of an extraordinary plasticity. They were associated with an intense kaleidoscopic play of colors. After about two hours this condition disappeared." Hofmann realized this was an extraordinary compound.

He described his second experimentation with the drug this way:

> vertigo, visual disturbances, the faces of those around me appeared as grotesque, colored masks; marked motoric unrest, alternating with paralysis; an intermittent feeling in the head, limbs, and the entire body, as if they were filled with lead; dry, constricted sensation in the throat; feeling of choking; clear recognition of my condition, in which state I sometimes observed, in the manner of an independent, neutral observer, that I shouted half insanely or babbled incoherent words. Occasionally I felt as if I were out of my body.

Uncertain what therapeutic value this new drug might have, Sandoz made it available on an "investigative" basis, suggesting that LSD, or Delysid, could help either patients affected by anxiety and obsession or psychiatrists seeking "insight into the world of ideas and sensations of mental patients." Not only were a small number of English, Canadian, and American psychiatrists fascinated with the potential of LSD, so was the CIA and the military. Official American pursuit of a "truth drug" or "mind control drug" dated back to 1942 and the creation of America's first intelligence service, the OSS. Wild Bill Donovan had inaugurated a top-secret committee that included Bureau of Narcotics commissioner Harry J. Anslinger to organize research into any promising pharmaceutical that could be used to advantage when interrogating spies, debriefing agents, or wreaking psychological havoc on enemies.

Marijuana, cocaine, heroin, morphine, ether, Benzedrine, ethyl alcohol, mescaline, all were tried with no great success on a range of human subjects, from CIA officers to prisoners—some aware of what was being tested, others not. An astonishing history of the CIA's experiments with LSD called *Acid Dreams*, based on tens of thousands of declassified government documents, shows that official enthusiasm for LSD really gained momentum in 1951 when small pilot studies looked highly promising. The agency came to believe that LSD was useful for " 'eliciting true and accurate statements from subjects under its influence during interrogation.' " As *Acid Dreams* relates, "For years they had searched, and now they were on the verge of finding the Holy Grail of the cloak-and-dagger trade. As one CIA officer recalled, 'We had thought at first that this was the secret that was going to unlock the universe.' "

The CIA began to bankroll seriously psychiatric research related to LSD, some of it bona fide, some fairly dubious. For instance, they underwrote research by the otherwise respected Dr. Harris Isbell at the Lexington Narcotics Farm, in which "certain patients—nearly all black inmates—were given LSD for more than seventy-five consecutive days. In order to overcome tolerance to the hallucinogen, Isbell administered double, triple and quadruple doses." Quite a questionable enterprise, promoting drug experiences among addicts at a federal facility dedicated to "curing" drug use. Especially when early researchers initially viewed LSD as a "psychotomimetic" or "madness-mimicking" agent. In short, subjects taking LSD were expected to experience temporary insanity.

In April 1953 CIA director Allen Dulles authorized a supersecret major drug and mind control program, code-named MK-ULTRA. Cal

Tech chemist Sidney Gottlieb, devoted in his spare time to square dancing and pet goats, was the agency's driving force in LSD research. Contracts were awarded (through such respectable fronts as the Josiah Macy Foundation, the Geschickter Fund for Medical Research, and certain federal agencies) for all kinds of LSD experiments. Typically, CIA contracts called for researchers to investigate how LSD could disturb memory, produce aberrant behavior that would discredit someone, alter sex patterns, help elicit information, make someone more suggestible, and last but not least, make someone dependent. Predictably, most of those used as human guinea pigs were unlikely to cause trouble: prisoners, mental patients, foreigners, and the terminally ill.

But the CIA officers working on the project also knowingly tested LSD on themselves, believing that such familiarity was useful. But soon the overt in-house experimentation shifted to the covert. LSD was slipped into drinks secretly on an impromptu basis to see what happened. One morning, a CIA operative realized his coffee had been spiked, and he panicked. He fled out into the streets of Washington. A colleague later described how the disoriented man felt "that every automobile that came by was a terrible monster with fantastic eyes, out to get him personally. Each time a car passed he would huddle down against a parapet, terribly frightened. It was a real horror for him. It was hours of agony."

This sort of irresponsible amateur research quickly claimed its first victim. In November of that year Dr. Frank Olson, an army scientist who specialized in biological warfare research, attended a three-day CIA conference at a Maryland hunting lodge at Deep Creek Lake. Dr. Gottlieb secretly spiked everyone's after-dinner drinks. Olson, forty-three, a congenial family man, responded badly and returned home deeply withdrawn. At work, his odd behavior caused his superiors to contact the CIA, which dispatched the despondent researcher up to New York to get help. A CIA-connected physician concluded after several weeks that Olson was stuck in a psychotic state brought on by the LSD experience. Arrangements were made to admit him to Chesnut Lodge psychiatric facility, near his home in Maryland. But on his last night in Manhattan, Olson reportedly committed suicide by jumping out the thirteenth-floor window of the Statler Hilton. A complete autopsy never was done and his widow and children would not find out the LSD aspects of his death for twenty years. In late 1994, forensic scientists who examined the exhumed body raised the possibility that Olson was murdered, perhaps because he was now viewed as a security risk.

Undeterred by such calamities, the CIA's Gottlieb decided to proceed with LSD testing on unwitting subjects. But now they would not be government officials but ordinary citizens. For this purpose, he recruited one of the Bureau of Narcotics' top agents, the fabled George Hunter White. Old OSS files had revealed that White already had tried out an earlier marijuana-based truth serum in the Donovan days. Now, with Anslinger's blessing, White rented a safe-house apartment down in Greenwich Village, which he fitted out with two-way mirrors and surveillance equipment. Then the personable White began hanging around the Village and inviting people back to his pad. There he sur-reptitiously gave them LSD and recorded their reactions. None of this was very sophisticated and it's hard to imagine the scientific value in such observations as "Gloria gets the horrors . . . Janet sky high." So often did the trips go badly that White nicknamed LSD "Stormy."

For uncertain reasons, White's safe-house operation was transferred to San Francisco in 1955, where it became even less professional and scientific. Code-named Operation Midnight Climax, this new "research" had White recruiting drug-addicted prostitutes, who were paid one hundred dollars a night to pick up unwitting men and bring them back to the apartment. There White, well-equipped with martinis, watched through a two-way mirror as the men reacted to the LSD-laced drinks and engaged in various sex acts. When not pursuing such dubious "research," White did function at times as a narcotics agent, or else irritated the neighbors with wild parties. This strange tax-supported scene proceeded unchecked until 1963, when a new CIA inspector general was appalled to discover the U.S. government was testing out a drug on innocent citizens known to cause psychotic breaks. Yet CIA director Richard Helms said the safe houses were necessary to provide "realistic testing" and "keep up with Soviet advances in the field." White went on his merry, kinky way until he retired in 1966. Thereafter he wrote a nostalgic letter to his longtime CIA supporter Gottlieb to say, "I was a very minor missionary, actually a heretic, but I toiled wholeheartedly in the vineyards because it was fun, fun, fun. Where else could a red-blooded American boy lie, kill, cheat, steal, rape, and pillage with the sanction and blessing of the All-Highest?"

Also floating across this surreal LSD shadowscape was an equally odd cold warrior named Alfred M. Hubbard, a tubby crew cut cloak-and-dagger type who had made millions as president of Vancouver's Uranium Corporation. A boy wonder inventor in his youth in Seattle, Hubbard seems to have taken up rum-running in the twenties and landed in prison. He was plucked from there for the purpose of smuggling American war matériel to the British during the earliest days of World War II. Once America entered the battle, Hubbard served in the OSS. After the war, he resurfaced in western Canada and made a fortune in uranium. Soon he had an island in Vancouver Bay, his own airplane, and a Rolls-Royce. It was in England in 1951 that Hubbard first experienced LSD provided by an English scientist. "It was the deepest mystical thing I've ever seen," he would later say. "I saw myself as a tiny mite in a big swamp with a spark of intelligence. I saw my mother and father having intercourse. It was all clear."

When Hubbard returned to Canada, he heard about a young English psychiatrist named Humphry Osmond, who was working on LSD and mescaline at a hospital in Saskatchewan. In 1952 Dr. Osmond had created a huge stir in the medical world by pointing out the similarities between the mescaline and adrenaline molecules, suggesting that schizophrenia might be a form of unintended self-intoxication. Hubbard was not the only layman piqued by Dr. Osmond's research.

Aldous Huxley, then living in Hollywood Hills, California, also had been tantalized when he read of Dr. Osmond's work with mescaline. The famous writer got in touch, and in May 1953 the two met when Osmond came to attend the annual meeting of the American Psychiatric Association. Huxley tagged along and amused himself by making obeisance at each of the frequent invocations of Freud's name. Huxley was too shy finally to say what he really wanted, which was to try mescaline personally. His wife, Maria, brought it up. Dr. Osmond had come prepared. He mixed the mescaline in a glass of water and handed it to Huxley. Then he stepped outside and hoped all would go well, for he did not want to be responsible for driving a world-famous writer over the edge. Huxley would later enthuse that he saw "eternity in a flower, infinity in four chair legs, and the Absolute in the folds of a pair of flannel trousers." "It was," the great novelist would write to his editor, "without question the most extraordinary and significant experience this side of the Beatific Vision." Huxley made clear in "The Doors of Perception" that this was not temporary insanity at all, but a mystical experience.

Two years later, when Huxley tried mescaline again, it was in the company of Cold Warrior Al Hubbard, whom he meanwhile had met through his friend Dr. Osmond. The two hit it off, and Huxley would write to Osmond, "What Babes in the Wood we literary gents and professional men are. The great World occasionally requires your services, is mildly amused by mine; but its full attention and deference are paid to Uranium and Big Business. So what extraordinary luck that this representative of both these Higher Powers should (a) have become so passionately interested in mescaline and (b) be such a very nice man." Later in 1955 Hubbard introduced a grateful Huxley to LSD.

Hubbard the cold warrior was an ardent Catholic who truly believed in the spiritual possibilities of LSD. He began steering Dr. Osmond away from the notion that LSD was merely a psychotomimetic, or a drug valuable only because it produced a form of temporary psychosis or madness. Instead, Hubbard argued that LSD could open new inner vistas and that physicians should view it as a potential tool for psychotherapy. Dr. Osmond was, in fact, much impressed with the energetic Hubbard's own experimental research project using LSD to treat hard-core alcoholics. The results were quite impressive (one third remained sober, another third drank less), and Osmond revised his thinking about LSD accordingly. In fact, it was Osmond who coined the word "psychedelic" in a correspondence with Huxley, when they agreed that the original term "psychotomimetic" was no longer apt. Osmond wrote, "To fathom hell or soar angelic/Just take a pinch of psychedelic." This new word, psychedelic, meant mind-manifesting.

The gung-ho, blustery Hubbard, oddly attired in a military-type uniform complete with side holster, now began his personal campaign to spread LSD. Using his own considerable fortune, this rich entrepreneur and onetime spy acted as an old-fashioned missionary to the influential, convinced he was remaking the world. He "promoted his cause with indefatigable zeal, crisscrossing North America and Europe, giving LSD to anyone who would stand still. 'People heard about it, and they wanted to try it,' he explained. During the 1950s and early 1960s he turned on thousands of people from all walks of life—policemen, statesmen, captains of industry, church figures, scientists. 'They all thought it the most marvelous thing,' he stated, 'and I never saw psychosis in any one of these cases.' "

California was a stronghold of early LSD research, and word spread quickly among the country's movers and shakers. Two West Coast psychiatrists traveled to Arizona in 1958 to supervise an LSD session for the powerful Henry Luce, founder and head of *Time*, and his wife, Clare Boothe Luce, then ambassador to Italy. Other early test subjects were such celebrities as writer Anaïs Nin and actor Cary Grant. In April 1959 the movie star relaxed on the pink submarine set of *Operation Petticoat* and explained to two baffled reporters that "I have been through a psychiatric experience which has completely changed me." Grant had taken something called LSD and he was now a much-improved person. That same year Allen Ginsberg also tried the drug all Hollywood was talking about. Recommended by a friend, he was given LSD at the Mental Research Institute in Palo Alto in 1959. In a drab hospital room crammed with machines, Ginsberg was subjected to the standard LSD research process of Rorschach tests, math problems, and other mental probings. A strobe light got him to worrying that "I would be absorbed into the electrical network grid of the entire nation. . . . I felt my soul being sucked out through the light and into the wall socket and going out." Not surprisingly, Ginsberg had little interest in soon repeating this awful sensation.

But meanwhile, LSD research elicited a great deal of interest and growing numbers of doctors and patients were involved. By 1965, "it was estimated that between 30,000 and 40,000 psychiatric patients around the world had received LSD therapeutically; and additional thousands of normal volunteers had received it experimentally." All told, about two thousand scientific papers on LSD's effects had been published. One persistent feature of the LSD experience, noted in these early days by psychiatrist Daniel X. Freedman at the University of Chicago's Pritzker School of Medicine, was what he dubbed "portentousness" or "the sense that something—even a trivial platitude—is fraught with a cosmic significance too profound to be adequately communicated."

And so when Michael Hollingshead appeared at Timothy Leary's imposing suburban mansion in early 1961, a tall, balding, amiable, mocking presence, bearing a mayonnaise jar of LSD in sugar paste, the drug already had quite a history. So much so that it is surprising Leary had not tried it already. Hollingshead lounged before the television and in his upper-class English accent urged the good professor to try a bit of hallucinogenic goop. But Leary demurred: "Everything I had heard about lysergic acid sounded ominous to me. . . . [It] was a laboratory product and had quickly fallen into the hands of doctors and psychiatrists. Then, too, I was scared. The sacred mushrooms were my familiar territory. I had them harnessed up to my brand of revelation and ecstasy. It was obvious the more powerful LSD swept you far beyond the tender wisdom of psilocybin." Leary also was preoccupied by his work and the growing rancor at Harvard. It was only when some frequent companion-voyagers to The Other World of psilocybin assured Leary that LSD was many other orders of magnitude more amazing that Leary relented. He was completely bowled over: "From the date of this session it was inevitable . . . that we would spend the rest of our lives as mutants, faithfully following the instructions of our internal blueprints." Twenty years later, Leary would write, "I have never recovered from that ontological confrontation. I have never been able to take myself, my mind, or the social world quite so seriously. . . . From that day I have never lost the sense that I am an actor, surrounded by characters, props, and sets for the comic drama being written in my brain."

When his psilocybin research colleague, Richard Alpert (later Ram Dass), saw the dazed and bedazzled post-LSD Leary, he was appalled.

Alpert found Hollingshead a dubious, debauched creature, and he did not like the ironic Englishman's sudden ascendance to guruhood. For Leary was an instant LSD convert, certain that he now had found a far superior hallucinogen, the true path to "spiritual awakening, and to artistic and political freedom." He became interested deeply in Buddhism and various Eastern religions as possible models for self-enlightenment.

By the summer of 1962 Leary had decided to test out a full blast, full-time assault on The Other World with several dozen followers at a remote Mexican seashore resort. The goal was deep self-knowledge and complete mass spiritual communion. Leary returned to Harvard that fall convinced he was on the right path to remaking the world. He organized something called the International Foundation for Internal Freedom, which promoted psychedelics as a basic human right. Leary told his old sponsor David McClelland, "We're through playing the science game." McClelland thought this a shame. "It tears my heart out to see what's happened to them. They started out as good scientists. They've become cultists."

All this was quite upsetting to Aldous Huxley, Humphry Osmond, and a host of psychiatrists who saw Leary jeopardizing all their judicious endeavors. When the elegant Huxley briefly swooped down on Harvard, he came away appalled. Leary, he wrote, "talked such nonsense . . . that I became quite concerned. Not about his sanity—because he is perfectly sane—but about his prospects in the world; for this nonsense-talking is just another device for annoying people in authority, flouting convention, cocking snooks at the academic world." One psychiatrist warned Leary that his new theatrics could well "do irreparable harm to the psychedelic field in general."

Harvard University finally lost patience with the psychedelic researchers and their ever-less scientific investigations. The Federal Drug Administration and local law enforcement officials were evincing too much interest. Amid riotous rumors of wild acid parties and a campus black-market in LSD-laced sugar cubes, Harvard fired Richard Alpert in May 1963 for giving LSD to an undergraduate. Leary showed no contrition at all, joking, "LSD is so powerful that one administered dose can start a thousand rumors." Harvard then fired Leary. Hitherto little known outside his own scholarly circles, Leary exploited his overnight fame to proselytize and gather new supporters. Exiled from academia, Leary and his followers regrouped down in the seaside resort in Mexico, only to be deported. In quick succession, they became persona non grata in two other Caribbean nations.

Finally they found a congenial retreat at a four thousand-acre estate known as Millbrook up the Hudson River Valley. Owned by William

Mellon Hitchcock, a twentyish stockbroker and heir to Gulf Oil, Millbrook featured a mile-long maple-lined drive up to a turreted sixty-four-room mansion surrounded by polo fields, fragrant pine woods, tennis courts, and a sylvan lake. A two-story chalet housed a bowling alley. Hitchcock's sister, Peggy, had been one of many influential New Yorkers charmed and beguiled by Leary. Comfortably ensconced in this rustic splendor, Leary, whose signature costume now became a white shirt, white slacks, red socks, and white sneakers, began to work on his grandiose visions of remaking America in some unspecified spiritual image. As Leary would tartly explain to an early and skeptical interviewer at Millbrook, "You're now sitting in a religious center. About 30 people are devoting their lives and energies to a full-time pursuit of the Divinity through the sacrament of LSD."

And there was no shortage of fascinated observers to this latest manifestation of that time-honored American phenomenon—the fervent, charismatic religious crusader preaching salvation. In 1964 one of the earliest alternative newspapers, The Realist, declared solemnly, "The future may decide that the two greatest thinkers of the 20th century were Albert Einstein, who showed how to create atomic fission in the physical world, and Timothy Leary, who showed how to create atomic fission in the psychological world." The disgraced Harvard professor had transformed himself into a modern version of the old fire-breathing preacher.

During this same period, out on the West Coast, an up-and-coming young writer named Ken Kesey was among those "normal volunteers" who discovered psilocybin and LSD by participating in psychological experiments, in this instance at the Menlo Park Veterans Hospital. Soon, he and other curious academics and writers were gathering regularly to use the drugs on their own, convinced that they were indeed on to something cosmic, important, and creative. Unlike Leary, who embarked on his psychedelic investigations with a reasoned agenda of helping people change through insight, Kesey and his crowd were far less directed, but just as enthused. This undirected enthusiasm eventually coalesced into a loose group that came to be known as the Merry Pranksters. They lived communally, favored odd, whimsical outfits, and aspired through LSD to live in "a place called Edge City, which was that part of the spectrum of being that lay between the ego, with its layers of conditioning, and the annihilating bath of the Void. To live in Edge City meant to live totally in the here and now."

Like the Beats, these new beings soon took to the road in quest of life and adventure, and to spread the new gospel of LSD. The Merry Pranksters proceeded east in a wildly painted ancient school bus with none other than Neal Cassady, old Beat and manic monologuist, piloting "this rolling affront to respectable behavior." The putative occasion was the imminent publication of Kesey's second novel, *Sometimes a Great Notion*, but also on the agenda was meeting up with the East Coast contingent of American lifestyle rebels, especially Kerouac and Leary.

By 1964, when Kesey and the Merry Pranksters in their Day-Glo bus rumbled up Millbrook's long driveway, the ragtag West Coasters found "a bunch of Ivy League eggheads walking around in robes and talking like comparative religion professors. Millbrook was a bore, and hostile to boot." Leary and his spiritual confreres were just as put off by this inarticulate, anarchic busload of youth, blithely advocating mass LSD trips for one and all without any advance preparation or guidance, no concern at all for all-important set and setting. The Pranksters completely disdained such hand-wringing as square and scoffed at Leary's notion that hallucinogens should be like alcohol—available, but licensed and dispensed in appropriate situations and settings. Kerouac was just as big a disappointment. He had retreated to the conservativism of his working-class youth, appearing at one Prankster party only long enough to carefully fold up an American flag tossed aside on a piece of furniture.

The Pranksters may have found the denizens of Millbrook dull squares, but the Dutchess County neighbors—initially friendly—had come to view the Millbrook crowd as beyond the pale. Again, as at Harvard, rumors floated forth of debauched behavior, sex orgies, constant drug use, and a willingness to welcome any curious young person into this nonstop house party. While Leary honeymooned in India with wife number two (a short-lived match) Millbrook spun out of control. One early enthusiast dropped by and was horrified to find Greenwich Village hustlers "lying naked and freaked out all around the mansion." A trip-all-the-time faction had taken over. Leary calmed things down when he returned, but he felt a need for a break from the continual hubbub, and in December 1965 headed south for Mexico with a new love, Rosemary, who would become wife number three, and his kids. At the Laredo border, Leary's daughter was caught with a small amount of marijuana, and Leary claimed responsibility. This was no small matter, for Texas had draconian laws on marijuana possession. So began Leary's numerous encounters and struggles with the American criminal justice system—including that in the Hudson River Valley. For when Leary returned from the ordeal in Texas, local law enforcement was gearing up.

As Leary's increasingly angry neighbors clamored for a crackdown, an ambitious Dutchess County assistant prosecutor named G. Gordon Liddy saw a chance to make a name. In April 1966, Liddy gathered a passel of deputies and staked out the mansion late one night, waiting for everyone to retire so he could lead a no-knock raid. Much to their disgust, the raiding party had to sit for hours in the damp bushes while the residents stayed up endlessly watching a film of a waterfall. Finally, when the house darkened, Liddy led the charge. Hearing the commotion, Leary emerged clad only in a shirt, and complained about this unconstitutional invasion. LSD and marijuana were found, but prosecutor Liddy's failure to give *Miranda* warnings got the case tossed. Undeterred, Liddy took to setting up roadblocks so that anyone coming to Millbrook was eyeballed stonily and questioned. By spring of 1967, Leary, with Rosemary and his two teenagers, decided he had had enough and decamped to California. There, once again, he was busted for marijuana.

By 1967 LSD had become available readily in virtually any large college campus or big city. As use mushroomed in certain locales, so did the casualties. Bellevue Hospital in New York City, close to Greenwich Village, was one of the first to notice the phenomenon of white middle-class youth flipping out on bad trips:

> In the 10-month period from March 1, 1965 to December 31, 1965, a total of 65 persons were admitted to the psychiatric division of Bellevue Hospital with acute psychoses induced by LSD. Prior to that time, LSD intoxication was rarely observed in that hospital. . . . [Fifty-two of these LSD cases were studied to yield the following:] Exactly half had taken LSD on only a single occasion; only 8 admitted to using it on more than 3 occasions. The predominant manifestation in 12 was overwhelming fear, and an additional 9 experienced uncontrolled violent urges including homicide attempts by 2 individuals. Four others were found running or sitting nude in the streets.

Of these 52 patients, 30 recovered within 2 days, 11 in about a week, 5 were followed incompletely, and 6 were in psychiatric care "for a prolonged period of time." In *Storming Heaven*, Jay Stevens estimates that for "every thousand people who took LSD, seven would suffer a breakdown."

Both California and New York moved to outlaw LSD, and in early 1966 the U.S. Senate convened hearings, inviting both Ginsberg and Leary to share their accumulated wisdom. Ginsberg, who by now had grown a great shaggy beard, wore a dark suit, tie, and wrinkled white shirt when he testified in the large marbled chamber under huge chandeliers. Chain-smoking Pall Malls, Ginsberg began, noted the *Washington Post*, by describing himself as a "man haunted by fear of death and a fear of women stemming from a frightening childhood with a mother who finally died in a mental hospital." In this era before it became commonplace for people to relate their deepest, most intimate experiences before complete strangers amid endless dissection of dysfunctional families, the hearing room clearly was taken aback by what one senator politely termed Ginsberg's "unique testimony."

Ginsberg went on to say that he had used hallucinogens about thirty times over the past fifteen years, trying to replicate his life-changing Blakean epiphany in East Harlem. "The whole universe seemed to wake up alive and full of intelligence and feeling." Ginsberg's larger point, generally, was that widespread LSD use would help the flowering of a more peaceful world.

Trying to relate to the politicians, Ginsberg told how he took LSD the day the unpopular with youth President Johnson was undergoing a gallbladder operation. Nonetheless, due to the influence of LSD, Ginsberg said, "I knelt on the sand surrounded by masses of green kelp washed up by a storm, and prayed for President Johnson's tranquil health. Certainly more public hostility would not help him or me or anyone come through to some less rigid and more flexible awareness of ourselves in Vietnam."

Leary, identified as the president of the Castalia Foundation, testified that he had used LSD or psilocybin 311 times over a period of six years. The so-called LSD crisis, declared Leary, "is not a crisis of peril but a crisis of challenge and promise. . . . There is nothing to fear from LSD. There is nothing to fear from our own nervous systems and from our own cellular structures. . . . The so-called peril of LSD resides precisely in its eerie power to release ancient, wise, and I would even say at times holy sources of energy, which reside in the human brain."

The senators, Leary made clear, were among the old fogeys for whom the word "drug" meant dope fiends, dope addict, crime. But the great wave of baby boomers swelling the nation's college campuses heard something else now when they heard "drug." To them it meant "positive things. It means possible growth, it means opening up the mind, it means beauty, it means in some cases a religious revelation. It may mean sensual awareness and enhancement of our nerve endings." Leary acknowledged the possibility of psychotic LSD reactions, but proposed legislation which would "license responsible adults to use these drugs for serious purposes, such as spiritual growth, pursuit of knowledge, or in their own personal development. To obtain such a license, the applicant, I think, should have to meet physical, intellectual, and emotional criteria." Much energy was spent wrangling over who was or was not an expert and what experts might or might not agree upon. But the crux of the matter—what was best for middle-class youth—was discussed in the final minutes of testimony.

Senator Christopher Dodd wanted to know if it was true, as the newspapers reported, that Leary was advising students to drop out of college if they couldn't find "LSD teachers" on campus. Leary qualified that somewhat, saying:

> I said that if students are seriously interested in expanding consciousness that they should get professors to teach them. If not, they should drop out of school and go someplace where they will find people who will take their interests and needs seriously. I suggested they go to India and find a philosopher or minister or a priest or someone who will help them go within rather than, as I think the American educational system is doing, focus on the outside. . . . Now this may sound reckless advice today, but it is the oldest advice that philosophers and religious leaders have passed on. Detach, drop out, find what is within.

The summer of 1967 in San Francisco was proclaimed the "Summer of Love," and LSD, now dubbed "acid," had spawned its own music—acid rock—identifiable fashions (tie-dye, anything from India or the East, sandals, long hair for men and women), and a loose philosophy that could be summed up as "sex, drugs, and rock 'n' roll." That autumn, Timothy Leary formed the League for Spiritual Discovery. LSD would be a weekly sacrament. "These ancient goals we define in the metaphor of the present—turn on, tune in, drop out." As Stevens recounts it, however, the spiritual message did not reach the masses: "LSD wasn't a trip to the Other World for these kids: it was mind-blowing fun, better than a fast car or a quick orgasm. . . . LSD was promoting a love of sensation, the more intense the better."

The Pranksters were just the vanguard of the middle-class masses who would soon play with the New Marginality and drugs. By 1965, half of America was under thirty, the first generation to come of age with television and the constant touting of instant gratification. The baby boom—the 75 million born between 1946 and 1957—provided a huge and gullible audience. Novelist Jeremy Larner observed that "students . . . are susceptible . . . to 'conspicuous consumption.' . . . [t]hey seek to consume pure experience. They hope that by . . . [taking drugs] they can create an external confirmation of the power and beauty they would like to feel within."

As Allen J. Matusow points out in his history, *The Unraveling of America*, "[H]ippies were only a spectacular exaggeration of tendencies transforming the larger society. The roots of these tendencies, to borrow a phrase from Daniel Bell, was a 'cultural contradiction of capitalism.' By solving the problems of want, industrial capitalism undermined the very virtues that made this triumph possible, virtues like hard work, self-denial, postponement of gratification, submission to social discipline, strong ego mechanisms to control the instincts."

As a generation experimented with drugs, many found them mindless and amusing. But for others there were bad trips and a certain burned-out anomie. Dedicated drug users did not evolve into higher human beings. After five or six years, Richard Alpert, one of the Harvard pioneers along with Leary, became disillusioned: "You came into the kingdom of heaven and you saw how it all was and you felt these new states of awareness, and then you got cast out again, and after 200 or 300 times of this, . . . an extraordinary kind of depression set in." Alpert eventually achieved non-drug-induced spirituality in India and became a guru, Ram Dass.

Leary airily brushed aside any concerns. "Even if the risks were fifty-fifty that if you took LSD you would be permanently insane, I still think the risk is worth taking, as long as the person knows that's the risk." In 1967 a middle-aged Allen Ginsberg urged every healthy person over fourteen to try LSD. Illegal drugs, "enlightenment," and the importance of being hip over being square were central tenets in the emerging counterculture.

Meanwhile, Ginsberg, who actively promoted various drugs as beneficial, banned their use on his own property. By 1961, his biographer writes, Ginsberg (in an act of utter hypocrisy) forbade drugs or alcohol on his Cherry Valley farm, a retreat purchased specifically "as a means of keeping [his lover] Peter away from the heavy drug culture so prevalent around their Greenwich Village apartment."

And then there were the casualties, those who spiraled down into the hard drug culture. Nicholas von Hoffman wrote a poignant column about a young hippie strung out on heroin: "She'd been so much a part of what she still called the psychedelic revolution, one of the San Francisco originals . . . one of many who'd put down smack, and made a superior division between her and her friends and the freaks who shot the white heroin into their bloodstreams."

Susan Gordon Lydon was another casualty, a talented sixties journalist who acquired a serious heroin habit. By the end of the seventies, Lydon would be "a shadow of the person I'd been. My inner self had been eroded so gradually over the years by the drugs that, without noticing it, I'd ceased to inhabit my own life or even my body. . . . I'd sought oblivion from pain, and I'd found it, but in the process I'd managed to obliterate myself." Lydon's neglected young daughter finally disowned her mother and moved out. "You don't come home," the girl said, "you don't take care of anything; all you care about is drugs."

All of this counterculture appropriation of drugs infuriated the cold warrior LSD apostle Al Hubbard, whose ardent proselytizing had caused him to neglect his now-withered business interests. By the mid sixties this onetime millionaire had become a special agent for the FDA, leading raids on underground acid labs. Reports *Acid Dreams*, "The Captain was particularly irked when he learned that LSD in adulterated form was circulating on the black market. To Hubbard this represented degradation of the lowest order. The most precious spiritual substance on earth was being contaminated by a bunch of lousy bathtub chemists." And despite the predictions of people like Leary and Ginsberg that serious LSD users would take a more benign and loving view of the world, Hubbard despised "weirdos—especially long-haired radical weirdos who abused his beloved LSD." In late 1968 this dislike had been channeled into a new professional role as a "special investigative agent" for the Stanford Research Institute. SRI was researching drug use by students and links between drugs and radical politics, fearing that the former was fueling the latter. Ironically, leftists were arguing about the same issue, but they complained that drug use defused political purpose.

After the peace, prosperity, and surface quiet of the fifties, America had entered a period of extraordinary upheaval. The sixties had begun hopefully, with President John F. Kennedy casting a glamorous glow amid a Camelot of liberals, academics, and young families playing touch football on the White House lawn. But the Cuban missile crisis and the Freedom Riders risking their lives in the South dramatically reminded the nation of its deepest problems: the Cold War and race. Then in 1963 the president was assassinated and America entered a decade of unremitting turmoil: one wrenching political murder after another, race riots and burning ghettoes, angry black militants, and escalating involvement in Vietnam matched by escalating opposition. Many Beats would date the end of their era to 1965, when the confluence of assassinations, civil rights, and Vietnam produced a politicized radical youth movement, swelled by the huge number of baby-boomer college students.

As for Leary, his sly, confrontational public manner stirred up nonstop trouble. He infuriated the antiwar and radicals movements by proclaiming that youth should eschew all politics and concentrate on psychedelics and dropping out. Then Leary declared his own candidacy for governor of California. It was the political silly season and Leary camped it up, posing with John Lennon and Yoko Ono in their bed-in. But the merriment came to an abrupt halt on April 23, 1970, when the California Supreme Court refused the right to bail while Leary appealed his conviction for marijuana possession. Leary, forty-nine, now a long-hair affecting the psychedelic look, was clamped in jail. Meanwhile, his Texas case, after many legal loop-de-loops, had resulted in a ten-year sentence in that unfriendly state. All Leary's various drug convictions combined loomed as a virtual life sentence. Desperate, his wife Rosemary arranged Leary's prison escape. Leary soon surfaced as an ally of the radical Weather Underground, which lauded Leary for "creating a new culture on the barren wasteland of what has been imposed on us by Democrats, Republicans, Capitalists and creeps."

Leary now began a bizarre period as a highly visible and public fugitive, fleeing with Rosemary first to Algiers, where he managed to quickly alienate the Black Panthers, and then to Switzerland, where he consorted with various high rollers. Then a new love convinced him to visit Kabul, Afghanistan, where he was captured in 1973 and brought back to the United States. Leary then infuriated his former friends and allies by turning informant. His cooperation meant he spent only three years in prison.

As illegal drug use became commonplace among middle-class whites, the small deviant drug subculture that had its origins in both the early Chinese opium dens and then the black hipsters of the jazz world had melded and completed its journey into the mainstream white culture. The two variables that always dictated the strength and size of America's illegal drug culture were now in full force: first, supply and availability. Drugs of all kinds were available readily (especially the new psychedelics, which were produced easily by any talented chemist). Whenever availability rises, so will use, abuse, and addiction. The second variable is demand, mediated by demography as well as zeitgeist. Demographically, half the country was young and the black northern slums were expanding. There, impoverished young blacks were truly on society's margins, while large numbers of middle-class youth played at being socially marginal.

A critical aspect further affecting demand is "learned experience." Dr. David Musto of Yale has long argued that we as a nation have had a cyclical learned experience with drugs (and also alcohol and tobacco). When the perils of drugs, abuse, and addiction become well known through firsthand experience, there is a natural "rejection of drugs as a result of popular experience with them." Demand and use then declines, even among the truly marginal. A tremendous naivete prevailed in the sixties among the middle class about the long-term consequences of drug use, i.e., a profound lack of "learned experience."

The new enthusiasm for drugs was observed with great concern by the government in Washington. In 1968, Narcotics commissioner Henry Giordano testified before Congress that

> the traffic in marijuana has increased sharply within the last three or four years. Many areas which were formerly almost free of drug abuse now report a small but persistent traffic, centering on the "hippie" elements and college campuses. Our reports show that more than 40 percent of the new marijuana users reported to the Bureau in 1967 were under the age of 21 years. Also seizures and arrests have sharply increased at the Federal level. In 1963, 6,432 pounds of marijuana were seized at borders and in the United States, and in 1966, 23,260 pounds were seized. . . . There were approximately 6,800 arrests in 1963, which have risen steadily each year to 23,952 in 1966.

The next year, an administration official noted uneasily:

> Local arrests for all types of illegal drug activity jumped to 34,309 in 1966 from 27,946 the previous year. Among juveniles, the increase was just short of 50 percent in nine cities. . . . California reported adult drug arrest data for the first six months of 1967 which showed an annual increase of 57.5 percent over the same period in 1966. Marijuana offenses were up 94.3 percent, and dangerous drug arrests 30.6 percent. Juvenile arrests rose to 5,735 from 2,146, an increase of 167.2 percent. Marijuana violations rose 181 percent and dangerous drugs 89 percent.

Most extraordinary, for the first time, America's illegal drug culture had avid advocates and spokesmen. The occasional lone voice who once bravely had defended the rights of old-style drug users not to be condemned as criminals had been completely superseded by self-confident young people declaring the absolute benefit and good of drugs in the quest of pleasure and self-enlightenment. When one scientist warned, "It is well established that no community ever achieved social or cultural progress" through drugs, the counterculture disdained this sage advice based on the historical record. People such as Ginsberg blithely preferred half-baked readings of the China experience, asserting, "There's an ancient tradition of very stable opium addicts in the Orient.

You can have a regular, stable life on opium." In fact, there was no such ancient tradition, but a recent imperialistic experience that had been much resisted, albeit unsuccessfully. But this was the New Age, when history and common sense could be turned on their heads.

And yet one heard here turn-of-the-century echoes, the familiar patent medicine penchant for proclaiming this elixir and that a cure-all for what ailed the body and mind. When Paul Krassner interviewed Leary for *The Realist* as early as 1966, Leary declared, "I predict that psychedelic drugs will be used in all schools in the very near future as educational devices—not only drugs like marijuana and LSD, to teach kids how to use their sense organs and their cellular equipment effectively, but new and more powerful psychochemicals like RNA and other proteins which are going to revolutionize our concepts of ourselves and education."

As Yippie Jerry Rubin declared, "Drug use signifies the total end of the Protestant ethic: screw work, we want to know ourselves. But of course the goal is to free oneself from American society's sick notion of work, success, reward, and status and to find oneself through one's own discipline, hard work, and introspection." It was perhaps typical of the hubris of the Age of Aquarius that the scornful but idealistic leaders of the young believed that once the genie of drugs was unleashed, they would dictate its use and consequences. Time would show how wrong they were.

CHAPTER 13

"Everybody Must

Get Stoned!"

— *"Rainy Day Women #12 & 35,"*
Bob Dylan, 1966

The city and suburbs of Baltimore, Maryland, allow us to see how abusing illegal drugs—once the deviant and stigmatized activity of a tiny number of people on the margins of society—became a widespread and almost mainstream activity in the 1970s and 1980s, openly celebrated by pop culture.

As World War II ended, Baltimore was the nation's sixth-largest metropolis, with a population of almost 950,000, a sprawling blue-collar town with mile upon mile of modest brick row-house neighborhoods. Despite a busy, bustling port connecting America's Midwest to the rest of the world, Baltimore rather prided itself on its provincialism. It had been settled in the eighteenth century by English Catholics and soon had a sizable community of free blacks. The town's generally conservative outlook was reinforced by the mid-nineteenth-century wave of well-off political refuges rolling in from Germany (H. L. Mencken's family came then), followed by far poorer immigrants from eastern and southern Europe—Poles, Czechs, Ukrainians, Russian Jews, Italians. None of these relatively established groups viewed with favor the influx of migration that began around World War II—poor whites from

Appalachia and poor blacks from the South, all uneducated folks seeking work at the port's flourishing docks, many shipyards, Beth Steel's Sparrow's Point complex, and numerous defense industries, such as Westinghouse and Martin Marietta.

It was in the city's black community that illegal drug use first appeared in Baltimore. One Calvin Johnson, nineteen, a black navy veteran back home from the war and living at his parents' house in west Baltimore, first encountered the small and still subterranean local drug scene on Pennsylvania Avenue. Fondly known as The Avenue, this wide street in the city's western section was the lively epicenter of black Baltimore, a traditional district of shopping, entertainment, nightlife, and vice. The Avenue was the heady scene of every kind of diversion, from fancy nightclubs to down-and-funky pool halls to prostitution. "In those days everything was flourishing," recalls Johnson, "Everyone had money after the war and people were having fun, fun, fun." The Royal Theater was one of the major stops on the black entertainment circuit and featured the country's greatest entertainers— Louis Armstrong, Fats Waller, Ella Fitzgerald, Nat King Cole, and such local stars made good as Cab Calloway and Billie Holiday. Joints such as Dreamland, Gamby's, and Ike Dixon's Comedy Club hopped to the hot sounds of musical prodigies such as Dinah Washington, Erroll Gardner, and Charlie Parker, and regularly booked such funny men as Pegleg Bates, Slappy White, and Butterbean and Susie.

It was on The Avenue that Johnson met his first hipsters in 1949, and with them found his niche: "I liked the hipsters' appearance. They were very slick. I liked the way they talked, the slang. You chose sides between the squares and the hipsters." The heroin, he would later explain, was just part of the "glamour" of hipsterdom. When Johnson talks about choosing sides between the hipsters and squares, one hears Leroi Jones's assertion that heroin appealed to the black proletariat because the "drug itself transforms the Negro's normal separation from the mainstream of society into an advantage. . . . It is one-upsmanship of the highest order. Many heroin addicts believe that no one can be knowledgeable or 'hip' unless he is an addict."

When Johnson surveyed the Baltimore he had returned to from wartime service, he felt deep anger that his patriotism had earned no greater respect or privileges. The memory forever rankled of the white soldiers on one troop train loudly declaring they couldn't wait to get to Washington, D.C., so " 'we can separate from these niggers.' " Says Johnson, "They thought I fought the war to let them come home and keep me down." But Johnson also felt adrift.

After World War II, despite the longtime presence of a significant

African-American community, Baltimore's racial attitudes were much like the rest of the nation's, hostile to those who did not kowtow to the city's racial rules—whether implicit or legislated. Blacks made up a fifth of the city's population in 1940, but occupied only one fiftieth of the city's area. In those industries and companies that employed them, blacks got the lowliest jobs. Juanita Jackson Mitchell, the aged matriarch of a black political clan, described the prewar Baltimore of her youth as a "living hell. You could not go to restaurants, movie theaters, or stores. We could not be policemen or firemen." *New York Times* columnist Russell Baker moved to Baltimore in the late 1930s as a teenager and recalls a Baltimore "as segregated racially as Johannesburg [South Africa]. Neighborhoods, schools, movie theaters, stores, everything was segregated. It was an all-white police force, and the *Sun* was an all-white newspaper."

However oppressive postwar Baltimore might be for blacks, to Calvin Johnson, nineteen, a black navy veteran, it was still preferable to the U.S. military. Johnson had returned home from World War II on the Greyhound bus one crisp spring dawn, having declined to reenlist for one overriding reason: "I didn't like the discrimination. During the whole war blacks were always segregated into the worst situations. I was a fireman first class in the South Pacific, working at a supply base in Espíritu Santo. If there were huts and mud for housing, we'd be in the mud. The only work you could do on navy ships up until 1944 was as a stewart's mate. I came home a person with no direction and feeling very bitter."

Johnson had experienced the usual Baltimore affronts: back-of-the-trolley seating in streetcars and segregated drinking fountains and bathrooms, complete with signs indicating "Colored" and "Whites." And once at a five-and-dime downtown with his mother, he had been ordered rudely away from a lunch counter. Moreover, he, like all Baltimore blacks of the era, knew that the big department stores extended the privilege of entrance only to the most refined black families. Still, Johnson's big, tight family largely had shielded him from racial indignities when he was growing up. And so it was in the U.S. Navy that he learned the harsh and galling truths of segregation and racism American style. Now, with the war over, Baltimore civil rights activists mocked the racial status quo in 1948 by organizing—of all unlikely events—an interracial tennis match in sylvan Druid Hill Park. The players were all promptly arrested for the crime of "integrated recreation."

Black veterans such as Johnson were very much part of the raised expectations described by Leroi Jones as a major psychological shift in black America, yet Johnson found nothing to satisfy his yearning for something better. The one thing he really loved was jazz and the new bebop, and so for several years he used his G.I. Bill money to go to music school and learn jazz piano. "But I was just playing games," he says many decades later. "That was not going to take me anywhere." When the veteran's benefits ended, Johnson took a job at an army depot, but "I wanted something more out of life, something to grab hold of me and get me out of the mud of routine." When nothing promising presented itself, no larger inspirational framework, no political or social movement that spoke to his hopes or his alienation, Johnson turned to Life Style as Statement—and heroin.

Calvin Johnson became part of a fast-growing Baltimore hipster underground that prided itself on its overall savoir faire. One longtime addict named Leroy explains that long ago scene: "Life was going out together—parties, clubs on the avenue, boosting [shoplifting]. Drugs were just part of that larger lifestyle. Your clothes and going to certain nightspots was very important. Part of the lifestyle was to look nice, to wear a necktie and a nice shirt. I didn't come from no broken home, and the thirty or so guys who were addicts right after the war, they didn't come from no broken home either." One of the rare black female addicts of the immediate postwar era recalls, "The lifestyle was to hang out where there was live entertainment and musicians, because a lot of the musicians who came into town used. You had women who were hustlers way before they were addicts, and they did a lot of shoplifting and passing bad checks [to pay for drugs]. By the fifties, though, most had turned to prostitution. And a lot of women hooked up with dealers because you could always be sure of having a shot." One needs to linger over the figure Leroy cites—"thirty or so guys"—to truly appreciate the minuscule number of hipster addicts and the amazing expansion of addiction in the coming decades.

As Calvin Johnson and others signed on to the hedonistic pursuits of the hipsters, Leroy estimates that the number of hipster-addicts grew from thirty to three hundred in five years. Another new convert, James, recalls the scene in 1950 when he discovered heroin:

> My gang of guys was on the progressive side. They were the best dressers, wore the best clothes, went to all the social functions, the jazz shows, the dances. I noticed they were sneaking off, and when I went with them out came a makeshift works, with eyedroppers, a used process spoon, and a piece of cotton. They cooked some substance out of little pills, which turned out to be heroin. A lot of neighborhood people shunned these guys, and so I was careful not to let my family know I was

hanging around with them. Many of the guys had jobs where they did some kind of hustle. Maybe they'd work at a clothing store or on a truck or in a grocery store. They'd always set aside [steal] something to sell.

And then you had the boosters and the burglars, guys that took pride in their hustles. Say they'd crack an automobile, steal a coat or a camera. These things would get him over for the day. He didn't need a great deal.

As one group of researchers observed: "Status in this subculture was derived primarily from criminal success, and it manifested itself in the argot used, style of dress, and general image projected to others. . . . Narcotics were used largely for their prestige value, since the user was regarded as being a special kind of person, or 'in the know.' . . . Addiction was not the result of an intolerable home life or the consequences of social deprivation; rather it appears to have been a by-product of a lifestyle that was consciously adopted."

As heroin became part of black Baltimore's hip scene, many felt obliged to try it. Recalls James, "Guys didn't want to be ostracized, to be called a square because they wouldn't try. They'd say you didn't know what you were missing, they'd ridicule you. Most of us were not strong enough to say this ain't for me. You wanted to be accepted by the group, and so out of curiosity you'd try it. And for most of us that was all it took to cut our hearts out and send us down the river for life. I only knew three people who tried drugs who didn't get involved." Even if the heroin was initially ancillary, purportedly part of a larger hip scene, eventually it always and insidiously became the central feature of these hipsters' lives. They always saw themselves as hipsters, but to the rest of the world they eventually were transformed into plain old junkies, people whose top priority and preoccupation was getting opiates into their veins.

Calvin Johnson recalls first snorting a capsule's worth of heroin in 1949 at a dance where Lester Young was playing. Johnson already had been smoking marijuana for a couple of years. "I was searching for something else in my life. I felt some kind of a void. And heroin filled that void." A year later, he was on the needle. "It was the high that superseded all else. It was the street of dreams that shunted everything else aside. This was now your master." Johnson's many brothers, honorably pursuing honest work and raising their own families, repeatedly warned him against drugs and the fast life. But Johnson paid no attention. Nor did he take any responsibility for a small daughter he had with a girlfriend, never even visiting the child. When over the years Johnson occasionally sought drug treatment, it was only under legal duress.

In this small-time drug scene, there were as yet no major pushers, no gangsters or organized crime types. Heroin was not introduced to Baltimore by criminal design, but almost certainly by New York blacks visiting the city—very possibly jazz musicians. Once the drug's pleasures and its (then small) potential for profit were known, some of the more enterprising local addicts traveled to Washington, D.C., or New York City to buy heroin that they would sell to their fellow addicts. They did not make any great money from this, but it allowed them to finance their own heroin habits. Says Hiram Butler, a retired black policeman who joined the Baltimore force in 1938 and worked the narcotics squad for part of his career, "Nobody had any idea then after the war that it would become so big or so bad."

The veteran addict Leroy confirms the small-time nature of this nascent drug culture, "Actually it was no big problem supporting your habit then because heroin was a dollar a cap. You needed about five dollars to support your craving. I learned all kinds of things from a few older fellows about robbing and that kind of thing. Most of these guys were boosting, shoplifting. It was the main source of income for heroin addiction. There were also a series of con games you could play, and I knew them all." At this early stage of Baltimore's drug culture, there were reportedly still certain observed rules of conduct. James asserts proudly, "In 1950 to '55, a black addict would not break into the home of anyone in his neighborhood. Nobody, absolutely nobody would do that. There was very strong integrity at that time. Except for one thing. If a black dealer got put into jail, everyone would just break their neck getting to his house to search it and see if anything was in it."

As heroin use and selling expanded beyond Pennsylvania Avenue and certain clubs, such as Dreamland and the Belmont pool hall, city authorities became concerned enough to appoint a Youth Emergency Council in March 1951, followed shortly by the establishment of a new police narcotics squad. Leroy feels the impetus for these actions was the city's first drug-related shooting in 1949. As he recalls it, "A fellow named Jimmy shot another guy at the Dreamland on Pennsylvania Avenue, then one of the few places you could get drugs in Baltimore. Jimmy had bought this stuff and he was not satisfied with the quality of it. He demanded reimbursement or more drugs, and the guy refused. So Jimmy shot him."

But newspapers of the day suggest that the galvanizing events were testimony before a local grand jury—one, by a federal narcotics agent, who declared marijuana use by local teenagers "almost out of hand" and, two, by a local policewoman who said "Negro teenagers in the Pennsylvania Avenue area were being given dope shots free 'in order to build up the habit.' " Probably just as alarming were a series of obviously drug-related crimes: an eighteen-year-old who raced into a men's clothing store, grabbed six suits, and fled. When caught by a foot patrolman, he confessed his plight. And then there were a series of brazen daylight holdups of downtown loan offices by a small group of addicts.

Baltimore police arrests reflect the soaring postwar levels of black heroin use. In 1942, seven blacks were arrested for narcotics. Ten years later that figure was 242. Hiram Butler, the pioneering black policeman, believed that in the late fifties a fair number of the fresh recruits to the addict life were newcomers from the South, those seeking a place in city life. And indeed, when the city surveyed several hundred arrested addicts in 1960, they found 30 percent had moved from elsewhere, mainly the South.

The Baltimore narcotics squad was launched in 1951 with Sergeant Joseph F. Carroll as its head. Described by a local paper as "200 trim pounds of fist, shoulder, and chest," Carroll immediately became a much feared presence around the avenue. Wearing dark suit, bow tie, and snap-brim hat, Carroll cruised in an unmarked car, keeping a hard eye out for drug activity. Stories soon circulated that Carroll had a special vendetta against addicts because his own father, also a Baltimore cop, had been killed by an addict. In fact, his father, also Sergeant Carroll, had been gunned down in front of Baltimore police headquarters on November 18, 1928, when a gunman wanted in New York City tried to shoot his way free of another policeman who had arrested him. If the gunman was an addict, the reports of the time do not mention it.

Seargeant Carroll the son gave no quarter, becoming a hated figure of authority to local addicts during his fifteen-year tenure. "Oh, man," remembers one, "he instilled fear in people, fear. We changed the way we operated. You couldn't deal out of your pockets no more. So we took it off the streets and into people's houses. Before there'd be an exchange right on the street. But Carroll, any time he saw you he'd frisk you down because he knew if he did it enough, he'd catch you dirty one of these times." In those days, the law allowed the narcotics squad to pick up addicts and detain them for seventy-two hours, more than enough for withdrawal to hit.

Once the three-man squad was organized, there was little more public hue and cry about drugs, in the white or black communities, for almost a decade. Carroll remembers virtually all the heroin addicts and dealers being black. And yet, "the black community never complained about the heroin problem. The ones who weren't involved didn't care." For just as black heroin addicts looked down on "square" people, the middle-class blacks looked down on the addicts. "It was a lower-class narcotic," explained Butler, the black cop. "It was a street form of narcotic. The real commoners used it." Certainly the *Afro-American*, a powerful voice in the Baltimore black community, paid little attention to the issue in these early years. When two black teenagers died mysteriously on the street one day in February 1950, the newspaper gave the deaths front-page play. But when the medical examiner's verdict of "heroin poisoning" came down, that was buried way in the back. One suspects that the newspaper perceived heroin as a lowlife issue deleterious (and irrelevant) to its readership of respectable blacks.

Moreover, in the fifties the relatively small number of black addicts had not yet begun to prey seriously on their own community. One might even say they served a certain purpose—supplying a steady stream of otherwise unaffordable material goodies. For shoplifting remained the favored means of paying for one's drug habit, and hot goods generally went for a third to a fifth of their value. Someone somewhere was buying shoplifted bargains. From his beat on Pennsylvania Avenue, Patrolman James Watkins watched the daily procession of hustlers back from a "boosting" outing at downtown department stores and shops. "They came back loaded down. They had regular booster coats and they could even take a small television between their legs. Belts with special hooks could hold two or three hams. They would even take orders from people for particular items—a tweed suit, whatever."

All through the fifties and early sixties, now Captain Carroll and his narcotics squad remained a feared force. One newspaper profile described how "from 9 to 10 each morning, five or six days a week, hopheads, pushers and informers come to pay homage to 'J.C.' . . . Carroll has a file of known narcotics users in the Baltimore area. He asserts he can get his hands on half of them in a few hours." Despite Carroll's deserved reputation for relentless enforcement, the city's addict population grew steadily. No amount of determined police work could change either the zeitgeist that deemed heroin hip or reverse the city's growing ranks of the poor and uneducated, fertile terrain for drug culture. "It was inevitable it would grow," says Johnson, "because of what drugs do. When you're high all your problems are solved. You are on top. And every person thinks they won't be like the others. They'll be able to control it."

Moreover, up until 1960 virtually no local treatment was available, save for ten beds in Spring Grove, a Maryland state hospital. But if treatment was in short supply up through the early sixties, drugs were not. Once sold only in select shady hangouts in west Baltimore, heroin now was being peddled in other city locales. For the first time, addicts could buy drugs in certain declining east Baltimore neighborhoods, or in south Baltimore. By 1964, police had on file more than a thousand names of known addicts. Of these, almost 700 were black men, 270 white men, 83 black women, and 35 white women.

But few of the whites were heroin addicts, simply because they did not have ready access to heroin. The coterie of black dealers were extremely leery of selling to whites, whose presence in highly segregated neighborhoods only attracted police notice. Instead, whites abused over-the-counter opiate-based cough syrups, forged prescriptions for drugs like dilaudid and morphine, conned doctors, or burglarized drugstores and physicians' offices in search of drugs. As researchers noted, "White addicts engaged primarily in crimes that yielded drugs, while black addicts focused upon crimes that generated cash to maintain an overall lifestyle that happened to include drugs."

Anthony Rizzi was one of a few dozen white addicts in the Baltimore of the late 1950s. Though he lived with his parents and younger sister in the middle-class Pimlico neighborhood, the sixteen-year-old Rizzi often hung around his grandmother's house in tough working-class Highlandtown in East Baltimore. And it was here that this high school sophomore, who did well academically and played basketball, baseball, and soccer, first tried drinking opiate-based cough syrup to get high. "The people who used the syrups were very elitist and condescending to anyone who drank alcohol," he recalls. "They weren't going to drink alcohol and get all sloppy. That's what drew me to the syrups, that euphoria without the sloppiness. And the few people I knew who did the syrups tended to be the better dressers, the good athletes. They felt they were hipper."

At first Rizzi could get high on one four-ounce bottle of cough syrup, which cost seventy-six cents. He continued during his sophomore year to do reasonably well in school and participate in sports. But by his junior year, he was up to four or five bottles of syrup a day and rarely at school, for studies or sports. "All the things kids normally do fell by the wayside," he recalls. Moreover, it was getting decidedly harder to buy syrup. When Rizzi had started you could walk into any pharmacy, pay for the syrup, sign a log, and walk out. Now, as pharmacists and the state got wise to what was happening, the whole procedure tightened up, until finally opiate-based syrups were no longer available over the counter in Baltimore. As cough syrups got harder to obtain, Rizzi was experimenting with morphine and heroin provided by the few other white addicts he knew.

"I remember the first time with heroin, these guys were telling me this would be the most wonderful feeling. They used an eyedropper and a needle to shoot me up. I didn't enjoy it, and it was another month or so before I tried it again. The problem with heroin for us was that it was very expensive. You had to be out stealing every day all day to finance a heroin habit. We used to go into stores and steal dozens of cartons of cigarettes. I never did it much because it was just such a difficult life. I got arrested with my friend Earl for stealing. I decided that stealing drugs directly made more sense. So I would go into pharmacies and just wait till the clerk went away from the counter."

Like the black heroin addicts, Rizzi, the white pharmaceuticals addict, also lived in fear of Captain Joseph Carroll and his narcotics squad. "They knew who used drugs. I was picked up eleven times for 'investigation,' as it was then known. They could detain you because they suspected you of using drugs and hold you seventy-two hours. Well, my poor mother and father were now going through an absolute nightmare. At 2 A.M. Captain Carroll would appear at our house and haul me off." Rizzi's first conviction came when a gas station owner caught him shooting up in the restroom. A sympathetic judge gave him five years probation. Rizzi also was sent for psychiatric treatment—to no avail. Six months later he was spotted stealing drugs from behind a pharmacy's counter. So well did Captain Carroll know the local addicts that the mere physical description of Rizzi sufficed. When they picked him up for questioning, he was found to possess drug paraphernalia. Since this was his second offense, he received a five-year prison sentence.

It was in 1960 that Calvin Johnson—with Captain Carroll after him for dealing—fled Baltimore for New York. By now Johnson had served two stints in state prison. "All dope fiends need to be in New York to know they've hit bottom," says Johnson. "In the shooting galleries there you see the most dirty, filthy shit—maggots, vomit, dirty cookers, dirty water. All they're ever thinking of is getting high. Before New York I just did dealing, but now I got into real criminal stuff." In 1963, a down-and-out Johnson came back to Baltimore, rejoining the fast-expanding ranks of addicts to resume a more provincial version of the fast life.

Throughout the sixties the addict population swelled, until the known number in the police file had more than doubled, from 1,084 to 2,338. And even that underestimated the true numbers. A 1969 *Drug Abuse Study* commissioned by the Maryland State Department of Mental Hygiene demonstrated that a great many addicts were unknown to local law enforcement. From 1951 to 1966 Baltimore City police records showed a total of about 4,000 known addicts. But a state study done in the late sixties identified almost 1,800 addicts previously undetected through checking state prisons, health agencies, and the state's psychiatric register.

When Anthony Rizzi emerged from state prison in 1965, the drug culture was "so much more pervasive and indiscriminate, it was a shock to me. I remember there were a bunch of guys who used to stand around with their cars outside a bowling alley on Park Heights Avenue. Now members of this group were using opiates. These were not people we had regarded as hip. Yet, here they were using drugs and all strung out." Rizzi himself soon relapsed, his connection a black friend from prison. It was only after he married and his daughter was born in late 1966 that Rizzi, now twenty-six, seriously reexamined his life. "It was really apparent that I was in a very precarious position, because if I was caught again I faced the possibility of a very serious sentence. And I felt guilty wasting money on drugs when the baby needed things." And so ten years after he first drank syrup and began his downward spiral, Rizzi signed up with the then experimental treatment of methadone maintenance. Of his friends who continued on in the fast life, he would say in the mid 1990s, "Bobby is dead of an OD, Paul is dead, Nicky dead of an OD, Buddy's alive but in prison, Earl is alive but in prison. And Guy runs an office supply place. He and I are the only ones who got out and did something with ourselves." Today Rizzi is an attorney.

But more than the sheer numbers of addicts was changing in Baltimore's full-time drug culture. As the ranks of the addicts swelled, and certain longtime addict-dealers went off to significant prison terms, black neighborhoods saw the rise of new, more ruthless heroin dealers, disparagingly known as the "profiteers." These were not enterprising addicts provisioning their fellow junkies with the all-important commodity—heroin—but tough guys who saw a chance to make a significant buck off a captive audience of consumers. As full-time dealers entered the scene, there was a dramatic increase over several years in the cost of heroin, from five dollars to twenty-five dollars a bag, and a notable drop in quality. No longer sold in capsules of about 5 percent purity, heroin came now in tiny glassine bags (the sort meant to be used by stamp collectors for stamps) containing God knew what.

But even more important perhaps for the existing drug scene, the new addicts coming on line were far younger and less skilled in financing the heroin habits that the profiteers were making more expensive every month. The new addicts were not seasoned military veterans or skilled hustlers who paraded their elegant wardrobes at swank clubs. The new addicts were increasingly highly troubled delinquents, the teenage products of broken families. From 1960 to 1970 the city of Baltimore's welfare population exploded, quintupling from 5,218 families with almost 18,000 kids to 26,666 families with 77,000 kids. Baltimore's black community always had been far poorer than whites (a median family income of $4,123 versus $6,390 in 1960), but now its family structure also began to crumble. And to Calvin Johnson, part of the reason was drugs. "When these people were using drugs, they couldn't earn a living, most of them, so they went on welfare. And their kids after them is on welfare too, because they don't know how to do anything. They're intertwined, drugs and welfare, a part of each other."

One of the original black addict-dealers recalls, "I went away [to prison] in '59 and came back in '65, and it was a different world when I came back. Some of the methods we used to support our habits had become obsolete to the generation of the sixties. They were nasty cats, man. They'd knock you on the head with a brick or something and take your money. Or they'd go into a bank with a pistol and hold people up. The younger generation just found it easier to use the gun than to use the cons. The gun became very prominent. They'd stick you up, take your money, and then be brazen enough to come back into the neighborhood the next day. Quite a few of the stickup guys were Vietnam vets. The Vietnam guys came back, gung-ho about hitting people and stuff. It was really frightening out there. It soon reached the point where human life didn't have much value. Guys were taking contracts on people, killing one another over ten dollars or fifteen dollars."

Soaring local crime statistics confirm this sense of criminality run amok. In 1948, when the city harbored less than a hundred heroin addicts, the Baltimore Police Department's annual report showed 1,765 burglaries. A burglary is a property crime—a thief has broken into a home or business to steal. In 1948 there were 3,873 larcenies, a crime category that covers any stolen property, including shoplifting. And then there were 402 robberies, or the taking of property through force—i.e., your typical street mugging or store holdup. By 1965, when the "now" generation of addicts hit the streets, those crime statistics would soar from 1948's 1,765 burglaries (break-ins) to 7,393 burglaries; from 3,873 larcenies (general stealing) to 17,436; and from 402 robberies (holdups) to 2,109. Over the next five years, as heroin addiction and overall drug use became even more epidemic the two most feared crimes—break-ins (burglary) and being mugged and held up (robbery)—rose manyfold. By 1970 burglaries had almost tripled, from 7,393 to 19,041, and robberies quintupled, from 2,109 to 10,965. In a twenty-year period, burglaries rose tenfold, while holdups and muggings soared almost thirtyfold!

One can probably safely attribute this huge surge in crime to the fast-spreading drug culture, because heroin addicts commit extraordinary amounts of crime to fund their habits, which are always growing. Addicts need ever-escalating doses of opiates to get high and stop feeling withdrawal symptoms. Moreover, addicts are not likely to put something by for tomorrow. If they score enough in a robbery to buy five bags of heroin, they will not carefully set aside four for the coming days. They will shoot up everything. And so they are on a constant treadmill of getting money and getting drugs.

Criminologist John Ball and Professor David Nurco researched the legal records of 243 longtime Baltimore addicts, and also interviewed them about their criminal activities. Over an eleven-year period "it was found that these 243 heroin addicts had committed more than 473,000 crimes. As measured by crime-days, the average addict committed over 178 offenses per year and almost 2,000 offenses during his post-onset lifetime. Although the predominant offense committed was [nonviolent] burglary and larceny (as with most populations of criminals), these addicts were also involved in a wide range of other crimes: drug sales, robbery, forgery, pimping, assault, and murder."

When one old-time dealer reemerged in 1965 from prison, he was amazed at how drugs had spread in the time he had been was gone. Certainly the state's own *Drug Abuse Study* showed that of about 900 drug addicts arriving in state prison in 1968, 70 percent had started using drugs since 1960. Recalls this dealer, "When I came back in '65 drugs was all over the city, little clusters. It wasn't centralized on Pennsylvania Avenue anymore. I think urban renewal had something to do with it . . . [and] this new young generation of addicts. When white people began moving out of certain neighborhoods and blacks moved in, they took their environment with them, including drugs."

James the longtime addict also observed the big changes in the black addict world when he emerged in the mid sixties from a prison stint: "The drug environment must have grown a thousand percent. Where once I saw one addict, now I saw ten." The old hipsters such as James and Leroy were not at all pleased by the appearance of this huge new generation of young black addicts, a group they disdainfully called the "now generation." Says James,

> These new addicts were kids born from broken homes, with no real mother, father, not enough love. So you took these kids with no real wholesome home, no good background, that's who was in the street.
>
> They started off drinking syrup [the same over-the-counter codeine cough syrups that were a staple for the white addicts] and then they migrated into hard drugs. This now demanded real money, and these kids had no knowledge of real hustling, none of the so-called arts of the older groups. This resulted in violence. How could he get one hundred dollars to take care of his habit? So the kid takes up a pistol and he begins to kill peo-

ple, by mistake. They just didn't know what they were doing. Then they began to snatch welfare recipients' checks, to snatch the pocketbook from some lady on the corner with a baby in her arms. If the baby falls and busts his brains, what do they care? They were desperate little animals. They were caught up in the rat race of that jungle they came out of and they didn't know no other way to get money. And there were no [drug treatment] programs available in Baltimore then. I think what added to the drug culture more than anything else was the social breakdown.

While the recollections of older addicts suggest that it was drugs alone that pushed the new young users into violence, Professor Nurco's extensive studies with Baltimore addicts show that most of these predatory addicts had been engaged in violent crimes before they started using drugs. They just became worse when addicted. Professor Nurco found that addicts fell into at least one of three categories: those who engaged in criminal activity (often violent) before discovering drugs and whose addiction encouraged more of the same; those who had little prior history of criminality but who steadily and skillfully committed nonviolent crimes once addicted and rarely were caught; and then a few who were addicted but controlled it enough to be part of the straight world and lead relatively upright lives. By the early seventies, heroin in Baltimore had become so expensive and so weak that addicts became known as "hope fiends." It was not so much the almost imperceptible high of this weak heroin that was addictive, but the "fast life" that revolved around the drug.

Throughout the postwar decades, the city of Baltimore was steadily growing poorer as both those better off and jobs migrated elsewhere, a decline that was almost assuredly exacerbated by the steadily expanding drug culture. Families of that era seeking to shield children from drugs could best accomplish that by moving. And the relentless criminal activities of local addicts exacted a steady and debilitating toll on community and commercial life. The Avenue declined precipitously as people feared to venture forth. How much shoplifting, how many holdups or nighttime break-ins could a business (or its customers) tolerate before it moved or shut down? In 1955, the city had 81 percent of the area's industrial plants and 58 percent of its manufacturing employment. By 1965 that had declined to 72 percent and 56 percent. And as Professor Nurco notes, "There's a relationship between poverty and addiction." So as the drug culture helped drive out "straight, square" society, the cycle of decline intensified, producing an ever poorer city. By 1970 a study found that in Baltimore almost 40 percent of black men between sixteen and twenty-five and 25 percent of white men were neither working or in school. Meanwhile, the exodus of hardworking, law-abiding citizens accelerated. From 1950 to 1975, the city's population shrank from 950,000 to 830,000.

Looking back on this period of rapidly expanding heroin addiction, Professor Nurco says, "First, there was widespread availability. And then you had the mood of the society in the sixties and the changing values that said this stuff was okay. Deviancy begets deviancy. If you have kids hanging around with kids who are deviant and there's open criminality in the home, you find it creates a constellation of deviancy. And the ultimate form of deviancy is narcotic addiction. The other thing we've observed, when you look at kids living on the same block exposed to the same opportunities to use drugs, is that the presence of the natural father is definitely a factor for those who reject drugs." With soaring illegitimacy and divorce rates and widespread addiction (addicts do not function well as husbands or fathers), many more children found themselves in homes without any father—much less their natural fathers—and therefore more vulnerable. Professor Nurco observed in a 1975 paper entitled, "Narcotic Abusers and Poverty," that "narcotic abusers under eighteen years of age have a greater likelihood of being on the Medicaid lists as members of a family on AFDC." Again, the poverty-welfare-drugs connection.

In 1950, the city of Baltimore had had two deaths from heroin overdoses, the two black teenagers who collapsed on the street. Over the next two decades, the city had become steadily poorer, until in 1970 12 percent of its populace was on welfare. As the city's fortunes declined, drug culture spread and became deeply entrenched, a destructive form of solace. In 1970, fifty-nine people died of drug overdoses, *thirty* times more than in 1950. Forty-four of these drug casualties were blacks: eleven teenagers, thirty-one adults between twenty and forty, and two over forty. Fifteen were white: two teenagers and thirteen adults aged twenty to forty. The words of James, one of the city's earliest black heroin addicts, haunt: "Out of curiosity you'd try it. And for most of us that was all it took to cut our hearts out and send us down the river for life." Rare was the acolyte of the full-time drug culture who found his or her way back up the river to a full and meaningful life. For as Johnson explained, "This [heroin] is your master now."

Up through the mid 1960s illegal drugs remained an inner-city phenomenon in Baltimore as elsewhere, a remote and irrelevant vice to white middle-class Americans placidly pursuing the good life in the nation's leafy suburbs. It was simply not a part of growing up white and upwardly mobile, not something that parents worried about. But all that was about to change drastically.

Milford Mill High School, just north of Baltimore, was the classic postwar suburban school, a low-lying brick box set amid athletic fields, the institutional equivalent of the suburban ranch house: no charm, no tradition, but attractive enough and well suited to its task. Opened in 1949 to educate the children of county farmers and the earliest suburbanites, by the early sixties Milford Mill's fluorescent-lit classrooms were swamped by the tidal wave of the postwar baby boom. French teacher Robert Rivkin, who taught at Milford Mill from 1963 to 1992, recalls, "About 75 percent of these kids went to a four-year college and practically all the students came from two-parent families where both mother and father had college degrees."

There were the perennial concerns about underage drinking and premarital sex, but in the fall of 1967 there was no concern whatsoever about drugs. Mindy Milstein Shuman, class of '68, remembers a happy ignorance: "When I first came into high school I had never heard of drugs." Robert Rivkin was probably typical of the teachers when he says that he was "totally unaware of the existence of drugs. I had heard of marijuana and heroin from stories I'd read in magazines and newspapers. But it was definitely all thug-underworld stuff to me at that time."

During the 1967–68 school year all that began to change. Tom Knoche, a Troy Donahue–handsome athlete and student government leader voted "most popular senior" of the class of '68, recalls that for him and virtually every other student in the school "drugs were all new. They were something you weren't supposed to do, really unacceptable behavior." Yet during that year smoking marijuana became more and more acceptable behavior. Milford seniors in the class of '68 all vividly remember that theirs was dubbed "The Class of Grass." In part this was playful allusion to the school's athletic fields being redone and reseeded, but it was mainly a reference to marijuana.

And while Mindy Milstein never used marijuana at Milford, she remembers nonetheless that 1967 clearly was delineated as a "drinking" class, while 1968 was a "smoking" class. "There was a lot of talk," she recalls. "People became more cavalier about it. There was no specific event that sticks in my mind, just this new realization during our senior year that there were now pot parties. I found it scary because I had a neighbor who was a college student and I had seen her go from marijuana to quaaludes in less than year, and she did not seem in good shape. I didn't want that kind of loss of control."

Knoche, referring to the morass in Vietnam and the ever tenser civil rights struggle, says, "Things were a mess and the message was 'Experiment, try things! Don't be a tight ass.' And so marijuana really came into its own. Our senior year we all knew it was around. I wasn't a user or into it, but I remember a couple of parties where I saw people smoking joints." Certainly these high school seniors were coming of age in an extraordinarily tumultuous time.

In the late sixties atmosphere of unrest and dissension, it is no wonder that the ambient message was, "Things are a mess. Experiment. Try things! Don't be a tight-ass." Moreover, as popular skepticism mounted about the official rosy pronouncements out of Vietnam, this filtered down into an all-round skepticism about any kind of government authority. Longtime official warnings and information about drugs—especially marijuana—were assessed in this newly skeptical light. For decades the Federal Bureau of Narcotics had been equating marijuana with heroin, describing it as a highly dangerous drug. Marijuana, declared the FBN again and again, might well drive you mad before leading you inevitably to heroin. Now students experimenting with grass found the initial experience was often giggles and euphoria. Remembers one junior from that year, "Friends who smoked grass or hash told me they weren't particularly harmful."

While students such as Knoche and Milstein and the vast majority of their classmates were only just hearing of marijuana for the first time in the 1967–68 school year, and perhaps trying it, a tiny coterie of Milford students—a few dozen in a high school of almost two thousand—were already deeply into illegal drugs. "I was wasted from day one of 11th grade," recalls Mike Gimbel, a wiry dark-haired boy who arrived at Milford Mill in the fall of 1967 as a junior. "I went varsity in drugs." Gimbel's enthusiasm for being high went back to eighth grade dances: "I found that getting drunk—usually Thunderbird wine—gave me confidence to be like my friends. It got me psychologically hooked on altering my senses."

By ninth grade, Gimbel had moved up to sniffing glue on the weekends. Then, in the summer of 1966, he went to Ocean City, a traditional Maryland teenage party spot. While others enjoyed the sun and surf, he was busy trying out various new drugs. Back home, young Gimbel appeared on the surface still to be engaged fully in normal teenage activities. He went to school each morning. Most Saturdays he worked for a sister-in-law's family at their pork stand in the bustling Lexington Market. But at school Gimbel was as high as a kite, and at his job he brazenly stole hundreds of dollars. "I used to come home smelling like a piece of bacon," he says, "but all this money was critical. It meant I could afford a car, and with the car and the money we could buy drugs and then get high."

Genteel ladies were the typical drug addicts of the late nineteenth century. In this drawing from a *McClure's* story, the woman on the left confesses that she became "habituated" when the doctor provided a stock of morphine to ease pain from "muscular rheumatism." (*McClure's* Magazine)

Patent medicines contained all manner of opiates and cocaine, but this was rarely revealed before the 1906 Food and Drug Act. The popular Mrs. Winslow's Soothing Syrup, its homey advertising from 1888 shown here, did not hint that the active ingredient was morphine. (Courtesy of William F. Helfand)

Sigmund Freud, in 1884 a little-known Viennese neurologist, began proselytizing cocaine ("this magical drug") as highly useful for treating a host of medical problems. His work, combined with Karl Koller's discovery of coca's anesthetic properties, unleashed a flood of interest. (Yale University Harvey Cushing/John Hay Whitney Medical Library)

By the turn of the century, opium dens were a fixture in many American communities and much patronized by the "sporting classes." Here a group of "swells" visits a den in New York City's Chinatown around 1905. (Brown Bros.)

Some of the first commercial products using cocaine were coca wines. One of the most famous was the French Vin Mariani. Mariani typically featured testimonials from kings, popes, and artists. Here Czech artist Alphonse Mucha has designed a postcard declaring, "The mummies themselves stand up and walk after drinking Vin Mariani." (Courtesy of William F. Helfand)

Coca-Cola was just one of dozens of "temperance" beverages that featured the stimulating cocaine rather than the "demon" alcohol. Others were Rocco Cola, Koca Nola, and Dope Cola. In 1903, Coca-Cola removed cocaine as an ingredient when the drug fell into disrepute. (Bettmann Archive)

TIRED? THEN DRINK *Coca-Cola*

IT RELIEVES EXHAUSTION

When the BRAIN is running under full pressure send down to the FOUNTAIN for a glass of

Coca-Cola

you will be surprised how quickly it will ease the Tired Brain—soothe the Rattled Nerves and restore Wasted Energy to both Mind and Body.
It enables the entire system to readily cope with the strain of any excessive demands made upon it.

AT ALL FOUNTAINS
ALSO IN BOTTLES 5c.

Other popular uses of cocaine (introduced by drug companies starting in 1885) were more medicinal, such as the cocaine toothache drops shown advertised here. The so-called catarrh powders, which were snuffed to relieve all variety of nasal congestion, contained 2 to 5 percent pure cocaine. Dr. Birney's and Dr. Grey's were two of the best-known brands; cocaine addicts were soon known as "Birney blowers" and "Grey men." (Courtesy William F. Helfand)

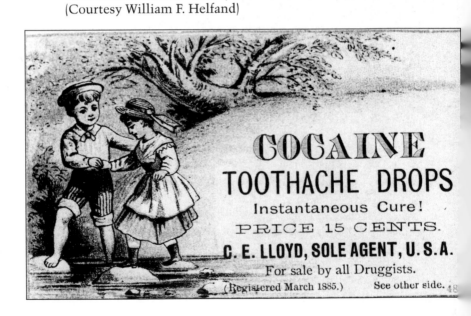

A man on the Bowery in New York City around 1910 shoots up cocaine. The alarming spread of lower-class cocaine and heroin addiction, with attendant antisocial behavior, led to stringent new drug laws. (Brown Bros.)

BĀYER
PHARMACEUTICAL PRODUCTS.

We are now sending to **Physicians** throughout the United States literature and **samples** of

ASPIRIN

The substitute for the Salicylates, agreeable of taste, free from unpleasant aftereffects.

HEROIN

The Sedative for Coughs.

HEROIN HYDROCHLORIDE

Its water-soluble salt.
You will have call for them. Order a supply from your jobber.

Write for literature to

FARBENFABRIKEN OF ELBERFELD CO.
40 Stone Street, New York,

SELLING AGENTS.

In 1898, the German pharmaceutical firm Bayer—well known for aspirin—introduced a new over-the-counter drug called Heroin. Highly effective for quieting coughs, Heroin was also touted as nonaddictive. (Courtesy DEA)

Mabel Normand was one of Hollywood's biggest stars in the silent movie era, a time when illicit use of cocaine and opiates was rampant in the film colony. Normand's career was one of many ruined by drugs. (MOMA Film Stills Archive)

Another major Hollywood star, Wallace Reid, was addicted to opiates. After his death in 1923, his wife, actress Dorothy Davenport (shown here), made and starred in *Human Wreckage*, a movie about the drug trade, as a "memorial" to her husband's struggle against his addiction. (MOMA Film Stills Archive)

Hollywood director William Desmond Taylor's murder in early 1922 was never solved. He actively opposed local drug dealers, leaving some reporters of the era convinced Taylor was a drug hit. (MOMA Film Stills Archive)

Criminal mastermind Arnold Rothstein transformed the New York underworld into big business. His final legacy was organizing international drug trafficking in the 1920s. This photo is from 1928, the year he was murdered. (Brown Bros.)

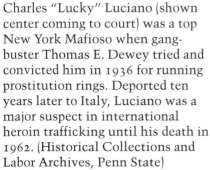

Charles "Lucky" Luciano (shown center coming to court) was a top New York Mafioso when gang-buster Thomas E. Dewey tried and convicted him in 1936 for running prostitution rings. Deported ten years later to Italy, Luciano was a major suspect in international heroin trafficking until his death in 1962. (Historical Collections and Labor Archives, Penn State)

Commissioner Harry J. Anslinger (right) ran the Federal Bureau of Narcotics with an iron fist from 1930 to 1962. He gloried in acting the tough cop, yet his real strength was as a drug diplomat at international conferences. (Historical Collections and Labor Archives, Penn State)

Musician (Milton) Mezz Mezzrow (left) was famous in Harlem for being the man who introduced marijuana beyond the tight circles of jazz in 1929. Mezzrow is best remembered not as a jazzman but as the author of *Really The Blues,* a minor classic about the black hepster world. (Rutger's Institute of Jazz Studies)

Charlie Parker, brilliant saxophonist and cocreator of the bebop style of jazz, had a serious heroin addiction. Other musicians and fans who worshipped Parker as a paragon of "hip" began using heroin as their badge of "cool." (Brown Bros.)

U.S. narcotics agent Andrew Tartaglino was among a handful assigned to Europe after World War II. In the early 1960s, he would help solve the Ambassador cases—important breakthroughs in the French Connection. Tartaglino then headed a major anticorruption investigation for the old Federal Bureau of Narcotics. (Courtesy of Andrew Tartaglino)

The French Connection became *the* source of heroin in the postwar years. Here John Cusack (center, wearing white top), a top federal narcotics agent, poses in the late 1950s with members of the French narcotics squad after a raid outside Paris. Cusack later led the successful effort to stop Turkish opium production and thereby ended the French Connection. (Courtesy of John Cusack)

Drs. Vincent Dole and Marie Nyswander together discovered and developed methadone maintenance treatment at Rockefeller University in the 1960s. Methadone maintenance remains one of the most successful methods of helping heroin addicts. (Courtesy of Rockefeller University)

A modern-day pieta by Angel Allende, *The Sorrow of a Mother*, depicts an East Harlem mother mourning her son, dead of a heroin overdose. Starting in the late 1950s, French Connection heroin became progressively more available in northern urban slums. (Museum of the City of New York)

LSD guru Timothy Leary, love beads and all, presides over a January 1967 "happening" in San Francisco's Golden Gate Park. A onetime Harvard academic, Leary would serve time in prison for drugs before returning to his favored role as party-going celeb and enfant terrible. (AP/Wide World Photos)

Allen Ginsberg, Beat poet and then counterculture leader, embraced the black hipster scene and drugs early on. However, Ginsberg and other whites like Timothy Leary preferred to promote drug use as part of a quest for higher consciousness. (UPI)

President Richard M. Nixon poses with Elvis Presley, who visited in late 1970 offering to help spread antidrug messages. Illegal drug use was exploding and the Nixon Administration often described it as "domestic problem number one." (Nixon Project, U.S. Archives)

The first Woodstock music festival in August 1969 showed how open and widespread illegal drug use had become among white middle–class Baby Boomers. The "grass shack" here sports a sign reading, "HAVE A MARIJUANA." (AP/Wide World Photos)

By the late 1970s, a whole paraphernalia industry arose to market drug-related wares. This early advertisement for a free-base kit alarmed drug experts, who knew that smoking cocaine was extremely addictive. Before drug paraphernalia was effectively outlawed, 300,000 such kits were sold. (Advertisement from *High Times*)

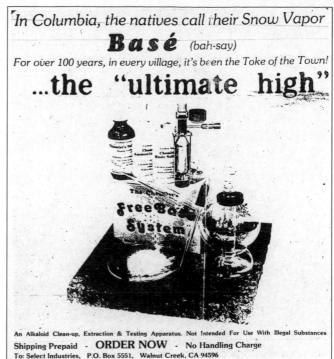

In Columbia, the natives call their Snow Vapor
Basé (bah-say)
For over 100 years, in every village, it's been the Toke of the Town!
...the "ultimate high"

An Alkaloid Clean-up, Extraction & Testing Apparatus. Not Intended For Use With Illegal Substances
Shipping Prepaid - **ORDER NOW** - No Handling Charge
To: Select Industries, P.O. Box 5551, Walnut Creek, CA 94596

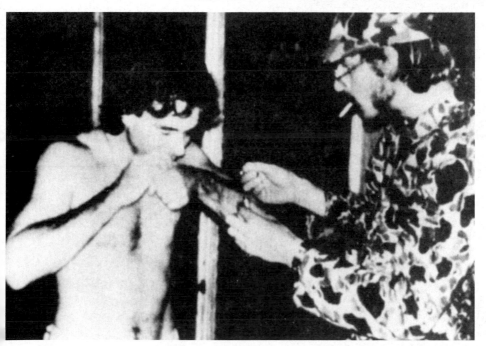

Colombian trafficker Carlos Lehder (left) samples cocaine in 1978. Lehder completely transformed the cocaine trade by smuggling in Colombian cocaine by the half-ton rather than the traditional five to ten kilos. He is serving life in prison. (U.S. Courts)

In the cartoon: "There is no widespread drug use in the White House, according to a high government official."

By the early 1980s, middle-class use of illicit drugs had become so commonplace that youthful White House staff felt free to indulge. The ensuing drug scandals sorely embarrassed the Carter White House, which became the butt of editorial cartoons like this one by Jeff MacNally. (Chicago Media Services)

First Lady Nancy Reagan hosts a "Just Say No" rally at the White House, May 22, 1986. While many derided Mrs. Reagan's campaign, her influence helped spread the vocal antidrug messages that led to big declines in drug use among kids. (Reagan Library)

The worst horror of the late 1980s crack epidemic was addicted women not caring that smoking could damage their own babies in utero. (Courtesy of Partnership for a Drug-Free America)

On September 29, 1989, the DEA made the most spectacular drug bust in American law enforcement history—confiscating twenty tons of cocaine and boxes and gym bags (shown here) holding $10 million in cash from an unguarded warehouse in San Fernando Valley, California. (Courtesy of the DEA)

A little girl stands with her mother, who has been arrested in a crackhouse raid. Those caught up in the crack subculture neglected, abused, and abandoned their children by the tens of thousands. Many are being raised by grandparents or foster care. (Marty Katz)

As the autumn of 1967 deepened to winter, Gimbel's basic outlook boiled down to: "The more serious drug I used, the more status. To me, marijuana was status because it was completely illegal. . . . I was completely on quaaludes most of eleventh grade."

Sometime during this high-all-the-time junior year, Gimbel and one or two other drug buddies began leaving school for a few hours and breaking into houses in their own tidy neighborhoods, secluded suburban ways with names such as Greenleaf and Hemlock: "People didn't lock their doors much in those days. And there was usually an open window somewhere. We'd be scared to death, but still a couple of times a week we were doing it." Despite all this, Gimbel managed to complete his junior year with Cs and Ds.

The summer of 1968 once again found Gimbel visiting Ocean City. While others frolicked in the rough Atlantic surf and worked on their tans, says Gimbel, "A friend introduced me to heroin for the first time." That summer was memorable not just for the personal story of Gimbel's ever-deeper descent into drug abuse, but also for the terrible political upheaval and mayhem abroad in the land. Bobby Kennedy was assassinated out in California, the Chicago Democratic convention degenerated into bloody street riots, and it was another tense summer in the nation's black slums. But this time Baltimore erupted, too. As shops were looted and torched all through the city's black west side, Governor Spiro T. Agnew called in the National Guard. It took almost six thousand troops and four days to quell the city's first "insurrection" since violent railroad strikes a century earlier. Craziness and despair were in the air.

At Milford Mill, "that summer of '68 seemed to change everyone," remembers Gimbel. "At school that fall everyone had moved up a notch. I was into heroin. The drinkers were into pot, and the pot smokers of the previous year were into acid [LSD]. Somehow that summer it was as if everyone's values changed, and their attitudes towards drugs. The culture was changing, we were going from this whole soul music about boy-girl love into music about revolution and being radical."

Popular music began to reflect the new world of mind-altering drugs, from the Beatles with *Sergeant Pepper's Lonely Hearts Club Band*, to the Rolling Stones shouting, "Get Off of My Cloud," Jefferson Airplane singing "White Rabbit," and Jimi Hendrix howling "Purple Haze." The film *Easy Rider* showed bad boys Jack Nicholson and Peter Fonda getting high. And so the popular culture of youth—above all the music—reflected a growing experience with altered drug states while further popularizing that interest.

Mike Gimbel soon found himself moving beyond marijuana, pills, and acid. Once his senior year began, Gimbel recalls, "I was doing heroin every day. A friend had a connection in the city, a couple of black guys in their mid twenties, these black brothers who lived in this house off Druid Hill Avenue." Every couple of days as the weather grew chilly and dusk descended earlier and earlier, Gimbel drove from his white suburban life to this staid-looking neighborhood in west Baltimore. Once Jewish, it was now black. Gimbel soon took to selling drugs in the northwestern suburbs to support his heroin habit.

Decades later, Gimbel recalled himself as having cut a swashbuckling figure in high school, a well-known person who was viewed as a highly hip and plugged-in guy. But classmates and teachers only vaguely remembered him, remarking, "Oh, yeah, he used to get in trouble—cutting class and stuff." There was no admiration. This is typical of the gulf between the addict's strangely glorified and self-important self-image and the rest of the world's indifference and/or low opinion of someone whose first allegiance is to drugs.

For Gimbel, "the revelation senior year was realizing I was addicted to heroin." Then one Saturday night at 2 A.M. Gimbel was driving in a black neighborhood downtown, heading home with a bag of heroin he had just purchased. Unable to wait, he stopped to shoot up then and there. The sight of a white teenager at that hour in that place caught the attention of some passing police. Gimbel, all of seventeen years old and a senior at an outstanding suburban high school, was arrested for possession of heroin. "They took me down and put me in a cell. I was pissing in my pants I was so scared. As you can imagine, this was a major eye-opener for Mommy and Daddy. A really good lawyer got me off. My parents sent me to a psychiatrist. But I was still using, and one day my father came home to find me with a needle in my arm." There ensued more not-very-productive visits to a psychiatrist.

By the time the class of '69 graduated, the Milford Mill teachers and administrators were beginning to understand that illegal drugs had arrived and could not be ignored or wished away. Almost unknown to the middle class several years earlier, drugs such as marijuana, LSD, speed, and various pharmaceutical uppers and downers were fast becoming commonplace. Faculty members later all would recall certain indelible events from this early period in the white recreational-drug culture. For instance, the first visit by Baltimore County police to discuss drugs at a faculty meeting. Recalls one teacher, "It was something of a traveling show. There were two officers and they had a whole pharmaceutical array under plastic. You could see what this stuff looked like. What marijuana looked like and smelled like." For the many experienced and veteran teachers on the Milford Mill staff this was a disconcerting event. Theirs was not an inner-city school burdened with juvenile delinquents; their school was for the best and the brightest. And yet here they sat, listening to policemen describe increasingly popular illegal substances.

Obviously, Mike Gimbel was an extreme case, a not-so-nice Jewish boy who spent his senior year at Milford Mill in a fog of heroin. One of the first suburban participants in the part-time, white recreational-drug culture, it did not take Gimbel and his friends all that long—just a few years—to spiral down and completely embrace the drug culture full time. While most of those who experimented and then stopped did fine, Gimbel and a few buddies got completely sucked in. They shucked all the advantages and expectations of their middle-class upbringings to live the fast life with like-minded addicts and pushers. Within a year of graduation, without school for structure, Gimbel had become the classic dope addict: staying high as much as possible, stealing, dealing, hustling, and ripping off everyone he knew, especially his family. Gimbel was arrested three more times on drug charges. Says his mother, "He drained us financially. We lost the house, he wrecked two cars that were not paid for. There were lawyers, there were psychiatrists."

Milford Mill High School saw its own drug problems escalate. The visit by Baltimore County police to describe various drugs had been distinctly disquieting. It gave formal voice to behavior never before encountered in this clean-cut suburban milieu. "Kids are natural explorers and risk takers," says Gunther Stern, who spent twenty years as a guidance counselor at Milford Mill. "And before this if you heard about a kid suddenly going downhill in school, you would look to see if the parents were having trouble or some other reason. But now there was always the possibility of drugs." By 1973 a survey of a nearby suburb, Howard County, would show that 40 percent of senior high school students reported some use of marijuana or hashish, with 7 percent admitting experience with heroin, methadone, or morphine. With white middle-class drug experimentation growing by leaps and bounds, tragedy soon ensued.

It came most dramatically at Milford Mill with the drug-related suicide of a loved and much admired student. The boy, described as "one of the most brilliant kids who went through this school," took LSD in 1971. Former English teacher Alan Lipsitz knew that for a lot of kids this was just another "means of experimentation. There was a lot of fascination with [Timothy] Leary apparently. But in this boy's case—he was especially young and innocent compared with his peers—he just completely freaked out. There were all these aftereffects. He was found just wandering on the beach at Atlantic City." French teacher Robert Rivkin recalls the boy as "one of my favorites, a star student." After the boy's bad trip, he was committed to Seton Hall in Washington, D.C. Says Rivkin, "I remember going down to take him some special fables from La Fontaine. I was hoping to get him interested again." Rivkin sighs as he dredges up ancient and painful memories. "He committed suicide by jumping out a window. He just never recovered from the LSD." In his history of LSD, *Storming Heaven*, Jay Stevens estimates that for "every thousand people who took LSD, seven would suffer a breakdown." This was one such casualty.

Angela Saxton, long head of guidance at Milford, found

> the denial of the parents in this whole matter incredible. We'd send someone home or even to the hospital because they were so nonfunctional, just bouncing off the walls. And the parents would send them back to school the next day with some note about how the child had just been very tired or on some medication. There was much more concern that SATs were not high enough or certain grades. I always remember one fourteen-year-old girl in ninth grade. She was part of a group that used to go hang out behind a supermarket off Liberty Road, where they apparently did drugs. One afternoon, this girl went into cardiac arrest and died. The mother never even admitted her daughter took drugs. I mean, these kids were always talking about love and peace and caring. And yet these same kids doing drugs at a party panicked when someone ODed and threw the kid out in the snow and didn't call an ambulance.

For years people like Allen Ginsberg, Timothy Leary, and other counterculture gurus had been proselytizing about the incomparable benefits of taking drugs and getting high. True populists, they somehow believed that most people were as highly educated and as spiritually hungry as they were. Moreover, the gurus overlooked the fact that their fame freed them from the constrictions of the mundane—whether appearing every day at a job (where being compos mentis was necessary to the safety and well-being of others) or simply attending high school. The reality was that few people were likely to have their lives dramatically changed for the better or even notably enhanced by getting high. Frequent altered states tend to interfere with ordinary responsibilities—whether school or job—and relationships. Yet for the moment young middle-class America heard only the siren call of these new, hip, and exciting substances.

CHAPTER 14

"The Problem Has Assumed the Dimensions of a National Emergency."

—President Richard M. Nixon,
June 17, 1971

On July 14, 1969, President Richard M. Nixon announced with great fanfare a "national attack on narcotics abuse." The message sent to Congress declared the explosion of drug use—juvenile arrests for drugs had risen by 800 percent between 1960 and 1967—a "growing menace to the general welfare of the United States." The president noted, "It is doubtful that an American parent can send a son or daughter to college today without exposing the young man or woman to drug abuse. Parents must also be concerned about the availability and use of such drugs in our high schools and junior high schools."

In tackling drugs, Nixon was engaging in something of a postwar presidential tradition. Back on November 2, 1951, President Harry Truman had become the first, officially declaring the "situation" with illegal drugs "of grave concern to me. Illicit narcotics peddling has recently risen sharply in volume. Moreover, drug addiction has reached serious proportions, particularly among some of the youth of our nation." Not only did Truman back the stiffer mandatory sentences of the 1951 Boggs bill as one useful antidrug measure, he also appointed an interdepartmental committee on narcotics (Treasury, State, Defense, Justice, Agriculture, and the Federal Security Agency) and entrusted it with a great many vague and ambitious goals. Naturally, the lead member of this enterprise was none other than Harry J. Anslinger, already commissioner of Treasury's Bureau of Narcotics for twenty-one years. Anslinger had no interest in having other departments nosing around his bailiwick. As far as can be discerned, the consummate bureaucrat successfully ensured that nothing more was heard from the interdepartmental committee.

Then on November 27, 1954, President Dwight D. Eisenhower took time out from a Thanksgiving golf vacation in Georgia to call for "a new war on narcotics addiction at the local, national and international level." The president appointed "a special Cabinet committee of five members to coordinate the campaign against illegal narcotics." They were charged with the fairly limited job of making a national survey of both addiction and law enforcement needs. The main upshot of their report was that Eisenhower backed the even tougher mandatory sentences of the Daniel's bill as an antidrug measure. Meanwhile, trafficking and addiction swelled rapidly through the late fifties, as Commissioner Anslinger assured official Washington all would be solved by the tougher mandatory sentences.

By the time John F. Kennedy took office in 1960, a small avante garde of urban middle-class kids was becoming intrigued by drugs, and even Anslinger could no longer convince anyone that heroin in the big northern cities was under control. (This was the year the Bureau of Narcotics discovered, to its dismay—via the first Ambassador case— how big heroin trafficking had grown.) As promised during his campaign, JFK quickly launched plans for the first-ever White House Conference on Narcotic & Drug Abuse, a two-day extravaganza attended by five hundred people—everyone from cops to governors to psychiatrists—in late September 1962. The meeting revealed the abysmal lack of knowledge about everything related to narcotics. Seeking concrete advice on how to proceed, the Kennedy White House appointed a full-fledged President's Advisory Commission on Narcotics and Drug Abuse on January 16, 1963. This time, with Anslinger retired, no one stood in the way of a serious survey of all aspects of the issue—law enforcement, treatment, and research (or lack thereof). In early November, Kennedy saw the thick document produced under E. Barrett Prettyman, retired chief judge of the U.S. Court of Appeals in Washington, D.C. The report still had not been released when JFK was assassinated three weeks later.

When Lyndon B. Johnson took over the presidency, he duly uttered appropriate expressions of concern about drugs and then had the Prettyman report—with its twenty-five recommendations—released in late January 1964. That done, White House aide Dean F. Markham, a one-time Harvard football lineman and longtime Kennedy insider, pondered the pros and cons of following through in any meaningful way. As he wrote in a memo that spring, "There is almost a public hysteria regarding the dope situation that even reaches into the areas of the country that have no real problem." The Prettyman recommendations ranged from the very simple and politically easy to the decidedly tough and complicated. The simple stuff involved the administration instructing federal executives to take "more aggressive action" and also appointing a special assistant within the White House to pursue the issue.

But other recommendations required far more political energy. A number were aimed at rectifying the information vacuum (one of Anslinger's most notable legacies), both through "a comprehensive research plan covering all aspects of narcotic and drug abuse [and] . . . a national reporting system to collect, collate, and analyze data." But Prettyman also took on the biggest, toughest issues. For instance, the commission proposed revamping the federal drug laws, doing away with the harsh mandatory sentences (especially for marijuana) of Boggs and Daniel. "The Bureau of Narcotics," wrote the commission, "maintains that the present severe penalties act as a powerful deterrent. The commission does not agree." A survey presented at the White House conference showed that more than 90 percent of federal prison wardens were against the mandatory sentences, as were more than 70 percent of federal district judges, more than 80 percent of probation officers, and about half of the U.S. district attorneys.

Even more drastic, Prettyman said the Bureau of Narcotics should be plucked from Treasury, relocated inside Justice, and made much bigger. (The bureau's top brass, meanwhile, were still insisting they didn't *need* any more than three hundred agents to do the job.) After considering the whole Prettyman report, White House aide Markham argued, "I feel that there is every advantage to be gained by continuing some sort of follow-up at the White House level, especially in view of the significance of this problem in certain regions of the country." Many of the easier recommendations were fulfilled and then a task force was appointed to wrestle with the more complicated matters.

Meanwhile, there was growing unease about the basic integrity and efficacy of the federal Bureau of Narcotics, the nation's frontline agency against international heroin trafficking. In 1964 Markham had mentioned that a "top official" in the Justice Department described FBN agents as "real bomb throwers" whose "rough-neck ways are going to cause some serious embarrassment to the Treasury Department and the Administration someday." About a year later, Markham was writing again of his concerns about the bureau, sparked this time by the arrest of the head of the FBN's Miami bureau on bribery charges. Markham urged "better control, since they [the Bureau] do not have to answer to anyone nor are they kept under a system of checks and balances. In addition to their methods of making cases, there has always been a rumor to the effect of bribes. . . . I wouldn't be at all surprised if some newspaper or magazine tries to run an exposé series on supposed abuses within the Federal Bureau of Narcotics."

On August 3, 1965, Markham's prophesy was fulfilled. His heart must have sunk as he scanned the screaming tabloid headline MOB SHAKE-DOWN in the *New York Journal-American*. A small-time drug dealer named Joseph Kadlub had been gunned down in a Brooklyn bar. Kadlub, however, was no ordinary crook, but an informer for the bureau. Moreover, fearing for his own life, Kadlub had gone to the *Journal-American* editors only weeks before to describe rampant corruption in local and federal narcotics enforcement. Kadlub had then recorded a number of incriminating phone conversations. And so Markham could read on the front page that Kadlub had established "how a federal narcotics agent was moving to shake down a Brooklyn man peddling narcotics for a large quantity of heroin that the agent himself was going to sell to a distributor in Harlem."

As a worried Markham wrote in a White House memo, the Kadlub case, plus the other in Miami, only confirmed "a great deal of confidential information given to us from municipal, state and federal sources concerning the internal operation of the Federal Bureau of Narcotics." For a decade, the Federal Bureau of Narcotics had, in fact, been growing ever more corrupt. Other law enforcement agencies such as Customs and the FBI avoided even sharing information with the FBN. And now the moment of reckoning had arrived.

Over in the Department of Treasury, assistant secretary David Acheson (patrician former U.S. Attorney for D.C. and son of Cold War mandarin Dean Acheson) had come to view the Bureau of Narcotics as a scandal waiting to erupt. He had tried, with no success, to convince Treasury Secretary Henry Fowler to foist the FBN on Justice before it embarrassed everyone at Treasury. With Anslinger gone, the bureau's top brass openly engaged in vicious infighting. Like juvenile tattletales, these grown men constantly sidled into Acheson's office with complaints against one another. Meanwhile, the second Ambassador case with Pardo-Bolland had shown Acheson that tons of heroin were flooding in while these higherups made war—not on drugs—but on each other. Moreover, Acheson was now hearing that the FBN was not just ineffective, but corrupt. In the wake of the Kadlub case, Acheson asked another Treasury agency, the IRS, to run quick discreet audits on everyone in the New York FBN office. The results were not reassuring. Certain agents were found to have deposited cash payments as large as seventy-five thousand dollars. Moreover, the IRS agents had little trouble using their own informers to make drug buys off corrupt FBN agents. Acheson now summoned Andrew Tartaglino, a veteran FBN agent who had made a name on the Ambassador cases, and dispatched him with four handpicked lieutenants to clean up the mess in New York.

Next Acheson discovered yet a further complication. As corrupt agents started jumping ship from the Bureau of Narcotics to avoid Tartaglino's probings, they were being hired by the Food and Drug Administration's new drug enforcement agency, the Bureau of Drug Abuse Control (BDAC), created in 1966 to police psychedelics, speed, and other such favorites of the burgeoning counterculture. Moreover, these two federal enforcement agencies were now squabbling over drug turf, adding another fractious voice to the longtime rivalry between the FBN and U.S. Customs. Faced with this mess, the Johnson administration decided the solution was to do what Prettyman's commission had proposed: move the Bureau of Narcotics over to the Justice Department. They further hoped to end the new rivalries between the bureau and BDAC by combining the two into one entity. In early 1968 Attorney General Ramsey Clark began the arduous process of pushing the reorganization through Congress. By April 8 of that year the new Bureau of Narcotics and Dangerous Drugs (BNDD) was born, a ward of Justice.

For thirty-two years Harry J. Anslinger had been Narcotics commissioner. Then for six years his lackluster clone, Henry Giordano, had run the show. Now Attorney General Ramsey Clark brought in a complete outsider, Charlotte, North Carolina, Police Chief John Ingersoll, to be the new director of BNDD. (The grandiose title of commissioner had been interred along with the bureau.) A graduate of Berkeley, the boyish-looking Ingersoll, thirty-nine, had served on the Oakland police force and worked with the International Association of Chiefs of

Police. It was for the IACP that Ingersoll had especially distinguished himself, doing "field studies" of various troubled departments. He himself had then overhauled the Charlotte police force to great acclaim. Ingersoll signed on with the Johnson administration mere weeks before LBJ announced he wouldn't run for a second term.

When Ingersoll walked into the mare's nest that was BNDD on Indiana Avenue, he found, aside from Tartaglino's big half-completed corruption investigation, a very odd mixture. "The two organizations—the Bureau of Narcotics and BDAC—were like night and day, even down to the way people talked and dressed. The Bureau of Narcotics was a very conservative organization where virtually everyone believed that marijuana was almost as bad as heroin. BDAC was just the opposite."

And while there were "pockets of brilliance" at BNDD, especially in investigative abilities, Ingersoll was amazed to find that no one at the old Bureau of Narcotics had ever sat down and performed the most rudimentary analyses of all its many cases: How might they be connected? Who were the trafficking gangs? How did they operate? Where did they operate? Where was most of the seized heroin entering the United States? Through what kind of smuggling operation? In cars? Airplanes? Ships? No one had ever made a systematic inquiry.

Nor had anyone at the postwar bureau pressed beyond the most elementary diplomatic initiatives to persuade our putative allies, the French, to crack down on the Corsicans. When LBJ's Task Force on Narcotics examined the whole drug situation, one of its major conclusions was that someone in authority should speak to the French: "The task force recommends that the U.S. Ambassador to France hold private discussions with the appropriate minister of France to convey the serious concern of the President over the illegal export traffic in heroin." As the task force noted with some amazement, "In fairness to the French, we are not aware that there has been any political discussion of this problem with the Government of France. . . . The matter would be raised . . . at a political level for the first time of which we have any knowledge."

When an obviously astonished Treasury Assistant Secretary Acheson discussed this with Narcotics Commissioner Henry Giordano in late 1966, the earlier bureau efforts were described. Giordano also gamely deconstructed the Gallic viewpoint:

> While the French are inwardly aware that they are not in spirit living up to their responsibility under the international narcotic treaties and in the community of nations, they outwardly take the position that the illicit production problem in their

country, which does not affect them, is artificially created by their accidentally being astride the route of the raw materials in the Near East and the market in North America. They overemphasize their transit position and conveniently overlook their actual position as a vast clandestine producer, a role created and sustained by their underworld which they also, for their purposes, tend to ignore.

To justify the lack of strength and effectiveness of their narcotics enforcement effort the Director of the Police Judiciaire has, on occasion, said the source and victim countries are the root and cause of the traffic while the transit countries are just accidentally caught in the middle.

Giordano explained that the bureau had pressed the French to do something through the United Nation and Interpol to no avail. Presumably Giordano was clinging to Anslinger's strategy of operating solo, for the bureau had sought little help from more powerful entities such as the State Department or White House. Not only Acheson, but Ingersoll, when he took over, found this baffling.

And then there was veteran agent John T. Cusack's imaginative ideas about getting the Turks out of opium growing, something no one at the bureau had given any serious support. For Cusack, the bureau's lead agent in Europe, the Rosal–Tarditi case had not been a surprise, "but it got me to thinking and was the spark that triggered the thought process about doing something in Turkey. That was the core of the problem and if we didn't control the raw materials in Turkey, the laboratories could be anywhere." Cusack first suggested in 1962 that Turkey—source of much Corsican morphine base—and the recipient of $3.5 billion in U.S. aid since 1948, ought to be more cooperative. Cusack pointed out "the complete lack of any real organized program on the part of the Government of Turkey to control the cultivation of opium and suppress the illicit traffic." A year later, in 1963, he would write Commissioner Giordano again:

Our intelligence indicates that at least 90 percent of the heroin entering New York is of French origin and smuggled either directly or via Italy by French violators in connivance with Mafia elements in Italy and the United States.

Information developed and investigations concluded by this office have repeatedly established that the bulk of illicit heroin originating in France is manufactured from morphine base produced in Turkey and Syria and smuggled from Beirut and Istanbul to Paris and Marseille. The origin of this morphine base is Turkish opium which continues to be diverted from legitimate production each year in vast, if not increasing, quantities.

Many years later, Cusack recalled, "I never received any response at all after transmitting this proposal to Bureau headquarters in January of 1963. In March of 1963 I received orders transferring me from Rome to Kansas City." Not exactly a promotion or a reward. For almost three years Cusack's proposal languished, ignored by Bureau of Narcotics higher-ups until David Acheson came into Treasury and revived it. Cusack, now back in Washington, was asked to brief Acheson, who thought the Turkish Opium Project a terrific and highly feasible idea. Acheson quickly brought it to the attention of the White House, and as a Treasury memo relates, by December 1965 Acheson had "worked out the broad outlines of a program of inspection, enforcement, crop control and crop substitution. In April 1966, Mr. Cusack visited Turkey briefly to advise the Embassy staff in its approaches to the Turkish Government. In May, Acheson headed the United States delegation to a CENTO working party on narcotics control." In fact, Acheson thought stopping opium at its origins was such a great idea, he recalls "that I thought 'Why not try the Golden Triangle, too?' I was all ready to send someone to Thailand, where there were rumors that the prime minister was personally involved, but the U.S. Ambassador there was completely against it. He said we couldn't afford to alienate Thailand and so we gave up." Negotiations with the Turks were still dragging on two years later when Ingersoll took over BNDD.

Ingersoll had inherited a corrupt, badly understaffed agency in a deep rut. At minimum a full *fifth* of the old bureau's agents were corrupt, actively colluding with major heroin traffickers and making major heroin sales themselves. It may well have been more, but investigations were not pursued on agents who decided to resign or retire. These disturbing findings were never released publicly, and so the worst corruption scandal ever uncovered in federal law enforcement passed by largely unnoticed by the press. As for those FBN agents who weren't actively corrupt, too many were just sloughing along, hewing to the decades-old rule that every FBN agent had to make two cases a month. Ingersoll put an end to that, declaring that the goal of the agency was not to make x number of cases, but to immobilize the source and distribution of illicit drugs. Aside from the turmoil of the corruption investigation, there were the difficulties of combining the bureau and BDAC and folding them into Justice.

Meanwhile, the Johnson administration was hearing in spring of 1968 from loyal Democrats such as Congressman Benjamin Rosenthal of New York that "our narcotics problem is growing by leaps and bounds, and only the most massive, well-coordinated and thoughtful effort will achieve any kind of results." Reports streamed in of the escalating drug problem. New York's chief medical examiner reported that drug overdoses for the first six months of 1968 had already reached 450, versus 670 for the entire previous year. (To put these figures into perspective: In 1950, there were a total of 57 ODs in New York City.) Nor was the drug problem confined any longer to the usual victims, the slum dwellers. In early June, the *New York Times* reported that venerable Columbia University was investigating student drug use after two freshmen were caught with heroin in a campus dorm.

Candidate Richard M. Nixon viewed the growing drug culture as part of the larger issue of law and order. Without a doubt the war in Vietnam and the half million U.S. soldiers mired there were *the* election issue. But for Americans who had watched twenty American cities being torched and sacked in the 1968 summer race riots, and who heard that drugs were everywhere, domestic law and order was also paramount. The rebellious baby boomers, the hipper media, and pop culture might be charmed by drugs, but parents were aghast. Employers had to worry about the consequences if workers (from the factory floor to the executive suite) followed the zeitgeist and made a habit of getting high.

Perhaps because of his sojourn as a private citizen in New York City, Richard M. Nixon believed, reported the *New York Times*, "that the narcotics problem and the high crime rate associated with it had become one of the foremost social problems in the United States and had to be stopped, whatever the cost." Consequently, when he took office, Nixon made crystal clear to his entire administration that quelling drugs was not just campaign rhetoric but genuinely a top priority. What had been middling priorities in the Johnson administration—getting the French to crack down, and the Turks and Mexicans out of opium—had risen to the top of the White House agenda.

No longer were those addressing the drug issue only lowly White House aides or assistant secretaries. Now they were people of the highest rank and power: the President, National Security Adviser Henry Kissinger, Secretary of State William Rogers, Defense Secretary Melvin Laird, Attorney General John Mitchell, presidential counselor Daniel Patrick Moynihan. Thus, in late September President Nixon ordered the departments of Justice and State to prepare recommendations for combatting heroin from abroad "regardless of foreign policy consequences." When Moynihan passed through Paris in August 1969 he told the number two man at the U.S. embassy (the ambassador was away) "of the Washington decision to make the international drug traffic a matter of highest priority in foreign affairs, and elicited both complete cooperation and genuine puzzlement. The minister knew almost nothing of the subject, and certainly had no inkling that his government back home was concerned about it."

But this was indeed the case, and significant high-level White House energy was devoted week in and week out to convincing our allies that the United States was now serious about curbing illegal drug traffic across our borders. As Moynihan would later write, "There was a quantum leap in the amounts of money, executive energy, and White House concern with the problem after 1969." The U.S. Secretary of State began to discuss opium poppies with the Turkish foreign minister. The U.S. Ambassador to France raised the heroin problem with the French foreign minister. American officials met with Mexican officials to launch a joint venture against drugs. In the fall of 1969 alone, Under Secretary of State Elliot Richardson and Attorney General John Mitchell submitted a report to the president "containing recommendations for an intensified international heroin control program." Congressional leaders were summoned to the White House to discuss narcotics. National Security Adviser Henry Kissinger convened the first meeting of the White House Task Force on Heroin "to prepare a detailed diplomatic scenario." Nixon wrote personally to newly elected President Pompidou of France, a far more friendly ally than his predecessor Charles de Gaulle. Pompidou agreed to more cooperation while disputing American assertions that 80 percent of heroin was Gallic. BNDD Director John Ingersoll was dispatched to France and Turkey for high-level meetings. All this unusual political activity aimed at drugs, commented one *Washington Post* editorial writer in early 1970, had the law enforcement types "a bit put out, and the diplomats a bit baffled. But a direction has been set."

As Daniel Patrick Moynihan tartly explained:

> Practices by friendly governments which would have been regarded as utterly intolerable had they extended to some recognizably political field, or had they been deleterious to the interests of a more visible class of people—people, to be blunt, known to the foreign policy establishment—such practices would have had the gravest and most immediate consequences for the practitioners. But so long as the only people being destroyed were far away and relatively invisible [i.e., poor slum

dwellers], these practices continued with barely the mildest demure.

In short, American foreign policy mandarins didn't give a fig about heroin as long as it was only destroying minority communities.

By spring of 1970, John Ehrlichman was reporting to the president, "we are making some major breakthroughs in securing French cooperation. . . . The French have assigned 50 additional agents to the suppression of the processing laboratories. . . . Ambassador [Arthur] Watson and his staff will continue to keep the pressure on." Meanwhile, the Turks were cooperating reluctantly, gradually reducing poppy cultivation from twenty-one provinces in the mid sixties to nine by late 1970.

In the midst of these serious affairs of state, there transpired some real theater of the absurd. The White House had decided to cultivate celebrities to be antidrug apostles, and just before Christmas of 1970 Elvis Presley came to the White House. Decked out in velvet pants suit with an open-necked silk shirt draped with gold jewelry, the rock 'n' roll star declared himself an ardent patriot and supporter of law enforcement much distressed by the drug problem. Presley presented the president with a .44 Colt automatic pistol. Rather taken aback, Nixon proposed Presley incorporate antidrug themes in his songs. As related by White House aide Egil Krogh, "Presley ended the interview by suggesting that they keep this meeting secret. Nixon responded, 'Absolutely! Don't tell anybody; preserve your credibility at all cost.' " (Despite the agreement to keep the meeting secret, an official photo was taken of Nixon and Presley that has become one of the most popular postcards sold in the National Archives gift shop.)

On the home front, the Nixon administration defused much youthful middle-class outrage over harsh drug laws simply by easing federal penalties for marijuana. As more and more white kids were caught experimenting with drugs—including the offspring of such eminences as the governor of New Jersey and the Democratic candidate for governor of New York—it seemed crazy to condemn mixed-up or curious youth to twenty years in jail for marijuana. Instead, first offenders for possession of—as opposed to selling—marijuana could be freed on probation and, if compliant, have their records wiped clean. These completely revamped drug laws—the Controlled Dangerous Substances Act of 1970—recognized that marijuana, the most popular baby-boomer drug, was certainly the least dangerous. Following the federal lead, marijuana use became a minor offense in a great many states. Drug liberals hailed this as an important repudiation of the much-reviled Anslinger hard line that had once equated grass to heroin in notorious articles such as "Marijuana, Assassin of Youth."

After all, when it came to drugs, anyone could see that marijuana was a relative side issue. For of the two flourishing drug cultures— recreational and full–time—the truly worrisome was the full-time heroin drug culture. And the reports there were alarming. In Washington, D.C., Robert DuPont, a Harvard-trained psychiatrist, had arrived in 1969 to work on local drug treatment just as the urban heroin epidemics of the late sixties really took off. Dr. DuPont was appalled to discover that in certain poor black neighborhoods in the nation's capital 10 percent of the young men were using heroin. And in a few badly hit areas, "more than a quarter of the males born in 1953 [as a for instance] became addicted to heroin." A New York study of one East Harlem block reported in late 1968 that "one-third of the teen-agers interviewed in the winter of 1965 have since become heroin addicts."

As if the full-blown heroin epidemic at home was not enough, now the Nixon administration was informed of a GI heroin epidemic shaping up in South Vietnam. As Professor McCoy describes in *The Politics of Heroin*:

> Previously unavailable in South Vietnam, suddenly no. 4 heroin was everywhere: fourteen-year-old girls were selling heroin at roadside stands on the main highway from Saigon to the U.S. army base at Long Binh; Saigon street peddlers stuffed plastic vials of 95 percent pure heroin into the pockets of GIs as they strolled through downtown Saigon. . . . With this kind of aggressive sales campaign, the results were predictable: in September 1970 army medical officers questioned 3,103 soldiers of the Americal Division and discovered that 11.9 percent had tried heroin since they had arrived in Vietnam and 6.6 percent were still using it on a regular basis. In November a U.S. engineering batallion in the Mekong Delta reported that 14 percent of its troops were on heroin. By mid-1971 U.S. army medical officers were estimating that about 10 to 15 percent, or 25,000 to 37,000, of the lower-ranking enlisted men serving in Vietnam were heroin users.

In short, the heroin epidemic in South Vietnam was now as bad as that in American ghettos.

By May 1971 administration officials could pick up the *Washington Post* and read, in a front-page article headlined, GI HEROIN SALES IN VIETNAM: CHEAP, FAST, IGNORED BY POLICE, how soldiers laughingly reported that heroin was still as readily available as ever: "You can go anywhere, ask anyone, they'll get it for you. It won't take but a few seconds." After all, said one army psychiatrist, many of the enlisted men were "like people in the ghettos, the scapegoats of society, hassled and harrassed by everyone around them. The way to forget is to take drugs and drugs are everywhere."

Early this same month Dr. Jerome Jaffe, a Chicago-based psychiatrist who had organized and established that city's much-admired drug treatment programs, got a call from the White House. The White House was calling wanting to know if Jaffe had any ideas about what to do with the Vietnam drug disaster. Dr. Jaffe thought the military should test everyone leaving Vietnam for drugs. Those who tested positive would be detained in Vietnam for several weeks to ensure they at least returned home drug-free. It had been observed that drug users tended to relapse when confronted by familiar environmental cues; so, the idea was to restrict drug memories and drug hunger to sultry, tropical Vietnam.

Some weeks passed, and then Dr. Jaffe was invited to Washington for a meeting on May 30 to discuss his ideas at the Pentagon. Expecting informal discussions with a few low-level research types, Jaffe was taken aback to find himself in a grandiose briefing room filled with generals and admirals. He recalls, "My informal assessment of the mean rank in the room was 2.75 stars per shoulder bar." Introduced as a consultant to the president, Dr. Jaffe outlined his proposal, which called for testing the urine of all departing troops:

> At first we were told it would probably be impossible to get urine specimens—to which I replied, "I cannot believe that the mightiest Army on earth can't get its troops to piss in a bottle." After some further discussion about potential adverse effects of the return of large numbers of untreated addicts from Vietnam to the United States, we were told, more or less, that D.O.D. [the Department of Defense] was looking into the matter and that by September something of the nature of what I proposed might be possible. With 1,000 men leaving each day, that amounted to a lot of inaction.

Dr. Jaffe forthrightly said as much, eliciting a ripple of surprised and disapproving murmurs. "I was unaware that such bravado born of sheer ignorance of protocol is not usually displayed in the briefing rooms of the Pentagon." In any case, Dr. Jaffe's chutzpah carried the day, and two weeks later drug-testing began in Vietnam.

What made the Vietnam heroin epidemic especially galling was that it was the work of our very own Southeast Asian allies, and to some degree the CIA. As Professor McCoy described it in his *Politics of Heroin*, the Central Intelligence Agency, in the course of cultivating anticommunist allies in the byzantine world of Southeast Asia, had allied itself to various tribal warlords in the Golden Triangle where Laos, Burma, and Thailand meet. With Western airplanes, helicopters, and boats to supplant mules and sampans, these longtime suppliers of local smoking opium now vastly expanded their poppy acreage and added high-grade heroin to their product line, ostensibly to fund their anticommunist insurgencies. Soon their new products found new markets, i.e., nearby South Vietnam, where hundreds of thousands of bored young American soldiers were fighting an unpopular war. By 1970 Golden Triangle heroin had flooded the South Vietnam market, causing a wave of addiction, first among GIs and then the Vietnamese.

The CIA connection went back a couple of decades to when it had backed nationalist Chinese army units along the jungly Burma-Chinese border in 1951. First sent to harry communist China, many of these Taiwanese troops never returned home. Instead they settled in and developed the indigenous opium trade from a small tribal matter into big business. A decade later, the CIA helped build Hmong tribesmen in northern Laos into a major army to fight against the Lao communists. Again, the traditional cash crop was opium, and as the local elites realized the possible profits of branching out into new markets, they did just that.

President Nixon was deeply unhappy about both the lack of significant progress at home vis à vis heroin and this whole new drug mess in the quagmire of Vietnam. For two hours on June 3, 1971, he fiercely lectured a handful of Cabinet members and staff. Notes from the meeting state: "President told group . . . crapping around will not be tolerated. . . . [W]e have tried to persuade our allies, Turkey and France, of the importance of heroin traffic to the U.S. We will be tough with our allies now and will put more emphasis on solving the problem, than on diplomatic niceties. . . . [The] President expressed concern that some of the public, especially some employers, view the Vietnam veteran as a ruthless killer and a junkie, and therefore he cannot get a job."

A week later Nixon presided over a similar laying-down-the-law meeting, this one attended by a host of top State Department officials, four Cabinet officers, CIA chief Richard Helms, and by the U.S. ambassadors to Thailand, Mexico, France, Turkey, Vietnam, and the United Nations. According to the briefing notes, the president planned to impress in forceful terms the absolute necessity for our foreign representatives to work constantly and energetically on solutions to the international opium/heroin problem. . . . You might explain the increasing Congressional pressure for drastic action. . . . [T]here is no alternative to using every possible lever which might be employed if there is a prospect that it might result in an effective elimination of opium/heroin sources. . . . As your closing comment, you might state that fighting the drug problem is a matter of the highest priority to you personally and the nation, and that you expect the fullest cooperation and support from all those present, and that you will not be satisfied with half-hearted action. You encourage every action which can be effective in stopping heroin from entering the United States.

Apparently, the CIA's assigned role in this full-bore effort was to "collect intelligence on dealers in Latin America and pass it to the officers of the Bureau of Narcotics and Dangerous Drugs." Predictably, it was a complete agency culture clash. The newly cleaned-up and reinvigorated BNDD was focused on arresting traffickers and diminishing drug traffic. Not so the CIA. As the new Latin America collaboration was launched, writes David Corn in his recent biography of a high-level CIA official, *Blond Ghost*, BNDD handed "over to the CIA their case files, lists of informants, and cable traffic." But BNDD soon discovered that the CIA had its own agenda. And it was not—despite President Nixon's orders—taking out traffickers, but gathering intelligence. So, using BNDD's leads, the CIA began recruiting "BNDD targets as CIA assets—and did so without telling the BNDD. . . . [In short, the CIA was now recruiting] the same people the drug agents were attempting to arrest."

In early June 1971—even as the bombshell of the Pentagon Papers was preoccupying much of the nation—President Nixon declared drug abuse "the number one domestic concern." A new, more realistic statistical method adopted by the Bureau of Narcotics and Dangerous Drugs had lifted the official estimate of the heroin addict population above three hundred thousand. Moreover, the White House believed that the "use of heroin by U.S. servicemen in Vietnam has allegedly reached crisis proportions and threatens to disrupt the Administration's Vietnamization policy."

In response, President Nixon announced a whole series of new endeavors: for starters, the appointment of Dr. Jerome Jaffe, the Chicago specialist in addiction and treatment, to take hold of the "demand" side of the problem through the new White House Special

Action Office for Drug Abuse Prevention, which would coordinate all federal drug education and research programs. Jaffe's basic premise was that if you had enough treatment, "no one could say he committed a crime to get drugs because he couldn't get treatment. I believed that only this way would our society make the distinction between the habitual criminal who happens to use illicit drugs but who would be involved in crime anyway, and those who in the absence of drug use and the high price of illicit drugs might have achieved a law-abiding, if unconventional social adjustment."

The Cabinet Committee on International Narcotics Control had been set up to oversee "efforts to fight the international drug traffic and to eliminate drugs at their source." All relevant embassies now had narcotics control coordinators. In Vietnam, the U.S. military was now giving every departing soldier a drug urinalysis test. Those who failed would enter mandatory thirty-day drug treatment. For Dr. Jaffe, the experiment proved very gratifying, for he had theorized that the mere prospect of a drug test would cause many soldiers who used but were not addicted to eschew heroin. And, indeed, this is just what happened. Month by month, the number of "positives" dropped, from an initial 10 percent to just under 2 percent six months later.

Despite such reassuring news, the situation in Southeast Asia was immensely embarrassing to an administration that was vehemently antidrug. And made more so by the testimony on June 2, 1972, of a then–Yale graduate student studying Philippine history named Alfred W. McCoy before a Senate committee. McCoy, twenty-six, a mild-mannered–looking academic, was describing his (at times) hair-raising researches into the politics of opium in France and Southeast Asia. McCoy had met a great many talkative and forthright opium players during eighteen months spent looking into the opium trade: retired French colonial military men who had long run the sub rosa opium monopoly in Indochina; peasant poppy growers up in the hills of the Golden Triangle; Laotian generals dominating the big-time trade; and Saigon street pushers loaded down with cheap, high-grade heroin.

McCoy laid it right out: "High government officials in Thailand, Laos, and South Vietnam are actively engaged in the heroin traffic and are protecting the region's powerful narcotics syndicates. Because the corruption in these countries is so systematic and narcotics traffic so lucrative, our political commitments to these governments inhibit and prevent any effective action to cut the flow of these illicit narcotics into the United States." Senators soon discovered that these general statements would be backed up in seven hundred detailed pages set to come out in a book from Harper & Row that fall.

McCoy continued:

> In a three-hour interview with me, General Ouane Rattikone [sic], former chief of staff of the Royal Laotian Army, admitted that he controlled the opium traffic in northwestern Laos since 1962. General Ouane also controlled the largest heroin laboratory in Laos.
>
> This laboratory produced a high grade of heroin for the GI market in South Vietnam and, according to the CIA, was capable of producing over 3,000 kilos of heroin a year. With the withdrawal of U.S. troops, the market for such heroin has shifted directly to the United States. Most of the opium traffic in northeastern Laos is controlled by Vang Pao, the Laotian general who commands the CIA's mercenary army.
>
> The Thai government allows Burmese rebels, Nationalist Chinese irregulars, and mercenary armies to move enormous mule caravans loaded with hundreds of tons of Burmese opium across Thailand's northern border.

Now not all of this was a complete secret. *Time* magazine, on September 8, 1967, had reported from the Golden Triangle when a mini–opium war flared up. A major Shan warlord ferrying his nine tons of raw opium to market had refused to pay eighty thousand dollars in tolls to the "outlaw remnants, some 3,000 strong, of Chiang Kai-shek detachments [that had] fled China in 1949 when the Communists took over." Reported the *Time* Correspondent (by no means a member of any radical form of American journalism), "Watching both antagonists from a hill were two companies of Royal Laotian infantry, ordered there by Laotian Commander in Chief Ouane Rathikoune, who depends heavily on his cut in the opium trade to buy the loyalty of his soliders. When Chan [the warlord] tried to cross the Mekong in barges, the Chinese opened fire with everything in their armory. The Laotian commander tried to negotiate a truce, and failing, withdrew to watch the melee."

What had seemed like amusing local color in 1967 was no longer quite so amusing now that people such as McCoy were charging that these vast mule caravans were ferrying drugs destined for Americans— whether in Vietnam or the United States. Also, McCoy was going beyond the local flare-ups to connect such native contretemps to the larger world of trafficking. As he told Congress, "U.S. agents working in Thailand claim that every major narcotics dealer in Thailand has a high-ranking 'adviser' on the Thai Police Force.

"In South Vietnam, the opium and heroin traffic is divided among the nation's three dominant military factions: President Thieu's political apparatus, Prime Minister Khiem's political organization, and General Ky's political entourage."

McCoy recited numerous damaging details and connections:

> Some of President Thieu's staunchest supporters inside the Vietnamese Army control the distribution and sale of heroin to American GI's fighting in Indochina. President Thieu's most important military adviser, Gen. Dan Van Quang, has been publicly accused by NBC of being the "biggest pusher" in South Vietnam. . . .
>
> American officials serving in Southeast Asia have a great deal of responsibility for the growth of the region's illicit drug traffic. American diplomats and intelligence agents have allied themselves with corrupt, indigenous groups without pressuring them to get out of the drug business.
>
> Throughout the mountainous golden triangle region, the CIA has provided substantial military support for mercenaries, rightwing rebels, and tribal warlords who are actively engaged in the narcotics traffic. And in Thailand, the CIA has worked closely with Nationalist Chinese paramilitary units which control 80 to 90 percent of northern Burma's vast opium exports and manufacture high-grade heroin for export to the American market.

CIA Director William Colby denied McCoy's assertions as "unsubstantiated." Yet six weeks later the New York Times reported on the front page that a Cabinet-level administration report had concluded that there was "no prospect" of stopping narcotics trafficking in Southeast Asia because "the corruption, collusion and indifference at some places in some governments, particularly Thailand and South Vietnam, precludes more effective suppression of traffic."

When the Church committee looked into these charges of complicity during Senate hearings, the agency's inspector general answered candidly, "The war has clearly been our overriding priority in Southeast Asia and all other issues have taken second place in the scheme of things. It would be foolish to deny this, and we see no reason to." However, the inspector general acknowledged concern about "agents and local officials with whom we are in contact who have been or may still be involved in one way or another in the drug business. . . . What to do about these people is a particularly troublesome problem, in view of its implications for some of our operations, particularly in Laos." So troublesome that the agency worried of "possible adverse repercussions for the Agency, if its relationship to certain assets were exposed."

In *Agency of Fear*, journalist Edward Jay Epstein argues that the Nixon administration hyped an imaginary heroin epidemic purely to justify creating new law enforcement entities that it could control. Epstein believes that the White House sought to organize its own domestic police unit and probably accomplished that with the hapless Office of Drug Abuse Law Enforcement (ODALE), which immediately embarked on all sorts of dubious midnight raids on innocent home owners.

But however certain Epstein was that the Nixonians were trying to organize their own private police apparatus, he was wrong to glibly dismiss the heroin epidemic as a White House PR ploy. For even as Nixon and his administration struggled to clamp down on drugs, *Newsweek* criticized the federal effort as "a step or two behind many cities and states of the U.S., which have been moving with galvanic speed to establish or reinforce a whole range of sometimes complementary, sometimes contradictory programs involving public hospitals, private agencies like Synanon, psychotherapy, anti-heroin drugs like methadone—plus more men on the narcotics squad."

In fact, the heroin epidemic was bona fide and terrifying. In 1961, when heroin addicts first became noticeable in the Charlotte Street neighborhood of New York's South Bronx, the forty-first Precinct reported 18 murders, 183 robberies, and 667 burglaries. As the full-time drug culture came to dominate the whole neighborhood, "On Charlotte and Minford they sold drugs like they were groceries," remembers one resident. "They used to carry the drugs upstairs in a baby carriage." By 1967 a local patrolman described the local addicts as a plague of locusts, swarming everywhere and just as destructive: "So many people OD'ed, we used to get them all the time in the hallways and vacant lots." By 1971 the forty-first Precinct had recorded five times as many murders, or 102, fifteen times as many robberies, or 2,632, and almost ten times as many burglaries, or 6,443. Junkies stripping apartment buildings—some of which they set afire to more easily extract copper pipe and other valuables—played a disastrous but crucial role in the ultimate abandonment of the Charlotte Street neighborhood.

Not only did this growing army of junkies undermine whole neighborhoods, their inability to serve as responsible husbands and fathers almost certainly enlarged the welfare roles. As Dr. DuPont wrote when looking at the Washington, D.C., heroin epidemic of the sixties:

> What became of the women? They were the individuals who in recent years ballooned the welfare roles in the District of

Columbia and other cities throughout the nation. From the beginning of the federal welfare program in the 1930's the typical welfare recipient was either a disabled individual or a woman who had been married but who had lost her husband (through death, imprisonment, desertion, etc.) and who raised her children with the help of the Aid for Families with Dependent Children (AFDC) program. This pattern changed in the late 1960's as thousands of young women, most of whom had never been married, went on AFDC.

Between 1961 and 1971 there was a rise in the total number of women receiving AFDC support in the District of Columbia from 5,000 to about 16,300.

In New York City the welfare roles had doubled, from half a million in the mid sixties to a million by 1970. Up until the early 1960s, new AFDC cases paralleled "almost precisely the unemployment rate for nonwhite males. Whenever the nonwhite employment rate went up . . . the number of new welfare cases went up. But in 1962–63, a remarkable thing happened: the number of new persons admitted to AFDC started going up even though the unemployment rate was going *down*." Many of the minority men who normally would have married and supported families were instead caught up in the fast life of heroin addiction. They fathered children, but they did not support them. The fast life and its credo of hipness actively scorned the very values that made steady family life possible.

Had heroin been so freely available only in places like Charlotte Street—the crumbling netherworlds of urban America—it's unlikely the Nixon administration would have been so exercised. But as Iowa senator Harold Hughes, identified as the leading congressional expert on addiction, said, once heroin "moved out of the black ghettos and into the suburbs and small towns and it moved right next door, that's when it became a crisis." By 1972 suburban citadels such as Long Island were reporting twenty-five heroin overdoses. *Newsday* provided details on who died:

Twenty were white; 23 were male; 17 were single; 24 were employed or were students; 17 died at home. Most of the victims lived with their parents. Four others died at the home of friends. One died in a hospital. Two were found in parked cars. One body was found lying on a roadside in Lake Success. . . . The average age of the victims was just under 23. . . . Of the 25 victims, all but one was listed as employed or as a student by

the county medical examiners. Their jobs were typical of suburban lower-middle-income employment: four were laborers,
two were clerks, one was a truck driver and another a barber.
There was a gym instructor and a computer programmer, a
maintenance man and a mechanic, a waiter, a restaurant
helper and a delivery man. Five were students.

And so career diplomats such as U.S. ambassador to Turkey William
Handley suddenly found themselves under direst pressure from the
White House to produce significant progress overseas. After five years of
gradual and reluctant concessions, the Turks—a military coup having
brought in a more pliant regime—suddenly agreed in mid June 1971 to a
complete ban on all growing of Turkish opium effective June 30, 1972. In
exchange, the United States anted up $37 million in aid. The White House
was jubilant and invited Prime Minister Nihat Erim to share the limelight
when the big announcement about the opium ban was made. But with the
escalating war in Vietnam and the unfolding drama of the secret Pentagon Papers, the country was too preoccupied to notice much.

While our allies the Turks—much beholden to U.S. economic and
military aid—had fallen finally into line by mid 1971, well timed for
the upcoming elections, our allies the French had not. Even though
U.S. Attorney General John Mitchell had flown to Paris that spring and
signed a cooperation agreement with French interior minister Raymond Marcellin for stepped-up drug enforcement, there was no sign of
anything happening. Not one heroin laboratory had been dismantled in
five years, and the heroin was still pouring out of Marseille.

Worse yet, the embarrassing Roger Delouette trafficking case that
unraveled behind the scenes in the spring and summer of 1971 strongly
suggested that the French counterpart of the C.I.A.—denizens of the
Cold War shadow world—were engaged actively in the very heroin
trade President Nixon was determined to stamp out. On April 5, 1971,
a rookie Customs agent at Port Elizabeth, New Jersey, was routinely
checking a white Volkswagen camper coming off the freighter *Atlantic
Cognac*. She noticed a loose screw on one of the floorboards, pried
opened the panel, and found ninety-six bags holding almost one hundred pounds of heroin. Not long after, a purported French businessman
named Roger Delouette presented himself at the pier to retrieve the
car. He was arrested promptly. Tall, modishly dressed, with classic
Cary Grant good looks, Delouette was escorted back across the Hudson River to his room in the Park Sheraton Hotel in Manhattan, where
he confessed all to agents from Customs, BNDD, and a French police
official stationed in New York.

Roger Delouette's story was astonishing. He forthrightly identified himself as one who had served on and off for twenty-five years as a member of the French counterpart to the CIA, the SDECE. Now forty-seven, Delouette had worked in Greece, Algeria, Cuba, and the Ivory Coast, all Cold War hot spots for the French. A war hero awarded the Croix de Guerre, he had a wife and six children, but had left them for his pregnant twenty-two-year-old mistress. His difficult domestic situation was exacerbated because he was no longer posted abroad, which meant a much-reduced pay check. Financially hard-pressed, Delouette earnestly had explained his plight in June 1970 to SDECE Paris chief Paul Ferrere, a.k.a. Paul Fournier.

As Delouette detailed in his confession:

> Around the 15th of December—maybe before then—he [Fournier] telephoned me to ask me if I would accept an assignment, a very special assignment which included certain risks. . . . On my agreement, he set up a meeting at the Café de Paris at the Champs Élysées." Delouette went to the café and met a mystery man "dressed in a very elegant manner and a very conservative manner. This man told me—first, I understood that he also belonged to the service. That is to say, when he referred to the service, he said "we" and "us." He told me that for special matters they needed to smuggle drugs to the United States.

The culmination of all this was that Delouette agreed to transport the drugs and was given about $5,500 in francs to buy a VW camper. On March 16, 1971, he helped hide heroin in the camper, and then the following morning dutifully drove to Le Havre and consigned the car to a shipping company. On April 4 he flew over on TWA. Delouette had been told he would be paid once he retrieved the camper and delivered it to a SDECE contact at the Park Sheraton in Manhattan. But Delouette found himself not sixty thousand dollars richer, but in handcuffs and under arrest on the pier at Port Elizabeth.

The U.S. Attorney for Newark, Herbert J. Stern, was flabbergasted and outraged. Here was a major heroin smuggler with absolutely no criminal record explaining that he was participating in an operation organized by a high official in French intelligence. When the French pooh-poohed Delouette's allegations, prosecutor Stern suggested that French judicial officials come to the United States and submit Delouette to a lie-detector test. If he passed all polygraph tests, said Stern, then the French should proceed against Paul Ferrere, a.k.a. Paul

Fournier, preferably extraditing him to Newark for trial. Eventually the French agreed to be present while Delouette took a lie-detector test, with the understanding that if he passed they would "proceed with an appropriate prosecution" of Fournier. By early October Delouette had passed two lie-detector tests. Amazingly, nothing of this—aside from the arrest—had yet made it into the newspapers.

As the struggle over the Delouette case went on quietly behind the scenes throughout the summer and early fall, a far more public dispute broke out. Known in France as L'Affaire Cusack, it began August 25, 1971, when the Marseille daily *Le Meridional—La France* published a series of exclusive interviews with BNDD's European chief, John Cusack, the same man who dreamed up the Turkish Opium Project. First off, Cusack accused the French of letting three or four major Marseille traffickers operate with virtual impunity, "thanks to their bank balances, social connections and considerations shown them, and because either they scare people, because people don't believe in their guilt or because informers fear reprisals." The French were incensed at such American gall, whereupon Cusack made various placating noises. But then BNDD director John Ingersoll reiterated all Cusack's charges on American television. The French national union of Customs agents jumped in, declaring, "There is a very influential underworld in Marseille which had and still has political protection."

Just as L'Affaire Cusack was subsiding, the Delouette case blew up in mid November, splashed across front pages throughout New York. Prosecutor Stern had flown to Paris November 5 to press for Fournier's extradition, only to be stonewalled by the French government. He returned to Newark and on November 14 announced a superseding indictment that included not just Delouette, but his superior, Paul Ferrere a.k.a. Fournier. All along, the French blandly had disavowed Delouette's claims to membership in SDECE, but in light of the indictment and what the French press now termed "cet épisode spectaculaire," Fournier was invited to testify before a magistrate. As he exited the grim, historic precincts of the Palais de Justice, Fournier, corpulent, with bushy eyebrows and a crew cut, grandly dismissed the whole matter. As for his accuser, Delouette, "C'est un personnage qui ne m'interesse pas." ("This is a person who bores me.") A news photographer on the scene had his film confiscated.

At this point, Delouette's onetime boss, Colonel Roger Barberot (by then retired and living in splendor in the fancy suburb of Neuilly), loyally stepped forward to say in a November 19 interview with Radio Luxembourg that Delouette indeed had worked for the French counterpart to the CIA, SDECE. Moreover, Barberot, a former ambassador to

Uruguay, stated that SDECE did traffic in drugs. *Le Figaro* and other major French papers realized that this was no longer a "banal affaire de drogue." Apparently the Pompidou administration had tried to clear SDECE of gangsters and other dubious elements, but Barberot the old Cold Warrior raised pointed questions about how successful the purge had been. There were tangled charges of double agents and treason.

Newark prosecutor Herbert Stern descended a second time upon Paris just as Barberot was stirring things up. In the French newspapers, Stern could read Fournier's arrogant challenge, "Si je suis coupable, M. Stern, prouvez-le." ("If I am guilty, Mr. Stern, prove it.") To which Stern, plagued by the stomach flu, replied that if Fournier were innocent he should have no fear of coming to America to stand trial. Once Stern had departed, Defense Minister Michel Debre brushed off the entire matter as "a bad novel that really belongs on page fifteen of a third-rate publication." Ultimately, Delouette served a short five years in U.S. prisons because he cooperated, while the French made clear their indifference.

But all that was about to change radically. Drug addiction was becoming a French problem. One member of the Marseille drug squad was quoted in the *New York Times* as saying, "In 1968 we knew personally every heroin addict in Marseille. In just two years the situation exploded on us. Now kids here are going straight to mainlining heroin with no waystops, no hash or L.S.D. along the way." Even more significant, the French army's rejection rate for drug addiction had been 3.2 per thousand. Over four years that rate had quintupled. France's two top police officials were ordered to "reorganize the antidrug drive completely and infuse it with new spirit." No longer would high French officials airly dismiss heroin as the problem of the source and victim countries. France now had its own junkie problem.

One retired French narcotics officer, Antoine Barbazza, remembered that when he was first transferred to Marseille in 1962, he had but a handful of colleagues. Then, in the mid sixties, a Chicago-style gang war broke out in the *milieu* between the Guerini brothers and a younger group of Corsicans. Barbazza says that the victors, the younger generation, ignored the old understanding about no trafficking of drugs to the French, especially the young. "We warned those fellows about continuing to sell drugs in France," he reminisces from his favorite café in a leafy Marseille neighborhood. "We told them we would come down on them like a ton of bricks. They didn't listen to us, and we came down." He slams the table. "We went from eight of us agents to eighty and we cleaned them out." Tellingly, trafficking sentences became much harsher. No longer would Corsican traffickers serve two or three years before returning to their lucrative craft. Now they were looking at ten to twenty years.

The French, when they care to be, are spectacularly efficient. Among those rounded up was "the evil genius of chemistry, Joseph Césari, when his laboratory was discovered in Aubagne" in March 1971. (Césari previously had been convicted in 1964 and had served a short sentence.) Why would this now older man return to his criminal métier as master heroin chemist when he was so notorious? Surely, he could retire on the millions he'd socked away safely in some Swiss bank account? But this shows no understanding for the harsh workings of the *milieu*. When arrested in 1964, Césari had lost many hundreds of kilos of morphine base and completed heroin that was the *milieu*'s. They expected to be repaid for their huge loss. To be able to repay his debt to the *milieu*, Césari apparently had no choice but to return to his highly dangerous line of work. It is not so surprising, then, that when he was arrested again in 1972, he hung himself in the infamous Les Baumettes prison rather than face the much longer prison term the new times called for and the prospect of once again being so deeply in debt to his criminal colleagues.

But even as the antitrafficking efforts at home and abroad became more genuine and focused, Nixon administration officials also pushed to find ways of diminishing demand for heroin. And so they had surveyed with enormous interest the advent of a new treatment called methadone maintenance pioneered in New York City. For decades, heroin addicts seeking help had had little option but to present themselves at the U.S. narcotics hospitals, either in Lexington or Fort Worth. A typical stay lasted several months. But even when addicts emerged drug free, there was no aftercare, and 90 percent relapsed within days, weeks, or months. In 1959 New York City, with an addict population in the tens of thousands, offered all of thirty-seven hospital beds to male addicts. For women addicts, there was nothing. Manhattan's Riverside Hospital program for adolescents had opened in 1952, but was so unsuccessful it closed in 1961. Instead, desperate New York addicts accepted thirty-day jail sentences from Magistrate's Court, so they could remove themselves from drugs. But in December 1958 the city's Corrections Department refused to accept this role any longer, saying addicts should be handled by hospitals. As the New York addict population swelled, so did the desperation of affected communities.

And so it was that a doctor named Marie Nyswander, who had served at the Lexington Narcotic Farm for a year in 1945, got drawn into the field of addiction. Originally Nyswander, a lithe blonde woman radiating nervous energy, had planned to specialize in orthopedic surgery, but when she returned to New York from Lexington she trained instead as a psychiatrist and psychoanalyst. By virtue of her brief service at Lexington, she was one of but three Manhattan private physicians with serious experience with drug addicts. "As people became more alarmed about the increase in addiction, we were more and more sought out in crises," she said. "The other two finally backed out of the whole problem. They wouldn't handle any addicts. I didn't throw up my hands, perhaps because I'm a woman and was therefore enough of a masochist to go on."

Once Dr. Nyswander became known as someone willing to deal with addicts, she "eventually became inundated with them. People would call me up and I'd assume the obligation, handling the addicts in whatever stumbling way I could because there was hardly anyone else. I had started by thinking there was only one solution—go to Lexington and stay there for four months." But after supervising several patients through opiate withdrawal in their homes, Dr. Nyswander became convinced of the then completely radical notion that addicts could be helped while living in their own communities. As at Lexington, treatment consisted of gradual withdrawal and then psychotherapy. However, patients had to come to terms with their addiction not in the drug-free environment of a hospital but in their own drug-saturated neighborhoods.

Dr. Nyswander's mother was an eminent public health professor who early on divorced her husband and went her own way. The fearless mother—who thought nothing of piloting small planes into the rural backwaters of Turkey or South America, where she worked—had raised a highly independent child. "There were never any bounds on me," Dr. Nyswander would say later. "I was very fortunate in the totality of freedom I had as a child. By the time I was eight, I'd go off for days in the mountains and my mother wouldn't worry because she knew I was thoroughly trained in mountain climbing." It clearly took such a strong, free, and inquisitive spirit to question the reigning assumptions about addiction and treatment.

Starting in 1960, Dr. Nyswander began coming twice a week to a bleak apartment with four locks in East Harlem, on East 103rd Street, to offer "storefront" psychiatry to neighborhood addicts. She was there at the invitation of the narcotics committee of the East Harlem Protestant Parish, a group actively trying to offer something to the burgeoning local addict population. The Reverend Norman Eddy, a Yale-educated dynamo, had arrived in the neighborhood in 1949 and by 1951 he had become "aware that mothers were very concerned that children were using this white powder. In our naivete, we didn't know anything about it." Over the next few years Reverend Eddy got a thorough education in the horrors of heroin, especially how little real help was available. When the heiress Doris Duke gave the parish twenty-five thousand dollars in 1958, the narcotics committee set up the storefront where Marie Nyswander came to practice several times a week, aided by a staff of social workers and therapists. Reverend Eddy worked there for five years, counseling more than two thousand addicts and their families.

Many decades later, a still-vigorous and active Norman Eddy mused back on those days while sitting in his study in a small, sturdily barred row house in East Harlem: "How did the addicts support their habits—which then might be a $5 bag one to five times a day? Well, some addicts would steal from everybody but their own family. Others would steal only from their family. Such a variety of patterns. Some specialized in second-story jobs. Others in holdups. A great many sold drugs to make money. We saw whole families where every one of five or six children became addicts. It was just endless, a real life of tragedy." Reverend Eddy summed up the situation for journalist Dan Wakefield: "At the end of five years we had file folders on more than two thousand addicts we had seen and tried to help. Of that whole number there were only eight people we knew about who had stayed off drugs for more than a year. So I think it's fair to say we had *no* influence."

As Norman Eddy and Dr. Nyswander struggled to provide help to addicts in East Harlem, Rockefeller University medical researcher Vincent P. Dole also found himself drawn to the issue. For some years Dr. Dole had commuted into Manhattan by train, struck by "the terrible contrast between suburban Rye, where I lived in a nice big home on the waterfront and saw lots of yachts, and Harlem and 125th Street. Even early in the morning the bars in Harlem would be open. Already there were abandoned buildings boarded up and you saw young people out on the streets not in school and up to no good. I began to inquire into what was going on and part of the story was obviously drugs. I thought it curious that there was no medical presence in this problem, the way there was with alcoholism."

A graduate of Harvard Medical School, Dr. Dole was a full professor heading his own department at the elite Rockefeller University. At age fifty he was a prominent researcher with a national reputation in lipid chemistry. As Dr. Dole asked around about narcotics, he discovered that his friend and distinguished colleague Lewis Thomas had been heading the N.Y. Health Research Council's Committee on Narcotics and was about to be away on sabbatical. Dr. Dole took over the post and devoted the next year to learning all he could about the problem of narcotics. He was struck by the extraordinary paucity of knowledge, especially clinical knowledge. One of the few things he read that impressed him was Marie Nyswander's 1956 book, *The Drug Addict as a Patient*, describing her outpatient work with addicts.

In a large Rockefeller office overlooking the East River, Dr. Dole, a tall graying man wearing a light-blue cardigan, corduroy pants, and black running shoes, recalls, "In 1962 I arranged for Marie Nyswander to come to lunch at Rockefeller here because she seemed to be the one doctor who had strictly hands-on clinical experience where the addicts were not confined in a hospital. It struck me how terribly tired she was. She had been working with addicts who had been offered counseling, group therapy, and social services. She was a compassionate, medically trained person and yet she really felt her efforts were not solving the problem. She was still failing." The relapse rate for those in Nyswander's outpatient treatment at the 103rd Street storefront was no better than for Lexington. Understandably, she was tired and discouraged.

Dr. Dole, new on the scene and morally outraged at medicine's abandonment of the field of addiction, invited Nyswander to come work with him at Rockefeller. He recalls, "I thought it was a privilege to work in a field that was so obviously important and where really nothing had been done." But first, recalls Dole, he prepared to defy the inevitable challenge by the Federal Bureau of Narcotics. Det Bronk, Rockefeller's president, agreed that addiction was a bona fide field for medical research and had the university's law firm, Milbank, Tweed, confirm that Dole and Nyswander had the right to engage in clinical research on addicts. Dole, meanwhile, who had "good friends in important places," lined up an "unofficial, unadvertised support group" to counter anticipated bureau attempts to shut them down.

Dole and Nyswander began their research very simply, by observing

> the effect of reasonable doses of narcotics given to people with a long-standing history of narcotic addiction. . . . We didn't have rigid guidelines: we simply accepted addicts that Marie Nyswander or others knew about, half a dozen at first. . . . We set up a schedule of different drugs and different doses, recording in a notebook how the addicts felt and looked, whether their voices and pupils changed, that sort of thing. It was really humdrum observational research. Most of these drugs were rather short-acting. In three or four hours the addict would be miserable and vomiting, needing another shot. The doses on which you could keep them comfortable kept going up and up; the addicts were never really satisfied or happy. It was not an encouraging experience.

One of the drugs they tried during these first weeks was morphine. Nyswander often had wondered if legalized morphine was not the solution. But when two addicts in the program were supplied enough morphine to keep them comfortable, Nyswander discovered that their daily tolerance rose so swiftly that this was simply impractical. "Also," she would explain later,

> on morphine the patients were rendered practically immobile. Much of the time they sat passively, in bathrobes, in front of a television set. They didn't respond to any of the activities offerred them. They just sat there, waiting for the next shot, . . . their interests ebbing and flowing with the morphine injections. I was confronted with an abysmal lack of knowledge of what to do next.
>
> And then there was an accidental circumstance. We switched them to methadone, a drug that had been synthesized during the Second World War by German chemists looking for inexpensive morphine substitutes. . . .
>
> The accident was this. We wanted to reduce the huge daily doses of morphine without subjecting the two patients to severe withdrawal symptoms. Methadone was a way to do that, but . . . we had to put them on equivalently high dosages of methadone, more than twice as large as is usually given when methadone is used to withdraw people from heroin.

While Nyswander sank into disappointed despair at the morphine maintenance debacle, Dr. Dole was noticing striking changes in the behavior of the same two patients now on methadone. Much to everyone's amazement, as the two addicts continued on methadone, whole new personalities and ambitions began to emerge. Eventually, both went back to school and, still taking methadone, got on with their lives.

Dr. Dole was only several weeks into this new research venture when an agent appeared from the Federal Bureau of Narcotics.

> I came into my office and there was this hard-jawed, crew-cut guy in a trench coat. He said to me, "You're breaking the law." And I replied, "Who are you?" He then identified himself as an agent for the Bureau of Narcotics and said he had reliable reports that I was giving drugs to addicts. I had been expecting this, of course, and I had prepared myself very thoroughly. The bureau, acting this way, had managed to intimidate every doctor who thought about doing something. Anyway, having consulted with the university and Milbank, Tweed, I was able to

say, "I understand the bureau's position because I have looked into it. I suggest you sue me."

The agent stood up and, talking out of the side of his mouth, said, "I'll see you later." It was the first time they'd had any doctor stand up to them. Three weeks later the agent was back. He said, "We've decided to let you do your research, but you have to report to us." I said, "No." So he left, but the bureau spread false rumors that we weren't conducting bona fide research. And later, they would go into our clinics and steal records.

The bureau responded by opening what became voluminous files on both Dole and Nyswander.

The bureau's attempted intimidation of Dr. Dole is slightly surprising. While long routine practice under Anslinger, this kind of bullying was in theory a thing of the past by the early sixties. And yet here was the bureau in 1963 trying to scare off the eminent Dr. Dole at the elite Rockefeller University from doing exactly the kind of basic research that had never been done and needed to be done.

Henry Giordano, commissioner during this period, never saw things that way. "Dole and Nyswander weren't curing addiction," he says, "they were maintaining addiction. Our position was that they weren't accomplishing anything at all." Giordano feels the FBN was quite justified in building files on Dole and Nyswander, for they were physicians engaged in "excessive prescribing of drugs."

For Marie Nyswander, who had striven mightily to rescue the junkies she counseled on 103rd Street and failed again and again, methadone was close to a miracle. Suddenly, many addicts she had known for years were freed of their heroin obsession and transformed into productive citizens. Unlike heroin, methadone is taken orally once a day, thereby liberating addicts from the nonstop hustle of finding drugs, shooting up, and nodding out three to four times a day.

One of Dr. Dole's favorite stories from this early period of experimentation was about a visit to Rockefeller by Harris Isbell, head of the Addiction Research Unit at Lexington. Dole had invited Dr. Isbell

> as part of a policy of trying to get others to support our work. . . .
> [Isbell] talked with the methadone group, asking them all sorts of
> questions. They responded, telling him what they were doing—
> many of them were going back to school, taking correspondence
> or evening courses. A couple of them had jobs in the daytime,
> reporting back to the ward at night. When he got done with this
> rather long talk and we had left the ward, he said to me, in a nice,

gentle way, "Well, Vincent, I'm sorry to tell you, but you're wasting your time. Those are not addicts." He left and I went back to the ward. Naturally these fellows were all particularly interested in this interview because they all knew him well from Lexington. When I told them what he had said, they all laughed and laughed. They said, "He sure didn't tell us that when we were at Lexington." Episodes of this sort convinced me of methadone's potential for rehabilitation.

Dole and Nyswander (who fell in love and then married) believed that prolonged heroin use produced permanent metabolic changes, and for that reason did not accept into their pilot program anyone who had used heroin for less than four years. Other criteria were a history of previous, failed treatment, voluntary participation, being older than nineteen, and absence of psychosis or other major medical problems. Dole and Nyswander stated from the beginning that they believed that the great bulk of opiate addicts using methadone would probably need to remain on high-dosage maintenance indefinitely. Their goal was simple: "Rehabilitation rather than withdrawal of the drug is the first target." And among the first twenty-two addicts who volunteered for methadone maintenance there was dramatic proof of rehabilitation.

As described previously, Dole had prepared himself carefully for the hostility of the Bureau of Narcotics. But he had never anticipated the extraordinary opposition to methadone maintenance by the medical establishment and the new drug-free therapeutic treatment communities such as Synanon and Daytop Village. From the medical establishment, the typical denunciation went like this: "I fail to appreciate how legalized addiction is any improvement over illicit addiction. Morally, in fact, it is much less defensible." Many doctors and the Bureau of Narcotics believed that methadone maintenance was simply unleashing another highly addictive opiate upon a drug-ridden society. The fact that many addicts maintained on this drug could refocus their energies on school and job and family was unpersuasive to these critics.

Sociologist Lewis Yablonsky, a board member of Synanon, vented his wrath in a *New Republic* article titled, "Stoned on Methadone," that featured numerous Synanon addicts comparing methadone with heroin or worse: "My own view is that the experimenters are openly giving addicts drugs to gratify their addiction. They are shifting the addict from heroin to methadone. . . . Dole and Nyswander's conclusion of cure would parallel the assertion that an alcoholic had been successfully removed from his addiction to gin and was now only using scotch."

Yet city administrators saddled with huge antisocial addict populations could not afford to dwell in such moral fastness. All they knew was that Dole and Nyswander were reporting high rates of patient retention with methadone maintenance, much reduced criminal activity, and significant social progress by motivated addicts. Dr. Dole remembers well his first discussion about the early promising results from a mere six methadone patients, in early 1965, with Dr. Ray Trussell, New York City's Commissioner of Hospitals: "I brought with me graphs and statistics of our work. I talked to him for a few minutes and, to my surprise, he picked up the telephone, called up Beth Israel Medical Center, said he was sending a doctor over, and he would like them to give me whatever I needed for my work. Then he said to me with a smile, 'This may be what I've been looking for for ten years.' "

By the fall of 1969, almost two thousand New York addicts were enrolled in methadone maintenance programs. Patients did not just swig a cup of Tang and methadone. They also were provided ample counseling and social services. The retention rate remained about 80 percent, while lifestyle changes were just as encouraging. Arrest rates fell dramatically, while employment and school attendance rose dramatically. A study of 544 New York male addicts on methadone showed that within "three months of starting methadone maintenance, more than half of the male addicts were productively employed or attending school. After a year the proportion rose to nearly two-thirds. . . . 'The greatest surprise has been this high rate of social productivity, as defined by stable employment and responsible behavior,' said Dr. Dole." Encouraged by such promising outcomes, by 1969 at least twenty-three cities had some form of methadone maintenance programs, often through individual doctors. In these early heady days of methadone maintenance, Dr. Jerome Jaffe, then a young psychiatrist, worked for a six-month stint in Dr. Dole's lab and became a convert to the possibilities of methadone, returning to Chicago in 1967 to launch a major methadone program. Unlike New York, Chicago accepted not just volunteers but those assigned by the courts as an alternative to prison. In 1969 Dr. Jaffe reported that addicts forced into methadone treatment did as well as those who came of their own volition. By 1970 New York City aggressively and successfully had expanded methadone maintenance to accommodate twenty thousand addicts.

Just as only a staunch anticommunist could have presided over détente, so only a law and order Republican such as Richard Nixon could have presided over the legalizing of a highly controversial and addicting member of the opiate family, in this case the synthetic opiate methadone—and then gone on to make it available to addicts through government clinics. Ever pragmatic and canny, the Nixon administration had checked out the methadone maintenance record and then had brought in Dr. Jerome Jaffe to push hard to establish, wherever needed, drug treatment clinics where methadone would be one of the choices. (A major motivation, says Dr. Jaffe, was Nixon's concern about returning Vietnam vets.)

In short, the Nixon administration was responsible for opening the first legal opiate clinics since the twenties. (Somehow, to this day, most Americans do not seem to realize that methadone is not some antibiotic or medicine that cuts off withdrawal. It is simply another synthetic opiate.)

By the mid seventies, under the continued prodding of the Nixon White House, eighty thousand methadone slots had been opened up. With drug treatment available nationwide on an outpatient basis, by 1972 it was possible to close that longtime monument to medical optimism, the Lexington U.S. Narcotics Hospital. There, despite high hopes, no cures had ever been achieved in the field of drug addiction.

Nonetheless, methadone maintenance did not become the magic bullet first envisioned. Dr. Vincent P. Dole (Marie Nyswander died in 1986) has thought about this a great deal, and he proffers a variety of reasons why methadone did not fulfill its early promise. Most important and most unanticipated has been the unrelenting hostility to maintaining addicts on methadone ad infinitum. For Dole the goal was social rehabilitation, but for the bulk of the drug treatment community, the goal was and remains being drug-free. Consequently, Dr. Dole believes that many, if not most, programs undermedicate addicts, providing insufficient methadone to truly stabilize them. Research bears him out. In general, higher-dose programs have better track records.

Then, because many heroin addicts are black, methadone became a racial issue, with some denouncing it as a white plot to enslave black addicts permanently. And although methadone has shown remarkably few side effects, its opponents continually bad-mouth it as hard on the body—the complaint was a vague "gets in your bones"—and this soon exacted a real toll, giving methadone a bad reputation among addicts, the very population that needed to be attracted. In 1976 Dole and Nyswander described incredulously one encounter with "a woman addict in jail, her veins obliterated and her body covered with ulcers from subcutaneous injections of contaminated heroin. [She] was asked whether she would like to apply for a methadone program. Her answer was negative because she felt that methadone would be bad for her health."

Moreover, many of the nation's three hundred thousand heroin addicts did not want to be liberated. They preferred what they called the "fast life." (As one treatment director remarked candidly, "Our clients like to be high. They don't want to go into treatment.") As anyone who works with addicts will confirm, a minority willingly seek help. Ironically, the addict community dedicated to the fast life joined the drug-free community in dumping on methadone as "taking your heart," meaning that those in methadone treatment no longer displayed the criminal hustle and savvy addicts so perversely prided themselves on.

Heroin addict Susan Gordon Lydon, who turned to methadone only when broke after losing her journalism job, said that at first

> methadone kept me feeling good enough that I didn't crave other drugs. But I was bored, I missed the excitement of running around copping, missed the hustle of dealing. . . . Getting on methadone to cure a heroin habit is like pulling yourself up on quicksand to keep from drowning in water. . . . When I looked at the people around me, bloated and sedated with legally sanctioned narcotics, I felt I was now associated with a truly hopeless segment of society. Toothless, battered, old before their time, these committed dope fiends resigned themselves to staying on methadone because it was just too painful to kick, worse than heroin.

Predictably, Lydon was soon mired again in the fast life of dealing and using prodigious quantities of drugs.

As the methadone maintenance programs expanded throughout the country, so did federal rules. Dole was astonished and angry, deeming this unexpected rule-making an

> unprecedented entry into the practice of medicine. If treating people with methadone is a medical process—like treating people with congestive heart failure with digitalis, or diabetes with insulin, or Addisonians with steroid hormones—then it constitutes a new phenomenon in medical practice to have some federal agency [the FDA], nonmedical at that, control medical decisions with detailed legislation. Rigid guidelines defined who could be treated, how long he could be treated, what dose he could be given, and what services, what reporting was needed, and what paperwork mandated. Anybody running a program became subject to unannounced inspections from the many agencies supervising it, putting physicians under the

threat of criminal prosecution if they hadn't followed the strict
regulatory guidelines. . . . The goal of treatment was not rehabilitation but abstinence.

Richard Lane, a director at the Baltimore Man Alive methadone
maintenance program, was himself on methadone for twenty-seven
years and he had heard all the arguments and put-downs. A few months
before he died of cancer in 1994, he said, "None of the addicts on
methadone like being on it. You think they like having to be tied to
this place? To check in regularly to get their dose? We'd like to see
everyone drug-free and abstinent, too. But for a lot of people, that's just
not practical."

To Dole it was not surprising in this atmosphere that first-year retention rates plummeted as low as 30 and 40 percent. But for those who do
stick it out, methadone is still demonstrably helpful. Three quarters of
those who remain in methadone maintenance stop using heroin and
commit far fewer crimes. A detailed study done by criminologist John
Ball in the 1980s of six treatment centers found that for those in treatment six months or longer criminal offenses dropped 80 percent. Those
who drop out of treatment swiftly return to all their old bad habits.

Throughout 1972 and 1973, the White House continued to maintain
the high-level pressure on allies and to orchestrate domestic antidrug
activities. Secretary of State Henry Kissinger appointed a senior advi-
sor and coordinator for international narcotic matters in April 1974,
thus firmly placing the power and panoply of State behind antidrug
efforts. Under the Nixon administration, overall federal spending on
the issue soared by an order of magnitude, from about $80 million in
FY 1969 to $730 million in FY 1973. Federally funded treatment cen-
ters grew from sixteen to almost four hundred. And then there was the
unanticipated good news on the Vietnam vet drug problem. Much to
every expert's amazement, those soldiers who had used heroin—even
heavily—in Asia showed little inclination to do so in the United
States. In September 1971 Dr. Jaffe had had researchers select a random
sample of 943 enlisted men leaving Vietnam. Of these, 495 were soldiers who had tested positive for opiates upon departure. And yet when
tracked down the following summer, virtually none of these hundreds
of veterans had continued to use heroin once back. This was extraordinarily good news, considering the hundreds of thousands of young men
who had served in Southeast Asia and were expected to return hopeless
junkies. It was also a dramatic demonstration of the influence of set
and setting on drug use and relapse.

By 1973, as Richard Nixon began his second term in the White

House, it was clear that the high-level attention to the heroin epidemic had paid off. Reports from every jurisdiction showed much reduced supply and decreasing addiction. One federal drug bureaucrat told Congress, "From 1972 through mid-1973 the street-level price of heroin in New York City quadrupled while the purity was reduced by one-half. In 1973 the rates of overdose deaths, drug-related hepatitis and property crimes, indicators of heroin addiction, declined throughout most areas of the United States for the first time in six years."

From the nation's capital, Dr. Robert DuPont, who had described the raging epidemic of the late sixties at a medical conference, now wrote:

> The heroin epidemic appeared to be waning. . . . The rate of death from heroin overdose peaked in the summer of 1971, when 29 deaths occurred in a 3-month period. Since then, heroin overdose deaths have decreased progressively. During 1972, there were only 20 heroin overdose deaths in the District of Columbia, all but two of which occurred during the first 6 months of the year. There has only been one heroin overdose death during the first 3 months of 1973. . . . Since June 1969 there has been a progressive decline in the purity of heroin available on the streets of Washington [from] more than 6 percent . . . [to] an all-time low of 2.1 percent.

From Connecticut, the director of preventive medicine at New Haven's Department of Health, wrote in *U.S. News & World Report*, "We have arrived at a turning point in the heroin epidemic. In New Haven, as in many other cities, overdose and death due to this drug have become a rarity, and the number of persons coming under care for detoxification is showing a sharp decline." The number of active heroin addicts had plummeted from 300,000 to 150,000 in twenty-four months.

In Baltimore, city government reported that its heroin epidemic had peaked in 1971, with heroin arrests declining from 2,900 in 1971 to 1,150 in 1973. The reasons given were an intensive police crackdown on major traffickers, much greater availability of drug treatment, and better drug prevention and education programs.

During its truncated second term, the increasingly beseiged Nixon administration focused largely upon survival and the obsessive quest to silence opponents viewed as enemies. Edward Jay Epstein argues that had Watergate not brought down the administration in August 1974, it intended to use the huge new Drug Enforcement Agency (DEA), staffed with former CIA agents, against its perceived domestic enemies. Epstein describes the White House push for an antidrug superagency as part of continuing efforts to control a "strong investigative arm for domestic surveillance. . . . It [would have] the authority to request wiretaps and no-knock warrants, and to submit targets to the Internal Revenue Service; and, with its contingent of former CIA and counterintelligence agents, it had the talent to enter residences surreptitiously, gather intelligence on the activities of other agencies of the government, and interrogate suspects."

While the Watergate scandal ended any such grandiose schemes, the Drug Enforcement Administration (DEA) came into being nonetheless in July 1973, a bureaucratic behemoth combining BNDD, Customs agents who did drug work, the ill-starred ODALE, something called the Office of National Narcotics Intelligence, and fifty former CIA agents. This consolidation brought together a great many groups and individuals who heartily disliked one another and proceeded to engage in destructive internecine warfare.

John Ingersoll, whose administrative and strategic abilities had refashioned BNDD into a reasonably effective agency, had resigned in disgust in mid 1973 at the strange political goings-on. Something else besides antidrug work seemed to be afoot. Ingersoll's departure was seen as a huge loss by those who worked for and with him. "He was just head and shoulders above every other person who ever held that job, with a foresight that surpassed anything before or since," said one longtime drug agent. "Basically Ingersoll was an honest person and that's why he wasn't head of DEA. If he had been, maybe we wouldn't have the drug problem we have today." So with the seasoned and much admired Ingersoll gone, the White House considered and rejected 150 candidates for head of DEA before settling on John Bartels, a Harvard-trained lawyer, whose few years at DEA were memorable largely for the even more vicious office politics.

On November 14, 1975, retired FBN commissioner Harry J. Anslinger died of heart failure. Eighty-three years old, blind, dependent on morphine to blunt his angina, Anslinger in his twilight years had surveyed the modern scene with puzzled outrage. How had he and his life's work become the subject of such ridicule? Forty-five years earlier, when he had taken over the new Federal Bureau of Narcotics, a powerful consensus had prevailed in American society that addicting and consciousness-altering drugs were bad. Hollywood, that great shaper and mirror of the popular zeitgeist, had decreed the topic tawdry and taboo. The one movie made after 1934 that dared address addiction, the 1955 film *The Man with the Golden Arm*, had portrayed drug users as desperate and depraved.

Now suddenly that powerful consensus had crumbled. The Establishment, confronted with two booming drug cultures—one peopled by middle-class youth fascinated by marijuana and psychedelics and the other by poor urban blacks hooked on heroin—had been forced to reconsider the old Anslinger hard line. Few could justify sending college students to ten-year jail terms for drug use—or heroin addicts either, for that matter.

In his twilight years, an aging Anslinger could only look on in angry amazement as the baby boomers gathered in Dionysian festivals pulsating with rock 'n' roll music to celebrate altered states. Or as mass circulation magazines such as *Playboy* promoted Timothy Leary pontificating on LSD ecstasy. On college campuses, student audiences watching the old antimarijuana film, *Reefer Madness*, roared with laughter. The popular culture portrayed drug use as fun and hip and meaningful—whether Robert Crumb's cartoon character Mr. Natural, the Rolling Stones singing "All my friends are junkies" in "Monkey Man," the Superfly films, or Cheech and Chong giggling away on the silver screen with their giant joints.

The older Establishment and governing classes responded to this sea change in the zeitgeist in surprising ways. Anslinger had summed up a decades-long consensus when he declared in the fifties, "We intend to get the killer-pushers and their willing customers out of selling and buying dangerous drugs. The answer to the problem is simple—get rid of drugs, pushers and users. Period."

But by the seventies, the problem no longer seemed so simple. Not to an ever more wealthy and liberal society devoted to consumerism and self-realization. After Baltimore City police raided Johns Hopkins University in late April 1969 and arrested numerous students, Maryland's most esteemed academic administrators (including Hopkins's president) took out a full-page ad in the *Baltimore Sun* to demand that Maryland reexamine state laws "pertaining to the possession, use and sale of the so-called drugs of abuse and addiction." The phrase "so-called" tells a great deal about the huge shift underway. By 1972, those stodgy champions of middle-class consumerism, Consumer's Union, essentially had proposed legalizing heroin and all other drugs. That same year, the Ford Foundation had funded the new Drug Abuse Council, which hoped to "encourage responsible drug using behavior." The council's youthful Fellows soon went public with their backing for legal heroin. This extraordinary volte-face by the Eastern Establishment, its endorsement of drug use as reasonable and even positive behavior, was an incredible sign of the times.

Dr. Jerome Jaffe, President Nixon's antidrug person in the White

House, says, "The president never shared with me why he had such strong feelings about drugs. I think he truly felt that drugs tore at the fabric of society. He was a student of history, and if you look over history, there has never been a situation where extensive drug use doesn't lead to the deterioration of social fabric and productivity."

PART IV

America's Third Drug Epidemic 1980–1995

"Cocaine: the champagne of drugs."
—NEW YORK TIMES, 1974

CHAPTER 15

"High on
Cocaine."

—Grateful Dead, 1970

In the 1977 film *Annie Hall*, the ever-nerdy Woody Allen character is a neurotic but successful comic; love interest Diane Keaton is a chanteuse on the rise. They are young adults living the highly examined good life in Manhattan. Deep into the amusing story of their complicated love affair, Allen and Keaton visit another couple. The man, a tweedy professional-looking sort with a thick mustache, sits on the couch matter-of-factly chopping up a small mound of cocaine. Everyone is urging a reluctant Allen to try the drug. He, meanwhile, is examining the friend's stash in an elegant box. Suddenly Allen sneezes and two thousand dollars worth of the white powder vaporizes into a useless cloud. This cinematic moment perfectly captured the late seventies zeitgeist, for all over America trendy baby boomers on the make were rediscovering cocaine, an all-but-forgotten turn-of-the-century drug.

Just as when cocaine first appeared in the 1880s and 1890s, a great many people had a great many nice things to say about the white powder, tempered with a few easy-to-ignore caveats. And so *Newsweek*'s "Life and Leisure" section (not its health or medicine section, mind you) described cocaine in 1971 as "the status symbol of the American middle-class pothead," mentioning along the way that "a year ago, the rock group The Grateful Dead popularized the fad of openly wearing a spoon around the neck." The inevitable newsweekly "co-ed" gushed, "Orgasms go better with coke," while the deputy director of Chicago's Bureau of Narcotics advised, "You get a good high with coke and you don't get hooked." And, of course, there was a knowing sprinkling of early cocaine history, tasty morsels about such early and brilliant users as Sigmund Freud and 1920s jazz musicians. Declared *Newsweek* brightly, "By last spring, *Rolling Stone* magazine was calling [cocaine] 'the drug of the year.' " Having generally established cocaine's winning pedigree—Freud, jazz, Grateful Dead, *Rolling Stone*—the newsweekly tossed in the requisite caveat. Even great drugs exacted casualties here and there, in this instance a musician who "blew his mind on 'snow' and ruined a brilliant career as a guitarist."

By the summer of 1972, *Rolling Stone*—the opinion-setting organ of the hipper boomers—ran its own quaint and amusing version of the history of America's "star-spangled powder." The opening paragraph, a huge blown-up quote from physician Paolo Mantegazza written in 1859 read, "Borne on the wings of two Coca leaves, I flew about in the spaces of 77,438 worlds, one more splendid than another. I prefer a life of ten years with Coca to one of a hundred thousand without it. It seemed to me that I was separated from the whole world, and I beheld the strangest images, more beautiful in color and in form than can be imagined." And of course there was the brilliant Freud, and all the funny stuff about Coca-Cola and its early rivals, and the patent medicines, and a few illustrations using the archaic ads of the long-gone catarrh powders.

Amid all the entertaining historical anecdotes and amusing trivia, the article conceded that cocaine was soon discovered to have "shall we say, drawbacks. . . . [S]ome people became slaves to the habit." Of course, it was pointed out that they were people like surgeon William Halsted, who was injecting two hundred times the modern pleasure-sized dose. (No mention was made of his three colleagues who failed to give up cocaine and were soon dead.) The message clearly came across that intelligent "recreational" users who snorted small amounts would not get into trouble. *Rolling Stone* blamed this delightful drug's earlier banishment from the American scene on "absurd laws about harmless drugs."

What this hip historical riff failed to reflect was the extensive medical and public health literature generated at the turn of the century by an increasingly alarmed nation. In 1888, when drug treatment took place at institutions with names such as the Home for Intemperate

Men, one proprietor described cocaine as "the very acme of pernicious appetite. . . . [The drug leaves] the willpower utterly wrecked, every lingering sense of personal honor and cleanliness destroyed, and but one madding desire—to use the awful drug at all cost, at any peril." A year later, a Detroit physician treated a young man suffering from hay fever in the usual manner, by prescribing cocaine to be snuffed. When five months had passed, a local druggist advised the doctor that the young man was using huge amounts of the drug. Reported the doctor, "the habit had gone too far to be easily eradicated, as the young man went on until he became temporarily insane, had to retire from his business, and be under strict supervision until the craving disappeared, a space of about three months."

Anyone who bothered to visit a decent medical school library could locate on the shelves the old *Surgeon's General's Guide to Medical Literature* (the first volumes in the indispensable *Index Medicus*). There, under the heading "cocaine," a researcher would find pages of turn-of-the-century articles, including a growing number devoted to cocaine's potential for toxicity and habituation. And even if the old medical and public health journals were not instantly on hand, interlibrary loan assuredly would produce the requested articles within a week or two.

The tone of these old articles often could be surprisingly bitter and personal. One New York doctor wrote in 1885 of how cocaine banished all sense of "physical and mental fatigue . . . as if by magic; the mind becomes excessively clear; ideas constantly flow and the faculty of speech seems especially exalted." But after prolonged usage different effects surface: a "debasing enslavement of the will, a general demoralization which is as diabolical as it is indescribable, and which tends rapidly towards depravity and to the debasement of everything that is degrading and ignoble in human nature. Habits of the most detestable character, a settled indifference to every interest in life, destruction of the most noble affections and affiliations. . . . [Cocaine is] the most powerful and devilish drug which it has ever been the misfortune of man to abuse." In the seventies no one was interested in such Victorian carping.

To appreciate the early stages of the boomer's love affair with cocaine, one has only to skim the literature of the 1970s, the so aptly named "Me Decade." A 1973 journal article ("Cocaine in Perspective") authored by doctors and staff of the Haight-Ashbury Free Medical Clinic set the typical tone: "The drug of aristocrats, kings, high priests, and highly articulate and creative men of many eras, [cocaine's] use has also been relegated to the lowest slaves and has been associated with social debasement of the most precipitous and pitiful nature. Now, in

1973, cocaine is enjoying renewed popularity among the affluent and the creative, especially in the music and entertainment fields. Called at various times snow, flake, girl, her, lady, blow, jam, happy trails, rock, nose-candy, the star-spangled powder, the gift of the sun god, heaven-leaf or just leaf, and the rich man's or the pimp's drug, cocaine is very much on center stage again." While the article acknowledged that cocaine "can lead to a profound and dangerous type of drug abuse," this sober warning was overwhelmed by paeans of praise not so different from those turn-of-the-century Parke-Davis ads about cocaine making the coward brave, etc. Concluded the Haight-Ashbury Clinic folk, "In its pharmacologic action, cocaine . . . reinforces and boosts what we recognize as the highest aspirations of American initiative, energy, frenetic achievement, and ebullient optimism even in the face of great odds."

This overheated effulgence characterized much of what was written about cocaine for the next decade. The words and especially the images of the time promoted cocaine as a safe, classy, and purely pleasurable drug historically used by brilliant, creative, and powerful people because it made you feel smart, energetic, and sexy. Still extremely expensive—an amount the size of a pea (enough for a few snorts) cost one hundred dollars—cocaine had become a major status symbol. True, some who used cocaine got in trouble, but the implicit message was that those who faltered were people who used untoward amounts of cocaine or went beyond the safety of snorting to shooting. In brief, a tiny minority of people who were not smart about their drug use.

The words and images associated with cocaine conjured up a world of glamour and wealth and power. A 1974 story in the highly influential and prestigious *New York Times Magazine* was typical. The headline was COCAINE: THE CHAMPAGNE OF DRUGS, while the first page illustrations were photos of three "users of the drug," those being the highly eminent Sigmund Freud, Sir Arthur Conan Doyle, and Pope Leo XIII. The big pop-out quote read, "For its devotees, cocaine epitomizes the best of the drug culture—which is to say, a good high achieved without the forbiddingly dangerous needle and addiction of heroin."

By the mid seventies, with cocaine use fast expanding among the glitterati and the educated elite, the first popular books appeared. *Cocaine: Its History, Uses and Effects* by journalist Richard Ashley was published in 1975 and totally reflected the times. He airily dismissed the early medical literature, putting great emphasis on the experiences of eighty-one users he could personally interview. All, he reported "agreed, as might be expected, that cocaine was a 'good' drug, and virtually all were certain it should be used in moderation. . . . No one reported experiencing depression or marked craving for cocaine when their supply ran out." Ashley conceded people could get into trouble with cocaine if you were "one of the very few who either lacks or fails to use his common sense." But with cocaine so expensive, users "reserved it for special occasions, much as they would an expensive wine."

Ashley also trotted out what would become a standard explanation for why American society had clamped down on cocaine the first time around. Not because it was a highly seductive, addicting drug whose use many people found impossible to control, but because of racism. Cocaine abuse during the first epidemic had initially been noticed in the southern states, states already obssessed with maintaining social control over their oppressed black citizens. It was not surprising that when blacks began using cocaine—which was described in contemporary accounts as "this greatest enemy of society and friend of the madhouse"—in nonwork situations, southern cities and states quickly began restricting access. But almost every state in the union (many of which had virtually no black residents) did the same, passing laws to restrict or ban cocaine. It was not racism that caused nonmedical cocaine use to be banned completely in the 1914 Harrison Act. It was the medical and societal consensus, based on three decades of accumulated experience, that cocaine was a highly risky and dangerous drug.

Historian Joseph Spillane, whose *Modern Drug, Modern Menace: The Legal Use and Distribution of Cocaine in the United States, 1880–1920* now stands as the most scholarly and thorough study of the first epidemic, concludes: "Three factors contributed to the view that cocaine use was extraordinarily risky: the ease and rapidity with which cocaine abuse developed in some users; the severe physical and mental effects of cocaine abuse, unlike anything encountered in opiate abuse; and the tenacity of cocaine abuse, despite the fact that it did not lead to a physical addiction."

The next major book of the 1970s was *Cocaine: A Drug and Its Social Evolution* by Harvard Medical School psychiatrist Lester Grinspoon and James B. Bakalar. Published in 1976, this was a far weightier and more serious enterprise than Ashley's, not surprising since the authors were academics at the nation's premier university. Nonetheless, the two professors were just as skeptical about the early cocaine literature and similarly enthusiatic about the drug, though their opinions were more judiciously and subtly presented. (After all, only a dozen years earlier Timothy Leary had been booted out of Harvard for being too loudly and blatantly pro-LSD.)

In their book's chapters on the turn-of-the-century cocaine experience, the two Harvard professors quoted a range of earlier literature about cocaine in such a way to make clear that these articles were unenlightened and almost certainly unscientific screeds that should be discounted. In citing a 1903 report by concerned pharmacists on fast-expanding cocaine abuse, Grinspoon and Bakalar wrote with apparent disbelief, "Nothing, the report says, is more baneful than cocaine. It turns upright men into thieves and liars."

In their section on "The Future," Grinspoon and Bakalar wrote, "The most significant sociological fact about cocaine today is that it is rapidly attaining unofficial respectability in the same way as marihuana in the 1960s. It is accepted as a relatively innocuous stimulant, casually used by those who can afford it to brighten the day or the evening."

Cocaine was linked constantly to the highest status items and images. Newsweek's 1977 take, "The Cocaine Scene," was illustrated with drawings of swanky people in evening clothes doing "lines," and the drug was likened to "Dom Perignon and caviar." The article described in breathless detail how "pinstriped Wall Street lawyers take it from 14-karat gold spoons at elegant parties." After all, "the accoutrements of the cocaine culture seem to be part of the kick. Some coke buffs wear neck chains with a razor blade and a tiny spoon dangling like amulets. Maxferd's, a San Francisco jewelry store, provides diamond-encrusted razor blades for $500 and custom-designed spoons that sell for as much as $5,000." The article asserted that "cocaine is not addictive and causes no withdrawal symptoms. Taken in moderation, cocaine probably causes no significant mental or physical damage and a number of researchers have concluded that it can be safer than liquor and cigarettes when used discriminately."

And then there was the Newsweek sidebar, "What the Doctors Say." Again the basic message was that cocaine was not addictive or particularly dangerous. New York psychiatrist Richard Resnick said, "It is rare to find people who use it in large quantities continuously." Best of all, Newsweek could report modern medical consensus; "For moderate users, the risks seem slight." (Of course, there was no suggestion that moderate users even could become immoderate users.) And if anyone wondered what constituted "moderate" use, in 1980 Harvard's Dr. Grinspoon would define "moderate use" in one of the nation's standard medical textbooks, the third edition of Kaplan's Comprehensive Textbook of Psychiatry, as snorting cocaine two to three times a week. And there medical consensus would remain until the mid 1980s.

By the time mainstream publications were celebrating cocaine in the mid seventies, it had become the de rigueur staple of a Hollywood once again awash in illegal drugs. The studio days were over, along with the old contracts that made drug use cause for firing. The Hays Office, which had enforced the prohibition of portraying drugs in movies, had withered away under competition from foreign films and television. By the 1970s, Hollywood was back to the highly public wild ways of the 1920s. In her harrowing autobiography, Oscar-winning producer Julia Phillips (*The Sting, Close Encounters of the Third Kind*) describes a zoned-out world of meetings and lunches and movie deals and parties and casual sex, all fueled by an ever more elaborate cornucopia of drugs.

A few typical excerpts from Phillips's sad memoir of a talent self-destructing: "I am still high from the party. Streams of names and semi-names have come to pay homage. I have done a fair amount of blow with a handsome young thing, heir to a fast-food fortune, in the bathroom, and he has given me this little package for the road."

Or this bitter memory of being backstage in New York at a Rolling Stones concert: "There is a smelly Israeli named Freddy who seems to be very important to everybody. He carries two medium-sized bottles filled with rock cocaine. He offers some to Goldie [Hawn] and some to me. Fuck you, Mr. Under-Assistant West Coast Promo Man. We turn him down; I've got my own. I always carry my own stash. It is usually better than whatever anyone else has got. It also establishes the rules. This is not a coke whore, it says."

A 1978 *People* magazine six-page spread on Hollywood "celebs" and the "new high" featured everyone from actor Jack Nicholson to country music star Waylon Jennings: " 'It's the '70s drug,' says a movie producer, . . . 'I think our generation is now more into productivity than creativity. . . . It comes with growing up a little. To take psychedelics, it takes three days—one to prepare, one to drop and one to recover. Who has that kind of time in this town? Coke is really easy—a toot here, a toot there. Of course, you have the occasional lost weekend when you do maybe a gram or two. . . . But it's a neat drug—makes you feel good, you can function on it. . . . It's getting bigger all the time."

Not long after, *Medical World News* ran a story titled, "Patching Hollywood's 'coke noses.' " Datelined Beverly Hills, the article began, "With some of the leading stars of the movie industry among the victims, chronic cocaine sniffers are coming down with holes in their nasal septums. And there is little agreement among ENT [ear, nose, throat] specialists and plastic surgeons about how to treat."

By 1978 producer Julia Phillips had moved on to smoking, also known as freebasing, cocaine: "I have the illusion that I am doing substantially less cocaine than if I toot it. My nose is very sore . . . and this pipe-smoking seems like a convenient method of intake.

"More important, the high is substantially more dynamic."

By the fall of 1979 this mother of a young girl has spent almost a year holed up in a room in her house, spending fifteen thousand dollars a week to smoke freebase nonstop and suffering convulsions. After a month at a treatment clinic, she relapses and proceeds to smoke her way through $120,000 of cocaine in three months. Faced with losing her child, she finally manages to stop, but dreams nightly of cocaine for years.

Whole movie and TV sets were deep in "snow," such that *TV Guide* blamed cocaine for the stupidity of American shows. Johnny Carson quipped at the 1981 Academy Awards, "The biggest money maker in Hollywood last year was Colombia. Not the studio, the country." A famous male star, for instance, is photographed looking fabulous with a gold razor blade (presumably for cutting "lines") dangling from a chain.

All through the 1970s—when popular culture and much of the main-line media presented illegal drug use as exciting, glamorous, and certainly normal—the United States experienced yearly rises in drug use, whether through experimentation, regular use, or abuse. This incredible national shift (wherein mind-altering drugs had become a commonplace of growing up) could be roughly charted, thanks to a new governmental measuring stick: the National Household Survey on Drug Abuse. The household survey was launched in 1971 and looked at four groups (12- to -17-year-olds, 18- to -25-year-olds, 26- to -34-year-olds, and those over 35) and their use of a whole range of abusable drugs—tobacco, alcohol, marijuana, cocaine, inhalants, hallucinogens, heroin, and the various psychotherapeutics available through prescription.

In the household survey, the most worrisome and important figure has been drug use within the "past month," because that identifies regular users and abusers. In its first report, issued in 1972, the survey found that 7 percent of the youngest cohort—those 12 to 17—reported smoking marijuana and hashish during the past month. Throughout the 1970s that figure rose again and again. In 1974 junior and senior high school kids smoking marijuana or hashish within the past month had almost doubled, to 12 percent, rising slightly in 1976 to 12.3 percent, rising noticeably in 1977 to 16.6 percent, and edging up again in 1979 to 16.7 percent.

For the cohort aged 18 to 25, past month marijuana use in 1972 was a surprisingly large 27.8 percent. By the end of the decade, that had escalated to an even larger 35.4 percent. In 1974, 3.1 percent of this group acknowledged past-month cocaine use. By 1979, that figure had *tripled*, to 9.3.

By the end of the 1970s illegal drug use had become commonplace and even rampant in the younger segments of the white middle class.

The general attitude was well captured by an advertisement run in *High Times* (a magazine described by Harvard's Dr. Grinspoon in his 1976 book as "the highly successful new publication that serves as the *Playboy* of the drug culture,") for that magazine's new *Encyclopedia of Recreational Drugs*. A lovely young woman sits on a sand dune, the picture of health. The ad copy reads,

> Sure, it's easy to close yourself off to experience, cover up, withdraw from life. Safe.
> But I choose life. I want to open up to sights, sounds, tastes, smells, feelings. . . . That's why I expose myself to drugs . . . sometimes. Let's face it. Who doesn't?
> But I also want to know what I'm doing. Really, I'm no fool. I want to know what it means . . . and all that. All the dope on dope, man.

The founder and publisher of *High Times* was a bizarre character who renamed himself Tom Forcade to shield his conservative Arizona family from the embarrassment of public kinship. A longtime drug smuggler, Forcade also was extremely active in radical Yippie politics and helped found various underground press services. He invented the Yippie act of throwing a pie at those they disliked in highly public, formal situations—such as congressional hearings or conferences. At one point, Forcade was indicted for conspiracy to bomb the 1972 Republican convention.

Publications such as *High Times*, which was launched in 1974, and *HiTimes*, *Rush*, and *Dealer*, sprang up to service, celebrate, and make a buck off the burgeoning middle-class drug culture. They all attracted much advertising from the fast-growing drug paraphernalia business—estimated to generate as much as $1 billion a year. "Head shops" brazenly opened in suburban malls and on streets near elementary schools and junior and senior high schools. These stores forthrightly hawked everything anyone might want or need to get high on every kind of illegal drug. Soon drug paraphernalia also could be found in record stores, liquor stores, and trendy boutiques. Respectable convenience stores began stocking rolling papers.

The paraphernalia business provided an important advertising base for the drug magazines. A typical ad would feature a bold headline: LOOKING FOR COCAINE PARAPHERNALIA? And then continue in small print:

> Cocaccessories that's all we sell. Not only do we carry a large selection of solid gold 14K gold bottles, spoons, straws, and

razors, but we also feature the largest collection of non-gold coca paraphernalia available from any one distributor anywhere in the world: from coke mirrors, mirror boxes, cutting plates and glass slabs, to strainers, pestles and spatulas, stashes, small and large scales, glass and metal straws, manitol, mannite, large jars, small vials, a complete line of informative books, test kits, razor blades and funnels . . . in short, all the tools of the trade. Whether you do a gram a month or an ounce or more, if you don't know about us by now, you should.

A complete catalog cost two dollars and could be ordered from Brother Bob Productions through a Hollywood, California, post office box.

One visitor to Washington in late 1979 described a duly licensed sidewalk vendor at the major downtown business intersection of 20th and K streets selling nothing but drug paraphernalia. He happily sold the woman nitrous oxide cartridges along with a gizmo to improve the high. "While I was there, a well-dressed man in his thirties bought a 'coke vial' as easily as if he were buying a pack of gum, two young girls (age 13 to 14) bought a bong [a water pipe used for smoking], and several people bought rolling papers. At the end of each sale, the vendor wished his departing customer, 'Happy Toking.' He's been on that corner for two and one-half years and described his business as 'pretty good.' "

A rising chorus among the nation's youthful educated and elite argued that using drugs to achieve altered states was a natural—even desirable—experience. Therefore, heroin, cocaine, and, above all, marijuana should be decriminalized, even made legal. To that end a new lobbying group, the National Organization to Reform Marijuana Laws (NORML) had set up shop in Washington in 1971. The Eastern Establishment, semiconvinced by the baby boomers' insistence that illegal drugs were no worse than the alcohol used and abused by the older generations, dutifully established the Drug Abuse Council in 1972 to consider this thorny matter.

The major financial backers were the Ford Foundation, the Carnegie, Kaiser, and Commonwealth foundations, and Equitable Life Assurance Society. One person on the new Drug Abuse Council's board of directors, Dr. Daniel X. Freedman, was a physician. Otherwise no one had any practical, hands-on experience with drug abuse and/or treatment. Of seven staff members, one was a practicing physician conversant with drug use and abuse. There was no scientist or researcher who had studied the physiological consequences of drug use. Over the next six years the council dispersed $10 million to a variety of groups and individuals who always seemed to favor decriminalization or legalization.

When the council's final report, *Facts About "Drug Abuse,"* was issued in 1980, it predictably advocated these pro–drug use stances. After all, the report said, "Medical experts generally agree that cocaine produces few observable health consequences in its users. . . . Recent American psychiatric and sociological studies have failed to substantiate the view that repeated cocaine use leads to physiological dependence or tolerance. . . . In this respect American cocaine use appears to resemble a common pattern in alcohol use in which fine wines or liquors are reserved for other than ordinary consumption." The council felt advocating abstinence from illegal drugs unrealistic. Moreover, it believed that "failure to distinguish between the misuse and the use of drugs creates the impression that use is misuse." In this national atmosphere that constantly insisted that youthful drug use was inevitable and no big deal, drug experimentation and use by the young rose again and again. After all, the adults were all saying it was completely normal to try drugs and to use drugs.

No less a person than the nation's new president, Jimmy Carter, had expressed exactly that belief in early August 1977 when he asked Congress to abolish all federal criminal penalties for those caught with less than an ounce of marijuana. The *New York Times* paraphrased the president's remarks: "Mr. Carter said he did not approve [of smoking marijuana] but suggested that most young people in the country had probably tried it at one time or another." In fact, the ever useful household survey showed that by 1977, 30.9 percent—a lot but certainly not "most"—of those 12- to 17-year-olds had smoked marijuana. Most of the nation's junior and senior high school age students had *not* tried marijuana. Yet the president's remark implied that trying marijuana was to be expected. What was true was that 59.9 percent of those aged 18 to 25 had smoked marijuana. Either way, it was an oddly morally relativistic stance for a highly public Christian.

The president proposed to Congress that pot possession be treated much like a traffic offense, with fines up to one hundred dollars. As the *New York Times* pointed out, the president's oldest son had been dismissed from the U.S. Navy for smoking marijuana. Moreover, his other sons acknowledged experimenting with pot. Peter G. Bourne, the president's youthful assistant responsible for drug policy, spoke to reporters also, saying the administration's drug abuse policy was aimed at being "realistic."

Bourne, a handsome and charming British-born psychiatrist, had been head of Georgia's drug program in 1971 when Jimmy Carter was governor. Bourne had earned his medical degree at Emory University in 1962, studied psychiatry, served in Vietnam, and then returned to Atlanta to teach at Emory. Before long, he was invited to establish a methadone maintenance program for the expanding ranks of that city's heroin addicts. Success there earned national attention, and Dr. Bourne was asked to join the Nixon White House. Dr. Bourne urged Carter to run for president in 1975. When Carter entered the White House, he appointed Dr. Bourne Special Assistant for Health Issues.

Just before assuming his White House role, Dr. Bourne had written, "The legalization or decriminalization of heroin is a politically unthinkable notion at the present time, it is an option that may well gain increasing attention in the next few years." Dr. Bourne constantly identified himself as a "realist" whose goals were to pursue "what's going to work. And that meant what would work to reduce deaths from drugs and reduce adverse consequences. In the case of marijuana, nobody had ever died from marijuana and lengthy jail sentences were worse than anything the drug could do." And so here Dr. Bourne was now in the White House, possibly in a position to effect exactly such a thing.

In another article, Dr. Bourne wrote, "Cocaine . . . is probably the most benign of illicit drugs currently in widespread use. At least as strong a case could be made for legalizing it as for legalizing marijuana. Short acting—about 15 minutes—not physically addicting, and acutely pleasurable, cocaine has found increasing favor at all socioeconomic levels in the last year."

With someone like this so close to President Carter, the enthusiasts for drugs and drug culture—as represented most publicly by attorney and professional Angry Young Man Keith Stroup, founder of NORML—had good reason to be delighted. And for a brief time, they were. After all, Dr. Bourne had gotten a decriminalization bill onto the congressional agenda and had conferred significant clout on NORML by his friendly relations with them. Other good folk had lined up behind NORML, too. After all, few reasonable people could argue that smoking or selling small amounts of marijuana was worse than murder, and yet there were significant horror stories of people with no criminal records condemned to decades in jail over a joint. As NORML's star ascended, Dr. Bourne was one of their friends and allies.

But then a cloud slowly settled over the chumminess between Bourne and NORML. In this period, when heroin was still viewed as the nation's most destructive illegal drug, Dr. Bourne was rather pleased to see how dramatically Mexico's new antipoppy campaign was reducing the heroin flow. Dr. Bourne enthusiastically briefed Vice President Walter Mondale that "heroin purity levels are currently at a five-year low, and retail and wholesale prices of illicit heroin have dramatically increased."

When NORML realized that the very spraying that was so efficiently wiping out Mexico's new opium poppy acreage also was wiping out Mexican marijuana, and possibly leaving what survived contaminated with the herbicide paraquat, director Stroup apparently felt double-crossed. NORML expressed its displeasure by filing suit against four federal agencies on March 13, 1978, arguing that "the Government failed to file an environmental impact statement assessing the potential hazards of smoking marijuana sprayed with paraquat."

Dr. Bourne was unmoved because by late May 1978 he could see the dramatic and positive effects of Mexico's spraying campaign. In 1975, 1,755 Americans had died from heroin overdoses. With heroin availability plummeting, only a *quarter* that many would die in 1978, thanks to Mexican eradication of the poppy crop. But NORML was not interested in the larger picture.

Years later, in an interview, Dr. Bourne also would suggest that the Carter administration's push for federal decriminalization (something that left the states free to make their own penalties) had undermined NORML's fund-raising abilities: "And so NORML was desperately casting about for ways to generate new income and they hit on paraquat. It was a completely fabricated issue. It was a way of saying to their constituency that the Carter people may have a new policy but now they're killing us. And they painted me as the bad guy." Also, in mid October 1977 Keith Stroup was busted for marijuana in Canada. Recalls Bourne, "Stroup was very angry with me that I wouldn't use my official position to help him in Canada." Then there was a Yippie "pieing" of a congressional aide at a 1977 NORML conference. When the White House expressed its disapproval in a letter to Stroup, he saw this as part of a plot to oust him. In July 1978 Stroup got his revenge.

The charming and cosmopolitan Peter Bourne, a bright, soft-spoken man who retains a British accent despite years in the United States, was very much a man of the times. And like much of the nation's young elite, Bourne, then thirty-eight, apparently felt free to "do his own thing," regardless of stated rules and laws. Dr. Bourne's downfall began on July 11, 1978, when a young woman walked into a Woodbridge, Virginia, pharmacy to fill a prescription for fifteen quaaludes written for "Sarah Brown." A Virginia State Pharmacy Board inspector there doing a routine inspection had mild suspicions about a prescription from a D.C. doctor being filled way out in the sticks. But when the doctor's phone number turned out to be disconnected, the police were called. It soon emerged that Dr. Bourne, a high White House official and the nation's drug policy chief, had written the prescription (using the fictitious name) for his assistant, one Ellen Metsky, who had complained of trouble sleeping. She in turn had given it to her roommate to fill.

Dr. Bourne was informed that his explanation—using a fictitious name to shield a White House employee from the stigma of using such drugs—left him on the wrong side of both state and federal laws. Moreover, quaaludes were well known as a much sought after recreational drug. Dr. Bourne seemed utterly stunned that such a "trivial" issue as writing false prescriptions for a much abused party drug could stir up such scandal.

It was at this vulnerable moment that Keith Stroup of NORML struck. Dr. Bourne already was receiving a fast and unpleasant lesson that public officials were expected to respect the letter and the spirit of the law. But he might, with sufficient contrition, have survived, for his friendship with the president went back to Georgia days. But now Stroup leaked the highly damaging fact that Dr. Bourne had "publicly used two illegal drugs, cocaine and marijuana, at a party given for 600 people by the National Organization for the Reform of Marijuana Laws." This was a major item on *Good Morning America* and the front page of the *Washington Post*.

The *Post* reported, "Bourne, who was then the president's chief adviser on health and drug abuse, inhaled cocaine into both nostrils through rolled up currency in a bedroom with about a dozen other persons, according to witnesses.

"In an interview yesterday, Bourne denied that he has ever used cocaine. 'I won't say that I've never used marijuana, but not since I've been in this job." That was the final blow. With that, Dr. Bourne's White House career came to an abrupt end.

Unable to leave bad enough alone, Dr. Bourne further stirred up trouble by saying to a reporter that "he believed there was a 'high incidence' of marijuana use among members of the White House staff . . . [and that] he was aware of the occasional use of cocaine by a few members of the White House staff. He did not identify them." And, he added, he was not the only staffer at the NORML party. "About half the White House staff was there that night, looking—well, looking as though they belonged."

Dr. Bourne denies to this day that he used cocaine at the NORML bash, though he acknowledged observing those around him partake. (Under the law, however, it is not use per se but possession or presence of a drug that counts.)

The entire episode forcefully reminded the elite baby boomers that while *they* might think drugs and altered states could be positive and should be legal, the vast majority of Americans vehemently disagreed. A deeply embarrassed President Carter, his administration the butt of endless political jokes and cartoons about "high" public officials, etc., felt compelled to warn his young, arrogant staff, "Whether you agree with the law or whether or not others obey the law is totally irrelevant. You will obey it or you will seek employment elsewhere."

The *Washington Post* proceeded to devote column upon column to the astonished reaction of inside-the-Beltway boomers to Bourne's fall from power for not obeying the drug laws. " 'You know, it's hard to believe,' said a former antiwar activist turned senator's aide, sitting before a coffee table holding the latest issue of the New Yorker, a formidable law dictionary and a small glass bottle of cocaine. 'When they talk about official Washington using drugs, they're talking about people like me.' "

So blatant had illegal drug use become that no one seemed to think it particularly strange during NORML's sixth annual conference the previous year that "several large-scale cocaine dealers set up informal hospitality suites at the Hyatt Regency Hotel where tired participants could drop by for some quick refreshment." The wonderful thing about cocaine, explained one Washington professional, was "it doesn't slow you down like marijuana. It lets you be ambitious with a buzz on."

One of the great ironies of the Bourne affair was that when Keith Stroup and NORML exacted their revenge, they also torpedoed their own cause. With Dr. Bourne's departure, the middle-class drug culture lost its highest-level ally. The Carter White House now viewed the whole drug issue as one giant hot potato. No Carter official was going to press Congress to make illegal drugs easier to get or use.

And this was not only because of the embarrassment of the Bourne affair. National surveys were showing an incredible escalation of pot smoking among junior and senior high school kids. In 1975 the government had started funding the High School Senior Survey to get full details on student drug use. By 1979 one in ten American high school seniors smoked pot daily. Parents and teachers watched with mounting alarm as nice normal kids retreated from school, from sports, from clubs, and all the usual teen activities. The "heads" clustered into hostile little groups of other users, no longer engaged in ordinary life, their maturing process on hold. (But since no one was dropping dead, public health experts saw all of this as unimportant. People were not dying, they were not seeking treatment. Therefore, pot was safe.) Once caught up in constant marijuana use, these kids often moved on to experiment with other, more dangerous drugs. In a national sample of 1,100 young men aged thirty who had never used marijuana, *one* went on to try heroin. In a sample of 1,400 who *had* used marijuana, about 10.6 percent also had used heroin. This was not true for those who had only dabbled briefly in marijuana, meaning less than ten times. However, of those who had by age thirty used marijuana a thousand times, 50 percent had tried heroin.

As parents began to understand that the constant celebration of drug use, the proliferating head shops, and the drug magazines were luring in ever younger middle-class kids, they rose up in fury. They organized themselves into groups and went after the politicians, the public health experts, head-in-the-sand schools, and the drug culture itself. Between the public outrage over Dr. Bourne and the gathering grassroots parents movement, the Carter White House chose to back off, leery of more damaging headlines and political cartoons. Unfortunately, the Carter White House also largely retreated from all aspects of the drug problem just as cocaine was gathering into a serious epidemic.

With the national infatuation with cocaine growing and the White House laying low, Congress took the lead. By now, of course, the accepted line on cocaine was that it was a safe party drug used by the best people. When drug use was mushrooming in the 1970s, the Ford White House had set up the Domestic Council Drug Abuse Task Force to assess "the current extent of drug abuse on America and present a number of recommendations." The ensuing September 1975 white paper had argued, "Not all drug use is equally destructive, and we should give priority in our treatment and enforcement efforts to those drugs which pose the greater risk, as well as to compulsive users of drugs of any kind."

And, predictably, cocaine was not seen as a problem drug. Guided by the National Institute on Drug Abuse (whose director then was Dr. Robert DuPont), the white paper reported, "The data indicate that cocaine is used for the most part on an occasional basis (several times a month or less); usually in the company of others; and it is likely to be taken in combination with alcohol, marihuana, or some other drug. Cocaine is not physically addictive. . . . Cocaine, as currently used, usually does not result in serious social consequences such as crime, hospital emergency room admissions, or death."

The white paper did concede in a footnote that the older literature suggested significant problems and that "the social cost could be considerably higher if chronic use began to develop." It also conceded that the "rate of increase of first use of cocaine is alarming." Nonetheless, the white paper, which would set the course of federal drug policy for the rest of the decade, declared cocaine a nonproblem: "Priority in both supply and demand reduction should be directed toward those drugs which inherently pose a greater risk—heroin, amphetamines (particularly when used intravenously) and mixed barbiturates." Cocaine was declared officially not worth worrying about.

Jerry Strickler, then an official in the DEA, vividly remembers going to the Ford White House to try and talk the task force into recognizing cocaine as a problem drug:

> We told them that the kinds of crimes being committed by people on cocaine were something very different and scary. Our agents had just not seen that sort of violence or edginess before. We were hearing about people going in to rob Mom and Pop grocery stores. They'd get the money and still turn around and kill these people. We hadn't seen that with people on other drugs. Cocaine was not something benign. We asked them to talk to some of the agents who were seeing what this stuff did to people. But their reaction was that I didn't have medical credentials and they weren't going to listen to me.

Part of the problem here was simply the means by which health care professionals and public health experts determined what constituted a problem. Morbidity and mortality were the usual measures. By those standards, the escalating use of cocaine by the middle class was just not worth worrying about. In any given year in the late 1970s, five to ten people might die from cocaine "poisoning," and typically these were couriers who had swallowed condoms with cocaine that had burst. If people weren't registering as visible casualties, it wasn't a public health crisis. "People just didn't know that much," remembers Dr. Bourne.

> It was just seen as not of much consequence compared to heroin. Prior to the advent of crack, the problems associated with cocaine were inconsequential. We spent enormous hours discussing cocaine. We talked and talked at this weekly meeting we had. Peter Bensinger from DEA would be there, Mathea Falco from State, Bob DuPont from NIDA, someone from CIA, and Bob Chasen from Customs. And we'd go over things, coordinating policy. Mainly we agreed we should try and keep the price up, because that kept it out of the hands of young people and limited use. But there was zero demand for treatment. And even if there were, we didn't have anything like methadone.

The Ford white paper did more than repeat the usual line about cocaine being a safe, recreational drug. It also focused federal law enforcement firmly away from cocaine just as trafficking was exploding. The White Paper suggested that "preference might be given to Mexico, which is an important source of both heroin and 'dangerous drugs,' rather than to Miami, where an agent is more likely to 'make' a cocaine or marijuana case." Strickler remembers that DEA agents were taken out of South Florida, where more and more cocaine was pouring in: "When agents down there developed cocaine cases, they were discouraged and told to make heroin cases. They'd say, 'We're swimming in cocaine.' But again and again, they were told, 'Cocaine is not a priority.' "

Within three years, South Florida was overwhelmed by violent Latin American traffickers smuggling in cocaine and marijuana. Murder and crime soared, and local law enforcement and politicians were pleading for help. Congressman Lester Wolff of New York and a few others visited the Sunshine State to hold hearings in early June 1978. They were stunned by the dimension of what they saw and heard. Before 1970, Customs rarely seized two hundred pounds of cocaine in a year. Now, exclaimed Congressman Wolff, "From October of 1977 through March of this year [1978] a six-man airport unit of the Dade County Public Safety Department has seized over 100 pounds of cocaine and 29 pounds of heroin. U.S. Customs marijuana seizures at Miami airport have gone from 20 pounds in 1975 to over 800 pounds thus far in 1978; from 37 pounds in 1975 to over 271 pounds of cocaine thus far in Miami airport alone."

The new DEA chief for Miami, Frederick A. Rody, Jr., had had about half a year to review the situation. He testified:

> South Florida has become inundated with marijuana and cocaine smuggling and trafficking. We serve as a gateway for the introduction of drugs from South America. . . . The dimensions of drug smuggling . . . and the associated economics involved are astounding. It is not unrealistic to say that the smugglers are better equipped, have more resources and financial backing than the entire law enforcement community. Of course, they do not have to play by the same rules and they are counseled by the best legal minds available.

Before leaving the state, the congressman fired off a telegram to the Carter White House requesting an emergency meeting and declaring Florida to be "in the midst of a catastrophic and overwhelming drug disaster. . . . The situation is so serious we must take immediate action to stem the tide of illegal drugs into the United States from the access point of South Florida."

In July 1979, the House of Representatives Select Committee on Narcotics Abuse and Control decided to hold anticocaine hearings to dispel "the general belief, especially among users, that cocaine is a safe and risk-free substance." In light of this stated aim, their choice of Harvard's Dr. Grinspoon as a witness is a bit odd, but he was a well-known expert. In that role, he reviewed the research literature generated in the previous five years, noting in his written statement that the older clinical literature was "sparse and affected by the limitations and prejudices of an earlier era."

In his testimony, Dr. Grinspoon duly acknowledged work that demonstrated the extreme reinforcing properties of cocaine in animals. "In experiments where unlimited access to intravenous cocaine is provided, animals will kill themselves by voluntary injections. In one recent experiment, for example, monkeys to whom intravenous cocaine was available 23 hours a day . . . developed hyperactivity, tactile hallucinations, ataxia, severe weight loss, tremors, and convulsions as they continued to inject the drug; they died within five days."

Nonetheless, explained Dr. Grinspoon in his oral testimony about the current situation, cocaine did not seem to be wreaking much havoc this go round because "people, generally speaking, don't use cocaine quite as recklessly as they did at the turn of the century and are more sophisticated about their use of it." Consequently, reassured Dr. Grinspoon, "At present, chronic cocaine abuse does not commonly appear as a medical problem, and there is little literature on treatment." All those boomers snorting cocaine twice or thrice weekly could be reassured by the eminent professor's testimony that he "could not persuade" himself that they were "very much at risk."

Dr. Robert Byck, a respected psychiatrist and pharmacologist at Yale Medical School, also testified at these same hearings. He had been engaged in laboratory studies of cocaine for five years. In his submitted, written congressional testimony, Dr. Byck said he found that America had responded to cocaine with "unreasoning fear" and "inappropriate regulation." He could see no sign that "cocaine causes an increase in aggression," though it was obvious that alcohol does. "There is no evidence that in the commonly used routes in the U.S., cocaine represents an acute or chronic health hazard of any significance, but there is no question that tobacco does."

However, when Dr. Byck appeared to testify in person, he was singing a very different tune. He had just returned from an international meeting on coca in Lima, Peru, and he was shaken badly. "I used to be in the same camp as Dr. Grinspoon appears to be, that is feeling unsure whether or not cocaine could ever be legalized. But in my more recent experience, I have come to the absolute, clear conclusion that it should not be legalized under any circumstance." The shaken Dr. Byck had seen the scary specter of Peru's coca paste smokers, addicts oblivious to all but another hit. He explained:

About three or four years ago . . . for reasons that are not clear, a number of people started smoking a material that was extracted from coca leaves, which they call "coca paste." It is really more cocaine than it is coca. A totally different use pattern then developed. Users could not take it or leave it. They smoked cocaine compulsively, just like the heroin user. When you smoke it you get very high very fast, and you then very shortly thereafter get a real crash, a feeling of depression and a tremendous urge to use the drug again. When people start smoking the material, they smoke cigarette after cigarette. And when they do that, they end up with a large total amount of cocaine in their bodies. They often become paranoid. They get somewhat crazy. They are fearful, they are anxious. Their heart rates go up; their blood pressures go up. Then they may progress to the point of psychosis, which we are presently investigating. . . .

It has been said in the past that cocaine is relatively safe. That is true for small amounts taken by nose. It is not true when the drug is smoked. When smoked the amount of cocaine in the blood goes up within a minute to levels that are higher than you get after an hour snorting cocaine. There is a rapid rise of cocaine in the blood. . . . [Smoking cocaine,] I think is an extremely dangerous habit. . . .

Here is a chance for the Federal Government to engage in an educational campaign to prevent a drug abuse epidemic. . . . This is a drug that is addicting in the traditional sense, and therefore, is one that we must pay attention to. I suggest that we act as follows: No. 1, find out about it; No. 2, establish some kind of collaboration with the media; and No. 3, show what happens when this drug is used, so we won't get an epidemic. We need our best minds to figure out how to do this without advertising the drug.

At this moment, the congressmen interrupted to say they had to go vote. When the hearing reconvened, Dr. Byck's impassioned testimony, an unequivocal scientific and medical call to arms over cocaine smoking, provoked no further discussion or apparent interest. In 1995 he would say, "It's always been bewildering to me that no one got the point."

And it was not as if cocaine smoking was some exotic foreign habit that could never find its way to the United States. Part of what had alarmed Dr. Byck was news through the scientific grapevine that *High*

Times had begun running a full-page ad for a kit to convert plain old cocaine into smokable freebase. The ad copy read, "In Columbia [sic], the natives call their Snow Vapor Base. For over 100 years, in every village, it's been the Toke of the Town! . . . the 'ultimate high.' " A large array of products were listed, including FreeBase-Tokers, Free-Base System (Kit), FreeBase Flash Torch, etc. The American drug culture now was promoting actively a product that would make it easy for intranasal users to become compulsive freebase smokers.

Yale's Dr. Byck was not the only one with disturbing news at that day's congressional hearing. When Dade County, Florida, medical examiner Charles V. Wetli testified, he provided the first contemporary reports that people could die from recreational snorting of cocaine. First published as a paper in the *Journal of the American Medical Association* that same month, Dr. Wetli's study described twenty-four deaths in his county from toxic reactions to cocaine, five from snorting. The medical examiner described five otherwise healthy young men who died after snorting cocaine. All the five using the drug "intranasally had a symptom-free interval of 30 to 60 minutes, after which they went into sudden unexpected grand mal–type seizures, with death occurring a few minutes later from respiratory collapse.

"The persons who died after snorting cocaine had also snorted the drug at least twice during the previous hour. The mechanism of death in all cases is one of respiratory collapse mediated by the effect of cocaine on the central nervous system."

But such warnings just did not penetrate the larger media celebration. In 1977, government surveys had shown 10 percent of young adults eighteen to twenty-five had used cocaine in the past year. Two years later that figure had doubled. Not so surprising when one saw how cocaine was portrayed constantly as a stimulating and empowering high, ideal for up-and-coming Yuppies eager to succeed and grab the good life. Certainly, the Washington go-getters had not slackened their cocaine use. Carter chief of staff Hamilton Jordan had been mired in a cocaine scandal. In September 1980 another Carter aide fell to cocaine charges, this time the president's national campaign manager, Tim Kraft, thirty-nine.

By mid 1981, conservative *Time* magazine would run a cover story titled, "High on Cocaine," with striking cover art—an elegant martini glass full of cocaine—that sent two powerful messages: cocaine was a class act, and it was as acceptable as alcohol. Now, reported the newsweekly, cocaine's use was spreading fast into the ranks of solid citizenry: "Today . . . coke is the drug of choice for perhaps millions of solid, conventional and often upwardly mobile citizens."

Of course, *Time* included the usual caveats about the drug's "darker side." There was the user quoted as saying, "After one hit of cocaine I feel like a new man. The only problem is, the first thing the new man wants is another hit." But in a sixteen-column story, only four columns were devoted to the downside of cocaine. The rest was a torrent of words and images linking cocaine use to smart, classy people who knew how to get ahead and have a good time.

Of course, places like *Rolling Stone* were as bullish as ever about cocaine. In November 1981, P. J. O'Rourke—identified as a former editor of *National Lampoon* and a writer of movies—penned a charming "Lessons in Modern Manners" about cocaine etiquette that proclaimed, "Cocaine makes us so intelligent, so quick, witty, charming, alert, well-dressed, good-looking and sexually attractive that it would be unthinkable to be rude under its influence."

Oh so droll, O'Rourke made various piquant references to "Indoor Aspen Lift Lines," "Granulated Money," and "Platinum Maxwell House" as he naughtily advised his readers to use as much cocaine as possible in social situations, so others "will be less inclined to destroy their mucous membranes, become psychotic, suffer heart palpitations or die from an overdose." He notes in the wryest of tones that the "detrimental" effects of cocaine "cannot be overstated. There was a washed-up musician who hung around a well-known New York nightspot mooching drugs. He turned into a dangerous psychopath and tried to bore several people to death. My own younger brother took too much of my cocaine, and the result was a painful bloody nose." A very funny piece of writing whose message was, as ever, that cool people used cocaine and did not get into trouble with it. At worst, you could become a cocaine bore.

The only scientist of this "We Love Cocaine" era to inveigh vocally and publicly against cocaine was Gabriel Nahas, a pharmacologist and professor of anesthesiology at Columbia University's College of Physicians and Surgeons. An outspoken critic of those who said marijuana was a "harmless giggle," Nahas was attacked constantly. Not only was he challenging the party line, but he tended to be abrasive and uncollegial. Nonetheless, he was invited to speak in 1982 at the California Conference on Cocaine. He describes the setting in Santa Monica as a "splendid oceanside hotel surrounded by gardens with palm trees and glowing hibiscus and where one could hear the intermittent sounds of the ocean breakers unfurling on the long, sunny beach."

Dr. Nahas was one who had read and believed the older literature. During his Santa Monica talk, he described how cocaine hijacked the pathways in the brain that induce pleasure and reward and was generally bleak about the effects of chronic cocaine use. He finished up by running a film showing monkeys self-administering cocaine until they went into convulsions. "My presentations received scant applause," he noted. The audience was not interested in hearing bad news about a safe, recreational drug.

Even less welcome then was Dr. Raoul Jeri, professor of neurology at San Marcos University in Lima, Peru. It was Dr. Jeri's patients who had so alarmed Yale's Robert Byck. Wrote Dr. Nahas, "In hesitant English and with the help of slides, Jeri described some of the damage wrought in South America by the epidemic use of cocaine paste which has been smoked since the early seventies. . . . Dr. Jeri summarized, 'Coca paste intoxication resembles a malignant disease featuring a gradual personality change which parallels the one observed in grave, incurable cases of dementia. I would like to warn the U.S. against the plague which has reached its border. . . . The trivialization of cocaine use is a curse on humanity.' "

Dr. Jeri's closing remarks were followed by an uneasy silence and then a few questions.

No one wanted to hear such downers. Especially the media, which was thrilled to discover that Timothy Leary was making the scene, even though no one had invited him. Good-looking and charismatic as ever despite his years on the lam and time in jail, Leary always was delighted to schmooze with the press. The questions were of the friendly, softball variety:

"I heard you say that there are no dangerous drugs. Is that true?"

"Well, that's my way of looking at it. The real problem with drugs is the stupidity of most users. Intelligent people are going to use drugs intelligently."

Another asked Leary to expound on cocaine. He said:

Obviously, cocaine is the drug of the day. Isn't it the seventh-largest business in the country? It's the drug of the 80's because this decade is facing the facts. We're in an age of realism and toughness. . . . [Cocaine] is well-adapted to our times. Of course the "narcs" who are cracking down on its use rant and rave about the dangers of that miserable substance, which is, in reality, a harmless substance. Amphetamines are much more dangerous, not to mention alcohol, the most common and harmful of all drugs. . . . [Cocaine's] a drug that causes euphoria, quite pleasant and sparkling like champagne. You feel powerful, as if you controlled the world—and intelligent, much more than you actually are. I've never turned down cocaine, except after midnight if I want a good night's sleep.

Even as Timothy Leary, his hair gone silver, his smile beaming and benign, expounded in 1982 on the delights of cocaine on the West Coast, a Manhattan clinical psychologist named Arnold Washton who ran a large heroin treatment clinic in East Harlem began to get Wall Street executives in three-piece suits walking in.

They would explain that they had a serious drug problem with cocaine and they couldn't find help. They had been to their private doctors, to therapists. They'd say, "I'm snorting cocaine and I can't stop. I'm not having any physical withdrawal but I have these terrible cravings and next thing I know I'm snorting again." They felt very foolish because wherever they had turned for help, they were told cocaine is a non-addicting drug and people did not get into trouble with it. The whole tenor of the times was that cocaine wasn't bad and if you were careful and didn't inject, you'd have no problems.

Not only were these high-powered people having trouble with cocaine, they said they had many friends in the same boat.

Drawing on his experience with other compulsive behaviors, Washton decided to treat the cocaine abusers like overeaters. "They were like patients on a diet. And part of the challenge was how to avoid the cues that clearly set off craving. So we had them on supervised urine testing, and then we would pair a couple of cocaine people together so they could provide mutual support, and we put groups of them in therapy together. It was obviously a whole different animal than the heroin addicts. Most of them were highly motivated and they did very well."

Dr. Washton's professional career had been spent largely working with hard-core heroin addicts, and so these Yuppie cocaine abusers were rather a shock. First, because they weren't supposed to have problems with cocaine. And second, because they presented an entirely new group of serious drug abusers. As word spread that Washton was interested and offering treatment, he began to get more and more phone calls from

desperate people who had never tried heroin, used needles, or even been arrested for a crime. These callers did not resemble the Harlem addicts at all. They were typically white, employed, middle-class people in their twenties or thirties who had good jobs, good incomes, intact families, and no prior history of drug addiction or psychiatric illness. Some were high-level executives, professionals, or entrepreneurs. Most were "baby boomers" who had used drugs occasionally or "recreationally" since late adolescence. They never thought they could become addicted, but now they had a serious problem: They were snorting cocaine, could not stop, and could not find professional help. It was well known that cocaine was not addictive, . . . and while these callers didn't experience any withdrawal from cocaine, using it was no longer a choice for them, it was an obsession.

It had taken most of these unhappy cocaine addicts about five years to arrive at their present predicament.

Having sighted this tiniest tip of the middle-class cocaine iceberg, Washton was curious just how bad it was.

I got the idea of a hotline, and got it listed as the N.Y. Cocaine Hotline. Then I asked some of the FM stations in Manhattan to run public service announcements for it at two, three, four in the morning, when all these cocaine users were crashing and feeling desperate. The hotline was just a telephone on my desk in the Harlem clinic hooked up to an answering machine. Anyway, I set this up in January of 1983 and flew down to Florida for a vacation. After a day, I called into the machine to check, and in one night the entire tape—one hundred messages—had been completely filled. I got on the next plane back to New York and had two more phones installed. Here was the first solid evidence that intranasal snorting could lead to cocaine addiction. Within two weeks I was on *Good Morning, America.*

Washton's cocaine hotline was bombarded by two to three hundred calls daily. Not only was he answering endless questions about cocaine, he began conducting interviews with those calling.

Most callers said that they felt unable to control their use, had failed repeatedly to stop using it on their own, and were often riddled with cravings and urges for the drug. Most earned over twenty-five thousand dollars per year and were spending six hundred dollars per week for cocaine. They complained of numerous cocaine-related problems, including depression, paranoia, loss of sex drive, panic anxiety, headaches, sinus infections, physical and mental exhaustion, weight loss, memory problems, financial problems, family problems, and job problems. Many had turned increasingly to other drugs—alcohol, tranquilizers, sleeping pills, even heroin—to alleviate the intolerable "crash" and other aftereffects of heavy cocaine use. Some had experienced seizures or became suicidal.

This was big and disturbing news. For a decade, the nation's medical and public health experts had been saying moderate intranasal cocaine use was safe. They had dismissed as unscientific and anecdotal all the turn-of-the-century medical and popular literature that had described vividly how insidious cocaine could be, how often cocaine use would escalate, and how easily cocaine hunger could fasten its merciless hold. No one in the 1970s had wanted to credit what the physicians of that earlier era—when the American public last had had easy access to the white powder—had to say. It went against everything everyone wanted to believe. Literature that old simply could not be useful or plausible. The modern experts again and again had insisted that rising cocaine use was of no concern. It was not a drug that caused physical dependence, it was being used carefully and in a sophisticated manner by the best people. Why worry?

And now, through the unlikely person of an East Harlem drug specialist, the most vocal and public experts were being shown to be completely, utterly, dramatically wrong. Cocaine was a highly addictive drug. Otherwise responsible, decent people who had used it recreationally, intranasally, moderately were finding their consumption gradually had escalated until they had become compulsive users. Ronald K. Siegel of UCLA observed in his studies of regular cocaine users that use escalated from one to four grams of cocaine a month in the first couple of years to one to three grams a week. Those who had begun recreationally were finding they had developed huge habits, their health was wretched, and they were stealing from their families, their employers, lying, betraying, for a white powder everyone said was energizing and fun and chic. This was not the benign, delightful substance celebrated in the pages of *Rolling Stone*.

Explained Dr. Byck many years later, "The most important thing about all the old literature is that Medline [a computerized listing of medical articles] started in 1966, and so no one looked at it." And even once doctors and scientists were aware of this older literature, "It wasn't taken seriously. It was viewed as uncontrolled, anecdotal. It was hard to get anyone to believe it." Ironically, Dr. Byck now cites a book published in Germany in 1926, Hans Maier's *Der Kokainismus*, as the best book ever written about cocaine. "It turned out that a tremendous amount was known about chronic cocaine abuse. Unfortunately, most people were not interested in the historical reality."

Dr. Robert DuPont, head of the the National Institute of Drug Abuse from 1973 to 1978, is quick to point out that in 1977 NIDA did release a study on cocaine that described cocaine as a "serious drug of abuse" and listed its potential side effects as "anxiety, insomnia, paranoid delusions and even death in rare instances." The *New York Times* found this surprising enough to run on the front page. Yet little more was made of it. There was no shift in the general perception that cocaine was a safe, fun drug.

Such occasional government warnings on cocaine as were issued largely were ignored, a legacy of the Anslinger years, when the government had ruined its credibility by using scare tactics. Anslinger long had insisted that smoking marijuana would soon turn you into a heroin addict and/or make you insane. Too many people discovered for themselves that these were alarmist lies. Today many studies have shown that those who frequently smoke marijuana *increase* their chances of further drug involvement, but that's a far cry from certain junkiehood or the asylum. And then when LSD came along, dire government warnings of mass chromosomal damage elicited similar skepticism. And so, even when the government did occasionally and timidly warn of adverse consequences of cocaine use, there was little inclination to pay attention.

The nation's highest and most vocal experts repeatedly said that cocaine was not addictive. They did warn it could potentially lead to psychological dependence. But what people *heard* was that cocaine was not addictive. The truth was that the drug experts themselves misunderstood what constituted addiction. "The problem we had as a nation, which very much focused on science, . . . was that we equated drug abuse with physical dependence," explained Dr. DuPont many years later. "I thought like that and everyone I knew thought like that. It was only in the mid-to-late seventies that I realized that addiction had nothing to do with physical dependency. It had to do with reward. . . . So some of the smartest people in the country totally misled policymakers and everybody else because of a fundamental misunderstanding of the nature of the problem."

Dr. David Musto, a physician and historian, had published the first scholarly, historical study of the nation's drug laws in 1973. Because heroin was then the big problem, his work focused mostly on opiates. Still, he was familiar with the cocaine history, and he would recall later that in the seventies

> many people, including some of the scientists, were so confident that cocaine was harmless that when I would mention what history had to say about cocaine they would tell me my sources weren't scientific. They were just case reports. There were no controlled studies of this business about violence, paranoia, and all other sorts of things. Those were just accounts. They didn't really study the matter the way we study it today. Even the people I spoke to who were aware of the history weren't concerned because they knew that cocaine was not a harmful substance. . . . Most people's view of history is that people were different back then so you can discount their experiences. They weren't like us. One gets the feeling that they think people in history were walking around in a kind of sepia-colored atmosphere.

And yet the cocaine experience presented one of those rare instances where historical analogy was completely valid. The human body had not changed in the course of the century. And neither had the drug. And yet somehow the experts had convinced themselves that the two situations were not comparable. As the drug experts of the 1970s watched the cocaine epidemic of the 1980s unfold around them, they belatedly realized that addiction was not solely a function of the classic symptoms of physical dependence on a drug—the model based on the familiar opiates such as heroin—but how "reinforcing" a drug was. When people (or monkeys) felt compelled to use a drug again and again, even though it was obviously wreaking havoc on their health and happiness, that meant the drug was a highly reinforcing, and therefore an addicting, substance.

Dr. Arnold Washton articulated this truer-to-life explanation of addiction in 1985: "The definition [of addiction] has three major components or identifying features. First is a lack of control over use; second is a craving and compulsion to use the substance; and third and perhaps most diagnostic, is continued use despite adverse consequences. I think with those three diagnostic criteria you have a definition that is of use to the practicing clinician to help somebody with a substance abuse problem."

It was only the extraordinary outpouring of cocaine-caused misery recorded by the new hotlines that forced the experts grudgingly to reconsider. As word of Washton's New York hotline spread through media attention, he began to get calls from cocaine users all over the country. Inundated, he decided to join forces with a psychiatrist and addiction specialist named Mark Gold. On May 6, 1986, they opened a national cocaine hotline, 800-COCAINE, located at the Fair Oaks Psychiatric Hospital in Summit, New Jersey. "It became clear that the cocaine epidemic was not restricted to New York," says Washton. "It was nationwide. The phones began to ring incessantly from the very first instant the Hotline went into operation. . . . Within the first three months the hotline had received calls from more than 37 different states in the U.S." The huge volume of calls—often reaching a thousand a day—led Washton and Gold to increase the number of incoming phone lines and provide twenty-four-hour staff. It was the hotline above all, says Washton, that revealed "how serious and widespread the cocaine problem had become without either the public or the professional community being sufficiently aware of it."

And so it was a cramped, windowless room in Fair Oaks Psychiatric Hospital with eight phones that provided the first detailed information about the middle-class cocaine epidemic. Five hundred cocaine abusers from the first one hundred thousand callers agreed to interviews. The average age was thirty. Two in three were men and most had been using cocaine between four and five years. Eighty-five percent were white. They were well educated, many being lawyers, doctors, educators, engineers. Four hundred and fifty had started cocaine with snorting. By the time they called, 306 were still snorting, 103 were smoking freebase, and 91 were injecting. They were using, on average, about six grams a week. In the week before calling the hotline they had spent $637 on cocaine.

Over 90 percent of those surveyed reported five or more adverse effects, including chronic insomnia (82%), chronic fatigue (76%), severe headaches (60%), nasal and sinus infections (58%), and disrupted sexual functioning (55%). The leading psychological problems (reported by 80%) were depression, anxiety, and irritability. Sixty percent also reported problems with paranoia, losing interest in nondrug activities or friends, and difficulty concentrating. Almost half (45%) said they had stolen money from employers, family, or friends to pay for their habits. Most were in debt from cocaine, and had mortgaged homes or squandered inheritances or trust funds. Thirty-six percent had taken to dealing, 26 percent had seen marriages or romances end because of cocaine, 17 percent had lost jobs, 12 percent had been arrested, and 11 percent had had automobile accidents. Sixty-eight percent had started using other drugs and alcohol to mediate the crash. So now they were involved deeply not just in cocaine, but tranquilizers, heroin, and/or alcohol.

The advent of the 800-COCAINE hotline marked the beginning of the end of an era that had romanticized and glamorized cocaine. Washton and Gold were quick to try and set the record straight about intranasal use. In a letter to the medical journal *Lancet* just months after the hotline opened, they wrote, "Contrary to popular belief . . . our findings demonstrate that intranasal users are not exempt from addictive patterns of use or from serious adverse consequences." From this period forward, the stories about cocaine became far more sober and somber. It had taken almost a decade, but middle-class Americans finally were discovering why authorities at the turn of the century had moved so strongly to end access to this seductive drug. The voices of caution grew louder and the news stories less celebratory as word slowly spread about the drawbacks of the seemingly perfect drug for the successful achiever. But a decade of great press is not overcome quickly. And with the wholesale price of a kilo plummeting from sixty thousand dollars in 1981 to fifteen thousand dollars in 1983, more and more Americans felt they could now finally try this fabulous drug. By 1985, fully a third of Americans aged 18 to 25 had used cocaine.

But as cocaine use exploded, the glamorous aspects of cocaine fast were giving way to what was often termed the drug's "darker" side. The cocaine casualties conspicuously began to pile up and the scandals to unfold in public. First and foremost had been the baby boomer's beloved funnyman, John Belushi. The ultimate hipster, he had entertained a generation with a wide range of hilarious schticks on TV and in the movies. On March 5, 1982, at age thirty-three he was found dead in a bungalow at Hollywood's Chateau Marmont Hotel. Belushi was not finicky about his drugs of abuse and indulged in anything and everything. But the fatal dose was a combination of heroin and cocaine. Now, Belushi's death was not *so* surprising. It was well within the Hollywood Babylon tradition, and Belushi was very much the wild and crazy guy.

But the next cocaine scandal was a different matter altogether. This time it was sports players, stars of the most sacred of American pastimes: baseball and football. In 1983, four Kansas City Royals, including onetime pitching sensation Vida Blue, went to jail over cocaine. Next, that same year, it was football players, as longtime rumors of high living proved to be true. Even those national icons the Dallas Cowboys were tainted by the great NFL cocaine scandal. Sportswriters were aghast when one football official conceded, "This problem is getting to the point where there could be a threat to the integrity of the game." One fullback speaking to reporters seemed puzzled by the brouhaha over cocaine: "I can't think of no one in the world who hasn't tried it once. You guys probably have."

By mid 1984 respected *New York Times* health columnist Jane E. Brody was warning her legions of Yuppie readers strongly against cocaine. Cocaine, she cautioned, could turn users into "impotent, emaciated, thieving, hostile, paranoid, groveling addicts who live for nothing more than another dose. It has ruined countless marriages, wiped out fortunes, destroyed careers and even claimed lives. Unfortunately, it is almost impossible to predict who will be able to control his or her use of cocaine and who will fall prey to its powerful addictive qualities. Without question, the number of users of cocaine is escalating with frightening rapidity across the country."

She warned further, "Cocaine is now known to cause fatal convulsions, respiratory failure and cardiac collapse, even at moderately high doses and in seasoned users."

The big novel of 1984, Jay McInerney's *Bright Lights, Big City*, reflected both the ever more rampant middle-class use of cocaine and the growing unease about the drug. The novel opens in a downtown New York club, where the unhappy protagonist is hoping to find a nice girl amid the shaved heads and black leather. He feels confused, upset: "All might come clear if you could just slip into the bathroom and do a little more Bolivian Marching Powder. Then again, it might not. . . . Somewhere back there you could have cut your losses, but you rose past that moment on a comet trail of white powder and now you are trying to hang onto the rush. Your brain at this moment is composed of brigades of tiny Bolivian soldiers. They are tired and muddy from their long march through the night. There are holes in their boots and they are hungry. They need to be fed. They need the Bolivian Marching Powder."

Many faithful readers of *Rolling Stone* must have been astounded in June 1984 when they flipped through the magazine to see an article with the huge headline: HOW TO GET OFF COCAINE. Hadn't the magazine just been extolling this wondrous drug? Now, here was a 180 degree reversal, all delivered in the magazine's standard Angry Young Man style. The article sternly declared, "Cocaine has enjoyed a far better reputation than it deserved. There is now a belated recognition that the drug is addicting. While cocaine doesn't produce the physical symptoms of narcotic withdrawal, continued use—by snorting, smoking and shooting—can lead to severe dependency. 'Addiction is compulsion, loss of control and continued use in spite of the consequences,' says Dr. David Smith, director of the Haight-Ashbury Free Medical Clinic in San Francisco."

The article took a reassuring tone with readers long conditioned to believe that the best and the hippest could take their drugs like men. *Rolling Stone* now counseled that it was okay to admit you couldn't handle drugs. The article declared firmly, "You're not a worse person for not being able to control your cocaine use. And you have lots of company."

But this sudden revisionism failed to immediately and fully penetrate the national psyche, still awash in a decade's worth of glamorous and glitzy cocaine images. It would take the shocking death of Len Bias, the University of Maryland basketball superstar, to squash truly the baby boomer's romantic illusions about cocaine. Len Bias: One day poised for NBA greatness and the extraordinary fame and fortune America bestows on its best athletes, the next day dead. Bias, a young man in the peak of physical condition, dead of cocaine-induced heart failure on June 17, 1986, while celebrating his signing with the Celtics.

One young *Washington Post* reporter covering the story expressed the general amazement: "Cocaine was still the perfect drug, a recreational drug that was not necessarily highly addictive. A bunch of doctors thought different. But for the most part we and most people who read the *Post* didn't realize that cocaine was a killer. So I guess that was our assumption. Could cocaine really kill a six-foot-eight, two-hundred-pound guy? Len was so huge, so substantial. It was unfathomable that something like that could have done him in."

The zeitgeist had been such that enthusiasts had been interested only in history's amusing tidbits about cocaine—Freud's early endorsement, its presence in Coca-Cola. No one (including the medical profession) seemed interested in the whole story, much less the downside. Yet less than a century earlier, numerous physicians had warned in American medical journals of the serious dangers of addiction to cocaine, and even of cocaine deaths just like Len Bias's. Typical of the latter was the 1891 report warning of the "lurking idiosyncrasy [of cocaine]. . . . Often the stout and robust man will fall before it, as by electric shock, while an enfeebled woman will endure with impunity almost any quantity." Or the doctor's report that a dental patient given a cocaine injection to numb his gums "died in convulsions in an hour, from probably the medicament entering the circulation immediately, and expending its full force on the heart." America had banned cocaine from all but medical practice in the first decade of this century because it was just too dangerous and seductive a drug. In 1910, President William Howard Taft had warned in his annual message to Congress, "Cocaine is more appalling in its effects than any other habit-forming drug used in the United States."

Just in case anyone doubted in 1986 that cocaine could fell the best and brawniest, the entire tragic Len Bias scenario was replayed prominently a mere eight days later. This time the dead superstar athlete was Cleveland Brown defensive lineback Don Rogers. Like Bias, Rogers died of cocaine snorted while partying. No one could kid themselves anymore that cocaine was benign. The hip and clever had to rethink cocaine. Smart people did not die for their high.

Once the baby boomers acknowledged the dark and dangerous side of cocaine, they reconsidered. And as they abandoned the drug in droves, the "champagne of drugs" began its ominous market transformation into the "Night Train of drugs," one aimed at the down and out. After all, those who grew rich trafficking in cocaine were not just going to sit back and do nothing when their middle-class market started shrinking.

The Colombian Cartels are "Far More Dangerous Than Any Criminal Enterprise in U.S. History."

—U.S. Senate Subcommittee on Terrorism, Narcotics, and International Relations, 1989

On the sweltering afternoon of July 11, 1979, a white-paneled Ford truck drove into the vast parking lot of Dadeland Mall, ten miles south of Miami. Surrounded by commuter communities of trim lawns and ranch houses, the mall was South Florida's largest. The Ford truck, "Happy Time Complete Party Supply" visible on one side, cruised through the acres of parked cars toward the small Crown Liquors store. Approaching from another direction in the shimmering heat was a white Mercedes-Benz sedan. The truck pulled up first at the curb, its engine idling. The two men in the Mercedes parked meanwhile, strolled into the liquor store, and ordered a bottle of Chivas Regal. As they stood waiting, two men emerged from the truck with guns drawn, a .380 Beretta automatic handgun and an Ingram MAC-100 machine pistol. They began firing wildly through the Crown doorway, killing the two customers and wounding the store clerk. Amid shrieks and shattering liquor bottles, the hit men ran back to their Ford truck, guns blazing. All told, sixty shots were fired in broad daylight at a busy mall. The dead men were eventually identified as a Colombian cocaine trafficker and his bodyguard.

In their excellent history of the rise of the Medellín cocaine cartel, *Kings of Cocaine*, Guy Gugliotta and Jeff Leen describe the Dadeland Mall murders and a turnpike machine-gun shootout in broad daylight the previous April as serving

> sudden and terrifying notice of the ascension of a new breed of criminal. The Colombian cocaine traffickers brought a stark savagery to Miami that U.S. lawmen had never before encountered. The Miami drug trade had been largely a marijuana importation industry run by American adventurers, hippie entrepreneurs, and CIA-trained Cuban exiles. They in turn were supported by mercenary drug pilots and a network of Cuban exile fisherman. . . . And although violence did occur, a certain decorum limited the nastiness. Now, the Age of Aquarius was over.

Cocaine was not new to Florida. Back in 1959, after Fidel Castro had triumphed in Cuba, the streams of wealthy refugees landing in Miami (for what they assumed would be a brief exile) tried to replicate their accustomed life style. Explained the *New York Times*, "In Batista's Cuba the rich snorted cocaine, while the poor smoked marijuana." And so the original cocaine traffickers of the sixties (when quantities were still small) were mainly Cubans catering to the expensive tastes of their own Latin community.

These traffickers included notable numbers of Cuban Bay of Pigs alumni. "Trained by the Central Intelligence Agency, defeated on the Cuban beaches, ransomed by the United States Government, . . . some of these Cubans drifted naturally into drug trafficking, putting to use their newly learned guerrilla techniques." Yet this was relatively small stuff, reflected by the fact that at no time in the 1960s did total U.S. cocaine seizures exceed one hundred kilos. One longtime federal narcotics agent always believed that the CIA in some way protected these early Cuban traffickers because the cocaine trade was a cheap way to keep the anti-Castro warriors happy. In Jonathan Kwitny's book *The Crimes of the Patriots*, he writes, "In south Florida, by the 1970s, police could scarcely arrest a dope dealer or illegal weapons trafficker without encountering the claim, often true, that the suspect had CIA connections. Perhaps the largest narcotics investigation of the decade [in Florida], the World Finance Corporation case, had to be scrapped after a year because the CIA complained to the Justice Department that a dozen top criminals were 'of interest' to it." (Until the CIA releases its files from this era—something it has steadfastly avoided—no one will know the full story.)

The traditional cocaine wholesalers in this early lucrative cottage industry were the Chileans. Enterprising Chilean criminals purchased coca leaf and paste in the primitive Andean highlands of Peru and Bolivia, brought it back to laboratories to refine it, and dispatched it north to the Florida Cubans, sometimes in the country's distinctive wicker wine bottles. As their product became more popular, the Chileans also began to employ Colombians as couriers, a move they would regret eventually.

What gradually transformed this small-time cocaine trafficking of the early sixties into something bigger by the late sixties was the presence in South America of French Corsicans on the lam. These Corsicans quickly made criminal common cause with the local smugglers known as *contrabandistas*—many based in Paraguay, many in Colombia—who had a long tradition of smuggling cigarettes, liquor, and electronics from North America into high tariff Latin American countries. "The French Corsicans operating out of South America," says former DEA agent Jerry Strickler, who worked on these cases, "came up with something new, and that was using the services of these *contrabandistas* to take their heroin north. The old-time smugglers were ferrying all these consumer goods south on their little planes or boats or what have you. Now, they would have something to fill the planes and their boats when they headed north." When Corsican drug trafficker August Ricord was active in Asunción, Paraguay, in the late sixties, his criminal colleagues were four Paraguayans, including one pilot, and a Brazilian. And when that French connection and other French-organized trafficking was broken up in the early seventies, the heroin (smuggled in first from France and then smuggled north by the *contrabandistas*) was replaced by locally available drugs, at first marijuana and then cocaine.

Wrote criminologist Peter A. Lupsha of the *contrabandistas*, "The organizational linkages to Florida, the Gulf, and the southeastern coastal states of the United States, the trafficking infrastructure . . . as well as the financial conduits and initial capital, were all in place from the earlier days of cigarette, coffee, and appliance smuggling. Contrabandista families . . . have been operating and feuding in Colombia for more than thirty years."

In Elaine Shannon's book about the Latin American drug trade, *Desperadoes*, she describes how these Colombian *contrabandistas* saw the fortunes being made off Mexican marijuana in the sixties and early seventies and moved to enter the field with better, more potent pot that could be marketed through Colombians on the eastern seaboard: "The only obstacle to the Colombian traffickers was the competition from Mexico. And that disappeared in 1977, thanks to the Mexican government's use in its eradication program of a herbicide called paraquat."

One is not surprised to discover that Corsican criminals and shady characters from onetime banana republics were busy trafficking in drugs. What was new and shocking in the sixties and seventies was the amazing assortment of ostensibly respectable middle-class Americans who had decided international drug trafficking was the career or part-time job for them. This was a historic and important shift, for well-educated, well-off Americans suddenly were devoting some of their considerable entrepreneurial energy to smuggling illegal drugs into their own country. Donald Steinberg, who started off selling pot in his small hometown of Carpentersville, Illinois, and quickly worked up in the 1970s to smuggling marijuana by the ton, would insist when finally arrested, "Marijuana doesn't hurt anybody. [Something plenty of families would angrily dispute.] We never saw ourselves as really doing anything wrong."

Many of the marijuana pilots were military veterans, solid family men who also rationalized their marijuana smuggling activities by saying this was an inocuous drug. Two of the pilots profiled in *Kings of Cocaine* were ex-marine and ex-navy pilots: "Marijuana, they reckoned, wasn't all that harmful, and people did want to smoke it." And then there was that tired American romance with outlaws and sociopaths that celebrated outwitting authority of any kind. In Robert Sabbag's tale of the early days of American middle-class cocaine smuggling, *Snowblind*, he observes that many in this era believed smuggling cocaine made one "some brand of counterculture hero, . . . a bold and dashing sort of figure."

How was American law enforcement to shield the public from illegal drugs—especially vulnerable teenagers—when middle-class adults were actively out to thwart them? A great many lawmen and women wondered this very thing as their investigations began to turn up not just the usual lowlifes, but presumably upstanding citizens. Fort Lauderdale's police chief complained in 1978, "We're finding more and more professional persons, doctors, dentists, lawyers, being involved in the importation of marijuana." Nor was middle-class trafficking restricted to marijuana. A Baltimore drug counselor recalls, "It was not uncommon at this time to hear of middle-class whites returning to Baltimore with heroin or opium secured in California, Mexico, Spain, or any of a number of Middle Eastern countries."

One of the major figures in *Kings of Cocaine* is just such a middle-class trafficker, a young man named George Jung. Raised in a well-to-do household on Cape Cod, he played football at college for a while, and then got caught up in sixties student politics and drugs in California. Jung and a boyhood friend had been piloting in marijuana from Mexico, making hundreds of thousands of dollars, until the law caught up with them. In 1974, while serving four years in Danbury Prison, Jung, by then thirty-two, met a Colombian named Carlos Rivas Lehder, twenty-five, also serving four years for marijuana trafficking.

Lehder was an odd duck. Offspring of a German engineer and a Colombian, he had come to New York as an adolescent with his divorced mother. By the time he landed up in Danbury, Lehder was a petty thief and small-time drug trafficker who idolized Che Guevara, John Lennon, and Adolf Hitler. Despite his unpromising situation, Lehder harbored big political dreams of becoming someone important back in Colombia, perhaps even president. Lehder's grand vision of political glory, however, required wealth. Consequently, he was fascinated that Jung had been transporting tons of marijuana using private planes. Up until now, cocaine usually was smuggled into the United States in small kilo lots. But Lehder saw no reason it couldn't be smuggled the way marijuana was—by the ton.

He proposed to Jung that when they got out, they smuggle cocaine instead of marijuana. It cost two thousand dollars a kilo in Colombia and it was selling in the United States for about fifty-five thousand dollars a kilo. Jung was more than game, figuring he could market the cocaine through his old marijuana network. From his California days he "knew plenty of people in the movie and record industries, stars and the like, who craved getting high. 'I figured that if the record industry and the movie industry were interested in it, they could promote the product through the greatest advertising medium there was,' Jung said years later. 'I saw what they did with marijuana in the 1960s.' "

As *Kings of Cocaine* points out, "Besides their connections, the two men had something equally important: the kind of inspiration that serves as a pivot for history. They were the first to recognize that the methods of marijuana smuggling could be married to cocaine."

By the summer of 1976 Lehder and Jung were out of jail and in the cocaine business, but not yet on the scale they dreamed of. Their first deal involved fifty kilos that Jung sold in LA to an old marijuana contact, a hip hairdresser with a Hollywood clientele. The cocaine sold like wildfire, and two weeks later Jung had $2.2 million in small bills. This made a huge impression on Lehder's supplier, a major cocaine producer back in the Colombian city of Medellín, one Pablo Escobar. The Colombians obviously had underestimated the baby boomers' gigantic appetite for cocaine. By the winter of 1976 Lehder and Jung had settled in tropical Miami, with its steady and growing supply of smuggled cocaine. Jung regularly flew west to LA, returning with suitcases full of cash.

In August 1977, Lehder's nefarious dream of transporting cocaine in huge lots, like marijuana, began to come true. A practicing attorney in Cape Cod who was also a pilot—one of those nice middle-class people who'd taken up trafficking on the side—agreed to fly down to Pablo Escobar's ranch outside Medellín, pick up 250 kilos, and fly back via Nassau to a remote strip in the Carolinas. Lehder and Jung each made five hundred thousand dollars. Jung meanwhile had become deeply addicted, inhaling five to eight grams of cocaine at a time. Lehder thought cocaine was poison, and he sternly admonished Jung against using it.

As the two partners got to know each other better, Lehder became more forthright about his political ambitions back home and his hatred of the United States, which he thought was "an imperialist police state. He told Jung that he hoped to flood the country with cocaine and disrupt America's political system and tear down its morality."

Lehder now bought a chunk of Norman's Cay, a charming sliver of an island with a long landing strip set in the aquamarine water of the Bahamas, a perfect base for air smuggling between Colombia, due south, and the United States, due west a mere 120 miles. All the longtime residents of Norman's Cay slowly were forced out, some at gunpoint. The Bahamian government blithely ignored the criminal takeover of part of its territory, thanks to huge bribes to well-placed officials.

Despite occasional, staged police raids, Lehder's business flourished, and he soon had six to eight pilots regularly flying quarter-ton loads of cocaine into remote landing strips in Florida, Georgia, Tennessee, and the Carolinas. Among these pilots were the ex-marine and ex-navy fliers, veterans of the marijuana trade. When asked to start flying cocaine, they insisted to their dubious families that "it wasn't like heroin, that nobody was going to die from it, and you didn't get addicted to it."

Carlos Rivas Lehder was just one of the more ambitious and successful of the hundreds of determined Colombian traffickers rapidly expanding the cocaine business. The Colombians had taken over from the Chilean wholesalers down in South America, largely thanks to the September 1973 coup that deposed elected president Salvador Allende and installed army general Augusto Pinochet Ugarte as president of Chile. Unlike Allende, Pinochet had no tolerance for cocaine traffickers and either jailed them or deported them to American justice. Pinochet had found convincing the American argument that once drug traffickers got rich enough, they would inevitably seek political power. Pinochet wasn't interested in nurturing future rivals. The few Chileans who escaped Pinochet's crackdown headed to Colombia to continue their trade. Their presence was short-lived. And so by the mid seventies the Colombians, already active in marijuana, had established a virtual monopoly over cocaine. They acquired the coca leaves from farmers in the remote mountain terrain of Peru and Bolivia, and refined the cocaine in their own jungle laboratories. The Andean city of Medellín, the nation's second largest, was home to most of the traffickers.

In the days when marijuana trafficking was picking up and cocaine was still smuggled in small kilo packages, tens of thousands of Colombians settled in Jackson Heights, Queens. A certain number came specifically to run the New York distribution networks. As the Colombian criminals dug in, their savage style shocked even the most hard-bitten American cops and criminals. In December 1975, reported *Harper's*,

> Colombian gangsters broke into the New York home of Oscar Toro, an expatriate Colombian who was making a fortune importing coke from his native land. The thugs stole $15,000 in cash, abducted Toro's ten-year-old son and seventeen-year-old baby-sitter, and hanged his five-year-old daughter with a length of nylon Christmas wrapping. The son and baby-sitter turned up nine days later, frozen solid, in an abandoned post office. Both had been bound and strangled, and the baby-sitter had been raped. Toro, who was away from his home at the time of the incident, was too good a businessman to offer any help to the police.

Murder and massacre were the standard MO of this new drug mafia. If they were double-crossed, cheated, or merely irritated, they responded with swift and savage violence. When trafficker Pablo Escobar was arrested in Colombia in 1976 with five other men for selling thirty-nine pounds of cocaine, the two policemen who made the case soon were assassinated. The case was then passed from one understandably nervous judge to another until all the documents conveniently disappeared from the courthouse.

The Colombian criminal style of wanton savagery had evolved during that nation's decades of vicious internecine warfare. Latin America was infamous for its oligarchical societies—where a small wealthy elite generally ran the government and lived like kings while the masses endured grinding poverty. Colombia's uneven distribution of wealth was worse than most places. "This is due, in part, to 'La Violencia,' " writes criminologist Peter Lupsha, "a period of violence and instability that racked the country between 1946 and 1953 and continued to take lives through 1959. It resulted in more than 200,000 deaths [Colombia's population in 1980 was 30 million] and left scars of normlessness and violence that have still not completely healed. Partly because of this period of violence, and partly because of geography, large areas of the country . . . have been largely outside government influence or control."

When the Colombian elite showed little inclination to reform the government or economy to create a more equitable society, a half dozen revolutionary guerrilla groups sprang up, backed by Cuba, the USSR, and China. Kidnapping, torture, and public attacks were standard operating procedure for the guerrillas. The security forces opposing them were equally brutal. Meanwhile, a scary urban underclass took hold in the dirt poor, debauched slums of Colombia's cities. The journalists who wrote *The Cocaine Wars* describe the Medellín vice district as "the easy recruiting ground of paid killers. Customers interested in a *trabajito*—'a little job'—can stop, literally, at any corner and recruit an assassin. Fees vary: $100 for an unfaithful lover; $20,000 for a government minister. The potential killer usually demands a photograph of the victim and asks about habits, place of work, and so forth, then, depending on the difficulty of the assignment, sets the price."

Small wonder, then, what with Colombia's murderous politics and its feral poor, the nation historically has had a homicide rate that makes the United States look like the peaceable kingdom. And pitifully few of the murders are ever solved by the country's notoriously feeble justice system. In the 1970s, New Yorkers were introduced to the Colombian way of death and dying, as drug feuds erupted ferociously in Jackson Heights. The massacred were predictably drug-dealing Colombians (and families, friends, and even pets with the misfortune to be around) on the outs with other drug-dealing Colombians. For Colombian criminals, it seemed, just killing your rival or enemy was not always enough. There were often additional ghoulish measures.

One Colombian military official would describe a favored form of revenge by traffickers as "necktie killings": "The target's throat is slit open so his tongue can hang through it like a tie. . . . It is a gruesome sight to see this—men, women, and children, all lined up in chairs like soldiers with their tongues coming out of their necks."

In Florida, meanwhile, the Cubans were experiencing the unique ruthlessness of the Colombian criminals. For when cocaine began to arrive by the quarter and half ton via air into Florida and other points in the south, the Jackson Heights Colombians and thousands still in Colombia headed for the Sunshine State. Why should they let the Florida Cubans run what was now the main show, getting fabulously rich off Colombian cocaine? As cocaine, drug money, and Colombians swamped Florida, so did violence. First the Colombians worked over the Cubans, and then the Colombians turned on one another.

By 1979 there was a drug killing a day in Miami. But it took the Dadeland Mall murders—executed in broad daylight in a busy, public, middle-class, all-American place—to drive home that the Colombian traffickers had arrived and they were indeed a new and vicious breed of criminal. And from there the violence escalated. In 1979 Miami had 349 murders. By 1981 murders had soared to 621. A quarter died from automatic weapons fire. Gun purchases were off the charts. From 1975 to 1980, 220,000 guns were sold in Dade County alone. In 1981, a record 66,198 guns were sold. And the consequences were very visible. One Miami resident said, "I see people walking down the streets openly carrying guns, some in their hands, others in their holsters. You don't dare honk your horn at anybody; you could end up dead." The Dade County Medical Examiner's Office had to rent a refrigerated hamburger trailer to hold the overflow of corpses.

Not only was the booming cocaine trade churning up bodies daily, it was distorting visibly the economies of southern Florida and Colombia. In David McClintick's complex tale of drug money laundering, *Swordfish*, he describes how

> the computers of the Federal Reserve System in Washington were generating numbers that at first seemed curious, then strange, then sinister. . . . In the thirty-sixth branch [Miami] the computers were detecting bizarre distortions. That branch alone was showing a *surplus* of $3.3 billion, a warp that was already huge and growing rapidly. The surplus had been $89 million in 1971, $924 million in 1974. By 1980 it would be $6 billion on its way to $10 billion. . . . And as experts at the Federal Reserve, the

Treasury, and the IRS began to peer behind the aggregate numbers, they grew even more concerned. Of the $68 million in cash
that a single Miami bank had deposited with the Federal
Reserve, 63 percent of it, $42 million, was in $20 bills, and
another 16 percent, $10.5 million, was in $100 bills. At another
bank, a customer from Colombia had walked in one day with
several aides and deposited $13 million in cash from an assort-
ment of suitcases, boxes, satchels, and shopping bags.

By 1980, the DEA estimated that Florida's illegal drug trafficking
had mushroomed to a $7 billion business, easily outstripping Florida's
largest legitimate industry—tourism, which earned $5 billion a year. To
handle this tidal wave of cocaine cash, legions of crooked bankers and
banks popped up to "launder" the bills for a tidy fee and move the
money wherever directed. By the early 1980s, the chairman of one
Florida bank admitted (off-the-record, of course) that "the reason so
many banks have opened offices here is because of the hot money, particularly drug money." It was not just American middle-class traffickers
who had decided it was okay to get rich bringing illegal drugs into their
own country. Bankers, lawyers, accountants, all kinds of ostensibly
respectable citizens actively were aiding and abetting the Colombians.

Veteran journalist Penny Lernoux described not only the notably lax
attitudes of many of Miami's more than one hundred banks, but also
Miami's dozens of foreign and out-of-state bank subsidiaries dealing
exclusively in overseas transactions. "As many as forty banks have
neglected to report cash deposits of $10,000 or more, as required by law.
The majority of those are small banks, known to cops and crooks as Coin-
o-Washers. At least four such banks are controlled by drug dealers."

As for the Florida nondrug economy, tourism declined as Miami
became infamous for its murder rate and the flood of drug money
inflated the costs of luxury property and services. A condo that had
been $300,000 could suddenly fetch $1 million as traffickers at every
level bid up prices and paid in cash. One U.S. Customs agent in South
Florida observed to Lernoux, "You know what would happen if we
really did our job here? If we were 100 percent effective we would so
drastically affect the economy that *we* would be the villains."

Indeed, when U.S. Customs Commissioner William von Raab
attended the annual meeting of the Florida Bankers Association in May
1982 and chastised "sleazy institutions who are intentionally profiting
from this dirty business," the furious bankers immediately moved to
adjourn the meeting. One yelled at von Raab, "You are using us as a
whipping boy."

Back in Colombia, about half of the $7 billion in marijuana and cocaine dollars was repatriated by hook or by crook. There, too, the narcodollars were fueling inflation of 30 percent, hurting average people. Again, Peter A. Lupsha: "Riots and violence across the nation, following an increase in bus fares, indicated the average Colombian's difficult position. Thus narcodollars have caused inequitable redistributions, have helped fuel inflation, and have tended to stretch and destabilize the nation's already frail economy."

Finally and inevitably, the scourge of cocaine reared its ugly head in an even more direct way. Colombia and the other Andean nations now began to experience their own serious drug problems, though they chose to say little about it. This new drug problem had nothing to do with the Andean Indians chewing coca leaves, a traditional practice that put the native Indians into a semistupified state to numb the effects of performing the arduous work of mining and high-altitude subsistence farming. This new cocaine problem was something called *basuco* (an acronym from the Spanish *pasta base de cocaina*), a coca paste that is an intermediate stage between the coca leaves and powdered cocaine and smoked in cigarettes.

In the 1970s, *basuco* became highly popular, first among Colombia's multitudes of poor, and then it spread into the middle class. "It was quickly realized that paste smoking [*basuco*] was far more serious than any other form of cocaine use," writes longtime drug researcher James A. Inciardi. For not only is smoking the most reinforcing way of using any drug because it gets to your brain in seconds, but the Andean paste still "contains traces of all the chemicals used to initially process the coca leaves—kerosene, sulfuric acid, methanol, benzoic acid, and the oxidized products of these solvents, plus any number of other alkaloids that are present in the coca leaf." Now, with each passing year, tens of thousands of Colombians were becoming caught up in smoking *basuco*, a form of cocaine capable of causing permanent brain damage. (It was *basuco* smoking, first seen by Yale's Dr. Byck in Peru in 1978, that had so transformed his previously benign view of cocaine.)

Back in Florida, the escalating anarchy unleashed by cocaine was made yet worse by Fidel Castro's authorization of the Mariel boat lift in spring of 1980. The 125,000 Cubans who fled Cuba on boats for Florida included about seven thousand hard-core criminals and felons specially sprung from prison, a Cuban communist bonus. These Marielitos went to work at what they knew best—murder and robbery and mayhem. When the FBI released its annual report on crime in the United States for 1980, Floridians were dismayed but not surprised to learn that six of the nation's top ten crime cities were in their state, with Miami holding the dubious distinction of number one. By 1980, crime in the South Florida counties of Dade, Broward, and Palm Beach had risen 41 percent in two years.

Of course, the Carter administration—adopting a super-low profile on the drug issue after the Bourne imbroglio—had provided no visible leadership on the growing cocaine problem. And so, Elaine Shannon describes in *Desperadoes* how "Federal officers responsible for drug enforcement and interdiction were overjoyed when Reagan took office [in January 1980]. They were soon disappointed: Reagan talked a good game, but despite his speeches bemoaning the threat of violent crime, when it came to more money for fighting crime, including drug traffickers, Reagan was as parsimonious as Carter." Every federal agency but Defense soon took a 12 percent cut. "DEA and Customs cars and airplanes were grounded. Money to make undercover buys ran out. One DEA office held a bake sale to pay for gasoline so night stakeouts could continue." From 1981 to 1986, federal funds available to fight drugs would shrink from $154 million a year to $117 million a year.

This fact of federal drug business as usual was sinking in with Miami's establishment just as *Time* ran a devastating cover story called, "Trouble in Paradise," that laid out in disturbing detail the extraordinary crime wave overwhelming South Florida. A Presbyterian pastor was quoted as saying, " 'My car has been broken into three times, my house has been robbed once, and my 15-year-old son was mugged.' His wife Robin, was mugged, shot, and severely wounded in a Coconut Grove shopping center." The story ran in late November, the start of the winter season. Tourist cancellations flooded in. And good corporate citizens such as Burger King made rumbling noises about relocating elsewhere, taking their "Burger University" with them. Miami's Anglo movers and shakers formed Miami Citizens Against Crime and decided the time had come to call in the cavalry. In December 1981 a formidable delegation of business leaders—led by Eastern Airlines chairman Frank Borman and Knight-Ridder newspapers chairman Alvah H. Chapman, Jr.—headed north to visit the Reagan White House and demand help.

And so came into being the Vice President's Task Force on South Florida, announced with great fanfare by the White House on January 28, 1982. George Bush donned a windbreaker and zoomed around the coastal waterways in zippy "cigarette" motorboats to demonstrate the White House's commitment to seriously beefing up federal law enforcement. Hundreds of additional feds were detailed down to South Florida. The U.S. Treasury contributed twenty analysts to start tracking drug money. And, for the first time ever, the armed services would be involved. Army helicopter gunships and navy surveillance planes were put on the case.

But the law enforcement problem went far deeper than manpower. In the early 1970s, the DEA had been focused resolutely on the heroin problem, and it had had notable successes, taking out the French connection. It had also been aware of the Colombians active in New York City and in 1974 had arrested eight major dealers and 112 lesser figures. Yet the DEA then saw U.S. judges give these Colombian cocaine dealers suspended sentences and deport them to deal with another day. Complained one agent, "We're a laughingstock." But after Jack Ingersoll's principled departure in 1973 just before the DEA reorganization was completed, the new agency had drifted along under a series of short-lived directors working for presidents—Ford and then Carter—with no great concern about the drug problem. Once again, the DEA had fallen back into its old obsession with producing nice-looking statistics—x number of buys, y number of arrests. No one was looking hard at what was happening in the drug culture or thinking imaginatively about how trafficking patterns were changing as a consequence. Nor about where traffickers were most vulnerable. And the DEA certainly wasn't making much use of the United Nations, a much maligned organization that had long been pivotal to American antidrug policy on the international front. On top of all this, the 1975 white paper had specifically directed that antidrug efforts focus on heroin, not cocaine. The bureaucracy had reacted accordingly. By the time the feds realized in the early 1980s that cocaine wasn't a flood but a tidal wave, the DEA and American law enforcement were way, way behind.

Slowly the DEA began to get some vague idea of who the Colombian cocaine kingpins were, but they had not figured out how they operated or how to cripple their enterprises. The sad state of U.S. cocaine intelligence was obvious when Pablo Escobar, a major cocaine producer, could walk into the American embassy in Bogotá in 1981 and get a visa to do business in Florida with no trouble. After a series of hearings about the Latin drug trade, Senator Joseph Biden would express the congressional consensus that "DEA and the Justice Department generally have achieved, as one Justice official admitted, a 'dismal record.' "

Nor was the situation quickly redressed. When Robert Stutman arrived in 1985 to take charge of the DEA's biggest office—New York—he could not believe how rudderless the operation was.

The office had not a clue as to who was buying or selling drugs or even at what price in the nation's largest drug market. For example, the office was unaware of what, if any, inroads the Medellín cartel had made into the New York cocaine market. Nor could it identify the top Asian heroin distributors. Yet drugs arrived in New York from everywhere but especially Hong Kong, Thailand, Colombia, Peru, Mexico, Turkey and Afghanistan. . . . Just one team of ten agents [among the ten teams in the office] had concentrated on developing cocaine cases, leaving the lieutenants of the Colombian cocaine barons, the most notorious of all dealers, free to come and go almost at their pleasure. This had gone on for almost ten years—since the day the Senate subcommittee recommended that while DEA not be disbanded, it focus on heroin, not the recreational drug cocaine. The cartels had used the time well.

Jack Ingersoll had insisted back in the early years of the 1970s, when he was head of BNDD, that seizures per se were not the point; understanding and disabling big international traffickers was. Now the DEA slowly began to return to that philosophy. And the means to that end were a trio of laws available since 1970 but little used: the Racketeer Influenced and Corrupt Organization law, (RICO); the Continuing Criminal Enterprise (CCE), a law specifically aimed at trafficking; and the Bank Secrecy Act (BSA). All of these highly complex laws allowed the government to nail people who never personally touched illegal drugs but were running the show. The first two let government seize "personal assets, whether these be cash, bank accounts, real estate, automobiles, jewelry and art, equity in businesses, directorships in companies, or any kind of goods or entitlements that are obtained or used for a criminal enterprise." The bank law required banks to report the cash deposit of ten thousand dollars or more to the IRS. Gathering court-usable evidence called for something more sophisticated than undercover buys-and-busts. Even once federal prosecutors understood the real-world value of this trio of laws, it took some time to figure out how to put together and try such cases.

One of the early efforts was a joint DEA-FBI probe of Florida banks launched in 1977 called Operation Banco. After a couple of years of plowing through bank and corporate records and hauling hundreds before a grand jury, Operation Banco yielded the first shadowy outlines of the Colombian traffickers. Operation Banco would be followed by Operation Greenback, which caught several major money launderers and forced Florida's nonrogue banks to start complying with the Bank Secrecy Act and reporting large cash transactions. It would take a great many more such operations before the DEA and the U.S. Department of Justice finally had a handle on what it was up against.

By then, the situation was out of control. In 1983, one year after the vice president's task force swooped down on South Florida and began making high-profile busts and cases, the wholesale price of cocaine in Miami *dropped* from fifty-five thousand dollars a kilo to half that. This was a clear-cut sign of massive glut even as American baby-boomer enthusiasm for the drug was growing strongly. If the plummeting kilo price couldn't convince the skeptics of the magnitude of the cocaine flood, the TAMPA bust did.

TAMPA was a two-jet Colombian cargo company in business since 1979. On March 9, 1982, U.S. Customs officers at Miami International Airport met one of TAMPA's Boeing 707s to conduct a routine check of a few dozen cardboard boxes that were being unloaded. The Customs manifest listed the cargo as blue jeans. The inspector jabbed a box with a screwdriver. Out trickled white powder. He tasted it. Cocaine. When the dockworkers saw this, they began to flee, understandably fearful that traffickers would materialize with machine guns to claim their wares. Drug agents from DEA and Customs poured in, and long into the night weighed and tested the purity of their booty. All were stunned. Almost two dozen big boxes held nothing but pure cocaine. It weighed in at almost two *tons*, four times the previous biggest seizure. Ten years earlier, cocaine seizures for the whole *year* had been eight hundred pounds, not even a half ton.

Back in Colombia, the Medellín traffickers responsible for this huge load were just hitting their stride. The previous summer the various drug dealers had been invited by the Ochoa clan, major cocaine producers along with Pablo Escobar, for a powwow at their vast cattle hacienda and family compound overlooking the lovely Caribbean waters near Barranquilla. Aside from an attractive, rambling tile-roofed house, the Ochoa ranch boasted a bullring, its own water system, powerful electric generators, and a new lake with an island slated to be populated with tigers and lions. Already, exotic African animals such as giraffes and elephants roamed the surrounding verdant meadows, presumably a puzzlement to the more traditional herds of cattle in residence. But perhaps the most relevant nouveau riche appurtenance was the five-thousand-foot-long paved runway, capable of handling commercial jetliners. For the Ochoas had a gigantic backlog of "product" and they had decided to start smuggling much of it themselves. They had used their new multimillions to purchase this big, remote tract, and had then installed a runway and hired a U.S. engineer to set up a sophisticated navigational and communications system. With that they could track the many flights that now began departing with steady, clockwork regularity. Just one Ochoa distributor would later say he moved nineteen *tons* of cocaine under this new setup.

Colombia's establishment tried hard not to notice the cocaine traffickers and their overnight hundreds of millions. No one questioned the flimsy stories of fortunes based on legitimate business. Initially this willful blindness may have represented the usual laissez-faire attitude toward enterprising *contrabandistas*. If idiot gringos wanted to use cocaine by the ton, why should this trouble Colombians? (Their own soon-to-be-huge drug problem had not yet penetrated public consciousness.) When a few officials and lawmen did dare challenge the drug traffickers, they were presented with a stark choice—silver or lead, meaning bribes or bullets.

By 1980 the Medellín traffickers had perfected their signature tactics of escalating terror. First there would be telephone threats—with specific mentions of wives, children, parents. A severed cow's tongue might arrive in the mail or appear outside one's door. Or murderous-looking thugs would blatantly shadow you to show they knew your habits and where you lived. Nor, as all soon learned, were these idle threats. If still the official refused to back off, the traffickers had him or her killed. In 1980 alone the traffickers assassinated seventeen policemen in Medellín, four judges, various businessmen, and the mayor's chief bodyguard. When eleven more judges received death threats, the whole Medellín bench of 180 judges and magistrates resigned en masse. They returned only when the country's president promised more police protection.

The following year, the traffickers further asserted their clout and willingness to terrorize when they took on the feared and shadowy guerrilla groups, who had been kidnapping wealthy Colombians with impunity for years. When the M-19 guerrillas snatched a young Ochoa daughter from her university on November 12, 1981, and demanded a $13 million ransom, they discovered a group even more ruthless than themselves.

The Ochoas promptly called a meeting in Medellín of all those active in trafficking, and 223 people appeared. In a land that had been rent by decades of La Violencia, the terror unleashed around Medellín was all too familiar. Squads of drug goons rampaged through the city and surrounding countryside looking for the young Ochoa woman. They broke into houses and shot anyone in their way. The prize trophy of this brutal manhunt was one of M-19's provincial leaders, a man who had eluded the army for years. Eventually, M-19 released the kidnapped woman, but not before exacting a half-million dollar ransom— not $13 million certainly, but a ransom all the same. This whole astounding vigilante episode publicly demonstrated two alarming points: The cocaine traffickers now had the money, men, and sheer moxie to challenge anyone who crossed them. And the Colombian government was utterly passive before this obvious threat to a democratic, civil society.

Invigorated by their highly public display of brute power, the Medellín traffickers began to collaborate more actively in the endeavor they cared most about: getting even richer and more powerful pushing cocaine. While often called a cartel, they did not set prices like a true cartel, but the Medellín traffickers did dominate the business and had it organized in classic vertical fashion. Now they worked on increasing productivity. Up through the early 1980s, Colombia's pure white cocaine powder had been produced by ragtag mom-and-pop laboratories that turned out five or ten kilos at a time. Now the cartel decided to modernize and increase many fold their production capacity. A large river island was purchased in the depths of Colombia's lush southern rainforest. By early 1983 the traffickers had ferried in hundreds of workers who cleared the island of trees and paved a runway. Once that was completed, a steady relay of cargo planes delivered the necessary building materials.

By summer of 1983 three separate compounds had been constructed on this tropical river island. The first was christened Tranquilandia. Here were found the executive offices, living quarters for one hundred people, several storage rooms for chemicals and supplies, and some adjacent workshops for automobiles and airplanes. But the real point of the island were the second and third camps, known as Villa Coca and Coquilandia, and the six additional airstrips. Here the Medellín traffickers began producing *twenty tons* of cocaine per *month*. There was constant airplane and helicopter traffic in, bringing raw coca base from Bolivia, ether and other chemicals necessary to the manufacturing process from America and West Germany, and food. These same planes then ferried out the steady tonnage of new cocaine powder. Such a huge and busy enterprise was certainly no secret, but the Ochoas and Pablo Escobar felt certain that no one in authority would bother them. And presumably Tranquilandia was not unique. Other comparably big, modern labs were almost certainly being built or in operation in other remote spots.

Colombia had a long and dishonorable history of rampant corruption that the traffickers happily exploited. Not only had their huge political donations been accepted during recent national elections, in 1982 Escobar himself had been elected as an alternate to the Colombian House of Representatives. Like his vicious cocaine colleagues, he preferred to cloak his true murderous self in the more decent guise of businessman-philanthropist. Don Pablo, as he liked to be called, underwrote a hospital and housing for the poor.

Medellín's other pioneering trafficker, Carlos Rivas Lehder, had by now abandoned Norman's Cay as too vulnerable and had returned to

his hometown of Armenia. The boyish Lehder was admired as a generous and successful businessman dedicated to developing a Bavarian-
style resort. In Colombia in 1982, everyone still seemed happy to
embrace the fiction that the narcotraffickers were just wonderful,
enterprising, patriotic Colombian go-getters.

Everyone, that is, except the United States. Official Washington and
all the federal agencies finally had woken up to the drug epidemic
being fueled by the growing blizzard of cocaine. The 1975 white paper
on drug abuse that had described cocaine as a nonproblem and directed
law enforcement to focus on heroin and Mexico was now thoroughly
discredited. In early 1983, when a new American ambassador was dispatched to Colombia, the White House had instructed: "We want you
to go down to Colombia to do anything and everything you can do
about the drug problem."

The nation of Colombia had very different priorities. When Belisario
Betancur had assumed the presidency of Colombia in August 1982, his
highest mission was convincing the numerous guerrilla groups to
come in from the cold and become regular politicians. He deeply
believed that this was a crucial first step to meaningful social reforms,
the kind of change that could close the vast gulf between Colombia's
few rich and many poor. Nor was anyone else in Colombia's political
establishment much concerned by the issue of drugs.

At first, the Medellín cartel did not worry about the new American
pressure. President Betancur had little interest in drugs and, more
important, he had stated that he would not enforce a bilateral extradition treatment first signed in 1979 by Colombia and the United States
and ratified in mid 1981 by each country. The treaty was notable
because Article 8 allowed native traffickers to be extradited to the
United States for trial. When American prosecutors realized they had
this powerful new weapon, they immediately began indicting every
Colombian trafficker they could and seeking extradition.

Even though Betancur showed no special interest or concern about
drug traffickers and refused to honor Article 8 on the principle of
national sovereignty, he did appoint Senator Rodrigo Lara Bonillo,
thirty-five, an aggressive reformer, as his justice minister in August
1983. By now, everyone in this traditionally corrupt society assumed
that the Medellín's hundreds of millions had been widely and deeply
spread around. Still, explained journalists Guy Gugliotta and Jeffrey
Leen in *Kings of Cocaine*, the establishment continued to believe that

> state power, when brought to bear, was infinitely stronger than
> cocaine power.

This was a miscalculation. Betancur himself was making it, ignoring the rot that had set into Colombian political institutions and the danger it posed to the integrity of his government. Politicians down the line were also making it. They had played footsie with the traffickers, taken their money, and pretended they didn't know where it came from or that it didn't matter. They didn't understand the extent of cartel influence. The cartel was not trying to buy favors with hot money; the cartel was trying to buy a government.

When Justice Minister Lara Bonilla began to crusade against the corruption caused by drug money, the Colombia media had a field day shredding the narcotraffickers' carefully constructed veneer of respectability. Traffickers who had gloried in their roles as respectable businessmen helping "develop" their country were suddenly exposed as murderous thugs who had become vastly wealthy trafficking in cocaine, assassinating anyone who crossed them. Moreover, no one kidded themselves anymore that drugs were just a gringo problem. Colombians could see plenty of *basuco* addicts in their own cities. Lara Bonilla now made Carlos Rivas Lehder, ostensibly respectable newspaper owner and Armenia's best known citizen, the first test case for extradition.

The U.S. attorney for middle Florida, Robert Merkle, had traveled to Bogotá the previous year to ask for Lehder's extradition. As far as Merkle was concerned, Lehder, who was under indictment in Jacksonville, Florida, was the evil genius who had transformed cocaine from a criminal enterprise pushing kilos to one pushing tons: "He was to cocaine transportation as Henry Ford was to automobiles." When the Colombia Supreme Court ruled in early September 1983 that the extradition treaty and Article 8 were constitutionally sound, Lehder dropped from sight and the order for his extradition proceeded for signature to President Belisario Betancur.

Lehder was an important figure in the early cocaine trade beyond his innovations in transport methods. It was Lehder, above all, who had recognized the vast untapped underground baby-boomer market for cocaine. Unlike the stay at home in Colombia traffickers, Lehder had spent the 1970s in the United States, watching the middle-class drug culture expand. It was Lehder and Jung's forays to Los Angeles that had demonstrated the gargantuan American appetite for the ideal drug of the seventies and early eighties—cocaine. Did U.S. baby boomers think mind-altering drugs were the greatest? Did they especially want cocaine, which everyone knew was safe and nonaddictive? Well, the cartel would be more than happy to supply them.

The Colombians had seen a tremendous criminal opportunity in the cocaine trade. They would supply a popular and much desired illegal commodity to the world's richest and biggest consumer market. To this end, the Colombians were prepared to move tons. And because they wanted to smuggle ton-size lots (versus the fifty to one hundred kilos of the French connection era) the Colombians, unlike the Mafia with heroin, would sell large lots of cocaine to anyone in America who had the money to buy. And so the Colombians drew into the corruption of the drug trade tens of thousands of new American players. And Carlos Rivas Lehder was a pivotal figure in this important and destructive shift. These thousands of new players would prove crucial when the middle-class markets began to shrink. Meanwhile, perhaps fittingly, Lehder had become addicted to his own product. He became known as a ranter and a raver, which made his fellow traffickers keep him more and more at a distance.

Once Colombian Justice Minister Lara Bonilla had Lehder on the run, he then targeted Pablo Escobar, a matter complicated by Escobar's being an alternate member of Colombia's House of Representatives. He had parlimentary immunity. Even as Escobar tried to cast the issue as one of imperialism, the newspaper *El Espectador* began to publish front-page stories about Escobar's 1976 arrest with thirty-nine pounds of cocaine and the ensuing murders of his arresting officers. It now came out that yet another officer connected with the case also had been murdered, this one only two years earlier, in 1981. The old Escobar case was reopened. Lara Bonilla kept up a steady assault on the reputation and activities of the cartel. Fleets of drug planes were denied flying permits. Most of the nation's soccer teams were revealed to be owned by drug barons. Politicians too cozy with the cartel were denounced.

Then came the raid on the cartel's modern processing lab churning out twenty tons of cocaine a month in the depths of the rainforest. On March 10, 1984, forty-two Colombian narcotics police took off in helicopters and planes and soon found what they were looking for—runways visible through the jungle canopy. When they landed at Tranquilandia, they found no one but a few dozen peon-level factory workers. As usual, some informant at the government ministry had alerted the cartel, giving everyone time to flee. The booty from three island compounds included, from Tranquilandia:

> 2,500 kilos of pure cocaine, 19 machine guns and rifles, hundreds of rounds of ammunition, 1 mortar, 7 portable radios, 27 military uniforms, 4 electrical plants, 1 motorcycle, 2 vehicles, 4 tractors, 55 drums of ether, and 3,000 units of other chemical ingredients

From Villa Coca:

> 4 fully equipped laboratories, 3,500 kilos of cocaine base, 30 more kilos of pure cocaine, 2,000 drums of ether, 4 small airplanes, and 1 helicopter

From Coquilandia:

> 5,500 kilos of cocaine, 15 laboratories, 4 electrical plants, 5,000 drums of ether, 3,500 plastic cans, etc.

It would take days to secure and assess the sheer amount of stuff. But once that was done, the cops poured the twelve tons of cocaine into the Yarí River, which turned whitish-gray as it sluggishly swirled the drug downstream. Somewhere in the compound stood one particular barrel of American ether—equipped with a homing device by the DEA, the beacon that had given the exact location of this cocaine complex.

The Medellín cartel had operated with such complete impunity since the mid 1970s that it obviously was shocked by Justice Minister Lara Bonilla's crusade against them. The cartel had so saturated Colombia's every institution with drug money and had so completely swallowed their own lies about their respectability, the traffickers seemed surprised to find themselves portrayed as criminals undermining their own people and nation.

Once it recovered from its shock, the Medellín cartel struck back with typical ferocity. Seven weeks after the Tranquilandia raid, Justice Minister Lara Bonilla came to the U.S. ambassador seeking a safe haven from the escalating threats on his life by the cartel. The United States agreed to spirit Lara Bonilla to the States until he could be appointed ambassador somewhere far away. Having arranged this, Lara Bonilla was heading home at dusk in his official Mercedes-Benz limousine when a Yamaha motorcycle pulled alongside in the rush-hour traffic. The young punk in the passenger seat pulled out a MAC-10 submachine gun and opened fire, instantly slaughtering Lara Bonilla. As the motorcycle roared off, the assassins flung a hand grenade at Lara Bonilla's bodyguards, who were shooting back furiously. At that instant, the speeding bike skidded out, killing its driver. The punk, who survived, admitted having been hired in Medellín to settle a drug score. The cartel had spoken.

President Belisario Betancur, who had till now studiously ignored the narcotraffickers while he concentrated on luring the guerrillas to the peace table, gathered his cabinet and went to the clinic where Lara

Bonilla's body lay. The cabinet then reconvened and met through the night. The next morning a grim Betancur declared a state of seige. Police fanned out across the nation, arresting hundreds of cartel members and confiscating their planes, car, trucks, and property. Betancur finally signed Lehder's extradition order, though Lehder was nowhere to be found. On January 5, 1985, the first four traffickers were dispatched to U.S. justice under Article 8.

As *Desperadoes* described it, "The Medellín traffickers publicly threatened to kill five Americans for every Colombian extradited to the United States." The U.S. ambassadors to Colombia and Bolivia were ordered home. A dynamited car blew up in front of the U.S. embassy in Bogotá. Then, "informants reported that . . . the hit list put American embassy officials first, wives and children of embassy officers next, then American businessmen and journalists. . . . A report reached Washington that the cartel had placed a $350,000 price on the head of [DEA Chief] Bud Mullen. Informants warned that the cartel was gunning for several other DEA officials." None of this came to anything, but it was typical of the climate of terror the cartel liked to churn up.

Meanwhile, many of the traffickers were holed up in luxury homes and hotels in Panama, where they had long been cosy with such government officials as Manuel Noriega, former head of the Panama Defense Forces and now president (following a much disputed election). From there the cartel made an abortive attempt to negotiate with Betancur. But slowly the traffickers all drifted back. Lara Bonilla had not been in his grave six months before Pablo Escobar, who had been indicted for the killing, felt free to go about Medellín as he pleased. On July 23, 1985, Escobar extracted his revenge on the Bogotá Superior Court judge who had had the gall to issue the murder indictment against Escobar. Five gunmen in a passing Mazda blew the judge away. As usual, no one was caught or charged. Nor was Escobar the only cartel member highly visible around Medellín. The cartel had assassinated a sitting cabinet minister, and they had gotten away with it. What still made them nervous was Article 8 of the extradition treaty. A handful of men they had worked with and knew had been handed over to American justice, and they were now beginning long, long prison sentences in the United States.

By the fall of 1985, the constitutionality of the extradition issue was scheduled to be argued before the full twenty-four justices of the Colombian Supreme Court. And it was here that the cartel now focused its malevolent energies. The justices, eminent jurists from old families, became astonished and then fearful as they experienced the

Medellín treatment. First came intimidating letters, some sent directly to homes. Then began the threatening phone calls. (Later it would come out that even President Betancur was getting telephone threats on his supposedly secure, private line.) But this was obviously too uncertain. The justices might still rule that extradition was constitutional and then what would the cartel do?

On November 6, 1985, the cartel launched an incredibly brazen preemptive assault. Several dozen M-19 guerrillas stormed in with heavy artillery at lunchtime and easily captured the Colombian Palace of Justice. By the time Colombian troops had surrounded and retaken the blocklike structure on Bogotá's central Plaza Bolívar at least ninety-five people were dead, including the Supreme Court's chief justice and eleven of the twenty-four justices. All the guerrillas were killed. Most of the documents for the extradition cases went up in the flames of the pitched battle. Nonetheless, the extraditions slowly continued. Escobar, Lehder, and the Ochoas were not captured, although frequently seen in Medellín. And the systematic terror continued, aimed at both officials who got in the cartel's way and other thugs. By 1985 Colombia had the highest murder rate in the world. In Medellín alone, 1,698 were killed. The next year, an especially nasty one, that figure more than doubled, to 3,500, or ten murders a day. Colombia, a country with one tenth the population of the United States, had eleven thousand murders to the U.S.'s sixteen thousand. And few of those in Colombia were ever solved.

On the face of it, the United States and the Reagan administration appeared to be going all out after the Colombian traffickers. Yet, as had been the case since the late 1940s—with the brief exception of the Nixon administration—so-called national security matters still took priority over reining in drugs. Our government had said and done little to press the French about their underworld producing heroin in the fifties and sixties. Out in Southeast Asia national security again had taken precedence as we ardently supported anticommunists who were also major opium traffickers. Now in Central America and Afghanistan the same dubious policy still prevailed. National security analysts long had insisted on viewing communism as a greater threat to the United States than widespread drug trafficking and abuse.

It soon became evident that the Reagan White House ardently embraced this dubious Cold War notion. The first obvious sign was the way the administration blithely ruined a major DEA cocaine trafficking investigation so it could embarrass the leftist Sandinistas and perhaps sway a congressional vote. This particular episode began in the spring of 1984 when longtime Louisiana drug smuggler Barry Seal "flipped" and agreed to work for the DEA, hoping to stave off several looming prison sentences. Such was Seal's status that he quickly hooked up with top members of the Medellín cartel, including Pablo Escobar, who was then laying low in Panama after the murder of Justice Minister Lara Bonilla. After various mishaps and delays, Escobar eventually commissioned Seal to pick up seven hundred kilos of cocaine from an airstrip in Nicaragua and fly it north to the States.

Seal's contact in Nicaragua was one Federico Vaughan, an aide to the Sandinista interior minister. On June 25, 1984, Seal flew a big military transport plane to a Nicaraguan airfield. As American spy cameras attached to the plane clicked away, Pablo Escobar, Federico Vaughan, and another major Medellín trafficker personally loaded the seven hundred kilos. Seal took off and returned the plane to Homestead Air Force Base. Seal's relationship with Escobar and the Medellín cartel was developing nicely, providing highly valuable intelligence. Escobar already had agreed to visit some Mexican airstrips with Seal to check them out. The DEA was making plans to arrest Escobar triumphantly when he was in Mexico, a major coup.

But the Reagan White House—for all the sincere talk about its commitment to combating the cartel—had a completely different agenda. Within a week of Seal's mission, which had captured Escobar and Vaughan photographically in the act, a U.S. Army general told a U.S. Chamber of Commerce audience in San Salvador that "the United States 'now had firm proof that the Sandinistas were actively and recently involved in drug trafficking, and the world would soon be given proof.' "

This kind of leaking to a small, isolated audience wasn't great, but the DEA and Seal felt they could ignore it and that Seal could continue his wooing of the Medellín cartel. And indeed, all was proceeding nicely until July 17, when the right-leaning *Washington Times* broke a front-page story detailing Seal's activities—not because of any interest in the drug cartel and cocaine, but because it made the Sandinistas look bad. The probable culprit—though he denies it—was the overzealous Lieutenant Colonel Oliver North, National Security Council staffer at a time when the Reagan administration was trying fervently to convince Congress it should fund the anti-Sandinista contras.

When the story broke, Barry Seal was flying a plane down to Mexico to meet cartel members at a ranch in the Yucatán. He was summoned desperately home. The Reagan administration's meddling destroyed the DEA's best prospect of bagging the actual cartel members. And by February 1985, Medellín had exacted its usual revenge: Seal was murdered by three cartel assassins in Baton Rouge. Moreover, there was never any real proof that Vaughan represented anyone but himself. No connections to other Sandinistas had been established, and the DEA refused to endorse Reagan administration statements smearing the Nicaraguan government as traffickers.

By late 1985, rumors began to circulate in Washington that more than the Sandinistas were playing dirty drug games in Central America. Now there was growing talk that the Reagan-backed contras were trafficking. It would take another two years before a CIA official would admit before a congressional committee that "a lot of people" in the contras were indeed "involved in cocaine smuggling." Once again, the foreign-policy makers had decided it best to overlook trafficking aimed at the United States when it helped underwrite anti-communists, in this case the contras fighting the leftist Sandinista government in Nicaragua. The Colombian cartels and their many contract workers found the contras useful allies and smugglers. A DEA official later would testify, "People on both sides of the equation [in the Nicaraguan war] were drug traffickers and a couple of them were pretty significant."

Eventually, the contra drug rumors became so rampant a Senate subcommittee under Senator John Kerry of Massachusetts began to investigate. The ensuing report concluded that it could find no

> evidence that the Contra leadership participated directly in narcotics smuggling in support of their war against the Sandinistas. . . . [But there was] substantial evidence of drug smuggling through war zones on the part of individual Contras, pilots who flew supplies, mercenaries who worked for the Contras, and Contra supporters throughout the region.
>
> There is also evidence on the record that U.S. officials involved in assisting the Contras knew that drug smugglers were exploiting the clandestine infrastructure established to support the war and that Contras were receiving assistance derived from drug trafficking. Instead of reporting these people to the appropriate law enforcement agencies, it appears that some officials may have turned a blind eye to these activities.

The whole contra scene

> served as a magnet for many individuals who exploited their activities on behalf of the Contras as a cover for illegal gun-running and narcotics trafficking. It appears that anyone or any organization was welcomed as participants in supporting the Contra cause. . . .

[N]arcotics traffickers were particularly astute in offering to assist the Contras in an effort to not only protect their operations, but also to avoid prosecution for their activities as well. This technique is known as "ticket punching." . . .

George Morales, the convicted cocaine trafficker, was quite candid that his primary motivation in providing support to Eden Pastora's organization was his belief that the CIA would actually intervene to assist him with his legal problems.

And what was anyone to make of the U.S. State Department's choice of four companies to "supply humanitarian assistance to the Contras"? Each and every one had been set up and was run by major traffickers. No one could explain to Senator Kerry how these four transport companies were selected. But, all told, they received about eight hundred thousand dollars in U.S. tax dollars. And, probably far more valuable, excellent "cover" for bringing in yet more tons of cocaine.

And then of course there was the severe embarrassment of our Panamanian ally, General Manuel Noriega, who was also a close partner of the Medellín cartel. It was no coincidence that Pablo Escobar and other cartel leaders headed to Panama to lay low after the assassination of Justice Minister Lara Bonilla. As Fred Kempe describes in *Divorcing the Dictator*:

> The cartel moved 120 people to Panama: accountants, bodyguards, lawyers, and families. Noriega provided them housing, advice, and even Panamanian passports. When Jorge Ochoa was arrested the following year in Spain, he and his family were traveling with Panamanian diplomatic passports. The cartel bosses who most needed security and secrecy rented U.S. officers' homes at Fort Amador, which had reverted to Noriega under terms of the Panama Canal Treaties. Others stayed in plush suites atop the Caesar Park Marriott Hotel.

The cartel had good reason to feel comfortable in Noriega's Panama. Since the summer of 1982 they had been paying Noriega one hundred thousand dollars each time a planeload of cocaine used a Panamanian airstrip. Then in 1983 they had cut a $5 million deal to establish a big cocaine refinery in Panama itself in "the thick of the El Sapo mountain range in Darien jungle, less than fifty miles from the Colombian border." Yet three weeks after Escobar and company had arrived in Panama, on May 21, 1984, this just completed facility had been raided, by Noriega's Panamanian Defense Forces no less, and now twenty-one cartel members were in Panama jails! Complaints by local Indians had filtered back to the American embassy. Noriega, working every side of the aisle, had decided to placate the DEA by giving them the cartel's new lab. Pablo Escobar was infuriated at the double-cross. He tried to contact Noriega, but the president conveniently had taken off to Israel and Europe on official business. Stymied, Escobar threatened to murder Noriega if he didn't make good. And, of course, by now, no one underestimated such threats.

Noriega's closest political aide, one Jose Blandon, a suave diplomat who heretofore had had no dealings with the cartel, was called upon to solve this threatening situation. Noriega, calling from Paris, instructed Blandon to travel to Cuba. There, he went directly to see Castro, whom he knew well. In *Divorcing the Dictator*, Kempe describes the meeting:

> Castro said "the Colombians" were enraged by the Darien raid. "And that's a dangerous situation—for Panama and for everybody." Castro didn't need to add for Blandon that Noriega also protected Cuba's myriad interests in Panama.
>
> "The cartel could transform Panama into a battle zone if Noriega causes it problems," he said, "It would be between the defense forces and the cartel."
>
> Blandon was surprised to hear Castro talk so knowledgeably about the cartel. He'd long suspected Noriega was in deep with drug interests, but he had long admired Castro. . . . Blandon had discounted reports of Cuba's ties to drugs as CIA propaganda.

Castro arranged for Blandon to meet a cartel representatative in Havana. The Panamanian diplomat humbly promised that Noriega would return the cartel's $5 million, free the prisoners, and give back the planes and helicopter seized at Darien.

Eventually, Noriega's activities became such an embarrassment that several higher-ups in the Reagan administration felt compelled to make a visit to the Panamanian president. Political analyst Joe Klein described how "CIA Director William Casey and National Security Adviser John Poindexter met with Noriega about the drug business in 1985—Casey 'winked at it,' and Poindexter 'read Noriega the riot act.' Noriega apparently figured this was gringo business as usual and took Casey's wink more seriously than Poindexter's lecture."

Meanwhile, in Florida, U.S. prosecutor Richard Gregorie would slowly amass sufficient evidence to bring a federal indictment against Noriega. In early February 1988, a Miami federal grand jury charged

Noriega with using his official position in Panama to "facilitate the manufacture and transportation of large quantities of cocaine destined for the United States and to launder narcotics proceeds." Specifically, they charged the general with accepting $4.5 million in payoffs for allowing two tons of cocaine to transit through Panama, and also with allowing the big Darien lab to be built.

The clash between national security and drug control was personified by U.S. Attorney Richard Gregorie, a highly seasoned and well-regarded drug prosecutor in Miami who finally resigned in disgust after eight years on the job. He told NBC in an interview, "I am finding the higher we go, the further I investigate matters involving Panama, high-level corruption in Colombia, in Honduras, in the Bahamas, they are concerned that we are going to cause a problem in foreign policy areas and that that is more important than stopping the dope problem. We are not being allowed to win this war."

Eventually, a deeply embarrassed United States would invade Panama on December 20, 1989, to roust out and capture Noriega. He was tried and found guilty in 1990 and imprisoned. But as his onetime political aide Jose Blandon—the one who negotiated in Cuba with the cartel—pointed out, the United States spent the 1980s fighting the wrong enemy in Latin America—communism rather than drugs: "You've been looking at Latin America through the wrong lens. . . . You've been obsessed with the left—the Sandinistas—when the real problem was the growing influence of the cartel, which was funding *both* sides in Nicaragua, corrupting Panama, buying key officials in other countries . . . and, of course, poisoning your children."

Nor were our Cold War national security obsessions limited to Central America. Just as the Reagan administration chose to ignore contra cocaine trafficking directed at the American market, so they also ignored Afghani-Pakistani heroin trafficking aimed at American markets. And, in doing so, they merely were continuing a policy started in the Carter administration. Dr. David Musto, the Yale University psychiatrist who had written a respected history of American narcotic laws, had joined President Carter's Strategy Council on Drug Abuse in 1977:

> Over the next two years, Musto found that the CIA and other intelligence agencies denied the council—whose members included the secretary of state and the attorney general—access to all classified information on drugs, even when it was necessary for framing new policy. The council's specific inquiries took years to produce "the sketchiest information" or "superficial responses." . . .

When President Carter reacted to the Soviet invasion of Afghanistan in December 1979 by shipping arms to the muja-heddin guerrillas, Musto's disquiet grew. "I told the council," he recalled, "that we were going into Afghanistan to support the opium growers in their rebellion against the Soviets. Shouldn't we try to avoid what we had done in Laos? Shouldn't we try to pay the growers if they will eradicate their opium production? There was silence." As heroin from Afghanistan and Pakistan poured into America throughout 1979, Musto noted the number of drug-related deaths in New York City rose by 77 percent.

By May 1980, Dr. Musto and a fellow council member were publicly expressing their dismay on the Op-ed page of the *New York Times*.

In the mid 1980s Vice President George Bush made an official visit to the Pakistan of General Mohammed Zia ul-Haq, by then a major source of heroin going to Europe and America. Our allies the Pakistanis generously had opened their nation to the CIA and its supposedly covert efforts to help the Afghani guerrillas fighting the Soviet forces in Afghanistan. No one seemed to mind that certain guerrilla groups—notably the fundamentalist Hekmatyar faction—were developing a brand new major heroin industry in collusion with high-level Pakistani officials.

Traditionally both Afghanistan and Pakistan had cultivated opium poppies. Some had been consumed locally, but most had been sold to the huge Iranian market. But with the revolution in Iran and the Russian invasion of Afghanistan in 1979, all that changed: "Opium cultivation became important for the war effort for its ability to raise cash. Guerrillas, peasants, and criminals would plant the poppies, and prune, irrigate and harvest them. The by-product would then be smuggled across the porous Pakistani border." By the mid 1980s Afghanis and Pakistanis happily were engaged in major league international heroin trafficking.

Of course, the United States was well aware of this. During the 1980s the DEA had seventeen agents in Pakistan: "European police who have worked closely with the DEA claim that U.S. agents have identified nearly forty significant narcotics syndicates in Pakistan. Yet in the past ten years [since 1978] not one single major syndicate has been broken up as a result of U.S. enforcement efforts. The only major network exposed in the last decade has been the Norwegian connection." And in that case General Zia's personal banker took the fall for other high-level government officials.

In McCoy's second edition of *The Politics of Heroin*, he notes,

> By 1988, there were an estimated 100 to 200 heroin refineries in the [north-west frontier] province's Khyber district alone. Trucks from the Pakistan army's National Logistics Cell 9NLC arriving with CIA arms from Karachi often returned loaded with heroin—protected by ISI papers from police search. "The drug is carried in NLC trucks, which come sealed from the [north-west frontier] and are never checked by the police," reported the *Herald* of Pakistan in September 1985. "They come from Peshawar to Pirpri, Jungshahi, Jhimpir where they deliver their cargos, sacks of grain, to government godowns [warehouses]. Some of these sacks contain packets of heroin. . . . This has been going on now for about three and a half years."

And just as the Andean nations trafficking in cocaine soon developed big drug problems, so did Pakistan. Up through 1980, Pakistan never had had a noticeable heroin problem. But as the hundreds of local heroin factories refined the black gooey opium into white powder, the drug became widely and cheaply available. "Unrestrained by any form of police controls, local smugglers also shipped heroin to Pakistan's own cities and towns. Addiction rose to 5,000 users in 1980, to 70,000 in 1983, and then, in the words of Pakistan's Narcotics Control Board, went 'completely out of hand,' exploding to more than 1.3 million addicts in less than three years." To put this into perspective, remember that the United States—always viewed as having the world's worst drug problem—then had a half million heroin addicts in a population of about 250 million. Pakistan had three times that number of heroin addicts in a population of about 70 million. And the problem had developed in less than a decade.

The same heroin that was enslaving Pakistanis in unheard of numbers was also streaming into the United States. Once again, our putative allies were busy sending a steady supply of addictive drugs our way. And so one cringes a bit to reread George Bush's acceptance speech for the Republican nomination: "I want a drug-free America. Tonight, I challenge the young people of our country to shut down the drug dealers around the world. . . . My administration will be telling the dealers, 'Whatever we have to do, we'll do, but your day is over. you're history." This was, of course, a member of an administration that secretly coddled traffickers on two continents while talking a good line at home.

In its final report on the contra-drug issue, the Senate Subcommittee on Terrorism, Narcotics, and International Relations had some useful warning words about international drug traffickers:

> The scale of the cartels' operations and the dimensions of their economic, political and military power make these organizations far more dangerous than any criminal enterprise in U.S. history. They have access to sophisticated weapons and intelligence. They have fielded their own armies and even have entered alliances with a variety of revolutionary groups and military institutions in the hemisphere. In many respects, they have taken on the attributes of sovereign governments.
>
> The United States government needs to recognize the enormous threat these organizations pose to the vital national interest of our country.

CHAPTER 17

"Now Everyone
Was Into
Smoking Crack."

—Susan Lydon,
TAKE THE LONG WAY HOME

In July 1985 the journal *Sociology & Social Research* featured an article in its Recent Social Trends column titled, " 'Rock' Sales in South Los Angeles." Written by two academics from the University of Southern California, it stated, "Throughout the Black residential areas of Los Angeles County, there has been a recent, dramatic increase in cocaine dealing. This has resulted in large part from the proliferation of cocaine 'rocks' and fortified 'rock houses' which, with certain refinements, constitute a new technology and organization for cocaine distribution.

"An increasing trend in the distribution system is the use of street gang members in various dealing roles."

The article explained that cocaine "rock" was a "pebble-sized crystalline form of cocaine base, obtainable currently for $25.00, an amount making it available to virtually any interested potential user. . . . Rocks are generally smoked through a pipe (water pipes are preferred), often with other substances such as marijuana or rum. They yield a brief but intense high. Rocks are easily manufactured, hidden, passed, and disposed."

Five months later, just after Thanksgiving, the *New York Times* ran a front-page story headlined, A NEW, PURIFIED FORM OF COCAINE CAUSES ALARM AS ABUSE INCREASES. The article warned that a "new form of cocaine is for sale on the streets of New York, alarming law enforcement officials and rehabilitation experts because of its tendency to accelerate abuse of the drug. . . . The substance, known as crack, is already processed into the purified form that enables cocaine users to smoke, or free-base, the powerful stimulant of the central nervous system."

New York City police reported raiding places called "crack houses" where "sales are made and users gather for smoking binges that can last for several days. . . . 'I talked to one woman there,' Lieutenant Creegan said, 'and it was almost like her mind was burned out. She told me all she does is do crack all day.' "

When the middle-class baby boomers first had rediscovered cocaine in the early 1970s, the new, hipper generation of drug experts generally had agreed that it was not a notably dangerous drug. After all, multitudes of young Americans were snorting powdered cocaine with no visibly disastrous public consequences. The 1975 Ford administration white paper said, "the data obtained from treatment programs and surveys generally reflect the fact that cocaine, as currently used, usually does not result in serious social consequences such as crime, hospital emergency room admissions, or death." But even during the 1970s, when cocaine was hyped as a glamorous, excellent drug for the up-and-coming Yuppie, the unconcerned experts always would interpose that caveat: "as currently used." Harvard's Dr. Lester Grinspoon, who had testified that he saw no big problem for those snorting two to three times a week ("I am unable to persuade myself that they are very much at risk.") did concede that "I am a little concerned about what would happen if the price of cocaine were less."

In 1981, the dean of LSD and marijuana research, Dr. Sidney Cohen, had written "if we were to be flooded with low cost cocaine one day, it could become a considerable scourge." Moreover, he warned, "smoked cocaine produces a state that is so overpowering that anyone can be swept into compulsive use. . . . Strength of character and psychological maturity are insufficient guarantees of noninvolvement with this substance. The best deterrents to date have been its cost and the poor quality of the available material."

Dr. Cohen was not writing about smoking crack, because it was unheard-of in 1981. However, he and other drug experts were already unhappily aware of a form of cocaine abuse around since the mid 1970s known as freebasing. Powdered cocaine was heated (often with a blow torch!) using various volatile chemicals to reduce it to a purer crystallized form. Once crumbled, it was smoked through a water pipe. This style of smoking cocaine really began to take off in 1979, thanks to the efforts of those good citizens—the drug paraphernalia industry. Knowing the drug culture's enthusiasm for things pure and organic, paraphernalia dealers cleverly marketed the new freebase kits with spiels like this: "Free-base is your favorite nasal stash with all the hydrochloride and most adulterants removed. This clean end product is as close to the natural state as it's been since it was harvested. The free-base is in an alkaline state and doesn't dissolve in water. It *must be smoked* and it's preferable to use a . . . water pipe since it's specifically designed for free-base. The advantage of free-base is that it will act much faster and stronger than snorting and save your nose from abuse."

Out in Los Angeles, UCLA psychologist and drug researcher Ronald K. Siegel, who favored aviator glasses, turtlenecks, and longish hair, watched with considerable concern the appearance of these paraphernalia ads in places such as *High Times*. After all, Siegel (a favored drug expert for *People*) provided treatment to certain Hollywood stars, and had observed firsthand producer Julia Phillips's severe freebase addiction. Siegel and others in the field knew too well that smoking a drug made it far, far more potent and addicting. Four years earlier, in 1975, Siegel had launched a longitudinal study of ninety-nine middle-class recreational cocaine users. While most were snorters, twelve (or 12 percent) were already familiar with smoking freebase.

Two years after Siegel launched his study, the first commercially developed freebase pipe became widely available throughout California. "The first free-base kit for extraction of cocaine free-base from cocaine hydrochloride was developed by Paraphernalia Headquarters of California in late 1978 and was introduced at the New York Fashion Show on January 4–7, 1979. At the same time, the first national advertisements for pipes and kits appeared in the January 1979 issue of *Paraphernalia Digest*, an industry trade journal with an approximate circulation of 15,000 in 1980."

By 1979, only sixty-one people of the original ninety-nine were still in Siegel's longitudinal study. But of these, twenty-four (or 40 percent) were now smokers of cocaine freebase. And, Siegel would write, "Most users reported being introduced to cocaine free-base smoking via paraphernalia advertisements and displays in head shops and other retail stores."

In December 1979, *Science News* became one of the first American publications to report the rising popularity of this new way of using cocaine: smoking it, a form of drug use that "almost always leads to severe abuse." Snorting cocaine was self-limiting, explained the magazine, because the drug is a "potent vasoconstrictor that slows down absorption in the nose even as it is being ingested. Maximum blood levels of the active ingredients thus reach a peak after 20 minutes to one hour following snorting or swallowing. When smoked, cocaine reaches maximum blood levels in two to five minutes."

Physicians might appreciate all this, but to the average person, the mere act of smoking just could not seem that dangerous. After all, one saw ordinary people smoking cigarettes every day. And within the drug culture, smoking marijuana was viewed as a mild, safe high. As one Bronx resident explained, "What happened was a lot of people said, 'Hey, another drug you smoke, so it can't be that bad.' " Yet this simple change in the "route of administration" so intensified and speeded up compulsive cocaine using that habits could be acquired in weeks and months, rather than the usual two to five years when you snorted powder. Moreover, the amounts consumed soared. While an active snorter might use two grams in a week, a freebaser could smoke that in one sitting and still crave more. The appeal for traffickers and dealers was obvious. Instead of customers spending two hundred dollars on cocaine in a week, they could binge their way through that in a day. The crack high lasted a mere fifteen minutes. So while a rock might appear cheap at five dollars, one was never near enough. Ten rocks would keep you high for only an afternoon.

After a powerful antifreebase article appeared in the LA Times in early 1980, a young woman wrote in with her own sad story: "I started doing free-base last June occasionally on weekends, then every weekend, and then it turned out to be every night. . . . I lost 25 pounds (my normal weight is 110) and my personality changed from a very happy young lady to a totally paranoid person." Then a friend died of a "free-base related heart attack." To avoid the temptations of drug-using friends, she moved from South Florida to LA. "The high is the best of highs, but a life being taken is just not worth it."

Meanwhile, the drug paraphernalia industry was pushing freebase kits as if cocaine smoking was just good, clean, organic fun. Paraphernalia Digest would report happily in its July 1979 issue that freebase kits, pipes, and accessories were the "hottest selling line for 1979." By 1980 the five major manufacturers reported selling almost three hundred thousand kits. But the hazards of this new drug-using fad caused even drug-loving Rolling Stone to run an article in May 1980 warning "Free Base—A Treacherous Obsession." People such as UCLA's Siegel, who really didn't believe in 1980 that snorting cocaine was worrisome, viewed smoking cocaine as "extremely hazardous." As disapproval grew, places such as *High Times* tried to display civic responsibility by banning freebase kit advertising. But after two months of losses, *High Times* reverted to its true mercenary nature and started running these ads again.

The vast majority of Americans were not plugged into the fads of the upper-middle-class drug culture. Nor did they read *High Times*. And, therefore, the first they heard of cocaine smoking and freebasing came when comedian Richard Pryor was burned badly on June 9, 1980. According to *Time*, Pryor ran shrieking from his suburban house "engulfed in flames. . . . His polyester shirt had melted onto his arms and chest, and he suffered third-degree burns from the waist up. . . . The Los Angeles police say Pryor told them he was 'free-basing' cocaine. This newly fashionable practice involves purifying the coke by mixing it with highly flammable ether, which, when it evaporates, leaves coke crystals that burn with a steady flame and are smoked through a water pipe." Apparently Pryor's fashionable freebase kit had exploded.

Despite such bad publicity, devotees of the drug culture clamored for freebase and the fabled high of smoking cocaine. The sudden skyrocketing demand for freebase in traditional urban drug markets was forcing dealers "to cook it up batch by batch for the customers, while they cooled their heels in the dealers' apartments—a level of sustained exposure to outsiders that dealers loathed." Longtime New York drug researcher Bruce Johnson later would explain, the drug dealers "tried to figure out an efficient way to create large batches of cocaine free-base and then package it in such a way that it could be sold at retail in a market they didn't necessarily interact with directly."

The production and packaging solutions these dealers were seeking may well have been passed along by someone from the Bahamas. For it was in those islands that crack first surfaced in any noticeable way in 1980. Gordon Witkin of *U.S. News & World Report*, who tracked crack's swift ascendance in a major cover story called "The Men Who Created Crack," reported that a huge glut of cocaine powder in the Bahamas had caused the price to drop by 80 percent. Faced with plummeting income, Bahamian drug dealers decided to offer a new product—rock cocaine that had to be smoked. Dr. James Jekel, a Yale Medical School epidemiologist who studied crack in the Bahamas, explained, "The pushers knew that crack addicts keep coming back for more and more, so figured, 'Let's create a demand by getting people to go to crack.' How did you get them to go to crack? They figured, 'Let's sell that and nothing else.' It was a marketing decision." The results were scary and pitiful. The Bahamian crack culture exploded and hundreds of emaciated, tattered addicts huddled for days on end in filthy rock houses, their lips and mouths burned and scabby from marathon sessions with their pipes.

In our ever more mobile and cosmopolitan world, people who had been to the Bahamas or Bahamians (or other Caribbean islands that soon learned how to make and use crack) then migrated to Miami or Los Angeles, carrying this drug know-how with them. When Miami police first busted a rock house in 1982 the scene was still reasonably respectable. "They didn't look like junkies. These were people with jobs—white, black, upper class, lower class, young girls. I remember thinking, 'What the hell have we got here?' They said they were doing rocks. They called it a 'rock house.' " But soon rock or crack had spread to the traditional drug markets of Miami's poor black neighborhoods, where this crystalline form of cocaine base sold for as little as five dollars. There local youths learned how to cook up crack from Caribbean immigrants and went into business.

Drug street researchers in New York City—always the nation's biggest market for illegal drugs—first had heard crack mentioned in December 1983. It would be another year before researcher Bill Hopkins, a former Bronx narcotics cop then working for the state, actually saw someone smoking crack. He recalls, "I learned for the first time it was done with baking soda, not ether. And I examined what he had, and it was in vials. I knew we had something new on the market." By 1985, crack was readily available throughout the city. And nowhere more so than northwestern Manhattan in Washington Heights, where the dominant Dominicans could comfortably do business in Spanish with their Colombian counterparts in Jackson Heights, and also sell to white suburbanites willing to risk a quick automotive dash off nearby highways.

Word spread swiftly through the middle-class drug culture about the superintense new kind of cocaine, and soon suburban cars were streaming off the bridges of upper Manhattan to check out crack. Writes Witkin, "When night fell, 'copping' zones like West 168th Streets or 174th Street and Amsterdam Avenue became choked with traffic. Some 70 to 80 percent of the consumers powering the market were white professionals or middle-class youngsters from Long Island, suburban New Jersey or New York's affluent Westchester County—all of whom could easily drive into the community."

By mid 1986, the National Cocaine Hotline had been up and running for more than three years. Dr. Arnold Washton, the hotline's creator, was amazed at the huge shift in calls. Looking back during the summer of

1986, he would say, "In September '85 we had not gotten a single call [on the cocaine hot line] about crack. Now [nine months later] 33 percent of all coke users who call are talking about crack addiction. The explosion has taken place in the past six to nine months. It's a true epidemic."

Eight years earlier, Yale psychiatrist Robert Byck had sat before the House Select Committee on Narcotics and made an impassioned plea that the nation's best minds figure out how to stave off cocaine smoking in the United States. What he had seen in Peru of the *basuco* smokers had been extremely alarming. Not one person displayed an iota of interest. "It's always been bewildering to me," Byck would say in 1995, "that no one did anything about it. There was just a complete failure of recognition of the problem. NIDA wasn't interested. Neither was anyone political. Nothing happened."

Susan Gordon Lydon, a nice Jewish girl from Long Island who had slid from the hip recreational drug culture into the lowest depths of the full-time drug culture in the 1970s, was part of the exploding crack epidemic. In the summer of 1986 she returned to Manhattan after three years away in Minneapolis, where she had tried but failed to stay off heroin. Back in New York, she found, "The drug scene had changed. Now everyone was into smoking crack. . . . 'Be careful now, baby,' my old friend Red Dog told me when I ran into him, 'these crackheads they got down here will cut your throat in a heartbeat. It ain't like it used to be here. Nowadays you can't trust nobody on the street." Soon, Lydon was smoking crack. "One night I met someone who showed me how to hit the pipe correctly, so that I heard the bells, and I fell in love."

As her heroin and cocaine use escalated, Lydon started selling her body. "I often found tricks on Delancey Street and brought them to a little hole-in-the-wall where you could pay seven dollars and rent a cubicle with a wash basin for twenty minutes. This was convenient for me because it was right near where they sold coke." She lost four jobs proofreading in as many months as her compulsive drug use made her late, completely absent, or too jittery to work well: "I'd come out of the bathroom covered with sweat, with my hands shaking and fingers blackened from resin, constantly looking over my shoulder from paranoia, and sit down at my desk to do a little proofreading. Ten minutes later I'd go to the downstairs bathroom and [get high again]." By September 1986—mere months since she had come home—Lydon described her "normal routine" as "copping coke on Stanton and Clinton, going around the corner to shoot it, turning tricks, running uptown for crack, etc., etc." Lydon, who prided herself on never having stolen from her parents (with whom she was living in their waterside suburban home), now began stealing cash.

For a good decade the Colombian cocaine cartels had been expanding furiously their production capacity to serve the seemingly insatiable American market. In 1974 already 5.4 million Americans acknowledged having tried cocaine at least once. Over the next decade, that figure would quadruple, until by the early 1980s about 22 million Americans, or one out of eleven, admitted having tried cocaine. Several million were regular users. The baby boomers had created a huge demand, snorting up ever more tons of cocaine, and the cartels had responded by planting and processing ever greater amounts of cocaine—from 25 tons in the late 1970s to 125 tons by the early 1980s. Stateside cocaine prices reflected the growing glut, as prices tumbled from $60,000 a kilo in the late 1970s to $15,000 to $20,000 in the mid 1980s. Moreover, purity in these cheaper kilos had risen from 35 percent to 60 or 70 percent.

But even as the expensive glamour drug of the seventies and early eighties became cheaper and more plentiful, the baby boomers' love affair began to cool. A great many users could look around at their friends and see that cocaine was not a benign drug. The cocaine hotline had reestablished—amid a fair amount of publicity—that cocaine was addictive. Even smart, theoretically disciplined users could and did get into big trouble. Skeptics who doubted the possible dangers of cocaine were hard put to ignore the one-two punch of Len Bias and Don Rogers dropping dead in mid 1986.

In fact, middle-class cocaine use among those 18 to 25 peaked in about 1980. That year, the household survey showed almost 20 percent had used cocaine in the past year, a figure that then began a steady decline throughout the 1980s. Heavy use, or use in the past month, declined even more dramatically in this cohort in the early 1980s. In 1979, 9.3 percent of those aged 18 to 25 had used cocaine in the previous month. By 1982, that had declined to 6.8 percent, rising to 7.6 percent in 1985 and then dropping to 4.5 percent in 1988. The older baby boomers, those 26 and over, however, continued their love affair with cocaine throughout the early 1980s, with 1985 the high-water mark. In 1985, 4.2 percent said they had used cocaine within the past year.

The cooling ardor of the mass of baby boomers made the advent of crack all the more fortuitous for the cartels. For just when cocaine was losing its panache with its core group of consumers—the middle-class boomers—it could be retargeted at the traditional illegal drug market: the inner-city poor. The middle class had created the demand and fueled the market. And as they pulled back, the cartels had no intention of packing up and going back home. They just refocused their drug on the have-nots.

By the mid 1980s, America's inner-city poor had become extremely vulnerable. There had developed a highly segregated underclass—largely minority—deeply alienated from mainstream society. Academics and public policy types argued over how and why this underclass formed, but clearly, starting in the 1960s, something had gone seriously awry. Ever since the New Deal created Aid to Families with Dependent Children (AFDC) in the 1930s, the number of families receiving welfare rose and fell in concert with the unemployment rates. When unemployment rose, so did AFDC; when it fell, so did AFDC. But starting in 1963, this seemingly logical connection became severed for good.

The 1960s were the most prosperous years the United States ever experienced, with the Gross National Product doubling in one decade. And yet even with unemployment low and the economy roaring along, the AFDC rolls exploded. Every major city experienced this. In 1960 3 million Americans were on welfare. By 1972, after a decade of unprecedented prosperity, almost 11 million were on welfare, and a disproportionate number were inner-city minority poor. The percentage of black children born out of wedlock rose steadily from 16.9 percent in 1966, passing 50 percent in 1980, while female-headed households doubled, hitting 60.6 percent in 1973. Arrest rates for black males between the ages of thirteen and thirty-nine rose by 49 percent between 1966 and 1974. As the social pathologies of the black urban poor mounted, their middle-class black neighbors fled. Illegitimacy, promiscuity, violence, drugs, crime, and little connection to daily work became hallmarks of the urban underclass. In certain swaths of the inner city a working husband–devoted father had become as rare as a whooping crane.

The steady disappearance of unskilled jobs that paid a family-supporting wage played a role in this escalating social disaster. In Elliott Currie's book *The Reckoning*, which examines the links between despairing poverty and drug abuse, he notes that "the bottom fifth of Americans lost about 12 percent in income between 1977 and 1990 while the top fifth gained over 30 percent—and the top 5 percent gained nearly 50 percent. . . . In short, a substantial part of the younger population, especially, saw its comparative fortunes plummeting."

However, it was not just declining opportunity. The hipster ethos played a role in exacerbating a bad situation. The hipster sneered at authority and denigrated the solid family man as a chump. The hipster goal was complete hedonistic freedom to seduce as many women as possible, to get as high as possible, make money from a hustle, not a job, and thereby be the coolest cat possible. A great many of the potential inner-city fathers and husbands of this era had opted to be hipster-hustler–drug addicts. AFDC, Medicaid, and food stamps underwrote the underclass male's abdication of spousal and parental responsibility. Entire populations had developed "an attitude."

By the time crack hit the inner city, the pathologies of the under-class had been deepening for two decades. Sexual promiscuity and teenaged single motherhood were the norm, as were second- and third-generation welfare. Doing well in already inadequate public schools was denounced as "being white." Steady, honest work—if it could be found—was derided. Crime and violence were accepted means for boys and young men to obtain "respect." Doing time in jail was a youthful rite of passage. It was hard to imagine how things could get much worse, but crack soon showed how it was all too possible.

The economics of crack were extremely simple. Most poor people had long viewed one hundred dollars (the going price) for a gram of powdered cocaine as too expensive. But make that gram into rock and the product appeared extremely affordable. That gram could be "transformed into any-where from 5 to 30 rocks. For the user, this meant individual rocks could be purchased for as little as $2, $5 (nickel rocks), $10 (dime rocks), or $20. For the seller, $60 worth of cocaine hydrochloride . . . could generate as much as $100 to $150 when it was sold as rocks." Cheap in price, attractive to heroin addicts worried about needles and AIDS, "crack" was instantly popular on the streets of the ghetto, the new fast-food of drugs.

For decades, heroin had been *the* famous and feared "hard" drug. Even the most prodrug publications, whether *Rolling Stone* or *High Times*, did not tout heroin. The drug had a well-deserved reputation for creating a habit that could enslave you quickly and ruin your life. Few people (aside from addicts) had any romantic illusions about heroin. There was nothing appealing about a full-blown junkie, especially since intravenous drug injection had been linked in the early 1980s to the terrifying and deadly new disease, AIDS.

When crack debuted as a street drug in 1985 and early 1986, it was so unknown it had no public reputation—except that it was a brand new variant of that fabulous, upper-class drug, cocaine. Moreover, crack could be smoked and the general public mistakenly assumed smoking was safer than needles. And so both the recreational and full-time drug cultures happily embraced crack, viewing it as yet another delightful way to get high, high, high.

By June 1986 *Newsweek* reported that crack had spread to seventeen major American cities and twenty-five states from coast to coast. While crack was indeed much cheaper than powdered cocaine, people soon learned that the drug habit it created was not. Crackheads, as they soon became known, discovered they were not satisfied with a ten dollars pipe or two. They compulsively binged until they ran out of money or collapsed into exhausted sleep. (Over half of New York crack addicts soon were spending more than one thousand dollars a month on crack. Much of this was funded by their own drug sales, meaning they were smoking their earnings. But a fair amount came from selling their worldly goods and then outright crime.) The women often turned tricks on the street or in the crack house, doing anything to get more crack. Men and women committed property crimes of every sort to get a few more dollars for another pipe. *Newsweek* reported that within six months of crack's appearance in New York City, "police believe it is the primary cause of an 18 percent jump in robberies early this year."

To appreciate how cocaine use soared among the urban underclass between 1984 and 1986, consider a Justice Department study testing the urine of men arrested in Manhattan for nondrug felony offenses. In 1984, 4,847 arrestees were tested. That year 42 percent tested positive for cocaine, 21 percent for opiates, 8 percent for methadone, and 12 percent for PCP. Two years later, with crack widely available, a far smaller but comparable sample were tested. This time 83 percent of the Manhattan arrestees tested positive for cocaine—twice the level of two years earlier—while the remaining drugs were pretty much the same. And it is worth remembering that this means cocaine had been used just within the previous two to three days, since it does not show up in urine otherwise.

This time around, the experts were right, and as they had warned, the world of crack was incredibly compulsive. While it attracted and ensnared a goodly number of experimenters—experts estimate 20 percent of powder cocaine users—many of those who became mired deeply tended to be longtime drug abusers like Susan Lydon. One New York study reported,

> The vast majority of crack addicts had prior histories of regular use of marijuana and/or cocaine, and a sizable minority were heroin injectors. In most cases, therefore, these drug abusers tended to add crack to their repertoire of drug consumption. Few reduced their heroin injections or cocaine snorting when beginning crack and what remission occurred was probably the result of spending much of their money on crack. . . . Crack abusers have higher intensities of use than most other drug abusers and the cost and frequency of crack use is much higher than for any other drug.

Longtime addicts whose other drug abuse had allowed some semblance of normal daily life were quickly lost to crack. They risked their jobs, their families. They engaged in dangerous and utterly degraded behavior. One Miami user/dealer was too obsessed with smoking to so much as change his pants for *five* months. He explained, "Everything is rocks, rocks, rocks, rocks. And to tell you the truth I don't even eat well for having all that money. You don't even want to have patience to sit down and have a good dinner. I could tell you rock is . . . I don't know what to say. I just feel sorry for anyone who falls into it."

Crack whores became commonplace. One Miami addict described being virtually imprisoned, and then raped when she balked at instantly providing some sexual favor: "After a while I got sick, and I was all bruised and looked so bad. . . . They just threw me out like I was just some piece of shit." Seasoned drug researcher and professor of criminology James Inciardi was shocked deeply by the new world of crack houses. He had been doing "street studies in Miami, Florida, for more years than I care to remember, and during that time I've had many an experience in the shooting galleries, base houses, and open-air drug and prostitution markets that populate the local drug scene. None of these prepared me, however, with what I was to encounter in crack houses."

The pure depravity of it was deeply disturbing: "I observed what appeared to be the forcible gang-rape of an unconscious child. Emaciated, seemingly comatose, and likely no more than fourteen years of age, she was lying spread-eagled on a filthy mattress while four men in succession had vaginal intercourse with her. Despite what was happening, I was urged not to interfere. After they had finished and left the room, another man came in, and they engaged in oral sex." Inciardi was told this was a "house girl," which meant "a person in the employ of the crack house owner. He gave her food, a place to sleep, some cigarettes and cheap wine, and all the crack she wanted in return for her providing sex—any type and amount of sex—to his crack house customers."

One New York girl named Ladeeta Smith, who had grown up in the Cypress Hills projects of Brooklyn, remembers that when crack hit, "Older people I respected started smoking and fighting and stealing right out in the streets." Then her mother succumbed and disappeared for days at a time. "I saw her high plenty of times. They'd start singing and dancing and acting all jolly. I was disgusted with her. I would walk past her like I didn't know her on the streets." Her mother had another baby, and as soon as she got home, she decamped in search of crack, leaving her young teenage daughter to raise the child.

While the new crackheads were crime-prone lost souls, even more terrifying were the youthful new drug dealers, the alienated young men of the underclass. While street-level drug dealing had been commonplace in the urban slums since the 1950s, the heroin players were relatively established. The American Mafias—Italian and then Chinese—maintained a monopoly on heroin's importation, while carefully selected neighborhood-based criminals took care of distribution. There was not a lot of room—even at the bottom—for newcomers.

Crack was a completely different story. Rapidly recognized as a wide-open free market arena, crack selling had no existing hierarchy. And unlike the Mafia and heroin, the cartel reps in Jackson Heights or back in Colombia were willing to sell to anyone. Making rocks was not too difficult, and swarms of customers—suburban and local—beseiged dealers clamoring for the drug. The *New York Times* would report in the fall of 1987 that in one previously sedate residential part of Queens alone

> dozens of new crack-dealing organizations have emerged to take advantage of the trade, the police say, and some are highly stratified groups with as many as 100 members.
>
> They generally buy their cocaine in Jackson Heights. . . .
>
> Increasingly, the police say, the dealing organizations of southeast Queens are armed with machine pistols, bullet-proof vests and electronic communications equipment. . . . [D]isputes over turf or punishment for betraying an organization often result in killings.

Ladeeta Smith of Brooklyn watched boys she had known since childhood take to the street corners, selling crack to the crowds looking for a high. If trouble was in the air, they'd warn her to go inside. The boys now carried guns and shot at boys from other projects. In all she would see eight friends die.

One fourteen-year-old dealer profiled by the *New York Times* described having three younger sisters, a father dead of an overdose nine years earlier, and a mother who was an on-again, off-again welfare recipient (and drug addict) who had him at fourteen. Now she had trouble making ends meet, what with her boyfriend in prison for selling drugs. The family refrigerator never had enough food in it, and the apartment often lacked electricity because his mother did not pay the light bill. When crack hit, he hustled out there, first for the older boys, then graduating to his own spot with his own gun. Eventually he was forced out by being arrested. But not before he was shot, leaving a permanent limp.

Even veteran drug researcher James Inciardi was taken aback by the youth and criminality of crack dealers in Miami. Inciardi located 254 kids—most not yet fifteen-years-old—deep into crack and crack deal-ing. Each of these kids—85 percent boys, 15 percent girls, 44 percent white, 40 percent black, and 16 percent Hispanic—had committed at least ten serious crimes or one hundred lesser crimes in the previous year: "These 254 youths were responsible for a total of 223,439 crimi-nal offenses during the twelve months prior to interview. Some 61.1 percent of these offenses were drug sales, 11.4 percent were vice offenses, 23.3 percent were property offenses, and 4.2 percent [98 crimes] were major felonies including robberies, assaults, burglaries, and motor vehicle thefts." Almost all the kids had been kicked out of school at some point, often because of selling drugs.

Especially amazing were the drug use histories of these kids. As Inciardi reported:

> They began their drug using careers at age 7.1 years with alco-hol experimentation and had been high by age 8. The majority (61.4 percent) proceeded to "regular use" (3+ times per week) of alcohol, at a mean age of 9 years. The onset of marijuana use began by age 10, followed by regular use of the drug by age 11. Moreover, *all* of the youths reported having used marijuana "regularly." Cocaine use occurred next in the progression, with experimentation by 98.4 percent of the sample at age 11.6 years, followed by regular use less than a year later.
>
> Experimentation with heroin, speed and prescription depressants was clustered in the early part of these juveniles' twelfth year, with only half moving on to the regular use of depressants, 20 percent reporting the regular use of heroin, and less than 5 percent using speed regularly. Some 96.9 percent reported experimentation with crack, however, at the mean age of 12.8 years, with the overwhelming majority of these moving on to the regular use of crack within but a few months.

These young dealers each consumed an average of eight thousand dollar-a-year's worth of crack!

But the early visions of fast, easy bucks in the crack trade turned out to be largely a delusion for the mass of young men working the street. The work was dangerous—guns and shootings were commonplace, as was debilitating addiction to your own product—while arrest and imprisonment were real threats. The violence was pandemic. One woman described how when two young men tried to horn in on a dealer's turf, the dealer walked right up and shot one in the testicles.

Anthropologist Dr. Ansley Hamid was one of numerous academics observing the New York crack epidemic. He and his colleagues saw a great many engaged in the street-level crack trade, but few making any real money. Moreover, he noted, "They don't have a Social Security number. They don't have health insurance. They don't have additional training. They always say they will get rich, but they don't get rich. They just get farther and farther away from a job." Even those making significant money had little understanding of how to accumulate wealth. These were impulsive young men—often with significant drug habits—and it was extremely important to project the right image.

Living in slum communities so isolated from the mainstream of work, these young dealers lack not only work role models but the normal network of contacts that other teenagers use. They can't get a summer job in their father's or mother's office or factory. Too many don't have fathers, and their mothers are on welfare, and so they have little idea how to go about looking for or finding a job. One dealer said, "I've never called a man 'Daddy.' I've never used that word. I don't even know what a daddy is."

By the late 1980s, the already embarrassingly high U.S. homicide rates reflected the Wild West atmosphere of crack-turf wars among dealers. In 1985, for instance, New York City had 1,384 murders, Washington, D.C., had 147. These figures were already several multiples of what they had been in the 1950s when the postwar drug culture was just getting going and most American families—black and white—still had fathers present in the home. By 1986 most American cities were in the throes of fast-rising mayhem. In New York, the murder toll rose from 1,384 to 1,461; in the nation's capital, from 147 to 197. A year later, the murder rate had increased yet again in both cities, now to 1,672 and 227. In March 1988, the *New York Times* wrote, "Young and violent drug gangs, in brutal territorial battles and in calculated campaigns to terrorize neighborhoods, are believed to be responsible for as many as 500 slayings in upper Manhattan in the last five years, according to law enforcement authorities." By 1989, New York City hit a record 1,905 homicides.

Crack cocaine created extremely violent new drug-dealing patterns, attracting thousands of young men with no better game plan in life. City neighborhoods that had once been relatively placid suddenly turned into twenty-four–hour drug bazaars. When these hordes of immature drug dealers acquired new high-powered weapons (so easily purchased thanks to lax American gun laws), you had a recipe for disaster. From 1985 to 1991 teenage male gun murders soared 154 percent, becoming the leading cause of death. "The drug dealers give the kids guns. Guns are the tools of their trade," explained one academic. Then "the young people dealing drugs started carrying their guns around with them, to school and in their neighborhoods, and then other teenagers began copying them. . . . [T]he process of younger and younger people arming themselves has become self-perpetuating." By the end of the 1980s, firearm homicides by black youths had risen to 68 per 100,000, eleven times that of white teenagers.

To put this into truly depressing perspective, compare the horrendous U.S. homicide rate for men aged 15 to 24 with that of other industrialized countries. Because of the astronomical rate for young blacks, the overall American rate in 1987 hit almost 22 homicides per 100,000 young men. In Scotland, that figure would be 5 homicides per 100,000 young men. In Austria, it was not even 1 homicide per 100,000 young men, but 1 for every 300,000 young men. This meant that for every 250 young black men being gunned down in the United States, *one* Austrian young man would be shot and killed. America had a long, ugly history of violence. The crack trade now fomented yet more violence in an already violent subworld.

Crack cocaine was completely new and worse in every possible way than the familiar illegal street drugs that had been around since the turn of the century. Researcher Inciardi recorded hair-raising descriptions of what he witnessed in Miami crack houses:

> a woman purchasing crack, with an infant tucked under her arm—so neglected that she had maggots crawling out of her diaper; a man "skin-popping" his toddler with a small dose of heroin, so the child would remain quietly sedated and not interrupt a crack-smoking session; people in various states of excitement and paranoia, crouching in the corners of smoking rooms inhaling from "the devil's dick" (the stem of the crack pipe); arguments, fist fights, stabbings and shootings over crack, the price of crack, the quantity and quality of crack, and the use and sharing of crack; any manner and variety of sexual activity—by individuals and/or groups . . . people in convulsions and seizures, brought on by crack use.

Crack addicts got very wired. They felt surges of energy and prowess that they blew off with varying levels of violence. Crack set off crime waves wherever it was sold because crack addicts needed steady infusions of money and were cranked up enough to take crazy chances.

There was a distinctly new and scary dimension to the crack epidemic: the women. Heroin, with all the needles, had never appealed much to women. Maybe 10 percent of heroin addicts were women.

Drug culture always had been mainly a male game. There was never much thought in either the recreational drug culture or the full-time drug culture about the consequences of drug-using on family life or on children. The drug culture was always about instant gratification and hedonism and being hip. Children, who require consistent twenty-four-hours-a-day care, constant love, and much hard work, did not fit in anywhere in that cosmos. Whether it was a onetime intellectual and Harvard professor such as Timothy Leary, who admitted completely neglecting his motherless teenaged children to pursue greater highs and better orgasms, or a literate but self-absorbed addict such as Susan Lydon, whose daughter finally sought refuge with others, or the decamped mother of Ladeeta Smith of Brooklyn, members of the drug culture rarely were thinking about anyone but themselves.

When poor women discovered crack, their already fatherless children paid a terrible price. The heroin drug culture had destroyed meaningful paternity; now crack removed many of the mothers. Female addicts accounted for about a third of those stuck on cocaine. The drug began to destroy what was left of family life among the nation's underclass. Beny J. Primm, a seasoned veteran of the sad fallout of New York's postwar drug culture, sounded the alarm: "It is such a devastating addiction that these people are willing to abandon food and water and child to take care of their crack habit."

In *The Promised Land*, Nicholas Lemann described one welfare mother's experience when her female set in a Chicago public housing project began smoking cocaine:

> By 1985, Juanita realized that she had become a drug addict . . . she smoked cocaine all through her pregnancy. Her brother Johnnie moved into her apartment and got on cocaine, too. . . . Just before Juanita was due to give birth, the usual crowd came over to smoke cocaine. . . . [Juanita] got to the point where she turned her public-aid identification card over to the dope man. When her check came, she would meet him at a local "currency exchange"—a storefront operation that received welfare checks directly from the public-aid department . . . —and turn all the money over to him in payment for her drug debts.

She sold her food stamps at seventy cents on the dollar, stopped paying her rent and electric bill, and began shoplifting regularly at downtown department stores. She stopped smoking cocaine only when a seizure landed her in the hospital. This was a woman with two small children and pregnant with a third.

Once upon a time, in the early decades of AFDC, families were assigned social workers whose role was to supervise and advise. But between the explosion in welfare numbers and the welfare rights movement (which viewed any oversight as an invasion of privacy), social workers no longer visited families or knew what went on. How many welfare checks went to buy drugs instead of supporting children? No one could say, but drug dealers referred to those days when welfare checks arrived as Mother's Day.

The huge escalation in female addiction was especially poignant for the affected children. At New York's Harlem Hospital, for decades about 5 percent of young mothers routinely had tested positive for heroin. In a typical year the hospital would request possible foster care for seventy-some drug-exposed babies. From August 1985 to August 1986 an ominous new trend surfaced. Now 15 percent of new mothers tested positive for cocaine (remember, this means using the drug within the previous two or three days). In 1986, the hospital referred three hundred newborns to social services, *quadruple* what it had been, mainly because of crack. Babies born with opiates in their system had never shown any long-term consequence once weaned off the drug. This was not so for those exposed in utero to cocaine.

A study at Kings County Hospital showed these babies were often premature and eight times as likely to be underweight. And far more vulnerable. Infant mortality rose in central Harlem from 16 deaths per 1,000 births in 1984 to an estimated 27 deaths per 1,000 births in 1986. This was not surprising once it was understood that when a woman was smoking crack, she was diminishing her fetus's oxygen supply. As crack addiction spread, Bronx-Lebanon Hospital saw the number of babies sent directly to foster care jump from 2 percent to 15 percent. When columnist Anna Quindlen visited that hospital's nursery, a nurse cautioned her about the crack-exposed babies: "They don't like it if you move too much. Some of them don't like it if you hold them either."

Pediatricians described those children most severely affected as suffering from

> seizures, cerebral palsy, or mental retardation. Most children have an array of symptoms that included hyperactivity, sudden mood swings, extreme passivity, apparent lack of emotion, slow language acquisition or mild speech impairment. Many, overwhelmed by stimuli like noise or piles of toys, have trouble interpreting verbal signals, are easily frustrated, find it hard to concentrate and learn something one day only to forget it the next.

Crack made heroin look like the good old days. The cocaine mothers were strangely cold. "My impression with cocaine is that the cocaine abusers don't care," said the chairman of Washington Hospital Center's neonatology unit. "The heroin mothers would come and they'd relate to their babies and learn how to take care of their babies. The coke mothers, they don't come. We often have to go out and really chase them down so they'll come and take their babies home." At first, experts came out with incredible and alarming figures of 375,000 crack babies a year, or one in ten births. Eventually, it was estimated in 1991 by the Center for the Future of Children that about 2 to 3 percent of American babies were exposed to cocaine in utero. This was still a shockingly high figure 75,000 to 100,000 annually.

The sad wreckage wrought by crack created legions of lost souls. Unwilling to use money for anything but more crack, they soon swelled the ranks of that group dubbed the "homeless." Advocates argued that inadequate low-income housing was the issue. And for some, this was surely so. But most of the homeless were either the mentally ill left to fend for themselves or drug addicts determined to preserve every dollar for drug purchases. In a major article on the issue, Christopher Jencks pointed out that

> 66 per cent of the single adults tested in New York's general-purpose shelters had traces of cocaine in their urine. In family shelters, the figure was 16 percent. . . . [H]eavy drug use makes marginally employable adults even less employable, eats up money that would otherwise be available to pay rent, and makes people's friends and relatives less willing to shelter them. . . . Drug use also makes it harder for the homeless to get back into conventional housing. . . . No one knows how many of the homeless could get off the streets if they stopped buying drugs and alcohol, but it is certainly safe to assume that many spend much of their income on such substances.

As if all these social disasters were not enough, then there was AIDS. In 1987, New York doctors began noticing a soaring number of babies born infected with syphillis. Once the rare, occasional case, in that year 160 babies were born infected. Reported the *New York Times*, "Doctors blame the rampant sexual activity of crack-addicted mothers." From there, it was just a matter of time before the sexually-transmitted disease was HIV. After all, crack research had revealed that a great many of those deeply hooked on crack were IV-heroin addicts, a major risk group for AIDS. They were now engaging in compulsive, decidedly unsafe sex in crack houses. By 1994, one half of those newly diagnosed as infected with HIV got it from intravenous drug abuse. For another fourth of those newly diagnosed, the HIV was "heterosexually transmitted." Four fifths of that fourth were women who had "sex with men who got infected when they injected drugs. Many had sex with these men during crack binges, or while they were abusing other drugs or alcohol, when they were not inclined to think about safe sex. . . . [A]s many as half of these women are crack addicts."

To put a human face on this sea of grim figures, there is the story of Ladeeta Smith, the Brooklyn girl who had watched her mother disappear into the netherworld of crack in the mid 1980s. In 1990 her mother was arrested, and Ladeeta and her two siblings were rescued from utter neglect by their maternal grandmother. Then, in 1991, Ladeeta learned that her mother, only thirty-nine years old, was HIV positive. Her mother's health deteriorated swiftly. She lost weight, her hair fell out, she became demented. By the time Ladeeta's mother went to a Bronx nursing home, her own daughter barely could recognize the emaciated woman covered with sores. In 1993, Ladeeta's mother died, leaving behind three minors with no one but a grandmother to see them to adulthood.

Or another face was that of Jennifer Torres, who was all of fourteen when her mother died of AIDS at age thirty-six, another casualty of the drug culture. A *New York Times* article described how Jennifer and her younger sisters long had lived with their grandmother because of the mother's drug addiction.

In a theater skit, Jennifer had a monologue with her dead mother. "AIDS didn't have to happen to you," she said. "You didn't have to die, but you preferred your friends, drugs, the streets, over me."

To see the bigger community picture, envision Frick Junior High School in Oakland, California, where the principal estimated in 1992 that more than half of the 750 students (virtually all black) did not live with a mother or a father any longer. The children apparently were extremely shamed by their state. When asked, they "avert their eyes and whisper that everything is fine at home long after their parents are lost to crack or locked in jail, and they are living with granma, auntie or a stranger." Understandably, these teenagers were suspicious, angry, and wounded. "They are distrustful of adults, greedy for attention and convinced that they must be worthless or their parents would not have left them."

Yet even as the full horrors of crack were understood and it acquired a reputation far more fearsome than heroin's, the criminal classes began moving the crack trade out of the big urban centers and across the nation. Two groups played pivotal roles: Jamaican posses and Los Angeles street gangs. Journalist Michael Massing described the highly violent Jamaican gangs as getting started during that Caribbean island's 1980 elections, which was marred by seven hundred fatalities. Once the posses had served their purposes of electoral intimidation, Jamaican authorities cracked down on them, and tens of thousands of posse members fled to the United States.

Drug culture magnifies and exacerbates existing social problems. The Jamaicans highlighted the very high price the United States was paying for its basic failure to control its own borders. After all, the Colombian traffickers busy in Miami and New York were almost certainly not possessors of valid green cards, nor were the Dominicans in upper Manhattan. Now, the Jamaicans were joining these other waves of illegal alien criminals to wreak havoc across the country. Similarly, lax American gun laws allowed all these foreign criminals to arm themselves better than local law enforcement, stockpiling Uzi machine guns and AR-13 assault rifles. These same lax gun laws also enabled the Colombians to export huge caches of weapons for their reign of terror back home.

Virtually every American town—no matter its size—always has had a "wrong side of the tracks," a neighborhood or community that is home to the local poor and troubled classes. The Jamaicans made it their business to introduce crack sales in these vulnerable populations. Massing described how, in New York State, Jamaicans were moving crack up Interstate 87, "hitting such tiny Hudson Valley towns as Newburgh, Kingston, and Saratoga Springs. In West Virginia, the posses have established crack houses in Martinsburg (population 13,000) and Charles Town (3,000). From there they have moved out along Interstate 81, shipping crack as far north as Chambersburg, Pa., and as far south as Roanoke, Virginia. . . . Today, Jamaicans are believed to control 35 to 40 percent of the nation's crack network."

Newsweek described how the Jamaican crack dealers invaded tiny Martinsburg, home of the Mountain State Apple Harvest Festival. Coming originally as migrant workers to pick apples and peaches at harvest time, many stayed on to deal coke and crack, creating an open-air drug supermarket mere blocks from the police station. Supplied by couriers shuttling between Washington, Miami, and New York, as many as fifty dealers could be found selling drugs brazenly in broad daylight.

The customers, pouring into Martinsburg from all over, were characterized by the local police chief as "all ethnic groups, age groups and every profession." Homicides shot up from the average one or two murders a year to twenty murders within eighteen months, as rival posses battled it out. Overwhelmed, local police called in the feds. In the fall of 1986, about two hundred agents cleared out twenty-six drug dens and arrested thirty-five dealers. The dealing quieted down considerably.

While the Jamaicans were spreading misery from the East Coast, from the West Coast descended the native-grown black gangs of Los Angeles. By the late 1980s black street gangs from LA had fanned out across the country. More than ten thousand gang members were said to be dealing drugs in some fifty cities from Baltimore to Seattle.

The crack epidemic well illustrates what happens when you have unprecedented availability of a drug combined with rising social marginality among poor and working-class people, as real income for all but the rich declined during the Reagan and Bush years. Finally, both of these factors were exacerbated by serious ignorance about the extraordinary perils of the drug in question. (Because crack was smoked, many equated it at first to marijuana.) While the middle-class and casual use of cocaine dropped significantly in the late eighties, a new core group of drug addicts developed. Moreover, as the recession deepened and lingered, cocaine use rose again. One NIDA official pointed out that rising drug use correlated rather well with rising unemployment, a telling demonstration of the importance of social marginality in drug culture.

In the wake of the nation's cocaine debacle, the nation's half-million heroin addicts were now joined by two million cocaine addicts. In 1900, one American in three hundred had been a drug addict. But many had been respectable people hooked through medical treatment. By World War II, the number of addicts had declined tenfold, to one in three thousand. After the heroin epidemic of the late sixties, the addiction figure rose to about one in four hundred, virtually all of whom could be classed as antisocial addicts. During the 1980s, the cocaine and crack epidemic added another two million to the ranks of the addicted. By 1992, one American in one hundred was a drug addict. In one short decade, the cocaine and crack epidemic had multiplied the misery fourfold.

"Coke Is Addicting, Health-Ruining, Home-Wrecking, and Worst of All, Career-Wrecking."

—Hollywood TV executive,
TV GUIDE, 1989

$\mathbf{A}$s the bad news about cocaine rolled in, the drug was undergoing a major public relations reversal. The media image of cocaine users as glitzy party-goers at Manhattan's Studio 54 was being superseded by scarifying footage of scuzzy crack-heads selling body and soul for one more pipe in the ghetto crack house. The glamour was gone. No longer was it Woody Allen flubbing the coke rituals or glittery stars sporting little spoons. Cocaine had become the drug of the poor, the affliction of depraved losers. By 1991 director Spike Lee presented cocaine as utterly corrupting in *Jungle*

Fever, a movie that took viewers into the nightmarish world of a Harlem crack house.

The deaths of Len Bias and Don Rogers, the violent spread of crack, the soaring legions of new addicts, the burned-out casualties of the long-gone Age of Aquarius, the growing use of drugs on the job and in the nation's military ranks, the idea that teenagers were high every day at school, the connection of drugs to AIDS—all these forced the country's young elite to reluctantly reexamine the counterculture zeitgeist that viewed drugs favorably. After almost twenty-five years, the baby boomers' romance with illegal drugs was beginning to sour.

Leading the way were not the baby boomers, however, but parents who had come of age just before drugs became rampant. These mothers and fathers now were worried deeply by widespread pot-smoking among their own adolesecent children. Typical were Pat and Bill Barton of Naples, Florida, who in 1978 discovered that their seventeen-year-old son and fifteen-year-old daughter were smoking marijuana daily. The boy was in trouble at school and had wrecked the family car; the girl's boyfriend was a dealer. Taken aback, the Bartons contacted all the parents of their children's friends. It soon became evident that Naples High School was awash with drugs, especially marijuana. In a two-week period, two hundred of the school's fifteen hundred students were photographed using, buying, or selling drugs.

The sad truth was that Naples probably typified high schools all over America. By 1980, the high-water mark for middle-class illegal drug use in the United States (with the exception of adult cocaine users), fully two out of three high school seniors had tried illegal drugs and more than a *third* used them regularly. While the majority of these young drug users were smoking marijuana, almost 6 percent were using heroin or cocaine. It is perhaps no coincidence that the worst year for overall drug use among high school seniors was also the year SAT scores hit bottom. (Scores dropped steadily from a combined average of 956 in 1969—when drugs arrived in most high schools—to 890 in 1980 when drug use peaked and was at its worst.)

In Atlanta, Georgia, another group of parents were astonished to realize their junior high school children were smoking marijuana. One mother had watched with growing concern as her son "gradually lost interest in both school and sports. He had trouble sleeping, his appetite was erratic, and he became moody and uncommunicative. Because David was her oldest son, for a while [his mother] clung to the belief that this behavior was a normal symptom of puberty."

Then one night the boy had a series of convulsions. The family pediatrician talked to the boy for a while and then "explained that the convulsions were probably caused by a marijuana joint laced with PCP. . . . He advised [the mother] to trust her observations that pot smoking was harmful to her son, and not to be intimidated by the benign image of marijuana projected by the media."

Soon, a group of Atlanta parents had organized into the DeKalb County Families in Action to confront this extremely youthful drug culture. Parents and teachers seeking information or help were appalled to find virtually everything written about illegal drugs, including and especially marijuana, had a conciliatory tone encouraging "responsible" use. And that popular culture music and movies treated drug use as hip and amusing. Not surprisingly, they encountered plenty of parents who preferred not to acknowledge what was going on. But slowly but surely Families in Action brought around the local schools. Then they took on the paraphernalia shops, convincing the Georgia state legislature to pass three laws that soon closed local head shops down.

And so was born the parents' movement known as Families in Action, grassroots groups completely opposed to the notion that teenagers would inevitably use drugs—or that using drugs was somehow liberating and beneficial. Students themselves, surrounded by the drug culture, were quite ready to question those assumptions. In 1979, a third of all high school students (not just seniors) had tried smoking marijuana. About half of that third continued to get stoned. Clearly, like a lot of parents and teachers, teenagers saw that kids who regularly used drugs often lost interest in school and extracurricular activities, and became aloof from non–drug-using family and friends.

The Atlanta parents found their best argument in the "gone" and "wasted" older teenagers who were involved deeply in drugs:

> The kids wondered about the hollow-chested, tired-looking teenage dealers who drifted in and out of their neighborhood. Was it the drug itself or the drug lifestyle that made them seem so lifeless and anemic? . . . Visions of 18- to 20-year-old "pot heads," still loitering around adolescent hangouts, haunted all their minds. . . . Their years of drug use had contributed to render them psychologically dependent, physically lethargic, academically impaired, and vocationally limited. They had not achieved the independence from childhood and parents that is the main task of adolescence. Because they were not able to cope with the more adult lifestyles and responsibilities of their nondrug-abusing peers, they resorted to the company of younger adolescents.

This time around no one was saying that smoking marijuana doomed users to becoming heroin addicts. Nor that pot would drive you crazy. Public health authorities tended to view marijuana as benign because it caused little obvious "morbidity and mortality." No one was dying (as they did with heroin) and no one was suffering any obvious physical ill effects. Yet for parents, that public health standard was not relevant. What they were observing in their kids was something that would be dubbed the "amotivational syndrome," or low-level zoning out. Marijuana gained a reputation for causing short-term memory loss. Parents also were observing a general alienation and loss of joy in living. Kids who were getting high every day obviously were not devoting those hours to more normal teenage activities—such as school work or athletics or drama club. Instead, they were spaced out. Drug culture veteran Mitchell Rosenthal, president of New York's Phoenix House, put it this way: "To grow, to develop, to achieve adulthood, adolescents must cope with the emotional storms and squalls of the troubled teen-age period. If they turn to marijuana, they establish a pattern of escaping rather than dealing with reality. They do not learn how to cope."

By the early 1980s, four thousand formal parent organizations all over America had modeled themselves after Families in Action. By 1980 one of the most active Georgia mothers, Sue Rusche, had entrée to the Carter White House, was a familiar media figure, and was bringing her antidrug views to a highly receptive Congress. When testifying before the Select Committee on Narcotics in 1979 on the booming drug paraphernalia industry, Rusche described such damning products as marijuana pipes disguised as Star Wars space guns, products obviously designed to appeal to kids. Or comic books "teaching the fine points of smoking dope and snorting cocaine. We are witnessing the emergence of an industry that glamorizes and promotes illicit drugs . . . [and] is developing a new market of illicit drug users—our 12- to 17-year-old children." In the wake of these hearings before the Select Committee and then the Senate Judiciary Committee, the U.S. Justice Department developed a model anti–drug-paraphernalia law, and in state after state the drug paraphernalia business soon found itself practically legislated out of existence. (Some hung on by doing mail order from the few states that did not enact the model law.)

Then director of NIDA Robert DuPont recalls, "With the help of the parents movement, I gained an entirely new perspective on the nation's drug problem: Tolerance towards marijuana use, which I had thought to be modern and scientifically based, was, I came to realize, both unreasonable and destructive." DuPont could see from household survey figures that teenage marijuana use was rising yearly in the 1970s.

Prompted by my new tutors in the parents movement I saw that something had gone terribly wrong with our national policy on marijuana. . . . In 1978 I became convinced, finally and firmly, that public support for decriminalization of marijuana use, which was then growing, was encouraging the normalization of marijuana use in America. That attitude shift from strict prohibition to greater permissiveness was itself contributing to the rising levels of the use of marijuana, especially by youth. The prospect of marijuana being used by youth at levels similar to, or even greater than, their levels of use of alcohol and tobacco was clearly contrary to the nation's public health interest. . . .

I also learned another painful lesson at that time. When it came to drugs, the "experts" whom I had come to rely on, the laboratory and other scientists, were just as vulnerable to fad and fashion in their ideas as everyone else. It was the American parents—not the scientists and certainly not the drug bureaucrats such as myself—who had seen the devastating effects of marijuana on their children and who played Paul Revere waking up the nation.

Determined to counter the prodrug forces, the grassroots parents groups opened a Washington office, the National Federation of Parents for Drug-Free Youth. They began "monitoring and fighting advertising and media messages that support or encourage drug use. . . . Numerous stores and retail firms have altered their marketing inventories as a result of the parents' influence. For example, a chain of retail shops no longer stocks magazines that promote drug use, and a department store chain has stopped selling products that are bought by young people to hide their drugs."

When Ronald Reagan took office in 1980, First Lady Nancy Reagan became a high-profile ally of the concerned parents, coining the much ridiculed "Just Say No" antidrug campaign. Yet here one had, for the first time in many a year, a high-level authority figure sympathetically urging children to eschew drugs and the zoned-out high for an active, engaged, interesting life. This was the ideal Reagan administration program. It articulated an anti-elite grassroots groundswell, cost virtually nothing, and gained much media attention. If much of that attention was media snobs making fun of Nancy Reagan, all the better. It just showed how out of touch they were with ordinary Americans. In 1982 the White House hosted several thousand parent-group leaders and reaffirmed its embrace of the drug-free philosophy. Moreover, the "Just

Say No" campaign dovetailed nicely with growing youthful disenchantment with drugs. Though it was not much noticed at the time, throughout the 1980s youthful drug use declined steadily, especially among the middle class.

Nor was it only parents who were demonstrating growing grassroots concern about the societal effects of illegal drugs. Another major group was employers, a natural Republican constituency. The first national publication to raise the issue had been the *Wall Street Journal* in a lead story back in 1970. The article related how New York Telephone was using "private plainclothesmen to detect employee dope-pushing rings. Recently, the agents uncovered a heroin ring operating in a company men's room. In the past year the utility has let go 50 to 60 employees who apparently were involved in narcotics."

Employers expressed concern that workers hooked on drugs "would not hesitate to steal to support the habit." The whole issue was so new, employers were still groping to get a handle on it. Some companies were described as using urine tests "as part of prehiring or annual physical examinations." But the primitive tests picked up only opiates, not marijuana use. The article warned, "The problem hasn't reached major proportions, but it clearly is growing swiftly and there is every indication that things will get a lot worse before they get better."

And indeed they did, as each successive year saw another wave of the drug-using baby boomers move into the world of work. By 1986, as adult middle-class cocaine use was peaking, *Time* ran a major cover story detailing the costs of on-the-job drug use. Aside from the obvious peril of theft by drug users needing money, they missed far more workdays and were three times as prone to injure themselves or someone else.

The article said that after a fatal 1983 air cargo crash at Newark airport, an autopsy on the pilot showed he had been smoking marijuana, perhaps while flying. In 1979 a Conrail employee high on marijuana missed a stop signal and crashed into another train, killing two people. In 1985, a New York air traffic controller who was injecting three grams of cocaine daily at work became confused and put a jumbo jet on a collision course with a small private plane. Disaster was averted only because the small plane swooped down at the last moment. Also in 1985 a computer operator at American Airlines high on marijuana failed to install a computer tape into the airlines reservation system. The company estimated that the eight hours the computer was down cost it $19 million. Gradually, corporate America began to see that drug use was not just a private matter, but an on-the-job hazard that was endangering lives and costing significant money.

One lawyer described "a stock-trading associate of hers who was sometimes guided in his decisions by stimulants. One day all his clients received telephone calls informing them that the world was coming to an end and that he was supervising their portfolios with that in mind. The world would end by water, said the financier, but the right people would turn into birds and escape. He and some of his clients already were growing feathers and wattles.

" 'Some gonna fly and some gonna die,' the broker intoned darkly to his startled customers." These were not words to reassure those whose savings were in this man's control.

Faced with growing evidence of drug-impaired job performance and accidents, some American businesses began in the late 1970s quietly screening job applicants by requesting urine tests. (By this time, tests could reasonably accurately detect not only opiates, but marijuana and cocaine use.) By the time *Time* ran its 1986 cover story, a *fourth* of the nation's Fortune 500 companies had resorted to this measure. They included Exxon, IBM, Lockheed, Shearson Lehman, Federal Express, United Airlines, TWA, and Hoffman-LaRoche. For those employees whose erratic behavior made it obvious they were high, employee-assistance programs began offering referrals to drug counseling and treatment.

Nor was it only American business that was grappling with drug-impaired employees. The U.S. military also was being pushed to confront the issue. The widespread use of drugs, especially heroin, by American soldiers in South Vietnam in the early 1970s was well known. There the military had been extraordinarily lucky. For it turned out that returning troops (forced to show themselves drug-free via urine tests before being allowed to come home) had exhibited little inclination to use heroin back in the States. And so the top brass apparently had deluded themselves that drug use had been some brief and unhappy aberration. Consequently, in late 1980, the Department of Defense had been shocked badly by a survey of armed services drug use. Marijuana use within the previous month among young servicemen had tallied up thus: army, 40 percent, air force, 20 percent, navy, 47 percent, and marine corps, 47 percent. Use of any drug (excluding alcohol) was 27 percent.

Unable to believe that almost half its young sailors were smoking marijuana and more than a fourth using others drugs, mainly cocaine, U.S. Navy brass in 1981 conducted anonymous urinalyses of 160,000 enlisted men aged 18 to 25. "The results," says Paul J. Mulloy, who directed the navy's antidrug program, "slammed home the truth: 47.8 percent of those tested had traces of marijuana metabolite in their urine." The navy immediately launched a series of ten actions to beef up antidrug actions and messages. These included everything from testing "all recruits at the accession point" to establishing "Alcohol and Drug Abuse Control Officer positions on all major staffs."

As all this was shaking out, a spectacular aircraft crash at night aboard the aircraft carrier USS *Nimitz* killed fourteen people and injured forty-two. The disaster was caught on film and shown repeatedly on television news. "As tragic as that was, autopsies revealed that cannabis was present in nine of the crew members working on the carrier's flight deck. The pilot of the jet aircraft, a reserve Marine Corps officer who was qualifying for night carrier operations, had been taking a prescribed antihistamine preparation (brompheniramine) without the knowledge of either his commanding officer or his flight surgeon." The monetary damage to aircraft of the May 26, 1981, crash was $53 million. Congress angrily demanded the military services get serious about drugs. This demand coincided with the marked improvement in drug-testing technology, a field the National Institute on Drug Abuse had targeted specially for development.

The navy announced that starting February 1, 1982, every officer and sailor was subject to unannounced random urinalysis that could detect cannabis, cocaine, barbiturates, amphetamines, PCP, and opiates. "Testing would also be extended to accidents, inspections, probable-cause incidents, and rehabilitation procedures. . . . Help would be provided to any member of the Navy, whether officer or enlisted personnel, who sought help in a nonmanipulative way. The help would be professional, and immunity from prosecution would be guaranteed unless manipulation was involved." Officers who tested positive would be dismissed with less than honorable discharges. Enlisted personnel would be given one more chance and then similarly booted.

While the navy was the most gung ho—because its members had the highest rates of drug use—the other military branches were also committed to urine testing as the best means of reducing drug use. By 1983, the U.S. military was conducting 10 million urine tests a year. Technical standards were established, and NIDA used these to certify all laboratories used for testing. All positive specimens were frozen and retained so servicemen and women could contest positive findings.

This huge and relatively novel undertaking was not without its serious screwups. *Time* reported that in the army "the program was developed so fast and handled so sloppily that it gave drug testing a bad name. Hundreds of soldiers claimed that they were falsely accused of being drug users because of inaccurate results. [The test was 2 percent inaccurate. Positives were routinely retested.]

"In July 1984, the Army admitted that in tests of 60,000 soldiers, about half of the urine samples had been mishandled. In many cases, samples were mixed up in the lab, and service members received results from specimens that were not their own."

Naturally, urine testing as a strategy for eliminating or reducing drug use was highly controversial. Who could be enthused about having to produce a little jar of personal fluid for people suspicious of your activities? Especially if that jar's contents could cause you to be denied employment or fired from your job? Lawyers—with the American Civil Liberties Union leading the way—happily leapt into the fray, and every aspect of drug testing was challenged ardently. Courts quickly agreed in the innumerable legal cases—especially in public sector jobs—that urinalysis constituted a "search" under the Fourth Amendment of the Constitution. On March 21, 1989, the U.S. Supreme Court ruled in two cases—the National Treasury's Employees Union v. Raab and Skinner v. Railroad Labor Executives Association—that drug testing was constitutional. The court ruled testing was a "reasonable search" in light of what was at stake—the ability of employers, coworkers, and the public to know that work sites were as safe as possible. Did anyone really want to be the innocent passenger in the jumbo jet heading for the private plane, thanks to the cocaine-high air controller?

While everyone (just about) can agree that those in such high-hazard jobs as directing jumbo jets or the military must be clean as a whistle, beyond that large gray areas lurk. This is especially because marijuana metabolites—the most frequently detected drug—remain in the body for weeks after use. A person could test positive but not be high at all. Thousands of disputes have worked their way through labor arbitration and the courts over just such questions. Nonetheless, as the measurable benefits of reduced drug use on the job have become incontestable, businesses and their employees have become resigned to this unappetizing but effective solution to those who think they can use illegal drugs and still do a good day's work. When Georgia Power Company instituted a comprehensive drug-testing program in 1981, accidents at its Vogtle nuclear power plant project were 5.4 for every 20,000 man-hours. By 1985, there had been a 90 percent decrease, to 0.49 per 20,000 man-hours. Southern Pacific Railroad experienced a 72 percent drop in the number of accidents; on-the-job injuries and sick days also were reduced. A Laurel, Maryland, paving and painting company saw its worker's compensation costs dive from one hundred thousand dollars a year to thirty thousand dollars after putting in a drug program. The impetus? A dump truck driven off a bridge, two that crashed into each other, a heavy equipment operator running down a foreman. The military reported that drug testing had helped cut drug use in half by 1986.

So, slowly but surely through the early 1980s, public antipathy and concern were building over the incredible, undermining spread of the drug culture. Many parents were unhappy, many employers were worried. When crack then took off in 1986, coinciding with the highly public deaths of college basketball star Len Bias and Cleveland Brown safety Don Rogers, the media went into an understandable feeding frenzy. "Suddenly," recalls journalist Elaine Shannon,

> newspapers, television shows, and magazines from *People* to *Sports Illustrated* to *Good Housekeeping* were packed with horror stories about cocaine abuse. It seemed that everyone wanted to "confess" an addiction: movie stars, teenagers, physicians, housewives, stockbrokers, and football players eagerly related intimate details of cocaine-ravaged lives. The CBS News contribution, *Forty-eight Hours on Crack Street*, earned the highest Nielsen rating of any documentary in the past five years. *Life* magazine's issue of October 1986 showed a young man puffing on a crack pipe. The headline read, "I AM A COKE ADDICT"—What Happens When Nice Guys Get Hooked.

The accumulated consequences of the drug culture finally were hitting home for tens of millions of Americans and their families. That year, a *New York Times*/CBS poll listed drug abuse as the "nation's leading overall concern."

By the summer of 1986, with midterm congressional elections looming, politicians plugged into the growing national alarm over drugs, especially cocaine and crack. Republican pollster Richard Wirthlin was one who put his finger to the wind in the spring of that year and picked up the rising grassroots worry. So far, Nancy Reagan had been the administration's antidrug apostle, visiting schools and urging children to say no to drugs. After Len Bias died, Mrs. Reagan had had an Op-ed piece in the *Washington Post* saying, "It's too late to save Len Bias, but it's not too late to save the young kids who idolized him. For their sake, I implore you to be unyielding and inflexible and outspoken in your opposition to drugs." This sort of talk made a great many sophisticated people roll their eyeballs. After all, everyone knew kids *would* try drugs. All this "drug-free" talk was simply unrealistic. Yet Mrs. Reagan had a shrewd appreciation for human motivation: restigmatizing drugs could serve as an important and powerful means of persuasion. The disdain of one's friends and family would be far more upsetting than the distant threat of law enforcement. Perhaps because Mrs. Reagan had been an actress, she understood the full power of media-generated messages.

In six years in office, Ronald Reagan never had made a single significant speech about drugs. Once, back on October 2, 1982, he had joined Nancy in making a radio broadcast against drugs. Now, as the public worry about cocaine rose by the month, it was decided that the president should jump on Nancy's bandwagon. Ever avuncular, President Reagan called a press conference at the White House on August 4, 1986. He said, "Starting today, Nancy's crusade to deprive drug peddlers and suppliers of their customers becomes America's crusade." The six stated goals were: a drug-free workplace; drug-free schools; ensuring public safety along with treatment for users; greater international cooperation; strengthened law enforcement; and expanding public awareness and prevention. The president made clear that he believed that drug testing "in both the public and private sectors was a key to curtailing the problem."

With that, the inside-the-Beltway war on drugs frenzy was launched in earnest. Throughout the 1980s, Democrats and Republicans in Congress had been badgering the White House to get interested in the problem beyond Nancy Reagan's "Just Say No" campaign. They especially wanted the Reagan administration to restore the deep budget cuts that had been made year after year in both drug-law enforcement and drug treatment.

From 1981 to 1986 federal drug law enforcement program funds had shrunk from $154 million per year to $117 million. "Who ever thought [Reaganites] would turn their back on law enforcement?" Ed Jurith, chief legal counsel to the Select Committee on Narcotics, rhetorically asked a journalist. "Even when Congress proposed money for law enforcement they tried to budget it out—and this was law enforcement, lock-them-up-and-put-them-in-jail kind of stuff." The Reagan administration sharply cut its antidrug law enforcement even as the cocaine epidemic was hitting, reducing DEA agents by almost half.

Drug treatment funding fared no better. The Reagan administration decided early on that drug treatment should be run by the states. This was a major shift, because the federal National Institute on Drug Abuse (NIDA) had funded and directed treatment ever since the Nixon administration rapidly had established treatment centers in the early 1970s. In 1981, federal drug treatment money, then $160 million, had not been increased at all during the recent highly inflationary years. The Reagan administration cut this figure by 25 percent and then bundled it into overall block grants also intended for treating alcoholism and mental health problems. Effectively, the federal government was both cutting its support and ceding its leadership role on drug treatment to the states. In 1981 the overall block grant figure dropped from $637 million to $492 million. The next year it took another hit, down to $432 million.

In light of these fiscal and political realities, one can appreciate how intensely galling it was to Democrats to watch as that master politician Ronald Reagan and his administration—which knowingly had cut back the nation's antidrug programs and displayed little concern—now virtuously launched a crusade against drugs. For Reagan had not stopped with his little White House speech about drug-free schools and jobs. He then had announced he would recall American ambassadors from "all the world's drug-producing countries to Washington next month for 'special consultations." And just to make sure the new message about the White House antidrug crusade got out, Reagan repeated it in a speech before the National Conference on Alcohol and Drug Abuse Prevention. Reagan promised that his administration would "strike at the heart of this monster."

By August 7, after President Reagan had inveighed publicly against drugs three times in six days, the *New York Times* described drugs as

> the No. 1 topic in Washington. . . . Mr. Reagan and leaders in both the Senate and the House seemed to be fighting to show who was the most concerned. And on Monday, as the House rushed to complete a multibillion-dollar anti-drug bill that was first planned only a week before, Dr. [Carleton] Turner's [a Reagan drug advisor] no-new-spending vow of three weeks ago became moot. . . .
>
> In the House, staff members said that the evolving omnibus anti-drug bill would cost $2 billion to $3 billion. Anti-drug bills that have lingered in committees for months or years are now passing out "in minutes," a Congressional aide said.

Journalist Elaine Shannon describes how on the issue of drugs, "the Congress went into a frenzy. No one wanted to be tarred soft on crime. . . . Republicans and Democrats scratched and clawed one another to offer more draconian amendments. On Sept. 11, by a vote of 392 to 16, the House approved a bill that was breathtaking in its scope, authorizing $6 billion over three years for both 'supply-side' interdiction and enforcement measures and 'demand-side' education and treatment programs." This was the Anti–Drug Abuse Act of 1986.

On September 14, a Sunday evening, President and Mrs. Reagan took to the televised airwaves together—a first—to reiterate their new joint crusade against drugs. Sitting together holding hands on a couch in the White House family quarters, they spoke to some of the most disturbing aspects of the drug culture. Nancy Reagan began by describing the special excitement of September "when we bundle our children off to school, to the warmth of an environment in which they could fulfill the promise and hope in those restless minds. . . .

"Today there's a drug and alcohol abuse epidemic in this country, and no one is safe from it—not you, not me and certainly not our children, because this epidemic has their names written on it."

She then invoked the newest and most tragic image the drug culture had yet produced—the crack-exposed newborns. She pulled out a clipping and read, "Listen to this news account from a hospital in Florida of a child born to a mother with a cocaine habit: 'Nearby, a baby named Paul lies motionless in an incubator, feeding tubes riddling his tiny body. He needs a respirator to breathe and a daily spinal tap to relieve fluid buildup on the brain. Only 1 month old, he's already suffered two strokes.' "

Her final message was especially for the young: "There's a big, wonderful world out there for you. It belongs to you. It's exciting and stimulating and rewarding. Don't cheat yourselves out of this promise. Our country needs you. But it needs you to be clear-eyed and clear-minded.

"Say yes to your life. And when it comes to drugs and alcohol, just say no."

President Reagan then rhetorically waved the flag, reminding the nation that the genuine sacrifices of earlier generations to preserve American freedom—especially those of World War II—were not made so Americans could squander that patrimony on getting high.

The next day, September 15, 1986, President Reagan issued Executive Order 12564 on the Drug-Free Federal Workplace. He called on all federal employees to eschew drugs and instructed each federal agency to set up programs to "test for the use of illegal drugs by employees in sensitive positions." This measure had been requested specifically earlier that spring by the President's Commission on Organized Crime: "After outlining the relation between organized crime and illegal drug use, the Commission turned towards solutions. Since attempts to limit the supply of drugs had failed, the Commission advocated a series of measures to decrease demand. In particular, it called upon government to 'provide an example of the unacceptibility of drug use.' "

The crack epidemic spread relentlessly across the country during the next several years, and America was reminded again and again of the high price cocaine exacted. Finally, by the late 1980s, even the baby boomers had become disgusted with the illegal drugs they had once so romanticized. UCLA psychologist Ronald K. Siegel, who had started following middle-class self-described recreational cocaine users in the mid seventies, had observed that by 1988—two years into crack and the Reagan War on Drugs—several longtime users "had stopped using cocaine. . . . Why did they stop? The users cited two factors: (1) the changing negative image of cocaine as a street drug and (2) the overall antidrug atmosphere promoted by the war on drugs."

That atmosphere was fostered not only by the horrific television images of crack and the general antidrug drumbeat of the print media, but by the first concerted advertising campaign against illegal drugs. For years popular culture had subtly and blatantly promoted and glamorized marijuana, cocaine, and hallucinogens. In 1987, the American Association of Advertising Agencies, inspired by the growing national revulsion against drugs, created a coalition known as the Partnership for a Drug-Free America. On March 5, 1987, the *Wall Street Journal* reported,

> Starting today, in what is being billed as the biggest public-service campaign since World War II, an advertising and media partnership is launching a war against illegal drugs. It has asked the nation's print and broadcast media to support the three-year effort by donating a staggering $500 million of ad space and time each year—millions more than even Coca-Cola Co. or Chrysler Corp. spends annually on advertising.
>
> The goal is to "convince people that drug usage is not chic, not acceptable, and is plain stupid," says Louis T. Hagopian, chairman of the New York–based ad agency N.W. Ayer.

It was rather jolting to see the American genius for marketing applied to antidrug messages. There was a baby bottle filled with crack, with the message: "Do crack while you're pregnant and your baby may be doing it for life." Or, "In a few days a lot of pot smokers will forget they read this." Or the photo filled with very young, wholesome white kids and the big bold headline: CAN YOU FIND THE DRUG PUSHER IN THIS PICTURE? Or an ad targeted at blacks, showing a brown hand holding crack vials with the huge statement: "Addiction is slavery."

With the steady barrage of heartbreaking crack and cocaine stories, the idea that illegal drugs were not chic finally was driven home to the baby boomers. In the spring of 1988, the *New York Times* reported with great seriousness, "In the world of high fashion, it's no longer fashionable to be high; . . . in the design rooms and executive suites where the major decisions are made, drugs are out of style." The new baby-boomer trend was natural living—eating healthfully and exercising often to stave off fast-encroaching middle age. "It's just not fashionable anymore to overindulge in anything, except exercise and good health," explained Halston.

A contributing editor to the highly trendy *Details* magazine declared, "I don't know anyone who does drugs anymore. People brag about getting up at six to go to the gym. Five and 10 years ago, no one was home before six."

Even the ever foolish, ever media savvy Timothy Leary knew better than to rhapsodize about cocaine. When *Vanity Fair* caught up with him in April 1988, Leary was on his fifth marriage and had transformed himself from "High Priest of the sixties into the Hollywood party person of the eighties." Leary—ever alert to the latest thing—had become enthralled with "interactive software and 'cyber-punk' computer-freak consciousness, . . . proclaiming that 'the psychedelic revolution was the forerunner of the Cybernetic Revolution.' " He designed software and also occasionally did stand-up comedy. *Vanity Fair* reported that "much of Leary's 'drug material' is *anti*-drug these days. He comes out sternly against kids using any kind of drug (including alcohol). He's always had an antipathy to 'linear' up-and-down drugs like coke and heroin, and in one of his stand-up appearances he did a scathing impression of an ex-cokehead."

As for LSD, *Vanity Fair* said that the "dream that [LSD] was the milk of human kindness, that all you need is love, ended in ruins; there's bitterness over the past." Leary explained that *he* still thought LSD a great drug, but as a high-living celeb Yuppie, "LSD is an enormous luxury I just can't afford now."

By early 1989, that ultimate Yuppie consumer magazine, *New York*, was running a service piece titled, "Fighting Back Against Crack." The story lamented crack and "its foul by-products: if not crack houses and street dealers or users, then crackhead crimes such as purse snatchings, car break-ins, burglaries, knife-point robberies, muggings, and murders." In the tradition of the city service piece, the article offered useful, practical advice on reclaiming neighborhoods. One downtown loft area was galvanized into action by the following episode: A woman had come down with her baby to get in her car. As she looked for her keys, "A crackhead ran up, grabbed the child, and raced across the street with the baby over his head, demanding five dollars. The woman started screaming. Luckily, a man walking up the street calmed the crackhead and retrieved the baby unharmed." Understandably, those who had contended with these addicts were unlikely to want to rush home and do drugs themselves. The whole scene had become tawdry and distasteful.

The advent of crack caused writer P. J. O'Rourke, who had once written so amusingly about cocaine when its reputation was still golden, to ponder the much changed drug scene. He freely acknowledged his own partaking of various illegal substances and lamented the fact that as a nation we were not serious about anything, including illegal drugs. He had the decency to understand his own baby-boomer role in this unhappy state of affairs: "If people like me—rich, white, privileged, happy—cannot even bother to abide by the legal standards of their freely constituted society, a society that has provided them with everything a civilization can be expected to provide, then those people deserve their drug problems and everybody else's drug problems, too. They deserve—*I* deserve—to have every crack addict in the country knocking on the front door saying, 'I lives here. Can I go in?' "

Of course Hollywood, like politicians and popular writers, carefully keeps an eternal finger to the cultural wind. By 1989, *TV Guide* was quoting a young network TV executive: "There's a tremendous difference in the way cocaine is viewed between now and six or seven years ago. Back then it was glamorous, fun, hip, cool. . . . Now it's all negative. Now coke is addicting, health-ruining, home-wrecking, and worst of all, career-wrecking."

The public health and medical literature on cocaine generated during the late 1980s was indeed a catalogue of disturbing article titles: "Cocaine/crack dependence among psychiatric inpatients"; "Cocaine danger on the road"; "Cocaine in breast milk"; "Cocaine-induced paranoia and psychosis proneness"; "Cocaine mothers imperil babies' brains"; "Cocaine-related death"; "Cocaine use, risk taking, and fatal Russian roulette"; "Is it schizophrenia or cocaine abuse?"

Among the many casualties of cocaine and crack should be included the nation's capital, Washington, D.C. Starting in 1986, longtime Mayor Marion Barry had begun snorting cocaine, then worked up to smoking crack, all accompanied by heavy cognac consumption. As he pursued getting high and getting laid (with others than his wife), wrote David Remnick in a *New Yorker* profile, "Barry depended more and more on his considerable abilities as a demagogue to cover up his, and the city's, decline; he played the race card when it suited him. And, all the while, everything got worse. The schools deteriorated. Deficits grew. The murder rate soared. The middle class fled. The tax base shrank." Open-air drug markets went from twenty precrack to *eighty* postcrack.

The *Washington Post* ran occasional stories that hinted at the mayor's steady descent into corrupt hedonism. Then in January 1990, near the end of Barry's third term, he was invited by a former model to meet her in Room 727 of the Vista International Hotel. There, while hidden law enforcement cameras whirred away, Mayor Barry was videotaped sharing a crack pipe while trying to seduce this woman. Wrote Remnick, "The Mayor, who had led rallies for schoolchildren urging them to stay off drugs, who had campaigned hard for the support of the clergy, turned out to be a liar and an addict." Barry was convicted on a narcotics misdemeanor and sentenced to six months in jail.

The Barry story played internationally, a major embarrassment to the United States. In Colombia, Barry's paltry sentence provoked public outrage. One senior Colombian official denounced the verdict, saying, "While Colombian judges put their lives on the line approving extradition, judges in the United States, faced with racial differences, soften their decisions to avoid political problems. . . . It weakens all of our arguments [for extradition]. While we endure terrorism here, they give in to racial pressure there." The Colombians again were trying to take on the traffickers, and in a single year, "hundreds of civilians, more than 200 policemen, half a dozen judges, a senator, and several investigative journalists have been killed in a terror campaign by the Medellín cocaine gangs." While it was absolutely true that the habits of millions of Americans just like Barry sustained the murderous cartels, the Colombians were culpable, too. As in America, drugs had magnified and made worse that society's weaknesses.

Ironically, even as the Marion Barry scandal shamed the United States, middle-class drug use was dropping steadily. By 1990, after a decade of "Just Say No," the steady rise of job-related drug testing, and the successful restigmatizing of illegal drugs, these social changes were having a notable effect in bringing down overall middle-class drug use. In 1979 a third of 12-to-17-year-olds reported having used illegal drugs in their lifetime. By 1990 that was down to 23 percent, or a fourth. Those teenagers who had used in the past month—the most important figure—was down even more sharply. In 1979, 17.6 percent of that age group had used in the past month. In 1990, it was 8.1 percent. Past month use for 18-to-25-year-olds for any illegal drug had been 37.1 percent in 1979. By 1990, it was 17.8 percent. For those 26 and older, past month use in 1979 had been 6.5 percent. In 1990, it was 4.6 percent.

The first household survey since 1988 found especially dramatic drops in youthful cocaine use. For those 12 to 17 years old, past month cocaine use had dropped from 1.4 percent to 0.6 percent. For those 18 to 25 years old, past year cocaine use had peaked in 1979 at almost 20 percent. By 1990, it was down to 7.5 percent. Past month cocaine use had dropped from 9.3 percent in 1979 to 2.2 percent in 1990. For those 26 and older, past year cocaine use had peaked in 1985 at 4.2 percent. By 1990, it was down to 2.4 percent. The high school senior survey ("Monitoring the Future") showed past year cocaine use had dropped from 12 percent in 1986 to 5 percent in 1990. The extent to which the drug culture had permeated society had been shown dramatically by early results from employee drug-testing programs. One of the first big labs offering tests, SmithKline Beecham Clinical Laboratories, found positives running at almost 16 percent in 1987. As the middle class increasingly shunned drugs, SmithKline saw that figure drop by 1994 to 7.5 percent, still significant. Drug use in the U.S. military, after almost a decade of testing had plummeted to the low single digits.

Yet even as the middle-class, mainly part-time, drug culture steadily was getting smaller and smaller—a major and important accomplishment—the full-time drug culture of crack pushers and addicts had expanded rapidly during the late 1980s. And it was this highly antisocial group that generated extraordinary problems. Illegal drugs—especially crack—magnified every single one of our nation's weaknesses. We always had had a propensity to violence. We always had had lax gun laws. The welfare system had created a subsociety of dependent, fatherless families marooned in inner-city slums. We had failed to enforce our own immigration laws. The United States long had tolerated far greater disparities in class and opportunity than other industrialized nations. We had not cared much as the working poor found fewer and fewer real jobs. And as P. J. O'Rourke pointed out, we were not serious about addressing any of these problems. Law-abiding Americans busy pursuing the American Dream just tried to move farther away into the suburbs.

Now drugs forced these bleak realities into the nation's living rooms. Who were these youthful pushers and ruthless traffickers? Who were these sad addicts? True, some were people like Susan Lydon, middle-class screwups who threw away all their advantages to glory in drug-taking, but the bulk of the hard-core, full-time addicts—those who bought about 75 percent of the illegal drugs—were the nation's down-and-outs. And many of the traffickers were foreign criminals—Colombians, Dominicans, and Jamaicans. The full-time drug culture—with all its corrosive violence and corruption, frenzied addiction, and crack babies—magnified our society's worst failures. The illegal drug culture forced us to pay attention to the underside of America—its collapsing inner cities, its longtime welfare class, the homeless, the free flow of criminal illegal aliens, the violence, the tens of millions of guns.

All these problems had been quietly but steadily getting worse. Now crack so intensified all of them that we could no longer ignore or rationalize them. We were used to a thousand murders a year just in one city—New York. But when that dreadful carnage doubled in five years, it could no longer be ignored. We had insisted that fatherless families were just another variant on domestic life. But even we could not put a positive spin on fatherless *and* motherless families. When batallions of inner-city young men entered the drug trade, we actually had to pay attention to what had happened to the working-class economy and acknowledge the moral collapse that led so many to willingly poison their own communities. Crack highlighted a whole constellation of long-standing, extremely difficult problems.

But the most immediate and pressing public concern was blatant and violent crack-dealing and the crime waves that rippled out all around it. In 1986 the Omnibus Anti-Drug Act put 70 percent of federal dollars into interdiction and law enforcement and 30 percent into treatment and prevention. But even this was something of a chimera. Just over a year later, the *New York Times* noted that the much touted $1.7 billion war on drugs was never actually fully funded. And so once the public was not watching, some "initiatives, like the 24 task forces to fight crack, evaporated entirely. . . . The Reagan drug war, in short, has turned into a squandered opportunity."

With crack continuing its relentless, highly televised spread into the nation's heartland, in 1988 Congress responded by fashioning yet another major antidrug bill. The Anti-Drug Act of 1988 *doubled* all antidrug funds—from $4.1 billion in fiscal year 1988 to $7.9 billion in fiscal year 1990. Not only did this pump much needed money into beefing up outgunned law enforcement, it gave the fields of treatment and prevention their first major infusions of money since the 1970s.

But just as important, the Democrats used the 1988 act to force the appointment of a national director of drug policy, a person immediately dubbed the drug "czar." Said Representative Charles B. Rangel, Harlem Democrat and head of the Select Committee on Narcotics Abuse and Control, "Now Congress and the American people will know who is in charge of dealing with the nation's drug crisis, because this individual will be responsible full time for developing and coordinating all aspects of our war on drugs."

George Bush assumed the presidency in 1989, when the crack epidemic was in full fury. (The Drug Abuse Warning Network, DAWN, data showed a twenty-eight-fold increase in hospital emergency room admissions for cocaine in just four years.) All through 1989 Republican National Committee polls showed drugs as the most important issue.

So, on September 5 President Bush went on television to give a much hyped speech, mainly memorable because the president waved a baggie full of crack that the DEA had arranged to buy across from the White House. The president reaffirmed that illegal drugs were domestic problem number one. Bush also appointed the hard-charging, high-profile former secretary of education, William Bennett, as his drug "czar," head of the congressionally mandated National Office of Drug Control Policy. As the Democrats had hoped, there was now someone in the administration at the cabinet level putting together an overall game plan who could be called to account.

Each year a detailed National Drug Control Strategy would be outlined, along with subsequent reports on what happened with all the plans and programs. How much money was spent? How many treatment slots created? Was someone able to do something about all those pregnant women using cocaine? How successful had border interdiction been? Was basic research progressing or producing anything? And so on and so forth.

William Bennett knew little about the drug problem, but he quickly established that he was a drug hawk. As he himself declared, "Two words sum up my entire approach: consequences and confrontation. Those who use, sell, and traffic in drugs must be confronted, and they must suffer consequences." Bennett was extremely gung ho about law enforcement and new prisons but seemed uneasy about treatment.

However, reporter Michael Massing pointed out, "Bennett never questions the efficacy of the criminal justice system. That system, like treatment programs, suffers from serious inefficiencies. Across the country, police chiefs, judges, and prosecutors are throwing up their hands, frustrated by their inability to contain, much less defeat, the drug trade." Bennett's faith in a mainly law enforcement solution was extremely ironic, given that those out on the front line, people such as DEA's Stutman in New York City and DEA head Jack Lawn in Washington, had been preaching the necessities of a more evenhanded approach. Reducing demand was integral, and it wasn't going to happen just through law enforcement.

The president of the U.S. Police Foundation explained the necessity of expanding beyond the traditional law enforcement repertoire in the United Nation's *Bulletin on Narcotics*: "More contemporary and promising approaches include community policing, problem-oriented policing, financially oriented investigations, increased international co-operation and a renewed emphasis on drug demand reduction."

Drug czar Bennett had spoken approvingly of a neighborhood group in Kansas City, Missouri, called the Ad Hoc Group Against Crime that had applied successfully neighborhood pressure to close one hundred crack houses in the course of a year. The group's leader, Alvin Brooks, told reporter Massing the community needed a tenfold increase in treatment that provided meaningful help once addicts were drug-free: "If people go back on the street and get a whiff of crack, without proper aftercare, they'll be back where they started." And that meant helping people find jobs and often some sort of housing. Meanwhile, Brooks was trying to open a swimming pool/rec center, a very reasonable goal. "Our kids have nowhere to go to swim, to sing, to dance. With nothing to do, they're vulnerable." Bennett's plan made clear he admired such local activism, for the drug czar rightfully was celebrating the courage and perseverance of the grassroots groups determined to maintain a decent, lawful atmosphere in their neighborhoods. These people were as fed up with drugs as the middle class. But federal antidrug strategy offered minimal money to underwrite exactly these sorts of much lauded efforts. As usual, America was not serious.

Like all epidemics, crack calmed down, usually about five disastrous years after it hit a locale. New York City had seen crack first arrive in 1985 and really take off in 1986. By 1991, the fury of the New York crack epidemic was ebbing, leaving in its wake a hard core of dedicated addicts and tens of thousands of crack-exposed babies. One twenty-six-year-old Harlem dealer had "started selling crack three years ago [in 1988, when] the craze for the smokable form of cocaine was still growing. It was not so much a matter of selling the drug as letting it be known that a supply was available and watching as customers snapped it up." But by the spring of 1991, this same dealer reported, "It's real slow now. Instead of 10 buyers, there might be three."

When a reporter visited a Harlem crack house in April 1991, the denizens said they did not know "anyone who had taken up the habit lately." The reporter was surprised to find present on this weekend afternoon a couple of ostensibly solid citizens who seemed able to hold jobs and control their crack smoking. But others hanging around were desperate cases. One was a thirty-three-year-old mother of three on welfare. "She started smoking crack five years ago, through the pregnancies of her two youngest. . . . It [crack] is on her mind from the moment she wakes. The 'thirsties,' the haunting desperate need for the drug shadow her every decision." Another woman, only twenty-three, had had three children by different fathers, two since she had taken up crack. She held up her crack pipe, saying, "This is my husband. He takes all my money." Another denizen was a big man just out of jail for drug dealing. He had binged for several days, was out of money, and had not slept: "Paranoia was taking over."

Wherever the scourge of crack had lit long enough, those who used soon became completely reviled. By mid 1990, even in the New York ghetto, "the smokable form of cocaine is gaining a reputation as a drug for losers." Several years of seeing firsthand what crack could do had sufficed. One young man described the demise of some older friends: "They're crackheads. They live on my block and they rob all the time; they rob off their best friends, their families. They're like fiends." One eighteen-year-old lifeguard described an older brother whose crack use and dealing landed him in prison. A nineteen-year-old sister had abandoned her baby to pursue crack. "I don't want to be like some people out there," the young man said. "They lose their homes because they're on it. I don't want to get involved with that." In the nation's meanest streets, the phrase "thirsty crackhead" had become a scathing insult.

But even as New York City emerged on the other side of the worst of the crack epidemic, other American communities were still suffering. The American impatience for instant results meant that by December 1990 *Time* already was running a story headlined THE LOSING WAR that gave brief snapshots of various afflicted cities and stated, "The nations's violent crime rate rose 10% in the first six months of 1990. Murders were up 8% in the first six months of the year and armed robbery rose 9%." When the bill came due for the huge Reagan-era deficits, and recession struck in 1990, Americans came to realize that their standard of living was visibly declining or stagnating. Basic sobriety seemed essential to reclaiming the nation's preeminence. Popular culture largely had shifted on the issue of drugs. For the first time since the 1920s, no drug elite was suggesting through music or movies or books that drugs and altered states were beneficial.

The unfortunately dubbed "war on drugs" gave the public the impression that there would be some intensive, determined major battles and then victory. Yet the historical experience from the first drug epidemic—which had not included the far more addictive crack—showed that shrinking antisocial drug cultures takes not a year or two or three or even four. It takes decades. And that success is contingent on adequate law enforcement, along with other social developments. It was important to "just say no." But it was equally important to have something to "just say yes" to.

Once baby boomers decided drugs were bad, they and the rest of the public seemed annoyed that the cocaine market did not just disappear. But the late 1980s and early 1990s saw continuous expansions in world coca and opium crops. Based on satellite and on-the-ground intelligence, the 1995 *National Drug Control Strategy* estimates that by 1993 Peru, Bolivia, and Colombia had produced some 700 or 800 metric tons of cocaine, of which 400 metric tons or so was smuggled into the United States. For the past decade, we have remained the major market, using about half of this particular drug. Of course, this flood of cocaine still arrives largely courtesy of the Colombians.

Up through the early 1990s, the Medellín cartel dominated, but its reign of relentless public terror against the government finally galvanized Colombian authorities to serious action. Carlos Rivas Lehder was extradited to the United States and languishes here in federal prison forever. Pablo Escobar (after escaping a deluxe prison) was gunned down in December 1993. The Ochoas wisely turned themselves in, received short sentences, and are presumed to operate a discreet version of their cocaine business from comfortable jail cells.

In the meantime, the Cali cartel moved into the breach. Having observed the fate of the savage, government-challenging Medellín cartel, Cali is more gentlemanly. But they will murder as necessary. When those working for Cali are arrested in the United States, they rarely cooperate because they say their family members will be killed. Nonetheless, Cali has not—so far—assassinated government officials, kidnapped their loved ones, or bombed public places and the national airlines to get their way. This kinder, gentler style of trafficking led a grateful government to make only the most occasional gestures of disapproval. In all of 1994 not one Cali member was arrested in Colombia. And so cocaine production, drug trafficking, and corruption proceeded merrily onward and upward. As many Colombian peasant families— some three hundred thousand—now make a living raising illegal drug crops as work in the coffee industry.

And so the cocaine continues to flood in. Since the late 1980s, American federal law enforcement routinely has seized one hundred metric tons of cocaine each year, a fairly respectable one quarter of what is estimated to come in. The most spectacular seizure remains that made on September 29, 1989, when the DEA received a tip and raided an unguarded warehouse in the San Fernando Valley. There they found *twenty* tons of cocaine, enough to fill two school buses. Also there were boxes and nylon gym bags filled with twenty dollars and one hundred dollar bills. When counted, it totaled $10 million. This dwarfed even the Tranquilandia raid in the heart of Colombia, cartel land. Yet in recent years price and purity have remained fairly constant. Clearly, the big expansion in law enforcement was not big enough.

While cocaine and cartels have hogged headlines, opium poppy crops have been surging steadily upward, doubling worldwide over the past decade. For 1993, the Office of National Drug Control Policy reported a total crop of 3,699 metric tons. (This would yield about 400 tons of heroin.) Unlike cocaine, for which we are the major market, with opiates we consume only 6 percent of the world crop. Plenty of other nations have opiate addict populations equal to or bigger than ours.

Far and away the biggest opium producer of the 1990s is Burma, or Myanmar, with 2,575 metric tons. Here the purported culprit is Jiao Khun Sa, a Shan Chinese tribal warlord who lives in an air-conditioned ranch house in the remote hills of the Golden Triangle. With his ten-thousand-man private force—the Shan United Army—to guard fields, refineries, and escort caravans, he has dominated the local opium and heroin trade for decades. A *Herald Tribune* reporter visiting Khun Sa in 1990 observed that the chain-smoking warlord had little illusion about his product. Any soldier in his army caught using heroin or opium was "subject to the death penalty after the requisite warning and a two-week jail sentence." Myanmar (and therefore Khun Sa) is largely responsible for the soaring heroin purity on America's meanest streets, for this southeast Asian nation has doubled its output since 1988 and now accounts for 60 percent of the heroin American addicts put in their veins.

The vast numbers of casual and occasional drug users has dropped way off, but that still leaves the 2.5 million hard-core users—the half million longtime and aging heroin addicts and the additional 2 million who have taken to crack. While some middle-class users have taken to trying the high-purity heroin, the biggest new consumers are the crack addicts who find it helps cushion the crash of binging. They are the heart of the problem, accounting for the bulk of drugs bought—maybe 60 to 80 percent. A serious crackhead can binge through many grams of cocaine in a day. Until that hard-core group gets smaller—whether through treatment or going to prison or dying out—the drug culture and the drug problem is not going to get much better. Crack cocaine had struck in 1986 just as the American middle-class romance with drugs was fast waning. It had created a massive new and complicated drug problem and highlighted our worst and most intractable social problems. It is not going to go away easily or cheaply.

CHAPTER 19

"You Have to

Pay Up Somewhere

Along the Line."

—novelist Robert Stone, 1986

As the United States confronts its drug culture in the 1990s, many Americans—especially the baby boomers—still remain ambivalent about illegal drugs. The days are gone when high-profile, middle-class drug enthusiasts extol getting high through powerful popular media. Yet for the elite of the baby-boom generation, there lingers this massive ambivalence. Why? Partly because many boomers feel that they enjoyed their flings with certain drugs, and even gained some insight into themselves and the world along the way. They are not certain why such interesting experiences should be illegal. What they fail to appreciate is that they represent a privileged and disciplined elite with a great many attractive options in life beyond drugs. While the middle-class cocaine epidemic proved to many a boomer that even they could get into deep trouble with drugs, the majority emerged unscathed.

The baby-boom ambivalence was showcased perfectly in a 1995 *New York* cover story on the drug trends of the trendy. The thirty-nine-year-old author apparently could not figure out whether to be bothered by well-to-do types doing heroin or to cheer on anything that challenged authority and shocked people. He proudly laid out his own participation in the drug culture as some sort of political statement. Even his purported regrets reeked of pure pride in doing naughty things:

> I could have done without that PCP. I would venture, too, that my brief Quaalude Period probably wasn't such a brilliant idea, if only I could remember something—anything—about it. Cocaine the night before that cross-country race in 1985? Sheer lunacy, never mind the fast time. Finally, I wish in retro-spect that the pile of discarded whippets outside our dorm win-dow all those years ago had been a lot smaller, and not just for appearance sake: By the time that particular nitrous-oxide craze had swept through campus, one of my classmates was dead of it.

One thinks of *The Great Gatsby*, where the careless rich indulged their pleasures, leaving behind the wreckage as they moved on. The upper middle class can mess around with drugs and think they're cute because experience and research show that the more well-to-do one is, the better educated, and the older, the less vulnerable one is to abuse and addiction. To drive this home, consider this extraordinary statistic: *Before* crack, a Harlem Hospital study found that "Harlem blacks were 283 times as likely to die from drug dependency as whites in the gen-eral population."

In short, not all are as lucky as the baby boomers. Leaders for the poor, the less privileged, and the very young rarely talk about drugs in that smart-alecky way and consistently have rejected legalization or decriminalization for a simple reason—they know their constituencies would be hit hardest. Tellingly, it has almost always been black leaders and the grassroots parent groups who have pressed Congress most to confront drugs. There is a certain accumulated folk experience that makes both these groups against any softening on drugs.

The elite boomer ambivalence about drugs has other sources. One is a lingering antipathy to authority. The feeling persists that somehow the government is still lying and exaggerating the perils of drugs. If the official policy is antidrug, then the boomer policy should be the oppo-site. Nor should one underestimate the powerful link between hipness and drugs. This has made it difficult for elite boomers, who still put great value on being hip, to completely repudiate drugs as necessary for the greater long-term good of society. The *New York* author admits he's given up drugs because he's the father of a young son. But he whines, "What a drag." Few baby boomers still openly sing the wonders of using drugs and getting high; at the same time they are extremely reluctant to concede that the squares and authority figures were right: The societal costs of widely available drugs clearly outweigh whatever pleasure and insight they provide to those who can handle them. Those baby boomers who feel they have benefited from drugs need to ask themselves, "Do our positive personal experiences outweigh the cumulative destructive consequences of the drug culture?" Frankly, one hopes the Me Generation can answer "No" and recognize what history shows—no society can progress and prosper with an active drug culture.

In an essay on American economic decline, writer James Fallows observes, "Most people, including economists off-duty, assume that there is a connection between the kinds of everyday behavior a society encourages and its stability and prosperity." A society that encourages or tolerates the use of illegal drugs does so at its own considerable peril. For as Fallows also points out, "there are two cultural traits that most successful capitalist economies have shared, however much the societies may differ in other ways. One is an emphasis on deferred gratification. . . . The other is some recognized link between individual and collective well-being."

Nothing better epitomizes instant gratification and its dangers than the drug culture. Obviously, one of the great attractions of marijuana, cocaine, hallucinogens, and heroin is that they instantly loosen or dissolve ordinary inhibitions and restraints. They immediately put users in an "altered state," oftentimes pleasurable. People under the influence of these drugs become notably less responsible and do things against their better judgment. And focused as drug users are on the personal pleasure of using drugs, they certainly have no thought for "collective well-being." An extreme but not so rare example is an AIDS activist who was HIV-positive. "I was resolved to practice safe sex, and my philosophy would not have allowed me to be unsafe," he said, "but using drugs and alcohol allowed me to have sex without condoms. It provided the excuse."

Fortunately drug use has now become unfashionable in boomer circles, an important reversal. For as the baby boomers move into positions of power in politics and business and the arts, the country needs their leadership to contain and shrink the drug culture. Once, as this history makes clear, marijuana, cocaine, and heroin were the almost exclusive province of the deviant, those people who chose to live on the antisocial margins of society. When drug use became normative and lost much of its stigma, it spread like wildfire, leaving us with the huge problem we have today. Viewing drugs as harmless or even redeeming has been part of an overall trend that Senator Daniel Patrick Moynihan trenchantly described as "defining deviancy down." Rather than confront our serious social problems—such as families without fathers or growing drug use—many chose to declare them normal. What was once outside the norm became acceptable. This proceeded to then make the problem even more widespread. The net effect of misguided elite baby-boomer tolerance and Cold War politics was to allow the drug culture—with its values of facile hipness, getting high, and instant pleasure—to flourish and become deeply entrenched, contributing strongly to the disintegration of families and even whole sections of certain cities.

Novelist Robert Stone is one of the very few members of the baby boom generation who has thought seriously about where all this began and where it has led:

> We old-time pot smokers used to think we were cute with our instant redefinitions and homespun minimalism. Our attention had been caught by a sensibility [that of hipsters] that a lot of us associated with black people. . . . Some of us were elitists who thought we had the right to get high because we were artists and musicians and consciousness was our profession and the rest of the world, the "squares," could go to hell. Others of us hoped the insights we got from using drugs like pot could somehow change the world for the better. . . .
>
> The first person I ever saw use cocaine was a poet I haven't seen for twenty-five years. It was on the Lower East Side, one night during the fifties, in an age that's as dead now as Agememnon. Coltrane's "My Favorite Things" was on the record player. The poet was tall and thin and pale and self-destructive and we all thought that was a great way to be. . . .
>
> Let me tell you I honor that man. I honor him for his lonely independence and his hard outcast's road. I think he was one of the people who, in the fifties, helped to make this country a lot freer. Maybe that's the trouble. Ultimately, nothing is free, in the sense that you have to pay up somewhere along the line.
>
> My friend the poet thought cocaine lived someplace around midnight that he was trying to find. He would not have expected it to become a commonplace drug. . . . He was the wild one. In hindsight, we should have known how many of the kids to come would want to be the wild ones too.

Robert Stone wrote the essay quoted here after an unnerving visit to Manhattan in the summer of 1986. As he walked almost the length of that island, he was distressed by the manifold signs of the cocaine epidemic—the men selling crack, the frenzied deals between buyers and dealers, the odd public behavior: "They're all loaded, I thought. That was my vision. Everybody was loaded on cocaine." As if that were not sufficiently disturbing, weeks later he was in a New England village by the sea. He was parked by the water and scanning his mail, when he became aware of another car parked next to his. In the front seat, two lovely teenage girls were snorting lines of cocaine openly. As they roared out of the little seaside lot, they practically smashed into an oncoming mail truck.

Long ago, middle-class intellectuals such as Robert Stone had tried to tap into what they saw as the more authentic lives of hipsters by appropriating certain parts of that world—including illegal drugs. But as the mass of ordinary and vulnerable people had taken up drugs—people with no interest in being artists, teenagers too immature to know who they were or what they were doing—when these people took up mind-altering substances, serious intellectuals such as Robert Stone had to reconsider. He had observed the whole journey of illegal drugs from outcast hipster poets in grungy Beat enclaves to wholesome girls in coastal villages doing lines. He felt no ambivalence on the issue. "Just say no," wrote Stone, ". . . because liberation starts from there." Any notion that mass use of illegal drugs would somehow be beneficial had proven a disastrous chimera.

Boomers could see that the American drug scene had become scary and pathetic, the source of crime and violence and personal tragedy. But many concluded that this was mainly the consequence of the drug laws, not the drugs. Therefore, they vaguely suggested, the solution to the drug problem was some form of legalization, a move strongly opposed by the vast preponderance of ordinary Americans. I recognize the boomer attitude well, because I subscribed to it before my own extensive research into the history of drug culture gradually convinced me that no society can afford to be conciliatory on drugs, much less supply them to its citizenry, especially in this era of ever more competitive world markets.

America's forgotten first opiate and cocaine epidemic teaches an extremely important lesson. The largely lower-class drug culture that society finds so alarming and repugnant—wherein addicts focus their whole existence around drugs and engage in antisocial behavior—was not created by criminalization of drugs. It existed *before* drugs were illegal, and indeed brought about antidrug legislation. Nor can one ignore the earlier historical experience of such diverse societies as China, Egypt, and Japan as they confronted addicting drugs. Each clearly concluded that no society could progress or move ahead if drugs became a significant presence. Alaska's brief experiment in decriminalizing even marijuana was rolled back by upset parents and employers.

History shows that successfully diminishing the drug culture (as America did before World War II) requires complete societal commitment. That is why the restigmatization of drugs is so important. Middle-class boomers who moan and whine about the lower-class drug problem should be aware that it was the huge boomer appetite for cocaine and the legions of boomer traffickers and dealers who turned a small problem limited to certain major urban areas into a huge and widely dispersed problem. Boomer hubris about drugs—especially cocaine—has played a significant role in landing us where we are.

Why have I—and virtually every other serious student of the American drug scene, whether historian, sociologist, or physician—concluded that legalization is bad policy? Basically because it is the drugs themselves—not the drug laws—that cause the bulk of social harm. One old friend said to me, "Drugs open up your dark side." Making illegal drugs more freely available and more normative will only multiply the drug disaster we already have in our midst. Many of the societal costs generated by the drug culture are caused by the drugs themselves, not the drug laws.

Dr. Herbert Kleber, respected psychiatrist, treatment expert, and veteran of the drug wars, describes the varying motivations and stances of the legalizers:

> Since current approaches have improved but not solved our drug problem, some people call for regulatory changes. Some do so from a misguided feeling of frustration: nothing is working, and the problem is getting worse. Others espouse the libertarian position: in a free society, people should be free to experiment with substances and suffer any consequences. Still others acknowledge that laws against the possession and sale of drugs may reduce their use but argue that such laws create more problems than they solve by leading to crime, violent drug wars, and wholesale imprisonment. The general thrust of all these arguments is that legalization would lead to decreased crime without a substantial rise in addiction and would therefore result in an overall benefit to society. Proposed schemes vary: legalize drugs completely and allow marketing similar to that of tobacco and alcohol, decriminalize personal use and

possession of drugs, or allow a medical dispensation of heroin
or cocaine to those already addicted.

Let's consider the current situation and the prolegalization arguments. First off, is the drug scene getting worse rather than better? Absolutely not. The middle-class drug scene—especially the young adult drug scene—is a fraction of what it once was. Those who pooh-pooh this as unimportant fail to understand that a society's basic character is set by the behavior of its middle-class citizenry. Today, the military is largely drug-free. Once almost half the soldiers and sailors tested positive for marijuana, while more than a quarter tested positive for other drugs, especially cocaine. Today, with drug-testing routinized within the armed forces, about 3 percent of soldiers, sailors, and officers test positive. That is a striking accomplishment. Similarly, many workplaces have managed to bring drug use way down through preemployment testing and offering treatment through employee-assistance plans. Of course, these sorts of quiet but important advances tend to be overlooked when drug dealers with Uzis are mowing down innocent children.

Truthfully, when discussing legalization what we're really talking about is crack cocaine. This is the drug that added a couple of million new addicts and tens of thousands of new drug dealers to our society, who in turn made for much new violence, crime, and disarray, and now cram our prisons and jails to bursting. If you hadn't had crack, the worst of the drug problem would be the half million heroin addicts— an aging cohort that has remained fairly stable for twenty years. Moreover, heroin addicts can be stabilized on methadone and were long supplied by reasonably well-behaved criminals.

All the new crack-related chaos and costs fueled libertarian fantasies. According to the libertarians, in a free society people should be free to experiment with substances and suffer any consequences. I will allow distinguished criminologist James Q. Wilson to answer this:

> The notion that abusing drugs such as cocaine is a "victimless" crime is not only absurd but dangerous. Even ignoring the fetal drug syndrome, crack-dependent people are, like heroin addicts, individuals who regularly victimize their children by neglect, their spouses by improvidence, their employers by lethargy, and their coworkers by carelessness. Society is not and never could be a collection of autonomous individuals. We all have a stake in ensuring that each of us displays a minimal level of dignity, responsibility, and empathy. We cannot, of course, coerce people into goodness, but we can and should

insist that some standards must be met if society itself—on which the very existence of the human personality depends—is to persist. Drawing the line that defines those standards is difficult and contentious, but if crack and heroin use do not fall below it, what does?

Probably the most distressing aspect of illegal drugs is how men and women who use them seem to lose much sense of responsibility to their own children. (What better illustration of how drugs open a "dark side"?) Heroin has certainly caused far too many lower-class men to neglect and abandon their offspring. And with the advent of crack, we have the horrifying spectacle of pregnant women smoking the drug, even though they are well aware that this is compromising their fetus's normal development. The upshot is that in the America of 1996 we now have a senior citizens organization called ROCKING, for Raising Our Children's Kids: an Intergenerational Network of Grandparenting. These are the relatives who stepped in when legions of crack addicts abandoned their parental duties. One New York pediatrician active in the group explained that "grandparents were taking care of grandchildren because of the introduction of crack to the community. . . . [T]here has never been anything like crack."

James Q. Wilson cites Douglas Besharov, who has been "following the effects of drugs on infants for twenty years. [Besharov] writes that nothing he learned about heroin prepared him for the devastation of cocaine. . . . Some crack babies have for all practical purposes suffered a disabling stroke while still in the womb. . . . Besharov estimates that about 30,000 to 50,000 such babies are born every year, about 7,000 in New York City alone."

No man (or woman) is an island. When drug addicts abandon children, the children will pay and so will the American taxpayer. The frequent prematurity of drug-affected children means longer, more expensive hospital stays. And once out in the world—whether with grandparents or foster care—the drug-affected babies are often supported through Social Security disability payments. Once enrolled in school, many require special classes. In a *Washington Post* story about the first wave of crack-affected children to enter school, it noted that Los Angeles spent fifteen-thousand dollars a year per drug-affected child in special programs, versus three-thousand dollars a child in regular classrooms. Is this situation caused by cocaine and its effect on people who abuse it or by the laws against cocaine?

But probably the reason most people toy with positive thoughts about legalization is they're tired of worrying about crime, by addicts or by dealers. It's horrible to walk out and find your car window smashed by addicts looking for something to steal. And it's downright scary to drive somewhere and realize that those thuggish young men with the hard stares are drug dealers flagrantly hawking their wares. Presumably they have guns and may well use them just as you're in the wrong trajectory. Drug dealers and their clientele all foster an aura of sordidness and menace. Many middle-class types may find buying drugs in the slums, or copping, part of the excitement and fun, but naturally they would be highly upset if this world got truly near theirs. (Of course, they help perpetuate it. Do they ever think of how their dollars enrich the murderous gangs?)

For many, then, the whole raison d'être of legalization would be to eliminate crime and antisocial behavior. Unfortunately, no one who knows the drug scene well believes this would happen. The antisocial behavior isn't caused by the drug laws, it's caused and/or exacerbated by the drugs. What researchers have learned since they began studying the phenomenon of addiction and the drug culture is that "while drug use tends to intensify and perpetuate criminal behavior, it usually does not initiate criminal careers. In fact, the evidence suggests that among the majority of street drug users who are involved in crime, their criminal careers were well established prior to the onset of either narcotics or cocaine use."

Researcher David Nurco, who has spent decades studying heroin addicts in Baltimore, certainly found that most addicts had engaged in criminality before falling in love with heroin. (Only 6 percent were not engaged in any kind of criminal activity at all.) Once hooked, addicts turned more heavily than before to drug dealing, shoplifting, and burglary to finance their habits. The most worrisome—about 7 percent of those studied—was the person the public most fears, the criminal who seems to enjoy committing violent crimes, is very active, and extremely dangerous. In this small group, each acknowledged committing about 900 crimes a year while hooked. But even *before* getting onto heroin, each had committed an average of 573 crimes per year. And even later, once off heroin, each committed 491 crimes a year. While drugs made them worse, they were active criminals who enjoyed committing crimes.

The legalizers will no doubt argue that even these violent criminals would commit many fewer crimes if they did not have to pay high prices for heroin. Well, let's look at England, where every effort has been made to provide heroin addicts with cheap legal drugs and keep addicts away from street dealers. Elliott Currie, in his thoughtful book *Reckoning*, writes,

As we have seen, British addicts could receive prescriptions for heroin from private doctors and, later, from carefully regulated medical clinics. But did addicts who could get heroin legally stop committing crimes? The evidence suggests that many did not—especially after the 1970s, when large numbers of poorer addicts emerged in Britain's cities. Thus a 1979 study of addicts who had been prescribed legal opiates at two London clinics concluded that "treatment for periods of up to 8.5 years had no effect on their overall crime rates." A more recent London study found that most addicts receiving either prescription heroin or methadone continued to commit crimes or to buy heroin in the illicit market.

The reasons that giving out free or cheap heroin and methadone do not necessarily produce completely law-abiding, much less model, citizens, explains Currie, is that "people use heroin not simply to satisfy uncontrollable physical cravings, but as part of their participation in a broader subculture that typically includes several kinds of crime and the use of several other drugs." In short, the fast life of drugs, crime, and general hedonism celebrates drug-taking as part of all-round antisocial behavior, including crime.

But still, let's say that making heroin and crack legal and therefore cheaper or even free would reduce the amount of crime committed per addict. Say, addicts now commit half the crime they once did, as is often true with those on methadone. Wouldn't that still be better? Think how great it would be if the United States crime rate were even *half* its present high rate?

The fallacy here is assuming that drug use would not balloon once drugs became more freely available. Drug use would only have to double—something that is not hard to imagine—and we would be back where we were because we would now have twice as many addicts, each commiting one half as many crimes. Again, let us look at what happened in England—always held up by the legalizers as some kind of beau ideal of a rational approach to drugs. Professor Wilson explains,

> Until the mid-1960's, British physicians were allowed to prescribe heroin to certain classes of addicts. (Possessing these drugs without a doctor's prescription remained a criminal offense.) For many years this policy worked well enough because the addict-patients were typically middle-class people who had become dependent on opiate painkillers. . . . There was no drug culture. . . .

All that changed in the 1960's. A few unscrupulous doctors began passing out heroin in wholesale amounts. . . . A youthful drug culture emerged with a demand for drugs far different from that of older addicts. As a result, the British government required doctors to refer users to government-run clinics to receive their heroin.

But the shift to clinics did not curtail the growth in heroin use. Throughout the 1960's the number of addicts increased—the late John Kaplan of Stanford estimated fivefold—in part as a result of the diversion of heroin from clinic patients to new users on the streets. . . . Many patients would use some of their maintenance dose and sell the remaining part. . . . As the clinics learned of this, they began to shift their treatment away from heroin and toward methadone.

Wilson concludes that by the late 1970s, when the number of American heroin addicts had risen tenfold, from fifty thousand to half a million (where it has remained stable), that "the number of British addicts increased by thirtyfold in ten years: the actual increase may have been much larger. . . . In the early 1980's the numbers began to rise again, and this time nobody doubted that a real epidemic was at hand. The increase was estimated to be 40 percent a year." The lesson here is that the more available heroin is, the more people will use it. Events in Pakistan show the same pattern. Pakistan had no noticeable problem with heroin, but it developed a huge problem in five years—1.3 million addicts—simply because heroin was widely available.

Moreover, those who propose legalization or making drugs more easily available to addicts in order to minimize crime somehow assume that once addicts have all the drugs they need, that will be that. But the pharmacology of the two "hard" drugs—heroin and cocaine—mitigate against any normalcy. Professor James Inciardi has spent decades hanging around addicts and drug scenes. He says, "Because heroin is a short-acting drug, with its effects lasting at best four to six hours, it must be taken regularly and repeatedly. Because there is more rapid onset when taken intravenously, most heroin users inject the drug. Because heroin has depressant effects, a portion of the user's day is spent in a semi-stupified state. Collectively, these attributes result in a user more concerned with drug-taking and drug-seeking than health, family, work, relationships, responsibility, or anything else." Crack cocaine is not a depressant, but a stimulant. Its serious devotees generally use it in a binging pattern. They snort or smoke for hours and even days to maintain the euphoria before collapsing into sleep. High doses of cocaine can bring on violent behavior, psychosis, strokes, and heart attacks. It's hard to imagine someone supplied with however much cocaine or crack they want making much of an employee for anyone.

So we might well supply addicts with large quantities of drugs, but it would certainly make them even less employable than they already are. And they would still need money to pay the rent and buy food, clothes, and other necessities. Where would this money come from if they did not work? At the moment, the U.S. taxpayer *already* provides sufficient money to underwrite illegal drug habits to about 250,000 addicts and alcoholics. How is this? Because Congress decided back in 1972 that if you were too drunk or strung out to work, then you were eligible for Social Security disability payments. Few addicts were aware of this until the 1990s, but once they were, then the numbers tripled. Two thirds of the $1.4 billion disbursed annually to this group in 1994 went straight to the addicts and alcoholics, who were not required to enter treatment to qualify for help. These monthly infusions of taxpayer cash were squandered largely on drugs and drink, say local social workers and treatment counselors, making it very difficult to get addicts into treatment. This federal cash for addicts may well end soon, since being revealed and denounced by Senator William S. Cohen of Maine.

To envision America with even more easily and cheaply available heroin and crack, just imagine even larger armies of homeless. Pete Hamill describes the unpleasant public consequence as experienced in the city with the nation's biggest drug culture, New York: "They are everywhere: rummies and junkies, most of them men, their bodies sour from filth and indifference. They sleep in subways and parks, in doorways and in bank lobbies. Some chatter away with the line of con that's learned in the yards of prisons. . . . Some are menacing and dangerous, their requests for handouts essentially demands." This segment of the so-called homeless want to preserve whatever funds they get from panhandling or stealing for one thing—a fix of drugs and alcohol. Even if drugs cost nothing, these people would still be noxious public burdens. And there would be many, many more of them, still panhandling and committing crimes.

But presume that despite all this, society still wanted to hand out drugs to addicts. There are yet other practical problems. The reality is that most hard-core drug addicts are polydrug abusers who simply want to get high. And because the body daily develops more tolerance for abused drugs, addicts must use escalating dosages to achieve euphoria. This is pharmacological reality. Will we hand out ever increasing doses of heroin and cocaine and whatever else is requested each week to individual drug abusers? If not, the addicts' ever growing appetites will not be satisfied and they will get supplementary fixes from street dealers.

If we do hand out increasing doses, what will happen when inevitably addicts die of overdoses? We live in a highly litigious society. It doesn't take much imagination to dream up all the possible lawsuits—from ODs to drug-exposed babies. Any policeman or emergency room doctor can attest that cocaine in large doses can incite psychotic, violent behavior. Are we prepared to be responsible for the behavior of those we supply with legal cocaine? The practical problems in providing these extremely destructive drugs are insurmountable.

And then, of course, there is the eternal refrain: Well, look at alcohol, it causes much more harm than drugs. Yes and no. Alcohol certainly causes many health-related problems and actual deaths. But this is again getting stuck in the public health mindset that only measures problems by "morbidity and mortality." This ignores the huge antisocial problems generated and exacerbated by drugs, because those don't register on public health measurements.

I pointed out in my introduction that alcohol is classed as a "moderately reinforcing" drug. Heroin and cocaine are "highly reinforcing." If all these substances were equally available, there would almost certainly be *more* drug addicts than alcoholics simply because of the more addicting nature of heroin and cocaine. Right now in this country we have about 10 million alcoholics. Why so many? Because this is a *legal* drug, one readily available throughout the nation—whether big city, suburb, or rural town. Although the sale of alcohol certainly comes under certain strictures and rules, you can almost always find a bar or a liquor store. We have five hundred thousand heroin addicts and 2 million cocaine addicts. Why so few compared to the less addictive alcohol? Because these are *illegal* substances. Finding them is not easy and certainly not safe.

A demonstration of how reinforcing cocaine is versus alcohol is seen in a one-year follow-up study done of sixty-five cocaine abusers treated at the Sierra Tuscon center in Arizona: "The population consisted primarily of single, male, white cocaine abusers with relatively short drug histories. Overall, 45 percent of the cocaine abusers treated in the program gave self-reports of achieving one year of abstinence successfully, compared to 75 percent of the alcoholics graduating from the program."

I find nothing hypocritical about limited and controlled access to alcohol. An important distinction between alcohol and the illegal drugs is that while it is possible to abuse all of them, anyone who is using drugs is seeking strictly to get high. This is not true with alcohol. On any given evening in America, tens of millions come home and unwind with a glass of wine or beer or a martini. Are they seeking to get high? Not if they're having one or two glasses. This commonsense distinction between how alcohol is used widely (to relax, for the pleasure of the taste of the stuff) and how illegal drugs are used (to get high) makes alcohol much more socially acceptable. Prohibition made clear that the majority of Americans wanted it that way. In states where the majority don't, they still have Prohibition. But there has never emerged a majority in this country asking to have the far more dangerous heroin and cocaine made legal. Even the "moderately reinforcing" marijuana never could garner a significant social movement.

It's really a shame that virtually all public debate about the drug problem is dominated by the phony issue of drug legalization or decriminalization. I say that because there is not the remotest political prospect that such a thing will ever come to pass. The reality is that the great mass of Americans rightly fear illegal drugs and want them kept as far away as possible. If that means violent drug markets are confined to (and ruining) inner-city neighborhoods and prisons are filled to bursting, middle-class Americans accept that price. All they know is heroin and cocaine are not available at the local mall. The highly public energy devoted to half-baked legalization proposals should be focused on shrinking the drug culture, especially the big hard-core drug population whose habits have become a major factor in the spread of AIDS.

Let us say that the United States decides to get *truly* serious about illegal drugs and banishing the drug culture back to the nether shadows whence it came. What would we need to do? History and experience show that law enforcement is key because availability greatly influences levels of drug use. What helped quell our first epidemic was successful law enforcement, international treaties, and widespread public revulsion against those who used and pushed drugs. The dismantling of the French connection in the early 1970s and the advent of methadone helped quell the second, largely heroin, epidemic.

Our third and most recent epidemic was fueled by crack, a far more addictive and pernicious drug. With the onslaught of crack, the number of committed addicts (not to mention drug dealers) *more* than quadrupled. Moreover, the crack trafficking apparatus is bigger, nastier, and more widespread. The antisocial crack culture of the 1980s overwhelmed the shrinking ranks of local and federal law enforcement, including our understaffed immigration services. The federal antidrug budget spent combating drugs—mainly crack—quadrupled, from about $3 billion in 1986 to $12.1 billion in 1994. This sounds like a huge increase, but contrast it with the tenfold increase in antidrug monies during the Nixon administration. The truth is, it was not enough, certainly not commensurate with the civic chaos created by crack. How do we know this, aside from our own gut sense that the country's been going downhill? Because the price and purity of cocaine has remained stable for the past decade, while the purity of heroin has soared. And because too many addicts cannot find treatment.

An equally depressing indicator is the continuing affront of flagrant open-air drug markets, with all the ensuing violence and public disorder. As long as drug dealers feel free to commandeer public space to shill their poisonous goods brazenly, we can see that local and federal law enforcement remains inadequate. Washington, D.C., had way too many open-air drug markets before crack—twenty—but once crack hit, that figure quadrupled to eighty. Places that never had had obvious drug problems suddenly had dozens or even hundreds of crack dealers openly milling about hawking their wares. Dealers took over wherever they thought they could dominate and intimidate, usually in poorer, minority neighborhoods. Just reestablishing minimal standards of lawful public order became a major challenge.

In Tampa, Florida, a black Baptist preacher and high school dean named Abe Brown watched horrified as crack ravaged his community. In June 1987, he could stand it no longer. He called a meeting at a local church and the 150 people formed Citizens for a Decent Community "to regain control of our neighborhoods." After a year spent bringing together black Tampa, Brown approached the white establishment demanding action and promising whatever cooperation was needed. First, abandoned buildings being used as crack houses were bulldozed. Then police began a steady process of arrests. But without a big enough force, the problem was just pushed from one place to another in the black neighborhoods. Then, on Christmas 1988 a white child was shot when her baby-sitter was trying to buy crack. The baby-sitter was sitting in her car when a dealer lunged to snatch her gold necklace. She resisted and his gun shots killed the child in the backseat.

Tampa decided it had to regroup, enlarge its police force, and develop a new strategy beyond mere arrests that pushed the problem from here to there. A QUAD squad (Quick Uniform Attack on Drugs) began meeting with community groups and discussing what was needed to drive out open drug dealing in 150 obvious "dope holes": "The QUAD squads taught citizens how to get vacant buildings condemned, lobby for more street lights, record license plates, identify car owners, and send letters advising 'Your vehicle was seen in an open-air drug market.' " The police pleaded for citizen help. It became clear many residents were afraid to put calls through to the police station, believing that dealers had spies there. Every QUAD cop was given a beeper. With confidentiality assured, hundreds of citizens began phoning in leads. The 1995 Drug Strategies' report, *Keeping Score*, reports that five years after Tampa embarked on this drive "two-thirds of the outdoor drug markets have been eliminated." This is progress, but not enough. One would venture to suggest that Tampa gladly would welcome still more police to close the remaining drug markets. But the police, in turn, need the wholehearted help of the community to succeed.

Regaining true control of our borders would go a long way toward reining in drug criminals. Colombians living and traveling here worked hard to flood our shores with cocaine, while Dominicans and Jamaicans operated the local franchises. Almost two thirds of heroin trafficking defendants in the United States are foreigners. Presumably most are here as illegal aliens. Our immigration services should focus forcefully on these groups. We have plenty of homegrown criminals, without having to host those from other countries.

While law enforcement is absolutely essential to maintaining civic order and discouraging the drug culture by choking local supply, there are other important tactics that can reduce demand. Back in the 1970s of the Nixon era we really began the process of systematically learning about the pharmacology of different drugs, tracking who the drug users were, looking at how drug use spread, studying treatment, and figuring out what did and did not work.

After twenty years, we now possess a great deal of useful information about illegal drugs. We know that the longer you can keep teenagers from using drugs, the less likely they are to become involved at some later age. Therefore, it is highly worthwhile to focus drug prevention efforts on junior and senior high schools. We know that when a whole community expresses its disapproval of illegal drug use, fewer people will partake. We know who is most vulnerable. We know that the longer someone is in treatment, the more chance of success he or she has.

But the sixty-four thousand dollars question is, how do we reduce the number of hard-core addicts, the real heart of the problem? It is well known in the drug world that most addicts will not seek treatment except under some sort of duress. Nor, for the most part, will they stick with it unless forced. One of the classic signs of addiction is that one abuses drugs even as common sense shows how horribly they are affecting your health and your life. However, in recent years research has yielded some interesting and meaningful news. First is that the majority of criminals are also drug users and/or addicts. This means a huge number of addicts pass through the criminal justice system, and while there they can be forced into treatment.

For years, those who ran the criminal justice systems—the courts, the prisons—insisted drug use was not that big a problem because to admit it would oblige the system to address it. Easier to ignore the fact that drug use by criminals was rampant outside as well as *inside* prisons. But then in 1984 the National Institute of Justice agreed to underwrite two small research projects that tested the urine of just-arrested criminals in Washington, D.C., and Manhattan for drugs. More than half—54 percent—tested positive, two to four times more than those arrested acknowledged when simply asked.

It's likely that nothing more would have come of all this except that the researcher who did the Manhattan work, Eric Wish, happened to sit next to James K. Stewart, director of the National Institute of Justice, on an airplane. Wish already had failed to get anyone at a series of federal agencies interested in expanding this testing to other cities. Stewart thought this was a brilliant way of showing the rampant drug use among the criminal classes. He put his agency's money and clout behind it.

And so, in 1987, the U.S. Justice Department launched a new nationwide survey known as DUF, for Drug Use Forecasting. Organized by Eric Wish, the survey conducted urine tests and follow-up interviews on those arrested for serious crimes in first a dozen and then later in twenty-four cities. The results were eye-opening, especially once the crack epidemic struck: "Between 53 percent and 79 percent of the men tested were found to be positive for at least one of ten drugs. Those levels were two to nine times higher than those in the general population." When cocaine use is tracked through DUF from 1987 through 1992, one sees how popular it remains with the criminal classes. Anywhere from a third to two thirds of those tested were positive for cocaine. Aside from allowing local cities to see what's happening with the hard-core local drug scene, DUF also makes clear that a huge number of addicts are cycling through the criminal justice system. This is exactly what that bureaucracy preferred not to acknowledge. For then, of course, a growing chorus began insisting, "What better time to address the drug problems of the criminal classes than when in the criminal justice system?"

In light of the DUF data on criminal drug habits, the second highly illuminating recent body of research is that even when people are forced into treatment—say, as a condition of parole or probation—they do as well as (and sometimes better than) those who enter voluntarily. Psychiatrist George Vaillant, who followed one hundred male addicts first admitted to the Lexington Narcotics Hospital in 1952, concluded that supervised parole worked so well for many of the addicts he followed "because it altered an addict's schedule of reinforcement. Parole required weekly proof of employment in individuals previously convinced they could not hold a job. It altered friendship networks. . . . Parole . . . provided an external superego and external source of vigilance against relapse. . . . Work provides structure to the addict's life and structure interferes with addiction." In part, coerced treatment works because those addicts are forced to participate longer than those who start on their own, lose interest, and drop out. Remember, if you look at everyone who begins a treatment program a year later, about 75 percent of those who started are gone. If the choice is drug treatment and clean urine tests for a year or time in jail, many find the will to resist drugs. Coercing criminals to stop using drugs shows real promise of reducing the hard-core addict population.

During the 1990s, a fairly steady stream of serious books has sifted through the growing mounds of research generated by the contemporary American drug problem. In 1992, Mark A. R. Kleiman of Harvard's Kennedy School published *Against Excess: Drug Policy for Results* and Mathea Falco, president of Drug Strategies, a Washington think tank, published *The Making of a Drug-Free America: Programs That Work*. The next year Elliott Currie published *Reckoning: Drugs, the Cities, and the American Future*. All these authors agree that in light of what we now know about criminals and drugs and treatment, we should be focusing a large part of our antidrug effort on the criminal justice system. It can produce bigger results for less bucks from the get go. Even if we all agree that drug possession should be punished, what says that punishment has to be incarceration at twenty-five thousand dollars a year in taxpayer money? Supervised probation is clearly much cheaper and appears more effective in changing behavior.

Drug courts—while still quite rare—are a much talked about tactic for keeping the hordes arrested for drug possession out of jail but off drugs. The most popularly cited drug court is the one that's been around the longest—in Dade County, Florida. Mathea Falco describes the Miami experience: "The Drug Court handles all first-time felony drug possession cases in Miami. . . . Among the 1,700 who have graduated from the program after a full year or longer, the rearrest rate is 3 percent. For those who have participated in treatment for shorter periods, the rearrest rate is 7 percent. This compares to rearrest rates of 30 percent for similar drug offenders who have not been through Drug Court."

A Justice Department study of the Dade County court makes clear the necessity of a big coercive stick—incarceration—to keep addicts involved in treatment. The Dade County Drug Court judge "often sends uncooperative clients to jail for two weeks if he feels they are capable of recovery but are simply not trying hard enough." How often is coercion needed? "About 6 out of 10 clients who eventually graduate from the program spend at least 2 weeks in jail for failing to cooperate—more time than they would have spent in jail if they had plea bargained the case. As many as 3 in 10 successful clients spend 4 or more weeks in jail where they receive continuing treatment." Just as noteworthy is that some defendants have become "virtual perpetual clients in the program. . . . Some clients who entered the program in 1989 [four years earlier] are still participating." The recourse to short jail stays for 60 percent of the "clients" shows how critical coercive power is in making addicts hang in there.

Mark Kleiman (*Against Excess*) suggests something far more ambitious than drug courts. He proposes that *all* prisoners and parolees in the criminal justice system (not just those arrested for drug use) be tested for drugs. Staying drug-free would be a basic expectation, with repeated failures punished on an escalating scale, "moving up through fines and hours of unpaid labor, personal curfew, brief periods of incarceration, and finally, referral back to court." Kleiman reports that this was successful in Santa Cruz, California, where even though many of the parolees could not find drug treatment programs, 95 percent of the drug tests came back clean and the burglary rate fell by more than a fifth. "The negative incentive provided by testing was apparently a sufficient aid to willpower even among longtime heroin users." The Washington, D.C., Superior Drug Court is testing actively which produces the best results with arrested addicts: sanctions alone, the old-style treatment programs, or a new, more intensive treatment program. It may turn out that the fear of landing in jail is as effective in stopping drug use as treatment. Coercion may turn out to be one of the most powerful tactics we have.

While it is rarely mentioned in discussions about our national drug problem, probably about half of all addicts are HIV positive or have AIDS. This means that ten years from now most of these people will be dead. If up-and-coming generations can be dissuaded from joining the drug culture, we could expect to see a significantly smaller core group of major drug abusers. It may be ghoulish to view AIDS as easing the drug problem, but in fact it will.

Because it seems so logical to focus the bulk of treatment efforts on the hard core, this approach now is being slowly incorporated into prison policy. After all, reducing hard-core addicts, who consume about three quarters of the supply, would signally reduce demand. Consequently, the Crime Contol Act of 1994 pushes for more drug courts far beyond the few dozen now operating, and many states are not waiting for federal dollars to move forward. The 1995 federal government's *Drug Control Strategy* also makes drug treatment for the incarcerated and paroled a major goal, citing (as does everyone in the field) two model treatment programs for imprisoned drug addicts: Stay'n Out in New York City and Cornerstone in Salem, Oregon. According to Mathea Falco, "rearrest rates for program graduates [of Stay'n Out] three years after their release are one-third lower than for inmates who did not participate in the program. . . . [Three years later] almost half the Cornerstone group had not been convicted of any crime, compared to one-quarter of the untreated group."

And as things now stand, there will be a great many candidates for drug treatment for the incarcerated, because our jails and prisons are overflowing with drug offenders. One of the continuing criticisms of the government's antidrug efforts is how drug arrests have over-whelmed the courts and prisons. Considering the huge number of people who threw themselves into the exploding crack culture, this was inevitable. Whoever dreamed so many Americans would rush to make a buck selling something they knew was so bad? (And whoever dreamed that a whole genre of music—gangsta rap—then would seek to glorify this criminal behavior destroying minority communities?) The local and state incarcerated populations have doubled over a decade, while the federal prisoners have tripled. All told, more than a million people are behind bars.

On the federal level, the number of prisoners has tripled in a decade mainly because of certain federal drug sentencing laws enacted in the late 1980s. Since 1989 (when the Supreme Court upheld the new guide-lines), federal judges who might once have given drug offenders super-vised probation or a year or two in prison now have no choice but to give sentences of five-, ten-, and fifteen-year stretches. And since parole for federal prisoners was eliminated in 1988, that means almost the whole sentence will be served, with a little time off for good behavior.

Former U.S. Deputy Attorney General Philip B. Heymann said in mid 1994 that there were "about 18,000 low-level drug offenders with no record of violence, no significant criminal record and no important connection to a drug organization . . . being held in Federal prisons for mandatory sentences of 5 to 10 years." These people were spending the same amount of time in jail as a kidnapper, a rapist, and only two or three years less than a murderer.

But the federal sentencing guideline that has aroused the greatest outrage is the ever more notorious one hundred-to-one disparity between crack and powdered cocaine. In 1988, Congress, responding to the fast-spreading crack epidemic, decided to make the possession of five grams of crack in federal cases punishable by a mandatory sentence of five years in prison. To get a comparable sentence for powdered cocaine, you would have to be caught with five hundred grams, or one hundred times as much. The U.S. Sentencing Commission points out that the real-life effect is that "retail-level crack cocaine dealers are being punished like wholesaler- and importer-level powder cocaine dealers." The other real-life effect is that a disproportionate number of young black men are serving federal time because 88.3 percent of those arrested in federal crack cases are black.

In Baltimore, which is about 60 percent black, 11,000 of 13,000 people arrested on drug charges in 1991 were black. Of the juveniles arrested that year, 1,304 were black and 13 were white. Some have complained that such figures show the justice system is racist. In fact, it sadly demonstrates the incredible collapse—familial, economic, and moral—of poor black communities. When crack hit, tens of thousands of young black men rushed to peddle drugs—and to arm themselves accordingly. In 1994, in *just* the city of Baltimore, 815 kids under the age of nineteen were shot. Forty-one of these kids died. (Hospital costs were almost $10 million.) All who deal deserve to be punished. As bad as crack is, it would be difficult to argue that it is one hundred times worse than powder, especially since you make crack from powder. The Sentencing Commission concluded the same thing, and proposed in a later report adjusting the sentences downward.

These sentencing policies mean the United States now has behind bars 519 people per 100,000 population, less only than Russia, which has 558. Singapore has 229, followed by Spain at 90 per 100,000, Germany at 80, and Denmark at 66. Endlessly locking up small-fry drug dealers and addicts for many years at twenty-five thousand dollars a year is not a good use of U.S. government money. Far better to incarcerate small-time, nonviolent drug offenders briefly, fine them, and then use supervised probation to coerce them into giving up drugs, going to school, engaging in community service, and otherwise becoming productive citizens. As the Albany, New York, Police Chief said in 1993, "Obviously we can't lock up the problem. That's what we thought previously. But we're locking up kids who are scambling for crumbs, not the people who make the big money."

The huge numbers of young black men in prison testifies to the profound (but predictable) failure of crumbling underclass communities mired in welfare and drugs to raise children properly. A profile of one AFDC mother, whose son was a crack dealer and daughter a drug addict and prostitute, noted that the mother, who also raised dozens of foster care children, "did not encourage or support the children in her care to do homework and she ignored their poor attendance and grades. None did well or enjoyed school; they saw no point in completing it. Virtually all children raised by Island dropped out of high school." There is no starker demonstration of why welfare must be reformed completely. Those who receive public money must be required to complete educations and then participate in the legitimate economy, if for no other reason than to connect their children to the world of school, jobs, and responsibility. While worthy programs can ameliorate some of the social disaster of the welfare underclass, only real reforms that squelch the welfare fast-life culture will effect bona fide change, i.e., marriage, responsible parenthood, and honest work. The harsh truth is that no program can ever replace the hourly, daily, weekly task of lovingly raising children who do well in school and look forward to a better future than using and/or selling drugs.

While all these policies should help steadily reduce the hard-core addict population, an equally important goal must be deterring teenagers from ever using drugs. So what do we know now about who's vulnerable? Potentially anyone can become caught up in drugs, and yet the reality is that some are more vulnerable than others. Who are they? Those with a family history of alcohol or drug abuse. Those from a disruptive home life without "clear, consistent rules." Those who experiment with drugs at a young age. Those who live where drugs are everywhere. Those who do badly in elementary school. Any one of these problems raises the probability of drug problems.

What do we know about prevention? We know it needs to start in the sixth or seventh grade when kids begin to experiment and care so desperately about being like everyone else. Mathea Falco describes in *The Making of a Drug-Free America* a handful of model programs that controlled studies show help lower drug use. Falco asserts that good prevention programs provide credible information about the dangers of alcohol, tobacco, and drugs. They also correct the mistaken notion that youthful drug use is widespread and teach practical strategies for resisting pressure to use.

Dissuading children from using cigarettes and alcohol, as well as marijuana, are extremely important for shrinking the drug culture. Why? Because extensive research shows a series of predictable sequential steps leading to use of illegal drugs by teenage. The work of Denise Kandel shows that this sequential pattern has held true over the decades and applies equally for rich and poor, urban and suburban and rural. Professor Kandel found that "adolescents are very unlikely to experiment with marijuana if they have not experimented previously with an alcoholic beverage or with cigarettes; very few try illicit drugs other than marijuana without prior use of marijuana." An important factor in whether youngsters become illegal-drug users is their age when they begin using cigarettes and alcohol.

As a society, we *can* discourage markedly the demand for illegal drugs. We can condemn illegal drugs consistently in no uncertain terms, a stance we *know* reduces use. We can use the criminal justice system to force prisoners and probationers to be drug-free. We can also train schoolchildren to reject tobacco, alcohol, and illegal drugs, while working to make all three much more difficult to obtain. All these are reasonable and important measures for gradually shrinking the drug culture and its voracious appetite for illegal drugs.

We also need to do all possible to diminish drug supply and the international drug traffic. Here in America, we must face up to the need for far more police and drug agents, so we can reclaim control (at minimum) of public spaces now ceded to drug dealers. As for the international side, the challenge is obvious when you take into account that in "the past decade worldwide production of illicit drugs has increased dramatically: Opium and marijuana production has roughly doubled, and coca production tripled."

As this book has made clear, since World War II, only the Nixon administration has given illegal drugs the high priority in our domestic and foreign policy that it deserves. Antidrug monies rose tenfold during the early 1970s. The French connection was smashed, crippling the heroin trade, and drug treatment was made available nationwide for the first time. With the excuse of the Cold War gone, the United States must once again treat drug traffic as a top policy issue, especially in the international arena. There should be no more mixed signals from government mandarins and knowing winks from CIA chiefs. Let us return to the morally straightforward days of FDR, when our government implacably opposed addiction and trafficking throughout the world. It is instructive what even small gestures of American ire can accomplish on the international front.

For instance, in mid 1995 Colombia suddenly began to arrest top members of the Cali cartel. Why? Because each year on March 1, the U.S. State Department releases with some fanfare its annual drug "certification" reports. Inflicted upon the State Department by Congress in one of its many moments of frustration, this hefty report serves primarily to embarrass publicly the world's narconations. Theoretically, it also could have real economic consequences. Explains the *New York Times*, "By law, if the State Department finds that a country is not cooperating on narcotics matters, it must cut off foreign aid and veto loans by the World Bank and other international institutions, unless it determines that there are 'vital national interests' to continue such aid."

The 1995 State Department report put Colombia for the first time on the uncooperating list: "Weak legislation, corruption and inefficiency hampered efforts to bring mid- and high-level narcotics traffickers to justice. No drug-related assets were forfeited, while already lenient sentences were further reduced pursuant to automatic sentencing reductions." Colombia may have been even more lax than in the past, but "vital national interests" were invoked to prevent aid cut off. Apparently this public rebuke sufficiently embarrassed the Colombians that they actually began to round up and arrest high-level Cali members in the summer of 1995. It remains to be seen how this might affect the drug trade.

If mere public censure by America could produce the arrests of major drug traffickers, what might unified, forceful international action gain? Once upon a time, drugs were viewed as largely an American problem. We had—and still do—the biggest and most antisocial addict population of the industrialized nations. *But*, in the past ten years, the rest of the world—especially Europe—has had the misfortune of starting to catch up with us.

Douglas Lipton has worked overseas extensively in recent years. "Where Europe was relatively drug free," he wrote in 1989, "they are now experiencing the most rapid growth of consumption-related problems anywhere. Italy, Spain, West Germany, and Great Britain are all experiencing this surge. Even Switzerland, which had been free of this scourge for many years, now says there are . . . thousands of addicts in their country." Because no European country has any organized way to measure drug use (like our household survey or DAWN), the European scene is extrapolated from medical and police reports.

The huge worldwide expansion in the production and abuse of illegal drugs has not gone unnoticed in the lofty councils of international affairs. Irving Tragen, a longtime American diplomat, claims in *Drugs and Foreign Policy* that "drugs now rank with peace, development, debt and environment at the top of the agendas of multilateral bodies." Slowly but surely, the previously indifferent governing classes finally may be realizing that drug traffickers and drug addiction pose serious threats to civil order and existing elites.

Peru, where 60 percent of the world's cocaine is grown, and Colombia, where it is grown and processed, long have heaped blame for the drug traffic on the United States, saying if we could control our domestic appetite for drugs, there would be no problem. But this ingenuously ignores the fact that sheer drug availability *develops* markets. Peru and Colombia have learned this basic drug culture fact the hard way. Since processed cocaine has become widely available there, both countries have developed large addict populations of their own.

In a 1991 *New Yorker* piece on Medellín, one couple described their son's terrible *basuco* habit: "He would come home so stoned, so crazy, that he would bang his head against the wall until we grabbed him and held him back. We'd tell him he was going to kill himself, but he would say that's what he wanted." He was soon into crime and, indeed, ended up dead. The parents reviewed for the reporter "the list of the kids in the neighborhood who had died or were on drugs. On some streets, they claimed, every household had at least one addicted son or—less frequently—daughter."

As Douglas Lipton observes, "The escalation of Latin America's own drug consumption problem, ironically and sadly, may become a solution to the problem there in the long term. These nations point to the United States as the culpable party—that is, if it weren't for the Americans' demand for drugs, there wouldn't be a problem—but now they are alarmed because their youth are rapidly becoming consumers of *basuco*, a cheap, ravaging, addictive and deadly product of the coca conversion process."

What then to do?

International treaties are in place—signed by major coca producers such as Colombia, Peru, and Bolivia—that require those countries to eradicate all illegal coca and opium poppies. Do we want to be serious about holding those countries to international law? Jack Cusack, the veteran narcotics agent who masterminded the highly successful Turkish opium crop eradication in the early 1970s, a key component of ending the French connection, is one who believes that crop eradication is still the way to go. He is highly critical of recent (and unsuccessful) U.S. drug policy overseas vis à vis eradication, because we have insisted on working solo.

Explained Cusack in an interview:

> I have been trying to sell the idea that the U.S. should form a coalition within the United Nations that would be the Group of Seven [United States, Canada, Japan, Britain, France, Germany, and Italy] plus four or five others. This group would create, finance, and control an earmarked fund limited strictly to reducing illicit production. Together—not just the U.S. by itself—this group would go to the producer countries and point out that they are not complying with UN conventions they

have signed. Remind them of their obligation. Offer recognized experts to provide technical assistance and funding. But before any funding, the country has to come to an agreement drawn up by the country's experts and the UN experts. No money until there are commitments and real progress. The idea is, you negotiate and you don't let up until you come to implementation. If they slam the door in our faces, then you have to do what you did with Iraq; you isolate them, make them pariahs in the international community.

We have put immense international pressure on Iraq because it tried to interfere with our oil supply (with the Gulf War) and Libya because it engaged in anti-American terrorism. I would wager that many Americans would view the deliberate producing of cocaine and heroin destined for our shores as equally heinous acts. Countries that fail to honor antidrug treaties they signed should be subject to international boycotts.

Thinking in a similar vein—that international drug trafficking is international and requires a less parochial approach—has led to proposals for an international drug court. One can see the potential immediately. The Colombian judiciary is understandably afraid to try drug cases because of endemic corruption and real threats to their lives. An international drug court would solve this. Cusack thinks the mass of Colombians would be more than glad to retrieve their country from the narcotraffickers and *basuco*. In 1983, when he was working for the House Select Committee on Narcotics, he traveled to Colombia: "We were staying at a hotel in Bogotá and eating in the dining room there. All evening, people came up to us asking if we were from the U.S. Congress. They welcomed us, saying, 'God bless you. The gangsters have taken over our country and are poisoning our children. They are destroying our country.' "

The U.S. government, operating on its own, in recent years has had little success with crop eradication. It has nonetheless applied some fresh thinking to other vulnerabilities of the international trafficking world. The upshot has been to zero in on money. People always can be replaced in the drug trade, but when money is gone, it's gone. Drug trafficking is basically about money, and so the hot new strategy of the 1990s has been pursuing and seizing drug profits, wherever they might be. The 1988 UN convention against illicit drug trafficking specifically criminalizes money laundering. Ratified by one hundred governments, the convention has been in effect since 1990. Slowly but surely signatory nations are passing laws to comply, making money laundering harder.

Switzerland, that bastion of bank secrecy, has changed its law to discourage drug money in its banks. It also has assigned, for the first time, an attaché in Washington, D.C., to work on money-laundering issues.

The First World slowly has come to view drug money and the power it confers on criminals a big enough threat to have organized its own money-laundering group, the Financial Action Task Force, in 1989. Many of the twenty-six member countries have revised their financial reporting laws based on the evaluations of outside experts. This task force meets regularly to discuss such "major issues as regulating wire transfers, standards for non-bank financial institutions, asset forfeiture and asset sharing, and the use of shell corporations, offshore banks and related entities to facilitate money laundering." It also has been traveling the globe preaching the virtues of catching money launderers and showing how this can be done. One incentive is sharing the seized assets. Since 1989, the United States alone has dispersed $34 million to cooperating foreign governments from assets seized in money-laundering cases.

As traffickers seek to evade the growing body of laws aimed at their ill-gotten gains, investigations against them have grown progressively more imaginative and sophisticated. In 1994, a DEA/IRS operation opened an offshore bank in Anguilla with the help of British authorities. Explains a State Department report, "The bank began taking drug traffickers' accounts in 1994. In addition, various undercover corporations were created to provide services such as loans, cashiers' checks, wire transfers, peso exchanges, etc. The Cali cartel also engaged the bank to sell three paintings, including a Picasso, a Rubens and a Reynolds, which were seized." This investigation, Operation Dinero, "targeted the illicit drug proceeds of the Cali Mafia, [and] resulted in 116 arrests in the U.S., Spain, Italy and Canada, the seizure of nine tons of cocaine, and the seizure of more than $90 million in cash and other property."

Another such case was Operation Primero: "The investigation centered on Universal de Cambios, a wire transfer business in Atlanta, which was allegedly one of the largest international money laundering organizations for the Cali cartel. . . . The indictment in Atlanta charged the defendants with laundering drug proceeds (by wire) from the U.S., Spain, France and Italy. The investigation resulted in the arrest of 91 persons in those three countries, and led to the seizure of $15 million in cash, 43 kilos of cocaine, and 250 pounds of marijuana."

In 1992, the U.S. Treasury Department established a task force called El Dorado in New York City that does nothing but go after drug money and launderers. Mainly a U.S. Customs/IRS venture, it also has staff from sixteen other agencies. The group has no trouble keeping busy.

Roosevelt Avenue in Queens, New York, writes Fredric Dannen in *The New Yorker*, "is the Wall Street of the drug trade, with literally hundreds of establishments that constitute a financial-service industry for the money launderers. The sheer number of *casas de cambio*, money trans-mitters, and travel agencies—all of which are used to wire money to South America—borders on the ridiculous. There are enough to serve ten neighborhoods of equal size but without a drug economy." In its first two years, El Dorado seized over $60 million in cash and assets, a por-tion of which went to participating agencies. One Treasury undersecre-tary explained, "When the people who handle your money start losing your money, that makes you very insecure. That's what I want. I want them [the traffickers] to be insecure, to be nervous, to be paranoid."

Rayburn Hess, the State Department's money-laundering expert, says, "We're not talking about creating a foolproof system. People will always figure out how to penetrate the financial systems. We just want to make it more difficult. We want to increase the probability of arrest. We want to make it more costly for the traffickers. And we want to make the case against this new breed of criminals, the money brokers who move money for a fee. If you go back ten years, we were worrying about some guy in Miami whose pants were held up with a rope going in with suitcases full of cash. Now, we're worrying about the overt and covert control of the financial system."

Hess has been urging unabashedly the major international banks to drop correspondent banks whose bona fides are not good, who are sud-denly awash in suspect cash. He says, "In the banking system, the ulti-mate weapon is not fear of sanctions by the U.S., but the threat of being excluded from the international payment systems." When Panama's new foreign minister went to Europe in 1995, he reportedly was stunned to hear from international bankers that his country's banks were viewed as havens for dirty money. Why he would be stunned is hard to imagine, since a prominent front-page story in the *Washington Post* on September 20, 1993, was headlined, PANAMA: A GATEWAY FOR COCAINE PROFITS, and described in some detail how Panama was "the most active center for cocaine 'money laundering' in the Western Hemisphere." Nonetheless, the unspoken threat by respectable inter-national bankers that they might be loathe to do business with Panama was enough to send the new government scurrying to clean up its act and actually pass meaningful money-laundering laws. This was some-thing never accomplished by years of American threats or the invasion and deposing of General Noriega.

The other vulnerability of the drug-trafficking syndicates is that they all need enormous quantities of what are called precursor and essential chemicals actually to turn the raw vegetable matter of coca leaves and opium poppies into the finished products—cocaine and heroin. The same 1988 UN convention against illicit trafficking that criminalized money laundering also has put global controls on the twenty-two chemicals used to make cocaine and heroin. These new mechanisms to counter money laundering and chemicals will take years to be up and fully functional. Again, no one deludes themselves that suddenly traffickers will be left high and dry without the chemicals they need. But it just makes trafficking that much more difficult and expensive and obliges chemical firms to know where their product goes. All through the 1970s and 1980s, it was legitimate American and European chemical companies that provided the products used in Colombia to refine cocaine. Under these new laws, such business dealings are illegal.

The possibilities of the new chemical control laws are illustrated by one raid made by the Colombian National Police in March 1994. While no arrests of any major traffickers were made that year, Colombian police did seize 1,754 metric tons of chemicals from Holanda Chemical International, enough to process 135.5 metric tons of cocaine.

If all this is discouraging, history reminds us that shrinking the drug culture requires not years of persistent effort, but decades. One must be content with slow and incremental improvements, which even our not very serious war on drugs can claim. The biggest cohort of hard-core drug abusers in America are currently in their thirties and forties. And probably close to half of these heroin and cocaine addicts are HIV-positive, which means that much of America's big addict population will die of AIDS in the next decade. Can we educate the up-and-coming generations to understand and fear the dark side of drugs? Or will our foolish romance continue?

Americans always have been seekers, a people driven to explore and somehow improve themselves and their world. The "pursuit of happiness," the fascination with frontiers physical and psychic, the quest to better oneself, all have been leitmotivs of American culture. It was perhaps inevitable that a people historically so enthralled with Possibility and Self would be drawn to such new and much touted substances as heroin and cocaine when they first became available at the turn of the century. Soon enough the dangers became manifest and that first American romance with drugs faded.

After World War II, marijuana and the psychedelics joined heroin and cocaine as drugs of abuse. This time drugs became firmly linked with hipness and the powerful forces of social rebellion. All over again, Americans had to discover painfully the ultimately corrosive quality of drugs—corrosive to self and society. Any thoughts that marijuana, LSD, heroin, or cocaine were modern elixirs that could somehow lift us en masse into a better place (or even provide just harmless fun) have proven a sad and costly chimera. Once again, the romance largely has faded.

The drug culture always will be with us in some form. The national challenge is to make that sad world as small and beyond-the-pale as possible, to push it back into the shadowy netherworld. We need to remember the terrible waste of those who became addicts, forfeiting the best of their youth and often their very lives. We need to challenge relentlessly those who glorify, proselytize, and traffick. And we need to keep at it year after year, decade after decade.

Chapter 1: "One Day You Find Yourself in Hell"

15 "the secret of happiness." Thomas De Quincey, *Confessions of an English Opium Eater* (Crescent Press: London, 1950), 258.
16 "confirmed opium eater." Ibid., 312.
16 "writhing, throbbing, palpitating." Ibid., 338–39.
17 crude opium imports. David Courtwright, *Dark Paradise* (Harvard University Press: Cambridge, Mass., 1982), 36.
17 "carelessness of physicians." Charles Terry, M.D., & Mildred Pellens, *Opium Problem* (Bureau of Social Hygiene: N.Y.C., 1928), 99.
18 "masturbation, photophobia." Courtwright, *Dark Paradise*, 48.
18 "more ladies to fall." Ibid.
18 Ella O'Neill story. Louis Sheaffer, *O'Neill* (Paragon House: N.Y., 1968), 21–22.
18 "I hate doctors." Ibid., 21.
19 "silken threads." R. B. Eubank, *Twenty Years in Hell* (Revelation: Kansas City, M.O., 1903), 18.
19 Keeley Institutes. Courtwright, *Dark Paradise*, 216.
19 "Cure for the Opium Habit." E. C. Huse, *The Therapeutic Gazette*, n.s. 1 (1880), 256–57.
19 "one such lucky hit." Sigmund Freud, *Cocaine Papers*, ed. Roby. Byck, M.D., (Stonehill: N.Y., 1974), 6.
20 "regularly against indigestion." Ibid., 7.
20 "recent issues of American newspapers." Ibid., 70.
20 "make the coward brave." Ibid., 367.
21 elixirs. L. Gomez, "Cocaine," *Life*, May 7, 1984, 57–64.

21   almost eleven tons. J. L. Phillips and R. D. Wynne, *Cocaine: The Mystique & The Reality* (Discus Books: N.Y., 1980), 56.

21   Holmes and cocaine. For an amusing and original essay on Holmes and Freud and cocaine, see David Musto's "Sherlock Holmes and Sigmund Freud: A Study in Cocaine," *Journal of the American Medical Association* (April 1, 1968).

22   W. A. Hammond. Byck, *Cocaine Papers*, 368–69.

22   New Neurological Society. "Cocaine and the So-called Cocaine Habit." *New York Medical Journal* (December 4, 1886): 637–39.

22   "Neither indifferent as to which." S. Nuland, *Doctors* (Vintage: N.Y., 1989), 396.

23   "abandoned himself entirely." W. Scheppegrell, "Abuse & Dangers of Cocaine," *The Medical News*, 73, 14, (October 1, 1898): 421.

24   newspapers and patent medicine. David Musto, *The American Disease* (Oxford University Press: N.Y., 1987), 93.

25   "The suffering." S. H. Adams, *The Great American Fraud* (AMA Press: Chicago, 1907), 115.

25   "while the daily newspapers." J. F. Spillane, "The Retail Druggist and the Transformation of Cocaine, 1885–1915," unpublished Paper, quoting from *National Druggist*, September 1905.

25   "every case of ptomaine." "House Votes To Expose Secrets of Drug Trade," *New York Times*, June 23, 1906, 3:1.

25   "operation of the new law," "A Fortnight Under The Pure Food Law," *New York Times*, January 13, 1907, pt. 3, 5:2.

Chapter 2: "Had the Dope Habit and Had It Bad"

26   "If opium habitués." J. R. Frisch, "Our Years in Hell: American Addicts Tell Their Story, 1829–1914," *Journal of Psychedelic Drugs* 9, no. 3 (July–September 1977): 204.

26   opium smoking. W. R. Cobbe, *Dr. Judas* (S.C. Griggs: Chicago, 1895), 10.

26   "Opium-smoking don't go." D. Griffin, "Opium Addiction in Chicago," *Chicago History* 6 (1977): 107–16.

27   "dreaming off the effects." "Opium Joints in the Black Hills," *Chamber's Journal* 65 (October 13, 1888): 654–55.

27   "sickening sight." "The Opium Habit in S.F.," *Medical & Surgical Reporter* 57 (December 10, 1887): 784–85.

28   "ruined morally." F. F. Kane, *Opium Smoking in America and China* (Arno Press: New York, 1976; reprint of 1882 edition), 1. On the early use of nondrug laws in San Francisco to discourage opium dens, see J. Baumohl, "The 'Dope Fiend's Paradise' Revisited: Notes from Research in Progress on Drug Law Enforcement in S.F., 1875–1915," *The Surveyor* 24 (June 1992): 3–12.

28   "dissolute-looking young." "Opium & Its Votaries," *The Californian* 1 (1892): 631–45.

28   "younger class of boys." Kane, *Opium Smoking*, 3.

29   twenty state legislatures. M. I. Wilbert and M. G. Motter, "Digest of Laws & Regulations In Force in the U.S. Relating to the Possession, Use, Sale, and Manufacture of Poisons & Habit-Forming Drugs," Public Health Bulletin No. 56, (Government Printing Office: Washington, D.C., 1912), 34. States specifically outlawing opium smoking and dens were Alaska, Arizona, California, Connecticut, Delaware, Idaho, Iowa, Minnesota, Missouri, Montana, Nevada, New Mexico, New York, North Dakota, Ohio, Pennsylvania, South Dakota, Utah, Washington, and Wyoming.

29   "its sole uses." " 'Opiokapnism' or Opium Smoking," *JAMA* 18 (June 4, 1892): 719.

29   "hot-beds of epidemics." J. Riis, *How the Other Half Lives* (Hill & Wang: N.Y., 1957), 2–3.

30   "condition of dreamy wakefulness." H. H. Kane, *Opium Smoking in America and China* (Arno Press; N.Y., 1976; reprint of 1882 book), 61.

30   Denver police raided a den. "The Golden 'Yen Hock,' " *Denver Daily News*, October 10, 1886, 2.

30   New York City's. Committee of Fifteen. Box 4 and 5, Rare Book and Manuscript Division, New York Public Library, Astor, Lenox, and Tilden Foundations.

31   "Splendid 'joints.' " S. Crane, *Prose and Poetry* (Library of America: N.Y., 1984), 853.

31 "Months earlier a doctor." Kate Jordan, "In the Gray Land of Drugs," *McClure's* 46 (December 1915), 22–24.

31 St. Louis. "Cocaine debauchery," *Eclectic Medical Journal of Cincinnati* 56 (1898), 464–65.

32 "utter debasement." C. W. Collins and J. Day, "The Eighth Deadly Sin," *Everyday Life* 4, no. 10 (July 1909): 1–3.

32 "state of depravity." "Cocaine Alley," *American Druggist & Pharmaceutical Record* 37 no. 12 (December 10, 1900): 1.

32 southern blacks. J. F. Spillane, "Modern Drug, Modern Menace: The Legal Use & Distribution of Cocaine in the U.S., 1880–1920" (May 1994 dissertation available through Rand Drug Policy Research Center publications): 246–53.

32 "extraordinarily severe work." "The Cocaine Habit Among Negroes," *The British Medical Journal* (November 29, 1902): 1729.

33 Lafayette Hotel. Luc Sante, *Low Life* (Vintage: N.Y., 1992), 150.

33 "a wonderful feeling." From the Papers of the Committee of Fourteen, Box 31, "Resume of Reports on Cabaret Situation 1917," p. 8, Rare Books and Manuscripts Division, New York Public Library, Astor, Lenox, and Tilden Foundations..

33 "extravagant feeling." G. K. Turner, "The City of Chicago," *McClure's* 28 no. 6 (April 1907), 582.

33 "a mood of well-being." C. W. Collins and J. Day, "Nightmare of Cocaine," *Everyday Life* (September 1909), 4–5.

33 "vivacious boy." Jane Addams, *Twenty Years at Hull House* (New American Library: N.Y., 1981), 212.

33 Gray's Catarrh. C. W. Collins and J. Day, "The Demon in the Bottle," *Everyday Life* (August 1909), 6–7.

33 Cocaine consumption was soaring. C. Moffett, "Rx Cocaine," *Hampton's Magazine* 26 (May 1911), 595–606.

34 Maltine Coca Wine. J.F. Spillane, "The Retail Druggist etc." 33.

34 "In every slum." C. W. Collins and J. Day, "Nightmare of Cocaine," *Everyday Life* (Sept. 1909), 4–5.

34 *Willie the Weeper*, Sante, *Low Life*, 148–49.

35 Courtwright has estimated. D. Courtwright, *Dark Paradise*, 25, 28.

35 Europe. M. I. Wilbert and M. G. Motter, "Digest of Laws," Public Health Bulletin No. 56, 14.

35 American Pharmaceutical Association. "Report of Committee on Acquirement of the Drug Habit," proceedings of the American Pharmaceutical Association 50 (1902), 567–73.

35 "Over 4,000 letters." "Snuffing Out the Cocaine Fiend," *Charities & the Commons*, 18 (April 13, 1907): 73.

36 diacetylmorphine. Trebach, *The Heroin Solution* (Yale University Press, New Haven, 1982), 39–40.

37 "the remedy was very prompt." M. Manges, "The Treatment of Coughs with Heroin," *New York Medical Journal* 68 (November 26, 1898): 768–70.

37 "habituation has been noted." M. Manges, "A Second Report on the Therapeutics of Heroin," *New York Medical Journal* 71 (January 13, 1900): 51–55, 79–83.

37 "prolonged use of Heroin." G. Pettey, "The Heroin Habit Another Curse," *The Alabama Medical Journal*, 15 (1903) 174–80.

38 "heroin is being used extensively." John M. B. Phillips,"Prevalence of the Heroin Habit," *JAMA* 59 no. 24 (December 14, 1912): 2146–47.

38 "sneak into hallways." "Caught Using Heroin," *NYT* (June 3, 1913), 18.

38 "Say Drug Habit Grips." "Say Drug Habit Grips the Nation," *NYT* (December 5, 1913).

38 "Leroy Street." Leroy Street, *I Was A Drug Addict* (Arlington House: New Rochelle, 1953), 13.

39 "mushroom growth." C. B. Farr, "Relative Frequency of the Morphine and Heroine Habits," *NYMJ* 101 (May 1, 1915): 892–95.

39 "without ambition." S. R. Leahy, "Some Observations on Heroin Habitués," *Psychiatric Bulletin of the New York State Hospitals* 8 (1915): 251–63.

39 "essentially a matter of city life." P. Bailey, "The Heroin Habit," *The New Republic* (April 22, 1916), 315.

Chapter 3: "Congress Should Take Immediate Action . . ."

41 Dowager Empress. J. P. Chamberlain, "Dope," *Survey* 42 (September 6, 1919) 797–98.

41 active federal involvement. D. F. Musto, *The American Disease* (Oxford University Press: N.Y., 1987), 26–31.

42 Elizabeth Washburn Wright. "Mrs. Wright, Narcotics Foe, Is Dead at 76," *Washington Post* (February 14, 1952).

42 "The habit of opium smoking." J. Spence, "Opium Smoking in Ch'ing China," in *Conflict & Control in Late Imperial China*, ed. F. Wakeman, Jr., and C. Grant (University of California Press: Berkeley, 1975), 146–48.

43 "1832 it was finally proven." Ibid., 150–51.

43 In 1840. H. H. Kane, *Opium Smoking in America and China* (Arno Press: N.Y., 1976; reprint 1882 ed.), 28.

43 "This domestic production." Spence, "Opium Smoking" (1840), 152.

43 "sots." F. J. Masters, "Opium & Its Votaries," *The Californian* 1 (1892), 640.

43 Elihu Root. Musto, *Disease*, 32.

44 "Our move to help China." Ibid., 39.

44 "large misuse of opium." U.S. Senate, A Report on the International Opium Commission and on the Opium Problem as Seen Within the United States and Its Possessions (compiler Hamilton Wright), 61st Cong., 2nd sess., 1910, S. Doc. 377, 51.

45 "perfectly absurd." Letter dated March 15, 1910, from Wright to Dr. Tenney. U.S. National Archives. RG 43 Wright Papers International Opium Conference, The Hague. File 1.

45 Foster bill. Musto, *Disease*, 41–48.

45 "I would hate to see." Bishop Brent to Wright, May 28, 1909. U.S. National Archives. RG 43. Wright Papers. International Opium Conference, The Hague, corresp. File 1.

45 "your earnestness." Bishop Brent to Wright, Jan. 24, 1911. U.S. National Archives. RG 43. Wright Papers. International Opium Conference. The Hague. Corresp. File 1.

46 "practice among solidery." R. M. Blanchard, "Heroin and Soldiers," *Military Surgeon* 33 (1913), 140–43.

46 "no man known," E. King, "The Use of Habit-Forming Drugs by Enlisted Men," *Military Surgeon* 39 (1916), 380–84.

46 "You are never happy." Bishop Brent to Wright, Sept. 21, 1910. U.S. National Archives, Washington, D.C., RG 43. Wright Papers. International Opium Conference, The Hague. Corresp. File 1.

47 "no individual has ever." House of Representatives *Registration of Producers and Importers of Opium, Etc.* 63rd Cong., 1st sess., 1913, H. R. 23, 3.

48 "Practically all of the addicts." H. C. Wood, "Some of the Results of the Harrison Anti-Narcotic Law," *J. of Am. Pharm. Assn.* 5 (1916): 1205–8.

49 Wright's bad relations. Memo dated June 14, 1914 from Wright to President Taft. U.S. National Archives. RG 43. International Opium Commission, The Hague. Corresp. Relating to Wright's Appointment. File 1.

49 "so carefully drawn." "Drug Users Seek Help," *New York Sun* (April 17, 1915).

49 "Now I was one of a band." L. Street, *I Was a Drug Addict* (Arlington House: N.Y., 1953), 101.

49 study of 130 habitués. C. B. Farr, M.D., "Relative Frequency of the Morphine and Heroine Habits: Based on Some Observations at the Philadelphia General Hospital." *New York Medical Journal* 101 (May 1, 1915): 892–95.

50 a second study from the same hospital. J. McIver, M.D., and G. E. Price, M.D., "Drug Addiction: Analysis of One Hundred and Forty-Seven Cases at the Philadelphia General Hospital," *JAMA* 66 (February 12, 1916): 477, 478.

50 Cleveland study. H. H. Drysdale, "Some of the Effects of the Harrison Anti-Narcotic Law in Cleveland (Analysis of Cases of Drug Addiction Treated in the Observation Department of the Cleveland City Hospital)," *Cleveland Medical Journal* 14 (1915): 363.

50 "I wish to state." P. Lichtenstein, "Narcotic Addiction," *NYMJ* 100 (1914): 965.

51 Jin Fuey Moy. Musto, *Disease*, 129.

51 a huge decline. Courtwright, *Paradise*, chap. 1

52 "no discussion of the subject." Musto, *Disease*, 132.

52 "according to the amount." A. S. Trebach, *The Heroin Solution* (Yale University Press: New Haven, 1982), 129.

52 New York City. "Fear Outbreak By Men Needing Drugs," *NYT* (April 10, 1919), 1.

53 sight-seeing buses. C. E. Terry, "Symposium on Narcotic Drug Addiction," *AJ Public Health* 11 (1921): 33.

54 "free-masonry of the drug addict." S. D. Hubbard, "The New York City Narcotic Clinic," *Monthly Bull. of the Dept. of Health City of NY* 10 no. 2 (February 1920): 33–47.

54 "One very peculiar." Ibid., 38.

55 New Haven. D. F. Musto, "A Follow-up Study of the New Haven Morphine Maintenance Clinic of 1920," *NEJM* 304 no. 18 (April 30, 1981): 1071–77.

55 "when the clinic opened." "Investigation of Narcotic Clinic at Houston, Texas," Houston IRS Agent to L. Nutt, March 26, 1920, Treasury Dept. Files, case 73221, available via FOIA D.E.A. to David Courtwright, who kindly lent them to me.

55 Shreveport clinic. C. E. Terry and M. Pellens, *The Opium Problem* (Bureau of Social Hygiene: N.Y., 1928), 863–72.

55 clinic effected no cures. Musto, *Disease*, 167–75.

57 "vast section of the country." U.S. House. *Prohibiting the Importation of Opium for the Manufacture of Heroin: Hearings Before the Committee on Ways and Means* 68th Cong., 1st sess., 1924. 49.

57 "familial ties." B. Dai, *Opium Addiction in Chicago* (Commercial Press: Shanghai, 1937), 186.

58 "more than 100 addicts." Street, *I Was a Drug Addict*, 4.

Chapter 4: "A Cinema Crowd of Cocaine-Crazed Sexual Lunatics"

59 Paramount Studios director William Desmond Taylor. R. Giroux, *A Deed of Death* (Knopf: N.Y., 1990).

60 Edward Doherty. Ibid.

60 Assistant District Attorney Tom Green. S. Kirkpatrick, *A Cast of Killers* (Onyx: N.Y., 1992), 30.

60 "Before she's through." R. Giroux, *A Deed of Death* (Knopf: N.Y., 1990), 114.

60 a couple of hundred silent movies. K. Brownlow, *Behind the Mask of Innocence* (Knopf: N.Y., 1990), 96–119.

61 "Publicity has thrown." C. F. Stokes, "The Problem of Narcotic Addiction of Today," *Medical Record* 93 (May 4, 1918): 757.

62 "vulgarians from the gutter." D. A. Yallop, *The Day the Laughter Stopped* (St. Martin's Press: N.Y., 1976), 145.

62 "cinema crowd." K. Anger, *Hollywood Babylon* (Delta Publishing: N.Y., 1981) 9.

62 "queens overnight." Berg, *Goldwyn* (Knopf: N.Y., 1989), 71.

63 "dark, windy days." B. Fussell, *Mabel* (Ticknor & Fields: N.Y., 1982), 108.

63 "pushers of dope." A. Loos, *A Girl Like I* (Viking Press: N.Y., 1966), 116.

63 "large estates." E. Doherty, "Land of Make-Believe is Only Too Real," *Chicago Tribune* (February 7, 1922), 2.

64 "kills all pain and worry." A. Crowley, *The Diary of a Drug Fiend* (University Books: New Hyde Park, N.Y., 1970; reprint of 1922 book), 57.

64 "The police were reticient." "Taylor murder," *NYT* (February 6, 1922), 1.

64 "to an eastern sanitarium." E. Doherty, "Suspect," *Chicago Tribune* (February 12, 1922), 2.

65 "Miss Normand." "Taylor Slain Guarding Her, New Theory," *Chicago Herald-Examiner* (February 12, 1922), 1.

65 "Let me furnish." E. Doherty, *Gall and Honey* (Sheed & Ward: N.Y., 1941), 200–1.

65 "There goes half a million," Fussell, *Mabel*, 170.

65 Olive Thomas. "Paris Authorities Investigate Death of Olive Thomas," *NYT* (September 11, 1920), 1.

66 *Vanity Fair*. "Happy Days in Hollywood," *Vanity Fair* (May 1922), 73.

66 "One day, Louis B. Mayer," A. S. Berg, *Goldwyn* (Knopf: N.Y., 1989), 9.

66 "cleaning house" B. Fussell, *Mabel* (Ticknor & Fields: N.Y., 1982), 145.

66 "With the brightening," *Vanity Fair* (May 1922), 73.

67 "tending to shock." Fussell, *Mabel*, 147.

67 "unsafe" Hollywood drug users. S. Hammond, "The Famous Addicts," *New York Post* (July 23, 1970).

67 "biggest box-office." Doherty, *Gall and Honey*, 201.

67 "It was HMC." Fussell, *Mabel*, 125.

67 "I'll either come out cured." Brownlow, *Mask of Innocence*, 111.

68 "Kliegeyes." "Wally Reid Victim of Studio Lights," *Toledo Blade* (October 21, 1922); "Reid Victim of Influenza," *Toledo Blade* (December 18, 1922).

68 "a queer coincidence." D. D. Reid, "From His Personal Stock," *L.A. Examiner* (January 3, 1923) (From Wallace Reid clipping file, Performing Arts Library, Lincoln Center, New York City.)

68 "Wally also adopted." Loos, *A Girl Like I*, 118.

69 " 'dope' parties in Hollywood." M. Starks, *Cocaine Fiends and Reefer Madness* (Cornwall Books: N.Y., 1982), 47.

69 "mysteriously worded telegrams." D. D. Reid, "From his Personal Stock," *Los Angeles Examiner* (January 3, 1923).

69 New York drug dealer. "$50,000 Drug Haul by Simon's Men," *NYT* (December 13, 1922), 28:1; "Fingerprints Revive Movie Dope Case," undated clip in Wallace Reid file at Performing Arts Library, Lincoln Center, New York City. This 1943 article identified Reid as one of Williams's clients.

69 trick golf club. Brownlow, *Behind the Mask*, 108.

70 "Illegal drug traffic." Starks, *Cocaine Fiends*, 55.

70 "It made her dirty." Ibid., 49–50.

70 "cocaine is habit-forming." Barry Paris, *Louise Brooks* (Knopf: N.Y., 1989), 367.

70 third scandal. Kirkpatrick, *Cast*, 110.

Chapter 5: "Arnold Rothstein, Financial Genius . . ."

72 Arnold Rothstein. Portrait drawn from Leo Katcher, *The Big Bankroll: The Life and Times of Arnold Rothstein* (Arlington House: New Rochelle, N.Y., 1959); "Rothstein, Round the Town" in Craig Thompson and Allen Raymond, *Gang Rule in New York*. (Dial Press: New York, 1940); "The Rothstein Era" in Virgil W. Peterson, *The Mob, 200 Years of Organized Crime in New York* (Green Hill Publishers: Ottawa, Ill., 1983); Alan Block, *East Side–West Side: Organizing Crime in New York 1930–50* (University of College Cardiff Press: Wales, 1980); Albert Fried, *The Rise and Fall of the Jewish Gangster in America* (Holt, Rinehart and Winston: N.Y., 1980); "The Rothstein Case: An Underworld Tale," *NYT* (October 6, 1929); "A Murdered Rothstein As Political Dynamite," *Literary Digest* 103 (October 19, 1929); 61–70.

73 "Broadway's greatest." "Rothstein, Gambler, Mysteriously Shot; Refuses To Talk," *NYT* (November 5, 1928), 1:6.

73 "Arnold Rothstein remained." "Victim Held Many Big Men in His Grasp," *New York American* (November 6, 1928), 2:1.

73 "Morgan of the Underworld." Jenna Weissman Joselit, *Our Gang: Jewish Crime and the New York Jewish Community, 1900–1940* (Indiana University Press: Bloomington, 1983), 146.

73 "from petty larceny." Arthur Goren, *Saints and Sinners: The Underside of American Jewish History* (American Jewish Archives: Cincinnati, 1988), 8.

73 "a gang of international criminals." "Banton Offers Immunity to Witness Naming Slayer; Federal Grand Jury To Investigate Possible Connection With Drug Ring," *NYT* (November 15, 1928), 31:8.

74 "went to the Mayor's table." L. Morris, *Incredible New York* (Random House: N.Y., 1951), 340.

74 Orthodox father Abraham. Katcher, *Bankroll*, 11–12.

74 sporting man. Joselit, *Our Gang*, 144.

75 Bribes to local officials. "Rothstein Dead, Keeping Silence as to Assailant," *N.Y. World* (November 7, 1928), 1.

75 Liberty bonds. "Arnstein Guilty with Four Others," *NYT* (May 5, 1921), 1.

76 "how to dress." A. Fried, *The Rise and Fall*, 109.

76 Black Sox scandal. E. Asinof, *Eight Men Out* (Holt: N.Y., 1987), 269.

76 shift from prewar America. Malcolm Cowley, in F. S. Fitzgerald, *The Stories of F. S.*

Fitzgerald: A Selection of 28 Stories with an Introduction by Malcom Cowley (C. Scribner's Son: N.Y., 1951), x–xi.

77 pilfering . . . heists. "Find Drugs in Bronx Valued at $25,000," *NYT* (October 27, 1921): 13:1. "Arrested in Drug Robbery," *NYT* (February 6, 1922), 6:2; Block, "Habitués," 405.

77 "confiscated opium." U.S. House, *Exportation of Opium: Hearings before a Subcommittee of the Committee on Ways and Means*, 66th Cong., 3rd sess., 1920–21, 53, 132.

78 one hundred thousand addicts nationwide. L. G. Nutt, "The National Narcotic Drug Situation Today," Prohibition Bureau, memorandum, February 20, 1928. Found in "Addiction Incidence" vertical file of the DEA Library in Pentagon City, Va.

78 buying narcotics on the Continent. Alan A. Block, "European Drug Traffic and Traffickers Between the Wars: The Policy of Suppression and Its Consequences," *Journal of Social History* 23, no. 2 (winter 1989): 315–38.

78 French police arrested him. State Department, Division of Far Eastern Affairs U.S. National Archives, RG 59, Lot 55, 607D name file suspected traffickers, 1927–42, Sidney Stajer, box 13.

78 Customs had confiscationed. U.S. Treasury Department. *The Traffic in Opium and Other Dangerous Drugs for the Year Ended June 30 1926* (G.P.O.: Washington, D.C., 1926), 3. And U.S. Treasury, *The Traffic in Opium and Other Dangerous Drugs for the Year Ended June 30 1928*, (G.P.O.: Washington, D.C., 1928), 21.

78 "bowling balls and pins." "Half-Ton of Drugs Trailed By Agents," *NYT* (July 13, 1926), 18:2; "Say 3 Smuggled $4,000,000 Drugs," *NYT* (January 28, 1927), 21:5; "Drug Smugglers Get Long Terms," *NYT* (February 24, 1927), 14:5.

79 personally attended the trial. "Unger Here to Face Drug Plot Charges," *NYT* (December 16, 1928), sec. 1, 6:1.

79 "sentence so severe." "Drug Smugglers Get Long Terms," *NYT* (February 24, 1927), 14:5.

79 "from Feb. 1." "Say 3 Smuggled $4,000,000 Drugs," *NYT* (January 28, 1927), 21:5.

79 "Legs" Diamond. Charles Webber to U.S. Attorney-General May 4, 1931, U.S. National Archives, RG 12, name file of narcotics traffickers, file no 12-51-21, on how to pursue Diamond and other traffickers.

79 Rothstein boldly posted. "Diamond Declared a Fugitive By Court," *NYT* (September 4, 1929), 31:3.

79 frenetic routine of Rothstein. "Rothstein Dead, Keeping Silent As to Assailant," *New York Herald Tribune* (November 7, 1928), 1:7.

79 "Do you know who." Quoting from report filed August 24, 1931, by Joseph A. Manning, Narcotics Agent in Charge, New York City, and included in Department of Justice file on Charles Webber, file no. 12-51-21, National Archives.

79 young Italian mobster. *People v. Luciano*. New York Municipal Archive. RG Manhattan DA's Papers. Series Title: People v. Lucky Luciano Trial testimony and Transcript, box 56, transcript pps. 5889–6069. Prosecutor Thomas Dewey has Luciano tell of his early career.

80 probation record. *People v. Luciano*.

81 "admitted lending money." "Legislative Inquiry on Rothstein Urged," *NYT* (December 10, 1928), 1:3.

81 Tuttle. "Charles H. Tuttle" obituary *NYT* (January 27, 1971), 40:1.

81 Will Rogers. "Murdered Rothstein," *Literary Digest*, 70.

81 "fell all over themselves." C. Thompson and A. Raymond, *Gang Rule in New York* (Dial Press: N.Y., 1940), 68–69.

81 directed a verdict of acquittal. "Judge Nott Directs Jury to Acquit McManus," *NYT* (December 6, 1929), 1:5.

82 "startling indications." "Mrs. Keyes Partly Identifies Gunman's Photo; Secret Files Expected to Link Slain Man with Many Underworld Affairs," *NYT* (November 22, 1928), 1:6.

82 Rothmere Mortgage Corporation. "$2,000,000 Narcotics of 'Rothstein Ring' Seized in Hotel Here," *NYT* (December 8, 1928), 1:1.

82 "lack of confidence." C. D. McKean, special agent in charge in NYC to Director J. Edgar Hoover, November 26,1928. The letter is the only correspondance in a small FBI file on Arnold Rothstein consisting almost entirely of newspaper clips and a bureau report on Katcher's biography.

82 "these folders." "Four Caught in Raids on Rothstein Ring," *NYT* (December 9, 1928), 1:4.

82 "This is biggest single raid." "Four Caught in Raids on Rothstein Ring; More Drugs Seized," *NYT* (December 9, 1928), 1:6.

82 Stephen G. Porter. "Unger Is Indicted," *NYT* (December 11, 1928), 26:2.

83 *Rochambeau.* "$4,000,000 Narcotics Seized Here, Traced to Rothstein Ring," *NYT* (December 19, 1928), 1.

83 In March 1929 four gangsters. "Seize 4 and Drugs of Rothstein Ring," *NYT* (March 6, 1929), 14:7.

83 $19,940 loan. "LaGuardia Reveals Vitale Got $19,940 Rothstein Loan, Magistrate Admits It," *NYT* (September 28, 1929), 1:1.

83 "If the Rothstein papers." "Two Scandals," *Literary Digest* 103 (October 19 1929): 61–70.

83 "three huge narcotic rings." "14 Taken in Roundup of 3 Narcotics Rings Linked to Rothstein," *NYT* (December 29, 1929), 1:6.

84 "how sinister." "Links Men 'High Up' to Huge Drug Rings," *NYT* (January 3, 1930); "Announce Seizure of Narcotic Ring," *NYT* (February 11, 1930), 28:1.

84 "Grand Jury Accuses." "Grand Jury Accuses Highest Officials in Narcotic Bureau," *NYT* (February 20, 1930), 1:5.

84 Colonel Levi G. Nutt. U.S. House, *Bureau of Narcotics:* Hearings on HR 10,561, House Committee on Ways & Means, 7–8 March 1930 71st Cong., 2nd sess., 75.

84 "We find no evidence." Ibid.

84 "could not get witnesses." Katcher, *Bankroll,* 298.

85 "Legs" Diamond. Gary Levine, *Anatomy of a Gangster: Jack "Legs" Diamond* (A.S. Barnes: New York,19??), 63–68. There are a variety of versions of what sparked the Rothstein–Diamond feud. George Carpozi, Jr., "Legs Diamond," *True Detective.* (September 1961), 57–77. "Rothstein Named in 5 Feud Murders," *NYT* (March 22, 1930), 1:7. Meyer Berger, " 'Legs' Diamond Slain in Sleep at Albany," *NYT* (December 18, 1931), 1:1.

86 "After Rothstein died," M. Berger, " 'Legs' Diamond Slain" (December 19, 1931).

Chapter 6: "The Days of the 500-Kilo Deliveries Have Passed"

87 SS *Alesia.* U.S. State Department National Archives. RG 59. Decimal Files 811.114 N16/Alesia/11/Box 4920. Also the criminal trial for this smuggling case is *U.S. v. Elias Eliopoulos,* U.S. Archives N.E. Region, Manhattan. RG 21 U.S. District Court for the Eastern District CR 39170.

88 SS *Milwaukee.* U.S. State Department National Archives. RG 59. Decimal Files 811.114 N16/Milwaukee/26/Box 4923. "3 Tons of Narcotics Seized on Pier Here," *NYT* (April 25, 1931), 1:5. Newspaper reports say three tons of narcotics were seized, but internal State Department files report half that much. These huge discrepancies among reports about the same seizure are constant, and one is uncertain what to make of it.

89 "very alert and intelligent." Wright to Walter H. Newton, June 26, 1930. From Herbert Hoover Presidential Library. Presidential Cabinet Offices-Treasury-End.-Narcotics Bureau.

90 "pointed out." Anslinger to Walter H. Newton September 23, 1930. Hoover Presidential Library. Presidential Cabinet Offices-Treasury-End.-Narcotics Bureau.

90 her to the Phillipines. A. Taylor, *American Diplomacy and the Narcotics Traffic, 1900–1939* (Duke University Press: Durham, N.C., 1969), 274.

90 "energy, zeal." Ibid., 304–5.

91 "mixture of new immigrants" H. J. Anslinger and W. Oursler, *Murderers* (Farrar, Straus & Cudahy: N.Y., 1961), 8.

91 "visiting in the house." Ibid.

91 "young pool player." Ibid., 8–9.

92 Black Hand. Ibid., 9–10.

92 "assistant to the Chief." John McWilliams, *The Protectors* (University of Delaware Press: Newark, Del., 1990), 28.

92 "uncovering a new Communistic." Anslinger to Franklin M. Gunther, May 2, 1924. Harry J. Anslinger Papers, box 3, file 16 Correspondence 1924, Pattee Library, Penn State University.

93 Anslinger was advanced to. J. McWilliams, *The Protectors* (U. of Del. Press: Newark, Del., 1990).

93 Stuart J. Fuller. "S. J. Fuller, Foe of Narcotics," *NYT* (February 4, 1941), 21:3. Also see Arnold Taylor, *American Diplomacy and the Narcotics Traffic 1900–1939* (Duke University Press: Durham, N.C., 1969), 270.

93 "established fact with Chinese politics." M. R. Nicholson, memorandum, "Survey of Narcotics Situation in China & the Far East," July 12, 1934. From Annex 18 to memo, p. 9. Anslinger Papers, box 10, file 3. Pattee Library, Penn State University.

93 "opium smoking shops." R. F. Fitch, "The Destroyer," *Opium a World Problem* 3, no. 4 (July 1930), 18.

94 "This was opium country." H. E. Salisbury, *The Long March* (Harper & Row: N.Y., 1985), 106.

94 "There is a brisk trade." M.R. Nicholson, memorandum, "Survey of Narcotic Situation in China and the Far East," July 12, 1923. From Annex V, p.1. Anslinger papers, box 10, file 3. Pattee Library, Penn State University.

94 "ostensibly respectable European firms" State Dept. U.S. National Archives RG 59 Lot 55 607D. Decimal File (1930–39) 800.114 N16/593/Box 4534. Press release dated February 25, 1935, of speech given by Fuller to Women's City Club of Washington, D.C.

95 Colonel Joseph W. Stilwell. T. M. Parsinnen and K. B. Meyer, "America and the World Market for Narcotic Drugs, 1919–1939" (paper given at the Organization for American Historians, Washington, D.C., March 1990), 1.

95 "to survey drug factories." A. A. Block, "European Drug Traffic and Traffickers Between the Wars," *JSocial History* 23, no. 2 (winter 1989), 317.

96 "France imported 251.5 tons." Block, "European Drug Traffic," 322.

96 Elias Eliopoulos. State Dept. U.S. Nat. Archives. RG 59. Lot 55 607D. Eliopoulos file, box 4. Also see Anslinger, *The Murderers*, chap. 5.

97 "end of August, 1930." U.S. State Dept. Nat. Archives. RG 59 Div. of Far Eastern Affairs, Lot 55 607D, names files. Elie Eliopoulos, file. box 4. From a statement made to Athens police in September 1932.

97 "tall, well-groomed." H. J. Anslinger, *The Protectors* (Farrar, Straus & Co.: N.Y., 1964), 6.

97 "startling tie-ins." Anslinger, Ibid., 24.

98 Committee of One Hundred. McWilliams, *Protectors*, 157.

98 "incessantly at it." Taylor, *American Diplomacy*, 271.

98 SS *Innoko* U.S. State Dept. Nat. Archives. RG 59 Decimal Files (1930–39). 811.114N16/Innoko.

99 "Señor Bacula's father." U.S. State Dept. Nat. Archives. RG 59 Lot 55 607D Decimal File 811.114 N16/2001, box 4918. Letter from American Embassy in Lima, Peru, to the Secretary of State, October 17, 1931.

100 Augie Del Gratio. U.S. State Dept. Nat. Archives. RG 59. Lot 55 607D, name files: Augie Del Gratio.

100 "I know for a fact." U.S. State Dept. Nat. Archives. RG 59 Lot 55 607D, name files. Undated statement of Seya Moses from Eliopoulos case file.

100 Sam Bernstein. This is from his testimony in the 1943 trial of the Eliopoulos brothers. U.S. Archives, Northeast Region, Manhattan. RG 21 U.S. District Court for the Eastern District of N.Y. Criminal case files CR 39188 Box 663. Trial transcript Vol. I, 191–240.

101 "I saw a lot of trunks." Sam Bernstein testimony in *U.S. v. Eliopoulos*. U.S. Archives/Northeast Region/Manhattan. U.S. District Court for the Eastern District. Criminal Case File. No. 39170, vol. I of testimony transcript.

101 "My privileged position." U.S. State Dept. Nat. Archives. RG 59. Lot File 55 607D name files. Statement of Elie Eliopoulos, September 21, 22, 23, 24, 1932, to Athens police.

102 George Z. Medalie, "Judge G.Z. Medalie Dies in Albany at 62," *NYT* (March 6, 1946). 27:1.

102 "New York has never." Anslinger to Geo. Z. Medalie, U.S. Atty, SDNY, Oct. 22, 1931. Anslinger Papers, Penn State. Correspondence File for 1931.

103 convention for the Limitation of the Manufacture. Taylor, *American Diplomacy*, chap. 9.

103 forty-two thousand tons. A. W. McCoy, *The Politics of Heroin* (Lawrence Hill:

Brooklyn, N.Y., 1991), 99; figures from International Opium Commission report, vol. 2, pp. 355–65, League of Nations annual report, 1935, 46–47.

103 "axe will fall." HJA to Kauffman, May 2, 1933. Anslinger Papers, Penn State, box 3, file 22. R. Kauffman correspondence (1933–58).

103 Henry Morgenthau, Jr. J. M. Blum. *Roosevelt and Morgenthau* (Houghton Mifflin: Boston, 1970), 8–9.

104 1934. Bureau of Narcotics *Traffic in Opium & Other Dangerous Drugs* (G.P.O.: Washington D.C., 1934), 29.

104 "To publicize the [narcotics] racket." "U.S. Drug Squad Inefficient?" *Inside Stuff* (February 15, 1935), 33. Anslinger Papers, box 7, file 16. Pattee Library, Penn. State.

104 checked himself into the U.S. Marine Hospital. Physician's report, April 10, 1935. FDR Library, Hyde Park. Morgenthau Papers. Correspondence box 206-207, narcotics smuggling.

105 "you must not worry." H. Morgenthau to HJA, April 18, 1935. Morgenthau Papers, Corresp. Box 206-207, narcotics smuggling. FDR Library, Hyde Park.

105 Lamar Hardy visited Morgenthau's. Treasury office. April 29, 1936, meeting described in Morgenthau diary, book 27, page 153. FDR Library, Hyde Park.

105 "seizures of narcotics." IRS. Palmer to Morgenthau, memorandum, December 21, 1936 (under cover of note to Morgenthau, January 7, 1937) from confidential files about people 1937. Morgenthau Papers, FDR Library, Hyde Park.

105 "not satisfied with the work." Morgenthau diary, August 18, 1936, book 30, 4. FDR Library, Hyde Park.

106 "the worst of all crimes." FDR to Jim Rowe, memorandum October 4, 1940. OF431/Narcotic File. FDR Library, Hyde Park.

106 "the agents under the direction." IRS memorandum, December 21, 1936. (Under cover of note, January 7, 1937, to Morgenthau.) Confidential files about people 1937. Morgenthau Papers. FDR Library, Hyde Park.

107 "fine law enforcement official." Anslinger, *Protectors*, 42.

107 "having a nice visit." Commander Thompson to Morgenthau, memorandum March 6, 1937. Morgenthau diary, book 58, 247. FDR Library, Hyde Park.

108 "We don't want any tourists." Commander Thompson to Morgenthau, memorandum March 31, 1937. Morgenthau diary, book 61, 347. FDR Library, Hyde Park.

108 "A good guess." Commander Thompson to Morgenthau, memorandum May 13, 1937. Morgenthau diary, book 68, 133. FDR Library, Hyde Park.

108 "The line of demarcation." Commander Thompson to Morgenthau, memorandum May 23, 1937. Morgenthau diary, box 69, 231. FDR Library, Hyde Park.

108 "There is no question." Commander Thompson to Morgenthau, memorandum June 2, 1937. Morgenthau diary, book 71, 170. FDR Library, Hyde Park.

108 "In using members of ships' crews." "Seizures Spur the Fight on Opium," *NYT* (March 14, 1937), sec. IV 10:3.

109 Bulgaria. "The Post Impressionist: Poison by the Ton," *Washington Post* (October 24, 1934). From Harry. J. Anslinger Papers, box 5, files 15 Scrapbook (1934–39).

109 "Monopolies are merely." "Money Out of Misery," *Washington Herald* (January 29, 1935), edit. page. From Anslinger Papers, box 5, files 14. Scrapbook (1935–37).

109 "did not suffer fools." B. A. Renborg, "The Grand Old Men of the League of Nations," *Bulletin on Narcotics* 17, no. 4 (December 1964): 9.

109 Bacula. "Dope Scandal Shakes France; Hold Diplomat," *Chicago Sunday Tribune* (June 12, 1938). Also Morgenthau diary. Bernard Wait to Morgenthau, memorandum July 25, 1938, on European drug situation, including breaking up of Bacula-Lyon gang. Book 134, 295–305. FDR Library, Hyde Park.

109 Katzenberg. "Leader of Narcotic Ring Is Sentenced to Ten Years in Prison and Fined $10,000," *NYT* (December 1, 1938), 2:3.

109 Shanghai. U.S. State Dept. Nat. Archives. RG 59. Dec. Files (1930–39) 800.114N16. Documents/145/Box 4535. League of Nations Advisory Committee on Traffic in Opium and Other Dangerous Drugs. *Summary of Illicit Transactions and Seizures* July 1, 1935. 8.

109 1,500 pounds of heroin. *Illicit Transactions & Seizures*, Report of the League of Nation's Advisory Committee on Traffic in Opium & Other Dangerous Drugs, April 1, 1938. U.S. State Dept. Nat. Archives. RG 59. Decimal File (1930–39), box 2525.

110 "small as to be." U.S. Treasury, *Traffic in Opium and Other Dangerous Drugs for the Year ended 1942* (G.P.O.: Washington, D.C., 1942), 14.

110 "Then I couldn't get." Courtwright et al., *Addicts*, 82. This speaker is Freida, a New York addict who began smoking opium in 1923.

110 "Sometimes you couldn't get opium," Courtwright et al., *Addicts*, 84. This speaker is a Chinese seaman.

110 "One reason . . . is the exacting price." Dai, *Opium Addiction*, 61.

111 The purity of street heroin. *Traffic in Opium for 1940*, 20.

111 "You didn't see no kids." Courtwright et al., *Addicts*, 105.

112 "chicken hatcheries." "Huge Farm Ready for Drug Addicts," *NYT* (May 19, 1935), sec. II 2:4.

112 "due to the confusion." W. S. Martin and I. Harris, "Drug Addiction and the U.S.P.H.S." (Proceedings of the Symposium Commemorating the 40th Anniversary of the Addiction Research Center at Lexington, Ky. (G.P.O.: Washington, D.C., 1978), 253.

113 "return to former associates." M. J. Pescor, "A Statistical Analysis of the Clinical Records of Hospitalized Drug Addicts," *Public Health Reports*, supplement no. 143 (1938): 21–22.

113 "general belief." Dai, *Opium Addiction*, 174.

113 "He will probably relapse." Pescor, "A Statistical Analysis," 23.

113 90 percent. Williams and Isbell, *Drug Addiction*, 212–13.

113 "There were no drugs." Courtwright et al., *Addicts*, 107.

114 "There was no heroin." Ibid., 193.

114 107th Street gang. "Big Opium Ring Is Smashed as 17 are Indicted," *New York Herald Tribune* (April 9, 1942), 36.

114 so many free beds. Williams and Isbell, *Drug Addiction*, 224–25.

114 Eliopoulos brothers. "Two Greek Refugees Indicted as Smugglers of $1,000,000 of Narcotics into U.S. in 1930," *NYT* (May 5, 1943), 29:2. Also see Anslinger, *The Murderers*, 71.

114 Newman brothers. Bureau of Customs weekly narcotics intelligence bulletin, May 3, 1940. U.S. State Dept. Nat. Archives. RG 59. Name files. Newman or Neiditch Bros.

114 "waged a diplomatic war." State Department Office of the Historian, "The United States & International Narcotics Control: An Historical Overview" (official paper, April 1983), 3.

Chapter 7: "The Sky Is High and So Am I"

119 "Heroin abuse became." J. Chambers, *Milestones I: The Music and Times of Miles Davis* (University of Toronto Press: Toronto, 1983), 139. This is LA pianist Hampton Hawes quoted (with no page cited) from his autobiography *Raise Up Off Me*. Hawes met Parker out west, became addicted, spent time in jail, and died at age forty-eight in 1977.

119 "It was the thing." Gitler, *Swing to Bop: An Oral History of the Transition in Jazz in the 1940s* (Oxford University Press: N.Y., 1985), 282.

121 "subordinating and disciplining." H. Finestone, "Cats, Kicks, and Color," *Social Problems* 5 (July 1957): 7.

121 "I am a man of substance." R. Ellison, *Invisible Man* (Signet Paperback: N.Y., 1953), 7, 16.

121 "conspicuous consumption." St. Clair Drake and H. R. Clayton, *Black Metropolis: A Study of Negro Life in a Northern City* (Harcourt Brace & Co.: N.Y., 1945), 389.

122 "vipers are always dangerous" M. Berger, "Tea for a Viper," *The New Yorker* 14 (March 12, 1938), 49.

122 "as respectable as Sunday morning." Mezzrow and Wolfe, *Really the Blues* (Citadel Press: N.Y., 1990), 5, 18.

123 "supply was drawn from." R. P. Walton, *Marijuana: America's New Drug Problem* (J.P. Lippincott: N.Y., 1938), 29–30.

123 "drug's peculiarly fascinating." Walton, ibid., 32.

123 "wasn't a sour note." M. Mezzrow and B. Wolfe, *Really the Blues* (Citadel Press: N.Y., 1990), 72–73.

123 "Louis gets high." D. Gillespie with Al Fraser, *to Be, or not . . . to Bop* (Da Capo: N.Y., 1979), 285. Also see D. Wakefield on Armstrong's influence, "Dope on the Downbeat," *Nation* (August 31, 1957), 92–93.

123 "turned me on." Gillespie, *to Be*, 283.

123 "There were two cliques," I. Gitler, *Swing to Bop: An Oral History of the Transition in Jazz in the 1940s* (Oxford University Press: N.Y., 1985), 279.

123 "It makes you feel good." A. Goldman, *Grass Roots: Marijuana in America Today* (Warner Books: N.Y., 1980), 94.

124 "[T]here was common agreement." Mayor LaGuardia's Committee on Marijuana, *The Marijuana Problem in the City of N.Y.* (Scarecrow Reprint Corp.: Metuchen, N.J., 1944), 12.

124 "Kaiser's was the crème." Interviewed by the author May 3, 1993, at Brightman's business, Stash Records, in Manhattan.

125 viper songs. P. Garon, "If Blues Was Reefers," *Living Blues* 1, no. 3 (autumn 1970), 13–18.

125 "vision of *high* culture." N. I. Huggins, *Harlem Renaissance* (Oxford University Press: N.Y., 1971), 10.

126 old piece of drug argot. D. Maurer, "Argot of the Underworld Narcotic Addict," *American Speech* 13 (October 1938), 179–82.

126 "wise, sophisticated." C. Calloway, *Cab Calloway's Cat-ologue* (rev. 1939 ed.)

126 Fitz Hugh Ludlow. E. M. Brecher, *Licit & Illicit Drugs: The Consumers Union Report on Narcotics, Stimulants, Depressants, Inhalant, Hallucinogens, and Marijuana—Including Caffeine, Nicotine, and Alcohol* (Consumers Union: Mt. Vernon, N.Y., 1972), 406–7.

126 "I've remembered your injunctions." Edward Homans to his fianceé, Frances Eells (1863). Letter 182 from box one of Homans family letters in Rare Books and Manuscript Division, NYPL, Astor, Lenox, and Tilden Foundations.

126 "scenes of the *Arabian Nights*." H. H. Kane, "A Hashish-House in New York," *Harper's* 67 (November 1883), 946.

126 "the hep cats." M. Berger, "Zoot Suit Originated in Georgia; Bus Boy Ordered First One in '40," *NYT* (June 11, 1943), 21:2.

128 "Negroes and lower class whites." R. J. Bonnie and C. H. Whitebread II, *The Marijuana Conviction: A History of Marihuana Prohibition in the U.S.* (University Press of Virginia: Charlottesville, 1974), 54.

128 "large numbers of boys." Walton, *Marijuana*, 31–32.

128 "disintegration of personality." A. Parry, "The Menace of Marijuana," *American Mercury* 36 (December 1935), 487–90.

128 "Is there any assistance?" Musto, *American Disease*, 223.

129 "it is an established fact." McWilliams, *Protectors*, 67.

129 "Marijuana: Assassin of Youth." H. J. Anslinger with C. J. Cooper, "Marijuana: Assassin of Youth," *American Magazine* (July 1937), 18–19, 150–153.

129 Marijuana Tax Act. Musto, *Disease*, 210–29.

129 "increasing volume of reports." Bonnie and Whitebread, *Marihuana Conviction*, 182–83.

130 "I sold reefers." Malcolm X with Alex Haley, *The Autobiography of Malcolm X* (Penguin Books: London, 1966), 187.

130 Louis Armstrong disdained. M. Jones and J. Chilton, *Louis: The Louis Armstrong Story 1900–1971* (Little, Brown: Boston, 1971), 114.

131 Addie Parker. G. Giddins, *Celebrating Bird* (Beechtree Books: N.Y., 1987), 26.

131 stick a needle in. Giddens, ibid., 46.

131 "I was working over 'Cherokee.' " R. Ellison, "The Golden Age, Time Past," in *Shadow and Act* (Random House: N.Y., 1964), 211.

132 "We used to play those records." I. Gitler, *Swing to Bop: An Oral History of the Transition in Jazz in the 1940s* (Oxford University Press: N.Y. 1985). This is musician Red Callendar speaking.

132 "A lot of cats." Ibid., 315.

132 "slop" Gillespie, *to Be*, 295.

132 "Bebop was the coup de grace." L. Jones, *Blues People* (Morrow: N.Y., 1963), 201.

133 "That's what you hear." S. Crouch, "Bird Land: Charlie Parker, Clint Eastwood, and America," *The New Republic* (February 17, 1989), 28. This is a quote from singer Earl Coleman.

133 "Bird was thin." "Interview with Gene Ramey," *Jazz Review* (November 1960).

133 "Bird came in late." Gillespie, *to Be*, 235.

133 "When you have a bad day." Gillespie, ibid., 291.

133 something highly exotic. Gitler, *Swing to Bop*, 279.

133 "to be like Bird." *Ibid.*, 281.

134 "I know a lot of cats," ibid., 174.

134 to storm Los Angeles. Giddins, *Celebrating*, 93.

134 "definitely the messiah." Watrous, "Man Who Defined Modern Jazz," *NYT* (Nov. 13, 1988), Arts & Leisure Section p. 26.

134 "I guess the only thing." R. G. Reisner, *From Bird: The Legend of Charlie Parker* (Da Capo: N.Y., 1975), 56.

134 "zenith of hipsterism." G. Sorrento, "Remembrances of Bop in N.Y., 1945–1950," *Kulchur* (Summer 1963): 76.

135 "strong and beautiful." J. Chambers, *Milestones I: The Music and Times of Miles Davis* (University of Toronto Press: Toronto, 1983), 139.

135 "A lot of guys died." Gitler, *Swing to Bop*, 287.

135 "Parker admitted ownership." Anslinger, *The Protectors*, 158.

136 "convicted of possession." John Cusack to Anslinger memorandum, November 7, 1951. Country files. 0660 France file 3. DEA. Pentagon City, Va.

136 "Diz, why don't you." Gillespie, *to Be*, 393.

136 attributed his death. D. Knight, 'The Night Charlie Parker Died,' *down beat* 47 (August 1980), 22.

136 "sense of rhythm." P. Watrous, "The Man Who Defined Modern Jazz," *NYT* (November 13, 1988), Arts & Leisure section, 26.

136 "This is something." Giddins, *Celebrating*, 101.

136 Lady Day. H. J. Anslinger, *The Protectors*, 152, 157.

137 Musicians' Clinic. C. Winick and M. Nyswander, "Psychotheraphy of Successful Musicians Who Are Drug Addicts," *Am. J of Orthopsychiatry* 31 (1961): 622–38.

137 "When I looked around." Dr. John (Mac Rebennack) *Under a Hoodoo Moon* (St. Martin's: N.Y., 1994), 37–39.

137 "I didn't even know." J. Hooper, "Stan Getz Through the Years," *NYT Sunday Magazine* (June 9, 1991), 78.

137 "Heroin had just about taken over." C. Brown, *Manchild in the Promised Land* (Signet Paperback: N.Y., 1965), 187, 189.

138 Three-block area of East Harlem. U.S. Senate. *Investigation of Organized Crime in Interstate Commerce: Hearings Before a Special Committee to Investigate Organized Crime in Interstate Commerce*, Part 14 82nd Cong., 1st sess. 1951, 264. The official testifying was New Yorker James R. Dumpson of the Welfare Council.

138 "Jaded on marijuana." "Narcotics and Youth," *Newsweek* (November 20, 1950), 52.

138 Detroit grand jury. U.S. Senate. *Investigation of Organized Crime* Part 14, 454. This "Report of the Federal Grand Jury at Detroit, Michigan, on Drug Addiction Among Teen-agers" was submitted as an exhibit during the hearings.

138 "could hear the throbbing." Sid Frigand, "Cop Poses As Addict in Fighting Dope Evil," *Brooklyn Eagle* (July 1, 1951).

138 new black addicts. John C. Ball and Carl D. Chambers, *The Epidemiology of Opiate Addiction in the United States* (Charles C. Thomas: Springfield, Ill., 1970), 200. The chapter on "Negro Opiate Addiction" traces black opiate addiction from 1935 to 1966, based on information obtained from addicts at Lexington.

139 twenty-year-old East Harlemite. Milton Lewis, "The Nation's Narcotic Problem," *New York Herald Tribune* (June 3, 1954), 1.

139 "invaded by literally thousands." David W. Maurer and Victor H. Vogel, *Narcotics and Narcotic Addiction* (Charles C. Thomas: Springfield, Ill., 1954), 258–61.

139 "common image." Harold Finestone, "Cats, Kicks, and Color," *Social Problems* 5 (July 1957): 8.

140 new black slums. Nicholas Lemann, *The Promised Land: The Great Black Migration and How It Changed America* (Knopf: New York, 1991), 117.

140 disturbing new twist. "Narcotics and Youth," *Newsweek* (November 20, 1950), 52–53; "New York Wakes Up To Find 15,000 Teen-age Dope Addicts," *Time* (January 29, 1951), 23; "Heroin and Adolescents," *Newsweek* (August 13, 1951), 51–52; Nathaniel L. Goldstein, New York State Attorney General, *Narcotics: A Growing Problem . . . A Public Challenge . . . A Plan for Action* (1951), a report to the State Legislature available at the New York City Municipal Reference Library.

2140 heroin epidemic. Carl D. Chambers and Arthur D. Moffett, "Negro Opiate Addiction" in *Epidemiology*, ed. Ball and Chambers, 180.

140 Federal Bureau of Narcotics. Federal Bureau of Narcotics, *Annual Report* (1958), 37.

Chapter 8: "His Fame Spread Throughout the World"

141 Luciano was being deported. M. Berger, "Deportation Set For Luciano Today," *NYT* (February 9, 1946), 15:1; "Pardoned Luciano on his way to Italy," *NYT* (February 11, 1946), 31:4.

141 1929 gangland "ride." Memorandum, May 27, 1939. "Lucky 1929 Ride," RG: Manhattan DA's Papers, subgroup: Lucky Luciano trial. Box 20: Luciano's deportation. N.Y. Municipal Archives.

142 "had had enough of the press." "Boss Stevedore Bars Reporters," *New York Herald Tribune* (February 11, 1946).

142 107th gang. Meyer Berger, "Harlem Is Called Narcotics Center," *NYT* (December 20, 1946). Anthony Marino and Art Smith, "Mafia in Harlem Rules Dope Racket," *Daily News* (December 20, 1946). Here Garland Williams is quoted as saying, "The East Harlem Mafia is now the most powerful of the five groups in New York City and northern New Jersey."

142 clutching in his left hand. "Masseria Shot," *NYT* (April 16, 1931), 1:2.

143 Waxey Gordon. Alan A. Block, *East Side–West Side: Organizing Crime in New York 1930–50* (University College Cardiff Press: Swansea, Wales, 1980), 68–75.

143 Dewey demurred. "Schultz is Next on Federal List." *NYT* (December 3, 1933), 35:3.

144 forcibly extradited. Hickman Powell, *Ninety Times Guilty* (Harcourt, Brace and Company: New York, 1939). The story of Luciano up through his conviction.

144 arrested nineteen times. Memorandum, January 19, 1946. RG: Manhattan DA's papers. Subgroup: Luciano trial. Box 20. Luciano's deportation. N.Y. Municipal Archive.

144 police had compiled virtually no. Luciano investigation, R.G. Manhattan DA's papers. Luciano trial, folder one. N.Y. Municipal Archive.

144 FBI were no more aggressive. File 54-404 on Charles "Lucky" Luciano from FBI's New York office obtained through Freedom of Information Act.

144 Staten Island grand jury. Memorandum, June 1, 1936, "Digest of Grand Jury Testimony of Lucky Luciano," R.G. Manhattan DA's Papers. Subgroup: Luciano trial. Deportation file. N.Y. Municipal Archives.

145 Luciano dressed for the Dewey trial. "Lucania Is Forced To Admit Crimes," *NYT* (June 4, 1936), 1:5.

145 "I never was a crumb." "Luciano Dies at 65," *NYT* (January 27, 1962), 1:6.

145 "Whenever possible" M. Berger, "The Great Luciano is at Last in Toils," *NYT* (April 12, 1936), 9.

145 Augie Del Gratio. J. C. McWilliams and A. A. Block, "All the Commissioner's Men: The Federal Bureau of Narcotics and the Dewey–Luciano Affair, 1947–54," *Intelligence and National Security* 5 (April 1990): 180. This article cites a memo noting that Del Gratio was one of the emissaries.

146 "counterespionage." Frederic Sondern, Jr., "Lucky Luciano's New Empire," *Reader's Digest* (September 1951), 64.

146 "aiding military authorities." "Dewey Commutes Luciano Sentence," *NYT* (January 4, 1946). In this news story, Luciano's lawyer, Moses Polakoff (who would represent Meyer Lansky during the Kefauver hearings in 1951), was reported as saying that "Luciano's . . . services were enlisted at the suggestion of Major Murray Gurfein of military intelligence, who had been a special prosecutor on Mr. Dewey's staff. Information the convict provided from his cell in Great Meadow Prison [a pleasanter place he had been moved to pending this cooperation] led to the locating of many Sicilian-born Italians who gave information of military value on conditions in Sicily." A more active participation is suggested by Tibor Koeves, "Lucky Luciano vs. the United Nations," *UN World* (August 1949): 36.

146 Luciano would be freed. "Dewey Commutes Sentence," *NYT* (January 4, 1946), 1.

146 four hundred agents investigating communists. R. G. Powers, *Secrecy and Power: The Life of J. Edgar Hoover* (Free Press: N.Y., 1987), 332–35.

146 FBI agent duly reported. Files dated May 17, 1946, from Lucky Luciano's FBI files provided under Freedom of Information Act.

146 Anslinger actively promoted this smear. J. C. McWilliams and A. A. Block, "All the Commissioner's Men," 171–92.

147 "Governor Dewey was quite disturbed." Hoover to aides, memorandum January 5, 1953. FBI file of Harry J. Anslinger. File No. 62-98715.

147 Luciano sailed off. F. Sondern, Jr., "Lucky Luciano's New Empire," 64; also U.S. Nat. Archives, name file on Lucania, Salvatore, in "Suspected Narcotics Traffickers." This Cuban episode marks the beginning of Luciano's State Department file.

147 Luciano had once again settled. Feder and Joesten, *Luciano Story*, 272. It was Narcotics Bureau supervisor Garland Williams who made this charge.

147 postwar seizure. "Drugs Seized on Liner," *NYT* (October 2, 1948); "Opium, Heroin Worth $1,000,000," *NYT* (January 8 1949), 1.

148 "The Italian [American] Underworld." Agent Anthony Piazza to N.Y. District Supervisor Garland Williams, memorandum Oct. 25, 1939, "Major Italian Narcotics Violators." Given to the author by former DEA employee John Bacon.

149 Garland Williams. McWilliams, *Protectors*, 160–61.

149 "narcotic law enforcement is actually non-existent." Williams to Anslinger, April 6, 1949. DEA Country Files. 0660 Italy, folder 2.

150 Trieste. C. Siragusa, *The Trail of the Poppy: Behind the Mask of the Mafia* (Prentice Hall: Englewood, N.J., 1966), 85–91.

151 Calascibetta. B. McGurn, "Luciano Linked to Major Figure in Italy Trial of Big Dope Ring," *New York Herald Tribune* (October 19, 1952).

151 "concrete evidence." Agent Charles Siragusa to Commissioner Anslinger, telegram, May 12, 1951. U.S. Nat. Archives, from name file of Lucania, Salvatore, "Suspected Narcotics Traffickers." RG 59. State Dept. Div. of Far Eastern Affairs.

151 sufficient cause to charge him. Feder and Joesten, *Luciano Story*, 284–302. Also, Charles Siragusa, *The Trail of the Poppy: Behind the Mask of the Mafia* (Prentice-Hall: Englewood Cliffs, N.J., 1966), 83–101.

151 "Who is this elegantly-dressed man." D. Goodman, *Villainy Unlimited* (Elek Books: London, 1957), 112.

152 "the Alfa concern." Report dated April 5, 1951. Country files. 0660 Italy, folder 4. DEA. Pentagon City, Va. Obtained through Freedom of Information Act.

152 "Italy appears to be." J. Jordon, "How Italy's Government Lets Heroin Flood U.S.," *Bluebook* (June 1955): 28.

153 "In view of the near-constant." Office of State Dept. Historian, "The U.S. and International Narcotics Control: An Historical Overview" (document dated April 1983), 3.

154 "a modest narcotics program." Office of State Dept. Historian, "U.S. and International Narcotics Control," 4.

154 "fabulous, fantastic career." Undated three-page manuscript titled "The Author," presumably written by Anslinger. File 9, box 4. Anslinger Papers. Historical Collections and Labor Archives, Pattee Library. Penn State University.

155 *Bluebook.* H. Jordan, "How Italy's Government Lets Heroin Flood U.S.," *Bluebook*, 24–31, 81–82.

155 "tremendous diversions." Harney to Anslinger, memorandum March 17, 1953. Country files. 0660 Italy, folder 5. DEA. Pentagon City, Va. Obtained through Freedom of Information Act.

156 "horrified to learn." State Dept. memorandum, June 8, 1955, RG 59, National Archives. Decimal files 1955–59, 411.65342/6-855.

156 "Apparently the situation was as new." Dulles to Lodge, secret letter. RG 59, National Archives, Decimal File 1955–59, 411.65342/6-955.

156 "there is no evidence." Secret Memo of Conversation dated June 21 and June 22, 1955, RG 59, National Archives, 1955–1959 Decimal File 811.53/6-2155. 2.

156 "quite a bombshell." Secret Memo of Conversation dated June 21 and 22, 1955, RG 59, National Archives, Decimal File 1955–59. 811.53/6-2155.

157 "has not, unfortunately." B. Renborg, "International Control of Narcotics," *Law and Contemporary Problems* 21, no. 1 (winter 1957): 102.

158 "had the Hearst." James Bennett oral history from JFK Presidential Library, 15.

158 "We'd like to concentrate." R. Carter, "Why the U.S. Doesn't Nab the Big Ones," unidentified N.Y. Newspaper clip dated August 8, 1952, from box 5/file 6/1948–57. Anslinger Papers. Penn State.

158 Scripps-Howard journalist. U.S. Senate, *Juvenile Delinquency (National, Federal and Youth-Serving Agencies): Hearings Before Subcommittee to Investigate Juvenile Delinquency in the U.S.* Part I, 83rd Cong., 1st sess., 1953, 248.

159 "flaxen-haired eighteen-year-old girl." H. A. Anslinger, *The Murderers* (Farrar, Straus & Cudahy: NY, 1964) 4.

159 "an unknown Chinese." From "Underworld Slaves" ms. Also, "Narcotic Case

Report," January 14, 1931, Cleveland, Ohio. Both in box 4/file 14. Anslinger Papers. Penn State.

159 "The total number of addicts." U.S. Senate. Anslinger testimony, before Senate Judiciary Subcommittee on Narcotics (June 2, 1955) . Anslinger Papers, box 1, file 10. Penn State.

159 "The Federal Bureau of Narcotics." D. Courtwright, H. Joseph, and D. Des Jarlais, *Addicts Who Survived* (Tennessee University Press: Knoxville, 1989), 332–33.

160 "Contrary to erroneous reports." H. J. Anslinger, "The Red Chinese Dope Traffic," *Military Police Journal* (1961). Anslinger Papers, box 12, file 8. Penn State.

160 "Heroin had been the thing." C. Brown, *Manchild*, 187.

161 implicated Luciano. Feder et al., *Luciano Story*, 273.

161 "Lucania maintains a brilliant standard." Naples police to Anslinger, translated report, August 24, 1947. "Charles Lucania" file in "Names Files of Suspected Narcotics Traffickers," RG 59. National Archives State Dept. Div. of Far Eastern Affairs.

161 "As a young man, we caught Il Capo." "Mafia & Smuggling," file 13, box 4. Anslinger Papers, Penn State.

162 describes smoking her first marijuana. U.S. Senate Special Committee to Investigate Organized Crime in Interstate Commerce, *Investigation of Organized Crime in Interstate Commerce*, Part 14, 82nd Cong., 1st sess, 1951, (GPO: Washington, D.C., 1951), 55, 451.

163 Eisenhower. "Eisenhower Asks Drug Use Study," *Herald Tribune* (November 28, 1954), 1.

163 Narcotics Control Act of 1956. Musto, *American Disease*, 230–33.

Chapter 9: "The Most Important Narcotics Smuggler's Haven . . ."

165 George Hunter White. A. A. Block and J. C. McWilliams, "On the Origins of American Counterintelligence: Building a Clandestine Network," *Journal of Policy History* 1, no. 4 (1989), 364.

165 "heavily built man." Derek Agnew, *Undercover Agent—Narcotics* (Souvenir Press: London, 1959), 112.

166 "During a state visit." A. McCoy, *The Politics of Heroin* (Lawrence Hill: Brooklyn, N.Y., 1991), 30.

166 Lord Rennell. McCoy, ibid., 35.

166 "a review committee." D. Eisenberg, U. Dan, and E. Landau, *Meyer Lansky* (Paddington Press: N.Y., 1979), 214–15.

167 "Certain 'undesirables.' " M. Pantaleone, *The Mafia and Politics* (Chatto & Windus: London, 1966), 169–70.

167 "An estimated 50 men." "Deportees Claimed Nucleus of Vast Narcotics Network," *Rome Daily American* (July 3, 1951). Luciano file released by DEA under Freedom of Information Act.

168 American consul general. U.S. Nat. Archives. U.S. consul in Palermo to State Department, Foreign Service dispatch, July 23, 1952. Both in Lucania, Salvatore, Name File, in "Suspected Narcotics Traffickers" RG 59. U.S. State Dept. Div. of Far Eastern Affairs.

168 Opium Protocol of 1953. House Subcommittee on Crime, Committee on the Judiciary, John T. Cusack testimony, *Drug Enforcement Policies Hearings* 97th Cong., December 10, 1981, 63.

169 "This is a hot port." Thompson to Morgenthau memorandum, March 31, 1937. Morgenthau diary, book 61, 347. FDR Library.

169 Marseille criminals. Newsday staff, *The Heroin Trail* (New American Library: N.Y., 1974). 74.

169 Spirito's fate. Derick Goodman, *Villainy Unlimited: The Truth about the French Underworld Today* (Elek Books: London, 1957), 91.

170 Spirito . . . a significant player. DEA, *Pilot Project III*. A confidential internal history and review of worldwide drug-trafficking patterns, 10–16. Given to the author.

170 "We were alarmed particularly." Senate Select Committee to Study Governmental Operations with Respect to Intelligence Activities. George Kennan testimony *Final Report*, Book IV, 94th Cong., 2nd sess., 1976, 31.

170 "secret operation." T. Barnes, "The Secret Cold War," *Hist. Journal* 24 no. 2 (1981): 413.

170 "The CIA, through its contacts." McCoy, *Politics of Heroin*, 60–61.

171 Marius Ansaldi. Goodman, *Villainy Unlimited*, 101–4.

171 another lab. "Illicit Traffic in Heroin," *Bulletin on Narcotics*, 5 no. 2 (April–June 1953): 48.

171 Police Judiaire Central. J. T. Cusack, "Response of the Government of France to the International Heroin Problem," in *Drugs, Policy & Diplomacy*, ed. L. Simmons and A. A. Said (Sage Pub.: N.Y., 1979), 249.

172 French Police "welcomed the participation." Ibid., 244.

172 "most important narcotics smuggler's haven." Charles Siragusa to Barrett McGurn, March 3, 1953, *Herald Tribune*. Country file 0660 France, file 3. DEA. Pentagon City, Va. Obtained through Freedom of Information Act.

172 "obstinate refusal." House Subcommittee on Crime of the Committee on the Judiciary, John T. Cusack testimony, *Drug Enforcement Policies, Hearings* 97th Cong., December 10, 1981, 64.

173 "No member of his family." Memo December 19, 1960. "Liaison with the Sûreté Nationale." Country Files. 0660 France. Folder No. 3. DEA. Pentagon City, Va. Obtained through Freedom of Information Act.

173 opium monopoly. McCoy, *Politics of Heroin*, 113–15.

173 "Desperately short of funds." Ibid., 131.

174 "Opium was a military objective," L. Bodard, *The Quicksand War* (Atlantic Monthly Press: Boston, 1967), 46.

174 "sold to local Chinese merchants." McCoy, *Politics of Heroin*, 135.

174 "Don't you have anything else." Ibid., 140.

175 "Born out of the Algerian turmoil." *Newsday* staff. *The Heroin Trail* (New American Lib.: N.Y., 1974), 128–30. Series ran from February 1–March 4, 1973 in *Newsday*.

176 "vaguely French antecedents." "The Boys at the Snow Leopard," *Time* (February 29, 1960), 35.

176 "watched from the side." Don A. Schanche, *Mister Pop* (David McKay: N.Y., 1970), 40.

176 "began splendidly." Bodard, *Quicksand War*, 79.

176 "Communist China is producing." "New Tactics Urged in Narcotic Battle," *NYT* (June 19, 1951), 1.

177 "There can be little doubt." U.N. Commission on Narcotic Drugs. *The Illicit Narcotic Traffic in the Far East*, remarks of H. J. Anslinger, April 1953. Anslinger Papers, box 1, file 8. Penn State.

177 "the greatest purveyor in history." "Peiping Narcotics Cited as U.N. Bar," *NYT* (August 1, 1955), 3:8.

177 "Communist heroin." U.S. Senate Judiciary Committee. Subcommittee to Investigate Internal Security. *Communist China and Illicit Narcotic Traffic*, 84th Cong., 1st sess., 1955, 3.

177 "narcotics smugglers named." D. C. Kinder, "Bureaucratic Cold Warrior: Harry J. Anslinger and Illicit Narcotics Traffic," *Pacific Historical Review* (1981): 169–91.

177 "international politics to distort." J. C. McWilliams, *The Protectors*, 152.

177 "politics in those days." Interview with Ingersoll in New York City. November 4, 1993.

178 "some large diversion." Anslinger to Siragusa, November 21, 1955. Country Files. 0660 France. Folder labeled Heroin Diversion. DEA. Pentagon City, Va. Obtained through Freedom of Information Act.

178 assured Anslinger. Siragusa to Anslinger, December 3, 1955. Country Files. 0660 France. Folder labeled Heroin Diversion. DEA. Pentagon City, Va. Obtained through Freedom of Information Act.

178 "closely allied to Corsican." Confidential memo dated March 20, 1963, written by Andrew Tartaglino. Country Files. 0660 France. Folder labeled Heroin Diversion. DEA. Pentagon City, Va. Obtained through Freedom of Information Act.

178 one Joseph Cesari. M. Denuziere, "Vie et mort de Jo Césari," *Le Monde* (April 1, 1972). Vertical file on Joseph Césari at *La Provencal-Meridional* newspapers in Marseille.

179 "One of the reasons." Dr. John, *Hoodoo Moon*, 38.

179 "Like all good cases." Interviews with Andrew Tartaglino, October 1993.

180 "essential oils." Miriam Ottenberg, *The Federal Investigators* (Prentice-Hall: Englewood Cliffs, N.J., 1962), 159.

180 Ambassador Rosal's Corsican connection. Miriam Ottenberg, *The Federal Investigators* (Prentice Hall: Englewood Cliffs, N.J., 1962), 157–68; Rosal and Tarditti. "Guatamalan Envoy Held As Smuggler," *NYT* (October 4, 1960), 1:2; Rosal case as described in confidential study. DEA, *Pilot Project Part III*. A confidential study of worldwide trafficking patterns given to the author, 32–40.

182 Bourbonnais began to talk. DEA, *Pilot Project III*, 38.

182 Cusack would testify. J. Cusack, "Response of the Govt. of France," 250.

183 "one and a half tons are smuggled." President's Advisory Commission on Narcotics and Drug Abuse (GPO: Washington, D.C., 1963), 8.

183 "five, and possibly ten, groups." U.S. House Committee on Foreign Affairs, *The World Heroin Problem*, 92nd Cong., 1st sess. (GPO: Wash., D.C., 1971), 8.

183 "Approximately 85–90%." "Report of the Task Force on Narcotics." File on Law Enforcement, Juvenile Delinquency, & Narcotics, Pt. 3. Office files of James Gaither, box 83. LBJ Library.

184 "such enormous quantities." Anslinger to Ambassador Herve Alphand, Oct. 21, 1960. Country Files. 0660 France. Folder No. 4. DEA. Pentagon City, Va. Obtained through Freedom of Information Act.

184 "almost all the heroin." Siragusa to Anslinger, memorandum, February 6, 1961. Country Files. 0660 France. Folder No. 4. DEA. Pentagon City, Va. Obtained through Freedom of Information Act.

184 "The minister [consul general]." Speer to Anslinger, memorandum, February 28, 1961. Country Files. 0660 France. Folder No. 4. DEA. Pentagon City, Va. Obtained through FOIA.

184 "I would be grateful." Dollon to Rusk, April 20, 1961. Country Files. 0660 France. Folder No. 4. Obtained through FOIA.

185 "there was no manpower." Jack Cusack memorandum, November 17, 1966. "Bilateral representations to France of the need for more effective domestic enforcement in France." Country Files. 0660 France. Folder No. 6.

185 "all normal law enforcement." Paris bureau memorandum, September 18, 1961. Country files. 0660 France. Folder No. 4. DEA. Pentagon City, Va. Obtained through Freedom of Information Act.

185 "take the position." Giordano, memorandum, October 14, 1966. *Report of Task Force on Narcotics*. File on Law Enforcement Juvenile Deliquent and Narcotics Office files of James Gaither, box 83. LBJ Library.

185 "he had highly placed friends." T. Tripodi, *Crusade: Undercover Against the KGB & Mafia* (Brassey's: N.Y., 1993), 186.

3186 "communist China and Cuba." "Narcotics Rise Laid to China and Cuba," *NYT* (June 1, 1962), 2:1.

187 took place in the sacristy. J. L. Meteya, "L'Enquete en France," *Le Figaro* (February 24, 1964), 1:13.

187 Uruguay's ambassador to Moscow. "Juan Aritzí—l'un des diplomates inculpes," *Le Figaro* (February 25, 1964), 3:17.

188 two old friends. FBN, *Traffic in Opium and Other Dangerous Drugs*, 1964 Annual Report. Also from "Project Pilot," Part III, Sepcial Report, DEA (No date, but sometime in mid 70s), 53–63; Bureau of Narcotics, *Traffic in Opium & Other Dangerous Drugs* 1964 Annual Report (GPO: Washington, D.C., 1965), 32–33. Also, "Diplomat Seized as Police Crack Heroin Ring Here," *NYT* (February 22, 1964), 1:1.

188 "[D]iplomats who enter the United States." State Dept. to Wm. J. Crockett, memorandum, March 27, 1964. Dept. of State File, JFK Library, Boston.

189 Michel Victor Mertz. *Newsday* staff, *The Heroin Trail* (Signet Paperback: N.Y., 1974), 114–15.

190 "These interventions." Cusack, "Response of the Govt. of France," 250.

Chapter 10: "Agents Were Engaged in Illicit Activities"

191 "This agent made the unforgivable error." U.S. Senate. *Federal Drug Enforcement: Hearings Before the Permanent Subcommittee on Investigations of the Committee*

of Government Operations Pt. I. From sealed Committee Exhibit 14A, an official DEA report on corruption, November 21, 1968, 94th Cong., 1st sess, 1975.

192 Edward J. Coyne. Interviews in spring 1991 and August 1993. Also see his congressional testimony.

195 "Mr. Speer was demoted." U.S. Senate, "Federal Drug Enforcement," 142.

195 FBN's Washington headquarters. Thomas A. Senate. Wadden, "We Put the Heat on Washington Dope Peddlers," *Saturday Evening Post* (October 3, 1953), 19–134.

196 "Because of arrest quotas." Senate. "Federal Drug Enforcement," *Hearings*. Pt. IV 94th Cong., 2nd sess., 906.

196 Corrupt agents. U.S. Senate. *Federal Drug Enforcement: Hearings*, 1975. Sealed memorandum, June 10, 1975; DEA corruption investigation report, November 21, 1968. Committee exhibit 14A.

197 five modest projects. Joint Committee of the American Bar Association and the American Medical Association on Narcotic Drugs, *Drug Addiction: Crime or Disease?* (Indiana University Press: Bloomington, 1961). This is the book version of the interim report.

198 "glaring inaccuracies." R. King, *The Drug Hang-up* (Chas. C. Thomas: Springfield, Ill., 1972). Rufus King was one of the members of the ABA joint committee.

198 "may well the crudest publication." B. DeMott, "The Great Narcotics Muddle," *Harper's* 224 (March 1962) 53.

198 "close supervision." Frederick G. Dutton to Hon. A. Gilmore Flues, memorandum, April 20, 1961. White House Name File (Harry J. Anslinger) at the JFK Library.

198 "The Narcotics Bureau." Benjamin DeMott, "The Great Narcotics Muddle," *Harper's* 224 (March 1962), 46–50.

198 "distinguished public health administrator." Stanley Meisner, "Federal Narcotics Czar: Zeal Without Insight," *The Nation* (February 20, 1960), 159–62.; DeMott, "The Great Narcotics Muddle," *Harper's*; Rufus S. King, "The Narcotics Bureau and The Harrison Act: Jailing the Healers and the Sick," *Yale Law Journal* 62 (1953): 736–49. Murtagh quote is from Meisner, "Czar," 162.

198 "a gas bag." "Anslinger Hits Back At Murtagh on Addicts," *NY Mirror* (May 26, 1959).

198 "Although many critics." S. Meisner, "Federal Narcotics Czar."

199 "just to get him." Jonnes, *We're Still Here*, (Atlantic Monthly Press, N.Y., 1986), 226.

199 10 percent of the cohort. L. Robins and G. Murphy, "Drug Use in a Normal Population of Young Negro Men," *Am. J Public Health* 57. no. 9 (September 1967): 1580–96.

200 "waste of time." Mott, "The Great Narcotics Muddle," 53.

200 "This conference can be." 'First White House Conference on Narcotic and Drug Abuse,' *Traffic in Opium and Other Dangerous Drugs* (GPO: Washington, D.C., 1962), 21–22.

200 "Most of the juvenile addicts." Anslinger, "The Facts About Our Teen-age Drug Addicts," *Reader's Digest* (October 1951).

201 CBS News's *New York Forum* Transcript of *NY Forum* on CBS (April 28, 1962). Anslinger Papers Box 1/file 8. Pattee Library, Penn State.

Chapter 11: "Burning for the Heavenly Connection"

205 "obscene and indecent writings." M. Schumacher, *Dharma Lion* (St. Martin's Press: N.Y., 1992), 254.

206 "a sweeping sense of exhilaration." Ann Charters, ed., *Dictionary of Literary Biography: The Beats: Literary Bohemians in Postwar America* Vol. 16, Pt. 1 (Gale Research Co.: Detroit, 1983), 158–59.

206 "In the very hour of achievement." Warren Susman, "Did Success Spoil The United States?" in *Recasting America*: Culture and Poltics in the Age of the Cold War, ed. Larry May (University Chicago Press: Chicago, 1989), 22–23.

207 "waiting for a prophet." Joyce Johnson, *Minor Characters* (Picador: London, 1983), 128.

207 "colored section." Jack Kerouac *On the Road* (Signet Paperback: N.Y., 1985), 148.

207 "One is Hip." N. Mailer, "White Negro: Superficial Reflections on the Hipster," *Dissent* (summer 1957): 278.

207 "greatly inferior." N. Polsky, "Reflections on Hipsterism," *Dissent* (winter 1958): 77–79.

208 "so antique a vision." James Baldwin, "The Black Boy Looks At the White Boy Norman Mailer," *Esquire* (May 1961), 104.

208 "the Beat thing." Peter Manso, *Mailer: His Life and Times* (Simon & Schuster: N.Y., 1985), 259.

208 "my nut-house record." William Burroughs, *Junky* (Penguin Books: New York, 1977; reprint with new introduction of 1953 original), xiv.

209 "crucial figure." Ted Morgan, *Literary Outlaw: The Life and Times of William S. Burroughs* (Henry Holt: N.Y., 1988), 123.

209 "I felt as though." Herbert E Huncke, *The Evening Sun Turned Crimson* (Cherry Valley Editions: Cherry Valley, N.Y., 1980), 115.

209 "the ordinary citizen's soul." The entry on "Allen Ginsberg" in Charters, *Beats*, 216.

209 "more with musical geniuses." Ann Charters, *Kerouac* (Straight Arrow Books: San Francisco, 1973), 220.

209 "consciously modeled." D. McNally, *Desolate Angel: A Biography of Jack Kerouac and the Beat Generation and America* (Random House: N.Y., 1979), 147–48.

209 "They called [marijuana]." A. Goldman, *Grass Roots: Marijuana in America Today* (Warner Books: N.Y., 1980), 113.

210 "the various drugs." Schumacher, *Dharma Lion*, 61.

210 "a year of evil decadence." Ibid.

210 "I tried it." W. S. Burroughs, *Junky*, xv.

210 "Using junk." Morgan, *Outlaw*, 121.

210 "He fit right into." Ibid., 139.

211 "I thought for many years." Miles, *Ginsberg*, 103.

211 "factualism." Morgan, *Outlaw*, 150.

212 "I saw my chance of escaping." Burroughs, *Junky*, 143.

212 "Like a guerrilla general." Johnson, *Minor Characters*, 114.

212 "My own antipathy." D. Wakefield, *New York in the Fifties* (Houghton Mifflin: Boston, 1992), 179–80.

213 "a suppressed cry." N. Podhoretz, "The Know-Nothing Bohemians," *Partisan Review* (spring 1958): 318.

213 "writing at all." J. Winn, "Capote, Mailer and Miss Parker," *The New Republic* (February 9, 1959), 27.

213 "a unique social formation." R. Jacoby, *The Last Intellectual: American Culture in the Age of Academe* (Basic Books: N.Y., 1987), 70.

213 Lawrence Lipton's exegesis. Lawrence Lipton, *The Holy Barbarians* (Julian Messner: N.Y., 1959), 283.

214 "Everything the shamans of jazz." Lipton, *Barbarians*, 180–81.

214 "I have seen God." P. O'Neil, "The Only Rebellion Around: But the Shabby Beats Bungle the Job in Arguing, Sulking and Bad Poetry," *Life* 47 (November 30, 1959), 117.

214 "Few outsiders realize." N. Polsky, *Hustlers, Beats, and Others* (Aldine Publishing: Chicago, 1967), 166.

214 marijuana smoking. Ibid., 172.

215 "not taken a bath." William S. Burroughs, *Naked Lunch* (Grove Press: N.Y., 1959), xi.

215 "Junk," he explained. Burroughs, *Naked Lunch*, xxxix.

215 *Life* had heaped scorn. O'Neil, "Only Rebellion," 122.

215 "a series of experiments." Miles, *Ginsberg*, 103.

216 "deliberate derangement." J. Ciardi, "Epitaph for the Dead Beats," *Saturday Review* (February 6, 1960), 13.

216 "always reminded us." Wakefield, *Fifties*, 219.

216 the most visible and vocal challenge. B. Ehrenreich, *The Hearts of Men: American Dreams and the Flight From Commitment* (Garden City, N.Y.: Anchor Press, 1983).

216 "Five narcotics detectives," "Police 'Beatniks' Aid Dope Raids," *New York Herald Tribune* (November 9, 1959).

Chapter 12: "One Pill Makes You Larger"

218 "three-story mansion." T. Leary, *Flashbacks* (Tarcher: Los Angeles, 1983), 36.
218 Leary's crew cut. J. Stevens, *Storming Heaven: LSD and the American Dream* (Perennial Library: New York, 1988), 123–32. Also, T. Leary, *Flashbacks.*
219 "how he devolved." J. Stevens, *Storming Heaven, 133.*
219 "axiom of psychology." Ibid., 134.
220 "Use Harvard's prestige," Ibid., 142.
220 "I'm the Messiah." E. Hyde, *On the Poetry of Allen Ginsberg* (University Michigan Press: Ann Arbor, 1984), 236.
221 "It seemed to us." Schumacher, *Dharma Lion,* 347.
221 "I spoke to Willem de Kooning." Stevens, *Storming,* 147.
221 "the effects of psilocybin." Schumacher, *Dharma Lion,* 348.
221 "Leary regaled me." D. Wakefield, *New York in the Fifties,* 172–73.
222 "stupifies the mind." Ibid., 174.
222 "Listen to us." Stevens, *Storming,* 148.
222 "wanted everyone to have." Leary, *Flashbacks,* 50.
222 "Leary wanted to spread." Morgan, *Literary Outlaw,* 367.
3223 "I experienced fantastic images." D. Solomon, ed., *LSD: Consciousness-Expanding Drug* (Berkeley Medallion: N.Y., 1966), 52.
223 "vertigo, visual disturbances." E. Brecher, *Licit & Illicit Drugs* (Consumers Union: Mt. Vernon, N.Y., 1972), 347.
224 Delysid. Stevens, *Storming Heaven,* 12.
224 "eliciting true and accurate." M. A. Lee and B. Shlain, *Acid Dreams: Complete Social History of LSD: The CIA, the Sixties, and Beyond* (Grove, Weidenfeld: N.Y., 1992), 14.
224 Isbell administered. Ibid., 24–25.
225 disturb memory. Stevens, *Storming Heaven,* 81.
225 "every automobile that came." Lee and Shlain, *Acid,* 30.
225 possibility that Olson was murdered. G. Tasker, "Inquiry into CIA Researcher's '53 Death Inconclusive," *Baltimore Sun* (November 29, 1994), B-1.
226 safe-house appartment. Lee and Shlain, *Acid,* 32.
226 White went on his merry. Ibid., 32–35.
226 Hubbard. Stevens, *Storming Heaven,* 54.
227 Hubbard first experienced. Lee and Shlain, *Acid Dreams,* 44–45.
227 The famous writer got in touch. Stevens, *Storming Heaven,* 46.
227 "What Babes in Wood." Ibid., 54.
228 "promoted his cause." Lee and Shlain, *Acid,* 50–51.
228 Cary Grant. Stevens, *Storming Heaven,* 64–65.
229 "absorbed into the electrical." Lee and Shlain, *Acid Dreams,* 59.
229 growing numbers of doctors and patients. Brecher, *Licit Drugs,* 350.
229 "portentousness." Ibid., 351.
229 "Everything I had heard." T. Leary, *High Priest* (New American Library: N.Y., 1968), 244.
229 "From the date of this session." Ibid., 256–57.
229 "I have never recovered." Leary, *Flashbacks,* 119.
230 instant LSD convert. Morgan, *Literary Outlaw,* 384.
230 "We're through playing science game." Stevens, *Storming Heaven,* 189.
230 "talked such nonsense." Ibid., 191.
230 "do irreparable harm." Ibid., 191.
230 "LSD is so powerful." Lee and Shlain, *Acid Dreams,* 88.
231 "You're now sitting in a religious." Timothy Leary, *The Politics of Ecstasy* (Ronin Pub.: Berkeley, 1990), 293.
231 "The future may decide." Paul Krassner, *Confessions of a Raving, Unconfined Nut* (Simon & Schuster: N.Y., 1993), 102.
231 Edge City. Stevens, *Storming Heaven,* 232.
232 "rolling affront." K. Bishop, "Down Electric, Kool-Aid Memory Lane," *International Herald Tribune* (November 7, 1990).
232 "bunch of Ivy League eggheads," Stevens, *Storming Heaven,* 235.
232 "lying naked and freaked out." Ibid., 258.

233 "In the 10-month period." New York Medical Society, "The Dangerous Drug Problem," *NYMJ* 22 no. 9 (May 5, 1966): 243–44.

233 "every thousand people." Stevens, *Storming Heaven*, 74.

234 "haunted by fear of death." J. M. White, "Senators Hear Ginsberg," *Washington Post* (June 15, 1966), A-1.

234 Ginsberg went on to say. U.S. Senate Judiciary Committee Special Subcommittee, *Narcotic Rehabilitation Act of 1966: Hearings*, 89th Cong., 2nd sess., June 14, 1966, 487–508.

234 Leary . . . testified that he had. *Narcotic Rehabilitation Act*, May 13, 1966, 239–58.

235 "turn on, tune in, drop out." Stevens, *Storming Heaven*, 326.

235 "mind-blowing fun." Ibid., 342.

236 "consume pure experience." J. Larner, "The College Drug Scene," *Atlantic* 216 (November 1965), 128.

236 " 'contradiction of capitalism' " Allen J. Matusow, *The Unraveling of America: A History of Liberalism in the 1960's* (Harper & Row: N.Y., 1984) 306.

236 "new states of awareness" R. Dass, *Be Here Now* (Crown Publishing: N.Y., 1971), chap. "Coming Down."

236 "I even if the risks." Leary, *Politics*, 299.

236 banned their use. Schumacher, *Dharma Lion*, 349, 543.

236 "So much a part" N. v. Hoffman, "The Haight Revisited," *Washington Post* (May 12, 1971), C-1.

237 "my inner self." Susan Lydon, *Take the Long Way Home*, (Harper S.F.: S.F., 1993), 169, 173.

237 "The Captain was particularly irked." Lee & Shlain, *Acid Dreams*, 199.

238 "a new culture." Ibid., 265.

239 "rejection of drugs." D. Musto, "Drugs in the '90s—1890s and 1990s: An Interview with David F. Musto," *Woodrow Wilson Center Report* 2, no. 3 (November 1990): 10.

239 "the traffic in marijuana," Commissioner's Feb. 27, 1968 statement before Congress. LBJ Library. WHCF. Box 16. Narcotics File.

239 "Local arrests for all types." memorandum, December 4, 1967. WHCF Box 16 HE 4-1 Narcotics File. LBJ Library.

239 "well established." Stevens, *Storming Heaven*, 199.

240 "There's an ancient tradition." Ed. Gordon Ball, *Allen Verbatim* (McGraw Hill: NY, 1974), 70.

240 "I predict that psychedelic drugs." Leary, *Politics*, 206.

Chapter 13: "Everybody Must Get Stoned"

242 "In those days." Interview with "Calvin Johnson" (not his real name) in 1986 in Baltimore.

242 "drug itself transforms." L. Jones, *Blues People* (Morrow: N.Y., 1963), 140.

242 The memory forever rankled. "Calvin Johnson." Interview with Johnson. 1986.

4243 "living hell." Interview with Juanita Jackson Mitchell, August 11, 1986.

243 "as segregated racially." R. Baker, *The Good Times* (Plume: N.Y., 1990), 77.

243 "didn't like the discrimination." Interview with "Calvin Johnson," September 16, 1994. He requested his named be changed.

244 "Life was going out," From taped interviews conducted with Baltimore heroin addicts in the mid seventies by Philip Stevenson and made available through Dr. David Nurco of Friends' Medical Science Research Center in Baltimore.

244 "lifestyle was to hang out." Interview of woman addict provided by Professor David Nurco of Friends Medical Science Research Center in Baltimore.

244 "My gang of guys were on the progressive side." Interviews from mid seventies courtesy of Dr. David Nurco, Friends Medical Service Center, Baltimore.

245 "Status in this subculture." D. N. Nurco, P. Stephenson, J. W. Shaffer, "Addict's Perceptions of the Availability and Distribution of Narcotics in Baltimore over Four Decades" (unpublished paper, June 29, 1982) Available through Friends Medical Research Center in Baltimore.

246 Youth Emergency Council. "Mayor Names Council to Combat Narcotics," *Baltimore Sun* (March 18, 1951). Available in Enoch Pratt Library, Maryland Room vertical file under "Narcotics."

247 30 percent had moved from elsewhere. M. Naver, "Narcotics Addiction Found Rising Problem," *Evening Sun* (April 3, 1961). (Available in Pratt Library vertical file, "Narcotics.") Statistics from the two U.S. Public Health hospitals—Lexington and Ft. Worth—confirm that in that era it was blacks in northern cities, not elsewhere, who were most prone to be hooked. As late as 1960, when 60 percent of blacks still lived in the South, only 5 percent of black addicts being treated came from that region. The country's ten most populous cities accounted for 70 percent of Negro addicts at the hospitals, even though only 40 percent of the black population lived in those cities.

247 "the black community never complained." Interview with Joseph Carroll, July 15, 1986.

248 "They came back loaded down." Interview with James Watkins, March 11, 1986.

248 captain Carroll. P. Sloyan, "Capt. Carroll of the Dope Squad" *Baltimore News-Post* (November 22, 1960). Available in Pratt Library vertical file, "Narcotics."

249 Anthony Rizzi. Interviews done in August and September 1994.

249 "White addicts engaged," Nurco, "Addicts' Perceptions," 6.

251 welfare population exploded. National Institute of Drug Abuse, "A Case Study—Narcotic Addiction Over a Quarter of a Century in a Major American City 1950–1977, NIDA Monograph Series" (1979), 7.

252 crime statistics would soar. Baltimore Police Commissioner's annual report to the governor of Maryland. Available in the Maryland Room of the Enoch Pratt Library.

253 "found that these 243 heroin addicts." J. Ball, L. Rosen, J. Flueck, D. Nurco, "Lifetime Criminality of Heroin Addicts in the U.S.," *Journal of Drug Issues* (Summer 1982): 225–39.

254 one of three categories. J. Shaffer, D. Nurco, et. al., "The Relationship of Preaddiction Characteristics to the Types and Amounts of Crime Committed by Narcotic Addicts," *Intl. J. of the Addictions* 22, no. 2 (1987), 153–65. Also, Nurco et al., "The Consistency of Types of Criminal Behavior Over Preaddiction, Addiction and Nonaddiction Status Periods," *Comprehensive Psychiatry* 30, no. 5 (September/October 89): 391–402.

255 neither working or in school. Nurco, "Case Study," 6.

255 "narcotic abusers." D. Nurco and E. Farrell, "Narcotic Abusers and Poverty," *Criminology* 13, no. 3 (November 1975): 389–98.

255 In 1970. B. Freed, "Heroin, Dilaudid and Methadone Overdoses killed 59 here in 1970," *Evening Sun* (January 26, 1971). Available in Enoch Pratt Maryland Room vertical file, "Narcotics."

256 "75 percent went to a four-year college." Interview with Robert Rivkin, August 1994.

256 "When I first came into high school." Interviews with Mindy Milstein Shuman, summer 1994.

257 "I was wasted." Interviews with Mike Gimbel, Summer 1994.

258 Baltimore erupted. "1,900 U.S. Troops Patrolling City," *Sun* (June 25, 1968), 1. Vertical file on "Riot, 1968, Baltimore," in Maryland Room of Enoch Pratt Library.

260 "He drained us." R. Henderson, "Drug Warrior," *Baltimore Sun* (November 10, 1991), "People" sec. front page.

260 Howard County. M. J. Clark, "Howard Study says 40% 10th, 12th grade students have used marijuana," *Baltimore Sun* (September 10, 1973). Clipping from Enoch Pratt Maryland Room vertical files, "Narcotics."

261 "every thousand." Stevens, *Storming Heaven*, 74.

261 "the denial of the parents." Interview with Angela Saxton, Summer 1994.

Chapter 14: "The Problem Has Assumed the Dimensions . . ."

262 "growing menace," "Text of Nixon's Message," *NYT* (July 15, 1969), 18.

263 "grave concern to me." Statement by the president, November 2, 1951. Bureau of the Budget Bill file. Papers of Harry S. Truman. Harry S. Truman Library.

263 "A new war on narcotics." "President Launches Drive on Narcotics," *NYT* (November 28, 1954), 1.

264 "almost a public hysteria." Markham to Lee White, memorandum April 1, 1964, WHCF HE-4 Box 14, File 11/22/63-8/23/64. LBJ Library.

264 "a comprehensive research plan." Markham to Lee White, memorandum, April 1, 1964. WHCF HE-4, box 14, November 22, 1963–August 23, 1964, 12. LBJ Library.

264 against the mandatory sentences. Task Force on Narcotics, Report, 1964 Folder, Law Enforcement, Juvenile Delinquency, and Narcotics, Office Files of White House Aide James Gaither, Box 83. LBJ Library.

265 "top official." Markham to Lee White, memorandum, April 1, 1964.

265 "better control." Markham to Lee White, memorandum, April 22, 1965. WHCF FG 110-12, Bureau of Narcotics, box 158. LBJ Library.

265 "how a federal narcotics agent." J. D. Horan and D. Frasca, "Mob Shakedown," *New York Journal-American* (August 3, 1965).

267 "In fairness to the French." Task Force on Narcotics, Report.

267 "While the French." H. Giordano to D. Acheson, memorandum, Oct. 14, 1966. *Report on Task Force on Narcotics*.

268 found this baffling. It is worth recalling that one Bureau higher-up, Wayland Speer, did actively inveigh against the French back in 1960–61, but his career was derailed soon thereafter by corrupt New York agents.

268 "complete lack of any." J. Cusack to H. Giordano, memorandum December 10, 1962, included as part of memorandum, from D. Acheson to J. Califano, December 13, 1965. In White House confidential files, box 11. Country File 296, Turkey. LBJ Library.

269 "Our intelligence indicates." J. Cusack to H. Giordano, memorandum, January 17, 1963, included in memorandum from D. Acheson to J. Califano, December 13, 1965. LBJ Library.

269 "worked out the broad outlines." J. P. Hendrick to H. Fowler, memorandum, April 16, 1968, in memorandum, Fowler to Ramsey Clark, May 4, 1968. White House confidential file, Country File 296, Turkey. Folder April 4, 1967–June 30, 1968. LBJ Library.

270 "our narcotics problem." Representative Rosenthal to Ramsey Clark, March 25, 1968. Folder on Narcotics and Drug Abuse Control–Transfer '68. Personal Papers of Ramsey Clark. LBJ Library.

270 "the narcotics problem." F. Belair, "U.S. Presses Pacts with 3 Countries in Fight on Heroin," *NYT* (January 1, 1969).

271 "regardless of foreign policy consequences," State Dept. Office of the Historian, *Chronology on International Narcotics Control, 1833–1980* Res. Proj. No. 1256-A (December 1981) 13.

271 "of the Washington decision." State Dept. telegram, December 3, 1973 from Moynihan. E.J. Epstein Archive. Box 11, File 8. Boston University.

271 "There was a quantum leap." Moynihan to State Dept., telegram, December 3, 1973 from Moynihan. Edward J. Epstein Archive. Box 11, Folder 8. Boston University.

271 "an intensified international heroin control." State Dept. Office of the Historian. *Chronology*.

271 "a bit put out." S. Rosenfeld, "U.S. Attacks Drugs at Sources Abroad," *Washington Post* (January 23, 1970).

271 "Practices by friendly governments." S. Rosenfeld, "U.S. Attacks Drugs," *Wash.Post*.

272 "making some major breakthroughs." J. Ehrlichman to RN, memorandum, May 23, 1970. WHCF Country: France, box 27, folder [EX] Co. 50, May 1, 1970–May 31, 1970.

272 "Presley ended the interview." Epstein, *Agency*, 153.

273 "more than a quarter of the males." R. DuPont, "Where Does One Run When He's Already in the Promised Land?" (paper presented at Fifth National Conference on Methadone Treatment, March 1973), 1395. Made available by Dr. DuPont.

273 "one-third of the teen-agers." D. Burnham, "Heroin Traps 33% on 'Addict Block'," *NYT* (October 13, 1968), 81:3.

273 "Previously unavailable in South Vietnam." McCoy, *Politics of Heroin*, 223.

273 "GI Heroin Sales," P. Osnos, "GI Heroin Sales in Vietnam," *Washington Post* (June 13, 1971), A-1.

274 "My informal assessment of the mean rank." J. Jaffe, "Looking back around the corner" (Proceedings of the thirty-eighth Annual Scientific Meeting, Committee on Problems of Drug Dependence, National Academy of Science National Research Council, Washington, D.C., 1976), 434. (Provided by Jaffe.)

275 "President told group." Nixon Project, summary of June 3, 1971, meeting. WHSF Krogh, box 32. Folder: Summary of President's Remarks. National Archives.

276 "impress in forceful terms." Memorandom to President Nixon, June 11, 1971. WHSF Krogh, box 31 Folder: Special Action Office for Drug Abuse Prevention, 1971.

276 new Latin America collaboration. David Corn, *Blond Ghost* (Simon & Schuster: N.Y., 1994), 258-60.

277 "could say he committed a crime." J. Jaffe, "Footnotes in the Evolution of the American National Response," *Brit. JAddictn* 82 (1987): 593.

277 "efforts to fight the international." Nixon Project, memorandum, Jan. 27, 1972, on drug enforcement programs. FG 17-16, file on ODALE/ONNI. National Archives.

277 every departing soldier. J. Jaffe, "Footnotes": 594.

277 politics of opium in France and Southeast Asia. Senate, Alfred W. McCoy speaking before Senate Foreign Operations Subcommittee (June 2, 1972), 699–702, 92nd Cong., 2nd sess.

278 "outlaw remnants." "Flower Power Struggle," *Time* (September 8, 1967). 22.

279 "corruption, collusion." S. Hersh, "Report to U.S. Sees No Hope of Halting Asian Drug Traffic," *NYT* (July 24, 1972), 1:7.

279 "The war has clearly been." Senate, *Foreign & Military Intelligence, Book 1: Final Report of the Select Committee to Study Governmental Operations with Respect to Intelligence Activities*, 94th Cong., 2nd sess. (GPO: Washington D.C., 1976), 229–31.

280 Epstein argues. Political scientist Patricia Rachal in her book, *Federal Narcotics Enforcement*, rebukes Epstein for slipshod research and concludes that "Epstein's conspiracy theory must be viewed with considerable suspicion."

280 Charlotte Street. J. Jonnes, *We're Still Here* (Atlantic Monthly Press: N.Y., 1986), 226–27.

281 "What became of the women?" R. DuPont, "Where Does One Run When He's Already in the Promised Land?" (paper presented to the Fifth National Conference on Methadone Treatment, March 1973), made available to the author.

281 new AFDC cases. J. Q. Wilson and R. DuPont, "The Sick Sixties," *Atlantic Monthly* (October 1973), 92.

281 "moved out of the black ghettos." "The Heroin Plague," *Newsweek* (July 5, 1971), 29.

281 "Twenty were white," Newsday staff, *Heroin Trail*, 303.

282 Roger Delouette trafficking case. Newsday staff, *The Heroin Trail*, 99–105. Also P. Hoffman, *Tiger in the Court* (Playboy Press: Chicago), 221–40.

283 "Around the 15th of December." This rather mangled translation of DeLouette's confession is from Paul Hoffman's *Tiger in the Court* (Playboy Press: Chicago, 1973), 225, the tale of career highlights from U.S. prosecutor Herbert Stern.

284 "proceed with an appropriate." M. Mintz, "Heroin Smuggler's Story," *Washington Post* (November 21, 1971) A-1.

284 L'Affaire Cusack. J. Randal, "Drug War Causes." Also A. Jaubert, *Dossier D . . . Comme Drogue* (Alain Moreau: Paris, 1974), 15–18.

284 "thanks to their bank balances." J. Randal, "Drug War Causes French-U.S. Spat," *Washington Post* (August 30, 1971), A-7.

284 "There is a very influential underworld." "Drug Rings Protected," *Washington Post* (September 12, 1971), A-14.

284 "C'est un personnage." D. Daville, "Le Colonel Fournier de SDECE C'Explique," *Le Figaro* (November 17, 1971), 1:11.

285 "banal affaire de drogue." "Le Colonel Barberot Met En Cause Le Fonctionnement de SDECE," *Le Figaro* (November 20–21, 1971), 3. J. Hess, "French Aide Backs U.S. in Drug Case," *NYT* (November 20, 1971), 1.

285 "a bad novel." G. LeBolzer, "Le gouvernment tient a s'affirmer etc," *LeFigaro* (November 25, 1971), 1.

285 "In 1968 we knew personally." L. Collins and D. LaPierre, "The French Connection—In Real Life," *NYT Sunday Magazine* (February 6, 1972), 51.

285 "We warned those fellows." Interview with the author in Marseille, June 1994.

286 Among those rounded up. M. Bouvier, "The Atlantic Narcotics Alliance," *Drug Enforcement* 2, no. 3 (Summer 1975): 23.

287 "As people became more alarmed." N. Hentoff, *A Doctor Among the Addicts* (Grove Press: N.Y., 1970) 69–70.

287 "There were never any bounds." Ibid., 60.
288 "At the end of five years." D. Wakefield, *New York in the Fifties*, 101.
289 "the effect of reasonable doses." D. Courtwright et al., *Addicts Who Survived: An Oral History of Narcotic Use in America, 1923–1965* (Tennessee University Press: Nashville, 1989), 334–35.
291 "as part of a policy." Courtwright et al., *Addicts Who Survive*, 336.
292 "rehabilitation rather than withdrawal." V. P. Dole, "In the Course of Professional Practice," *NYS J Med* 65, no. 7 (April 1, 1965): 929.
292 "I fail to appreciate." *JAMA* (March 14, 1966)
293 "My own view." L. Yablonsky, "Stoned on Methadone," *New Republic* 155 (August 13, 1966), 16.
293 "I brought with me graphs." D. Courtwright, et al., *Addicts Who Survive*, 340.
293 "three months of starting methadone." E. M. Brecher, *Licit & Illicit Drugs* (Consumers Union: Mt. Vernon, N.Y., 1972), 144.
294 higher-dose programs. J. Ball and A. Ross, *The Effectiveness of Methadone Maintenance* (Springer-Verlag: N.Y., 1991).
295 "a woman addict in jail." V. Dole and M. Nyswander, "Methadone Maintenance Treatment, A Ten-Year Perspective," *JAMA* 235 no. 19 (May 10, 1976): 2119.
295 "methadone kept me feeling." Lydon, *Long Way Home*, 156.
295 "unprecedented entry." Courtwright et al., *Addicts Who Survived*, 341.
296 A detailed study done. Ball and Ross, *The Effectiveness of Methadone* 241.
296 Vietnam vet drug problem. L. Robins et al., "Narcotic Use in S.E. Asia & Afterward," *Archives of General Psychiatry* 32 (August 1975): 955–61.
297 "From 1972 through mid 1973." House, "The Effectiveness of Turkish Opium Control," Jerry Jenson of DEA speaking before House Committee on International Relations, 94th Cong., 1st sess., September 11, 1975 (GPO: Washington, D.C., 1975), 65.
297 "The heroin epidemic appeared to be waning." R. L. DuPont and M. H. Greene, "Dynamics of a Heroin Addiction Epidemic," *Science* 181 (August 24, 1973): 716–21.
297 "We have arrived at a turning point." H. H. Neumann, "The Tide Has Turned," *U.S. News & World Report* (July 16, 1973), 48.
297 In Baltimore. P. Gilbert, "Use of Heroin in City Found Past its Peak," *Evening Sun* (April 12, 1974). Vertical file on Narcotics in Maryland Room of Enoch Pratt Library.
298 "strong investigative arm." Edward J. Epstein, *Agency of Fear: Opiates and Political Power in America* (G.P. Putnam's Sons, N.Y.: 1977), 252.
299 "pertaining to the possession." "Open Letter to Gov. Mandel (advertisement)," *Evening Sun* (May 1, 1969). Vertical file on Narcotics in Maryland Room of Enoch Pratt Library.

Chapter 15: "High on Cocaine"

301 "status symbol of the American middle-class pothead." "It's the Real Thing," *Newsweek* (September 27, 1971), 124.
304 "Borne on the wings." C. Perry, "The Star-Spangled Powder," *Rolling Stone* (August 17, 1972) 24, 26.
305 "the very acme of pernicious appetite." Charles A. Bunting, *Hope for the Victims of Alcohol, Opium, Morphine, Cocaine and Other Vices* (Christian Home Building: N.Y., 1888), 71.
305 Detroit physician. J. B. Mattison, "Cocaine Dosage and Cocaine Addiction," *Peoria Medical Monthly* 7 (1886–7): 532–42.
305 "physical and mental fatigue." Letter from Dr. J. K. Bauduy, *NYMJ* 42 (1885) 339–43.
305 "The drug of aristocrats." G. Gay, M.D., C. Sheppard, M.D., et. al., "Cocaine in Perspective" *Drug Forum* 2, no. 4 (Summer 1973): 409–29.
306 COCAINE: THE CHAMPAGNE OF DRUGS. A. Crittenden and M. Ruby, "Cocaine: The Champagne of Drugs," *NYT Sunday Magazine* (September 1, 1974), 14–17.
306 "agreed, as might be expected." R. Ashley, *Cocaine: Its History, Uses & Effects* (St. Martin's Press: N.Y., 1975), 156–57.

307 "one of the very few." Ibid., 123.

307 "reserved it for special occasions." Ibid., 124.

307 "Three factors contributed." J. Spillane, *Modern Drug, Modern Menace* (Rand Drug Policy Research Center: Santa Monica, Ca., 1994), 108.

308 "The most significant sociological fact." L. Grinspoon and J. Bakalar, *Cocaine: A Drug & Its Social Evolution* (Basic Books: N.Y., 1976), 64–65.

308 highest status items. R. Steele, "The Cocaine Scene," *Newsweek* (May 30, 1977), 20–25.

309 harrowing autobiography. J. Phillips, *You'll Never Eat Lunch in This Town Again* (Signet: N.Y., 1992), 179.

309 Rolling Stones. Ibid., 213–14.

309 "more into productivity." "In showbiz, the celebs with a nose for what's new," *People* 9 (January 16, 1978), 16–21.

309 "coke noses." "Patching Hollywood's 'coke noses,'" *Medical World News* 19 (April 3, 1978): 81–82.

309 "I have the illusion." Phillips, *Lunch*, 390,

310 By the fall of 1979. Phillips, ibid., 418.

311 Household Survey. NIDA, *National Household Survey on Drug Abuse Highlights 1990* (ADAMHA: Washington, D.C., 1991), 68–71.

311 "the highly successful." Grinspoon and Bakalar, *Cocaine*, 64.

311 "Sure, it's easy to close." Ad for *High Times Encyclopedia* in June 1979 issue.

311 Tom Forcade. Patrick Anderson, *High in America* (Viking: N.Y., 1981), 174–75.

312 "Cocaccessories." Ad in *High Times*, June 1979, 29.

312 licensed sidewalk vendor. U.S. House of Representatives Select Committee on Narcotics Abuse and Control, *Hearing on Drug Paraphernalia*, 96th Cong, 1st sess., November 1, 1979 (GPO: Washington, D.C., 1979), 85.

313 "Medical experts generally." Drug Abuse Council, *Facts About Drug Abuse* (Free Press: N.Y., 1980), 185–87.

313 "failure to distinguish." Ibid., 5.

313 abolish all federal criminal. J. Wooten, "Carter Seeks to End Marijuana Penalty," *NYT* (August 3, 1977), 1.

314 "The legalization or decriminalization." P. Bourne, "It Is Time to Reexamine Our National Narcotics Policy," *Urban & Social Change Review* 9, no. 2 (summer 1976): 5.

314 "what's going to work" Interview with Dr. Bourne, March 10, 1995.

314 "Cocaine . . . is probably." Musto, *American Disease*, 265.

315 "heroin purity levels." Bourne to Mondale, memorandum, January 18, 1978. Subject: Mexico. Box 28 WHCF Bourne. Carter Presidential Library, Atlanta, Ga.

315 NORML expressed its displeasure. "Marijuana Group Sues," *NYT* (March 14, 1978), 18:6.

316 "the president's chief adviser." F. Barbash and E. Walsh, "Carter Aide Resigns," and R. Shaffer, "The Cocaine Incident," *Washington Post* (July 21, 1978) 1.

316 " 'high incidence' of marijuana use." J. Wooten, "Carter Drug Aide Quits," *NYT* (July 21, 1978), A-8.

316 "About half the White House staff." J. Wooten, "Statements by Bourne," *NYT* (July 22, 1978), 7:1.

317 "Whether you agree." H. Johnson, "Revolution: Drugs' Acceptance," *Washington Post* (July 30, 1978), A-3.

317 " 'You know, it's hard to believe,' " L. Darling. "The Drug Set," *Washington Post* (July 30, 1978), 1.

5317 a national sample. U.S. Senate Hearing on Subcommittee on Criminal Justice of Committee on Judiciary, *Drug Paraphernalia and Youth*, 96th Cong., 2nd sess., November 16, 1970 (GPO: Washington, D.C., 1980), 9.

318 "Not all drug use is equally." Domestic Council on Drug Abuse Task Force, *White Paper on Drug Abuse* (GPO: Washington, D.C., 1975), 6.

318 "The data indicate." Domestic Council, ibid., 25.

318 "Priority in both supply." Ibid., 98.

320 "preference might be given." *White Paper*, 34.

320 "From October of 1977," U.S. House, *Hearings on Cocaine and Marijuana Trafficking in S.E. U.S.*, Select Committee on Narcotics Abuse and Control 95th Cong., 2nd sess., June 9, 10, 1978 (GPO: Washington, D.C., 1978), 104.

320 "South Florida has become inundated." House, "Cocaine Trafficking," 71.
320 "midst of a catastrophic." House, "Cocaine Trafficking," 105.
321 "the general belief." House Select Committee on Narcotic Abuse and Control *Hearings on Cocaine: A Major Drug Issue of the Seventies*, 96th Cong., 1st sess, July 26, 1979, 45.
321 Byck . . . also testified. House, *Hearings on Cocaine*. July 26, 1979.
322 The shaken Dr. Byck. House, *Hearings on Cocaine*. 61–63.
323 "intranasally had a symptom-free." House, *Hearings on Cocaine*, 71. See also, C. V. Wetli, "Death Caused By Recreational Cocaine Use," *JAMA* 241, no. 23 (June 8, 1979): 2519–22.
323 a cover story titled. M. Demarest, "Cocaine: Middle Class High," *Time* (July 6, 1981).
324 "Cocaine makes us so intelligent." P. J. O'Rourke, "Lessons in Modern Manners," *Rolling Stone* (November 12, 1981), 20–22.
325 "splendid oceanside hotel." G. Nahas, *Cocaine: The Great White Plague* (Eriksson: Middlebury,Vt., 1989), 128.
325 "In hesitant English," Ibid., 133–34.
325 Leary was making the scene. Ibid., 140.
325 Leary to expound on cocaine. Ibid., 140–41.
326 Manhattan clinical psychologist. Telephone interview with Arnold Washton, January 20, 1995.
327 "desperate people." A. M. Washton, *Cocaine Addiction* (Norton: N.Y., 1989), 1.
328 "Most callers said." Ibid., 2.
328 use escalated from R. K. Siegel in "Cycles of Cocaine Use & Abuse" in *Treating Drug Problems* Vol. 2, ed. D. Gerstein and H. Harwood (National Academy Press: Washington, D.C., 1992), 308.
329 "a serious drug of abuse." L. Charlton, "A Major Federal Study of Cocaine," *NYT* (July 7, 1977), 1.
330 "many people, including some of the scientists." David Musto, "America's Response to Drug Use: Lessons From the Past" (edited transcript from Center for Substance Abuse Speaker Series, January 1992), 18. Available through the Center for Substance Abuse Research, University of Maryland, College Park.
330 "The definition [of addiction] has three major components." New York State Division of Substance Abuse Services, *Cocaine Symposium Update* (document of meeting, March 7, 1985), 14.
331 "became clear that the cocaine epidemic." A. S. Washton, "Cocaine, Drug Epidemic of the '80s," in *The Cocaine Crisis*, ed. D. Allen (Plenum: N.Y., 1985), 48.
331 first detailed information. Washton, "Cocaine," in *Cocaine Crisis*.
332 "Contrary to popular belief." A. M. Washton, et al., "Intranasal Cocaine Addiction," *Lancet* (December 10, 1983): 1374.
332 price of a kilo plummeting. "Snow Blizzard," *Time* (September 12, 1983), 23.
333 NFL cocaine scandal. P. Axthelm, "Cocaine Crisis in the NFL," *Newsweek* (July 25, 1983), 52.
333 "impotent, emaciated." J. Brody, "Personal Health," *NYT* (May 23, 1984), C 6:4.
333 "All might come clear." J. McInerney, *Bright Lights, Big City* (Vintage Original: N.Y,. 1985), 1–2.
333 "Cocaine has enjoyed a far better reputation." I. Mothner, A. Weitz, "How to Get Off Cocaine," *Rolling Stone* (June 7, 1984), 29.
334 "Cocaine was still the perfect drug." L. Cole, *Never Too Young to Die* (Pantheon: N.Y., 1989), 94.
334 "lurking idiosyncrasy." L. C. Anderson, "Observations on the Use of Cocaine," *NYMJ* (October 3, 1891): 370.
334 "died in convulsions." R. Haynes, "The Danger of Cocaine," *Medical News* (July 7, 1894): 14.

Chapter 16: The Colombian Cartels

337 "sudden and terrifying notice." G. Gugliotta and J. Leen, *Kings of Cocaine* (Harperpaper: N.Y., 1990), 14–15.
337 "In Batista's Cuba." J. Markham, "Florida Is Becoming Drug Traffic Center," *NYT* (May 1, 1972), 1.

338   total U.S. cocaine seizures. J. Maher, "Erythroxylon coca: a lecture" (DEA: Washington, D.C., 1986), 61.

338   "police could scarcely arrest a dope dealer." J. Kwitny, *Crime of the Patriots* (Norton: N.Y., 1987), 96.

338   August Ricord. DEA, *Pilot Project III* (internal document), 300–4.

339   "organizational linkages to Florida." P. A. Lupsha, "Drug Trafficking: Mexico & Colombia in Comparative Perspective," *Journal of International Affairs* 35, no. 1 (spring/summer), 1981, 104.

339   "The only obstacle." E. Shannon, *Desperadoes* (Viking: N.Y., 1988), 71–72.

339   "Marijuana doesn't hurt anybody." "Trouble in Paradise," *Time* (November 23, 1981), 30.

339   "wasn't all that harmful." Gugliotta and Leen, *Kings*, 76, 78.

339   "brand of counterculture hero." R. Sabbag, *Snowblind* (Picador: London, 1978), 102.

340   "more and more professional." House Select Committee on Narcotics Abuse & Control, *Hearings on Cocaine & Marijuana Trafficking*, 95th Cong., 2nd sess., June 9, 10, 1978, 40.

340   One of the major figures. Gugliotta and Leen, *Kings*, 39.

341   "imperialist police state." Ibid., 55.

341   Norman's Cay. P. Eddy et. al., *Cocaine Wars*, 154.

341   "wasn't like heroin." Gugliotta and Leen, *Kings*, 78.

342   "Colombian gangsters." D. Owen, "Boycott Cocaine," *Harper's* 265 (December 1982), 18.

343   Escobar was arrested. "Colombia's Kings of Coke," *Newsweek* (February 25, 1985), 20.

343   " 'La Violencia.' " P. Lupsha, "Drug Trafficking," 103.

343   "easy recruiting ground of paid killers." P. Eddy, H. Sabogal, S. Walden, *The Cocaine Wars* (Norton: N.Y., 1988), 29–30.

344   "necktie killings." Inciardi, *Drug Wars II* (Mayfield: Mtn. View, Calif., 1992), 217.

344   "I see people walking down the streets." "Trouble in Paradise," *Time* (November 23, 1981), 26.

344   "the computers of the Federal Reserve." D. McClintick, *Swordfish* (Pantheon: N.Y., 1993), 27–28.

345   "the reason so many banks." P. Lernoux, "The Miami Connection," *The Nation* (February 18, 1984), 186–98.

345   Customs agent. Ibid.

345   von Raab attended the annual meeting. J. Morley, "Contradictions of Cocaine Capitalism," *The Nation* 249 (October 2, 1989), 343.

346   "violence across the nation." Lupsha, "Drug Trafficking," 107–8.

346   "realized that paste smoking." J. Inciardi, *Drug Wars II*, 110.

347   crime in South Florida. G. Jaynes, "Fla. Seeks Explanations & Cures as Crime Mounts," *NYT* (October 18, 1980), 28.

347   "overjoyed when Reagan took office." Shannon, *Desperadoes*, 81.

347   From 1981 to 1986, federal funds. L. Cole, "Prisoners of Crack," *Rolling Stone* (February 9, 1989), 134.

348   "We're a laughingstock." N. M. Adams, "Cocaine Takes Over," *Reader's Digest* (May 7, 1975), 87.

348   sad state of U.S. cocaine intelligence. Gugliotta and Leen, *Kings*, 138.

348   "DEA and the Justice Department." Shannon, *Desperadoes*, 78.

349   "The office had not a clue." R. Stutman, *Dead on Delivery* (Warner: N.Y., 1992), 147–49.

349   "personal assets." Inciardi, *Drug Wars II*, 234.

350   wholesale price of cocaine. Gugliotta and Leen, *Kings*, 113.

350   TAMPA bust. Ibid., 115–119.

350   Ochoa ranch. Ibid., 135–36.

351   traffickers had him or her killed. Shannon, *Desperadoes*, 90.

351   M-19 guerrillas. Gugliotta and Leen, *Kings*, 149–61; P. Eddy, et al., *Cocaine Wars*, 289.

352   Tranquilandia. P. Eddy et al., *Cocaine Wars*, 290–92.

353   "go down to Colombia." Gugliotta and Leen, *Kings*, 170.

354   "state power, when brought to bear." Ibid., 175.

354   "He was to cocaine transportation." P. Eddy et al., *Cocaine Wars*, 189.

355 raid on the cartel's. Ibid., 297.

357 "traffickers publicly threatened." Shannon, *Desperadoes*, 171.

358 highest murder rate. Gugliotta and Leen, *Kings*, 425–26.

359 "firm proof." Ibid., 279.

360 contras were trafficking. Senate Commission on Foreign Relations. Subcommittee on Terrorism, Narcotics and International Operations, *Report on Drugs, Law Enforcement, & Foreign Policy*, 100th Cong., 2nd sess. (GPO: Washington, D.C., 1989), 38.

360 "People on both sides." Senate Foreign Relations Comm., ibid., 39.

360 "evidence that the Contra leadership." Senate, ibid., 136.

360 "evidence on the record." Senate, ibid., 124–25.

361 "The cartel moved 120 people," F. Kempe, *Divorcing the Dictator* (Putnam: N.Y., 1990), 186.

362 "El Sapo mountain range." Ibid., 184.

362 "Castro said." Ibid., 197–98.

363 "CIA director William Casey." J. Klein, "The Man Who Knows Too Much," *New York* (January 15, 1990), 12.

363 "facilitate the manufacture." Kempe, *Dictator*, 254–55.

363 "I am finding the higher we go." *Senate, Drugs, Law Enforcement & Foreign Policy*, 123.

363 "You've been looking at Latin America." Klein, "The Man," 12.

364 "Over the next two years, Musto." McCoy, *Politics of Heroin*, 436–37.

364 publicly expressing their dismay. J. H. Lowinson and D. F. Musto, "Drug Crisis & Strategy," *NYT* (May 22, 1980), A-35.

364 "Opium cultivation became important." S. B. MacDonald, "Afghanistan's Drug Trade," *Society* 295 (July–August 1992): 64.

365 "European police." L. Lifschultz, "Inside the Kingdom of Heroin," *Nation* 247 (November 14, 1988), 496.

365 "100 to 200 heroin refineries." McCoy, *Politics of Heroin*, 454.

366 "I want a drug-free America." Lifschultz, "Kingdom of Heroin," 496.

366 "The scale of the cartels' operations." *Senate, Drugs, Law Enforcement & Foreign Policy*, 134.

Chapter 17: "Now Everyone Was Into Smoking Crack"

367 "Throughout the Black residential." M. W. Klein, C. L. Maxson, " 'Rock' Sales in South Los Angeles," *Sociology and Social Research* 69 (July 1985): 561–65.

368 "new form of cocaine." J. Gross, "A New, Purified Form of Cocaine," *NYT* (November 29, 1985), 1.

368 "the data obtained from treatment." Domestic Council Drug Abuse Task Force, *White Paper on Drug Abuse* (GPO: Washington, D.C., 1975), 24.

368 "I am unable to persuade myself." House Select Committee on Narcotics Abuse and Control, Hearings on *Cocaine: A Major Drug Issue of the Seventies*, 96th Cong., 1st sess., July 24, 26, October 10, 1979 (GPO: Wash., D.C., 1980), 51, 54.

368 "if we were to be flooded." S. Cohen, M.D., *Cocaine Today* (American Council for Drug Education: Rockville, Md., 1981).

369 "Free base is your favorite." R. K. Siegel, "Cocaine Smoking," *JPsychoactive Drugs* 14, no. 4 (October–December 1982): 290.

369 "The first free-base kit." Siegel, "Smoking," 290.

369 "Most users." Ibid., 289.

370 rising popularity. "Smoking Cocaine," *Science News* 116 (December 1, 1979): 373.

370 "I started doing free-base." "Freebase Takes Away a Friend," *LA Times* (March 14, 1980).

370 free-base kits. Siegel, "Cocaine Smoking," 289–94.

371 "engulfed in flames." "Richard Pryor," *Time* (June 23, 1980), 10.

371 "cook it up batch." G. Witkin, "The Men Who Created Crack," *U.S. News & World Report* (August 19, 1991), 47.

371 "tried to figure out." Ibid., 47.

372 "When night fell." Ibid., 49.

373 "In Sept. '85, we had not gotten." J. V. Lamar, "Crack & Crime," *Newsweek* (June 16, 1986), 20.

373 "The drug scene had changed." S. Lydon, *Take the Long Way Home* (Harper: S.F., 1993), 203–8.

374 tried cocaine at least once. E. H. Adams and N. Kozel, "Cocaine Use in America," *Cocaine Use in America: Epidemiologic & Clinical Perspectives*, Research Monograph 61 (NIDA: Washington, D.C., 1985).

374 25 tons in the late 1970s. "Crack & Crime," 19.

374 peaked in about 1980. "Selected Tables from the National Household Survey," (NIDA: Washington, D.C., October 1, 1992).

375 highly segregated underclass. N. Lemann, *The Promised Land* (Knopf: N.Y., 1991), 282–83.

375 examines the links. E. Currie, *The Reckoning* (Hill & Wang: N.Y., 1993), 138–39.

376 economics of crack. Inciardi, *Drug Wars II*, 113.

377 more than one thousand dollars a month on crack. B. Johnson, "The Crack Era in NYC," ms., February 19, 1991, 5. (Available at University of Maryland Center for Substance Abuse Research in College Park.)

377 "police believe." E. D. Wish, "Crack & Crime," 16.

377 Justice Department study. E. D. Wish, "Drug Use Arrestees in Manhattan," Narcotic & Drug Research Paper. NYC February 12, 1987. (Available at the University of Maryland's Center for Substance Abuse Research in College Park.)

377 "The vast majority of crack." J. Johnson, et al., "Crack Abusers & Noncrack Abusers," *JDrug Issues* 24, no. 1 (winter 1994): 128–29.

378 "Everything is rocks, rocks, rocks." J. Inciardi, *Drug Wars II*, 117.

378 "After a while I got sick." Ibid., 122.

378 "forcible gang-rape." J. Inciardi and A. Trebach, *Legalize It?* (American University Press: Washington, D.C., 1993), 178.

378 "Older people I respected," F. Lee, "With No Parents, Ladeeta, 18, Presses on," *NYT* (April 6, 1993), 1.

379 "dozens of new crack dealing organizations." P. Kerr, "A Crack Plague in Queens," *NYT* (October 19, 1987), 1.

379 take to the street corners. Lee, "With No Parents," *NYT*.

379 fourteen-year-old dealer. Isabel Wilkerson, "Legacy of Guns and Killing Lives On," *NYT* (December 13, 1994), A-1.

380 "began their drug-using careers." J. Inciardi and A. Pottieger, "Kids, Crack, & Crime," *JDrug Issues* (1990).

380 largely a delusion. G. Kolata, "Despite Its Promise of Riches," *NYT* (November 26, 1989), 1.

381 "They don't have a Social Security." Kolata, Ibid. 1. The low-level street dealers were not very different than the middle-class mid-level dealers profiled by sociologist Patricia Adler in *Wheeling and Dealing* (Columbia University Press: N.Y., 1985). She observed that after three or four years, "in between episodes of intensive partying, veteran dealers and smugglers were struck by anxiety. . . . Eventually, the rewards of trafficking no longer seemed to justify the strain. It was at this point that the straight world's formerly dull ambience became transformed (at least in theory) into a potential haven."

381 U.S. homicide rates. T. E. Johnson, "Urban Murders," *Newsweek* (February 9, 1987), 30; "Slaughter in the Streets," *Time* (December 5, 1988), 32.

381 "Young and violent drug gangs." S. Raab, "Brutal Drug Gangs Wage War," *NYT* (March 15, 1988), B-1.

382 teenage male gun murders. F. Butterfield, "Teen-age Homicide Rate Has Soared," *NYT* (October 14, 1994), A-22:8.

382 homicides by black youth. N. Peirce, "The Odds that Lafayette Rivers," *Baltimore Sun* (April 1, 1991), 7A.

382 other industrialized countries. "U.S. Homicide Rate for Young Men," *Baltimore Sun* (June 27, 1990), 9A. From a study by Lois A. Fingerhut in June 27, 1990, *JAMA*.

382 "a woman purchasing crack." Inciardi and Taylor, *Legalize It?*, 178.

383 "By 1985, Juanita realized." Lemann, *Promised Land*, 293–94.

384 New York's Harlem Hospital. P. Kerr, "Crack Addiction: The Tragic Impact," *NYT* (February 9, 1987), B-1.

384 babies were often born. Ibid., B-1.

384 Infant mortality rose in Central Harlem. L. Cole, "Prisoners of Crack," *Rolling Stone* (February 9, 1989), 64.

384   "They don't like it." A. Quinlen, "With These Babies," *Intl. Herald Trib.* (October 10, 1990), 11.
384   "seizures, cerebral palsy," S. Chira, "Crack Babies Turn 5, and Schools Brace," *NYT* (May 25, 1990), 1.
385   "My impression with cocaine." L. Duke, "Drugs Get Choke Hold," *Washington Post* (January 18, 1988), 1.
385   2 to 3 percent of American babies exposed. "Estimating the Number of Substance-Exposed Infants," *The Future of Children* 1, no. 1 (Spring 1991). This is the journal of the Center for the Future of Children, Los Altos, California.
385   "66 per cent of the single adults." C. Jencks, "The Homeless," *New York Review of Books* (April 21, 1994), 26.
386   "Doctors blame." P. Kerr, "Addiction's Hidden Toll," *NYT* (June 23, 1988), 1.
386   By 1994. G. Kolata, "New Picture of Who Will Get AIDS," *NYT* (February 28, 1995), C-3.
386   "To put a human face." M. Navarro, "Left Behind By AIDS," *NYT* (May 6, 1992), B-1.
386   Frick Junior High School. J. Gross, "Collapse of Inner-City Families," *NYT* (March 29, 1992), A-1.
387   Jamaican crack dealers. M. Miller, "A Jamaican Invasion in West Virginia," *Newsweek* (March 28, 1988), 24.

Chapter 18: "Cocaine Is Addicting, Health-Ruining, . . ."

390   Barton of Naples, Florida. E. C. Brynner, "New Parental Push Against Marijuana," *NYT Sunday Magazine* (February 10, 1980), 51.
390   SAT scores. August 25, 1994, College Board, New York City, 10.
390   "gradually lost interest in both school." M. Manatt, *Parents, Peers, and Pot* (NIDA: Washington, D.C., 1979), 4.
391   "The kids wondered." Ibid., 15–17.
392   "To grow, to develop." Brynner, "New Parental Push," 37.
392   "teaching the fine points of smoking." House Select Committee on Narcotics, *Drug Paraphernalia*, 96th Cong., 1st sess., November 1, 1979 (GPO: Washington, D.C., 1980), 4.
392   "With the help of the parents' movement." R. L. DuPont, *The Selfish Brain* (American Psychiatric Press: Washington, D.C., 1995).
393   National Federation of Parents. R. A. Linblad, "A Review of the Concerned Parent Movement in the USA," *UN Bulletin on Narcotics* 35, no. 3 (1983): 48.
394   "private plainclothesmen." A. Malabre, "Heroin, Marijuana Use By Workers, Applicants," *Wall Street Journal* (May 4, 1970), 1.
394   the costs of on-the-job drug use. J. Castro, "Battling the Enemy Within," *Time* (March 17, 1986), 52–61.
395   "a stock-trading associate." R. Stone, "A Higher Horror of the Whiteness," *Harper's* 273 (December 1986), 52.
395   Department of Defense had been shocked. P. Mulloy, "Winning the War on Drugs in the Military," in *Drug Testing: Issues & Options*, eds. R. H. Coombs and L. J. West (Oxford University Press: N.Y., 1991), 92.
396   "slammed home." Mulloy, ibid., 93.
396   "As tragic as that was." ibid., 94.
396   "Testing would also be extended." Mulloy, Ibid., 96.
396   "the program was developed so fast." Castro, "The Enemy Within," 57.
397   urine testing as a strategy. R. Angarola, "Substance-Abuse Testing in the Workplace: Legal Issues & Corporate Responses," in *Drug Testing: Issues & Options*, eds. R. H. Coombs and L. J. West (OUP: N.Y., 1991), 155–89.
397   Georgia Power Company. *Washington Post* (May 5, 1986), B-8.
397   Southern Pacific Railroad. J. M. Walsh and J. G. Trumble, "The Politics of Drug Testing," in *Drug Testing: Issues & Options*, eds. R. H. Coombs and L. J. West (OUP: N.Y., 1991), 33.
398   Laurel, Maryland, painting and paving company. J. Treaster, "Testing Workers for Drugs Reduces Company Problems," *NYT* (October 10, 1993), A-1.
398   "newspapers, television shows." Shannon, *Desperadoes*, 371–72.

399 "Starting today, Nancy's crusade." R. Timberg, "Reagan Opens Drug Drive with request for testing," *Baltimore Sun* (August 5, 1986), A-2.

399 "Who ever thought [Reaganites]." L. Cole, *Never Too Young To Die* (Pantheon: N.Y., 1989), 171.

400 Reagan administration cut this figure. K. J. Besteman, "Federal Leadership in Building the National Drug Treatment System," in *Treating Drug Problems* vol. 2, eds. D. Gerstein and H. Harwood (National Academy Press: Washington, D.C., 1992), 63–85.

400 "the No. 1 topic in Washington." J. Brinkley, "Competing for the Last Word on Drug Abuse," *NYT* (August 7, 1986).

400 "Congress went into a frenzy." Shannon, *Desperadoes*, 377–78.

401 "bundle our children off to school." G. Boyd, "Reagans Advocate 'Crusade' on Drugs," *NYT* (September 15, 1986), 1.

401 Drug Free Federal Workplace. C. Zwerling, "Current Practice and Experience in Drug and Alcohol Testing in the Workplace," *Bulletin on Narcotics* 45 no. 2 (1993), 158.

402 "had stopped using cocaine." R. K. Siegel, "Repeating Cycles of Cocaine Use and Abuse," in *Treating Drug Problems* V. 2, eds. D. Gerstein and H. Harwood (National Academy Press: Washington, D.C., 1990), 289–316.

402 "Starting today, in what is being billed." J. Lipman, "Media & Ad Firms Join Forces to Launch Major Anti-Drug Campaign," *WSJ* (March 5, 1987).

402 "Do crack while you're pregnant." Partnership for a Drug-Free America, "Creative Round-up, 1990–1991."

403 "In the world of high fashion." W. Hochswender, "In Fashion World, the Trend is Away From Drugs," *NYT* (May 16, 1988).

403 "High Priest of the sixties." R. Rosenbaum, "Back in the High Life," *Vanity Fair* (April 1988) 134–144, 154.

403 reclaiming neighborhoods. E. Pooley, "Fighting Back Against Crack," *New York* (January 23, 1989), 29–39.

404 "If people like me—rich, white." P. J. O'Rourke, *Parliament of Whores* (Vintage: N.Y., 1991), 122.

404 "There's a tremendous difference." G. Dillow, "Hollywood's Drug Scene—How Bad Is It Now?" *TV Guide* 37 (August 19–25, 1989), 4–8.

404 "Barry depended more and more." D. Remnick, "The Situationist," *The New Yorker* (September 5, 1994), 87–88.

405 "While Colombian judges put their lives." D. Farah, "In Colombia, Outrage at Barry Verdict," *Intl. Herald Tribune* (August 13, 1990), 3.

405 In 1990. NIDA, *National Household Survey on Drug Abuse Highlights 1990* (NIDA: Washington, D.C., 1990), 68–70.

407 "initiatives, like the 24 task forces." "President Reagan's Drug Bust," *NYT* (November 13, 1987), A-38:1.

407 "Now Congress and the American people." J. Johnson, "Reagan Signs Bill to Curb Drug Use," *NYT* (November 19, 1988), A-9:1.

408 "Two words sum up." M. Massing, "The Two William Bennetts," *New York Review of Books* (March 1, 1990), 29–33.

408 beyond the traditional law enforcement. H. Williams, "Drug Control Strategies of U.S. law enforcement," *Bull. on Narcotics* 42, no. 1 (1990): 27.

409 "started selling crack." J. Treaster, "Crack Dealer Feeds a Family & Habits of Fewer Addicts," *NYT* (May 16, 1991), 1.

409 "anyone who had taken up the habit." J. Treater, "In a Crackhouse," *NYT* (April 6, 1991), A-1.

410 "smokable form of cocaine." G. Kolata, "For Some Poor N.Y. Youths, Crack is Now a 4-Letter Word," *Intl. Herald Trib.* (July 24, 1990), 3.

410 various afflicted cities. E. Shannon, "The Losing War," *Time* (December 3, 1990), 46.

411 As many Colombian peasant families. J. Brooke, "Drug Graft in Colombia is Rife," *NYT* (August 14, 1994), 6.

411 Twenty tons of cocaine. S. Mydans, "Vast Drug Cache & $10 Mil Discovered," *NYT* (September 30, 1989), A-1.

412 Khun Sa. P. Smucker, "In Burma's Shan State, Warlord is One-Man Heroin Cartel," *International Herald Tribune* (November 1, 1990).

Chapter 19: "You Have to Pay Up Somewhere Along the Line"

414 "I could have done without that PCP." G. Kalogerakis, "Stoned Again," New York (May 1, 1995), 45.

414 "Harlem blacks." Currie, Reckonings, 188; C. McCord and H. Freeman, "Excess Mortality in Harlem," NEJM 322 (1990): 173–77.

415 "Most people, including economists." J. Fallows, "Wake Up, America!" New York Review of Books (March 1, 1990), 14.

415 "I was resolved to practice." M. Signorile, "HIV-Positive and Careless," NYT (February 26, 1995), E-15.

416 "We old-time pot smokers." R. Stone, "A Higher Horror of the Whiteness," Harper's 273 (December 1986), 51.

418 "Since current approaches." H. D. Kleber, "Our Current Approach to Drug Abuse—Progress, Problems, Proposals," NEJM 330 no. 5 (February 3, 1994): 362.

419 "The notion that abusing drugs." J. Q. Wilson, "Against the Legalization of Drugs," Commentary 89, no. 2 (February 1990), 23.

420 ROCKING. S. Rovner, "Calling Granny 'Mom,' " Washington Post (April 24, 1995), D-5.

420 "following the effects of drugs." Wilson, "Against Legalization," 23–24.

420 fifteen thousand dollars a year per drug-affected child. M. Norris, "And the Children Shall Need," Washington Post (July 1, 1991), A-1.

421 "while drug use tends to intensify." J. Inciardi, Legalize it?, 186.

422 "As we have seen, British addicts." Currie, Reckoning, 177.

422 "Until the mid-1960's." Wilson, "Against the Legalization," 22–23.

423 "Because heroin is a short-acting." Inciardi, Legalize, 172.

424 Social Security disability payments. "Tax Dollars Aiding & Abetting Addiction: Social Security Cash Benefits to Drug Addicts & Alcoholics," Investigative Staff Report of Senator William S. Cohen, February 7, 1994.

424 "They are everywhere: rummies." P. Hamill, "City of the Damned," Esquire (December 1990), 65.

425 Sierra Tuscon center. M. D. Anglin and T. H. Maugh, "Ensuring Success in Interventions with Drug-Using Offenders," in Drug Abuse: Linking Policy & Research, special volume, ed. Eric Wish, Annals of the American Academy of Political and Social Science (Sage: Newbury Park, 1992).

427 Tampa. E. Methvin, "Tampa's Winning War on Drugs," Reader's Digest 139 (July 1991), 56–60.

428 two thirds of heroin traffickers. U.S. Sentencing Commission, Cocaine & Federal Sentencing Policy: A Special Report to Congress, 157. Available through National Institute of Justice, U.S. Dept. of Justice.

429 tested the urine of just-arrested. R. DuPont and E. D. Wish, "Operation Tripwire Revisited," in Annals ed. E. Wish, Drug Abuse, 91–111.

429 "Between 53 percent and 79 percent." J. Reardon, The Drug Use Forecasting Program (National Institute of Justice: Washington, D.C., 1993), 13, 23.

430 "because it altered an addict's schedule." G. E. Vaillant, "What Can Long-term Follow-up Teach Us About Relapse & Prevention of Relapse in Addiction?" Brit.JAddiction 83 (1988): 1153–54.

430 "The Drug Court Handles." M. Falso, The Making of a Drug-Free America (Times Books: N.Y., 1994), 140.

431 How often is coercion. National Institute of Justice, Miami's 'Drug Court': A Different Approach (National Institute of Justice: Washington, D.C., 1993), pamphlet available through the NIJ.

431 far more ambitious. M. Kleiman, Against Excess (Basic Books: N.Y., 1992), 195. And Kleiman, "Fight Crime, Seriously," NYT (July 23, 1992).

432 "rearrest rates." Falco, Drug-Free America, 134–35.

432 "about 18,000 low-level." P. Heymann, "Billions for New Prisons?" NYT (July 9, 1994), A-19.

433 "retail-level crack cocaine dealers." U.S. Sentencing Commission, Cocaine & Federal Sentencing Policy (February 1995), xiii, 161, 198.

433 11,000 of 13,000 people arrested. N. West, "Young City Black Men: 56% in Trouble," Baltimore Sun (September 1, 1992), A-1.

433 now has behind bars. N. Kristof, "Japanese Say No to Crime," NYT (May 14, 1995), A-1.

433 "Obviously we can't lock up." "Is the drug war racist?" *USA Today* (July 23–25, 1993), 2.

434 "did not encourage." E. Dunlap and B. Johnson, "The Setting for the Crack Era: Macro Forces, Micro Consequences (1960–1992)" *JPsychoactive Drugs* 24, no. 4 (October–December 1992): 313.

434 handful of model programs. Falco, *Drug-Free America*, 44–45.

435 "adolescents are very unlikely." D. Kandel and K. Yamaguchi, "From Beer to Crack: Developmental Patterns of Drug Involvement," *AJ Public Health* 83, no. 6 (June 1993): 851–54.

435 "past decade worldwide production." ed. R. Perl, *Drugs & Foreign Policy* (Westview Press: Boulder, Colo., 1994), ix.

436 "must cut off foreign aid." S. Greenhouse, "U.S. Says Colombia Refuses to Cooperate in Drug War," *NYT* (March 2, 1995), A-3.

436 "Weak legislation, corruption." U.S. State Dept. *International Narcotics Control Strategy Report* (State Dept. Pub., April 1995), 81.

436 "Where Europe was relatively drug-free." D. Lipton, "Drug Control Abroad," unpublished ms. lent by the author. 1989, 66.

437 "He would come home so stoned." A. Guillermopietro, "Letter From Medellín," *New Yorker* (April 22, 1991), 100–1.

437 "escalation of Latin America's." Lipton, "Drug Control Abroad," 66.

439 "major issues as regulating wire." U.S. State Dept. *International Narcotics Control Strategy*, State Dept. Pub., (March 1995), 488.

439 dispersed $34 million. State Dept., *Narcotics Control*, 486.

439 "The bank began taking drug traffickers'." State Dept., *International Narcotics Control Strategy* 1995, 483.

439 Operation Primero. State Dept., ibid., 484.

440 "Wall Street of the drug trade." F. Dannen, "Colombian Gold," *New Yorker* (August 15, 1994), 29–30.

441 Colombian National Police. State Dept., *International Narcotics Control Strategy*, 460.

Trends in the Percentage of Persons Reporting Any Illicit Drug Use 1979 to 1993

The National Household Survey on Drug Abuse began in the early 1970s. This longitudinal chart starts in 1979 (when most drug use nationwide peaked) and then shows the gradual decline, and the worrisome recent rises in youthful drug use. The most important indicator is use in "past 30 days" because that reveals regular use, as opposed to experimentation.

Age of respondent and recency of drug use	YEAR							
	1979	1982	1985	1988	1990	1991	1992	1993
12–17								
ever	34.4	28.0	29.7	24.7	22.7	20.1	16.5	17.9
past year	27.3	22.0	23.3	16.8	15.9	14.8	11.7	13.6
past 30 days	18.5	13.2	14.9	9.2	8.1	6.8	6.1	6.6
18–25								
ever	69.8	64.5	63.7	58.9	55.8	54.7	51.7	50.9
past year	49.7	43.4	41.0	32.0	28.7	29.1	26.4	26.6
past 30 days	37.4	30.8	25.1	17.8	14.9	15.4	13.0	13.5
26 AND OLDER								
ever	23.2	24.8	31.7	33.7	35.3	36.0	36.0	37.3
past year	10.3	12.1	12.7	10.2	10.0	9.4	8.3	8.9
past 30 days	6.6	7.8	8.0	4.9	4.6	4.6	4.1	4.1
ALL AGES 12 AND OLDER								
ever	33.3	32.3	36.7	36.6	37.0	37.0	36.2	37.2
past year	19.5	18.7	18.6	14.1	13.3	12.7	11.1	11.8
past 30 days	13.7	12.2	11.6	7.3	6.4	6.3	5.5	5.6

Note: Any illicit drug use includes use of marijuana, cocaine, hallucinogens, inhalants (except 1982), heroin, or nonmedical use of sedatives, tranquilizers, stimulants, or analgesics. The exclusion of inhalants in 1982 is believed to have resulted in underestimates of any illicit use for that year, especially for 12–17 year olds. Prior to 1979, data were not totaled for overall drug use and instead were published by specific drug type only.
Source: National Household Survey on Drug Abuse

S E L E C T E D
B I B L I O G R A P H Y

Those interested in American drug culture will find useful material in the following locales and publications.

Most of the research material collected in the course of writing this book having to do with addicts, drug culture, and public policy will be deposited in the archives of the National Library of Medicine in Bethesda, Maryland. All the drug-trafficking material will be deposited at the National Security Archive in Washington, D.C.

The Drug Enforcement Administration has an excellent library at its Pentagon City, Virginia, headquarters. Its holdings go back to the twenties and include not only such basic official documents as congressional hearings and the Treasury Department's annual report, *Traffic in Opium and Other Dangerous Drugs*, but a wide selection of books. It also offers unique vertical files containing voluminous clipped material. The DEA also dispatched to the Records Center (at the U.S. Archives in Suitland, Maryland) an extraordinary collection of old documents. However, viewing these requires Freedom of Information Act permission.

The personal and a few official papers of Commissioner Harry J. Anslinger, who presided over the Federal Bureau of Narcotics (the predecessor agency to the DEA) from 1930 to 1962, are now in the Harry J. Anslinger Papers compilation at the Historical Collections and Labor Archives, Pattee Library, Pennsylvania State University, University Park, Pennsylvania.

Out in San Francisco, the private Fitz Hugh Ludlow Memorial Library has extensive holdings in books, periodicals, and images on the drug culture. For more than a decade, however, the library has been without a home and inaccessible.

The State Department's Division of Far Eastern Affairs' papers in the National Archives are a treasure trove of voluminous material about international drug trafficking and policy from the 1920s to just after World War II.

The National Security Archive in Washington, D.C., has been compiling an archive on U.S. drug policy from the 1970s to the 1990s. The archive, housed in the George Washington University Library, will include newly declassified government documents from the Nixon administration on.

For recent research on drug use, visit the Center for Substance Abuse Research at the University of Maryland, College Park. Their library and catalogued vertical files of journal articles are outstanding. The U.S. Department of Justice's National Institute of Justice issues an excellent catalogue that includes much material on drugs and crime.

READINGS

Anyone interested in the field would do well to begin with Dr. David F. Musto's *The American Disease: Origins of Narcotic Control* (1987). The standard work on the history of American narcotics laws, this was first published in 1973 and provides detailed analysis up to the 1930s. Subsequent events receive intelligent but cursory treatment.

Two important books about early addicts and their worlds are by David Courtwright. The first, *Dark Paradise: Opiate Addiction in America Before 1940* (1982), is an excellent epidemiologic study that shows the changing profile of drug addicts. This has a superb bibliography. The second Courtwright book, written with Herman Joseph and Don Des Jarlais, is *Addicts Who Survived: An Oral History of Narcotic Use in America, 1923–1965* (1989). Aged methadone patients describe early drug subculture. Bingham Dai's *Opium Addiction in Chicago* (1937) remains the preeminent study of addiction in a major American city. A good first-person account of old-time addicts is Leroy Street's *I Was a Drug Addict* (1953). Mezz Mezzrow's book, *Really the Blues* (1946), is a minor classic about the hepster life.

Historian Joseph F. Spillane has written an excellent dissertation on cocaine called *Modern Drug, Modern Menace: The Legal Use and Distribution of Cocaine in the U.S., 1880–1920.* Published in 1994, it is available through the Rand Corporation's Drug Policy Research Center. A useful compendium of early cocaine literature is to be found in *Cocaine Papers* edited by Robert Byck (1974).

Another useful work for historians is Charles E. Terry and Mildred Pellens's *The Opium Problem* (1928), a bibliographic listing of work on drugs. It's worth knowing that Terry preferred to view typical addicts as genteel.

Probably no aspect of drug culture is murkier than that of trafficking. The standard account of early U.S. diplomatic efforts to curb the worldwide drug trade is Arnold H. Taylor's *American Diplomacy and the Narcotics Traffic, 1900–1939* (1969). The State Department also publishes its own histories. John C. McWilliams's *The Protectors: Harry J. Anslinger and the Federal Bureau of Narcotics, 1930–1962* (1990) is both a biography of Anslinger and the agency. Alfred W. McCoy's revised *The Politics of Heroin* (1991) details Cold War trafficking policy and patterns. On the rise of the cocaine cartels, the best account is Guy Gugliotta and Jeff Leen's *Kings of Cocaine* (1989). A more scholarly and more recent book is *Drug Trafficking in the Americas* edited by Bruce M. Bagley and William O. Walker (1995).

For a sense of the middle-class drug culture of the sixties and seventies and the surrounding politics, read Tom Wolfe's *The Electric Kool-Aid Acid Test*, Jay Stevens's *Storming Heaven: LSD and the American Dream* (1987), and Patrick Anderson's *High in America* (1981).

More than one hundred research monographs put out by the National Institute for Drug Abuse are a gold mine of scholarly information on virtually every aspect of drug use, addiction, treatment, and prevention.

For discussion of the situation in the early 1990s, see Mark A. R. Kleiman's *Against Excess* (1992) and Mathea Falco's *The Making of a Drug-Free America* (1994).

Government Documents

Domestic Council Drug Abuse Task Force. *White Paper on Drug Abuse* (GPO: Washington, D.C., 1975).

U.S. House of Representatives. "Cocaine: A Major Drug Issue of the Seventies," *Hearings Before the Select Committee on Narcotics Abuse and Control*, 96th Cong., 1st sess., July 1979.

U.S. Congress. "Cocaine & Marijuana Trafficking," *Hearings Before the House Select Committee on Narcotics Abuse and Control*, 95th Cong., 2nd sess., June 9, 10, 1978.

U.S. Department of State, Office of the Historian. "The Role of the Department of State in International Narcotics Control, 1840–1961." Research Project No. 1256-B (December 1981).

U.S. National Archives, State Department Division of Far Eastern Affairs. Name File of Suspected Narcotics Traffickers, 1927–1942 Record Group 59, Lot 55 607D.

Books and Articles

Anderson, Patrick. *High in America*. Viking: N.Y., 1981.

Anslinger, Harry J. *The Traffic in Narcotics* (Funk & Wagnalls: New York, 1953).

———. with Courtney Ryley Cooper. "Marijuana, Assassin of Youth." *The American Magazine* (July 1937): 18–19, 150–153.

———. and Will Oursler. *The Murderers: The Story of the Narcotic Gangs*. Farrar, Straus & Cudahy: New York, 1961.

Bagley, Bruce, and William O. Walker. *Drug Trafficking in the Americas* (Transaction: New Brunswick, N.J., 1995).

Bailey, Pearce. "Heroin Habit." *The New Republic* 6 (April 22, 1916): 315–16.

Ball, John C., and Carl D. Chambers. *The Epidemiology of Opiate Addiction in the United States* (Charles C. Thomas: Springfield, Ill., 1970).

Block, Alan. "The Snowman Cometh: Coke in Progressive New York." *Criminology* 17 (May 1979): 80.

———. "European Drug Traffic and Traffickers Between the Wars: The Policy of Suppression and Its Consequences." *Journal of Social History* 23, no. 2 (Winter 1989): 315–38.

Bonnie, Richard J., and Charles H. Whitebread II. *The Marihuana Conviction: A History of Marijuana Prohibition in the United States*. University Press of Virginia: Charlottesville, 1974.

Brecher, Edward M., and the editors of *Consumer Reports*. *Licit and Illicit Drugs: The Consumers Union Report on Narcotics, Stimulants, Depressants, Inhalants, Hallucinogens, and Marijuana—Including Caffeine, Nicotine, and Alcohol*. Consumers Union: Mt. Vernon, N.Y., 1972.

Brownlow, Kevin. *Behind the Mask of Innocence*. Knopf: N.Y., 1990.

Byck, Robert, ed. *Cocaine Papers*. Stonehill: New York, 1974.

Charters, Ann, ed. *Dictionary of Literary Biography: The Beats: Literary Bohemians in Postwar America*. Vol. 16, Pts. 1 and 2. Gale Research Co.: Detroit, 1983.

Courtwright, David. *Dark Paradise: Opiate Addiction in America Before 1940*. Harvard University Press: Cambridge, 1982.

———. Herman Joseph, and Don Des Jarlais. *Addicts Who Survived: An Oral History of Narcotic Use in America, 1923–1965*. University of Tennessee Press: Knoxville, 1989.

Dai, Bingham. *Opium Addiction in Chicago*. Commercial Press: Shanghai, 1937.

De Quincey, Thomas. *Confessions of an English Opium Eater*. Crescent Press: London, 1950.

"Drugs in the '90—1890s and 1990s: An Interview with David F. Musto." *The Woodrow Wilson Center Report*. 2 no. no. 3. November 1990: 10.

Falco, Mathea. *The Making of a Drug-Free America*. Times Books: N.Y., 1994.

Feder, Sid, and Joachim Joesten. *The Luciano Story*. David McKay: N.Y., 1954.

Gillespie, Dizzy, with Al Fraser. *to Be, or not . . . to Bop*. Da Capo: N.Y., 1979.

Giroux, Robert. *A Deed of Death*. Knopf: N.Y., 1990.

Gitler, Ira. *Swing to Bop: An Oral History of the Transition in Jazz in the 1940s*. Oxford University Press: N.Y., 1985.

Goldman, Albert. *Grass Roots: Marijuana in America Today*. Warner Books: N.Y., 1980.

Gugliotta, Guy, and Jeff Leen. *Kings of Cocaine*. HarperPaper: N.Y., 1990.

———. "The New York City Narcotics Clinic and Differing Points of View on Narcotics Addiction." *Monthly Bulletin of the Department of Health of New York City* 10, no. 2 (February 1920).

Hubbard, S. Dana, M.D. "Municipal Narcotic Dispensaries." *Public Health Reports* 35 (March 26, 1920): 771.

Inciardi, James. *Drug Wars II.* Mayfield: Mtn. View, Calif., 1992.

Johnson, Joyce. *Minor Characters.* Picador: London, 1983.

Joint Committee of the American Bar Association and the American Medical Association on Narcotic Drugs. *Drug Addiction: Crime or Disease?* Indiana University Press: Bloomington, 1961.

Katcher, Leo. *The Big Bankroll: The Life and Times of Arnold Rothstein.* Arlington House: New Rochelle, N.Y., 1959.

Kinder, Douglas Clark. "Bureaucratic Cold Warrior: Harry J. Anslinger and Illicit Narcotics Traffic." *Pacific Historical Review* 50 (1981): 169–91.

———. and William O. Walker. "Stable Force in a Storm: Harry J. Anslinger and the United States Narcotics Foreign Policy, 1930–1962." *Journal of American History* 72 (1986): 908–27.

Kleiman, Mark A. R. *Against Excess.* Basic Books: N.Y., 1992.

Leary, Timothy. *The Politics of Ecstasy.* G.P. Putnam's: N.Y., 1968.

———. *Flashbacks.* Tarcher: L.A., 1983.

Lewis, David Levering. *When Harlem Was in Vogue.* Knopf: N.Y., 1981.

Lipton, Lawrence. *The Holy Barbarians.* Julian Messner: N.Y., 1959.

McCoy, Alfred. *The Politics of Heroin: CIA Complicity in the Global Drug Trade.* Lawrence Hill: Brooklyn, N.Y., 1991.

McNally, Dennis. *Desolate Angel: A Biography of Jack Kerouac and the Beat Generation and America.* Random House: N.Y., 1979.

McWilliams, John C. *The Protectors: Harry J. Anslinger and the Federal Bureau of Narcotics, 1930–1962.* University of Delaware Press: Newark, 1990.

———. and Alan A. Block. "All the Commissioner's Men: The Federal Bureau of Narcotics and the Dewey-Luciano Affair, 1947–54." *Intelligence and National Security* 5 (April 1990).

Maurer, David W. "The Argot of the Underworld Narcotics Addict." *American Speech* 11, no. 2 (April 1936): 117.

Mayor's Committee on Marijuana. *The Marijuana Problem in the City of New York.* Scarecrow Reprint: Metuchen, N.J., 1944.

Mezzrow, Milton, and Bernard Wolfe. *Really the Blues.* Anchor Books: Garden City, N.Y., 1972; reprint of 1946 Random House edition.

Miles, Barry. *Ginsberg: A Biography.* Simon and Schuster: N.Y., 1989.

Morgan, Ted. *Literary Outlaw: The Life and Times of William S. Burroughs.* Henry Holt: N.Y., 1988.

Musto, David F., M.D. *The American Disease: Origins of Narcotic Control.* Oxford University Press: N.Y., 1987.

Parssinen, Terry M. *Secret Passions, Secret Remedies: Narcotic Drugs in British Society 1820–1930.* Institute for the Study of Human Issues: Philadelphia, 1983.

Polsky, Ned. *Hustlers, Beats, and Others.* Aldine: Chicago, 1967.

Reisner, Robert George. *From Bird: The Legend of Charlie Parker.* Da Capo: N.Y., 1975.

Renborg, Bertil A. "The Grand Old Men of the League of Nations." *Bulletin on Narcotics* 16, no. 4 (October–December 1964): 9.

Russell, Ross, *Bird Lives: The High Life and Hard Times of Charlie (Yardbird) Parker.* Charterhouse: N.Y., 1973.

Shannon, Elaine, *Desperadoes.* Viking: N.Y., 1988.

Siragusa, Charles. *The Trail of the Poppy: Behind the Mask of the Mafia.* Prentice-Hall: Englewood Cliffs, N.J., 1966.

Starks, Michael, *Cocaine Fiends & Reefer Madness: An Illustrated History of Drugs in the Movies.* Cornwall Books: N.Y., 1982.

Stevens, Jay. *Storming Heaven: LSD and the American Dream.* Perennial Library: N.Y, 1988.

Street, Leroy. *I Was a Drug Addict.* Arlington House: New Rochelle, N.Y., 1953.

Taylor, Arnold H. *American Diplomacy and the Narcotics Traffic, 1900–1939: A Study in International Humanitarian Reform.* Duke University Press: Durham, N.C., 1969.

Terry, Charles E., and Mildred Pellens. *The Opium Problem.* Bureau of Social Hygiene: N.Y., 1928.

Walton, Robert P. *Marijuana: America's New Drug Problem.* J.P. Lippincott: N.Y., 1938.

Wilbert, Martin I., and Murray Galt Motter. "Digest of Laws and Regulations in Force in the United States Relating to the Possession, Use, Sale, and Manufacture of Poisons and Habit-forming Drugs." *Public Health Bulletin* no. 56. G.P.O.: Washington, D.C., 1912.

Manuscripts and Typescripts

Keire, Mara. "High Living: Drugs and the Hollywood Scandals, 1920–1923." American History Seminar Paper. Johns Hopkins University, 1991.
Parssinen, Terry M., and Kathryn B. Meyer. "America and the World Market for Narcotic Drugs, 1919–1939." Paper given at the Organization of American Historians. Washington, D.C., March 1990.

ACKNOWLEDGMENTS

My principal debt is to John Higham, now professor emeritus at the Johns Hopkins University, who took on a writer ingrained with the habits of journalism and, exhibiting great patience, molded her into a historian. It always has been a pleasure and an honor to be his student.

I have worked on this history for the better part of a decade. During those years many people and organizations generously extended time, energy, and backing to see this book (which draws on my Ph.D. dissertation but is expanded vastly) to fruition. The Johns Hopkins history department always was welcoming and collegial. Susan Berresford of the Ford Foundation, introduced to me by Mitchell Sviridoff, supported my research at the very beginning. Robert Curvin at Ford, through Susan, continued that much appreciated support. The LBJ Foundation underwrote an important research trip to the presidential library in Austin. The National Endowment for the Humanities funded a year's worth of writing in 1994.

Early on, historian David Courtwright was a regular and extremely generous critic and correspondent. Michael Aldrich and Michael Horowitz of the Fitz Hugh Ludlow Memorial Library in San Francisco directed me to numerous sources of material, as did Ronald Walters, Mara Keirie, Kathy Jacob, and Terry Parssinen. John C. McWilliams, biographer of longtime U.S. Narcotics Commissioner Harry J. Anslinger, introduced me to other scholars in the field. David Nurco kindly shared his trove of taped interviews with postwar addicts, and made available reprints of his extensive research into addiction. Archivist Dane Hartgrove at the U.S. Archives in Washington, D.C., provided guidance with the State Department files, while Morton Goren, head librarian at the U.S. Drug Enforcement Administration, repeatedly extended assistance. During a half year when I was living in Munich and writing, Lewis A. Erenberg, there as a Fulbright scholar, was always helpful with talk and ideas. Historian Joseph F. Spillane. who works on cocaine, has been a stimulating colleague. Thanks are also due to Alan A. Block for sharing his files, to Douglas Lipton for providing a manuscript of his overseas experiences, and to Eric Wish for access to the outstanding library of the Center for Substance Abuse Research at University of Maryland, College Park. Without the endlessly efficient Inter-Library Loan staff at Johns Hopkins's Eisenhower Library, I could never have written this book.

A number of longtime federal narcotics agents and officials were indispensable in sharing information and documents. I am particularly indebted to Andrew Tartaglino, Edward Coyne, John Cusack, John Bacon, John Ingersoll, Jerry Strickler, and Wayne Rocques. Former and present National Institute of Drug Abuse officials also have extended help. Many thanks to Dr. Robert Dupont and Dr. Jerome Jaffe. At the State Department, I thank Jeffrey A. Soukup for providing copious documents. Kate Doyle at the National Security Archive helped with a critical Freedom of Information Act appeal to the DEA and shared her files. At the DEA, I am grateful to Tom Wingate for finally producing long-awaited material and to Rogene Waite for all-round efficient help.

In France, Ivan Rioufol, director of documentation at *Le Figaro*, generously opened that newspaper's archives. In Marseille, *Figaro* correspondent Jose D'Arrigo graciously introduced me to Omar Sharif of *Le Meridionale*, who was my guide to the city's old drug culture and also arranged access to his paper's archives. In Paris, national archivists at various ministries and librarians at the Bibliothèque Nationale were helpful.

Many thanks to collector William Helfand for providing illustrations from his fascinating trove of pharmaceutical materials.

Often, when I traveled for research purposes, family and friends extended bed, board, and sometimes baby-sitting. Thanks to my parents, Lloyd and Lyn Jonnes; my in-laws John Ross, Clare Romano, and Tim Ross; Heidi and Costas Syropoulos for repeated hospitality at Penn State; and in New York, Peggy and Bob Sarlin, Deborah and Christopher Buck, and Amy Dunkin. Other family and friends have been good-humored as year after year I was still writing this book.

Thanks to those who spent time reviewing certain chapters or the entire book manuscript: Andrew Tartaglino, Nancy Eskridge, David Nurco, and John Ball.

Fellow writer and friend, Robert Kanigel, started the book writers' dinners that have been a source of good fun and practical advice for all of the years I've been working on this history. I am further indebted to Rob for introducing me to Joy Smith, my original Scribner editor, an enthusiastic supporter who helped shape the early chapters. Her excellent colleague Hamilton Cain then saw the book to completion. Every writer should be blessed with such editors.

Special appreciation goes to my agent, Tom Wallace, a steady friend and adviser who provided much useful encouragement and counsel.

Finally, much love and deepest thanks to my husband, Christopher A. Ross, who has been here through it all, cheering me on. And then there is my darling daughter, Hilary, whose sleep habits and good nature made much writing possible and life a joy.